The Law Applicable to Cross-border Contracts involving Weaker Parties in EU Private International Law

María Campo Comba

The Law Applicable to Cross-border Contracts involving Weaker Parties in EU Private International Law

Springer

María Campo Comba
Erasmus School of Law
Erasmus University Rotterdam
Rotterdam, The Netherlands

ISBN 978-3-030-61480-5 ISBN 978-3-030-61481-2 (eBook)
https://doi.org/10.1007/978-3-030-61481-2

This Springer imprint is published by the registered company Springer Nature Switzerland AG.
The registered company address is: Gewerbestrasse 11, 6330 Cham, Switzerland

Acknowledgements

This book is the product of my four years of research as a PhD student at the University of Groningen (Netherlands). It is also the result of a four-year-long learning process, with many challenges and experiences and which has only been possible thanks to the support, help and advice of numerous people, whom I honestly would like to thank. The successful completion of my PhD thesis, and its adaptation to become this book, is thanks to them.

First, I would like to thank my PhD supervisor, Prof. Dr. Mathijs ten Wolde, for giving me the opportunity to pursue this project and for supporting and inspiring me during all the research process. His close supervision, advice and encouragement were essential to the writing of my PhD dissertation and also to the professional and personal development reached during these past four years.

I am also thankful to my co-supervisor, Prof. Dr. Rafael Arenas García, whose feedback and insights were deeply helpful in the development of this project. In particular, my visits to the Universidad Autónoma de Barcelona became crucial for me to develop new insights and reach a more complete understanding of certain complex matters.

My gratitude also goes to the members of the Assessment Committee, Prof. Dr. Charlotte Pavillon, Prof. Dr. Sixto Sánchez Lorenzo and Prof. Dr. Miguel Gardeñes Santiago, for dedicating their time and effort in reviewing my work. Furthermore, I would like to thank the University of Groningen and, specifically, the personnel of the Graduate School of Law, for allowing me to pursue this project, providing all the necessary help and support during the whole process, always with the kindest responses.

I would further like to thank my colleagues on the Private International Law section of the University of Groningen, which have been a constant support during the past years. I would like to state my admiration to both their professional and personal skills, which I had the luck to get to know through the years. Although the writing of a PhD thesis might sometimes be a lonely path, having a friendly, calm and supportive work environment indeed makes the difference. I am especially grateful to those colleagues, such as Beibei and Nischa, who, after long conversations over work and non-work, important and also irrelevant matters, struggles and experiences together, have made this experience really enjoyable.

I am also greatly thankful to the good friends I have made in this city, Groningen, whose support and friendship have made it possible for me to have the strength to carry on this research and also, when necessary, to forget about it and focus on what is really important in life. Marta, Cassia, Elias, Raouf, Amr and Mo, who have been here with me in Groningen for a long time, and many others who left the city, such as Nuria, Cosmin and Bego, and others who arrived later, such as Carmen and Giulia: without all of you, this would not have been possible. I am grateful for having met you, for having become your friend and for all the great moments we have shared together. During these years, among the working weeks and fun weekends in a country that used to be foreign to us, we have made each other grow and made Groningen feel like home to us. To all of you, and the rest of the Groningen family I have not mentioned, thank you.

A very special thank you to a very important friend from this Groningen family and someone who has been with me since the very beginning of this project, my partner, Joshua. During the good and not-that-good moments that led to finishing this book, including some self-doubt ones, his support and trust made me continue to pursue what I wanted. If it were not for all the pushes, support and trust he placed on me, I believe the writing of this thesis would have not been possible.

I am also very grateful to my university and hometown friends: Oriana, who, in fact, during our LLM studies together, planted in me the idea of pursuing a PhD; Cris and Rober, who, since we studied together in Santiago, have pushed me and trusted me to reach all the academic and professional objectives I aimed for; Laura, Lucía, Andrea, Ánxela and Paula, whose love and support I have unconditionally since we grew up together.

Finally, I am deeply thankful to my family, especially my mother, my father, my brother and my aunt. Without any doubt, it is thanks to their efforts and their love and care that I am here today. Gracias.

Contents

Chapter 1
Introduction

Private international law (PIL)[1] involves the question of which law applies to a legal relationship in cases that have connections with more than one legal order. For example, how is it determined which is the law applicable to a consumer contract with cross-border elements? The two main methods that have been used over the years to answer this type of question are the unilateral method and the multilateral method.[2] The former involves determining the spatial reach of a rule to determine its applicability, having as a starting point the norm itself. The multilateral method entails designating the applicable law, having as a starting point the legal relationship and assigning it to a particular legal order through objective connecting factors, regardless of whether the legal order designated is the law of the forum or a foreign law. The multilateral method has gained popularity in Europe since the late nineteenth century.[3] Nowadays, the conflict of laws system is characterised by the existence of a plurality of methods since after the 1960s, the exclusivity of the multilateral method was questioned, and the need for flexibility and adaptation to the social and legal reality of the time was demanded.[4] Still, the current conflict of laws

[1]The discipline of private international law is generally referred to as conflict of laws within common law jurisdictions (e.g. US, England etc.). While both terms are often used indistinctively, when the author refers along this book to 'conflict of laws rules' or 'conflict rules' she is specifically referring to the rules determining the applicable law.

[2]Siehr (2017) and Basedow (2017).

[3]The multilateral method had almost completely displaced the unilateral approach by the beginning of the twentieth century in Europe. It is shown, for example, in the deliberations of The Hague Conference on Private international law, which between 1893 and 1904 adopted seven international Conventions. During the preparatory works of the first sessions, the adoption and predominance of Savigny's conflict of laws multilateral approach became obvious (HCCH Publications, *Actes et documents de la Première à la Septième sesión (1952)). Doctrine, case law and codifications of PIL in Europe followed in its majority the multilateral method since the end of the nineteenth and beginning of the twentieth century.* Gutzwiller (1923, 1929), and Nolde (1936).

[4]González Campos (1996), pp. 5239–5242; Mayer (1985), p. 129; Audit (1984), p. 219.

M. Campo Comba, *The Law Applicable to Cross-border Contracts involving Weaker Parties in EU Private International Law*,
https://doi.org/10.1007/978-3-030-61481-2_1

system is mainly based on the multilateral approach, and it also includes the principle of freedom of choice of law by the parties, the doctrine of overriding mandatory rules and special conflict rules that provide special connecting factors for weaker contracting parties and protect them to a certain point from the risks of party autonomy.[5]

After the Treaty of Amsterdam (1999) and the Treaty of Lisbon (2009), Europeanisation of PIL has enormously intensified, and the numerous legislative acts enacted prove the importance acquired by PIL in the last two decades in the European Union (EU), contrasting with the opposite situation of the previous years. Regarding conflict of laws in contractual obligations, the first instrument unifying them was the 1980 Rome Convention on the law applicable to contractual obligations,[6] then replaced by the Rome I Regulation on the law applicable to contractual obligations,[7] which is now in force. However, while conflict of laws in contractual obligations is already regulated by the Rome I Regulation, including some special rules for consumer and employment contracts, some EU directives dealing with substantive matters include some rules that have implications for PIL and have a unilateral conflict of laws basis. The different approaches taken by the different conflict rules in these areas make the system incoherent. Should the EU directives provide for their own criteria of applicability in a unilateral manner, or are the current conflict rules sufficient and adequate?

In the context of the EU, there are intra-EU situations, within the Member States, and extra-EU cases, which involve elements from one or more non-Member States. EU law is concerned with whether rules might impose a restriction or disadvantages on the internal market, while PIL traditionally serves international legal transactions in a wider manner and not just in the intra-EU context.[8] The multilateral conflict of laws system was originally based on the equality of all legal systems.[9] It makes sense that when different legal systems share common legal values, or even common standards, like in the case of the EU Member States, conflict of laws rules should promote equality between these different national legal systems.[10] However, when legal systems do not share similar legal values and important interests are at stake, such as consumer or employee protection, the situation is different. In this context, the case where a French consumer contracts with a German business (intra-EU situation) can be considered different from a French consumer contracting with a Puerto Rican principal (extra-EU situation) as the latter situation faces the risk of

[5] Ten Wolde and Henckel (2012), pp. 12–26.

[6] Convention on the Law Applicable to Contractual Obligations of the 19 June 1980 [1980] OJ L266/1, consolidated version [1998] OJ C27/34.

[7] Regulation (EC) No 593/2008 of the European Parliament and of the Council of 17 June 2008 on the law applicable to contractual obligations (Rome I) [2008] OJ L177/6.

[8] However, since the entry into force of the Treaty of Amsterdam, which gave the EU the legislative competence regarding PIL, EU PIL also serves the EU purposes, and does not necessarily have to follow the same logic than traditional national PIL rules. González Beilfuss (2004), p. 118.

[9] Boele-Woelki et al. (1998), p. 205.

[10] See the 'scale of Ten Wolde' in Ten Wolde (2013), pp. 574–576.

non-application of European standards that normally—in its own market—would be applicable to a consumer in this case. Thus, conflict rules, when regulating these type of situations, should be consistent and alive to the different risks for the protected weaker parties and the correct functioning of the internal market. They should have as a purpose legal certainty and predictability of connection, respect the legitimate expectations of the parties, as well as find the appropriate solution to the particular situation.[11]

In this context, this book aims at analysing the coherence between EU PIL, in particular the Rome I Regulation on the law applicable to contractual obligations, and EU secondary law instruments harmonising conditions regarding consumer, employment and other weaker parties' contracts.

1.1 Research Questions

The primary focus of this book concerns the interaction between EU private international law (EU PIL)—specifically conflict of laws rules—and EU secondary law regarding weaker contracting parties. In the last years, the relationship between private international law (PIL) and European Union law (EU law) has received a significant amount of attention from scholars.[12] The rationale behind these two areas of law differs: while EU law is concerned with maintaining and developing an area of freedom, security and justice, for which the proper and effective functioning of the internal market is essential, PIL is, in principle, not concerned with EU law objectives or substantive aims.[13] Under the traditional PIL system in Europe, conflict rules generally focus on the centre of the legal relationship and, in the case of contractual relationships, generally designate the law most closely connected to the contract. That is, conflict rules will point to that law without giving decisive importance to the fact that it is the law of the forum, the law of a Member State or a foreign law.[14] Despite the different rationales, in order to achieve the EU objectives, EU PIL and EU law should be in harmony.

[11]Stone (2014), pp. 289, 290; Plender and Wilderspin (2015), p. 35; De Miguel Asensio (2005), pp. 82, 83.

[12]For example: Remien (2001), Francq (2005), Basedow (2006), Kuipers (2012), Kramer (2015) and Mathieu (2015).

[13]Kuipers (2012), pp. 10, 11. Title V of the TFEU is devoted to the area of freedom, security and justice, of which judicial cooperation in civil matters (article 81 TFEU) is an essential part.

[14]The traditional multilateral PIL approach is characterised by the neutral and rigid multilateral conflict rule that relates the abstract legal relationship to the law more closely connected. However, during the last third of the twentieth century, new adjustments in relation with material objectives—such as the protection of weaker contracting parties, among others—were included in order to adapt the traditional approach to the new needs and interests of the society and the state. Arenas García (2008), p. 88.

On the one hand, weaker party protection is essential for the EU internal market at both social and economic levels. The EU has enacted numerous secondary law instruments, principally directives, providing for substantive rules regarding consumer and employment contracts, as well as regarding other contracts involving weaker parties (insurance, agency etc.). On the other hand, conflict rules determine the law applicable to a legal relationship in a cross-border situation; in this case, they would determine the law applicable to a cross-border consumer contract or cross-border employment contract. If as a result of the operation of the conflict rules a non-EU law is applicable, the substantive protective rules of the EU directives are not applied. Therefore, both areas of law must be coordinated.

Thus, the main question of this research is whether EU conflict rules and EU secondary law are well coordinated regarding the protection of weaker contracting parties and, if not, how they could be in harmony with each other. As a result of this main enquiry, several other questions arise.

1. How Do Traditional Principles of Conflict of Laws Relate to the Requirements of the Internal Market for the Realisation of the EU Objectives Regarding the Protection of Weaker Parties Such as Employees, Consumers Etc.?

The modern European PIL system is mainly based on the Savignian multilateral conflict of laws approach, which consists in designating the applicable law through objective connecting factors based on the legal relationship, regardless of whether it is the law of the forum or a foreign law. The original Savignian model has been revised, methodological purity has been rejected and numerous criteria and principles have been added, such as the weaker party protection principle or the doctrine of overriding mandatory rules, but it is still the basis of our conflicts method in Europe.[15] The Rome I Regulation on the law applicable to contractual obligations, which is the unified EU PIL instrument containing conflict rules to determine the law applicable to contracts, is mainly based on the multilateral conflict of laws approach.

The influence of the Europeanisation process on PIL is relevant. With the Treaty of Amsterdam in 1999, the European Community acquired a comprehensive competence in the area of judicial cooperation in civil matters, including the adoption of several measures in order to promote compatibility of the rules applicable in the Member States in relation to conflict of laws and jurisdiction. A step further was taken with the Treaty of Lisbon, which in its Title IV, with the heading 'Area of Freedom, Security and Justice', allows the EU to act in the area of judicial cooperation in civil measures, *in particular, when necessary for the functioning of the internal market* (article 81 TFEU). EU PIL cannot be seen anymore as an area outside the European legal system, and regardless of the former tension between PIL and EU law, they should be in accordance with the same objectives, that is towards

[15] Ten Wolde and Henckel (2012), pp. 9–11.

market integration. The reason underlying the use of the current PIL method and its adequacy for both intra-EU and extra-EU situations shall be studied.[16]

Essential for the purposes of this book is the party autonomy principle in PIL, or freedom of choice of law. The principle of party autonomy is uncontested in the area of contractual obligations and is one of the cornerstones of the Rome I Regulation (recital 11 Rome I), but it is also acknowledged that the freedom of choice of law requires regulation, especially when it works to the detriment of one of the parties to the contract, like a consumer or an employee.[17] EU directives concerning contracts involving weaker parties mainly aim at protecting private interests; however, it is arguable that, in some cases and up to certain extent, public interests are also at stake (e.g. ensuring undistorted competition). The Rome I Regulation ensures the application of overriding mandatory provisions, which are those aimed at protecting public interests, regardless of the law applicable to the contract. This is the existent unilateral inroad in the multilateral system of the Rome I Regulation and the biggest limit to party autonomy. However, there is a large debate as to whether rules protecting weaker parties—including those deriving from EU directives—can fall under the definition of overriding mandatory rules, threatening the principle of party autonomy.[18]

2. When and How Should PIL Ensure the Applicability of EU Directives on Weaker Party Protection?

The introduction of a new body of law such as EU law brings back basic PIL questions, such as when an EU consumer or employment directive should be applicable in an international situation or whether the existent multilateral conflict rules are adequate to determine its applicability. Directives are not directly applicable but need to be implemented into the national law of the Member States. In the majority of the cases, directives are minimum harmonising directives, which means that they set minimum standards that Member States can choose to improve when implementing them into their national law. As a result, there is a minimum EU common standard set by the directive that all Member States respect, and still different standards among Member States, since they can improve the minimum. From an EU point of view, we can find intra-EU situations, where the situation is only connected with Member States, and extra-EU situations, where the situation is connected not only with the EU but also with some third country or countries.[19] It is in the latter situation where it should be determined when and how PIL should

[16]This topic is discussed in several occasions during this study, such as in Sect. 4.2 and Chap. 3, or Sect. 5.2, leading to a general discussion and conclusion in Chap. 7.

[17]Recital 11 Rome I recognises that '(t)he parties' freedom to choose the applicable law should be one of the cornerstones of the system of conflict-of-law rules in matters of contractual obligations'. Regarding party autonomy in the Rome I Regulation: Heiss (2009), Symeonides (2010), Maultzsch (2016) and Mills (2018).

[18]This topic will be object of discussion during this book, and it is specifically addressed in Sect. 3.3.1.

[19]Ten Wolde (2013), pp. 577–579; Kuipers (2012), p. 222.

ensure the international applicability of a specific directive. It is in this specific regard where EU law and PIL seem to not have reached an understanding. On the one hand, according to our current PIL understanding, the Rome I Regulation determines the law applicable to a contract in a cross-border situation; if this law is the law of a Member State, the protection of the relevant directive is applicable as implemented by the law of that Member State. On the other hand, some EU directives—specially the second generation of EU consumer directives—include a so-called scope rule that interferes with PIL. Scope rules generally provide for the application of the protection provided by the directive when the situation is closely connected with the EU. The technique used by these rules affects PIL because they seem to adhere to a unilateral PIL approach to determine the applicability of the directive by determining the applicability of the instrument without referring to foreign law, clashing with the multilateral nature of the Rome I Regulation. In addition, the existence of scope rules spread around directives disrupts the aim of unifying conflict of laws of the different Member States regarding contractual obligations in one instrument—the Rome I Regulation. Moreover, these rules refer to the application of the directive and not national law, but Member States have to implement these rules into their national legislation; the broad drafting of scope rules gives place to different interpretations when implementing these rules among the national laws of the Member States, adding more uncertainty to the situation.[20] Finally, not all directives contain scope rules, but some are silent about their applicability and others refer to the Rome I Regulation. While many PIL scholars defend the point of view that the application of the directives should depend on the operation of the Rome I Regulation, the fact that certain directives intend to cover a broader scope of application should be taken into account in considering whether the current drafting of the existent conflict rules needs to be more EU focused.

3. Are the Current EU PIL Conflict of Laws Rules and PIL Method Adequate to Ensure the EU Objectives Regarding Weaker Contracting Parties, or Is There a Call for a Different PIL Method?

Under a PIL multilateral approach, a consumer contract between a Dutch consumer and a German professional is not different from a consumer contract between a Dutch consumer and a Brazilian professional. However, from the point of view of EU law, the situations completely differ from each other: while in the first case the application of the EU standards is generally ensured, in the second case there is the possibility that the EU standards are not applied when the EU intended those standards to be applicable, thereby disrupting the smooth functioning of the internal market. The Rome I Regulation provides for mechanisms on weaker party protection, especially regarding consumer and employment contracts, which are governed by special provisions. However, they are considered insufficient in some cases to ensure the applicability of EU mandatory provisions contained in directives. While the doctrine of overriding mandatory rules has been defended for those cases, it is

[20] The problematic around the existence of scope rules in directives is discussed in detail in the context of EU consumer directives in Sect. 4.1.

questionable and dangerous to generalise the use of overriding mandatory rules as a mechanism to ensure the application of provisions deriving from EU directives protecting weaker parties. Such general use would jeopardise the current PIL system. A balance and mutual understanding between all the interests and principles involved, both from PIL and EU law, is necessary, taking into account the PIL values, the need of protection of weaker contracting parties and the special needs of the internal market. In this regard, it has to be pointed out that regarding the PIL method, methodological purity (i.e. purely multilateral method or unilateral method) is not realistic nor desirable; no contemporary PIL system is purely multilateral or purely unilateral.[21]

1.2 Structure of the Book

In order to answer the aforementioned questions, this book is divided into seven chapters.

The first chapter, which is the current chapter, introduces the research topic and research questions, addressing the objective and importance of this research.

The second chapter includes an analysis of the rationale behind weaker party protection in EU PIL. First, it is necessary to identify which are those referred to as 'weaker contracting parties' in the context of PIL and then explain why they need special protection in substantive law and PIL. Special focus is put on consumers and employees as the traditional structural weaker contracting parties both in this chapter and in the rest of the book. While EU PIL also contains special rules for insurance policyholders and, to a certain extent, passengers, these parties will be mentioned within the category of 'other weaker parties in a contract', together with other possible weaker parties (agents, franchisees etc.). Both consumers and employees are paradigmatic weaker parties in a contract, are protected by similar conflict rules and have a similar interaction with EU directives. In the meantime, insurance policyholders are not always a weaker party in an insurance contract, and the conflict rules that were previously scattered among the insurance directives are now superseded by one provision in the Rome I Regulation on the law applicable to contractual obligations. There is also a new provision protecting passengers based on the wish to protect them as consumers, but the position of the commercial carrier is respected and plays a big role in it, limiting its protective effect. Thus, although these other weaker parties will be mentioned throughout the book and analysed in Chap. 6, the main focus of the book is on consumer and employment laws, which are essential areas for the EU and its internal market, at both economic and social levels.

Chapter 2 will also contain a discussion regarding why ordinary traditional conflict rules do not respond to the specialities of consumer contracts and individual employment contracts. In this regard, the importance of the principle of party

[21] Symeonides (2005), pp. 433–434.

autonomy will be highlighted, as well as the need to limit such a principle in order to prevent a possible abuse by 'stronger' counterparties. The need for special connecting factors in conflict rules dealing with these special contracts is also explained. In addition, a comparison of the existing possible mechanisms of protection of weaker parties in PIL is conducted, discussing the different manners legal systems have in order to deal with party autonomy and special connecting factors regarding weaker contracting parties. Finally, the role of the EU regarding consumer and employee protection is studied to the extent that it affects the current EU PIL rules.

The third chapter focuses on the Rome I Regulation on the law applicable to contractual obligations and its mechanisms of protection of consumers and employees. The provisions that determine the law applicable to consumer contracts (article 6 Rome I) and employment contracts (article 8 Rome I) are objects of analysis, as well as the relevant case law. Moreover, the mechanism of overriding mandatory rules (article 9 Rome I) is examined. Relevant questions such as whether overriding mandatory rules can be used as a mechanism of protection of weaker contracting parties or whether, as a result, the rules deriving from the EU consumer and employment directives can be considered as having overriding mandatory character will be analysed. In addition, art. 3(4) Rome I, which ensures the application of EU mandatory law when all the relevant elements of the situation are located within the EU and parties have chosen a non-EU law as applicable, will also be object of study.

The fourth chapter deals with the relationship and coordination between the EU consumer directives and the Rome I Regulation. In order to do that, the existent inconsistencies and gaps regarding the interaction between EU consumer directives and the Rome I Regulation are described. Then intra-EU conflicts of laws between Member States in relation to the implementation of the EU consumer directives are discussed, to later focus on EU consumer directives and extra-EU conflicts of law, especially referring to the international scope of the EU consumer directives in PIL terms. This chapter aims at answering how to achieve better consumer protection in the EU while respecting PIL values. The available PIL methods and their convenience are discussed.

Similarly, the fifth chapter focuses on the relationship and coordination between the EU employment directives and the Rome I Regulation. A similar analysis to the previous chapter regarding the scope of application of the directives in the context of the current EU PIL is conducted. This chapter will focus on the Acquired Rights Directive, which contains a 'scope rule' similarly to some of the EU consumer directives. In addition, it will deal with the law applicable to employment contracts in the context of a temporary posting of workers. The Posted Workers Directive will be analysed, in relation to which overriding mandatory provisions play an important role. Again, the available PIL methods and their convenience are discussed.

The sixth chapter examines what the situation is regarding other weaker contracting parties and the Rome I Regulation. To a lesser extent than with regard to consumers and employees, EU PIL, and specifically the Rome I Regulation, extends the protection to passengers and some insurance policyholders. In addition, other contractual parties can often have a weaker contracting position in their contract (such as franchisees, distributors or commercial agents). This chapter aims to analyse the interaction between special (and less protective) conflict rules and general conflict rules of the Rome I Regulation with the EU secondary law instruments that contain mandatory provisions protecting weaker parties other than consumers and employees.

Finally, the seventh chapter includes the reflexions and conclusions resulting from this research.

References

Arenas García R (2008) El Derecho Internacional Privado (DIPr) y el Estado en la Era de la Globalización: la vuelta a los orígenes. Cursos de derecho internacional y relaciones internacionales de Vitoria-Gasteiz:19–94

Audit B (1984) Le Caractère Fonctionnel de la Règle de Conflit. Collected Courses Hague Acad Int Law 186:223–397

Basedow J (2006) European private international law of obligations and internal market legislation-a matter of coordination. In: Erauw J et al (eds) Liber Memorialis Peter Sarcevic-universalism, tradition and the individual. Sellier, European Law Publishers, München:13–24

Basedow J (2017) Private international law, methods of. In: Basedow J et al (eds) Encyclopedia of private international law. Edward Elgar Publishing, Cheltenham, pp 1402–1407

Boele-Woelki K et al (1998) Dutch private international law at the end of the 20th century: pluralism of methods. Netherlands reports to the fifteenth international congress of comparative law (Conference report), pp 203–227

De Miguel Asensio P (2005) Conflictos de Leyes e Integración Jurídica: Estados Unidos y Unión Europea. Anuario Español de Derecho Internacional Privado 5:43–102

Francq S (2005) L'Applicabilité du Droit Communautaire Dérivé au Regard des Méthodes du Droit International Privé. LGDJ, Paris

González Beilfuss C (2004) Relaciones e Interacciones entre Derecho Comunitario, Derecho Internacional Privado y Derecho de Familia Europeo en la Construcción de un Espacio Judicial Común. Anuario Español de Derecho Internacional Privado 4:117–186

González Campos J (1996) El Paradigma de la Norma de Conflicto Multilateral. In: Estudios Jurídicos en Homenaje al Profesor Aurelio Menéndez. Civitas, Madrid, pp 5239–5270

Gutzwiller M (1923) Der Einfluss Savignys auf die Entwicklung des Internationalprivatrechts. Kommissionsverlag : Universitäts-buchh. Gschwend, Tschopp & Co, Freiburg

Gutzwiller M (1929) Le Développement Historique du Droit International Privé. Collected Courses Hague Acad Int Law 29:287–400

Heiss H (2009) Party autonomy. In: Ferrari F, Leible S (eds) Rome I regulation: the law applicable to contractual obligations in Europe. Sellier, European Law Publishers, München, pp 7–16

Kramer XE (2015) The interaction between Rome I and mandatory EU private rules- EPIL and EPL: communicating vessels? In: Stone P, Farah Y (eds) Research handbook on EU private international law. Edward Elgar Publishing, Cheltenham, pp 248–284

Kuipers J-J (2012) EU law and private international law: the interrelationship in contractual obligations. Martinus Nijhoff Publishers, Leiden

Mathieu B (2015) Directives Européennes et Conflits de Lois. LGDJ, Issy-les-Moulineaux

Maultzsch F (2016) Party autonomy in European private international law: uniform principle or context-dependent instrument? J Priv Int Law 12:466–491

Mayer P (1985) Le Mouvement des Idées dans le Droit des Conflits de Lois. Droits 2:129–143

Mills A (2018) Party Autonomy in Private International Law. Cambridge University Press, Cambridge

Nolde B (1936) La Codification du Droit International Privé. Collected Courses Hague Acad Int Law 55:299–432

Plender R, Wilderspin M (2015) The European private international law of obligations, 4th edn. Sweet & Maxwell, London

Remien O (2001) European private international law, the European community and its emerging area of freedom, security and justice. Common Market Law Rev 38:53–86

Siehr K (2017) Private international law, history of. In: Basedow J et al (eds) Encyclopedia of private international law. Edward Elgar Publishing, Cheltenham, pp 1391–1401

Stone P (2014) EU private international law, 3rd edn. Edward Elgar Publishing, Cheltenham

Symeonides SC (2005) Accommodative unilateralism as a starting premise in choice of law. In: Rasmussen-Bonne H et al (eds) Balancing of interests: Liber Amicorum Peter Hay. Verlag Recht und Wirtschaft GmbH, Frankfurt am main, pp 417–434

Symeonides SC (2010) Party autonomy in Rome I and Rome II from a comparative perspective. In: Boele-Woelki K et al (eds) Convergence and divergence in private international law- Liber Amicorum Kurt Siehr. Eleven International Publishing, The Hague, pp 513–550

Ten Wolde MH (2013) The relativity of legal positions in cross-border situations: the foundations of private interregional law, private intra-community law and private international law. In: A commitment to private international law – essays in honour of Hans van Loon. Intersentia, Cambridge

Ten Wolde MH, Henckel KC (2012) European private international law- a comparative perspective on contracts, torts and corporations. Hephaestus Publishers, Groningen

Chapter 2
The Rationale Behind the Protection of Weaker Contracting Parties in EU PIL

Modern PIL instruments generally contain a special regulatory regime applying to weaker contracting parties, specifically for consumers and employees, which are generally seen as the typical structural weaker parties in a contract. These special PIL rules are more favourable to the interests of consumers and employees than to those of their counterparties.

The history of weaker party protection in PIL can be described as short and easy in comparison with the lengthy and complicated history of PIL in general. In fact, the special PIL rules are a reflection of the existing legal framework in national substantive law that has been adapted to ensure that any advantage of the contracting party with the strong position in the contract will remain without effect.[1] Substantive national laws only started to introduce special weaker party rules in the last century.[2] The state started to increasingly intervene in certain areas limiting party autonomy based on several reasons. The main reason, although not the only one, consisted in correcting the imbalance of contracts containing weaker parties.[3] Since most of the special substantive law on weaker party protection constitutes mandatory law, PIL rules also need to be adjusted in order to avoid their circumvention. But who are these weaker parties in need of such a special protection? Why are they considered to be in a weaker position than their contractual counterparty?

---

[1] Rühl (2011), Grusic (2015), pp. 17–55.

[2] After the Second World War and the subsequent economic growth, the necessity of protection of the consumer started to become evident. Companies were growing in length and complexity, together with the offer of goods and services to consumers. The speech of President Kennedy on 15 March 1962, where he actually points out the need for the protection of consumers in the market, is iconic in this regard. This consumer protection ideology would have its reflection in Europe in the 1970s. Arenas García (1996), p. 41.

[3] The intervention of the state in private relationships between individuals is based on a plurality of reasons or criteria and economic or political interests, going beyond the solely protection of the weaker party. Pocar (1984), p. 352, 353.

M. Campo Comba, *The Law Applicable to Cross-border Contracts involving Weaker Parties in EU Private International Law*,
https://doi.org/10.1007/978-3-030-61481-2_2

Both national law of the Member States and EU law provide for mandatory rules on weaker party protection. In addition to the substantive national law regarding consumer and employment contracts that Member States have developed since the twentieth century, the EU has enacted numerous legal instruments in that regard. Thus, the EU has developed its own consumer and employment policy, which is implemented into the legal framework of the Member States.[4] Consumer contract law, at both the domestic and EU levels, has been developed in an incremental manner, until the point that it has become an increasingly dense and intricate body of law in which cross-border consumer contracts are the more complex part. In the area of EU PIL, the fundamental problem of inconsistency of the EU consumer acquis with the conflict rules of the Rome I Regulation remains to be solved. The European Commission has made numerous efforts to make the European consumer acquis more coherent. Specifically, the European Commission has been especially active regarding the harmonisation of consumer law: there are over 90 EU directives dealing with consumer protection matters. Since the majority of the directives are of a minimum harmonising nature, several calls of the European Parliament in favour of a European Civil Code incited an animated academic debate. The discussion over unification or full harmonisation of EU contract law or, in other cases, of EU consumer law has been intense, and the literature over it is extensive.[5] The role of PIL would be seriously reduced if unification of substantive law would happen. However, apart from the unlikeliness of this situation, PIL would still be necessary in extra-EU situations. In fact, it will be argued in this chapter that EU PIL rules are at least as adequate as unified substantive law is in order to regulate cross-border consumer contracts in the EU.

The situation regarding employment law differs in the sense that Member States are more reluctant to confer legislative freedom on the EU because of the wide diversity of regulatory techniques and objectives relating to employment issues in the different countries.[6] Thus, some important areas of employment are left to domestic law, such as protection against unfair dismissal, and other areas are directly outside the competence of the EU, such as payment, right of association or right to strike.[7] Leaving aside the areas of fundamental rights, fundamental freedoms and

[4]The legal basis of EU consumer policy is found in Articles 4(2)(f), 12, 114 and 169 of the Treaty on the Functioning of the European Union (TFEU) and Article 38 of the Charter of Fundamental Rights of the European Union. Article 114 TFEU is the legal basis for harmonisation measures aimed at establishing the internal market. Regarding EU social and employment policy, the legal basis is found in Article 3 of the Treaty on European Union (TEU) and Articles 9, 10, 19, 45–48, 145–150 and 151–161 of the Treaty on the Functioning of the European Union (TFEU).

[5]For example: Collins (2008), Micklitz (2009), Boele-Woelki (2010), Twigg-Flesner (2012), Weatherill (2013), Halson and Campbell (2013), Twigg-Flesner (2016).

[6]The existent legal diversity is due to the unique social, political economic and cultural roots of the Member States. For example, while in the Nordic countries most of the important areas are regulated by collective bargaining, France or Spain have comprehensive regulations regarding employment issues, besides collective bargaining. Grusic (2015), p. 3, 4.

[7]Riesenhuber (2012), p. 26, 27.

equality, EU employment law is mostly laid down in secondary legislation, especially in directives, which, besides having a minimum harmonisation approach, do not cover all areas of employment law. Still, overall, EU employment law is considered as a 'coherent whole' since it does cover large areas of regulatory employment law.[8]

EU PIL needs to respond to the necessities of both these weaker parties and the EU internal market in that regard. Are ordinary traditional conflict rules able to respond to the specialities of contracts involving weaker parties? Party autonomy is one of the cornerstones of EU PIL regarding contractual obligations.[9] As the stronger party, a company or an employer would be able to introduce in the consumer contract or individual employment contract a choice of law clause unilaterally. This clause might indicate a law with a low standard of protection for consumers or employees. Weaker contracting parties need some mechanism of protection against the threats that party autonomy brings.[10] The law applicable in the absence of choice should neither be determined by the general connecting factors, but adequate and protective connecting factors need to be designated. Around the globe, we find different PIL mechanisms that offer protection to weaker contracting parties, ranging from a complete prohibition of party autonomy to a more flexible approach, like providing for a more protective law, as well as a variety of connecting factors in the absence of choice of law. Which mechanism seems to respond better to the necessities of these special contracts?

In this context, this chapter will, first, identify which are the contracting parties that are considered weaker in EU PIL. It will be analysed why consumers and employees are in need of special protection in substantive law and PIL. A definition of what is understood by consumers and employees in need of special protection in EU PIL will be given. Also, other weaker parties and other possible weaker parties are identified and defined.

Second, it will be argued why ordinary traditional conflict rules do not respond to the specialities of consumer contracts or individual employment contracts. Party autonomy is a well-established principle in EU PIL according to which parties are free to choose the law applicable to their contract. Freedom of choice of law brings numerous advantages to the contractual relationship. However, when one of the parties to the contract is in a clear weaker contracting position, such as consumers and employees, party autonomy needs to be limited. In addition, it will also be explained that when parties have not chosen the law applicable to their contractual relationship, the regular connecting factors are not completely adequate in relation to consumer and employment contracts.

---

[8]Ibid., p. 26.

[9]Recital 11 Rome I Regulation states that '[t]he parties' freedom to choose the applicable law should be one of the cornerstones of the system of conflict-of-law rules in matters of contractual obligations'.

[10]On the limits to party autonomy in choice of law: Mills (2018), pp. 455–490. Also, regarding the specific limits to party autonomy for the protection of weaker contracting parties in the Rome I Regulation, see Chap. 3 of this Book.

Third, the role of the EU regarding consumer and employee protection will be analysed to the extent that it affects the EU PIL rules. An overview of the EU policies and strategies concerning consumer and employee protection will be given, as well as a summary of the development of the EU legislation and competences in that respect. The specialty of EU PIL rules on consumer and employment contracts lies in the fact that, besides ensuring compliance with certain mandatory rules of the Member State in question, they also need to adapt to the EU necessities. Most EU legislation on consumer and employment contracts is laid down in EU directives that have a minimum harmonising nature, which means that Member States have to transpose the minimum protection standard required by the specific directive but can also improve that standard. As a result, the rules and the protection standard differ from one Member State to another. At the same time, there is a minimum EU protection standard versus a potentially lower standard by a third country. Therefore, EU PIL rules need to be aware of the EU consumer and employment strategies and substantive legislation. On the other hand, this chapter will also make reference to the debate regarding the unification of EU contract law and will defend unified and coherent EU PIL rules as a better alternative.

Finally, this chapter will analyse the different mechanisms for the protection of consumers and employees in PIL existent in different jurisdictions around the world. That is, it has been submitted that party autonomy needs to be limited, but how and to which extent? Not all jurisdictions use the same mechanism. In the same way, the different existing protective conflict rules dealing with the law applicable in the absence of choice of law in consumer and employment contracts will also be the object of analysis. The advantages and disadvantages of the existing mechanisms will be described in order to ascertain which ones can be considered more adequate for the protection of weaker contracting parties in PIL.

2.1 Identification of Weaker Contracting Parties in EU PIL

The EU PIL instruments relating to contracts in civil and commercial matters (i.e. Brussels I bis Regulation,[11] regarding jurisdiction and recognition and enforcement, and Rome I Regulation,[12] regarding the applicable law) provide for specific rules for special categories of contracts involving presumably weaker parties. Section 4 (Articles 17–19) of the Brussels I Regulation, regarding jurisdiction and enforcement, and Article 6 Rome I Regulation, regarding the law applicable, contain special rules concerning consumer contracts, having as a principal objective the

[11]Regulation (EU) No 1215/2012 of the European Parliament and of the Council of 12 December 2012 on jurisdiction and the recognition and enforcement of judgments in civil and commercial matters (OJ L 351/1).

[12]Regulation *(EC)* No 593/2008 of the European Parliament and of the Council of 17 June 2008 on the law applicable to contractual obligations (*Rome I*) (OJ L 177/6).

protection of the consumer in cross-border situations. In the same manner, Section 5 Brussels I bis Regulation (Articles 20–23) and Article 8 Rome I Regulation contain specific rules referring to individual employment contracts, with the main aim of protecting the employee as the weaker party of the contract.

Consumers and employees are regarded as the paradigmatic example of a weaker party in a contract. The information asymmetries between the parties to the contract and the economic or social dependence of the weaker party towards his or her counterparty are the characteristic reasons that justify the mandatory character of the substantive consumer and employment law of the Member States and also at EU level. EU PIL ensures that the application of mandatory consumer or employment law is not circumvented due to the stronger contractual position of the professional or the employer.

EU PIL instruments also contain special rules regarding insurance contracts and contracts of carriage. The protection is extended to passengers and some insurance policyholders, although to a lesser extent. Moreover, it is also possible to identify some contracting parties that could be regarded in some cases as having a weaker bargaining position in a contract but do not enjoy special protection under the EU PIL rules. This can be the case of franchisees, distributors, commercial agents and even some small businesses.[13] However, this study is principally focused on consumer and individual employment contracts since consumers and employees are evident weaker parties in need of substantive and PIL rules ensuring their rights.

Below, an overview of the rationale behind the need for protection of consumers and employees will be given, as well as a general definition of consumer and employee in EU PIL terms and a reference to other possible weaker parties.

2.1.1 The Necessity of Protection of Consumers

2.1.1.1 Rationale Behind Consumer Protection

Consumer protection policies and consumer rights are nowadays established in most of the contract law of countries around the world. The concept of consumer protection became generalised in the second half of the twentieth century as a necessary limit to freedom of contract, and it was recognised in the majority of national laws. In the majority of Western and Nordic European countries, the concept of 'welfare state' became popular in the 1960s and 1970s and led to an interventionist approach concerning consumer protection. The interests of

[13]Generally, commercial parties are more reluctant to be considered as having a weaker position in the market because of the fact of being commercial, and often lack special legal protection. A paradigmatic example is, in the context of carriage of goods by sea, the existence of obvious bargaining disparities between ship owners and carriers, which have the majority of bargaining power, and, on the other hand, cargo owners and receivers, which are in need of special protection despite being commercial parties. In this regard: Salmerón Hernríquez (2016).

consumers were considered as necessary to achieve satisfactory market conditions.[14] In general, consumers are seen as vulnerable market participants that need to be protected against the market forces, and although this approach might differ between European countries (e.g. France traditionally with a more paternalistic approach vs. the Netherlands with a more free market approach), they all agree on the necessity of consumer protection and the need to correct the imbalance between professionals and consumers in the market.[15] For example, the former different treatment of protection from standard contract terms in consumer contracts among Member States illustrates the very different approaches existent before the drafting of a uniform EU legislation (Unfair Contract Terms Directive).[16] This is also a paradigmatic example of the need for consumer protection. When the European countries started to recognise the need for consumer protection and the necessity of controlling standard contract terms in the 1970s, legislation and practices differed very much among them.[17] Besides different legislative techniques, one of the main discussions concerned the scope of application of the control over unfair contract terms: in general, some countries deemed that all contracts between consumers and professionals should be the object of control, while others considered that all the contracts containing standard contract terms should be the object of control.[18] While the first ones focused on the concept of consumer, the second ones had to focus on the concept of standard contract terms.[19] The debate consisted on which scope of application is adequate to the legislative control. The control of standard contract terms or potential unfair contract terms constitutes a limitation to freedom of contract, which is essential, and thus the legislative control has to be proportionate and justifiable.[20] Freedom of contract is based on free and voluntary consent. If a contract clause is standard and not negotiated, the consumer is not freely giving its

[14]For example, in Germany, the reform in 1965 of the UWG (German Unfair Competition Act) already introduced the right to bring an action to court to consumer organisations, becoming the pillar of German consumer law together with the AGBG (Standard Contract Terms Act) of 1976. The Netherlands, from the 1970s onwards, actively enacted several laws and regulations aiming at consumer protection, such as the introduction of misleading advertisement in the Dutch Civil Code, and by the 1980s most rules on consumer rights (e.g. consumer sales, standard contract terms, consumer credit etc.) were recognised in the Dutch legislation. Since the end of the 1980s, it would be European legislation that would promote the adoption of consumer legislation in the different Member States as transposition of EC directives. For an explanation on the early national developments of consumer law in Western Europe, see Cseres (2005), pp. 158–170; Haupt (2004).

[15]Cseres (2005), p. 170.

[16]Council Directive 93/13/EEC of 5 April 1993 on unfair terms in consumer contracts (OJ 1993 L 95/29).

[17]A comparative analysis of the different pieces of legislation and the practices of the Member States and several other European states before the implementation of the Unfair Contract Terms Directive is found in Hondius (1987).

[18]Águila-Real (1998), p. 54.

[19]Ibid., p. 54.

[20]Ibid., p. 56.

consent. Voluntary consent is a necessary part of freedom of contract. A consumer is not expected to read the small letter of the contract.[21]

In consumer law, the national legislator seeks to protect consumers from an abuse of the freedom of contract resulting from the inequality in bargaining power between the consumer and the professional. In order to do that, substantive consumer rights are reflected in mandatory consumer contract regulations. Consumer law consists of mandatory rules that guarantee that the contracting parties will not circumvent the legislative rules to the detriment of the consumer, the obligation of information disclosure, measures regarding the safety and quality controls of goods and services, indebtedness, dispute resolution etc.[22] In a cross-border situation, those consumer rights also need to be protected, and that is why the concept of consumer protection is also present in PIL.

Why are consumers considered 'weaker' than their counterparty? Traditionally, a weaker position is explained by the lesser bargaining power of the consumer, who is in an inferior position to defend his or her interests against the professional. The disparities are found in the relationship between the consumer and professional when it comes to bargaining power, knowledge/information and resources.[23] Consumers know less about contracts and about the products and their quality than the professionals do, and therefore they find themselves in a weaker bargaining position. Information asymmetries consist of the impossibility or difficulty of acquiring relevant information for the transaction, and in the case of consumers, difficulty to assess the conditions and quality of the products or services before the conclusion of the contract. In addition, consumers do not have the economic capacity to individually asses every contract they enter into.[24]

Moreover, when talking about cross-border transactions, the consumer might be in more need of protection than in domestic cases since the language, the other party or the rules might be foreign to the consumer.[25] Regarding the latter, there are costs related to the legal fragmentation in international transactions, that is costs associated to the fact that different legal systems are involved. While entering into transactions in an international market brings many benefits and possibilities to consumers in comparison with their national market, being able to have more opportunities to find the most satisfactory options for themselves, it also brings 'risks of internationality', as Garcimartín refers to (*riesgos de internacionalidad*).[26] A party to an international

[21]Besides that, even in the case contract terms were negotiated individually, it does not guarantee that the consumer has the sufficient knowledge of the market and of the possible terms. This is, individual negotiation of a contract would not ensure consumer protection neither, but only a transparent market would. Thus, the consumer does not need protection only against unfair terms, but also against other possible inequalities. Ibid., p. 58, 59.

[22]Cseres (2005), p. 156.

[23]United Nations Conference on Trade and Development (UNCTAD) (2016) Manual on Consumer Protection, p. 2.

[24]Rühl (2011), pp. 572–573.

[25]Devenney and Kenny (2012), p. 239.

[26]Garcimartín Alférez (2002), p. 128, 131.

transaction does not have the security that the rights deriving from its own legal system are the same as the ones deriving from other foreign legal systems or the security that the rights derived from a legal system can be recognised and implemented in others. The risks involve having to go to a foreign country to start legal proceedings, to obtain evidence, to ask for the recognition or enforcement of a decision or to gather information and adapt the conduct to a foreign law. These risks have to be assumed by one of the parties to a cross-border contract.[27] PIL normally allocates the costs derived from these risks to one of the parties. In the case of consumer contracts, when the risks of internationality are created by a foreign professional when approaching the consumer in the consumer's country, those risks and costs should be borne by the professional.[28]

In order to achieve economic efficiency in the market, professionals should engage in fair competition, provide consumers with information about the products, ensure quality and safety standards and offer compensation to consumers if problems arise. At the same time, consumers should act reasonably and acquire products with the quality required and at the best price, be well informed about those products or services and be aware of the remedies available.[29] Nevertheless, this is not the case in practice. On the professional's side, they will do what is better for their business, even though sometimes that requires some abuse toward their weaker counterparty. On the consumer's side, although it is normally expected that the consumer has given preferences and makes rational choices, it is not expected that a consumer will review standard contract terms or fully understand them. Moreover, consumer behaviour is complex, and while the traditional approach is the rational choice model, on which economics and law have based their theories on consumer protection for many years, a more psychological-based approach has been introduced in the last years which deviates from the standard economic theory and introduces the notions of bounded rationality, bounded willpower and bounded self-interest.[30] In general, the rational choice model presumes that individuals act in a manner that benefits and maximises their own welfare, and therefore they compare the costs and benefits of an action before taking a decision, they look for the necessary information, they are able to process and understand such information and, finally, they have stable preferences.[31] However, it has been shown in several studies that consumers' behaviour is often not rational and factors such as emotions, overconfidence or the context itself might have an influence and make the behaviour of the consumer 'irrational'.[32] Therefore, it is argued that consumers are in need of protection not only because of their lack of information but also because there are cases in which

[27]Ibid., pp. 131–133.

[28]Ibid., p. 144, 147.

[29]United Nations Conference on Trade and Development (UNCTAD) (2016) Manual on Consumer Protection, pp. 2–4.

[30]Schüller (2012), pp. 129–142.

[31]Rühl (2011), p. 582.

[32]Schüller (2012), pp. 129–142.

they do not act rationally, and it would be irrational to act rationally (e.g. reading the terms and conditions before every purchase).

In addition to the objective of economic efficiency in the market, consumer protection measures, when achieving bargaining equality between consumers and professionals, contribute to social justice. In a contemporary society, consumer rights are part of the social rights that individuals are entitled to.[33]

Regarding consumer transactions in PIL, the weaker position of the consumer is evidenced in view of the law applicable to the consumer contract. While professionals are normally aware of which law will benefit them, consumers do not know which law the professional wishes to apply. Professionals will invest in gathering information regarding the expected benefits of the application of certain law, while consumers will know about the quality of the law only after the problems occur, after the conclusion of the contract.[34] It might be of little use protecting the consumer with national (or EU) substantive law if a professional can, by inserting a jurisdiction or choice of law clause, escape the application of such protective provisions of the consumer's law.

The traditional PIL method, the multilateral method proposed by Savigny, rests on value-free connecting factors: the conflict rule designates the law of a particular country where the legal relationship should be localised through objective (value-free) connecting factors, regardless of the interests of the parties, the difference in power balance of the parties or the substantive value of the law designated.[35] This method, contrarily to the situation in Europe, was never a complete success in the US.[36] In the US, since the 1950s, promoting justice and defending substantive

[33]United Nations Conference on Trade and Development (UNCTAD) (2016) Manual on Consumer Protection, p. 2, 3.

[34]Rühl (2011), p. 574.

[35]Friedrich Carl von Savigny played a definitive role in the development of private international law in the European continent. The German jurist made his great contribution to the subject in the eighth and last volume of *System des heutigen Römischen Rechts* (System of Modern Roman Law) in 1849 (von Savigny 1849). The eighth volume (Berlin, 1849) of *System des Heutigen Römischen Rechts* constitutes a treatise on the conflict of laws in itself. An English translation is found in von Savigny (1869).

[36]From the nineteenth to the mid-twentieth centuries, the theoretical foundations of the conflict of laws system in the US were principally laid down by the conflict of laws theories of Joseph Story (1779–1845) and Joseph H. Beale (1861–1943). As a really general overview, Joseph Story followed Ulrich Huber's axioms and the notion of comity, although he also accepted alternative conflict methods (Story 1846). On the other hand, Joseph Beale rejected the notion of comity and substituted it with the vested rights theory (Beale 1935). It has to be noticed that while Story laid down the broad basis of the traditional American conflict of laws, it was Beale who created an actual conflict of laws system. Beale considered that conflict of laws should be founded in two principles: territoriality and vested rights. He claimed that all laws were territorial and admitted very few exceptions to that, and to justify the application of foreign law, he defended that the forum would acknowledge the fact that a right was created by foreign law and then recognise that right under the forum law. The main criticisms of this theory were that it gave no discretion at all to the judge to refuse the application of foreign law, while with Story's theory the opposite happened, and it sometimes led to the application of a law of a state that had a really vague contact with the case.

policies have become the aim of conflict rules. The so-called conflict of laws revolution changed the previous approach in the US.[37] However, it did not contain specific reference to consumer protection as such. They were the European countries that took the lead in considering consumer protection in PIL.[38] Although there was no clear event such as conflict of laws revolution in Europe, the growth of the consumer society and the development of the protection of human rights after the war had also its reflection in PIL. Since the 1960s, the law has started to pay special attention to regulating and protecting the rights of the consumer, and gradually consumer law became a separate area from other areas of commercial law, which led to having separate PIL rules for this area as well.[39] The first EU PIL instrument, the 1968 Brussels Convention on jurisdiction and the enforcement of judgments in civil and commercial matters,[40] did not originally contain any special jurisdiction rule concerning consumer contracts. In the first version of the Convention in 1968, Section 4 referred to 'jurisdiction in matters related to instalment sales and loans'. It was not until the reform of the Convention in 1978[41] when Section 4 became 'Jurisdiction over consumer contracts' and introduced special jurisdiction rules for consumer contracts. Thus, it can be seen that by the time the Brussels Convention was drafted, countries did not yet conceive special jurisdiction rules for consumer

---

Besides the criticisms that these systems received, the First Restatement in 1933, which took Beale's rationalisation, was further criticised as rigid, and eventually not only authors but even judges departed from the traditional system, giving place to the movement known as the American conflict of laws revolution. Symeonides (2016), pp. 54–57, 94, 95; Juenger (1993), pp. 29–31; Nadelmann (1961).

[37]One of the main authors of the modern American conflict of laws approaches was Professor Brainerd Currie (1913–1965) and his governmental interest analysis (Currie 1963). He considered that a conflict of laws should be solved on the basis of whether the states involved would have an interest in applying their law to the dispute or, in other words, whether these states have a 'governmental interest' in the outcome of the case. In order to ascertain that interest, it would be necessary to examine the content of the substantive law and then determine whether, according to the purpose of the rules, there is a wish for that law to be applicable. Currie proposed a modern version of the unilateral method in which he determined the applicable law by defining the spatial reach of the substantive laws, like the statutists, but unlike them, he considered that this should be done through an ad hoc judicial interpretation of the purposes and policies underlying these rules to discern the interest in its applicability, rather than classifying the laws as personal or real. The concept of state interests became popular among most of the modern conflict of laws theories in the US, and both doctrine and judicial authorities recognised this notion. As a result, most of the approaches developed in the US followed, at least in part, a unilateral approach (although note that the Restatement (Second) of Conflict of Laws (1971) contains a combination of both multilateral and unilateral approaches). Symeonides (2015).

[38]Tang (2009), p. 5.

[39]Ibid., p. 5.

[40]1968 Brussels Convention on jurisdiction and the enforcement of judgments in civil and commercial matters [OJ (1972) L 299/32].

[41]Council Convention on the accession of the Kingdom of Denmark, Ireland and the United Kingdom of Great Britain and Northern Ireland to the Convention on jurisdiction and the enforcement of judgments in civil and commercial matters and to the Protocol on its interpretation by the Court of Justice (Signed on 9 October 1978) (78/884/EEC).

contracts, but they already included specific regulations regarding specific special areas, such as instalment sales, where the buyer was perceived as being in a weaker position.[42] Regarding special rules on the applicable law, the firs conflict rules on consumer contracts were enacted in the 1970s: Section 41 of the Austrian Act on Private International Law[43] and Article 5 of the 1980 Convention on the Law Applicable to Contractual Obligations (Rome Convention)[44] included a separate provision regarding applicable law for consumer contracts.[45] Other national codifications around Europe soon followed them (e.g. in the 1980s, Article 120 of the new

[42]Arenas García (1996), p. 41, 42.

[43]Gesetz über das internationale Privatrecht – IPR-Gesetz [Federal Act on Private International Law] of 15 June 1978, BGBl. No 304/1978: *§ 41. (1) Verträge, bei denen das Recht des Staates, in dem eine Partei ihren gewöhnlichen Aufenthalt hat, dieser als Verbraucher besonderen privatrechtlichen Schutz gewährt, sind nach diesem Recht zu beurteilen, wenn sie im Zusammenhang mit einer in diesem Staat entfaltete, auf die Schließung solcher Verträge gerichteten Tätigkeit des Unternehmers oder der von ihm hiefür verwendeten Personen zustande gekommen sind. (2) Soweit es sich um die zwingenden Bestimmungen dieses Rechtes handelt, ist eine Rechtswahl zum Nachteil des Verbrauchers unbeachtlich.*

[44]*Convention 80/934/EEC on the law applicable to contractual obligations opened for signature in Rome on 19 June 1980 [1980] (OJ L 266).* Article 5 Certain consumer contracts:

1. This Article applies to a contract the object of which is the supply of goods or services to a person ('the consumer') for a purpose which can be regarded as being outside his trade or profession, or a contract for the provision of credit for that object.
2. Notwithstanding the provisions of Article 3, a choice of law made by the parties shall not have the result of depriving the consumer of the protection afforded to him by the mandatory rules of the law of the country in which he has his habitual residence:
   - if in that country the conclusion of the contract was preceded by a specific invitation addressed to him or by advertising, and he had taken in that country all the steps necessary on his part for the conclusion of the contract, or
   - if the other party or his agent received the consumer's order in that country, or
   - if the contract is for the sale of goods and the consumer travelled from that country to another country and there gave his order, provided that the consumer's journey was arranged by the seller for the purpose of inducing the consumer to buy.
3. Notwithstanding the provisions of Article 4, a contract to which this Article applies shall, in the absence of choice in accordance with Article 3, be governed by the law of the country in which the consumer has his habitual residence if it is entered into in the circumstances described in paragraph 2 of this Article.
4. This Article shall not apply to:
   (a) a contract of carriage;
   (b) a contract for the supply of services where the services are to be supplied to the consumer exclusively in a country other than that in which he has his habitual residence.
5. Notwithstanding the provisions of paragraph 4, this Article shall apply to a contract which, for an inclusive price, provides for a combination of travel and accommodation.

[45]Rühl (2011), p. 570.

Swiss Act on Private International Law[46]). Nowadays, consumer protection conflict rules are present in many of the legal systems around the world.[47] In the EU, Article 6 of Rome I Regulation on the law applicable to contractual obligations is the special protective conflict rule regarding consumer contracts.

It is true that consumer law is characterised by a lack of cases since most of the disputes arising out of consumer contracts are small claims, and thus parties consider it unreasonable to bring the dispute to court. Of course, if parties do not bring the case to court, PIL issues do not have to be considered. However, first of all, this is not always the case, and some contracts might involve a large value (e.g. contracts regarding timeshares, package holidays, credit sales etc.).[48] More importantly, the law must ensure legal certainty and that the expectations of the parties are met, regardless of the number of claims. Also, the law plays a role in preventing disputes to arise. The consumer policy of the company will in part depend on legal pressure. This means that when it is difficult for the consumer to sue, the company will have less pressure to provide for a favourable consumer policy, while if PIL rules favour the consumer and put the company at risk of being sued and the application of a law favourable and familiar to the consumer is ensured, then the company will be eager to provide good customer service in order to solve the dispute before going to court.[49]

2.1.1.2 Definition of Consumer in the EU PIL Context

There is no international or uniform legal definition of consumer. Different legal regimes draw the limit between a commercial contract and a consumer contract and between customer and consumer in a diverse manner. For our purpose, we will

---

[46]Bundesgesetz über das Internationale Privatrecht [Federal Act on Private International Law], of December 18, 1987, AMTLICHE SAMMLUNG [AS] 120 (1988) (Switz.) [Swiss Private International Law Act]: Article 120:

1. Contracts pertaining to goods or services of ordinary consumption intended for a consumer's personal or family use, provided such use is not connected with the consumer's professional or business activity, are governed by the law of the state of the consumer's habitual residence:

    a. if the supplier received the order in that state;
    b. if the contract was entered into after an offer or advertising in that state and if the consumer performed in that state the acts required to enter into the contract; or
    c. if the consumer was induced by the supplier to go to a foreign state for the purpose of delivering the order.

2. No choice of law is allowed. [English translation provided in *Commentaire romand, Loi sur le droit international privé, Convention de Lugano, edited by Andreas Bucher with Helbing&Lichtenhahn, Basle]*

[47]See Section 4 of this Chapter (4.2).

[48]Tang (2009), p. 11, 12.

[49]Ibid., p. 12.

define the term 'consumer' in the context of EU law, more specifically in the context of EU PIL, where 'consumer contract' is to be defined as an independent and autonomous concept. According to the European Court of Justice (ECJ), the terms consumer and professional must 'be given an autonomous and uniform interpretation throughout the Union. . ., and in order to ensure compliance with the objectives pursued by the European legislature in the sphere of consumer contracts, and the consistency of European Union law, account must be taken, in particular, to the definition of "consumer" in other rules of European Union law' .[50]

Since the existence of a special provision for consumer contracts is based on the inequality between the parties to the contract, the characteristics of the parties are relevant to identify a contract as a consumer contract. In EU PIL, for a contract to be considered as a consumer contract, the consumer must be an individual acting outside his or her trade or profession, while his/her counterparty (the professional) should be acting within the course of his/her business or profession.[51] These types of contracts are normally referred to as business-to-consumer contracts (B2C contracts).

The Consumer Acting Outside His or Her Trade or Profession

There is no common definition of consumer in EU law, and there are also differences among the definitions used in the national law of the Member States (partly as a result of the transposition of EU consumer directives into national legislation).[52] However, the vast majority of the definitions of 'consumer' found in EU legislation, despite being phrased in a different manner, refer to the consumer as a natural person who is acting for a purpose outside the scope of his or her trade or profession.

The origin of this wording is to be found in Article 13 of the Brussels Convention after the revision of 1978, later reproduced in Article 5(1) Rome Convention, and from there it spread into the European consumer acquis.[53] Nowadays, this is the notion found in the majority of EU consumer directives and in the Brussels I bis Regulation and the Rome I Regulation. It is a negative definition since it requires that a consumer act *outside* the scope of a business.[54]

[50]Case C-508/12 *Walter Vapenik v Josef Thurner* [2013] ECLI:EU:C:2013:790, paras 23 and 25.

[51]These requirements are found in Article 17 Brussels I bis Regulation and Article 6 Rome I Regulation.

[52]Since a large part of the EU consumer directives follow a minimum harmonisation approach, many Member States extended the scope of their consumer protection law beyond the definition of consumer under EU Law.

[53]Article 5(1) Rome Convention reads: 'This Article applies to a contract the object of which is the supply of goods or services to a person ("the consumer") *for a purpose which can be regarded as being outside his trade or profession* (. . .)' (emphasis added).

[54]On the contrary, Article 2(a) CISG, for instance, gives a positive definition of the consumer by excluding sales 'of goods bought for personal, family or household use'.

It is clear that in the context of EU PIL, the consumer shall conclude the contract for a purpose outside his or her trade or profession. However, it is necessary to clarify some uncertainties arising from this concept:

- Although in some legal instruments it is admitted that the consumer can be a legal person, in the context of EU PIL it is clear that only a natural person or individual can be a consumer. In *Benincasa v Dentalkit*,[55] the ECJ already held that the term consumer in Article 13 Brussels Convention covered only a private final consumer, and 'consequently, only contracts concluded for the purposes of satisfying an individual's own needs in terms of private consumption come under the provisions designed to protect the consumer as the party deemed to be the weaker party economically'.[56] In *Idealservice*,[57] in the context of Directive 93/12 on unfair contract terms in consumer contracts, the ECJ clearly stated that only natural persons could be consumers. This approach is now clarified by the definitions of consumer given in the Brussels I bis and the Rome I Regulations, which refer to the consumer as a 'natural person'.
- Another uncertainty regarding the concept of consumer acting outside his or her trade or profession comprises whether a party who contracts outside his/her trade or profession at the time of concluding the contract but uses the object of the contract for his/her trade or profession in the future is a consumer.[58] The ECJ also addressed this issue in *Benincasa v Dentalkit*, in the context of Article 13 Brussels Convention, where it was held that a consumer should conclude the contract outside any trade or professional activity or purpose, whether present or future.[59] Even if one of the parties, at the time of concluding the contract, is in a weaker position than that of its counterparty, it is not sufficient to receive protection as a consumer. The ECJ held that '[t]he specific protection sought to be afforded by those provisions is unwarranted in the case of contracts for the purpose of trade or professional activity, even if that activity is only planned for the future, since the fact that an activity is in the nature of a future activity does not divest it in any way of its trade or professional character'.[60] Thus, a consumer should be understood as someone contracting for a purpose outside his/her trade or profession at the moment of contracting and also outside the trade or profession that he or she would have as a result of the contract.

Doubts arise regarding profit contracts that are concluded by a person acting outside his or her trade or profession, for example a case involving the purchase of frozen stallion sperm for the purpose of breeding horses by a person whose normal

[55]Case C-269/95 *Benincasa v Dentalkit* [1997] *ECR* I-3767.

[56]*Benincasa v Dentalkit*, para 17.

[57]Joined Cases C-541/99 *Cape Snc v Idealservice Srl* and C-542/99 *Idealservice MN RE Sas v OMAI Srl* [2001] *ECR* I-09049.

[58]Tang (2009), p. 22.

[59]*Benincasa v Dentalkit*, paras 17 and 18.

[60]*Benincasa v Dentalkit*, para 17.

profession is a gardener. This was a case brought against the Austrian courts,[61] where the court did not question the fact that it was not the normal professional activity of the purchaser. Since it is a contract for profit, the consideration of such a contract as being for private purposes, as held by the ECJ in the *Benincasa* judgment, is very doubtful.[62]

On the other hand, the situation of a customer partially acting within and outside its trade or profession might also create doubts. Contracts with a 'mixed purpose' (i.e. for a goods or services to be used both inside and outside a person's trade or profession) pose the question of whether the customer can be regarded as a consumer. This occurs especially in cases of self-employed persons who purchase objects for dual purposes (e.g. a computer). The ECJ took a specific approach in this regard in the *Gruber v Bay Wa AG* case[63] in the context of the Brussels I Regulation. In this case, a farmer, Mr. Gruber, bought building materials for the replacement of the roof of his farm house, where he also lived with his family (62% of the floor for family use and the 38% left for business purposes). The ECJ took a restrictive approach by classifying contracts with mixed purposes as non-consumer contracts, with the exception that the business purposes are so minor as to be insignificant. Only those in a weaker position should be afforded protection, and the general weaker position of the buyer does not exist when he buys for his trade or profession, even partially.[64] In its reasoning, the ECJ emphasises the weaker position of the consumer ('inasmuch as a contract is entered into for the person's trade or professional purposes, he must be deemed to be on an equal footing with the other party to the contract, so that the special protection reserved by the Brussels Convention for consumers is not justified in such a case'),[65] as well as the restrictive interpretation that the negative definition of consumer implies.[66] In order to determine when the purpose for trade or profession is to be regarded as negligible, the ECJ suggests to take into account the content, nature and purpose of the contract and the circumstances in which it was concluded.[67] This approach contrasts with the traditional understanding, according to which the predominant purpose of the contract was considered as decisive.[68] Nowadays, this predominant purpose test is to be found in other instruments of EU consumer law, such as in the Consumer

[61]OGH, 25 October 2000–8 Nd 502/00.

[62]Wilderspin (2016), p. 460.

[63]Case C-464/01 *Gruber v Bay Wa AG* [2005] ECR I-439.

[64]*Gruber v Bay Wa AG*, para 39.

[65]*Gruber v Bay Wa AG*, para 40.

[66]*Gruber v Bay Wa AG*, para 43: 'That interpretation is supported by the fact that the definition of the notion of consumer in the first paragraph of Article 13 of the Brussels Convention is worded in clearly restrictive terms, using a negative turn of phrase ('contract concluded ... for a purpose. . .outside [the] trade or profession') (. . .)'.

[67]*Gruber v Bay Wa AG*, para 47.

[68]The Giuliano-Lagarde Report regarding the Rome Convention considered it as a consumer contract if the person was acting primarily outside of his or her trade or profession. Giuliano-Lagarde Report [1980] OJ C282/1, 23.

Rights Directive.[69] However, the ECJ approach is considered more consistent with the requirements of predictability and certainty regarding jurisdiction and applicable law.[70]

More recently, in the *Schrems* case,[71] the ECJ confirms the restrictive interpretation of the aforementioned judgments and, on the basis of this interpretation, determined whether Mr. Schrems, a Facebook user with habitual residence in Austria, was to be considered a 'consumer' and thus fell under Article 15 Brussels I Regulation (now Article 17 Brussels I bis Regulation).[72] Mr. Schrems used the Facebook account only for personal purposes under a false name, utilizing it solely for his private activities. However, he later also opened a Facebook page in order to report to Internet users on his legal proceedings against Facebook Ireland, his lectures, his participation in panel debates and his media appearances, as well as to call for donation of funds and to publicise his books (about legal proceedings against alleged infringements of data protection by Facebook). The ECJ explained that, taking into account the nature and objective of the contract, a user of digital social media can rely on his status as a consumer 'only if the predominately non-professional use of those services, for which the applicant initially concluded a contract, has not subsequently become predominately professional'.[73] Since, on the basis of previous case law (such as *Gruber* and *Benincasa*), a 'consumer' is defined by contrast to an 'economic operator', regardless of his knowledge or information, the expertise acquired by the consumer regarding those services or his assurances given for representing the rights and interests of the users of those services cannot deprive him of the notion of consumer; otherwise, this would prevent an effective defence for the rights of the consumer.[74] Therefore, the ECJ concluded that '(...) the activities of publishing books, lecturing, operating websites, fundraising and being assigned the claims of numerous consumers for the purpose of their enforcement do not entail the loss of a private Facebook account user's status as a "consumer" (...)'.

In addition, it is questionable whether it is necessary that the supplier knows, or ought to have known, the status of the consumer. To the question of whether it is necessary that the professional has been aware of the purpose for which the contract was concluded, the ECJ in *Gruber* held that the court seized, when determining if a contract was concluded outside the purpose of trade or profession, '(...) must not take account of facts or circumstances of which the other party to the contract may

[69]Recital 17 of the Consumer Rights Directive states that 'in the case of dual purpose contracts, where the contract is concluded for purposes partly within and partly outside the person's trade and the trade purpose is so limited as not to be predominant in the overall context of the contract, that person should also be considered as a consumer'.

[70]Plender and Wilderspin (2015), p. 237, 238; Calliess (2015a), p. 169.

[71]Case C-498/16 *Maximilian Schrems v Facebook Ireland Limited* [2018] ECLI:EU:C:2018:37.

[72]*Maximilian Schrems v Facebook Ireland Limited,* paras 29–32.

[73]*Maximilian Schrems v Facebook Ireland Limited*, paras. 29, 37, 38.

[74]*Maximilian Schrems v Facebook Ireland Limited*, paras. 39, 40.

have been aware when the contract was concluded, unless the person who claims the capacity of consumer behaved in such a way as to give the other party to the contract the legitimate impression that he was acting for the purposes of his business'.[75] According to the ECJ, a person cannot claim the status of a consumer if they have negligently created the impression that they were acting in the course of a business (e.g. by using a company letterhead or address). In such cases, the 'consumer' is renouncing to the special protection afforded to him or her by the EU PIL provisions.[76]

Finally, the ECJ in a recent case clarified that the requirement of a consumer acting outside its trade or profession can be fulfilled regardless of the knowledge or expertise about the subject matter of the contract.[77] In the context of Article 17 (1) Brussels I bis Regulation regarding jurisdiction, the Czech Supreme Court referred to the ECJ the question whether a natural person acting outside her trade or profession who engages in trade on the FOREX (foreign exchange) market can be regarded as a consumer within the meaning of Article 17(1) of the Brussels Regulation or whether, by reason of the knowledge and expertise required to engage in that trade, the complex nature of the contract at hand ('financial contract for differences' (CFD)), and of the risks involved, that person should not be considered a consumer. The ECJ replied that the natural person must be classified as a consumer within the meaning of that provision if the conclusion of that contract does not fall within the scope of that person's professional activity, and the special factors above named are irrelevant in that regard. In addition, The fact that a natural person would fall under a different term other than a consumer under EU directives because of those other factors (in this case, that person is a 'retail client' within the meaning of Article 4(1)(12) of Directive 2004/39/EC) and the fact that contracts involving financial instruments fall outside the scope of Article 6 Rome I Regulation, regarding the law applicable to consumer contracts, are both in principle irrelevant in terms of the concept of consumer under Article 17 Brussels I bis.

[75] *Gruber v Bay Wa AG*, para 54.

[76] *Gruber v Bay Wa AG*, paras 52–53: 'That would be the case, for example, where an individual orders, without giving further information, items which could in fact be used for his business, or uses business stationery to do so, or has goods delivered to his business address, or mentions the possibility of recovering value added tax.

In such a case, the special rules of jurisdiction for matters relating to consumer contracts enshrined in Articles 13 to 15 of the Brussels Convention are not applicable even if the contract does not as such serve a non-negligible business purpose, and the individual must be regarded, in view of the impression he has given to the other party acting in good faith, as having renounced the protection afforded by those provisions.'

[77] Case C-208/18 *Jana Petruchová v FIBO Group Holdings Limited* [2019] ECLI:EU:C:2019:825.

The Status of the Other Party: The Professional Acting Within the Course of His or Her Trade or Profession

To be regarded as a consumer, it is necessary that the counterparty of the consumer is acting within the course of his or her trade or profession. This means that the consumer would not be in a weaker position against the seller if the latter is acting outside his/her trade or profession (e.g. a person selling second hand his or her old phone to another person, both presumably with the same bargaining position and information). Contrarily to the definition of consumer, this is a positive definition since it is of relevance that the provisions protecting the consumer are applicable only when the person is in the position of a professional and, therefore, knows the existence of determinate risks involved due to the application of mandatory consumer protection rules.[78]

The counterparty of the consumer is referred to in different terms around EU legislation (e.g. 'trader', 'supplier', 'seller', 'vendor' etc.). Thus, unlike the term consumer, the counterparty of the consumer has no established terminology within the consumer acquis. Since the EU consumer directives used this variety of terms, which might create confusions, it was suggested that the conceivable formulations to refer to the consumer's counterparty are 'business' or 'professional'.[79] The Rome I Regulation uses the term 'professional'.

Regardless of the terminological incoherence, the meaning of the concept in the EU consumer acquis does not change: the professional is a person acting in the exercise of his or her trade or profession. Therefore, a private individual who is selling his/her bicycle second hand to another individual is not considered a professional. In such a contract, both parties are outside the course of their trade or profession, which means that none of them is a professional and neither a consumer under EU PIL.

As in the case of the concept of 'consumer', the ECJ must make an independent autonomous interpretation according to the EU PIL instruments and having regard to alternative descriptions of the consumer counterparty described in other EU consumer law instruments, unless there are strong signs that it would not be appropriate.[80] In contrast to the consumer, the professional can be a natural or a legal person.

The definition of professional requires to determine which was the trade or profession at the time of concluding the contract and whether the contract was concluded on the course of such a trade or profession. In most of the cases, it is clear what constitutes the trade or profession of a person. Both commercial (e.g. merchants, craftsmen etc.) and professional activities (such as lawyers, architects etc.) are covered by the definition, while the economic activities of the employees are excluded. However, individuals also sell things or provide services while this does not constitute their 'official' profession, and sometimes it is difficult

[78]Hondius et al. (2008), p. 145.

[79]Schulte-Nölke et al. (2008), p. 349.

[80]McParland (2015), p. 536.

to draw the line regarding whether this might constitute a (maybe part-time) commercial or professional activity. It is generally suggested, following the Draft Common Frame of Reference (DCFR),[81] that the decisive criterion is the exercise of an independent or self-employed activity.[82] The avocational business should then be delineated from a simple hobby, and the overall impression of the appearance at the market is crucial. Also, the durability or economic sustainability shall be taken into account.[83] For example, a person that sells some second-hand items on the Internet from time to time would not constitute a professional; however, if that person sells a substantial amount of used products and on a regular basis, it could indeed be considered a professional.[84] The regularity of trade or the accumulation of stock may indicate the existence of a commercial activity. It is not necessary the intention to make a profit. Thus, a lawyer working on a pro bono basis or a non-profit organisation offering goods or services in the market to compensate the loss created by a non-commercial activity can be considered as professionals.[85] The key factor in these cases is the appearance in the market in the role of a business. Moreover, the professional does not necessarily have to receive money in return for his or her products or services to be considered a professional (e.g. an Internet provider that offers information or other services to consumers for free but is still rewarded indirectly by selling consumer information to other parties, for instance).[86]

On the other hand, the fact that a client (subjectively and mistakenly) believed that he or she was dealing with a professional in the exercise of his/her trade or profession when he/she was not has no relevance, except if it was due to the misleading conduct of the other party. If the 'non-professional' claimed to be operating in the course of his/her trade or profession (maybe because he/she wanted to benefit from avoiding his/her 'amateur' position), he/she may have to face the consequences of being considered as a professional.[87]

[81]Principles, Definitions and Model Rules of European Private Law: Draft Common Frame of Reference (DCFR). Prepared by the Study Group on a European Civil Code and the European Research Group on Existing EC Private Law (Acquis Group). *Principles, Definitions and Model rules of European Private Law: Draft Common Frame of Reference (DCFR).* München: Sellier. European Law Publishers (2008).

[82]Calliess (2015a), p. 166.

[83]Ibid., p. 166.

[84]On a discussion based on some German consumer law decisions, it has been stated that, while a retired person restoring classic cars on the weekends and selling them from time to time should be considered as a hobby and not a commercial activity, a housewife selling a substantial quantity of second-hand items on eBay on a regular basis would qualify as a professional (even if not registered as a power seller). McParland (2015), p. 537; Calliess (2015a), p. 166.

[85]McParland (2015), p. 537; Calliess (2015a), p. 166.

[86]Calliess (2015a), p. 166.

[87]McParland (2015), p. 538. According to the ECJ in the Gruber judgment, a person cannot claim to be a consumer if he or she has – negligently – created the impression that he/she was acting in the course of his/her trade or profession (see above Sect. 2.1.1.2, the consumer acting outside his or her trade or profession). Logically, the misleading conduct of a person leading the consumer to believe

2.1.2 *The Necessity of Protection of Employees*

2.1.2.1 Rationale Behind Employee Protection

> In its inception it is an act of submission, in its operation it is a condition of subordination, however much the submission and the subordination may be concealed by that indispensable figment of the legal mind known as the 'contract of employment'. The main object of labour law has always been, and we venture to say will always be, to be a countervailing force to counteract the inequality of bargaining power which is inherent and must be inherent in the employment relationship.[88]

This is the iconic definition that Kahn-Freund provided in 1967 for the employment relationship and still referred to nowadays in employment law manuals.[89] This definition evidences the consequences derived from a liberal model where employment protection law did not exist: submission, subordination and inequality of bargaining power.

As to inequality of bargaining power, the employer generally has superior resources (larger capital, legal advice, experience in the market etc.). While this is also a characteristic feature of the relationship between professionals and consumers, in the case of employment contracts there is also the factor that workers would normally require immediately an income while employers can generally wait for a better offer with only a risk of reducing profits. Although that is not always the case, and an employer might need urgently a workforce or an employee has unique skills, the most common situation is that the employer offers work on a 'take it or leave it' basis.[90] Employees find themselves in a situation of economic and/or social dependence on the employer. First, employment is their source of income, and, second, employment is also relevant for the personal development and social status of a person.[91] As to the submission feature, employees submit to the standard terms of the employment contract, to which they do not pay enough attention or simply do not understand, giving more importance to issues such as working environment or promotion opportunities, absent in the contract. As to the subordination aspect, this is the key feature of the employment relationship. The employment contract has an authority structure, in which, in return for payment, the employer bargains for the right to issue directives and direct the employee to perform productively. The employee gives the consent to obey the employer's instructions.[92] Thus, the aforementioned characteristics of the employment relationship require special legislation for employment contracts.

---

that he/she is acting in the course of his/her trade or profession should also face the same consequences.

[88]Kahn-Freund (1967).

[89]Collins et al. (2019), p. 51; Cabrelli (2018), p. 162; Collins (2010), p. 6.

[90]Collins (2010), p. 6, 7.

[91]Rühl (2014), pp. 344–345.

[92]Collins (2010), pp. 9–11; Collins et al. (2019), pp. 51–53.

Freedom of contract would generally lead to unfavourable employment terms for employees due to the imbalance between the employer and the employee in the labour market, and that is why substantive law contains mandatory provisions aimed to protect the employee as a weaker contracting party (rules regarding minimum remuneration, maximum working hours and minimum rest periods, minimum paid annual holidays, health and safety, equality etc.). In the nineteenth century, with the rise of freedom of contract, employment contracts were understood as general contracts, in which the contracting parties would be equal before the law and would exercise their free will. However, it seems nowadays obvious that this treatment did not bring equality but put in evidence the inequality in the bargaining power of the parties due to the socio-economic dependence of the employee on the employer.[93] A special regulation of the contract of employment was demanded. Some justified this necessity on the lack of equality of the bargaining power of workers and employers, which led to a market failure. However, some claim that the inequality of barganing of workers entered was in fact due to the operation of a competitive labour market rather than the result of a market failure.[94] The purpose of national systems in regulating contracts of employment was not to intensify the competitive nature of the labour market but rather to prevent the outcome of competitive market by serving distributive purposes and to protect workers.[95] Legal systems approached this distributive regulation of contracts of employment in two ways: the first approach consisted of legislation imposing compulsory terms and obligations on contracts of employment (e.g. minimum wage rules, maximum working hours etc.); the second approach consisted of restructuring the labour market through the creation of collective bargaining, which strengthened the bargaining position of the employees and thus resulted in an improvement in the terms of the employment contracts. The second approach is a type of self-regulation, which in fact might lead to the setting of higher standards than the ones imposed by legislative measures and adapt to the precise circumstances of the business or sector. Member States have used both techniques to different extents and in diverse ways. This study will not enter into the regulation of collective agreements. It will only focus on the regulation of individual employment contracts.

During the twentieth century, an autonomous concept of employment contract was developed, together with protective legislation. With the main goal of compensating the imbalance of the employment relationship, European countries developed their national legislation on labour law. In addition, the modern European legal regulation regarding employment aims to integrate economic and social policies.[96] In the last decades, the internationalisation of markets led to a continuous increase in the existence of employment contracts with cross-border elements. Transnational employment relationships are nowadays common: workers commuting to a place of

[93] Veneziani (2009), p. 100 et seq.

[94] Collins (2001), p. 211.

[95] Ibid., p. 211.

[96] Grusic (2015), p. 22.

work in their neighbouring country, employers posting workers to a foreign place of work, companies seeking out employees abroad or even workers whose job is of a cross-border nature (lorry drivers, aircrew members, offshore installations etc.). In those cases, PIL needs to respond to the needs of substantive employment law. Substantive employment law aims to achieve a balance between the private interests of the parties to the employment contract but also pursues social policy goals, containing thus rules of public character. However, I will focus on the private dimension of employment protection, whose peculiarities are to be reflected on PIL rules.

As it has been already mentioned, PIL aimed to be 'neutral': the traditional multilateral approach proposed by Savigny decided which law was applicable through the abstract legal relationship and connecting factors, finding the legal system to which the legal relationship 'belonged'. Thus, under Savigny's traditional approach, which enjoyed exclusivity in Europe until the second half of the twentieth century, the protection of employees was a task of the applicable substantive law. In Europe, the evolution of European conflict rules for employment contracts started with the publication of the Draft Convention on the law applicable to contractual and non-contractual obligations in 1972,[97] which provided that in the absence of choice of law, the law applicable to employment contracts would be the law of the country of habitual place of work and that the choice of law could not undermine the mandatory rules of that law.[98] It is remarkable that the Draft Convention did not include a similar provision regarding consumer contracts.[99] Also, at the same time, a proposal for a Regulation on the law applicable to employment relationships was published in 1972, amended in 1976, and intended to determine the law applicable for employment contracts performed within the European Economic Community

[97]*Preliminary Draft Convention on the Law Applicable to Contractual and Non-Contractual Obligations*, xiv/398/72-E, Rev: 1 (1972).

[98]Articles 2(3) and 5 of the Draft Convention. According to Article 2(3), the choice of law in employment contracts could not affect the mandatory provisions protecting the employee that were in force in the country of the habitual place of work of the employee. Then Article 5 stated:

> In the absence of an express or implied choice of law, contracts of employment shall be governed by the law of the country
>
> (a) in which the employee habitually carries out his work;
> (b) in which the establishment which engaged the employee is situated, if the employee does not habitually carry out his work in any one country;
>
> unless in all the circumstances it is clear that the contract of employment is more closely connected with another country.

[99]However, already in that time, the lack of such special rule was criticised, and the inclusion of a similar limitation to party autonomy in the case of consumer contracts, plus the application of the law of habitual residence of the consumer to certain consumer contracts, were already claimed by Ole Lando (1974), p. 6, 19-21-33.

(ECC).[100] However, a Convention establishing uniform rules on the law applicable to contractual obligations, including employment contracts, was preferred to a regulation only covering intra-Community cases. The Rome Convention on the law applicable to contractual obligations was signed in 1980, including in Article 6 a specific rule for employment contracts, regardless of whether the place of work was inside or outside the ECC. Nowadays, modern PIL instruments contain special rules regarding employment contracts based on the objective of protection of employee as a weaker contractual party. Recital 23 Rome I Regulation declares that, with regard to contracting parties considered as weaker, they should be protected by conflict rules that are more favourable to their interests than are general rules. Thus, the objective is to achieve justice and fairness in international employment contracts by favouring the interests of the employee as a weaker contracting party.[101] In the EU, Article 8 Rome I Regulation is currently the special protective conflict rule regarding individual employment contracts.

2.1.2.2 Definition of Employee in the EU PIL Context

In broad terms, individual employment contracts are contracts between an employee and an employer under which the employee needs to perform the service promised while the employer gives a remuneration in return. The term 'individual employment contract' excludes any provisions of collective labour law (e.g. collective bargaining agreements).

The characterisation of a contract as an employment contract depends largely on the interpretation of the term 'employee'. Among the national laws of the Member States, the classification of a contract of employment differs and reflects diverse notions of the concept of employee, which can also vary depending on the nature of the substantive law protection involved. However, the differences are not that big, and, in a comparative perspective, many common characteristics can be found in the definition of employee among the Member States.

In Europe, a distinction is made between an employee and a self-employed person, or, in other words, a distinction is made between those who are employed and provide their work under a contract of employment and those who are 'self-employed' who enter into contracts to perform work or services for others. It is characteristic of numerous Member States that the relevant criteria of the notion of employee are to be found in case law rather than to provide for a statutory definition. While German case law considers an employee as personally dependent of his or her employer, who has the right to issue directives, French courts emphasise on a relationship of legal subordination, and the UK defines the employee by questioning

[100] Proposition de Reglement (CEE) du Conseil relatif aux dispositions concernant les conflicts de lois en matière de relations de travail à l'interieur de la Communauté, 23 mars 1972 [1972] OJ C 107/8.

[101] Grusic (2015), p. 18.

whether he/she worked under the counterparty's 'control' (the so-called control test).[102] A big common element for many Member States is the criterion of the employer having the right to issue directives, as well as the element of subordination. The ECJ considers that an employment relationship is an employment contract but if the subordination requirement is not satisfied, then it is a contract of services: 'any activity which a person performs outside a relationship of subordination must be classified as an activity pursued in a self-employed capacity for the purposes of Article 52 of the Treaty'.[103]

In the case of EU PIL, the term 'employee' must be defined autonomously, taking into account the intention of the regulation involved and EU law. That is, the definition must be consistent with the instruments of EU PIL (Rome regime and Brussels regime) and aligned with other relevant provisions of EU law and the case law of the ECJ.[104] The case law developed an autonomous interpretation derived from the *Lawrie-Blum* case,[105] in the context of Article 45 Treaty on the Functioning of the European Union (TFEU) on the free movement of workers. The court held that 'the essential feature for an employment relationship (...) is that for a certain period of time a person performs services for and under the direction of another person in return for which he receives remuneration'. This definition has been widely adopted in other areas of labour law among EU directives (e.g. Working Time Directive[106]) and case law (e.g. *Martínez Sala* case[107] regarding equal pay). It has to be noticed that the ECJ also stated that the definition of worker in EU law varies depending on the area where the definition is to be applied.[108] However, it is likely that the main features of the definition of employee in the sense of Article 45 TFEU, defining the employee as a person who performs services for and under the direction of another person for a certain period of time in return for a remuneration, are to be considered in the context of EU PIL regulations.

Therefore, it is submitted that an employee in the EU PIL context is a natural person performing services for and under the direction of another person, for a period of time and in return of remuneration. Also, services should be real and genuine and have some economic value.[109] An employee is to be under the direction and control of his or her counterparty, and there is a relation of subordination between them rather than consisting of a commercial transaction with an independent service provider. Thus, the broad definition from the *Lawrie-Blum* case should

[102]McParland (2015), p. 636, 637; Franzen and Gröner (2015), p. 220, 221.

[103]Case C-268/99 *Aldona Malgorzata Jany & Others v Staatssecretaris van Justitie* [2001] *ECR* I-08615.

[104]McParland (2015), p. 637, 638; Franzen and Gröner (2015), p. 220.

[105]Case C-66/85 *Lawrie-Blum v Land Baden-Württemberg* [1986] ECR I-2121.

[106]Directive 2003/88/EC of the European Parliament and of the Council of 4 November 2003 concerning certain aspects of the organisation of working time (OJ 2003 L299/9).

[107]Case C-85/96 *María Martínez Sala v Freistaat Bayern* [1998] ECR I-2691.

[108]Case C-256/01 *Debra Allonby v Accrington & Rosendale College et al.* [2004] ECR I-873.

[109]McParland (2015), p. 641.

be applied to the concept of individual employment contract in the Brussels I bis and Rome I Regulations. By following a broad definition rather than a narrow one, it is ensured that anyone covered by the national mandatory legislation as an employee would also be likely to be covered by the special EU rules on jurisdiction and applicable law. Also, by taking a too narrow approach, the special PIL rules might lose their purpose since it could allow employers to avoid their protection.[110] The ECJ in the context of the Brussels Convention, although it did not define the term employee as such, seems to support this broad definition: '(. . .) contracts of employment, like other contracts for work other than on a self-employed basis, differ from other contracts – even those for the provision of services – by virtue of certain peculiarities: they create a lasting bond which brings the worker to some extent within the organisational framework of the business of the undertaking or employer, and they are linked to the place where the activities are pursued, which determines the application of the mandatory rules and collective agreements'.[111] The ECJ did not define in that case the term 'employee' but gives some guidance. It refers to the subordination between the employee and employer and the bond of the employee with the business of the employer. It refers to work done other than on a self-employed basis, which seems to exclude those genuinely self-employed.[112]

A broad definition would ensure that the 'false self-employed' is considered as an employee in terms of application of the protective EU PIL rules. 'False self-employed' persons have been defined as 'employees who are disguised as self-employed in order to avoid the application of some specific legislation (for example, labour or fiscal regulations) which is considered unfavourable by the employer. Another example is the case of self-employed persons who are economically dependent on a sole (or main) customer.'[113] This description has been given by the General Advocate Wahl and confirmed by the ECJ, who held: 'On a proper construction of EU law, it is only when self-employed service providers who are members of one of the contracting employees' organisations and perform for an employer, under a works or service contract, the same activity as that employer's employed workers, are "false self-employed", in other words, service providers in a situation comparable to that of those workers, that a provision of a collective labour agreement, such as that at issue in the main proceedings, which sets minimum fees for those self-employed service providers, does not fall within the scope of Article 101(1) TFEU.'[114]

[110]Merrett (2011), p. 76.

[111]Case C-266/85 *Hassan Shenavai v Klaus Kreischer* [1987] ECR 239.

[112]Merrett (2011), p. 68.

[113]Case C-413/13 *FNV Kunsten Informatie en Media v Staat der Nederland* [2014], Opinion AG Wahl ECLI:EU:C:2014:2215, para. 52.

[114]Case C-413/13 *FNV Kunsten Informatie en Media v Staat der Nederland* [2014] ECLI:EU:C:2014:2411. In this case, the ECJ uses the term 'false self-employed' in connection with free competition as regulated in Article 101 TFEU.

Although the existence of an authority relationship is an important factor to distinguish an employee or a 'false self-employed' person from a self-employed person, there are other important elements to take into account. In comparison with an employee or a 'false self-employed' person, a self-employed person is characterised by freedom and flexibility in determining his or her time schedule and the place and contents of his/her work.[115] Another characteristic is that a self-employed person runs a commercial and financial risk, while employees and 'false self-employed' persons do not. Moreover, forming part of the employer's economic unit is of relevance to be considered an employee (or a 'false self-employed' person). Therefore, the relevant elements to determine whether a person is an employee, self-employed or false self-employed are whether there is legal subordination between the parties, whether there is financial and commercial risk and whether the person is involved or forms part of the business of the employer.[116]

2.1.3 *Other Weaker Parties in a Contract*

While consumers and employees constitute the paradigmatic example of weaker contracting parties under EU PIL, the protection afforded by the EU PIL rules is not limited to them, although to a lesser level the protection is extended to passengers and some insurance policyholders. Moreover, even when special rules protecting a weaker contracting party in EU PIL rules on civil and commercial matters only include consumers, employees, insurance policyholders (or other beneficiaries) and passengers, other contractual parties can be considered weaker parties in need of protection (such as franchisees or commercial agents). European legal instruments harmonising substantive rules of contract law protect other individual private parties' interests by setting a minimum common level of protection among the Member States and thus cover other (weaker?) contractual parties that do not enjoy a special protection under EU PIL rules.[117]

2.1.3.1 Passengers

In the case of a contract of carriage of passengers, passengers are considered a weaker party. A special protective rule is provided regarding the law applicable to these contracts (Article 5(2) Rome I Regulation), although regarding jurisdiction and

[115]The ECJ considers that an assessment of all circumstances of the case is always necessary when determining whether there is an authority relationship between the employer and employee. In the case *FNV Kunsten Informatie en Media* Case *v Staat der Nederland*, the ECJ gave more importance to the freedom that a working person has to choose his or her time schedule and the place and the contents of his/her work rather than to the authority relationship.

[116]Verhulp (2017), p. 6, 7.

[117]Lazić (2014), p. 100.

enforcement the general rules apply. The recognition of passengers as a weaker party in EU PIL is recent as before the Rome I Regulation, there was not a special conflict rule for contracts of carriage of passengers since no difference was made between carriage of goods and carriage of passengers. At the same time, they were excluded from the special provision for consumer contracts on the basis that contracts of carriage of passengers 'cannot adequately be dealt with by application of the law at the consumer's habitual place of residence: Cross-border carriage, especially for the conveyance of passengers, usually involves a large number of consumers from different countries. Therefore, application of the consumer's law would require the carrier to comply with different protective laws at the same time. It is evident that this is neither feasible nor desirable.'[118] However, the passenger might as well be in the same weaker position as a consumer (the passenger is a consumer in the general meaning of the term), and it is considered as a weaker party. The difference lies in the emphasis on the interests and expectations of the carrier. Although the enactment of a special provision protecting the passenger is driven by a wish to protect him or her as a consumer, the position of the commercial carrier is respected and plays a big role in it. The Rome I Regulation tried to reach a compromise between the interests of the passenger and the interests of the carrier.[119]

The rationale behind the protection of passengers is the same as the rationale behind the protection of consumers: they are in a weaker position in respect of their counterparty due to an imbalance regarding bargaining power, knowledge/information and resources. In fact, passengers can generally be regarded as consumers, although in EU PIL terms they are excluded from the special rules on consumers. The same goes for some insurance contracts. Recital 32 Rome I Regulation provides:

> Owing to the particular nature of contracts of carriage and insurance contracts, specific provisions should ensure an adequate level of protection of passengers and policy holders. Therefore, Article 6 [regarding consumer contracts] should not apply in the context of those particular contracts.

In the same manner as between consumers and professionals, information asymmetries exist between passengers and carriers. It is difficult for the passengers to acquire relevant information about the conditions and quality of the service of transport before the conclusion of the contract. Moreover, in cross-border cases, the language, the other party or the applicable law might be foreign to the passengers.[120] In the case of the law applicable to the contract, carriers will be aware of which law will benefit them: they can invest in gathering information regarding the expected

[118]Max Planck Institute for Foreign Private and Private International Law (2007), p. 276.

[119]In fact, the special rule for contracts of carriage of passengers of the Rome I Regulation is harshly criticised because of trying to meet the interests of both the passenger and the carriage and instead not ensuring protection to the passenger and limiting flexibility to carrier. See, for example, Fentiman (2016), p. 444.

[120]Devenney and Kenny (2012), p. 239.

benefits of the application of certain law. On the other hand, a passenger will know about the quality of law only after problems occur after the conclusion of the contract.[121] The application of general EU PIL rules can lead to the circumvention of mandatory rules that protect the passenger in substantive law and which application is in accordance with his or her legitimate expectations.

2.1.3.2 Insurance Policyholders (or Other Beneficiaries)

Insurance policyholders are not always a weaker party in an insurance contract. EU PIL distinguishes between contracts where the policyholder needs special protection and contracts where there is no need for such protection. Specifically, a distinction is made between contracts on large risks, contracts on mass risks and mandatory insurance contracts. Only the two latter categories are considered to need special EU PIL rules regarding weaker parties' protection. On the other hand, contracts for large risks, as defined in the EU legislation, are mostly relevant for business-to-business (B2B) contracts as they normally regard large industrial and transport business operations. Therefore, it is assumed that the policyholders insuring large risks are not in need of special protection since they have sufficient bargaining power, capacity and resources to negotiate the terms of the contract.

Contracts that do not qualify as contracts for large risks are referred to as contracts for mass risks. Both B2C and B2B contracts and those of different types of insurance can fall within this category. Customers ensuring smaller risks are more likely to be in a weaker position since it is unlikely that they will have the necessary information, resources or capacity to negotiate the terms of the contract and to deal with foreign laws. Thus, special EU PIL rules are necessary in order to avoid a potential abuse from the insurer and a circumvention of the mandatory law protecting the policyholder.

EU PIL rules offer an extra degree of protection and mandatory character in the case of mandatory insurance contracts, namely when Member States impose an obligation to take out insurance. In that case, the protection is not only in the policyholder's interest but mainly for overriding public policy reasons, which underpin the decision to impose a mandatory insurance cover in the first place.

2.1.3.3 Other (Possible) Weaker Parties Not Covered by EU PIL Rules

As referred to above, the term weaker party in EU PIL generally regards consumers and employees and, to a lesser extent, insurance policyholders and passengers. However, there are other parties that could be regarded as having a weaker bargaining position in a contract. This can be the case of franchisees, distributors, commercial agents and even some small businesses. National substantive rules, and

[121] Rühl (2011), p. 574.

even EU legal instruments harmonising or unifying substantive rules of private law, offer protection to some of these other parties' interest.

Therefore, these parties can be regarded as weaker parties in the substantive level and thus enjoy special protection, but this special protection is not reflected at the EU PIL level, which means that the 'strong party' of the contract could intentionally avoid the application of that special protection in a cross-border situation as a consequence of the operation of the general EU PIL rules. It is not very clear why protection is afforded to some weaker parties and not to others who in other contexts are viewed as weaker parties as well.

For instance, in the case of commercial agents, it is true that where consumers and employees must be protected against a choice of law and its negative consequences, it is argued that the need for protection of agents becomes less obvious. Firstly, agents are usually better informed and experienced. Secondly, in the current international practice, commercial agents are often organised as corporate bodies having more than one principal. Nevertheless, when the commercial agent is a natural person having only one principal, his or her situation is highly comparable as the one confronted by an employee and, therefore, subject to possible abuse from the principal.[122] Due to the possible imbalance on the bargaining power between the agent and its principal on the agency contract, the principal may impose the terms of the contract, including a choice of law clause. The principal, aware of the legal diversity in this area, may wish to elude the national legislation that afford a level of protection to the agent, in order to be more economically efficient and become more competitive within its operating market. Therefore, the agency contract may contain a choice of law clause referring to a non-Member State law which does not set the minimum standards of protection in favour of the agent as the Commercial Agents Directive[123] does. As a consequence of this behaviour, it can be considered that the internal market may suffer a negative impact as it promotes distorted competition. Furthermore, the direct consequence would be for the commercial agents as they will be unprotected against eventual abuses from their principal. As it has been said, these were precisely the negative effects that the Commercial Agents Directive aimed to eradicate. However, commercial agents do not enjoy special EU PIL protective rules.[124] In the majority of the cases, a commercial agent will not be in need of protection but rather will act as a corporation in equal bargaining position as its principal.

---

[122]Verhagen (2002), p. 153; Kuipers (2012), p. 217.

[123]Council Directive 86/653/EEC of 18 December 1986 on the coordination of the laws of the Member States relating to self-employed commercial agents (OJ 1986 L 382/17).

[124]During the drafting of the Rome I Regulation, there was an extensive discussion about the inclusion of a special provision regarding commercial agents. See Article 7 Proposal for a Regulation of the European Parliament and the Council on the law applicable to contractual obligations (Rome I) COM/2005/0650 final (Rome I); Max Planck Institute for Foreign Private and Private International Law (2007), pp. 298–311. However, the ECJ has 'filled in the gap' in this regard through case law (see Chap. 6).

The same arguments can be used in the cases of franchisees, distributors and, especially, small businesses: although in some cases they might be in an imbalanced position in the contract, it is argued that in general they would be better informed and experienced than the protected consumers and employees, and therefore in those cases the principle of party autonomy would prevail over their need of protection.

2.2 EU PIL Principles and Weaker Parties: The Importance and 'Dangers' of Party Autonomy and the Need for Special Protective Connecting Factors

This section aims to explain why ordinary traditional conflict rules do not respond to the specialities of consumer contracts or individual employment contracts. First, the unequal position of the parties questions the adequate application of party autonomy in contracts involving one weaker party. Party autonomy is one of the most important principles in modern EU PIL, and the freedom of the parties to choose the law applicable to their contract is generally acknowledged. However, it is thought that, as the stronger party, a company or an employer would be able to introduce in the consumer contract or individual employment contract a choice of law clause unilaterally. This clause might indicate a law with a low standard of protection for consumers or employees.

On the other hand, when parties do not choose the law applicable to the contract, the general conflict rules apply, which traditionally would determine the law applicable based on the existence of certain connections between the case and the territory. The use of objective connecting factors ensures that the law applicable would be the law of a country that has a substantial (and, ideally, the closest) connection with the dispute. However, the application of that law might be against the interests of the consumer since, in general, the law having the closest connection to the contract would be the law of the place of establishment of the company. The neutral and objective connecting factor is not suitable for consumer contracts. In the same manner, the use of the general objective connecting factors might not lead to the adequate applicable law to employment contracts.

Thus, this section will first highlight the importance of party autonomy in PIL, especially regarding contractual obligations, and then refer to some necessary restraints on the use of this freedom of choice of law by the parties, especially regarding consumer and employment contracts. Then the need for special connecting factors regarding the law applicable to these special contracts in the cases where parties did not choose the law applicable will be explained.

2.2.1 *The Importance of Party Autonomy and the Need for Limits*

Party autonomy, as the power of individuals to arrange their legal relationships according to their own interests, stands nowadays as a basic principle for international contracts worldwide. It encompasses in the area of PIL the notion that parties to a contract have the freedom to choose the law governing their legal relationship, and it is considered one of the leading concepts in contemporary PIL.[125] Accordingly, in the contemporary conflicts theory, it is believed that the applicable law should be determined by the will of the parties.[126] The law agreed by the parties will therefore replace the law otherwise applicable to the contract.

To a large extent, the European systems of PIL rest on the attitude that legal systems are equivalent.[127] Party autonomy rests on the same theoretical premises as in an increasingly international society, it has to be respected that legal systems provide for different values, and especially in the area of contract law where parties enjoy a general freedom of disposition, it can be said that 'no jurisdiction has a monopoly of excellence in contract law'.[128]

Although the concept of party autonomy has evolved over the time, it is said to have been explicitly recognised as a connecting factor in PIL in the sixteenth century by Charles Dumoulin.[129] Nevertheless, it is argued that Dumoulin was just referring to the will of the parties as an argument to apply the law of the place of performance

[125]In words of the recognised PIL scholar S. Symeonides: 'The widespread endorsement of party autonomy has become one of the unifying principles of contemporary PIL, although differences remain about the modalities and limitations of this autonomy.' Symeonides (2014), p. 346.

[126]Mandery (2014), p. 17.

[127]This is especially true regarding intra-EU situations, where the fact that it is known that other Member State laws will be based on similar legal values plays a role. But still when the law of a third country is involved, if a country insisted on the absolute application of its own law in an international scenario, that would not be accepted by the other countries involved and that country would see its role in international commerce reduced. It is true that in that kind of situations, the basis for the application of a foreign law would to some extent depend upon the relationship between the countries involved, but in an area such as contract law, where substantive law contains moderately few mandatory rules, a value-neutral multilateral conflict of laws method prevails, at least as a starting point, within the European legal systems. See the 'scale of Ten Wolde' in Ten Wolde (2013), pp. 575–579; De Boer (1996), p. 280.

[128]Verhagen (2002), p. 144; Watt (2010), p. 261.

[129]Charles Dumoulin (1500–1566), French scholar adherent to the statutist theory of the conflict of laws, referred to the will of the parties in order to determine the law applicable to international marriages according to the law of the habitual residence of the husband rather than where the marriage took place. In this sense, see Basedow et al. (2012), p. 190, 191. Nevertheless, it can be opened to discussion whether the concept of party autonomy was already known in the ancient world. Broadly speaking, after the decline of the Roman Empire, the application of different laws was dependent upon the ethnicity of the parties, but this practice resulted over the years in the manipulation of the applicable law by the parties by declaring their belonging to a specific ethnic group. It can be argued therefore that by accepting this practice, courts already recognised implicitly the party autonomy concept. This approach is explained in Juenger (1993), p. 10.

and not as an independent connecting factor as we understand it nowadays. In the same way, several authors of the sixteenth and seventeenth centuries used the currently known party autonomy concept as an argumentative aid in their reasoning.[130] It was Mancini (1817–1888)[131] who claimed party autonomy as an independent principle of PIL, and together with the economic and political liberalism on the late nineteenth century and the beginning of the twentieth century, it proved to be successful.[132] Although the political climate during the war periods in the twentieth century led to an increased regulation of the sovereign State, and therefore to a decline of the liberal concept of party autonomy, it became well accepted again together with the increase of international trade.[133] Freedom of choice of law was generally accepted in contractual obligations among the European countries already in the 1960s, and it was definitely recognised with its incorporation in the Rome Convention. Article 3(1) Rome Convention allowed the parties to choose the law of any state to govern their contract, and its success led to maintaining party autonomy in the Rome I Regulation as the cornerstone of its conflict of laws mechanism.[134] Party autonomy is without any reservation one of the most important achievements in the development of PIL in the twentieth century, its strengthening and development being one of the current and future tasks of PIL, both in Europe and worldwide.[135] Moreover, the role of party autonomy in European PIL is nowadays well rooted and goes beyond the area of contractual obligations. The European PIL instruments are increasingly accepting party autonomy in areas where it used to be

[130]For example, Ulrich Huber (1636–1694), in *De Conflictu Legum*, relied on the will of the parties to connect contracts to the law of the place of performance; as well as Dumoulin, his reasoning was also in relation with a situation where marriage took place in a country and cohabitation took place in another country, prevailing the law of the latter place. See Nygh (1999), pp. 190–192.

[131]Mancini is best known for the fact that he stated, broadly speaking, that it was for the law of the nationality to govern the legal relationships of the individuals; nevertheless, in the situations where the regulation of the issues was left to the parties and not to the State, parties should have freedom to choose the law applicable to these affairs. This is an explicit recognition of party autonomy. Ibid., p. 8.

[132]Among Europe, courts and academics were divided on their opinions. For example, French, English and German courts used to be more favourable in respecting the will of the parties, whilst courts in other states and a large number of scholars argued that parties should not be able to avoid the applicability of the law otherwise applicable. Rühl (2007), p. 153,154; Basedow et al. (2017), p. 191.

[133]Nygh (1999), pp. 3–13; Mandery (2014), p. 44, 45; Rühl (2007); Basedow et al. (2012), pp. 190–192.

[134]Recital 11 Rome I Regulation states that party autonomy is one of the cornerstones of the conflicts system of the Rome I Regulation; in addition, the ECJ has elevated this principle from being 'a' cornerstone to 'the' cornerstone of the instrument (Case C-184/12 *United Antwerp Maritime Agencies (Unamar) NV v Navigation Maritime Bulgare [2013]* EU:C:2013:663, para 49). Plender and Wilderspin (2015), p. 133, 134; Calliess (2015b), p. 77; Mankowski (2016), p. 103.

[135]Heiss (2009), p. 7; Leible (2011), p. 215.

excluded and, therefore, recognising its importance in a wider way than Member States traditionally did.[136]

This is due to the undeniable advantages it encompasses and the prominent role it plays in the globalised world.

First of all, the use of party autonomy provides legal certainty and predictability to the legal relationship in question, avoiding at the same time the unforeseeability that sometimes arises from the determination of the applicable law based on the objective application of the conflict of laws rules and preventing the possibility that different courts may answer the question of the applicable law in different ways, which could lead to an unexpected result and create legal uncertainty in comparison with the precision of what could have been freely agreed upon by the parties.

Second, the parties, by exercising their freedom of choice of law, are able to pursue their more convenient interests and are able to agree on what is more satisfactory for themselves or their legal relationship. In the context of international trade, there are countless situations that may lead the parties to become interested in a law apparently not related to the contract. Factors as familiarity, neutrality, reputation or simply the most convenient law for their transaction may be decisive for the parties to choose the law applicable to their contract. Party autonomy therefore allows a proper regulation of individual cases.[137]

Third, as a natural consequence from that legal certainty, a great economic efficiency is achieved by reducing the costs of determining the applicable law, as well as preventing any possible costs arising from a possible unexpected solution to their controversies.[138]

All the aforementioned has to be placed in the context of the ideological, economic and political environment of today's globalised society and the idea of welfare state.[139] Freedom of choice of law is commonly seen as the conflict of laws

[136]Party autonomy in choice of law has also been recognised in the Rome II Regulation on the law applicable to non-contractual obligations (Regulation (EC) No 864/2007 of the European Parliament and of the Council of 11 July 2007 on the law applicable to non-contractual obligations [2007] (OJ L 199/40)), in the Rome III Regulation (Council Regulation (EU) No 1259/2010 of 20 December 2010 implementing enhanced cooperation in the area of the law applicable to divorce and legal separation, [2010] (OJ L 343/10)), in the Maintenance Regulation (Council Regulation (EC) No 4/2009 of 18 December 2008 on jurisdiction, applicable law, recognition and enforcement of decisions and cooperation in matters relating to maintenance obligations [2009] (OJ L 7/1)), in the Succession Regulation or Rome IV Regulation (Regulation (EU) No 650/2012 of the European Parliament and of the Council of 4 July 2012 on jurisdiction, applicable law, recognition and enforcement of decisions and acceptance and enforcement of authentic instruments in matters of succession and on the creation of a European Certificate of Succession [2012] (OJ L201/107)), or in the Matrimonial Property Regulation (Council Regulation (EU) 2016/1103 of 24 June 2016 implementing enhanced cooperation in the area of jurisdiction, applicable law and the recognition and enforcement of decisions in matters of matrimonial property regimes [2016] (OJ L 183/1)). Regarding a reflexion about party autonomy in the different EU PIL instruments: Maultzsch (2016).

[137]Basedow et al. (2012), p. 190; Belohlávek (2011), p. 666.

[138]Mandery (2014), p. 17; Leible (2011), p. 215; Carrascosa González (2012), Ortiz Vidal (2012), p. 55, 56.

[139]Ortiz Vidal (2012), p. 56.

expression of the freedom of contract.[140] In national law, it is accepted that parties should freely determine the terms and content of their contracts, within the limits of the mandatory laws of the country. Thus, if parties can decide on their contractual obligations in national law, it makes sense that they can also do so on the international level. In fact, parties enjoy more autonomy on an international level since no state can effectively control international contracts.[141] Parties have the possibility to choose the court and the law applicable and avoid the applicability of the rules that they do not wish to be applied to their contract. They can even manipulate the situation to avoid otherwise applicable mandatory law, even when the possibility to choose the applicable law is limited. That is, parties can manipulate the connecting factors by, for example, choosing the place of conclusion of the contract, place of performance etc. In these cases, since states cannot control de facto international contracts, they would have to recognise it *de iure*.[142] In addition, the forum legislator cannot impose the forum law to an international contract with relevant connections to other laws in the same manner as he or she will apply his/her law to a contract that has exclusive connections to the forum. In these situations, a restraint in the regulatory authority is necessary, and thus private parties should enjoy a larger autonomy to regulate their contract on an international plane than on an exclusive national one.[143]

Therefore, throughout party autonomy, the parties would create the appropriate legal framework for the development of their activities, endowing at the same time their legal relationship with legal certainty, predictability and economic efficiency and adapting their behaviour to that chosen law. As a consequence, international trade becomes more attractive, and international harmony of decisions, by making sure that every court will decide upon the chosen law, is also promoted.[144] It should also be noted that, apart from the direct advantages to the parties, party autonomy is also an incentive to national legal orders to ensure that their rules are attractive for the parties and thus prevent them from avoiding the applicability of their rules by choosing a more favourable law; therefore, party autonomy enhances competition between legal orders.[145]

Thus, it is not surprising that the Rome I Regulation on the law applicable to contractual obligations (Rome I Regulation) states in its Recital 11 that *the parties' freedom to choose the applicable law should be one of the cornerstones of the system of conflict-of-law rules in matters of contractual obligations.*

This instrument provides in Article 3(1) that the contract shall be governed by the law chosen by the parties and, therefore, recognises the freedom of choice of the

140 Mandery (2014), p. 17.
141 Kuipers (2012), p. 49.
142 Nygh (1999), p. 2.
143 Kuipers (2012), p. 50.
144 Ibid., p. 50.
145 Basedow et al. (2012), p. 190.

parties in similar words than its predecessor, the Rome Convention.[146] Parties are completely free to choose any state law. A specific relation between the chosen law and the contract is not necessary; that is, party autonomy, in principle, operates in its entirety.[147]

According to the European Court of Justice (ECJ), party autonomy is essential for the correct functioning of the internal market, being a significant concept for the freedom of movement of goods, services, capital and persons, as it was determined in the judgment *Alsthom Atlantique* from 24 January 1991.[148]

Besides all the advantages that party autonomy entails, the exercise of party autonomy may sometimes become problematic as parties choose the law most suitable to their interests, regardless of the existence of some higher interests at stake.[149] Therefore, legislators need to impose restrictions on the exercise of party autonomy in some situations. For example, the European legislator imposes several restrictions on party autonomy in the Rome I Regulation.

Firstly, there is the evident limitation regarding public policy in Article 21 Rome I, which introduces the so-called *exception de ordre public.* According to this provision, the court can avoid the application of any provision of the law designated by the parties when it is contrary to the public policy of the forum. It is only where essential legal values of the forum are undermined that the public policy exception will be justified.[150]

Secondly, due to the importance of the public interests at stake, Article 9 Rome I ensures the application of the so-called overriding mandatory provisions, which must be of internationally mandatory application regardless of the law applicable to the contract and whether this was the result of the choice of the parties or not, as in the case of the public policy provision. Overriding mandatory provisions are defined in Article 9 (1) as

> provisions the respect for which is regarded as crucial by a country for safeguarding its public interests, such as its political, social or economic organisation, to such an extent that they are applicable to any situation falling within

---

[146]Except for one minor textual change in relation to the implicit choice of law, the concept of party autonomy has remained the same. According to the Rome Convention, an implicit choice must be proved 'with reasonable certainty' by the terms of the contracts or the circumstances of the case, whereas Rome I says it should be demonstrated 'clearly'. The former left room for more interpretation, and in this sense the Rome I Regulation limits the courts' discretion to determine when there has been an implied choice of law by the parties. Willem Vernooij (2009), p. 72; Heiss (2009), p. 7; Wilderspin (2008), p. 263.

[147]Ortiz Vidal (2012), p. 73,74; Leible (2011), p. 217; Garcimartín Alférez (2008), p. 63.

[148]Case C-339/89, *Alsthom Atlantique SA v Compagnie de construction mécanique Sulzer SA* [1991] ECR I-107. See Belohlávek (2011), p. 665.

[149]Garcimartín Alférez (2008), p. 63.

[150]Leible (2011), p. 232; Renner (2015), pp. 395–411; Stone (2018), pp. 485–487; Belohlávek (2011), pp. 1935–1938.

their scope, irrespective of the law otherwise applicable to the contract under this Regulation.

Therefore, these provisions express a national public interest in a wide sense and are to be enforced regardless of the otherwise applicable law in international situations. It must be noted that legal certainty and party autonomy could be seriously undermined if Member States indiscriminately consider their domestic mandatory rules as internationally mandatory in order to take precedence over the law chosen by the parties, and therefore this limitation should be interpreted narrowly.[151]

Thirdly, there are two special situations where the European legislator deals with the scope of party autonomy. These are the purely internal situations and intra-EU situations, under Article 3(3) and Article 3(4) Rome I, respectively.[152] These both provisions have a clear purpose of fighting against abuse of law.[153] In both cases, the aim is to prevent the parties from artificially relating the contract to any country to which it lacks any connection when they do it with the only intention to avoid the application of the mandatory national or European provisions. Pursuant to Article 3 (3) Rome I, when a situation is only connected to one single Member State, the choice of a foreign law by the parties should not affect the application of the domestically mandatory provisions of the national law. In the same manner, pursuant to Article 3(4) Rome I, if the situation is only connected with one or several Member States, the choice of a non-Member State law by the parties will not affect the application of the mandatory EU law. This provision is also a potential vehicle for the safeguarding of the interests of contractual parties as they will be prevented from avoiding the applicability of mandatory provisions originated in European directives in intra-EU situations, and consequently the proper functioning of the internal market is ensured. The non-application of those rules would precisely frustrate the main objective of European directives, which is to harmonise the rules regulating transactions between market participants operating within the EU.[154]

Finally, special safeguards are imposed in order to guarantee the protection of the considered contractual weaker parties. Of course, there is a big risk that parties abuse their autonomy to the detriment of the party with less bargaining power, who sees a choice of law imposed on him or her. In the Rome I Regulation, within this classification, we find consumer contracts (Article 6 Rome I), individual employment contracts (Article 8 Rome I), both already protected in the Rome Convention, and – to a lesser extent – also transport contracts (Article 5 Rome I) and insurance contracts (Article 7 Rome I). The limitations are imposed in the manner that in the former two categories, the parties can make a choice of law in a conditioned manner, meaning that it cannot deprive the consumer or employee of the protection afforded

[151] See discussion over overriding mandatory rules in Chapter 3.3.

[152] Mankowski (2016), pp. 374–426; Stone (2018), pp. 426–429; Calliess (2015b), pp. 104–108.

[153] Lagarde (2006), p. 337.

[154] Van Bochove (2014), p. 147; Verhagen (2002), p. 140.

to them by the mandatory provisions of the law which would have been applicable in the absence of choice. In the two latter categories, parties only have the option to choose the applicable law to their contract among several pre-established options.

As it has been submitted, the protection of the contractual party with a clearly weaker bargaining position is recognised in most contemporary legal systems. The intention of limiting party autonomy when one of the parties in the contract is considered as weaker is to prevent the 'strong' party from abusing its position by invoking a law that eventually would be disadvantageous for the other party.

While professionals will be aware of which law will benefit them, consumers do not know which law the professional wishes to apply. Professionals will invest in gathering information regarding the expected benefits of the application of certain law, while consumers will know about the quality of the law only after the problems occur after the conclusion of the contract.[155] In the case of consumer contracts, a choice of law clause will most probably be contained in the general terms and conditions of the professional, and that choice will usually always be the law where the professional has his or her habitual residence (familiarity with the law is one of the principal reasons for choosing a certain law). However, it can also be a law with lower consumer standards chosen on purpose. National instruments of consumer and employee protection are usually mandatory contract law (parties cannot change it by agreement, and thus freedom of contract is limited) and differs among states. When the national legislator enacts consumer law or employment law protecting consumers or employees from an abuse of contractual freedom, the substantive rights established in the form of national mandatory law should also be protected in a cross-border situation in certain occasions.

In addition to the rationale behind special PIL rules, which aim to ensure the applicability of substantive protection of the objectively applicable law, the Rome I Regulation also needs to adapt to the needs and objectives of the internal market. While PIL rules around the world limit party autonomy in order to protect weaker parties from a possible abuse, EU PIL faces a different situation. Part of the national consumer and employment mandatory rules are the transposition of EU directives. Directives clearly distinguish between intra-EU situations and extra-EU situations: a consumer or employee operating within the internal market, or with strong connections with the Member States, is different from a consumer or employee with non-relevant connections to the EU and not operating within the internal market. However, the special conflict rules for consumer and employment contracts of the Rome I Regulations do not make such a distinction. Mandatory rules at EU level are increasing, and it will be seen that the 'neutrality' of PIL does not always respond to the requirements of the internal market.

Although the increase of mandatory regulation in the private arena is notorious both at national and European levels, it is generally agreed that party autonomy is still the basic principle of international contracts. Party autonomy is the rule, and its

[155] Rühl (2011), p. 574.

limitations and safeguards are the exceptions.[156] Nevertheless, it is also true that the stressing mandatoriness of the EU directives may threaten the prevalence of the will of the parties, promoting the application of mandatory EU law serving the necessities of the internal market.[157]

2.2.2 *The Law Applicable in the Absence of Choice of Law: The Need for Special Connecting Factors for Weaker Parties*

Many times, discussions about conflict of laws in contractual obligations focus on the principle of party autonomy and its limits. However, it is also necessary to refer to the principles governing cases where the parties have not chosen the law applicable to their contract. Mandatory rules protecting the weaker parties that cannot be deviated from by agreement belong to the law applicable in the absence of choice.

The Rome Convention embodied the principle of the closest connection in order to determine the law applicable to a contract in the absence of choice of law.[158] Article 4 Rome Convention provided as a general rule, in the absence of choice, for the applicability of the law with the closest connection to the contract and contained a general presumption according to which it was to be assumed that the law with the closest connection was the law of the party that rendered the most characteristic performance of the contract (i.e. the party that delivered the goods or rendered the service, for instance).[159] Concerning the justification of this presumption, in the

[156]Verhagen (2002), p. 135.

[157]Kuipers (2009), p. 1524; Verhagen (2002).

[158]Plender and Wilderspin (2015), p. 176; Stone (2018), pp. 441–445; Magnus (2016), pp. 270–272. The conflict rules among the Member States before the Rome Convention varied and used diverse connecting factors for the law applicable to a contract in the absence of choice of law. However, it could be observed that many Member States had a preference for a flexible approach that allowed the judge to consider the decisive connecting factor depending on the contract and circumstances of the case. After analysing the different solutions found in the legislation and case law of the Member States, the solution of Article 4 Rome Convention was adopted. Giuliano-Lagarde Report on the Convention of the law applicable to contractual obligations [1980] OJ C282/1, 19-20; Ibid., p. 271, 272.

[159]Article 4(1) of the Rome Convention stated that '[t]o the extent that the law applicable to the contract has not been chosen . . ., the contract shall be governed by the law of the country with which it is most closely connected'. Article 4(2) Rome Convention supplemented that provision stating that 'it shall be presumed that the contract is most closely connected with the country where the party who is to effect the performance which is characteristic of the contract has. . . his habitual residence'. Article 4 Rome I Regulation contains instead specific rules depending on the type of contract (sale of goods, contract f services, contract relating to a right in rem in immovable property or to a tenancy of immovable property, franchise contract, distribution contract etc.), where the connecting factor is also referring to the place of the party effectuating the characteristic performance, and then it provides that in case the law cannot be determined according to those specific

Giuliano-Lagarde report it was stated that 'the idea that this performance refers to the function which the legal relationship involved fulfils in the economic and social life of any country. The concept of characteristic performance essentially links the contract to the social and economic environment of which it performs part.'[160] In addition, the aim of the presumption was to improve the predictability of the law applicable to the contract, identifying the country most closely connected.[161] This approach, in principle, disregards the possible regulatory interests of the country of performance of the contract and rather focuses on the personal effects of the contract on the parties (such as the obligation to render performance or pay damages in case of breach of contract).[162] The use of the connecting factor of the place of the party rendering the characteristic performance of the contract is especially useful when the mutual obligations created by a contract were to be performed in different countries, avoiding the uncertainty.[163]

By following this approach, the 'risk of internationality' is generally assumed by the purchaser of goods or services or the party receiving the characteristic performance. This is the party that will have to deal with the application of a foreign law. The general costs deriving from the 'internationality' of the contract referred to above in this chapter are reduced when the law of the party performing the characteristic performance is applicable.[164] First, the party rendering the characteristic performance is more affected by the law applicable to the contract since, in general, legal systems impose specific regulations with regard to the characteristic performance (e.g. special contractual regimes for the sale of goods, loans etc.). Delivering goods or the provision of services can be complicated performances that require specific and detailed regulations, while the performance of payment is a simple transaction.[165] Besides more specific regulation, characteristic performance is more often the object of public law measures, and the application of both private and public laws of the same country to a contract reduces possible adaptation or

rules or there is a law manifestly most closely connected, the law most closely connected will be applicable.

[160] Giuliano-Lagarde Report [1980] OJ C282/1, 20. The Report also clarifies that the innovative idea of Article 4(2) Rome Convention was not completely unknown to some specialists and was in fact found in legal writings and certain case law of the time (Vischer, *Internationales Vertragsrecht*, Bern, 1962, 89-144, containing a table of decisions in this regard; also, judgment of 1 April 1970 of the Court of Appeal of Amsterdam, in *NAP NV v Christophery*). Giuliano-Lagarde Report [1980] OJ C282/1, 20, ft 38.

[161] Plender and Wilderspin (2015), p. 177.

[162] Solomon (2007), p. 1715. The Giuliano-Lagarde report states that '[t]he submission of the contract, in the absence of a choice by the parties, to the law appropriate to the characteristic performance defines the connecting factor of the contract from the inside, and not from the outside by elements unrelated to the essence of the obligation such as the nationality of the contracting parties or the place where the contract was concluded'. Giuliano-Lagarde Report [1980] OJ C282/1, 20.

[163] Plender and Wilderspin (2015), p. 177.

[164] See above Sect. 2.1.1.1.

[165] Garcimartín Alférez (2002), pp. 149–151.

coordination costs.[166] In addition, the party carrying out the characteristic performance would tend to conclude more than one contract (e.g. a business) for the same purposes. Applying different laws for every contract will strongly disturb that party. The connecting factor of 'habitual residence of the party rendering the characteristic performance' promotes efficiency since that party will be able to conduct its trade or business under the same legal regime. Also, it is not generally necessary for a business to insert a choice of law clause since the law applicable in the absence of choice already leads to its national law.[167] On the other hand, the application of the law of the party rendering the characteristic performance results in a reduction of the general costs of legal information since this party would also require more legal information for the transaction.[168]

Article 4 Rome I Regulation follows a similar rationale as its predecessor. However, in order to address the concerns about legal certainty and with the aim of providing highly foreseeable rules, Article 4(1) Rome I introduces specific rules with different connecting factors for eight different types of contracts, most of which correspond to the result that would have been reached by applying the characteristic performance approach. In most of the cases, the objective connecting factor is the habitual residence at the time of the conclusion of the contract of the party designated by the rule, which is normally the one rendering the characteristic performance of the contract (exceptions: place where immovable property is located or place where an auction takes place). Thus, in practice, courts were already generally following these rules in the context of the Rome Convention.[169] Article 4(2) Rome I then states that when the law applicable to the contract cannot be designated by the previous specific rules, the law most closely connected to the contract is applicable, and then Article 4 (3) Rome I introduces an escape clause for situations where there is a manifest closest connection with other laws. Article 4(1) Rome I lies in the assumption that the designated law is generally the law most closely connected to the contract.[170] The rules of Article 4(1) Rome I are not rigid rules since Article 4(3) Rome I allows the judge to apply a different law if it is manifestly connected closer to the contract.

However, the approach followed by Article 4 Rome I is not considered to be appropriate for all categories of contracts, and there are a number of categorical exceptions for which the application of the law of the party rendering the characteristic performance is not suitable. The typical exception concerns consumer contracts and employment contracts since in contracts involving weaker parties, the application of that general connecting factor structurally favours the economically stronger

[166]Ibid., p. 150.

[167]Solomon (2007), p. 1716.

[168]Garcimartín Alférez (2002), p. 150.

[169]Plender and Wilderspin (2015), p. 186 et seq.; Magnus (2016), p. 270, 271.

[170]Magnus (2016), p. 269.

party.[171] To counterbalance the difference between the bargaining position of the parties, specific connecting factors are provided.

In the case of consumer contracts, consumers are generally protected in most jurisdictions by the application of the law of the country where the consumer has his or her habitual residence. In the Rome I Regulation, Article 6(1) provides for the application of that law in the absence of choice. If the general rule of Article 4 (1) Rome I was applicable, the connecting factor will be the habitual residence of the seller or of the provider of services. The mandatory rules of the consumer habitual residence would therefore not be applicable. The same can be said as in a situation of choice of law: when the national legislator enacts mandatory consumer law protecting consumers, the substantive rights established in the form of national mandatory law should also be protected in a cross-border situation.

A similar system for the protection of the weaker party is provided with regard to individual employment contracts. However, in this case, the employee is the party effectuating the characteristic performance, and thus the application of the objective connecting factor would lead to the application of the law of the habitual residence of the employee. In the Rome I Regulation, Article 8 primarily refers to the law of the country in which the employee habitually carries out his or her work. The place of habitual work is considered as most closely connected to the employment contract, and in general, both the employee and the employer are familiar with it. Moreover, the place where the employee habitually carries out his/her work will often coincide with his/her habitual residence. The country where the employee habitually carries out his/her work has the most interest in applying his/her mandatory rules ensuring employment rights and conditions.[172]

2.2.3 *Protection of Consumers and Employees in Cases of Pre-contractual Liability*

It is necessary to mention a special situation where consumers or employees can also lose their protection due to the applicable law. Articles 6 and 8 Rome I do not include cases outside the material scope of the Regulation. Article 1(2)(i) Rome I excludes from the scope of the Regulation cases arising out of pre-contractual negotiations. Which is the law applicable to the obligations arising from pre-contractual dealings in case of consumer and employment contracts?

For example, pre-contractual obligations may arise when a consumer receives a post-mail or email from a foreign company stating that he or she is the winner of a prize and then a contract is not successfully concluded or when the professional, before the conclusion of a contract, does not fully disclose the necessary

---

[171] Guardans Cambó (1992), p. 323 et seq. regarding consumer contracts and 405 et seq. regarding individual employment contracts.

[172] In that regard, see below Sect. 2.4.

information. Or when a person receives a very promising job offer in a different country but when he or she has quit his/her current job and moved and bought a house in the new country, the new employer decides not to conclude the new employment contract. This type of cases would fall under the category of pre-contractual liability or *culpa in contrahendo*.[173] Pre-contractual liability or *culpa in contrahendo* is a liability arising due to a harmful conduct that occurs during the formation period or negotiation phase of a contract.[174] The law applicable in a cross-border situation becomes very relevant since it is not a harmonised area and legislation differs among Member States, it being possible that the professional or employer would be liable according to the law of a country and not liable according to a different national law.

In continental Europe, the concept of *culpa in contrahendo* is not unified, and depending on the country, it covers different situations. Pre-contractual liability may be caused by several circumstances, which generally consist of infringement by one of the parties of information duties or false information or omission of essential information about the object of the contract during the preparatory negotiations; negligent causing of physical injury by a party to the other party's person or property during the course of the negotiations; dropping off of negotiations without just cause, causing the other party important patrimonial or business damages; or invalidity of the contract caused by one of the parties.[175] Normally, in the case of consumer and employment contracts, pre-contractual liability would be related to information duties or breaking-off negotiations.

The categorisation of pre-contractual liability as a contractual or extra-contractual matter differed among the different national legislation. Nowadays, pre-contractual liability has been qualified by the EU legislator as an extra-contractual matter. Already the ECJ dealt with this problem of categorisation in the context of the 1968 Brussels Convention in the *Tacconi* judgment.[176] In the *Tacconi* decision, the ECJ held that actions covered by Article 5(3) Brussels Convention (actions based on tort, delict or quasi-delict) could be distinguished from actions covered by Article 5 (1) Brussels Convention (actions based on contract) by answering whether an obligation was assumed freely by one party towards another.[177] The ECJ stated that there was not a freely assumed obligation in the case of a breach of a rule that required the parties to act in good faith during the negotiations and, as a result, they

[173]The terminology used in the different jurisdictions differs, mainly referring to pre-contractual liability or *culpa in contrahendo*. Here, I refer to both terms indistinctively, regardless of the differences that exist between what the terms englobe in some jurisdictions.

[174]Hage Chahine (2012), p. 452.

[175]Moura Vicente (2013), p. 54; Arenas García (2007), pp. 320–322.

[176]Case C-334/00 *Fonderie Officine Meccaniche Tacconi SpA v Heinrich Wagner Sinto Maschinenfabrik GmbH (HWS)* [2002] ECR I-07357.

[177]Tacconi, para 23.

understood the action concerning pre-contractual liability as a matter relating to tort, delict or quasi-delict under Article 5(3) Brussels Convention.[178]

Thus, the law applicable to pre-contractual liability is determined by the Rome II Regulation on the law applicable to extra-contractual obligations.[179] The Rome I Regulation, in Recital 10, makes clear that 'obligations arising out of dealings prior to the conclusion of the contract are covered by Article 12 of Regulation (EC) No 864/2007. Such obligations should therefore be excluded from the scope of this Regulation'.

The Rome II Regulation introduced Article 12 as a novelty, clarifying the law applicable in such cases, which before the entering into force of the Regulation were solved by case law and doctrine.[180] The EU legislator decided to introduce a specific conflict rule in the Rome II Regulation on the law applicable to extra-contractual obligations as an autonomous concept.[181] In this regard, Recital 30 Rome II refers to two examples of *culpa in contrahendo*: violation of the duty of disclosure and breaking off of contractual negotiations. Article 12 Rome II reads:

1. The law applicable to a non-contractual obligation arising out of dealings prior to the conclusion of a contract, regardless of whether the contract was actually concluded or not, shall be the law that applies to the contract or that would have been applicable to it had it been entered into.
2. Where the law applicable cannot be determined on the basis of paragraph 1, it shall be:
   (a) the law of the country in which the damage occurs, irrespective of the country in which the event giving rise to the damage occurred and irrespective of the country or countries in which the indirect consequences of that event occurred; or
   (b) where the parties have their habitual residence in the same country at the time when the event giving rise to the damage occurs, the law of that country; or
   (c) where it is clear from all the circumstances of the case that the non-contractual obligation arising out of dealings prior to the conclusion of a contract is manifestly more closely connected with a country other than that indicated in points (a) and (b), the law of that other country.

Focusing on the first paragraph, the provision refers us to the law that applies or would have been applicable to the contract if concluded. Therefore, in cases of breaking off of negotiations of a consumer contract or individual employment contract or violations of the duty of disclosure, for example, Article 12 Rome II allows the application of the laws designated by Articles 6 and 8 Rome I. Therefore, the special conflict rules protecting certain consumer and employment contracts extend their protection to the pre-contractual negotiating period of the contract. Thus, weaker contracting parties are granted protection also before the conclusion of the contract, in accordance with national legislation that provide for protection to

[178]Tacconi, paras 25 et seq.

[179]Regulation (EC) No 864/2007 of the European Parliament and of the Council of 11 July 2007 on the law applicable to non-contractual obligations (Rome II) (OJ 2007 L 199/40).

[180]Moura Vicente (2013), p. 54, referring for a deeper analysis to: Moura Vicente, *Da responsabilidade pré–contratual em Direito internacional privado* (Coimbra, 2001).

[181]Recital 30 Rome II.

consumers and employees during the pre-contractual phase.[182] However, in practice, it can be under some circumstances difficult to predict whether the situation would fall under the special circumstances of a specific provision or not. For example, in the case of consumers, it could be that at the time of the breaking off of negotiations, the circumstances required by Article 6 Rome I to be considered a protected consumer contract are not present in the case. However, while in the context of Article 5 Rome Convention the requirements became more problematic in this case, the requirements of Article 6 Rome I can be easily fulfilled prior to the conclusion of the contract. That is, one of the cases where Article 5 Rome Convention became applicable was when, in the country of habitual residence of the consumer, the conclusion of the contract was preceded by a specific invitation addressed to the consumer or by advertising and the consumer had taken in that country all the steps necessary for the conclusion of the contract. Before the conclusion of the contract, the latter requirement could have not been determined. However, the requirements of Article 6 Rome I do not provide for circumstances that cannot be predicted as such before the conclusion of the contract.[183]

2.3 Consumers and Employees in the EU Internal Market

EU Member States have provided, in different degrees, for consumer protection in their domestic law since the 1960s. Following a similar policy and in order to prevent the existent disparities between national laws from becoming an impediment to achieving the internal market, the EU started to enact directives harmonising national laws. Until recently, these EU consumer directives have generally followed a minimum harmonisation technique, leaving the option to Member States to grant a more beneficial and extensive protection to consumers. Thus, they set minimum consumer standards in the internal market. Although these directives approximate national laws, they do not solve the problem of disparities of national legislation. This is one of the reasons why the Consumer Rights Directive[184] has adopted a maximum harmonisation approach, and this seems to be the new trend of the EU legislator. Thus, in the current EU consumer acquis, there are a big number of directives regulating topics such as unfair contract terms, distance selling, package travel, consumer rights etc.; following minimum and maximum harmonisation approaches; and establishing mandatory consumer provisions at EU level.

[182]Hage Chahine (2012), p. 524.

[183]Arenas García (2007), p. 17.

[184]Directive 2011/83/EU of the European Parliament and of the Council of 25 October 2011 on consumer rights, amending Council Directive 93/13/EEC and Directive 1999/44/EC of the European Parliament and of the Council and repealing Council Directive 85/577/EEC and Directive 97/7/EC of the European Parliament and of the Council (OJ 2011 L304/64).

The EU attitude towards employee protection differs from the consumer protection approach since the 'social' dimension – rather than the competition and economic integration one – is of major importance. The main purposes of EU employment legislation have been the removal of obstacles to the free movement of workers, elimination of discrimination and prevention of potential negative consequences to the creation of a common market (e.g. social dumping or a regulatory race to the bottom).[185] Nowadays, the Treaty of Lisbon emphasises the social dimension. The EU lays down numerous directives in the diverse areas concerning employment (e.g. protection from discrimination, health and safety; protection during business changes; posting of workers; etc.)[186] Besides having a minimum harmonisation approach, directives do not cover all areas of labour law. Thus, domestic regulation of cross-border employment remains still of major importance. Because of the importance of the interests involved and the disparities existent between the laws of the Member States, they are more reluctant to agree on EU common rules in the area of labour law.

EU PIL rules on consumer and employment protection need to be aware of the existing EU substantive legislation and policies in that regard in order to be coordinated with it and vice versa. The fact that directives take a minimum or maximum harmonisation approach, or the debate regarding unification of EU contract law, indeed affects EU PIL.

Therefore, in order to ascertain the role of the EU regarding consumer and employee protection and how it affects PIL, this section will briefly define the EU policies and strategies concerning consumer and employee protection, as well as a summary of the development of the EU legislation and competences in that respect, to then discuss the advantages and disadvantages of the unification of EU contract law versus the operation of PIL rules.

2.3.1 The EU Consumer and Employment Legislation and Policy: An Overview

2.3.1.1 An Overview of EU Consumer Policy

The vast part of the legislative activity regarding consumer contracts conducted by the EU has been pursued towards economic integration in the internal market and achieved by harmonising the laws of the Member States. In the subject areas where Member States transfer their regulatory competence to the EU for the harmonisation of the subject matter, the EU chooses the standards of consumer protection. But what regulatory technique is the most appropriate? Should there be a level playing field left to the Member States to set stricter rules than the ones provided by the

[185] Grusic (2015), p. 2.

[186] For more detailed explanation and examples of specific directives: Leighton (2010), p. 29, 30.

directives? By shortly reviewing the development of the consumer policy of the EU, a better understanding of the consumer protection objectives of the EU, and of the current situation, can be achieved.

Under the Treaty of Rome, which was agreed in 1957 and entered into force in 1958, there was no specific legal base regarding consumer protection, and only few incidental references were made to the position of the consumer in the EEC legal framework.[187] These explicit references did not constitute an attempt to develop a structure of consumer rights, but rather it was understood that the consumer would simply benefit from a more efficient market than the process of integration would develop.

In the 1970s, Member States had already developed different consumer protection laws. Those with a French law basis focused on consumer information and consumer contract law. Common law countries rather focused on the law of product safety and competition law. German-law-oriented countries just covered specific areas of consumer protection, while the Nordic countries had already a well-developed consumer protection law.[188]

Following the trend, from the 1970s onwards, and despite lacking a specific type of consumer policy or legal basis for consumer protection at an EEC level, initiatives in the field of consumer protection were taken by the EEC. The inauguration of a consumer protection policy in the EEC came with the Council Resolution of 14 April 1975 on a preliminary programme of the European Economic Community for a consumer protection and information policy.[189] In the Programme for consumer protection and information policy of 1975, it was recognised by the Commission that consumers are a weaker party and their interests must be protected. The need for providing detailed information to the consumers was emphasised, and some basic consumer rights were demanded: the right to protection of health and safety, the right to protection of economic interests, the right of redress, the right to information and education and the right of representation. It was proposed that it was necessary to intervene and end the equality of contracting parties in consumer sales. The rationale followed by the Commission was based on the paradigm of the rational consumer who only requires adequate information to achieve his or her adequate role in the market. In the second Programme in 1981,[190] the same approach was confirmed by the Commission, and, in addition, consumer protection was recognised as a means to achieve the objectives of the internal market.[191] A third Council Resolution took place on June 1986,[192] regarding the future policy for the protection and promotion of consumer interests, expressed within the context of internal market policy.[193] The

[187]Weatherill (2013), p. 3, 4.

[188]Cseres (2005), p. 195.

[189]OJ 1975 C-92/1.

[190]OJ 1981 C-133/1.

[191]Schüller (2012), p. 126, 127.

[192]OJ 1986 C-167/1.

[193]Weatherill (2013), pp. 7–9.

Commission considered that national consumer laws affected market integration and thus must be taken into account for ECC policy.

Later, in 1987, consumer protection became an independent policy objective with the adoption of the Single European Act of 1987.[194] Even though it still did not provide for a specific legal basis, it considered consumer policy as a complement to the process of market integration and required the Commission to take action to ensure a high level of protection in the areas of health, safety, the environment and consumer protection. A consolidation of the former policies was attained in the 1989 Council Resolution regarding future priorities for relaunching consumer protection policy.[195]

During that period, not only soft law measures were taken. Several consumer directives were adopted during the mid-eighties on the basis of Article 100 of the Treaty Establishing the European Community (EC Treaty) (subsequently Article 94 EC, now Article 115 TFEU), which had as requisite a direct link with the common market, with the intention to safeguard the economic interests of the consumers: Directive 84/450 on misleading advertising,[196] Directive 85/374 on product liability,[197] Directive 85/577 on contracts negotiated away from business premises[198] and Directive 87/102 on consumer credit.[199] Once the Single European Act entered into effect, the then Article 100a (subsequently Article 95 EC, now Article 114 TFEU), used for the adoption of measures approximating national laws with the objective of establishing the internal market, became the legal basis for the subsequent consumer law directives. Thus, much of EU consumer law is tied to the internal market.

The Maastricht Treaty 1992 incorporated a specific legal basis for consumer protection measures. The Treaty contained a special title on consumer protection (Title IX). Its Article 129a (later 153 in the Treaty of Amsterdam, now Article 169 TFEU) provided:

> The Community shall contribute to the attainment of a high level of consumer protection through:
>
> (a) measures adopted pursuant to Article 100a in the context of the completion of the internal market;
> (b) specific action which supports and supplements the policy pursued by the Member States to protect the health, safety and economic interests of consumers and to provide adequate information to consumers.

[194] Single European Act (SEA) OJ 1987 L 169/1.

[195] OJ 1989 C-294/01.

[196] OJ 1984 L 250/17, repealed by Directive 2006/114/EC (OJ 2006 L 376/21).

[197] OJ 1985 L 210/29.

[198] OJ 1985 L 372/31, repealed by Directive 2011/83/EU (OJ 2011 L 304/64).

[199] OJ 1987 L 42/48, repealed by Directive 2008/48/EC (OJ 2008 L 133/66).

Thus, it was for the first time recognised that the Community had the power to act in order to protect consumers either as an internal market policy or as a supporting policy of the Member States' actions.

The Amsterdam Treaty brought an important revision of the title on consumer protection. Article 153 Treaty of Amsterdam (now 169 TFEU) largely modified and improved its predecessor. Article 153 recognised consumer rights (instead of consumer interests), applicable to both internal and non-internal market measures. Specifically, it was required that the Community contributed to promoting the right of consumers to information and education and to organise themselves in order to safeguard their interests. Also, consumer protection requirements had to be taken into account in defining and implementing other Community policies and activities. Moreover, the Community was required to take measures both supporting the internal market objective and supporting and monitoring the policy pursued by the Member States.[200] The Treaty of Nice maintained the changes adopted by the Treaty of Amsterdam.

During this second phase, in which the need to protect the consumer became linked to the establishment of the functioning of the internal market, a big number of directives regarding consumer protection were enacted, such as Directive 90/314/EEC on package travel,[201] Directive 93/13/EEC on unfair contract terms,[202]

---

[200](1) In order to promote the interests of consumers and to ensure a high level of consumer protection, the Community shall contribute to protecting the health, safety and economic interests of consumers, as well as to promoting their right to information, education and to organize themselves in order to safeguard their interests.

(2) Consumer protection requirements shall be taken into account in defining and implementing other Community policies and activities.

(3) The Community shall contribute to the attainment of the objectives referred to in paragraph 1 through:

(a) measures adopted pursuant to Article 95 in the context of the completion of the internal market;

(b) measures which support, supplement and monitor the policy pursued by the Member States.

(4) The Council, acting in accordance with the procedure referred to in Article 25174 and after consulting the Economic and Social Committee, shall adopt the measures referred to in paragraph 3(b).

(5) Measures adopted pursuant to paragraph 4 shall not prevent any Member State from maintaining or introducing more stringent protective measures. Such measures must be compatible with this Treaty. The Commission shall be notified of them.

[201]Council Directive 90/314/ECC of 13 June 1990 on package travel, package holidays and package tours (OJ 1990 L 158/59), now repealed and replaced by Directive 2015/2302/EU (OJ 2015 L 326/1).

[202]Council Directive 93/13/EEC of 5 April 1993 on unfair terms in consumer contracts (OJ L 95/29.

Directive 94/47/EC on timesharing,[203] Directive 97/7/EC on distance selling,[204] Directive 98/27/EC on injunctions,[205] Directive 99/44/EC on the sale of consumer goods and associated guarantees[206] or Directive 2002/65/EC on distance marketing of financial services.[207] These Directives are generally characterised by taking information disclosure measures as a means to protect the consumer and having a minimum harmonisation approach, meaning that they set a minimum standard for the development of consumer policy, allowing Member States to adopt more protective rules.

Traditionally, Member States have followed a more interventionist approach regarding consumer policy than the EC, which until that point opted for a less paternalistic line based on information disclosure as the most important mechanism for consumer protection.[208] It seems so far that the EC focused on market integration, and therefore the market and competition issues acquired more importance than did social issues. Meanwhile, the Member States' consumer law was more based on the concept of social welfare, and the consumer was considered the weak party who needs to be protected by national regulation. The EC put such an emphasis not on the consumer as the weaker party but on the responsibility of both market parties, and thus it provided for the adoption of information provisions rather than corrective legal measures.[209] This information model is based on the existence of a rational and independent consumer who is reasonably informed and able to act according to his or her interests and who can facilitate the establishment of the internal market.[210]

The string of directives adopted up to this period are of a minimum harmonising nature (except Directive 2002/65/EC on distance marketing of financial services). This means that directives allow Member States to adopt rules more favourable to the consumer than the ones provided in the directive itself. As it is already known, directives need to be transposed into national law, and when doing so Member States have the choice in deciding the means to achieve the results required by the directive,

---

[203]Directive 94/47/EC of the European Parliament and the Council of 26 October 1994 on the protection of purchasers in respect of certain aspects of contracts relating to the purchase of the right to use immovable properties on a timeshare basis (OJ 1994 L 280/83), now replaced by Directive 2008/122/EC (OJ 2009 L 33/10).

[204]Directive 97/7/EC of the European Parliament and of the Council of 20 May 1997 on the protection of consumers in respect of distance contracts (OJ 1997 L 144/19), repealed by Directive 2011/83/EU (OJ 2011 L 304/64).

[205]Directive 98/27/EC of the European Parliament and of the Council of 19 May 1998 on injunctions for the protection of consumers' interests (OJ 1998 L 166/51) repealed by Directive 2009/22/EC (OJ 2008 L 110/30).

[206]Directive 1999/44/EC of the European Parliament and of the Council of 25 May 1999 on certain aspects of the sale of consumer goods and associated guarantees (OJ 1999 L 171/12).

[207]Directive 2002/65/EC of the European Parliament and of the Council of 23 September 2002 concerning the distance marketing of consumer financial services and amending Council Directive 90/619/EEC and Directives 97/7/EC and 98/27/EC (OJ 2002 L 271/16).

[208]Cseres (2005), p. 20, 21.

[209]Ibid., p. 111, 112.

[210]Ibid., p. 220.

as well as providing only the protection established by the directive or improving it. The result of this minimum harmonisation approach is that instead of creating a uniform EU consumer law, there are as many consumer laws as there are Member States. Minimum harmonisation approximates national rules and diminishes the differences between national consumer laws of the Member States, creating a minimum threshold of protection for the consumer, adjusting the degree of diversity existing between the consumer regulations of the different Member States. The reasoning behind this approach towards EU consumer law lies in two main arguments. Firstly, in a cross-border situation, even in an intra-EU situation, two or more national laws collide, and one has to govern the transaction. In this context, consumer law is in its majority considered as mandatory law, and thus national or EU consumer law cannot be circumvented by choosing the law of another country as applicable to the transaction. The differences existing between the consumer laws of the Member States could be an obstacle to cross-border transactions within the internal market since the parties, especially the traders, might not be aware of the levels of protection that their customers might enjoy.[211] Secondly, on the side of the consumers, the differences between the consumer laws of the Member States create a lack of confidence when contracting across the border due to the uncertainty regarding the protection they might receive when purchasing goods or contracting services abroad.[212] Harmonisation of the main areas of consumer law helps to remove, or reduce, these obstacles to cross-border transactions within the internal market.

However, the Consumer Policy Programme for 2002–2006[213] encouraged minimisation on the variations in the consumer protection rules among the Member States that 'create fragmentation of the internal market to the detriment of consumers and business' and thus provided for the review and reform of the existent EU consumer directives. The Commission increasingly considered minimum harmonisation as inadequate and promoted a shift towards maximum harmonisation, where the EU would have the regulatory responsibility in the field covered by the particular measure and Member States would not be able to set stricter standards. The debate between the adequacy of minimum or maximum harmonisation as a means to regulate consumer law protection in the EU has been intense and is still the object of discussion. Since it brings direct consequences to the EU PIL regulation of the law applicable to consumer contracts, as a conflict rule would become useless in an intra-EU cross-border situation in the case of a maximum harmonisation scenario, the debate between minimum and maximum harmonisation will be the object of study in a separate section.[214]

Nevertheless, the shift to the intended consumer policy has not resulted in a maximum harmonisation approach on all EU consumer directives enacted since

---

[211] Twigg-Flesner (2012), p. 8, 9.

[212] Ibid., p. 8, 9.

[213] COM (02) 208, OJ 2002 C-137/2.

[214] See below Sect. 2.3.2.

then. There have been some directives enacted with a maximum harmonisation approach, such as the Unfair Commercial Practices Directive,[215] the Consumer Rights Directive[216] (although its material scope was reduced in order to accept its maximum harmonisation scope) and the new Package Travel Directive.[217] However, the Consumer Credit Directive[218] or the Timeshare Directive,[219] for example, were enacted with a minimum harmonisation approach. The 2002–2006 and 2007–2013 consumer policy strategies included as their main objectives high common level of consumer protection, effective enforcement and involvement of consumer organisations in EU policies, empowering consumers, enhancing welfare and protection from risks that consumers cannot cope with individually.

Since the Treaty of Lisbon, the primary law for consumer protection policy in the EU has been Articles 4(2)(f), 12, 114(3) and 169 of TFEU and Article 38 of the Charter of Fundamental Rights. Article 169 TFEU, titled Consumer Protection, states:

> 1. In order to promote the interests of consumers and to ensure a high level of consumer protection, the Union shall contribute to protecting the health, safety and economic interests of consumers, as well as to promoting their right to information, education and to organise themselves in order to safeguard their interests.
> 2. The Union shall contribute to the attainment of the objectives referred to in paragraph 1 through:
>
>   (a) measures adopted pursuant to Article 114 in the context of the completion of the internal market;
>   (b) measures which support, supplement and monitor the policy pursued by the Member States.
> 3. The European Parliament and the Council, acting in accordance with the ordinary

---

[215] Directive 2005/29/EC of the European Parliament and of the Council of 11 May 2005 concerning unfair business-to-consumer commercial practices in the internal market and amending Council Directive 84/450/EEC, Directives 97/7/EC, 98/27/EC and 2002/65/EC of the European Parliament and of the Council and Regulation (EC) No 2006/2004 of the European Parliament and of the Council ('Unfair Commercial Practices Directive') (OJ 2005 L 149/22).

[216] Directive 2011/83/EU of the European Parliament and of the Council of 25 October 2011 on consumer rights, amending Council Directive 93/13/EEC and Directive 1999/44/EC of the European Parliament and of the Council and repealing Council Directive 85/577/EEC and Directive 97/7/EC of the European Parliament and of the Council ('Consumer Rights Directive') (OJ 2011 L 304/64).

[217] Directive 2015/2302 of the European Parliament and of the Council of 25 November 2015 on package travel and linked travel arrangements, amending Regulation (EC) No 2006/2004 and Directive 2011/83/EU of the European Parliament and of the Council and repealing Council Directive 90/314/EEC (OJ 2015 L 326/1).

[218] Directive 2008/48/EC of the European Parliament and of the Council of 23 April 2008 on credit agreements for consumers and repealing Council Directive 87/102/EEC (OJ 2008 L 133/66).

[219] Directive 2008/122/EC of the European Parliament and of the Council of 14 January 2009 on the protection of consumers in respect of certain aspects of timeshare, long-term holiday product, resale and exchange contracts (OJ 2009 L 33/10).

legislative procedure and after consulting the Economic and Social Committee, shall adopt the measures referred to in paragraph 2(b).

4. Measures adopted pursuant to paragraph 3 shall not prevent any Member State from maintaining or introducing more stringent protective measures. Such measures must be compatible with the Treaties. The Commission shall be notified of them.

Article 169 supplements Article 114 of the TFEU, which contemplates the adoption of measures approximating national laws with the objective of establishing the internal market and indicates that regarding consumer protection, the Commission will take as a base a high level of protection. Most of the EU consumer directives are in fact enacted on the basis of the latter provision rather than on the former one. Consumer protection requirements must be taken into account in defining and implementing other EU policies and activities according to Article 12 TFEU, and Article 38 of the Charter of Fundamental Rights of the European Union provides that Union policies shall ensure a high level of consumer protection.[220]

In 2012, the Commission adopted the European Consumer Agenda, which explains the EU consumer policy to follow up to 2020. Among its objectives we find maximisation of consumer participation and transactions in the market, and its key points include improving consumer safety, enhancing knowledge of consumer rights, strengthening the enforcement of consumer rules or integrating consumer interests into the key sectoral policies.[221]

Regarding the existent EU secondary law, there are nowadays more than 90 EU directives that deal with issues related to consumer protection. The consumer acquis is complex and occasionally inconsistent. Although for this study we only refer to the directives that have a bigger impact regarding cross-border consumer contracts, the current scenario of directives dealing with consumer matters includes both minimum and maximum harmonisation directives, with different regulatory techniques and regarding cross-border issues or not necessarily.[222]

The most common regulatory technique used by EU consumer directives consists in requiring that the consumer be provided with specified information about the eventual transaction. This approach is aimed at improving transparency in the pre-contractual phase and is frequently complemented by the requirement of a 'cooling off' period within which the consumer is allowed to exercise his or her right to withdraw from the contract.[223] This approach minimises the intervention with private autonomy since it does not interfere in the substance of the contract.

[220] Jana Valant, 'Consumer Protection in the EU. Policy overview' EPRS I European Parliamentary Research Service, September 2015.

[221] Communication from the Commission to the European Parliament, the Council, the Economic and Social Committee and the Committee of the Regions. A European Consumer Agenda - Boosting confidence and growth. COM(2012) 225 final.

[222] In this regard: Weatherill (2013), De la Rosa (2003).

[223] Weatherill (2013), pp. 92–94.

This technique promotes an 'informed consumer' without diminishing the choice. It supports the consumer in the pre-contractual and post-contractual phases and attempts to improve the bargaining process: the consumer, with a clearer appreciation of what is on offer, will be able to negotiate a deal closer to his or her preferences. Cooling-off periods offer a fallback protection. However, these procedures are funded on the rational consumer rationale, assuming that the consumer has the capacity to process the information that is supplied to him/her and react rationally to it, and that is not always the case. Moreover, another criticism lies in the failure to address substantive unfairness. Even if the consumer is supported by mandatory information disclosure, he/she might not be able to get a fair deal due to the imbalance of bargaining power. This regulatory approach is followed by the Consumer Credit Directive, Payment Services Directive, Timeshare Directive, Package Travel Directive or Consumer Rights Directive.

Another regulatory technique would consist of using the law to address the fairness of the contract. Although freedom of contract is restricted, the purity of contractual freedom is not consistent with current modern market conditions. This technique is used, for example, in the Directive on Unfair Contract Terms, Directive on Consumer Sales and Guarantees or Consumer Rights Directive.

Thus, we can observe that there is no comprehensive and consistent regime for EU consumer contract law. The EU rules supplement national consumer law, which evolves unaffected by the EU in the areas not covered by the EU directives or even in those areas covered by directives with a minimum harmonisation nature. The scenario is at least chaotic, consisting of several directives dealing with specific types of contracts, directives in the context of cross-border commercial transactions and some others not necessarily (e.g. off-premises contracts, credit). In addition, not all directives follow the same regulatory regime.

It has to be kept in mind that the EU has its own agenda, on which Member States do not always agree. In addition, the development of EU consumer law previously mentioned is characterised by a massive production of consumer directives, which also affects the current scenario. In this regard, according to Weatherill, the consumer law acquis is chaotically shaped because of political accident.[224]

2.3.1.2 An Overview of EU Employment Policy

EU employment law has been developed in different phases, from a market liberal approach to the current system of social accommodation. The need to complement economic integration with a 'social dimension' and the acquisition of competences by the EU characterise the development of the EU employment legislation and policy.

From the Treaty of Rome until the 1970s, the body of EU employment law consisted mainly of few rules of primary law (provisions on free movement and

[224]Ibid., p. 141.

equal pay between men and women) and some supplementary secondary legislation.[225] These measures were based on the liberal approach, which considered that the building of a common market would bring economic progress, from which consumers and employees would benefit. The employment provision on equal pay, for example, was motivated not by social policy reasons but rather by competition reasons: companies from Member States that paid women the same wages as men could suffer from a competitive disadvantage within the market.[226] By the end of the 1970s, concerns about structural imbalances in Europe led to the rise of a social dimension to the internal market. In 1974, the Council adopted the first Programme of Social Action.[227]

The first sex discrimination directives were enacted during the 1970s, as well as the first directives on collective redundancies, transfer of undertakings and employer insolvency. The Single European Act (SEA) 1986 introduced provisions for the harmonisation of health and safety conditions at work. During the 1980s, the need for a social policy accompanying the economic integration project was recognised. This policy change was reflected in the Community Charter of Fundamental Social Rights of 1989,[228] which, albeit not legally binding, was of considerable importance for the upcoming legal development; in fact, a vast part of EU employment legislation enacted since then has referred to the Community Charter.[229]

With the entry into force of the Treaty of Maastricht, Member States agreed on the Social Policy Protocol, which provided for additional competences in the area of social policy and thus made it possible to implement the Social Charter.[230] The Council was endowed with the power to adopt directives laying down minimum requirements in several new sectors, which would then be binding on all Member States (except the UK, which opted out).

The Treaty of Amsterdam integrated the Social Policy Protocol into the EC Treaty with some minor changes, making it thus applicable to the UK as well. Important new directives, such as the Directive 2000/43/EC on equal treatment between persons irrespective of racial or ethnic origin and Directive 2000/78/EC on a general framework for equal treatment in employment and occupation, were soon adopted.

With the turn of the millennium, a shift of policy can be appreciated: focus was placed on the combination of ideas of flexibility in the labour market and employment security as a means to achieve economic efficiency and competitiveness. Legal instruments on part-time, fixed-term, and temporary agency or telework were

---

[225] Riesenhuber (2012), p. 18.

[226] Ibid., p. 18.

[227] Social Action Programme COM(73) 1600 24 October 1973.

[228] *Community Charter of Fundamental Social Rights* - Draft. COM (89) 471 final, 2 October *1989.*

[229] Riesenhuber (2012), p. 19, 20.

[230] Directives adopted on the basis of the Protocol include: European Works Council Directive (94/45/EC) now replaced by the revised directive (2009/38/EC); Parental Leave Directive (96/34/EC) now replaced by Directive 2010/18/EU; and the Part-time Work Directive (97/81/EC).

enacted. In the 2006 Green Paper 'Modernising Labour Law to Meet the Challenges of the 21st Century', the EU presented that approach as 'Flexicurity', which was not well received and therefore not further pursued.[231]

The Treaty of Lisbon allowed for further progress in consolidating the social dimension of European integration. The Treaty of Lisbon emphasises social objectives. The Charter of Fundamental Rights is given the same binding force as the Treaties. The Charter recognises rights such as workers' right to information and consultation, as well as the rights to collective bargaining, fair and just working conditions, social security and social assistance.

Sources of EU employment law are both primary and secondary laws of the EU. The EU Treaty (TEU) and the Treaty on the Functioning of the European Union (TFEU) have ensured, since the Treaty of Lisbon, an internal market where the fundamental freedoms, open market economy and free competition are guaranteed (Articles 3(2) and 3(3) TEU and 119 TFEU). Among the fundamental freedoms, the free movement of workers is the most important for EU employment contract. However, freedom of services and freedom of establishment are also of relevance (e.g. when a national labour law affects those rights). Also, free movement of goods can play a role (e.g. when a labour dispute restricts cross-border commerce). Article 157 TFEU containing the principle of equal pay is also relevant.

Leaving aside the areas of fundamental rights, fundamental freedoms and equality, EU employment law is mostly laid down in secondary legislation, especially in directives. As it is known, directives lay down goals, usually as minimum standards, which have to be achieved by the Member States. Domestic implementations differ among the Member States, which can normally improve the minimum standards provided by the respective directive. For example, the European Working Time Directive entitles workers to receive an annual paid leave of 20 days, but some Member States have adopted a more beneficious regime for the workers. In accordance with Article 153 TFEU, the EU adopts directives that set minimum requirements for working and employment conditions and informing and consulting workers.

There are EU employment directives in the following areas: protection from discrimination at work on grounds of sex; protection from discrimination on other protected grounds (race/ethnicity, disability, sexual orientation, age and religion and belief); health and safety at work; protection during business changes (redundancy, mergers/acquisitions and outsourcing changes); freedom of movement for workers to obtain jobs or be seconded across the EU and to establish businesses in other parts of the EU, along with supportive measures, such as mutual recognition of qualifications and skills, provision of information and consultation with employees and/or their representatives in addition to the requirements relating to redundancies and transfers; rights for some atypical/non-standard workers, such as part timers,

[231] Riesenhuber (2012), p. 22, 23.

teleworkers, fixed-term workers and agency temps; and 'family friendly rights', such as maternity rights and parental leave.[232]

Besides having a minimum harmonisation approach, directives do not cover all areas of employment law. Thus, domestic regulation of cross-border employment remains still of major importance. Legal diversity within the EU is very noticeable. For example, Nordic countries such as Denmark and Sweden are known for regulating most of the important issues by collective bargaining at different levels. On the other hand, France, for instance, has a comprehensive and detailed regulation (although also high levels of collective bargaining).[233] The legal diversity in the area of employment law among Member States is the main reason for the exclusion of some very important areas of labour law from the EU competences (e.g. unfair dismissal, right to strike etc.) or the lack of regulation regarding some other issues because of the difficulty to reach agreements among the Member States. Because of the importance of the interests involved, Member States have a special interest in regulating employment law matters themselves.[234] However, it is also an area of utmost importance for the well functioning of the EU internal market.

The current phase of development has been defined as one of 'consolidation'.[235] While EU employment law is focused upon cross-border matters and the well functioning of the internal market, genuine employment protection is provided by the national law of every Member State.[236] In this regard, important attempts from the Commission to make amendments on this area have been withdrawn due to the lack of agreement. For example, that is the case of the Proposal to amend the Working Time Directive 2003/88/EC,[237] as well as the Proposal for a Regulation on the exercise of the right to take collective action within the context of the freedom of establishment and the freedom to provide services.[238]

Developments through EU law in some areas of labour law regarding employee protection are therefore very difficult to achieve, and although there is still room for the improvement of minimum standards, EU employment law is nowadays more

[232]For more detailed explanation and examples of specific Directives: Leighton (2010), p. 29, 30.

[233]Grusic (2015), p. 3, 4.

[234]Riesenhuber (2012), p. 26, 27.

[235]Ibid., p. 24.

[236]Ibid., p. 24.

[237]Proposal for a Directive of the European Parliament and of the Council amending Directive 2003/88/EC concerning certain aspects of the organisation of working time (COM/2004/0607 final), and later Amended proposal for a Directive of the European Parliament and of the Council amending Directive 2003/88/EC concerning certain aspects of the organisation of working time (COM/2005/0246 final).

[238]Proposal for a Council Regulation on the exercise of the right to take collective action within the context of the freedom of establishment and the freedom to provide services (COM/2012/130).

focused on cross-border matters. Among some of the recent legislative projects, we can highlight the adoption of the revision of the Posted Workers Directive.[239]

EU employment law is a complex area because of the importance of the interests involved, both at national and EU levels. The existence of different levels and sources of regulation makes difficult the determination of the applicable law in cross-border situations.

2.3.2 *Unification of EU Contract Law vs. EU PIL Rules as the Best Regulatory Technique for Consumer and Employment Contracts*

A vast quantity of cross-border contracts in the EU have connections exclusively with two or more Member States. They are purely intra-EU contracts, happening within the internal market. Therefore, the issue of harmonisation of substantive law within the internal market receives special attention from the EU Commission and legal scholars. The incremental growth of the programme of legislative harmonisation in the area of contract law during the last decades brings the debate of what should be the best manner to address contract law in the internal market. On the one hand, some have defended the necessity of creation of a much more systematic structure within this area through the elaboration of a European Civil Code.[240] They defend that unification of contract law will benefit the functioning of the internal market. On the other hand, the opposite view defends Europe's legal diversity based on the argument of a deep existent cultural diversity, and thus reject any attempt that goes beyond minimum and fragmentary harmonisation, contending for fewer harmonisation initiatives at European level.[241] In between these extremes we find many other options and initiatives. However, this section is intended not to describe all the initiatives and attempts in harmonising this area but to highlight the benefits and disadvantages of the unification or maximum harmonisation of contract law versus the operation of PIL. Thus, only a brief overview of the main harmonisation attempts in this area and the current situation will be given before evaluating the necessity and adequacy of harmonisation in the EU.

---

[239]Directive (EU) 2018/957 of the European Parliament and of the Council of 28 June 2018 amending Directive 96/71/EC concerning the posting of workers in the framework of the provision of services (OJ 2018 L 173/16).

[240]For example: Collins (2008) and Hartkamp and Von Bar (2011).

[241]Weatherill (2013), p. 188, 189.

2.3.2.1 A Brief Overview of the Attempts of Full Harmonisation or Unification of EU Contract Law

Harmonisation of contract law has been on the agenda for years. Several calls of the European Parliament in favour of a European Civil Code incited an animated academic debate. During the 1990s, working groups were established with the intention to develop common principles among the private laws of the Member States that could lead to further harmonisation of contract law (e.g. the Pavia Group, the Study Group on a European Civil Code (Von Bar Group) and the Research Group on EC Private Law (Acquis Group)). Also, the Lando Commission, which was already set up in 1980 with the aim of finding common rules of private law among the EU, published the first part of the PECL (Principles of European Contract Law) in 1995.[242] The PECL are non-binding rules on contract law. Due to their optional character, their functions are restricted, but they still could be chosen as applicable (neutral) law by the parties to a contract or serve as a model for legislators or for the EU institutions when drafting laws or even as a model for a European Code of Contracts.[243] The PECL does not include aspects of EU law. The Acquis Group later filled that gap and published in 2008 the Principles of Existing EC Contract Law (ACQP).

The European Commission has been especially active regarding harmonisation of contract law. In 2001, the Commission issued a Communication on European Contract law,[244] considering four options for subsequent action in the area of contract law: 1) no EU action, 2) promotion of the development of principles of contract law that would lead to greater convergence of national law, 3) improvement of the quality of the existing legislation and 4) adoption of a new comprehensive legislation with the form of a European Code (either replacing national law or as an optional instrument). In February 2003, the follow-up Action Plan on a more coherent European Contract Law revealed the outcome of the process of consultation. Preference was on the second and third options, disregarding the extremes. The Commission's response was twofold: first, the Commission aimed to review the legislative consumer acquis and remedy the deficiencies in the EU consumer directives; second, the Commission proposed the adoption of a Common Frame of Reference (CFR).

Regarding the revision of the consumer acquis, the Commission went through a deep review of the functioning of the EU consumer directives and identified as main problems the absence of a common interpretation of relevant terms and the use of 'minimum' rules.[245] The Commission aimed at applying a common approach and reduce national diversity by switching from a model of minimum harmonisation to a

[242] Part II in 2000 and part III in 2003. Commission on European Contract Law, Lando et al. (2003).

[243] Kuipers (2012), p. 246, 247.

[244] COM (2001) 398.

[245] Green Paper on the Review of the Consumer Acquis COM (2006) 744.

maximum harmonisation one. Eight EU consumer directives were reviewed.[246] However, the Proposal for a Directive on Consumer Rights in October 2008 considered only the replacement of four of those Directives (regarding doorstep selling, unfair terms, timeshare and distance sale). This project was proved to be overambitious, and the turning of those four Directives into a maximum harmonisation directive turned to be not politically realistic. The Consumer Rights Directive,[247] adopted in 2011, kept the maximum harmonisation model, but its scope was reduced to replace only two of the Directives (regarding doorstep selling and distance contracts) of the eight that were in the original review agenda.

Regarding the Commission's idea to adopt a Common Frame of Reference, the planned intention for the Common Frame of Reference was to identify the best solutions to be taken into account in national practice, the EU acquis and relevant international practice. It would set out common fundamental principles of contract law, definitions and model rules, and thus it would be available to the Commission as a 'toolbox' when preparing proposals to improve the existing EU contract law or for the drafting of new instruments. A draft CFR was delivered to the Commission in 2007 and published in 2009; however, it was to be treated and referred to as an *academic* Draft Common Frame of Reference (DCFR). The DCFR has to be distinguished from the CFR originally called for by the Commission in its Action Plan. The DCRF is a comprehensive body of detailed rules on European private law. The DCFR contains principles that underpin the model rules, definitions of terms used in the model rules and model rules on a number of areas of private law. Some even consider it as a European Civil Code in all but in its name.[248] However, most defend its nature as an academic project providing for insights in the area of EU contract law. The DCFR has been the subject of extensive criticism, principally due to its shape as a closed and comprehensive body of specific rules.[249]

Nowadays, the DCFR is available to deepen knowledge of European private law and as source of inspiration and reference for European and national legislators, as well as the European Court of Justice and national courts when tasked with resolving a novel or difficult question in the field of private law covered by the DCFR. As Kuipers states, '[t]he DCFR is another milestone on the road towards a larger convergence between the European legal systems. It is however unclear where that road will lead to.'[250]

---

246 Directives 85/577 (about doorstep selling), 90/314 (regarding package travel), 93/13 (unfair contract terms), 94/47 (timeshare), 97/7 (distance contracts), 98/6 (indication of prices), 98/27 (injunctions) and 1999/44 (sale).

247 OJ 2011 L304/64.

248 Hesselink (2009), p. 923.

249 Jansen and Zimmermann (2010).

250 Kuipers (2012), p. 249.

The Commission also referred in some occasions to the possibility of adopting an 'optional instrument' of contract law at EU level.[251] This eventually resulted in the Proposal for a Regulation on Common European Sales Law (CESL).[252] The CESL would be a second regime for each Member State, like an overall 29th regime for the EU. Its use was intended to be optional, depending on the will of business and consumers to choose it as applicable rather than other national law, and it would be limited to cross-border contracts regarding B2C contracts and B2B contracts where one of the parties was a small or medium-size enterprise. This EU ambition towards codification, even though an optional document, did not come through, and the issues covered by the CESL are currently governed by EU Directives (the Consumer Sales Directive (CSD), Consumer Rights Directive, Unfair Terms Directive and e-Commerce Directive). All four, with the exception of the Consumer Rights Directive, are minimum harmonisation instruments.

The improvement of the EU Directives regarding their drafting and internal coherence does not affect the conflict of laws system in intra-EU situations. Neither would have done it the adoption of an optional instrument since differences between the legal systems of the Member States would continue to exist. In fact, in the preamble to the Rome I Regulation, it is stated that in the event that the EU adopted rules of substantive contract law, including standard terms and conditions, such instrument could provide the possibility that parties could choose those rules as applicable to the contract. Such a 29th regime would therefore be like another law that the parties could choose to apply.[253]

However, the gradual harmonisation in the EU contract law does diminish the role of Rome I, especially if the EU legislator decides to systematically pursue the maximum harmonisation approach like it has been done lately in the area of EU consumer law. Such a trend could lead to the substitution of national consumer policy by an EU *acquis*. The options of maximum harmonisation or a Civil Code would indeed significantly limit the role of the Rome I Regulation. If the contract law of the Member States was unified, no conflict rules for intra-EU cases would be needed.

Nevertheless, such a unification does not seem to be a realistic option. Besides the political reluctance of the Member States to the unification of contract law in the EU

[251]E.g. in the Commission's Communications of 2001 (COM (2001) 398), of 2003 (COM (2003) 68), and of 2004 (COM (2004) 651).

[252]Proposal for a Regulation *of the* European Parliament and of the Council on a Common European Sales Law (COM/2011/0635 final).

[253]However, the optional code could also be construed as an alternative to Rome I, preventing thus the application of the latter instrument, which would mean that the special conflict rules protecting the consumers and employees would also be circumvented. While it might seem easier to choose to apply the optional code and do not worry about the different levels of protection of the different national laws, it would not seem feasible that Member States would agree to such a regime after the efforts to protect consumers and employees in choice of law cases. Of course, this would also depend on the protection afforded to the weaker parties by the optional instrument. Kuipers (2012), p. 254, 255.

and to the maximum harmonisation approach in most of the areas, the desirability and feasibility of such options are also the object of discussion.[254] First, regarding the desirability of an EU unified contract law instrument, it has to be pointed out that there are areas of contract law, such as international sales law, where an EU codification would bring more difficulties by creating more layers to the existent regulatory regimes. For example, an EU codification could be contradictory to the UNIDROIT Principles.[255] The field of international commercial contracts between professionals is benefited by a low intervention and flexible legal solutions such as soft law solutions or universal principles such as the UNIDROIT Principles.[256] Second, concerning feasibility, with regard to the competence of the EU, there is no explicit legal basis in the TFEU that recognises the power of the EU to act in the area of contract law. A potential Civil Code or Contract Code should then be based on a general law making competence. Article 114 TFEU could provide a legal basis if the adoption of such a code would be necessary for the functioning of the internal market since that provision allows the EU to adopt 'measures for the approximation of the provisions laid down by law, regulation or administrative action in Member States which have as their object the establishment and functioning of the internal market'. However, Article 114 should not be interpreted in a too broad manner.[257] In fact, it is generally agreed that the EU does not have the competence to adopt such a comprehensive code.[258] The possibility of sector-specific codes is more likely, especially regarding consumer contracts, a field in which the EU has vast legislation.[259]

2.3.2.2 Advantages and Disadvantages of Unification of EU Contract Law: Defending EU PIL as the Best Current Option to Regulate EU Consumer and Employment Contracts

If feasible, is unification or maximum harmonisation of contract law the best option for the better functioning of the internal market? Can there be a truly EU internal market without a comprehensive legal framework at EU level? The discussion over unification or full-harmonisation of contract law or consumer law is intense, and the literature over it is extensive. Many authors put into question the arguments behind those initiatives. The criticisms towards the transaction cost argument and the

---

[254] Weatherill (2013), pp. 199–203.

[255] Sánchez Lorenzo (2003), pp. 377–379.

[256] Ibid., p. 379. At the same time, Sánchez Lorenzo stated that this inconvenient did not involve consumer contracts, for which a EU common instrument would still be a good option.

[257] Kuipers (2012), p. 250, 251.

[258] Regarding some reflexions about the question of legislative competence, see Weatherill (2013), pp. 199–203; Kuipers (2012), pp. 250–253.

[259] Regarding specifically the unification of EU consumer law, see, for example, Hesselink (2007), Rutgers and Sefton-Green (2008).

'consumer confidence' argument are numerous and fierce and destroy the foundations on which EU bases the need of unification or maximum harmonisation.[260] On the other side of the balance, other authors also fiercely defended the benefits of unification of contract law and proposed many ways to achieve such a purpose. In this regard, the work of Collins seems remarkable.[261] In short, he submitted that the EU could not evolve into an effective system without the creation of a cohesive community (or transnational legal society), for which the common private rules are necessary, since private relationships are the root of a social order. That community requires an economic and social constitution that will give shape to a particular economic and social system that would promote Europe-wide values of fairness and social justice. According to this author, the EU has failed to establish such an integrated transnational legal society which would have led to a common European identity. He claims that by harmonising the basic rules and institutions governing social interaction in civil society (i.e. private law), the EU could evolve to such an integrated community.[262] The European Civil Code according to Collins

---

[260]See, for example, Halson and Campbell (2013), Wilhelmsson (2004).

[261]Collins (2008).

[262]Collins summarises his propositions regarding a European Civil Code in the following manner (Ibid., p. 1, 2.):

(1) The European Union today is a political structure without a community. It is a system of government for a continent, but this territory is fragmented into many political and cultural communities. Although nation states have pooled some of their sovereign powers in the institutions of the European Union, at the level of everyday social interactions, national borders still present serious obstacles to the formation of a single community – a transnational civil society. Because the European Union does not rest on a deeply integrated civil society, its political union often proves fragile and dysfunctional, to the detriment of all sovereign powers in the institutions of the European Union, at the level of everyday social interactions, national borders still present serious obstacles to the formation of a single community – a transnational civil society. Because the European Union does not rest on a deeply integrated civil society, its political union often proves fragile and dysfunctional, to the detriment of all.

(2) Any successful community or social order is rooted in the bonds established through commonplace social interactions. In its basic elements, a cohesive civil society evolves through working together in productive activities, through exchanges of goods and services, and by the establishment of private associations, family relations, and all the different kinds of connections formed between ordinary people in their daily lives. In modern societies, private law – principally the laws of property, civil wrongs and contracts governing relations between citizens – helps to channel these relationships, to stabilise expectations and sometimes to correct disappointments and betrayals.

(3) Once established, these relations of civil society form the bedrock out of which political communities and shared identities arise. Through the long-term repetition of these social interactions of civil society, there emerges a belief on the part of the participants that they are members of the same community and share a common identity. Comprising a single people, an integrated community, they require and accept political union – a single governance structure – as well.

(4) The European Union, however, lacks such a dense set of connections between peoples. It has failed to establish an integrated transnational civil society out of which a common

would be founded on respect for social and economic rights. Instead of conceiving such a code as a complex body of detailed rules, the author considers that, to be legitimate and effective, an EU Civil Code would have to encompass principle-based regulation, a framework of normative standards for an integrated legal community or transnational legal society.[263] This idea seems attractive, since it has a strong emphasis on the society and social rights, but even more burdensome and 'utopic' than the projects pursued by the EU institutions or other working groups. Indeed, it seems more realistic to focus on the possibility of a full harmonisation of EU consumer law, an area where the EU has already achieved many legislative advances.

On the one hand, the benefits of the unification approach have to be recognised. The principal argument in this regard consists of the reduction of the transaction costs in cross-border trade, benefiting the internal market. The EU normally refers to the removing of barriers that hinder the correct and smooth functioning of the internal market to justify the drafting of common or harmonised rules in different legal areas, especially in contract law and consumer law. According to the 2010 Green Paper on options for European Contract Law,[264] the difference between the national laws can constitute barriers to the internal market. Those differences might entail additional transaction costs and legal uncertainty for business. Therefore, full harmonisation would help to eliminate those barriers and benefit consumer confidence and allow to 'take full advantage of the internal market'.[265] Thus, it is generally claimed that diversity among the different Member States' laws distorts competition in the market. According to that line of reasoning, full harmonisation or unification of the rules in contract law would constitute a reduction of the costs of pursuing business. The 'costs of internationality' would be avoided while operating within the internal market. That is, compliance with foreign legal requirements,

---

European identity could be constructed. The protection of fundamental economic freedoms by the European Treaties – the free movement of goods, services, capital and labour – created elements of a European civil society by giving citizens the right to engage in commerce across borders. The additional regulatory interventions of the Single Market initiative reduced further the barriers between national communities. These measures removed some of the most conspicuous obstacles to cross-border trade such as quotas, tariffs and prohibitions. But a more comprehensive and inclusive transnational civil society requires more extensive support.

(5) It is necessary to adopt common legal principles. By harmonising the basic rules and institutions governing social interaction in civil society, Europe can enable the evolution of a transnational civil society community. In short, as Napoleón foresaw, the European Union needs to work towards uniform laws: an integrated body of legal principles to govern all the different kinds of relations formed by citizens in a civil society.

[263] See, for example, Collins (2006, 2008).

[264] Green Paper from the Commission on Policy Options for Progress Towards a European Contract Law for Consumers and Businesses, COM (2010) 348 final.

[265] Green Paper from the Commission on Policy Options for Progress Towards a European Contract Law for Consumers and Businesses, COM (2010) 348 final. See also Halson and Campbell (2013), p. 101.

standards, mandatory rules etc. might prevent businesses to engage in cross-border transactions since they can be very costly. The costs of seeking appropriate information and foreign legal systems might prevent businesses to engage in cross-border trade.[266] Moreover, it is difficult to anticipate the different results in the different stages of the contract, the legal means and the costs of solution, and in case a dispute arises, the costs of specialised lawyers in cross-border cases are most likely not affordable to medium and small enterprises. Because of the costs of cross-border commerce, it would be large companies that could benefit from diversity among legal systems.[267]

In addition, it is also considered that consumer confidence is damaged by the uncertainties of the legal aspects of a cross-border transaction. The 'consumer confidence' argument considers that consumers are prevented from entering into cross-border transactions because of the differences between national laws since they would not be confident that they would receive adequate protection outside their own market. The consumer attitude to cross-border trade would constitute an important barrier to the well functioning of the internal market.[268] EU Consumer Directives refer to this argument in their recitals as a justification for harmonising the specific area of consumer law they cover. For example, Recital 5 of the Consumer Sales Directive (99/44/EC) reads:

> the creation of a common set of minimum rules of consumer law, valid no matter where goods are purchased within the Community, will strengthen consumer confidence and enable consumers to make the most of the internal market.

Recital 3 of the Directive on the Distance Marketing of Financial Services (2002/65/EC) refers to consumer confidence on Recitals 3 and 5, first stating that

> (...) a high degree of consumer protection is required in order to enhance consumer confidence in distance selling

and then providing that

> [b]ecause of their intangible nature, financial services are particularly suited to distance selling and the establishment of a legal framework governing the distance marketing of financial services should increase consumer confidence in the use of new techniques for the distance marketing of financial services, such as electronic commerce.

---

[266] Riesenhuber (2012), p. 303.

[267] Mattei (1997), p. 538; Weatherill (2013), p. 205.

[268] Gómez Pomar (2008), p. 7, 8; Twigg-Flesner (2011), p. 4.

In the Unfair Commercial Practices Directive (2005/29/EU), Recital 4 refers to the existence of different national rules on unfair commercial practices, which create barriers for traders and consumers and which

> "make consumers uncertain of their rights and undermine their confidence in the internal market";

also, Recital 13 states that

> in order to support consumer confidence the general prohibition [in Art.5] should apply equally to unfair commercial practices which occur outside any contractual relationship between a trader and a consumer or following the conclusion of a contract and during its execution.

Finally, Recital 6 of the Consumer Rights Directive (2011/83/EU) provides that

> [c]ertain disparities create significant internal market barriers affecting traders and consumers. Those disparities increase compliance costs to traders wishing to engage in the cross-border sale of goods or provision of services. Disproportionate fragmentation also undermines consumer confidence in the internal market.

According to Recital 7, legal certainty would be considerably increased through the full harmonisation of consumer information and the right of withdrawal in distance and off-premises sales, which would boost cross-border sales.

Therefore, it is generally believed that unification of contract law within the internal market would reduce transaction costs and increase consumer confidence on the internal market. In addition, one of the reasons calling for a different approach consisted in the existence of problems derived from the minimum harmonisation approach by the directives. It is argued that the minimum harmonisation technique has failed to provide a suitable legal framework, especially in the area of EU consumer law, and therefore a different alternative is needed.[269] EU consumer directives only deal with some aspects of consumer law and also have to be implemented into national law of the Member States. Minimum harmonisation directives allow national legislation giving effect to the directive to go further and make possible for Member States to retain existing national law without major change if it was already matching (or exceeding) the minimum standards required by the directive. This approach is criticised because it has not been able to create a coherent or consistent body on consumer law but rather has given rise to different sets of rules on unfair contract terms, doorstep selling and so on per Member State. Minimum harmonisation directives approximate national laws and reduce the differences between the different standards existent among the Member States. Legal diversity is not eliminated. The continuing diversity is mainly due to the incoherence

[269] Twigg-Flesner (2011), p. 5, 6.

within the existing directives (e.g. inconsistencies when transposing directives into national law due to the different language versions), the regulatory gaps existent in the directives and filled by the Member States in different methods or the reliance on minimum harmonisation clauses.[270] Unification of consumer law or contract law would solve the problems related to the minimum harmonisation approach of directives.

Nevertheless, it can also be argued that legal diversity would not completely disappear, neither would the transaction costs deriving from it. Even if law in the books became the same among the Member States, the law in practice would still be different. Courts, legal procedure, legal environment etc. would still differ, and businesses would still have to adapt to the foreign market traditions. As a result, the costs of legal diversity for businesses would not drop dramatically within the internal market.[271]

The aforementioned 'consumer confidence' argument is also highly disputed.[272] It can be argued that the reluctance of consumers to shop abroad is explained by many other factors that have more relevance to their behaviour than the possibility of application of a foreign law (language, for example, or accessibility in general) and that cannot be easily solved though legal regulation. It has been argued that this argument has been used in an excessive manner as a justification for harmonisation measures by the EU and then as a justification for the need for the unification of consumer law or contract law.[273] A close understanding of the expectations of consumers and the consumer culture is necessary, and that varies among Member States. In addition, unification would probably lead to less protection for the consumers of some Member States (especially Nordic countries). At the same time, the consumers of some countries would gain protection; others would lose more, which, at least for the latter, would not increase consumer confidence in the internal market.[274]

Regarding the argument of legal diversity, legal diversity is not necessarily bad from an economic perspective. In general, EU consumer directives claim that diversity among national contract law regimes distort competition within the internal market. However, this statement has not been satisfactorily proven.[275] Such an assumption would mean that all the differences between the private laws of the Member States would be an impediment to the functioning of the internal market and should be eliminated. Nevertheless, the example of the United States shows that the

[270] Ibid., p. 5.

[271] Gómez Pomar (2008), p. 7.

[272] See in this regard: Wilhelmsson (2004) and Twigg-Flesner (2016).

[273] Wilhelmsson (2004), p. 336, 337.

[274] Ibid., pp. 317–337; Twigg-Flesner (2016).

[275] Evidence of the costs of legal diversity seems hard to acquire. Data provided by the Commission in this regard is criticised as being 'piecemeal', showing just *some* firms detrimentally affected by *some* types of legal diversity, but without analysing across sectors or regarding the size of the companies. Weatherill (2013), p. 205, 206.

achievement of an integrated market is not dependent to such a big extent on the unification of legislation.[276] In fact, unification can be damaging as well. An EU uniform law could easily become static since a single Member State would not be able to change it. Meanwhile, both local preferences and legal standards will probably change and evolve over time. Moreover, the consumer preferences or needs and the legal culture among Member States also differ, and unification would not be able to reflect that. That is, for instance, what is considered an unfair trade practice in one Member State might be considered a common one in another Member State.[277]

In the area of contract law, if legal diversity is maintained, Member States will develop better solutions adapting to the wishes and needs of private parties. Since market participants can freely move around Member States, they would choose for the one offering the best solutions. This could lead to a race to the top: Member States would learn from each other, which would lead to better and more efficient rules. Eventually, the most efficient set of rules would dominate within the market, and thus the contract law in the EU would converge towards the most efficient solution.[278] However, in the areas of contract law where mandatory rules play an important role, like in the cases involving weaker contracting parties, the situation is different. In those cases, national preferences and levels of protection tend to differ among the Member States. For example, in the case of consumer law, competition for the best legal system entails that consumers and traders can move around the Member States at no cost and are fully informed about the content of the legal systems in force in the Member States, so they choose the most efficient and the most beneficial for them. Indeed, consumers are not in such a situation. Most frequently, consumers would be ignorant regarding the comparative advantages of other legal systems. Costs of relocation are high; there are cultural differences, different languages etc. In the same way, the opposite scenario of a 'race to the bottom' in which Member States with better protective rules would lower their standards to compete with Member States that have lower social standards and thus are more attractive to companies does not seem likely. First, legislators would find it too costly, and, second, a regime with stricter standards is considered more beneficial to businesses in the long term since the obligation to comply with higher standards might cause technological improvements, resulting in a competitive advantage. Although unification of consumer law would avoid such a risk, it could also prevent the parties from the economic advantages of legal diversity. EU PIL allows parties to a contract to choose the law applicable to their contract and thus benefit from a more favourable legal system for their interests. In the case of contracts involving weaker parties, EU PIL rules ensure that the mandatory rules of the country of the consumer or the employee are applicable, protecting them from a possible abuse of their counterparties.

[276] Koetz (2012), p. 8.

[277] Kuipers (2012), p. 262.

[278] Ibid., p. 260.

Since this study is focused on the protection of weaker parties, which are areas where mandatory rules are more present than dispositive rules, special attention is necessary. Full harmonisation is mainly called for in the area of consumer law, although there has also been some – less successful – calls regarding EU labour law.[279] However, as it has been submitted, the introduction of a common regulation with the exact same protection in all Member States might be beneficial to some countries but prejudicial to others. Thus, the setting of EU minimum standards is still an option and can be, in fact, the good option. However, that would require improvement in the implementation of the EU directives by the Member States and the coordination of the rules and scope of EU directives with the EU PIL rules. If the current implementation and coordination gaps are solved, unified EU PIL rules would be able to ensure that the minimum EU mandatory standards are respected when necessary in cross-border extra-EU situations and at the same time ensure legal diversity between Member States. Therefore, the use of EU PIL rules would preserve legal diversity and, at the same time, ensure that the consumer enjoys an adequate protection, benefiting from legal diversity: the law applicable to the consumer contract is the law of the country of habitual residence, and parties can only choose another applicable law if it grants the same standards of consumer protection as or higher ones than the law of habitual residence of the consumer (Article 6 Rome I). In intra-EU situations, when the existent conflict rules are according to the values and objectives of the EU, parties benefit from legal pluralism among the Member States. Thus, it can be said that the problem lies in legal predictability rather than in legal diversity.

Taking into account all the aforementioned, I consider that harmonisation up to a certain extent of EU contract law, especially regarding EU consumer law, seems necessary for and beneficial to the EU internal market. There are certain values regarding consumer and employee protection that need to be ensured at EU level in order to avoid distortions, affecting both the economic and social structure of the EU. However, full harmonisation, at the current moment, might be a step too far, bringing, in general, more burdens than advantages. Still, in the area of EU consumer law, important and beneficial achievements have been made. It is true that unified EU PIL rules do not achieve equivalent result as do unified contract law rules in the internal market; however, they are not contrary techniques but complementary.[280] In my opinion, in order to achieve a correct protection of consumers and employees within the EU internal market, both partial harmonisation and EU PIL rules should play an important role. If EU PIL rules are sufficiently adapted to the objectives of the internal market and coordinated with EU substantive law, legal certainty and flexibility within the market would be achieved. EU PIL is presented as the best solution provided that conflict rules in contract law (Rome I Regulation) are effectively coordinated with the EU directives protecting weaker parties and vice versa. In that manner, EU PIL can deal with cross-border contracts within the internal market

---

[279]Collins (2006).

[280]Sánchez Lorenzo (2003), p. 365, 366.

without bringing disadvantages to the proper functioning of the internal market, and at the same time it brings more advantages than a situation of unification or full harmonisation.

2.4 Mechanisms of Protection of Weaker Parties in PIL

The peculiarities that substantive consumer law and employment law present are also reflected in private international law. Once it has been determined that certain contracting parties are in need of some protection, the next question regards how this protection can be best achieved.

The protection of weaker contracting parties is in our time an inherent part of most PIL systems. However, there are many different ways to deal with the necessities of weaker contracting parties in PIL terms. Nowadays, the majority of legal systems have implemented multilateral conflict rules in consumer and employment matters. Only a few states still keep a unilateral approach, especially regarding employment contracts, due to the private and public interests at stake, and thus define the scope of the application of their own employment regulations (e.g. Article 11 Russian Labour Code[281] provides that domestic labour laws are mandatory on all employers within the Russian territory, including employment relationships of foreigners).[282] A unilateral approach in employment contracts was also accepted in some European countries before the enactment of the Rome Convention; for example, some English statutes expressly defined their territorial scope of application, and if a case felt within it, the application of foreign law would be overridden; also, German courts used to determine the application of domestic labour law in a particular case.[283] It is also remarkable that, even nowadays, the Spanish Workers' Statute (*Estatuto de los Trabajadores*)[284] contains a very controversial provision in Article 1(4), which is of a unilateral nature but which is in fact a rule determining the territorial scope of Spanish labour laws.[285] However, in general, the multilateral PIL

[281] Labour Code of the Russian Federation of 31 December 2001, Federal Law No 197-FZ of 2001.

[282] Fornasier (2017), p. 1682.

[283] Grusic (2015), p. 41.

[284] Real Decreto Legislativo 2/2015, de 23 de octubre, por el que se aprueba el texto refundido de la Ley del Estatuto de los Trabajadores ("BOE" núm. 255, de 24/10/2015).

[285] Article 1(4) states: 'The Spanish labour legislation will be applicable to the work provided by the Spanish workers hired in Spain to the service of Spanish companies abroad, without prejudice to the public order rules applicable in the place of work. These workers will have, at least, the economic rights that would correspond to them in working in Spanish territory' [translation by the author] (*La legislación laboral española será de aplicación al trabajo que presten los trabajadores españoles contratados en España al servicio de empresas españolas en el extranjero, sin perjuicio de las normas de orden público aplicables en el lugar de trabajo. Dichos trabajadores tendrán, al menos, los derechos económicos que les corresponderían de trabajar en territorio español*). Although this rule should have been displaced by the Rome Convention and later by the Rome I Regulation on the law applicable to contractual obligations, it is still contained in the last version of the Spanish text,

method gained terrain even in these areas of law, and thus the majority of PIL rules we find are of a multilateral character, which take into account the possible applicability of a foreign law.

The existing general rules regarding party autonomy and the law applicable in the absence of choice are modified in the case of consumer and employment contracts. It has been submitted that weaker contracting parties need some mechanism of protection against the threats that party autonomy brings. In this regard, the options range from the extreme method of prohibiting party autonomy altogether to a more flexible approach like providing for a more protective law. On the other hand, the law applicable in the absence of choice should neither be determined by the general connecting factors, but adequate and protective connecting factors need to be designed. Thus, this section will describe the main options and mechanisms that exist that deal with and restrict the freedom of choice of law in consumer and employment contracts, as well as the existing protective conflict rules dealing with the law applicable in the absence of choice of law in consumer and employment contracts.

2.4.1 *Party Autonomy and Protection of Consumers and Employees: The Options*

It has been submitted that party autonomy is a general principle in PIL relating to contractual obligations almost all around the world. However, when important interests are at stake, like in the cases of consumer and employment laws, the weaker contracting party would see itself at a disadvantaged position if the stronger party was to freely choose the law applicable to the contract. As a result, most legal systems restrict the freedom of choice of law in these cases.

In consumer contracts, the discussion regarding party autonomy was brought up as soon as the consumer protection movement became widespread in the legal systems around the world in the 1960s and 1970s. Since then, most legal systems have restricted party autonomy in consumer contracts in one way or another, and consumer protection in PIL has become an integral part of the different national PIL regulations.[286]

In employment law, the discussion regarding the treatment of an employment contract as a normal contract with the possibility of the parties choosing the law applicable was brought up early on. The main argument against party autonomy in employment contracts was evidently the inequality of bargaining power, with the risk that the employer could impose the application of a law with lower standards in employment protection than the law of the country of the place of work.

keeping the controversy about its function and relationship with the mentioned EU instruments. In this regard, see, for example, Fotinopouplou Basurko (2004) and Llobera Vila (2016).

[286] Rühl (2011), p. 570.

Nevertheless, a growing number of European countries started to recognise party autonomy in these cases, although in a very limited manner.[287] For example, in the Netherlands, party autonomy was permitted but with a statutory exception in some cases of unfair discharge.[288] In Spain, while also allowing party autonomy in general, there was a statutory provision that required the application of Spanish law when there were some specific strong connections to Spain.[289] With the Rome Convention, the possibility of choosing the law applicable in employment contracts, with limitations, was generalised among the European states.

Despite the differences of rationale between consumer protection and employee protection in substantive law, the threats of party autonomy in PIL are similar (i.e. in general terms, the danger that the strong party chooses as applicable to the contract a law with low standards of consumer or employee protection). Thus, the manner of treating party autonomy in PIL in consumer and employment contracts is the same in this regard.

There are several ways to restrict party autonomy which bring different advantages and consequences. Essentially, party autonomy can be completely excluded, limited to specific legal systems or limited as to its effects.

2.4.1.1 Exclusion of Party Autonomy

The complete exclusion of party autonomy is an exceptional and straightforward measure. This drastic solution is found, for example, in Switzerland in the case of consumer contracts: according to Article 120(2) of the Swiss Act on Private International Law, choice of law is excluded in consumer contracts. Also, exclusion was found in the Proposal for the Rome I Regulation (Article 5 Proposal Rome I). Regarding employment contracts, this measure can also be found in China, where Article 43 of the Chinese Private International Law Act also does not admit party autonomy in labour contracts.

By eliminating the possibility to choose the law applicable to the contract, consumers and employees do not have to fear that their counterparties will choose the law with the lowest protection standard. Moreover, legal certainty is definitely enhanced since it is clear that parties are not allowed to choose the law applicable. Therefore, consumers and employees can easily predict the rights and obligations derived from the contract and receive the protection of a law they are familiar with. In addition, the contracting parties and the courts do not have to engage in a complex

[287] Krebber (2000), p. 517, 518.

[288] Regarding party autonomy, *Hoge Raad*, decision of June 8, 1973, N.J. Nr. 400 (1973); regarding its limitation, Article 6 B.B.A.

[289] Regarding party autonomy, Article 10(6) Código Civil; regarding its limitation, Article 1 (4) Estatuto de los Trabajadores.

process as compared to other models that limit party autonomy, and as a result this solution provides for legal certainly and reduces transaction and litigation costs.[290]

However, this model would set aside all the advantages that party autonomy brings, and has been harshly criticised.[291] While it seems logical to reduce the professional's or employer's choice of law in order to avoid a potential abuse, the exclusion of party autonomy also brings consequences upon the consumer or employee. Firstly, consumers and employees see themselves deprived of the eventual benefits of choosing the law: what if their chosen law is more beneficial to them? The main criticism of this model rests on the difficulty to rightly defend the interests of the weaker party since it might exclude the application of a law more favourable than the law applicable in the absence of choice.[292] Moreover, the fact that these contracts involve parties with unequal bargaining power does not necessarily mean that the choice will be done unilaterally and in detriment of the weaker party; even if it is, it is more probable that the choice would refer to the application of a law familiar to the professional or the employer (e.g. law of the domicile of the business or law where the employer is established), which can be either more beneficial or detrimental to the weaker party than the law otherwise applicable in the absence of choice.[293] Also, this approach might impair cross-border commercial activities, making businesses concentrate on their own national market. For example, in the case of consumer contracts, professionals might have to adjust the contract to a foreign law, which would be reflected in higher costs for the goods or services. Moreover, professionals might even refuse to provide their services or sell their goods in some countries due to the applicable law.[294] Furthermore, the exclusion of party autonomy also excludes the possible benefits deriving from the competition among legal systems, which can lead to a more protective national legal system where non-national professionals are at a disadvantage, which would result in an increase of prices and thus a disadvantage to the local consumers. Party autonomy is also an incentive to national legal orders to ensure that their rules are attractive for the parties and thus prevent them from avoiding the applicability of their rules by choosing a more favourable law.[295]

Therefore, even if this option might enhance legal certainty, the complete exclusion of party autonomy seems to bring more disadvantages than benefits to the parties.

---

[290] Rühl (2011), pp. 592–594.

[291] Among others, Lando and Nielsen (2007), p. 39, 40; Guardans Cambó (1992), p. 324; Calliess (2015a), p. 163, 164.

[292] Guardans Cambó (1992), p. 324.

[293] Tang (2007), p. 128, 129.

[294] Rühl (2011), p. 595.

[295] Basedow et al. (2012), p. 190.

2.4.1.2 Limitation to Specific Legal Systems

A second option, less drastic than completely excluding party autonomy, consists in limiting the freedom of choice of law to certain legal systems. This model can consist of a broad or narrow approach: it can limit the choice to either any law with sufficient connection to the contract or a number of specific laws. An example of a broad approach can be found in the US Uniform Commercial Code, where, regarding consumer contracts, a choice of law is not effective unless the transaction holds a reasonable relation to the country designated.[296] We also find an example of this model in a narrow approach, regarding employment contracts, in the Swiss Act on Private International Law, in which Article 121(3) limits the choice of the parties to the law of the country of habitual residence of the employee or to the law of the country in which the employer has the place of business, domicile or habitual residence.[297]

Although this model provides for more flexibility for the parties, while avoiding the choice of a law that is not sufficiently connected with the contract, I consider it also brings more downsides than advantages.[298] First of all, this model will only ensure a minimum protection to weaker parties if the laws provided ensure it; it can happen that a law with some connections to the contract provides for little or no consumer or employee protection at all. In this regard, if a listed law or a law sufficiently connected provides for a low protection, limiting party autonomy becomes useless since the objective was to prevent the stronger party from taking advantage of its counterparty by choosing a more detrimental law. Thus, this option would only be effective if the choice of law is limited to laws of countries that are members of a federation or part of a union that enjoys the same or similar legal framework, such as the US or the EU; in these cases, the EU Member States share the same minimum standards of protection, and therefore it would not be so relevant if the law applicable is that of one Member State or another.[299] However, this model would just work in an intra-EU context and not towards third states. The EU Green Paper on the conversion of the Rome Convention into the Rome I Regulation,[300] when considering the existing possibilities to update the rule on the law applicable to consumer contracts, referred to this model. In one of the options, a limited choice of law was suggested, allowing only the choice of the law of the country where the business is established. However, for the choice to be valid, it would have to be required that the business proved that the consumer had made an informed choice and that the consumer had the information on all rights and obligations conferred on him or her by the law of the business' habitual residence, such as the right of

[296]UCC, Sections 1–301(e)(1); Tang (2007), p. 114.

[297]Grusic (2015), p. 39, 40; Nygh (1999), p. 156.

[298]In the same opinion, Grusic (2015), p. 40; Rühl (2011), p. 592 et seq.

[299]Rühl (2011), p. 594.

[300]Green Paper on the conversion of the Rome Convention of 1980 on the law applicable to contractual obligations into a Community instrument and its modernisation COM (2002) 654 final.

withdrawal, the duration, the terms of the guarantee etc. If these conditions were not met, the court would have to apply the law of the consumer's habitual residence or the mandatory provisions of that law. Also, this option would only be applicable to businesses domiciled in Member States, while those with domicile in a third country would be subject to the mandatory provisions of the country of habitual residence of the consumer when they choose another applicable law.[301]

This solution seems problematic. Primarily, regarding the requirement to provide information concerning all the rights and obligations conferred on the consumers by the chosen law, it seems difficult to determine which information to provide since consumer law is rather complex and might involve several laws and issues. More importantly, even if businesses were to provide all the relevant information, it is unlikely that consumers would actually read it and, if so, understand it. It does not seem feasible to ask consumers to compare their own law with the chosen law.[302]

Finally, regarding both consumer and employment contracts, another disadvantage lies in the fact that the strong party of the contract might be able to influence the choice of law by influencing the connecting factors; for example, in cases referring to the law of the place of the habitual residence or place of business of the employer, this place can be chosen by the employer due to its low employee protection. In addition, in the same manner as the previous model excluding completely party autonomy, it deprives the weaker parties of the enjoyment of a more beneficial law to their situation.

2.4.1.3 Limitation of the Effects of Party Autonomy

A third option encompasses curtailing the effects of party autonomy, without neither excluding it or limiting it to certain laws. The parties can choose the law applicable to their consumer or employment contract, but this choice cannot deprive the consumer or employee of the protection provided by the law applicable in the absence of choice. This is the model used in the European Union. Article 6 Rome I, regarding consumer contracts, and Article 8 Rome I, regarding individual employment contracts, allow the parties to choose the law applicable to their contract as long as it does not deprive the consumer or employee of the protection afforded to him or her by the mandatory provisions of the law which, in the absence of choice, would have been applicable. Regarding consumer contracts, this model is also followed, for example, by Japan, Korea, Turkey and the US.[303] Also, regarding employment

[301] Green Paper on the conversion of the Rome Convention of 1980 on the law applicable to contractual obligations into a Community instrument and its modernisation COM (2002) 654 final, p. 32. Tang (2007), pp. 115–117.

[302] Ibid., p. 116, 117.

[303] Article 11(1) Japanese Private International Law Act, Section 27(1) Korean Private International Law Act, Article 1212(1) Russian Civil Code and Article 26(1) Turkish Private International Law Act, Section 187(2) Restatement (Second) of the Conflict of Laws. Rühl (2011), p. 589, 590.

contracts, this solution is found in the US.[304] However, the US model for consumer and employee protection differs from the preferential law model of the EU since it is a determined fundamental public policy doctrine. Employee and (most of) consumer protection rules are considered an expression of fundamental policy, and according to Section 187(2)(b), the

> application of the law of the chosen state would be contrary to a fundamental policy of a state which has a materially greater interest than the chosen state in the determination of the particular issue and which (...) would be the state of the applicable law in the absence of an effective choice of law by the parties.

That is, consumers and employees are protected against a choice of law that violates a fundamental public policy of the law applicable in the absence of choice.[305] In the same manner as in the EU, courts engage in a comparison between the law chosen by the parties and the law applicable in the absence of choice; however, while in the EU when the law chosen is less favourable than the mandatory rules of the law objectively applicable then a mix of both laws applies (i.e. the law chosen plus the better mandatory protection of the law applicable in the absence of choice), in the US the law chosen would be completely set aside and the law in the absence of choice would govern completely the contract.

This model enhances predictability of results and legal certainty, allowing the parties to choose the law applicable to their contract. At the same time, consumers and employees do not lose the protection afforded to them by the law objectively applicable to their contracts. The preferential law model allows parties to choose the law applicable to their consumer or employment contract and at the same time ensures that they are not deprived of the protection afforded to them by the law applicable in the absence of choice. In case the law chosen provides lower protection than the mandatory provisions of the law in the absence of choice, these mandatory provisions will be applicable. It is a compromise between freedom of contract and weaker party protection. Thus, it respects the parties' preferences by not excluding party autonomy but rather allowing the choice of law that would benefit the weaker contracting party. In contrast to the option of completely excluding party autonomy, in which consumers and employees see themselves deprived of the eventual benefits of choosing the law, according to this model only those consumers and employees who agree to a lower standard of protection see themselves deprived of the freedom of choice of law. In addition, the other party to the contract is also benefited since this approach allows the standardisation of the legal relationships with its consumers or employees.[306]

However, this approach also has some downsides and has been initially criticised due to the *depeçage* resulting from it, as well as owing to the information costs

[304] 187(2)(b) Restatement (Second) of the Conflict of Laws. Grusic (2015), p. 42, 43.

[305] Rühl (2011), p. 591; Grusic (2015), p. 42, 43.

[306] Palao Moreno (2016), p. 583.

resulting from the obligatory analysis of a foreign legal system.[307] Criticisms around the fractioning of the law applicable to the contract or *depeçage* have been overcome nowadays, at least in the EU context, where the Rome I Regulation even refers to the possibility of *depeçage* in Article 3 Rome I regarding party autonomy.[308]

Still, this approach is characterised by the difficulty of application, especially complicated in practice.[309] The preferential law approach requires parties and courts to compare the law chosen and the mandatory rules of the law applicable in the absence of choice; in some versions, it can even require courts to combine both laws. In this regard, two main difficulties arise: the determination of mandatory rules and the issue of comparison. 'Mandatory rules' are defined as rules that cannot be derogated from by agreement. They are provisions of a legal order whose mandatoriness is only internal and not international, especially those aimed to protect the weaker party; they are part of the domestic legal system.[310] However, it is still a vague concept since it varies from country to country, and, as a result, it might create difficulties regarding the predictability of their application in a specific situation.[311] On the other hand, a comparison between two different laws also becomes burdensome. Since the mandatory rules of the law in the absence of law only become applicable when they are more beneficial to the weaker party, the court must compare in order to decide which law is preferential to the consumer since that process cannot be made in abstract. This comparison is not always easy, and it entails several dangers. For example, in the case of a consumer contract, the law of the country of the habitual residence of the consumer recognises to consumers the right to withdraw from a contract within 14 working days of receipt, while it requires professionals to reimburse the money within 90 days; at the same time, the law chosen by the parties only gives 7 days to withdraw from the contract, but it requires professionals to reimburse the money within 30 days.[312] Or in the case of an employment contract, one law provides for the right to payment upon dismissal but not the right to claim reinstatement, while the other law provides for the latter right but not the right to monetary compensation.[313] The comparison should not result in the practice of cherry picking, by which a combination of preferential rules from both laws are combined with the result of a protection that none of the laws aims to provide; it should neither result in a practice under which the consumer always wins.[314] It is generally agreed that the comparison should be based on the implications for the individual case and attending to the overall level of protection of

[307]Gamillscheg (1983), pp. 306–320; Palao Moreno (2005), p. 328.

[308]Article 3(1) Rome I provides that '(. . .) parties can select the law applicable to the whole or to part only of the contract'. Gardeñes Santiago (2008), p. 404, 405.

[309]Ibid., pp. 405–407.

[310]Concerning the definition of mandatory rules, see Chapter 3.3.1.1.

[311]Tang (2007), pp. 122–124; Calliess (2015a), p. 189.

[312]Tang (2007), p. 125.

[313]Nygh (1999), p. 158.

[314]Calliess (2015a), p. 189, 190.

each legal order for the claim at issue; nevertheless, it is indeed a troublesome process.[315]

In conclusion, it is true that the application of the preferential law approach is complicated in practice; nevertheless, an overview of the different possible models to protect the weaker parties against party autonomy shows that it is not possible to ensure consumer and employee protection, grant party autonomy and avoid complex rules simultaneously.[316]

2.4.2 The Existing Connecting Factors in the Absence of Choice of Law

The law applicable in the absence of choice must also be considered specifically for these cases since the general conflict rules are not designed for contracts having a weaker party. Generally, this law is the most relevant for the party protected, the law that this party would reasonably expect to be applicable.

2.4.2.1 Law Applicable to Consumer Contracts in the Absence of Choice

Regarding the law applicable to consumer contracts in the absence of choice, it is generally agreed in most legal systems that the appropriate connecting factor is the habitual residence of the consumer. Thus, in most jurisdictions around the world, the law applicable to the consumer contract is the law of the habitual residence of the consumer. For example, this conflict rule is found in the EU in Article 6(1) of Rome I, Article 120(1) of the Swiss Private International Law Act, Article 11(2) of the Japanese Private International Law Act, Article 1212(2) of the Russian Civil Code, Article 26(2) of the Turkish Private International Law Act etc. Also, the law of the country of the habitual residence of the consumer is the law applicable to consumer contracts under the Restatement (Second) of Conflict of Laws. Despite the fact that there is no specific rule providing that contracts in general are subject to the law of the party who receives the goods and services (Sections 189 to 197) and since the consumer is normally that party, the result would lead to the applicability of

---

[315]Ibid., p. 190; Gardeñes Santiago (2008), p. 407. This process becomes even more complicated when the determination, comparison and possible application of the mandatory rules of the law applicable in the absence of choice is not done *ex officio*. For example, according to Article 11(1) of the Japanese Private International Law Act, it is the consumer who must declare and prove the content of the mandatory rules of the law of his or her place of habitual residence (which is the law applicable in the absence of choice). In the same manner, it is generally common in the US that parties must prove foreign law. Rühl (2011), p. 592.

[316]Rühl (2011), p. 598.

the law of his or her habitual residence, without the need for specific provisions dealing with consumer contracts.[317]

Since, in general terms, the consumer contract will be for the supply of goods or services for personal, household or family use, it seems natural that the connecting factor for the law applicable is the place where the consumer lives and would most likely receive and use the services or goods.[318] From the point of view of the consumers, they are more familiar with the law of their habitual residence, and it can be guessed that they have a better access to information about that law. The application of the law of the habitual residence of the consumer corresponds to reasonable expectations from the consumer, while the professional can also predict that when he or she targets the market of a different country, the consumer law of that country would apply.

In addition, the application of the law of the consumer's habitual residence prevents a possible abuse from the professional. Even if there is no choice of law, the professional could influence the applicable law if, for example, a non-protective conflict rule was applicable. If the law of the place of habitual residence of the seller or the provider of the services (i.e. the professional in this case) was applicable, the professional could determine this law by moving the seat of the company, for instance.[319]

Moreover, since most countries also assign the jurisdiction of the court of the consumer's habitual residence in the case of consumer contracts, the application of the law of that country avoids a split of jurisdiction and applicable law. Therefore, the court does not need to engage in the burdensome task of applying a foreign law, which will also increase the chance that the consumer has his or her rights enforced correctly.[320]

2.4.2.2 Law Applicable to Employment Contracts in the Absence of Choice

There have been various options developed regarding the determination of the law applicable to employment contracts in the absence of choice. The diversity of conflict rules in this area is due to the different approaches in the law applicable to contracts regarding the determination of the law applicable in the absence of choice and the different situations to which these rules have to adapt. Some solutions are based on flexible connecting factors while others on hard rules; some focus on the interests of the parties, while others give more importance to public interests.[321] Some authors have even suggested that courts should take into account all legal

[317] Rühl (2011), p. 598, 599.

[318] Nygh (1999), p. 160.

[319] Rühl (2011), p. 599, 600.

[320] Ibid., p. 600.

[321] Morgenstern (1984), pp. 21–43; Grusic (2015), p. 44, 45.

orders related to the employment contract and decide among them for the most favourable law to the employee.[322] However, it is the law of the place where the work is performed that is generally considered to be the most appropriate for the majority of 'typical' employment relationships.

In a typical employment relationship, in which the employee works and lives for the entire period of employment in one place, which is also where the employer is established, the application of the law of the habitual workplace is the most common in most jurisdictions. In the EU, Article 8 Rome I includes the country in which or from which the employee carries out his or her work as its main connecting factor in the absence of choice of law. In the same manner, other jurisdictions also refer to the law of the habitual place of work (e.g. Article 21(3) Japanese Private International Law Act, Article 27(2) Turkish Private International Law Act, Article 121(1) Swiss Private International Law Act, Section 196 Restatement Second of Conflict of Laws, Article 41 Chinese Private International Law Act etc.).[323] Since the employee works and resides in the same place where the employer is also established, there is generally no need to consider another law. The employee is entitled to the rights that the law which is most familiar provides, while the employer is ensured that all employment contracts with the employees working in the same place are subject to the same law. Thus, both parties benefit from it. Regarding public interests, the protective national legislation of a country is normally directed to the employees habitually working in that country and to their employers. Moreover, the courts of that place would normally have jurisdiction, and they will be able to apply their own law.[324]

Determining the law of the habitual place of work as applicable suggests that the law applicable to the employment contract does not change in cases where the employee is temporarily posted abroad. Nowadays, it is common that employers expect their employees to be mobile, either to acquire knowledge and experience or to contribute to their work on establishments abroad on a temporary basis. Since the habitual place of work does not change, the law applicable to the contract usually remains the same. However, it seems logical that the country to which the employee is posted might also have some interest in the application of some terms of its labour law, such as mandatory provisions regarding health and safety, minimum wage, non-discrimination etc., with the intention to protect local employers and employees from competition from abroad.[325]

On the other hand, not all transnational employment relationships are traditional employment relationships, and thus the adequacy of the application of the law of the

[322]However, if that was the case, it would be extremely burdensome to compare all the laws related, some of which might even have a very weak relation with the contract and no interest in regulating the employment relation. At the same time, this possibility would bring a high level of legal uncertainty due to the number of possible laws involved, making it very difficult to the parties and the court to ascertain the law applicable. See Grusic (2015), p. 44, 45.

[323]Fornasier (2017), p. 1688.

[324]Ibid., pp. 1687–1689; Grusic (2015), pp. 44–46.

[325]In this regard, see Chapter 5.3.

country of habitual place of work is sometimes doubtful. In some cases, the place where the employer is established is used as a connecting factor to determine the law applicable to the employment relationship. This connecting factor is used in addition to the habitual place of work in many jurisdictions (e.g. Article 8(2) Rome I Regulation, Article 43 Chinese Private International Law Act, Article 12(2) Japanese Private International Law Act, Article 121(2) Swiss Private International Law Act, Article 27(3) Turkish Private International Law Act). It seems that the place where the employer is established is a connecting factor less suitable to protect the interests of the employees. Firstly, it might lead to fortuitous results; for example, in the case of large multinational companies, with numerous offices and agencies in different countries, the place where the employee was hired might be the result of a coincidence. Secondly, the place of establishment of the employer might be easily manipulated, and in that manner the employer could be located in a country with a low standard of protection of employees on purpose. However, there might sometimes be good reasons to apply the law of the country where the employer is established due to the nature of the employment relationship. In the case of transnational companies, specialist employees, or management or advisory personnel, are often transferred from one of the countries where the employer does business to another. If the employment contract is governed by the law of the principal place of business, it avoids having to consider a different law every time an employee is transferred, which is beneficial to the employer and can be reasonably expected by the employee.[326] Also, it has to be noticed that this connecting factor is normally used when it is not possible to establish the habitual place of work of the employee; i.e., it works as a subsidiary of the connecting factor of the habitual place of work.

Employment relationships without a habitual place of work might be problematic from the private international law point of view. These are cases where the employee carries out his or her work in several countries or when the territory where the work is carried out does not belong to any country.[327] Typical examples of the first scenario are international transport workers (e.g. seamen, aircrew members or lorry drivers), in which regular assignments abroad are performed and there are at least two countries where the work is habitually performed.[328] Also, some commercial representatives, which act in different countries and wherein the centre of their activity has not been established, belong to this category. Regarding the second scenario, which is not found very often, an example could be temporary employment at offshore installations, such as an oil platform.[329] The law of the place of establishment of the employer is the common conflict rule in these cases, although there are other widespread solutions, such as the laws of the countries of the ship's flag,

---

[326]Grusic (2015), p. 46.

[327]In the EU, the ECJ has referred and provide solutions to these cases in several judgments. In this regard, see Chapter 3.2.2.

[328]Grusic (2015), p. 48; Morgenstern (1984), p. 28.

[329]Morgenstern (1984), p. 32.

the law of the country where the aircraft is registered or the law of the place from which the work is performed.[330]

All the mentioned connecting factors look for the most closely connected law to apply to the employment relationship. However, due to the diversity of factual circumstances, it might be the case that the employment relationship is more closely connected to a different country than the one indicated in the applicable conflict rule. Conflict rules regarding employment contracts must be flexible enough to take into account the important interests involved. In this regard, many jurisdictions include an 'escape clause' that allows courts to disregard the law designated by the other connecting factors and apply instead the law that is most closely connected to that specific case. This escape clause can be found in the EU in Article 8(4) Rome I, Article 67(2) Tunisian Private International Law Act or Article 27(4) Turkish Private International Law Act.[331]

The use of this clause is justified when all the elements of the employment relationship are located in one country except the habitual place of work or by the common nationality of the parties or the common place of habitual residence. A clear example would be when a company based in one country hires an employee domiciled in the same country to work indefinitely in a foreign country where the standards of employment protection are lower than in their home country; in this case, courts would rather apply the law most closely connected, which would be the law of the home state rather than the law of habitual place of work, which offers lower standards of protection.[332]

References

Águila-Real JA (1998) Cláusulas Abusivas, Cláusulas Predispuestas y Condiciones Generales. Anuario Jurídico de La Rioja 4:53–70

Arenas García R (1996) Tratamiento Jurisprudencial del Ámbito de Aplicación de los Foros de Protección en Materia de Contratos de Consumidores del Convenio de Bruselas de 1968. Revista Española de Derecho Internacional 48:39–69

Arenas García R (2007) La Regulación de la Responsabilidad Precontractual en el Reglamento Roma II. Anuario Español de Derecho Internacional Privado 7:315–339

Basedow J et al (eds) (2012) The Max Planck Encyclopedia of European private law. Oxford University Press, Oxford

Basedow J et al (eds) (2017) Encyclopedia of private international law. Edward Elgar Publishing, Cheltenham

Beale JH (1935) A treatise on the conflict of laws. Baker, Voorhis & Co., New York

Belohlávek AJ (2011) Rome Convention - Rome I Regulation. Juris Publishing, Inc., Huntington

Boele-Woelki K (2010) Unifying and harmonizing substantive law and the role of conflict of laws. Brill, Leiden

Cabrelli D (2018) Employment law in context. Oxford University Press, Oxford

[330]Grusic (2015), p. 48; Morgenstern (1984), pp. 28–32.

[331]Fornasier (2017), p. 1963.

[332]Ibid., p. 1962, 1963.

Calliess G-P (2015a) Article 6. Consumer contracts. In: Calliess G-P (ed) Rome regulations. Commentary, 2nd edn. Kluwer Law International, The Netherlands, pp 155–193

Calliess G-P (2015b) Article 3. Freedom of choice. In: Calliess G-P (ed) Rome regulations. Commentary, 2nd edn. Kluwer Law International, The Netherlands, pp 76–108

Calliess G-P (2015c) Rome regulations. Commentary, 2nd edn. Kluwer Law International, The Netherlands

Carrascosa González J (2012) La Autonomía de la Voluntad Conflictual y la Mano Invisible en la Contratación Internacional. Diario La Ley 7847

Collins H (2001) Justifying European employment law. In: Grundmann S et al (eds) Party autonomy and the role of information in the internal market. De Gruyter, Berlin, pp 205–224

Collins H (2006) A Workers' Civil Code? Principles of European contract law evolving in EU social and economic policy. In: Hesselink MW (ed) The politics of a European civil code. Kluwer Law International, The Hague, pp 55–71

Collins H (2008) The European Civil Code: the way forward. Cambridge University Press, Cambridge

Collins H (2010) Employment law, 2nd edn. Oxford University Press, Oxford

Collins H et al (2019) Philosophical foundations of labour law. Oxford University Press, Oxford

Cseres KJ (2005) Competition law and consumer protection. Kluwer Law International, The Hague

Currie B (1963) Selected essays on the conflict of laws. Duke University Press, Durham

De Boer TM (1996) Facultative choice of law: the procedural status of choice-of-law rules and foreign law. Collect Cours Hague Acad Int Law 257:223–427

De la Rosa FE (2003) La Protección de Consumidores en el Mercado Interior Europeo. Granada, Comares

Devenney J, Kenny M (eds) (2012) European consumer protection. Theory and practice. Cambridge University Press, Cambridge

Fentiman R (2016) Article 5: contracts of carriage. In: Magnus U, Mankowski P (eds) Commentary - Rome I Regulation. Verlag Dr. Otto Schmidt, Köln, pp 441–452

Fornasier M (2017) Employment contracts, applicable law. In: Basedow J et al (eds) Encyclopedia of private international law. Edward Elgar Publishing, Cheltenham, pp 1679–1703

Fotinopouplou Basurko O (2004) Consideraciones en torno al Art. 1.4 del Estatuto de los Trabajadores. Acerca del Sistema de Fuentes del Derecho Internacional Privado. Revista del Ministerio de Trabajo e Inmigración 52:49–60

Franzen M, Gröner N (2015) Article 8. Individual employment contracts. In: Calliess G-P (ed) Rome Regulations. Commentary, 2nd edn. Kluwer Law International, The Netherlands

Gamillscheg F (1983) Rules of public order in private international labour law. Recueil des Cours 181:285–347

Garcimartín Alférez FJ (2002) La Racionalidad Ecónomica del Derecho Internacional Privado. Cursos de derecho internacional y relaciones internacionales de Vitoria-Gasteiz:87–154

Garcimartín Alférez FJ (2008) The Rome I Regulation: much ado about nothing? Eur Legal Forum:61–80

Gardeñes Santiago M (2008) La Regulación Conflictual del Contrato de Trabajo en el Reglamento Roma I: una oportunidad perdida. Anuario Español de Derecho Internacional Privado 8:387–424

Gómez Pomar F (2008) The harmonization of contract law through European rules: a law and economics perspective. Indret: Revista para el Análisis del Derecho 4:2

Grusic U (2015) The European private international law of employment. Cambridge University Press, Cambridge

Guardans Cambó I (1992) Contrato Internacional y Derecho Imperativo Extranjero. Aranzadi, Pamplona

Hage Chahine N (2012) Culpa in Contrahendo in European private international law: another look at Article 12 of the Rome II Regulation. Northwest J Int Law Bus 32:451–540

Halson R, Campbell D (2013) Harmonisation and its discontents: a transaction costs critique of a European contract law. In: Devenney J, Kenny M (eds) The transformation of European private

law harmonisation, consolidation, codification or Chaos? Cambridge University Press, Cambridge, pp 100–130
Hartkamp A, von Bar C (2011) Towards a European civil code. Kluwer Law International, Alphen aan den Rijn
Haupt H-G (2004) The history of consumption in Western Europe in the nineteenth and twentieth centuries. In: Hartmut K (ed) The European Way. European societies in the 19th and 20th centuries. Berghahn Books, New York, pp 161–185
Heiss H (2009) Party autonomy. In: Ferrari F, Leible S (eds) Rome I Regulation: the law applicable to contractual obligations in Europe. Sellier, European Law Publishers, München, pp 7–16
Hesselink MW (2007) European contract law: a matter of consumer protection, citizenship, or justice? Eur Rev Priv Law 15:323–348
Hesselink MW (2009) The common frame of reference as a source of European private law. Tulane Law Rev 83:919
Hondius E (1987) Unfair terms in consumer contracts. Molengraaff Instituut voor Privaatrecht, Utrecht
Hondius E et al (2008) Principles of European law: sales contract. Sellier, European Law Publishers, München
Jansen N, Zimmermann R (2010) A European Civil Code in all but name: discussing the nature and purposes of the draft common frame of reference. Cambridge Law J 69:98–112
Juenger FK (1993) Choice of law and multistate justice. Martinus Nijhoff Publishers, Dordrecht
Kahn-Freund O (1967) A note on status and contract in British labour law. Mod Labour Rev 30:635–644
Koetz HD (2012) Contract law in Europe and the United States: legal unification in the civil law and the common law. Tulane Eur Civil Law Forum 27:1–16
Krebber S (2000) Conflict of laws in employment in Europe. Comp Labor Law J Policy J 21:501–542
Kuipers J-J (2009) Party autonomy in the Brussels I Regulation and Rome I Regulation and the European Court of Justice. Germ Law J 10:1505–1525
Kuipers J-J (2012) EU law and private international law: the interrelationship in contractual obligations. Martinus Nijhoff Publishers, Leiden
Lagarde P (2006) Remarques sur la Proposition de Règlement sur la Loi Applicable aux Obligations Contractuelles (Rome I). Revue critique de droit international privé 95:331–349
Lando O (1974) The EC Draft Convention on the law applicable to contractual and non-contractual obligations: introduction and contractual obligations. Rabel J Comp Int Priv Law 38:6–55
Lando O, Nielsen PA (2007) The Rome I proposal. J Priv Int Law 3:29–51
Lando O et al (eds) (2003) Principles of European contract law. Kluwer Law International, The Hague
Lazić V (2014) Procedural Justice for 'Weaker Parties' in cross-border litigation under the EU regulatory scheme. Utrecht Law Rev 10:100–117
Leible S (2011) La Importancia de la Autonomía Conflictual para el Futuro del Derecho de los Contratos Internacionales. Cuadernos de Derecho Transnacional 3:214–233
Leighton P (2010) EU employment law: a practical guide. Thorogood Publishing Ltd, London
Llobera Vila M (2016) El Artículo 1.4 ET a la Luz de la Jurisprudencia Comunitaria en Materia de Ley Aplicable al Contrato de Trabajo Internacional. Revista de Derecho Social 73:127–148
Magnus U (2016) Article 4: applicable law in the absence of choice. In: Magnus U, Mankowski P (eds) Rome I Regulation-commentary. Verlag Dr. Otto Schmidt, Köln, pp 263–441
Mandery M (2014) Party autonomy in contractual and non-contractual obligations. Peter Lang, Frankfurt
Mankowski P (2016) Article 3: freedom of choice. In: Magnus U, Mankowski P (eds) Rome I Regulation - commentary. Verlag Dr. Otto Schmidt, Köln, pp 87–263
Mattei U (1997) A transaction cost approach to the European Code. Eur Rev Priv Law 5:537–540
Maultzsch F (2016) Party autonomy in European private international law: uniform principle or context-dependent instrument? J Priv Int Law 12:466–491

Max Planck Institute for Foreign Private and Private International Law (2007) Comments on the European Commission's Proposal for a Regulation of the European Parliament and the Council on the law applicable to contractual obligations (Rome I). RabelsZ Bd71

McParland M (2015) The Rome I Regulation on the law applicable to contractual obligations. Oxford University Press, Oxford

Merrett L (2011) Employment contracts in private international law. Oxford University Press, Oxford

Micklitz H-W (2009) The targeted full harmonisation approach: looking behind the curtain. In: Howells GG, Schulze R (eds) Modernising and harmonising consumer contract law. Sellier, European Law Publishers, München, pp 47–84

Mills A (2018) Party autonomy in private international law. Cambridge University Press, Cambridge

Morgenstern F (1984) International conflicts of labour law. A survey of the law applicable to the international employment relation. International Labour Office, Geneva

Moura Vicente D (2013) Culpa in Contrahendo in European private international law. Anuario Español de Derecho Internacional Privado 13:53–72

Nadelmann KH (1961) Joseph Story's contribution to American conflicts law: a comment. Am J Legal Hist 5:230–253

Nygh PE (1999) Autonomy in international contracts. Oxford University Press, Oxford

Ortiz Vidal MD (2012) Ley Aplicable a los Contratos Internacionales y Eficiencia Conflictual. Granada, Comares

Palao Moreno G (2005) Las Normas del Derecho Internacional Privado de Origen Comunitario en Materia de Contrato Individual de Trabajo, ante los Retos de la Integración Europea y la Globalización. Anuario Español de Derecho Internacional Privado 5:309–334

Palao Moreno G (2016) Article 8: individual employment contracts. In: Magnus U, Mankowski P (eds) Rome I Regulation - commentary. Verlag Dr. Otto Schmidt, Köln, pp 577–599

Plender R, Wilderspin M (2015) The European private international law of obligations, 4th edn. Sweet & Maxwell, London

Pocar F (1984) La Protection de la Partie Faible en Droit International Privé. Collected Courses Hague Acad Int Law 188:339–394

Renner M (2015) Article 21. Public policy of the forum. In: Calliess G-P (ed) Rome regulations. Commentary, 2nd edn. Kluwer Law International, The Netherlands

Riesenhuber K (2012) European employment law. A systematic exposition. Intersentia, Cambridge

Rühl G (2007) Party autonomy in the private international law of contracts: transatlantic convergence and economic efficiency. In: Gottschalk E et al (eds) Conflict of laws in a globalized world. Cambridge University Press, Cambridge

Rühl G (2011) Consumer protection in choice of law. Cornell Int Law J 44:569–601

Rühl G (2014) The protection of weaker parties in the private international law of the European Union: a portrait of inconsistency and conceptual truancy. J Priv Int Law 10:335–358

Rutgers JW, Sefton-Green R (2008) Revising the consumer acquis: (half) opening the doors of the Trojan Horse. Eur Rev Priv Law 16:427–442

Salmerón Hernríquez JA (2016) Freedom of contract, bargaining power and forum selection in bills of lading. Ulrik Huber Institute for Private International Law, Groningen

Sánchez Lorenzo S (2003) La Unificación del Derecho Contractual Europeo Vista desde el Derecho Internacional Privado. In: Derecho Patrimonial Europeo. Thomson-Aranzadi, Cizu Menor (Navarra), pp 363–381

Schüller B (2012) The definition of consumers in EU consumer law. In: European consumer protection. Theory and practice. Cambridge University Press, Cambridge

Schulte-Nölke H et al (eds) (2008) EC consumer law compendium. Comparative analysis. Universität, Bielefeld

Solomon D (2007) The private international law of contracts in Europe: advances and retreats. Tulane Law Rev 82:1709–1740

Stone P (2018) Stone on private international law in the European Union, 4th edn. Edward Elgar Publishing, Cheltenham

Story J (1846) Commentaries on the conflict of laws: foreign and domestic, in regard to contracts, rights, and remedies, and especially in regard to marriages, divorces, wills, successions, and judgments, 3rd edn. Little, Brown

Symeonides SC (2014) Codifying choice of law around the world: an international comparative analysis. Oxford University Press, New York

Symeonides SC (2015) The choice-of-law revolution fifty years after currie: an end and a beginning. Univ Ill Law Rev 2015:1847–1921

Symeonides SC (2016) Choice of law. Oxford University Press, Oxford

Tang ZS (2007) Parties' choice of law in e-consumer contracts. J Priv Int Law 3:113–136

Tang ZS (2009) Electronic consumer contracts in the conflicts of laws. Hart, Oxford

Ten Wolde MH (2013) The relativity of legal positions in cross-border situations: the foundations of private interregional law, private intra-community law and private international law. In: A Commitment to private international law- essays in honour of Hans van Loon. Intersentia, Cambridge, pp 569–581

Twigg-Flesner C (2011) 'Good-bye harmonisation by directives, hello cross-border only regulation?' - a way forward for EU consumer contract law. Eur Rev Contract Law 7:235–256

Twigg-Flesner C (2012) Comment: the future of EU consumer law – the end of harmonisation? In: European consumer protection. Theory and practice. Cambridge University Press, Cambridge, pp 6–20

Twigg-Flesner C (2016) The importance of law and harmonisation for the EU's confident consumer. In: Leczykiewicz D, Weatherill S (eds) The images of the consumer in EU law. Hart, Oxford, pp 183–202

United Nations Conference on Trade and Development (UNCTAD) (2016) Manual on Consumer Protection

Van Bochove LM (2014) Overriding mandatory rules as a vehicle for weaker party protection in European private international law. Erasmus Law Rev 7:147–157

Veneziani B (2009) The Employment relationship. In: Hepple B, Veneziani B (eds) The transformation of labour law in Europe. A comparative study of 15 Countries 1945–2004. Hart, Oxford, pp 99–128

Verhagen HLE (2002) The tension between party autonomy and European Union law: some observations on IngmarGB Ltd v Eaton Leonard Technologies Inc. Int Comp Law Q 51:135–154

Verhulp E (2017) The notion of 'Employee' in EU law and national laws. The European Centre of Expertise (ECE) in the field of labour law, employment and labour market policies

von Savigny FC (1849) System des Heutigen Römischen Rechts. Veit und Comp, Berlin

Savigny FC von (1869) Private international law. A treatise on the conflict of laws, and the limits of their operation in respect of place and time (trans: William Guthrie). T. & T. Clark, Edinburgh

Watt HM (2010) "Party Autonomy" in international contracts: from the makings of a myth to the requirements of global governance. Eur Rev Contract Law 6:250–283

Weatherill S (2013) EU consumer law and policy, 2nd edn. Edward Elgar Publishing, Cheltenham

Wilderspin M (2008) The Rome I regulation: communitarisation and modernisation of the Rome Convention. ERA Forum:259–274

Wilderspin M (2016) Article 6: consumer contracts. In: Magnus U, Mankowski P (eds) Rome I Regulation - commentary. Verlag Dr. Otto Schmidt, Köln, pp 453–490

Wilhelmsson T (2004) The abuse of the 'confident consumer' as a justification for EC consumer law. J Consumer Policy 27:317–337

Willem Vernooij N (2009) Rome I: an update on the law applicable to contractual obligations in Europe. Columbia J Eur Law Online 15:71–76

Chapter 3
The Rome I Regulation and Its Mechanisms of Protection of Consumers and Employees

Party autonomy is the cornerstone of the Rome I Regulation on the law applicable to contractual obligations.[1] Freedom of choice of law is considered as an extension of freedom of contract and is now well rooted in the area of contract law in EU private international law (EU PIL).[2] In the Rome I Regulation, as a general rule, the objective connecting factors will only apply when the parties have not made a choice of law. Article 3(1) Rome I allows the parties to the contract to choose the law of any state as the law governing their contract. In a cross-border contract, a Dutch seller and a Spanish buyer are free to choose German law to govern their contract, even when the situation has no connections to Germany. Moreover, the depeçage, or choice of a law to govern only a part of the contract, is also permitted, although it is highly debated whether the contract should be divisible into different parts in those cases.[3] Parties also have the freedom to change the law applicable to their contract at any moment. That is, parties can agree on a different law (or choose a governing law if they did not do it in their contract), for example when the dispute has already arisen. In addition, the choice of law can be express or implicit. This means that the

[1]Recital 11 Rome I Regulation refers to party autonomy as one of the cornerstones of the system of the Rome I Regulation; moreover, the ECJ refers to party autonomy as 'the' cornerstone of the instrument (Case C-184/12 *United Antwerp Maritime Agencies* (*Unamar*) *NV v Navigation Maritime Bulgare [2013]* EU:C:2013:663, para 49).

[2]In addition to the field of contract law, party autonomy has also been extended and increasingly recognised in other areas in EU PIL, especially during the last years. In the area of non-contractual obligations, article 14(1) Rome II Regulation recognises the freedom of choice of law of the parties. Even in the areas of family law and succession the possibility to choose the applicable law is recognised: first, the 2007 Hague Maintenance Protocol which came into force through the Maintenance Regulation among most Member States; then, article 5 Rome III Regulation recognises that married couples can choose the law applicable to their divorce and separation. Finally, article 22 of the Succession Regulation affords the deceased a (unilateral) choice of law regarding the succession rights resulting from the death.

[3]Kuipers (2012), p. 46.

M. Campo Comba, *The Law Applicable to Cross-border Contracts involving Weaker Parties in EU Private International Law*,
https://doi.org/10.1007/978-3-030-61481-2_3

choice can be expressly stipulated by the parties, but it can also be implied by the terms of the contract and all the circumstances of the case. In order to consider that there is an implicit choice of law, the genuine intention of the parties in that regard must be established with a reasonable degree of certainty, taking into account all the circumstances of the case.[4] Party autonomy, at least in the area of contracts, is widely recognised and accepted in EU PIL. The discussion is focused on its extension and its limits. Thus, it is also acknowledged that the freedom of choice of law requires regulation, especially when it works to the detriment of one of the parties to the contract, like a consumer or an employee.

Protection of weaker parties is one of the principles underlying the current EU PIL and widely present in the Rome I Regulation. The Rome I Regulation provides for several mechanisms for the protection of weaker contracting parties which constitute a limit on party autonomy. Also, special connecting factors are established to determine the law applicable in the absence of choice for those contracts that are considered to be imbalanced. The weaker contracting parties that enjoy special protection in the Rome I Regulation are consumers involved in a consumer contract falling under the conditions required by article 6 Rome I and employees part of an individual employment contract according to article 8 Rome I.

On the one hand, when there is a choice of law, the danger of party autonomy is similar in the case of consumer and employment contracts, entailing the possible threat that the strong party chooses as applicable to the contract a law with low standards of consumer or employee protection. Thus, both articles limit party autonomy in the same manner, providing for the application of the provisions that cannot be derogated from by agreement of the law objectively applicable to the contract. On the other hand, in the absence of choice of law, both articles provide for special connecting factors. Article 6 Rome I, in the case of consumer contracts, provides for the application of the law of the country of habitual residence of the consumer. The application of the law of habitual residence of the consumer corresponds to the reasonable expectations of the consumer, and, at the same time, the professional can also predict that when he targets the market of a different country, the consumer law of that country would apply. In addition, the application of the law of the consumer's habitual residence prevents a possible abuse from the professional: if the general connecting factors of article 4 Rome I would apply to the consumer contract, they will most probably lead to the application of the law of the country of the seller or service provider (the professional in this case), which means that the professional could determine this law by moving the seat of the company, for instance.[5] In the case of employment contracts, article 8 Rome I primarily refers to the law of the country in which the employee habitually carries out his work. The place of habitual work is considered as most closely connected to the employment

---

[4]For commentaries regarding party autonomy in the Rome I Regulation, see, for example: Mills (2018); Rühl (2007); Calliess (2015a); Mankowski (2016); Plender and Wilderspin (2015), pp. 133–174; Krvavac and Belovic (2014).

[5]Rühl (2011), pp. 599, 600.

contract, and, in general, both employee and employer are familiar with it. Moreover, the place where the employee habitually carries out his work will often coincide with his habitual residence. The country where the employee habitually carries out his work has the most interest in applying its mandatory rules ensuring employment rights and conditions.[6]

However, articles 6 and 8 Rome I are not the only mechanisms that the Rome I Regulation has in order to ensure the application of mandatory law protecting weaker contracting parties. Article 3(3) and (4) Rome I limits party autonomy with the aim of preventing parties from artificially relating the contract to any country to which it lacks any connection, with the only intention of avoiding the application of the mandatory national or European provisions. Pursuant to article 3(3) Rome I, when a situation is only connected to one single Member State, the choice of a foreign law by the parties should not affect the application of the domestically mandatory provisions of the national law. In the same manner, pursuant to article 3(4) Rome I, if the situation is only connected with one or several Member States, the choice of a non-Member State law by the parties will not affect the application of mandatory EU law. This provision is also a potential vehicle for the safeguarding of the interests of contractual parties as they will be prevented from avoiding the applicability of mandatory provisions originated in EU directives in intra-EU situations.

In addition, article 9 Rome I ensures the application of the so-called overriding mandatory provisions, which must be of internationally mandatory application regardless of the law applicable to the contract. Overriding mandatory provisions are defined in article 9(1) as

> provisions the respect for which is regarded as crucial by a country for safeguarding its public interests, such as its political, social or economic organisation, to such an extent that they are applicable to any situation falling within their scope, irrespective of the law otherwise applicable to the contract under this Regulation.

However, whether this provision can be used as a mechanism for the protection of consumers, employees and other weaker parties is highly discussed.

Thus, this chapter will focus on those specific mechanisms that the Rome I Regulation provides for the protection of weaker parties, especially of consumers and employees:

[6] In this regard, Sect. 2.4.2.

- Firstly, article 6 Rome I regarding consumer contracts will be the object of analysis. Not all consumer contracts fall under the conditions required by article 6 Rome I, and as a consequence, those contracts outside its scope of application will be subject to the general rules of the Rome I Regulation and will not enjoy the special protection ensured by article 6 Rome I. Both the scope of application and connecting factors of article 6 Rome I regarding consumer contracts will be analysed.
- Secondly, article 8 Rome I concerning the law applicable to individual employment contracts will be examined.
- Thirdly, article 9 Rome I regarding overriding mandatory rules will be the object of analysis. Specifically, the role of overriding mandatory rules regarding the protection of weaker parties will be debated.
- Finally, article 3(4) Rome I will also be described as a mechanism for the protection of weaker parties within the EU.

3.1 The Law Applicable to Consumer Contracts: Article 6 Rome I

Consumers have a weaker economic and legal position vis-à-vis professionals, and the protection designed to balance out this inequality needs to be reflected in PIL. The principle of consumer protection is reflected in the area of EU PIL regarding the law applicable to cross-border consumer contracts in article 6 Rome I. National legislators, and the EU legislator, enact mandatory consumer contract provisions that restrict the freedom of contract and create substantive consumer rights; these rights need to be protected in cross-border situations.

Already the Rome Convention included a special conflict rule protecting consumers (article 5 Rome Convention). Due to its narrow scope of application and other inconsistencies, article 6 Rome I introduced changes. Article 5 Rome Convention covered only 'certain consumer contracts', namely those 'the object of which is the supply of goods or services' and those 'for the provision of credit for that object'. PIL interprets the supply of goods and services in a narrow contractual understanding of the concept (not extended to almost every economic activity), and as a result, the scope covered by article 5 Rome Convention was inconsistent with the scope that the EU directives on consumer protection intended to cover.[7] Moreover, the challenges of the growth of electronic commerce also called for a new rule.

When modernising the Rome Convention, EU PIL was aligned regarding consumer contracts, and article 6 Rome I was drafted in coordination with articles 15–17 Brussels I Regulation (now articles 17–19 Brussels I bis Regulation). Recital 7 Rome I makes express reference to the synchronisation between both Regulations:

[7]Case C-70/03 *Commission of the European Communities v Kingdom of Spain* [2004] ECR I-9657. In this regard, see Sect. 4.1.1.3.

the substantive scope and the provisions of this Regulation should be consistent with Council Regulation (EC) No 44/2001 of 22 December 2000 on jurisdiction and the recognition and enforcement of judgments in civil and commercial matters (Brussels I) and Regulation (EC) No 864/2007 of the European Parliament and of the Council of 11 July 2007 on the law applicable to non-contractual obligations (Rome II).[8]

3.1.1 Conditions of Application of Article 6 Rome I

Article 6 Rome I applies to consumer contracts entered into on or after 18 December 2009. As to the personal scope, a consumer under article 6 Rome I needs to be a natural person who is acting for a purpose outside the scope of his trade or profession. At the same time, the professional needs to be a person (natural or legal) acting in the exercise of its trade or profession. The notion of consumer and professional needs to be interpreted autonomously and independently according to the object and purpose of the Regulation.[9]

The complexity of article 6 Rome I lies in the specific requirements necessary for its applicability. Since not all 'consumers' or 'customers' are in need of protective PIL rules, article 6 Rome I limits its scope of application. Under the Rome Convention, the applicability of the rule was subject to the difference between passive consumer and active consumer. The passive consumer, who is approached by a professional to enter into a contract, might not be aware of the international character of the situation (e.g. he does not know whether the professional is located in the consumer's country or not). Conversely, the active consumer, who enters into a contract by its own initiative with a business in a foreign country, is aware of the internationality of the contract. Therefore, the reasonable expectation of the passive consumer, as well as of the business that intentionally directs his activities to that country, is the law of the consumer's home country to be applicable, while the active consumer who approaches a business in a foreign country can reasonably expect that his own law will not be applicable.[10] Both the Rome I Regulation and the Brussels I Regulation changed this approach. Article 6 Rome I intends to prevent contracting around mandatory consumer regulations as a result of the operation of the conflict rules in the cases where the contract has a close connection to the home country of the consumer. To determine the applicability of article 6 Rome I, we can distinguish between material and territorial requirements.

[8]Regarding the coherence principle in EU Private International Law: Sánchez Lorenzo (2018).

[9]See Sect. 2.1.1.2. for a more exhaustive definition of consumer and professional within the EU PIL.

[10]Calliess (2015b), p. 157.

3.1.1.1 Material Requirements

Article 6 Rome I applies to

> a contract concluded by a natural person for a purpose which can be regarded as being outside his trade or profession ('the consumer') with another person acting in the exercise of his trade or profession ('the professional') [...]

as long as the contract falls within the scope of such activities. The material requirements necessary in a contract to be considered a consumer contract under article 6 Rome I are fulfilled when:

- The professional party pursues commercial or professional activities.
- The consumer does not act within its commercial or professional activities.
- The contract falls within the scope of such activities.
- The contract does not fall within the material exclusions of article 6(4) Rome I.

Thus, article 6 Rome I applies to all types of contracts concluded between a professional and a consumer, except those specifically excluded.[11] Article 6 Rome I applies without prejudice to articles 5 and 7 Rome I (contracts of carriage and insurance contracts, respectively), which are dealt with in specific provisions due to the particular nature of those types of contract.[12]

The two first points have been previously the subject of analysis.[13] Regarding the third point, it is required that the contract falls within the scope of 'such activities'. In this regard, recital 25 states that

> [...] provided that the consumer contract has been concluded *as a result* of the professional pursuing his commercial or professional activities in that particular country [...],[14]

which requires a nexus between the activities and the conclusion of the contract. This requirement should not be interpreted strictly since in cases of advertisement in media, for example, it would be very difficult to prove the link between the directed activity and the conclusion of the contract. Moreover, the consumer does not need to establish the existence of a causal link, and it is also not necessary that the professional advertise the specific product or service acquired by the consumer, but only a general relation to the business is sufficient.[15]

---

[11] By contrast to article 5 Rome Convention, which only applied to contracts for the sale of goods, supply of services or provision of credit for that purpose.

[12] Recital 31 Rome I.

[13] Section 2.1.1.2.

[14] Italics provided by the author.

[15] Case C-190/11 *Daniela Mühlleitner v Ahmad Yusufi and Wadat Yusufi* [2012] ECR I-0000.

Article 6(4) Rome I provides for a list of excluded contracts.[16] The exception in point (a) regards a contract for the supply of services to be supplied entirely outside the consumer's country of habitual residence. Although included in the definition of consumer contracts within the Brussels I bis Regulation, it is excluded from article 6 Rome I on the ground that, in such cases, the consumer cannot reasonably expect the protection of his own law.[17] A clear example is a contract for the provision of hotel accommodation or a language course. In those cases, it is understood that the consumer 'cannot reasonably expect the law of his state of origin to be applied ... The contract is more closely connected with the State in which the other contracting party is resident, even if the latter has performed one of the acts described in paragraph 2 (advertising, for example) in the State in which the consumer is resident.'[18] This rationale is questionable in some aspects. Especially, it is inefficient the fact that it is not parallel with article 17 Brussels I bis Regulation and thus might lead to a situation where the court of the country of the consumer has to apply a foreign law. For this provision, it is essential to distinguish contracts for the provision of services from contracts for the sale of goods, including issues regarding mixed contracts or a third category of contracts. In this regard, it has to be noticed that the concept of contract 'for the supply of services' in EU PIL is not as broad as in other areas: the ECJ in *Falco Privatstiftung*[19] held that the notion of service required some activity or active conduct from the service provider and, thus, is not synonymous to the concept of services within the meaning of article 49 of the EC Treaty.[20] Moreover, to be excluded by article 6(4)(a), the service has to be provided *exclusively* in a country different from the country of the consumer. Service is rendered where the provider performs the activities and, when applicable, where the consumer receives the results. In cross-border services, these places could be different countries (e.g. an Internet service provider situated in one country, while the consumer

---

[16] Article 6(4) Rome I:

> (a) a contract for the supply of services where the services are to be supplied to the consumer exclusively in a country other than that in which he has his habitual residence; (b) a contract of carriage other than a contract relating to package travel within the meaning of Council Directive 90/314/EEC of 13 June 1990 on package travel, package holidays and package tours (15); (c) a contract relating to a right in rem in immovable property or a tenancy of immovable property other than a contract relating to the right to use immovable properties on a timeshare basis within the meaning of Directive 94/47/EC; (d) rights and obligations which constitute a financial instrument and rights and obligations constituting the terms and conditions governing the issuance or offer to the public and public take-over bids of transferable securities, and the subscription and redemption of units in collective investment undertakings in so far as these activities do not constitute provision of a financial service; (e) a contract concluded within the type of system falling within the scope of Article 4(1)(h).

[17] Giuliano-Lagarde Report [1980] OJ C282/1, 24.

[18] Ibid.

[19] Case C-533/07 *Falco Privatstiftung and Thomas Rabitsch v Gisela Weller-Lindhorst* [2009] *ECR* I-03327.

[20] Wilderspin (2016), p. 468.

downloading the content of the website is in another country).[21] The place of performance is considered to be the place where the service is completed and passed to the customer. However, in the case of the exception of article 6(4)(a), it is clear that the service is just excluded when the consumer has to travel abroad in order to receive the service, and in such a case the service will be performed and the results received outside the country of the consumer.

Article 6(4)(b) Rome I excludes a contract of carriage other than a contract involving a package travel as defined by Directive 90/314/ECC on package travel, package holidays and package tours (now repealed by Directive (EU) 2015/2302).[22] All kinds of carriage, whether by air, sea, rail or land, are excluded, irrespective of whether the contract of carriage is for the passage of goods or persons and of whether the carriage is free or not.[23] The drafting of this norm has been criticised.[24] Article 2 (1) Package Travel Directive defines a package as a combination of accommodation, transport and/or other tourist services. Thus, a package could be a combination of accommodation (e.g. hotel) and a tourist service (e.g. sailing), without transport, and in this case it could fall at the same time under the previous exception of article 6(4) (a) (i.e. services that are provided exclusively in a country other than the country of the consumer). Following an interpretation parallel to the Brussels I Regulation, it is understood that the exception of article 6(4)(b) is a *lex specialis* in regard to the other exceptions of article 6(4) Rome I.[25]

Article 6(4)(c) excludes from the scope of consumer protection contracts relating to rights in rem in immovable property (e.g. contracts for the sale or donation of real estate, mortgage contracts etc.) or tenancies of immovable property other than timeshare contracts. The ratio of this exclusion is that such contracts are normally subject to the law of the place where the real state is situated, to which they are most closely related.[26] The importance of the connection between immovable property and the territory where the immovable property is located is shown in article 4(1) (c) Rome I and article 24(1) Brussels I bis, which, respectively, use as connecting factor the place where the property is located to determine the law applicable and point to the court of the place where the property is situated as the exclusive jurisdiction for contracts relating to rights in rem in immovable property or more than 6-month tenancies of immovable property. Article 4(1)(d) and article 24(1) provide as an exception that a tenancy of up to 6 months for private use (e.g. holiday

[21]Calliess (2015b), p. 183.

[22]Directive (EU) 2015/2302 of the European Parliament and of the Council of 25 November 2015 on package travel and linked travel arrangements, amending Regulation (EC) No 2006/2004 and Directive 2011/83/EU of the European Parliament and of the Council and repealing Council Directive 90/314/EEC (OJ 2015 L 326/1).

[23]Ragno (2009), p. 140.

[24]Ibid., p. 141.

[25]Article 15(3) Brussels I Regulation (now article 17(3) Brussels I bis) provides: 'This Section shall not apply to a contract of transport other than a contract which, for an inclusive price, provides for a combination of travel and accommodation.'

[26]Wilderspin (2016), p. 470; Calliess (2015b), p. 185.

house) is most closely connected to the country of common habitual residence of the tenant and landlord. The main issue regarding article 6(4)(c) is that parties are then allowed to freely choose the law applicable to contracts relating to rights in rem in immovable property or tenancies of immovable property according to article 3 (1) Rome I, deviating from the conflict rules of article 4(1)(c) and (d). As a result, since article 6 Rome I cannot ensure the applicability of the mandatory rules of the place where the property is located when it comes to the protection of private tenants, it is uncertain whether these norms could apply as overriding mandatory rules according to article 9 Rome I.[27]

Timeshare contracts within the meaning of Directive 94/7/EC, now repealed by Directive 2008/122/EC,[28] are not subject to this exception. The definition of a timeshare contract under the new Directive is simplified, and it is defined as 'a contract [...] under which a consumer [...] acquires the right to use one or more overnight accommodation [...]'.[29]

This exception creates the uncertainty of whether all timeshare contracts fall under the scope of article 6 Rome I or whether those that could fall under other exceptions at the same time (i.e. timeshare contracts that are essentially contracts for the provision of services excluded by article 6(4)(a)) would be excluded. That is, the broad definition of timeshare contracts includes contracts for the provision of services that could be supplied exclusively in a country other than the consumer's country of habitual residence and thus also fall under the exception of article 6(4) (a).[30] It can be considered that the legislative intent and objective purpose of the rule is to include any timeshare contract covered by the Directive in the scope of article 6 Rome I, article 6(4)(c) being a *lex specialis* over article 6(4)(a) regarding all contracts covered by the Timeshare Directive, even if they do not relate to a right in rem in or a tenancy of immovable property.[31]

The next exception refers to financial instruments, public issuances or offers and public takeover bids and the subscription and redemption of units in collective investment undertakings. Article 6(4)(d) excludes

> rights and obligations which constitute a financial instrument and rights and obligations constituting the terms and conditions governing the issuance or offer to the public and public take-over bids of transferable securities, and the subscription and redemption of units in collective investment undertakings in so far as these activities do not constitute provision of a financial service.

---

[27]Calliess (2015b), p. 185.

[28]Directive 2008/122/EC of the European Parliament and of the Council of 14 January 2009 on the protection of consumers in respect of certain aspects of timeshare, long-term holiday product, resale and exchange contracts (OJ 2009 L 33/10).

[29]In accordance with article 18 of the new Timeshare Directive, references made to the repealed Directive shall be understood as references to the new one.

[30]Wilderspin (2016), p. 471.

[31]Ibid., p. 471; Calliess (2015b), p. 185.

This exclusion, as well as the previous and the following one, was not included in the Rome Convention. In this case, that is due to the fact that, while article 5 (1) Rome Convention was not applicable to the sale of securities, article 6 (1) Rome I extended the scope to all contracts.

It first has to be clarified that this exclusion affects only financial instruments (i.e. the rights and obligations that derive from a financial instrument) and not contracts that have as object a financial instrument. Article 6(4)(d) is complex and has to be read together with recitals 26, 28, 29 and 30 Rome I. Recital 30 states that financial instruments are those referred to in the Markets in Financial Instruments Directive (MiFID),[32] which provides for a list including transferable securities, money-market instruments, units in collective investment undertakings (UCITS), options, futures, swaps and any other derivative contracts, credit default swaps (CDS) or financial contracts for differences.[33] The ratio of this exception is to prevent any negative effects that could arise from the application of two different laws as a result of the operation of article 6 Rome I. It is of importance that some aspects of transactions of financial instruments are governed by a single law and thus must be excluded from article 6 Rome I (which can lead to the application of two different laws to the consumer contract).[34] That is, financial instruments are rights and obligations that are normally fungible and standardised products, which, as a consequence, should be governed by a single law, not always being possible if they fall under article 6 Rome I. Also, if the law applicable to the financial instrument was dependent on the country of habitual residence of the holder who fell under the definition of consumer, financial markets would not work properly.[35] However, despite these risks on which this exception is justified, its practical relevance or even its necessity is questioned, firstly, on the basis of the existence of the general exceptions of article 1 Rome I in paragraphs 2(d), (f) and (h), already excluding obligations under negotiable instruments, questions governed by the law of companies and constitution of trusts and the relationship between settlors, trustees and beneficiaries. Secondly, a consumer in practice is very rarely involved in a direct manner in the referred international transactions but rather invests through his domestic bank.[36]

The last exclusion of article 6(4) Rome I regards contracts concluded within a multilateral system bringing together or facilitating the bringing together of multiple third-party buying and selling interests in financial instruments. Normally, consumers are not admitted to directly participate in those systems, and contracts

---

[32]Now Directive 2014/65/EU of the European Parliament and of the Council of 15 May 2014 on markets in financial instruments and amending Directive 2002/92/EC and Directive 2011/61/EU [2014] (OJ L 173/349).

[33]Article 4 MiFID referring to Section C of Annex 1.

[34]See recital 28 Rome I. Calliess (2015b), p. 186.

[35]Garcimartín Alférez (2009), pp. 90,91.

[36]Ragno (2009), pp. 224,225; Calliess (2015b), p. 186. For some more detailed comments regarding financial instruments and the Rome I Regulation see, for example: Garcimartín Alférez (2009).

mentioned in article 6(4)(e) usually comprise persons acting for professional or commercial purposes in their own names.[37]

3.1.1.2 Territorial Requirements

For article 6 Rome I to be applicable, besides the material requirements previously mentioned, some territorial requirements need to be met. Article 6 Rome I is applicable when (a) the professional pursues his activities in the Member State of the consumer's habitual residence or (b), by any means, directs such activities to that Member State (article 6(1) Rome I). That is, the so-called targeted activity test, which was first provided by article 15(1)(c) Brussels I Regulation in order to adapt the private international law rules to a more technological neutral approach, is introduced in the Rome I Regulation.

The interpretation of point (a) does not bring specific difficulties. A physical presence of the professional in the country of the consumer is required. This point refers to situations where the professional has its place of central administration or principal place of business according to article 19(1) Rome I outside the country of the consumer, but the contract was concluded, according to article 19(2) Rome I, through the operations of a branch, agency or any other establishment (or they are in charge of the performance of the contract) located in the country of the consumer. Article 6(1)(a) Rome I is applicable not only when the establishment of the professional in the country of the consumer is permanent but also where the professional, or his agents, employees, or representatives are temporarily in the consumer's country (e.g. a stand at a trade fair) and solicit a consumer contract there.[38] Also, it is sometimes defended that a situation falls under article 6(1)(a) Rome I when the professional provides on a regular basis services in the country of the consumer or when the professional arranges the journey of the consumer to a foreign country in order to induce the conclusion of a consumer contract.[39] It is not sufficient for the application of this article, however, fact that the professional enters in the country of the consumer after the conclusion of the contract for the performance of the contract if the contract itself was not solicited in the country of the consumer.[40]

The interpretation of point (b), which requires the professional to direct his activities to the country of the consumer, is more complex. Article 6(1)(b) Rome I is applicable where the professional (or his employees, or staff in general, and affiliates) was not physically present in the country of the consumer to induce the conclusion of the contract but by any means directed his commercial or professional activities to that country in order to conclude contracts with consumers from that country. The concept of 'directed activity' or 'targeted activity' was introduced by

---

[37]Ragno (2009), p. 225; Calliess (2015b), pp. 187,188.

[38]Calliess (2015b), p. 175.

[39]Ragno (2009), p. 228.

[40]Calliess (2015b), p. 176.

the Brussels I Regulation with the aim of adapting the rules for the growth of communication technologies and distance selling, especially with regard to electronic commerce.[41] In reference to consumer contracts, recital 24 Rome I states that

> [...] the conflict-of-law rule should make it possible to cut the cost of settling disputes concerning what are commonly relatively small claims and to take account of the development of distance-selling techniques. Consistency with Regulation (EC) No 44/2001 [now Regulation No 1215/2012 –Brussels I bis-] requires both that there be a reference to the concept of directed activity as a condition for applying the consumer protection rule and that the concept be interpreted harmoniously in Regulation (EC) No 44/2001 and this Regulation [...].

However, because of its intended broad approach, it has to be said that the concept of 'directed activity' sometimes comes as rather vague and thus needs to be interpreted.

Article 6(1)(b) Rome I encompasses many situations in which the professional makes himself known to the consumers of another country through, for example, telephone calls, television broadcasts, paper advertising etc. Nowadays, one of the main ways and the most controversial one is through Internet websites. Commercial websites can be viewed generally in almost every country, and that creates different risks. First, this can result in companies obtaining businesses of consumers from countries that they have not targeted and thus facing the risk of a foreign court or a foreign law being applicable, and, second, a consumer might be subject as well to those risks without even leaving his house. Although these risks are not exclusive to electronic commerce, they are more common due to the big and increasing amount of Internet transactions worldwide.

The ECJ has clarified the meaning of 'directed activities' in numerous cases.[42] The following case law can be highlighted.

The joined cases of *Pammer* and *Alpenhof*[43] concerned the interpretation of the concept of 'directed activities' in the context of article 15(1)(c) and (3) of the Brussels I Regulation (now article17(1)(c) and (3) Brussels I bis Regulation). In the first case, Mr. Pammer, with habitual residence in Austria, booked a voyage by freighter from Italy to the Far East via the Internet through a company with a seat in Germany. In his view, the description of the website did not correspond to the conditions of the vessel, and Mr. Pammer decided to claim payment of the balance

---

[41] Ragno (2009), p. 228.

[42] The ECJ rulings related to article 17 Brussels I bis—ex article 15 Brussels I- must also apply for the purposes of article 6 of the Rome I Regulation. Recital 14 Rome I expresses that '(....) Consistency with Regulation (EC) No 44/2001 requires both that there be a reference to the concept of directed activity as a condition for applying the consumer protection rule and that the concept be interpreted harmoniously in Regulation (EC) No 44/2001 and this Regulation (...)'.

[43] Joined cases C-585/08 *Peter Pammer v Reederei Karl Schlüter GmbH & Co. KG* and C-144/09 *Hotel Alpenhof GesmbH v Oliver Heller* [2010] ECR I-12527.

and interest before an Austrian court. The Austrian court referred a preliminary ruling to the ECJ asking (1) whether the 'voyage by freighter' constituted a package travel and (2) whether the fact that an intermediary's website can be accessible on the Internet is sufficient to consider that activities are being 'directed' to the Member State of the habitual residence of the consumer. The ECJ answers the first question in the affirmative: a contract of transport including, for an inclusive price, a combination of travel and accommodation falls into the concept of package travel. Given the similarity of the second question with the question brought in the *Alpenhof* case, the ECJ responded to them jointly. In the second case, the dispute arose between Hotel Alpenhof, a company located in Austria operating the hotel with the same name, and Mr. Heller, with habitual residence in Germany. Mr. Heller saw the hotel's website and booked a number of rooms through email. After saying that he had problems with the quality of the hotel's services, Mr. Heller left without paying, and Hotel Alpenhof brought an action against him before an Austrian court. The preliminary question brought to the ECJ was whether the fact that a website could be consulted on the Internet was sufficient to find that an activity is being 'directed' within the meaning of article 15(1)(c) Brussels I Regulation. Thus, it needed to be ascertained on the basis of which criteria a trader using a website can be considered as directing his activities to the Member State of the consumer and whether the fact that such a website is accessible in the Member State of the consumer is sufficient to consider that. The ECJ, since the Brussels I Regulation did not define the concept of activity directed to the Member State of the consumer's country, stated that this concept must be interpreted independently, by reference to the system and the objectives of the Regulation.[44] Although this provision has the intention to protect consumers, this protection is not absolute, and consequently the ECJ considered that the trader must have manifested its intention to establish commercial relations with consumers from one or more Member States (including the Member State of the consumer).[45] It follows that it is necessary to determine whether, before the contract was concluded, there was evidence showing that the professional had the intention to do business in the Member State of the consumer. The ECJ held that it must be apparent from the website and the overall activity of the professional that, before the conclusion of any contract with the consumer, the trader envisaged doing business with consumers domiciled in one or more Member States, including that of the domicile of the Member State in question. In order to consider that the website is inviting the consumer to contract, national courts can take into account a non-exhaustive list of evidence: 'The following matters, the list of which is not exhaustive, are capable of constituting evidence from which it may be concluded that the trader's activity is directed to the Member State of the consumer's domicile, namely the international nature of the activity, mention of itineraries from other Member States for going to the place where the trader is established, use of a language or a currency other than the language or currency generally used in the Member State in which the trader is

[44] *Pammer and Alpenhof*, para 55.

[45] *Pammer and Alpenhof*, para 75.

established with the possibility of making and confirming the reservation in that other language, mention of telephone numbers with an international code, outlay of expenditure on an internet referencing service in order to facilitate access to the trader's site or that of its intermediary by consumers domiciled in other Member States, use of a top-level domain name other than that of the Member State in which the trader is established, and mention of an international clientele composed of customers domiciled in various Member States. It is for the national courts to ascertain whether such evidence exists.'[46]

Although recital 24 Rome I expresses that the language or currency used by a website does not constitute a relevant factor in order to consider that a website is directing its activities to a determinate Member State, the ECJ did not follow that guideline and made clear that foreign language and currency do constitute factors to take into account when considering whether a website is inviting a consumer to contract.[47]

Finally, it has to be highlighted that the mere accessibility of the trader's website in the Member State of the customer is not sufficient.

The ECJ in the *Emrek* case[48] clarified whether or not there is a need for a causal link between the commercial or professional activity directed to the Member State of the consumer's habitual residence via a website and the conclusion of the contract. In this case, Mr. Emrek, with habitual residence in Germany and who was looking for a second-hand motor vehicle, learned from acquaintances of Mr. Sabranovic's second-hand motor vehicle business located in a French town close to the German border. Mr. Sabranovic's shop had a website containing the details of his business, including French telephone numbers and a German mobile telephone number, with their respective international codes. Mr. Emrek went to the premises of the undertaking in France to conclude a written contract for the sale of a second-hand motor vehicle. Subsequently, Mr. Emrek filed a claim against Mr. Sabranovic under the warranty before German courts. The preliminary questions referred to the ECJ were (1) whether in cases in which the trader's website is directed to the Member State of the consumer it is required that the consumer be induced to enter into the contract by the website and thus the website has a causal link with the conclusion of the contract and (2), in the case that causal link is required, whether is it necessary that the contract be concluded at a distance. Regarding the first question, the ECJ explains that the essential condition for article 15(1)(c) Brussels I Regulation is that of the professional activity directed to the member State of the consumer, and that condition is satisfied in this case. The addition of an unwritten condition requiring a causal link between the existence of the website and the contracting would be contrary to the objective of protecting the consumer and would give rise to problems of proof.[49] Therefore, the ECJ concludes that there is no need for a causal

[46] *Pammer and Alpenhof*, para 93.

[47] Wilderspin (2016), pp. 476–478; Plender and Wilderspin (2015), pp. 249–252.

[48] Case C-218/12 *Lokman Emrek v Vlado Sabranovic* [2013] ECLI:EU:C:2013:666.

[49] *Emrek*, paras 23–25.

link between the means employed to attract the consumer and the conclusion of the contract. That is, even if the consumer knew about the business from a friend and not through the website, it does not affect the applicability of the provision. Regarding the second question, the ECJ already gave answer to it 1 year before in the *Mühlleitner* case.[50]

The *Mühlleitner* case concerns the possible limitation of the concept of 'directed activities' to distance contracts, also in the context of article 15(1)(c). In this case, Ms. Mühlleitner, with habitual residence in Austria, when searching the Internet for a car was directed to an offer of Autohaus Yusufi, a partnership established in Germany. Ms. Mühlleitner contacted the business through the telephone number stated on the website, which contained an international dialling code, in order to obtain more information. However, she went to Germany to sign the contract of sale and received the vehicle. Subsequently, because she considered that the vehicle was defective, she brought proceedings in an Austrian court for rescission of contract. The preliminary question brought to the ECJ regarding this case was whether the application of article 15(1)(c) Brussels I Regulation (the concept of 'directed activity') required that the contract between the consumer and the undertaking be concluded at a distance. There is no express mention to such a requirement in the regulation, and the ECJ considers that the addition of such a non-written condition would run counter to the objective of protecting the consumers of the provision in its 'new, less restrictive formulation'.[51] According to the ECJ's reasoning, the essential condition for the application of the provision in question is that relating to a commercial or professional activity directed to the state of the consumer's domicile, and both the establishment of a contact at a distance and the reservation of goods or services at a distance, like in this case, or the conclusion of the contract at a distance in other cases, are indications that the contract is connected to the activity.[52] Thus, the ECJ concluded that it is not necessary that the contract between the consumer and the trader be concluded at a distance.

In relation to e-commerce and the concept of directed activities, the new Geo-Blocking Regulation,[53] which entered into force on 22 March 2018 in the EU as part of the Digital Single Market strategy, includes certain obligations that might have an effect on the concept of directed activities under article 6 Rome I. The Geo-Blocking Regulation deals with the obstacles that traders create when blocking or limiting access to online interfaces (websites, apps etc.), goods or services or when discriminating for reasons related to payment. Certain geo-blocking obstacles are sometimes used by traders to avoid engaging in commercial relations with

[50]Case C-190/11 *Daniela Mühlleitner v Ahmad Yusufi and Wadat Yusufi* [2012] ECLI:EU:C:2012:542.

[51]*Mühlleitner*, para 42.

[52]*Mühlleitner*, para 44.

[53]Regulation (EU) 2018/302 of the European Parliament and of the Council of 28 February 2018 on addressing unjustified geo-blocking and other forms of discrimination based on customers' nationality, place of residence or place of establishment within the internal market and amending Regulations (EC) No 2006/2004 and (EU) 2017/2394 and Directive 2009/22/EC (OJ 2018 L 60I/1).

customers from other Member States in order to protect them from divergent legal environments, the legal uncertainty involved, risks involving the applicable consumer protection laws, environmental or labelling laws, taxation and fiscal issues, delivery costs or language requirements. However, in other cases, traders artificially create internal barriers within the internal market that hamper the free movement of goods and services, resulting in a restriction of the rights of the customers and preventing them from benefitting from a wider choice and under optimal conditions. It is considered that these types of unjustified geo-blocking practices, together with factors such as legal uncertainty, language or consumer protection and confidence, contribute to the low level of cross-border contracts within the EU.[54] The Geo-Blocking Regulation clarifies which of those obstacles or different treatments cannot be justified within the internal market and bans these unjustified geo-blocking practices in the EU.

Geo-blocking elements helped to ascertain whether the activities of the trader were directed to some specific countries and not to others, which cautioned consumers located in these other countries against contracting with that trader and avoided risks for the professional since it was clearer to which countries he directed his activities (risks of litigating in the country of habitual residence of the 'consumer' and having the law of that country as applicable). Since many geo-blocking elements are now banned by the Geo-Blocking Regulation, article 1(6) of the Geo-Blocking Regulation clarifies that where a trader, complying with the provisions of the Regulation, does not block or limit access to an online interface or redirects the customer to a different version of it, does not apply different conditions of access to goods and services or does not reject specific commercial transactions or applies different payment conditions to those transactions, he should not be considered as directing his activities to the Member State of habitual residence of the consumer.[55] That is, the trader's compliance with the different requirements of the Geo-Blocking Regulation should not constitute grounds to consider that a trader is directing activities to the consumer's Member State. Thus, article 1(6) Geo-Blocking Regulation protects the position of the trader against the consequences of directing activities to the Member State of the habitual residence of the consumer.

---

[54] Recitals 1 and 2 of the Geo-Blocking Regulation.

[55] Specifically, article 1(6) provides that '...where a trader, acting in accordance with Articles 3, 4 and 5 of this Regulation, does not block or limit consumers' access to an online interface, does not redirect consumers to a version of an online interface based on their nationality or place of residence that is different from the online interface to which the consumers first sought access, does not apply different general conditions of access when selling goods or providing services in situations laid down in this Regulation, or accepts payment instruments issued in another Member State on a non-discriminatory basis, that trader shall not be, on those grounds alone, considered to be directing activities to the Member State where the consumer has the habitual residence or domicile. Nor shall that trader, on those grounds alone, be considered to be directing activities to the Member State of the consumer's habitual residence or domicile, where the trader provides information and assistance to the consumer after the conclusion of a contract that has resulted from the trader's compliance with this Regulation.'

However, the idea that the Geo-Blocking Regulation establishes what is relevant with regard the interpretation of articles 17(1)(c) Brussels I bis and 6(1)(b) Rome I can be debated. When a trader concludes contracts on a regular basis with customers located in a specific country through a website with an international setting (e.g. in English language and price in euros), the regularity of conclusion of contracts with clients from a specific country can be a factor indicating that the trader is directing his activities to that country. The concept of 'directed activities' has been interpreted in a broad manner by the ECJ, and the list of factors that indicate whether a website is directing activities to the Member State of the consumer is numerous and non-exhaustive. Thus, in practice and despite the clear wording of article 1(6) of the Geo-Blocking Regulation, it might not be that easy to differentiate between relevant factors indicating that the trader is directing his activities to the Member State of the consumer and factors that are just a consequence of the requirements of the Geo-Blocking Regulation. It has to be considered that many traders will have to adapt their websites in order to comply with the requirements of the Geo-Blocking Regulation. So far, in that situation, if they were not directing activities to other Member States until that moment, article 1(6) Geo-Blocking Regulation ensures that adaptation to the requirements of the Regulation does not change the previous situation, and therefore traders do not have to comply with the consumer protection rules of other Member States. A different scenario would be when a trader, as a result of the requirements of the Geo-Blocking Regulation, grants access to his products to consumers from all Member States and, in addition, decides to consequently expand his business to other Member States, adapting his website and business to such an expansion, and the professional has the clear intention of directing his activities to other Member States. However, a trader, when adapting the business' website to the requirement of equal access to goods and services of the Geo-Blocking Regulation, might decide to add in the website an English language option and show the prices in euros (when this is not his country's language or currency) just to facilitate such an access but without any intention to actually target consumers of another Member State. Will granting access and, as a result, offering the website in a foreign language (e.g. English, a widely spoken language among the Member States) mean that the trader is targeting other specific markets? Will traders have to comply with consumer protection law of other Member States?

In practice, article 1(6) of the Geo-Blocking Regulation can be interpreted in a manner that favours the trader, restricting the interpretation of the concept of directed activities. At the same time, it can also be argued that if a trader, as a result of the obligations of the Geo-Blocking Regulation, is legally 'bound' to serve consumers in a certain country, the analysis of the criteria that determine the trader's intention to direct commercial or professional activities to such country might become blurred, despite the clarification of article 1(6) of the Ge-blocking Regulation. In order to ensure legal certainty, courts should be in the future more cautious in the analysis of the criteria that determine the trader's intention to direct his activities and take into account all the circumstances of the case, especially the existence of the requirements of the Geo-Blocking Regulation. That is, legal certainty for traders and consumers might require a more careful examination of the *Pammer* and *Alpenhof* criteria when assessing whether the website of a professional is directing commercial activities to consumers of another Member State, taking into account all the circumstances of the case and, specifically, the existence of the requirements of the Geo-Blocking Regulation.

3.1.2 The Law Applicable to Consumer Contracts Under Article 6 Rome I

When the previous requirements are not met, it means that the contract is not considered a consumer contract under the definition of article 6 Rome I, and thus the general rules of the Rome I Regulation will be applicable to that contract. Where all the previous requirements are met, which means that the consumer contract has a close connection to the country where the consumer has his habitual residence, article 6(1) Rome I provides that the contract shall be governed by the law of the country of habitual residence of the consumer. The place of habitual residence is to be interpreted according to article 19 Rome I, which in paragraph 3 states that the relevant point in time to determine the habitual residence shall be the time of the conclusion of the contract.

However, article 6 Rome I also recognises the exercise of party autonomy. This conflict rule does not differ as much as expected from article 5 Rome Convention. Article 5(2) Rome Convention provided that

> a choice of law made by the parties shall not have the result of depriving the consumer of the protection afforded to him by the mandatory rules of the law of the country in which he has his habitual residence.

Radical changes were suggested in the debate regarding the conversion from the Rome Convention to the Rome I Regulation due to the criticisms received by the so-called preferential law approach.[56] The main criticism consisted in the complexity of such an approach: first, it is difficult to determine which mandatory rules bring a higher level of protection, and it has to be determined on a case-by-case basis; second, the exact division between non-mandatory rules, mandatory rules and overriding mandatory rules is complicated; and, third, the mix of provisions of two different legal systems might lead to a 'cherry-picking' problem (i.e. choosing the most favourable rules from both legal systems and mixing them). Also, taking into account that most consumer contracts involve small claims, these complexities were

---

[56]Green Paper on the conversion of the Rome Convention of 1980 on the law applicable to contractual obligations into a Community instrument and its modernisation (COM(2002) 654 final) pp. 30–32.

criticised as extremely burdensome in comparison with the claims involved.[57] As a consequence, the Commission Proposal did not recognise at all the possibility of choice of law of the parties but only stipulated the law of the country of habitual residence of the consumer as applicable. Although indeed simple, this approach completely excluding party autonomy was criticised: the choice of law would probably be a law with which the professional is familiar with, such as the law of his place of establishment, which can be either more beneficial or detrimental to the weaker party than the law otherwise applicable in the absence of choice; also, excluding party autonomy may impair cross-border commercial activities since the professional might want to focus on the national market.[58] A compromise between weaker party protection and party autonomy is desirable, respecting the parties' preferences and keeping a minimum level of consumer protection, benefiting both parties. Following the preferential law approach, in contrast to the option of completely excluding party autonomy, only those consumers agreeing to a choice of law with a lower standard of protection see themselves deprived of the freedom of choice of law. At the same time, the professional is also benefited since this approach allows the standardisation of the legal relationships with its consumers.[59]

Thus, the final version of the Rome I Regulation determines that consumer contracts falling under article 6 Rome I are governed by the law of the country of habitual residence of the consumer, except when there is a choice of law by the parties, in which case the chosen law is applicable as long as it does not deprive the consumers of the protection provided by the mandatory rules of the law otherwise applicable. Article 6(2) Rome I provides:

> *Notwithstanding paragraph 1, the parties may choose the law applicable to a contract which fulfils the requirements of paragraph 1, in accordance with Article 3. Such a choice may not, however, have the result of depriving the consumer of the protection afforded to him by provisions that cannot be derogated from by agreement by virtue of the law which, in the absence of choice, would have been applicable on the basis of paragraph 1.*

By taking this approach, the legislator adopted a hybrid system that reconciles the principle of party autonomy with the need for consumer protection. The rationale behind the preferential law approach consists in the idea that the mandatory rules of the country of the consumer already provide for a minimum protection to the consumer, and there is no reason to hinder the parties from agreeing on a higher level of protection.

---

[57] Calliess (2015b), p. 163, referring also to Max Planck Institute for Foreign Private and Private International Law (2004), p. 52 et seq.

[58] Regarding the advantages and criticisms of the option completely excluding party autonomy, see Sect. 2.4.1.1.

[59] Regarding the advantages and disadvantages of the preferential law approach, see Sect. 2.4.1.3.

The choice of law has to be made in accordance with article 3 Rome I; that is, it has to be established that a choice of law agreement was formed under article 3 (1) and 3(5) Rome I. In a consumer contract, the choice of law will generally entail an express choice of law clause contained in the contract, usually in the general terms and conditions of the professional. Moreover, it will generally refer to the law of the country of habitual residence of the professional. It has to be noticed that a standard choice of law clause will not generally come as a surprise or will be considered not transparent due to the international character of a cross-border consumer contract. However, in this regard, the ECJ in *Verein für Konsumenteninformation v Amazon EU Sàrl*[60] has made a decision regarding the general terms and conditions of a contract containing a choice of law for the law of the Member State in which the company is established. This case concerned Amazon EU, a company established in Luxembourg, which, among other activities, via a website with a domain name with the extension.de (amazon.de) addressed consumers residing in Austria, concluding electronic sales contracts. Until 2012, the general terms and conditions of the contracts contained a clause providing a choice of law for Luxembourg law. The ECJ concluded: 'Article 3(1) of Council Directive 93/13/EEC of 5 April 1993 on unfair terms in consumer contracts must be interpreted as meaning that a term in the general terms and conditions of a seller or supplier which has not been individually negotiated, under which the contract concluded with a consumer in the course of electronic commerce is to be governed by the law of the Member State in which the seller or supplier is established, is unfair in so far as it leads the consumer into error by giving him the impression that only the law of that Member State applies to the contract, without informing him that under Article 6(2) of Regulation No 593/2008 he also enjoys the protection of the mandatory provisions of the law that would be applicable in the absence of that term, this being for the national court to ascertain in the light of all the relevant circumstances'.

One of the main complexities of the preferential law approach is the comparison between the chosen law and the law otherwise applicable to the consumer contract (i.e. the law of the country of habitual residence of the consumer). It is considered that the mandatory norms of the country of the consumer are to be applied not jointly and cumulative but alternatively to the applicable rules of the chosen law, and thus a comparison of the results of both needs to be made in order to determine which ones are more beneficial to the consumer.[61] It is generally considered that the comparison needs to be made on the basis of the concrete claim at issue, attending to the general

[60]Case C-191/15 *Verein für Konsumenteninformation v Amazon EU Sàrl* [2016].

[61]The wording of article 6(2) Rome I is 'the choice may not have the result of depriving the consumer of the protection afforded to him...', while the wording of article 3(3) says that 'the choice of the parties shall not prejudice the application'. Because of this different wording, it is interpreted that under article 3(3), the mandatory rules are applicable in any case and the chosen law works as an incorporation by reference, while from the wording of article 6(2) and its purpose of protecting the legitimate expectations of the consumer, an alternative choice between the mandatory rules of the chosen law and the law otherwise applicable needs to be made. Plender and Wilderspin (2015), p. 260; Calliess (2015b), p. 190.

results in the individual case, since it would be impossible to the judge to decide in abstract which law is better. 'Cherry-picking' is not allowed, and thus the consumer cannot pick preferential norms from both legal systems involved and combine them to come up with a result that none of those laws intend to provide. Therefore, the comparison has to refer to the mandatory consumer provisions of both legal systems involved and get an overall view of the level of protection that each legal system provides to the consumer in the specific case in order to apply either the mandatory protection of the chosen law or the law of habitual residence of the consumer.[62]

This process needs to be kept impartial in order to avoid a kind of 'Robin-Hood principle', under which the consumer as the weaker party would always win.[63] A balance between consumer protection and impartiality in the legal process is difficult to maintain, and thus when applying article 6 Rome I, its purpose needs to be kept in mind: the legitimate expectations of consumers need to be protected against a possible abuse of the professionals, which would deprive them of the protection afforded to them by their country. However, it is not intended to create an overprotective system in which the consumer would always get the best solution ever, ignoring legal certainty and the legal expectations of both parties.

3.2 The Law Applicable to Individual Employment Contracts: Article 8 Rome I

The protection of employees as weaker parties in individual employment contracts is reflected in EU PIL regarding the law applicable to the contract in article 8 Rome I Regulation. Article 8 Rome I has article 6 Rome Convention as precedent and is drafted in a very similar manner, although with several improvements. Both provisions share the objectives of protection of the worker as the weaker party to the contract and the determination of the most closely connected law to the employment relationship.[64]

Regarding its scope of application, article 8 Rome I only applies to individual employment contracts, and therefore it does not cover collective labour law issues, such as collective bargaining agreements. Under the Rome I Regulation, the term individual employment contract needs to be interpreted autonomously, taking into account the intention of the Regulation and relevant EU law. An individual employment contract is a contract between an employee and an employer, according to which the employee must perform the service promised and the employer gives in exchange the agreed remuneration. The EU has developed an autonomous definition of the term 'employee' from an EU perspective in reference to the freedom of movement of workers in article 45 Treaty on the Functioning of the European

[62] See Sect. 2.4.1.3.

[63] Calliess (2015b), p. 190.

[64] Giuliano/Lagarde Report.

Union (TFEU): an employee is a person who performs services for and under the direction of another person for a certain period of time in return for a remuneration. This definition can be taken into account for the interpretation of the term 'employee' under article 8 Rome I, although with certain reservations.[65] In general, according to the definitions of the different Member States and the definition in article 45 TFEU, it can be stated that the criteria of the employer having the right to issue directives and the employee as a person who fulfils work for the employer due to a contractual obligation are of major importance for the definition of individual employment contract.

Individual employment contracts concluded after 17 December 2009 are governed by the law as determined by the conflict rules under article 8 Rome I. This provision allows a limited choice of law by the parties and provides for different connecting factors in order to determine the objectively applicable law.

3.2.1 Choice of the Law Applicable to the Individual Employment Contract

According to article 8(1) Rome I:

> An individual employment contract shall be governed by the law chosen by the parties in accordance with Article 3. Such a choice of law may not, however, have the result of depriving the employee of the protection afforded to him by provisions that cannot be derogated from by agreement under the law that, in the absence of choice, would have been applicable pursuant to paragraphs 2, 3 and 4 of this Article.

Therefore, choice of law agreements only operate in favour of the employees. However, employers insert such choice of law agreements in their employment contracts anyway on the basis of several grounds. For example, employers might be unaware of the operation of article 8(1) Rome I, or the cross-border contract might have been initially a domestic contract with a choice of law of domestic law that was left unchanged when becoming an international contract. Also, in the case of permanent posting of workers to another country, there might be a choice of the law of the country of origin. Moreover, employers might also decide to include a choice of law clause with the intention of discouraging employees from pursuing a claim, expecting that when a dispute arises and the employee reads such a clause in the contract, he will be discouraged from pursuing the claim and ignore the fact that he could still enjoy the protection granted by the objectively applicable law.[66]

---

[65] For more details regarding the definition of 'employee', see Sect. 2.1.2.2.

[66] Grusic (2015), pp. 154, 155.

Like in the case of consumer contracts, a limited choice of law is allowed in individual employment contracts. The mandatory provisions of the law objectively applicable are the minimum protection to which the employee is entitled in the case of a dispute regarding a cross-border individual employment contract. When parties have chosen the law applicable to their employment contract, the judge must first determine which law would be objectively applicable according to the following paragraphs of article 8 Rome I and subsequently compare that law to the chosen law to conclude whether the chosen law offers the same or a better protection to the employee than the mandatory provisions of the objectively applicable law. Thus, it is necessary to identify the relevant mandatory provisions and then compare which ones offer a better protection to the employee.

Which are the relevant mandatory rules? First of all, 'provisions that cannot be derogated from by agreement' are to be distinguished from the narrower category of 'overriding mandatory provisions' (recital 37 Rome I). Article 8(1) Rome I only refers to the provisions of the law objectively applicable, which parties cannot exclude by agreement. Second, article 8(1) Rome I refers not to all mandatory provisions of that law but only to those concerning the protection of employees. The article specifically refers to the provisions protecting the employee ('. . .choice of law may not . . . have the result of depriving *the employee of the protection afforded to him* by provisions that cannot be derogated from by agreement. . .').[67] Labour legislation in most of the EU countries constitutes one of the most important sources of mandatory provisions. Protective statutory provisions such as provisions against wrongful dismissal, working hours and vacations, protection of employees in a business transfer etc. fall within that category.[68] Collective agreements also contain mandatory provisions that sometimes are relevant for the purposes of article 8 (1) Rome I, especially when the state extends the application of a collective agreement to additional employers and employees, giving it a status similar to legislation.[69]

On the other hand, it is not that easy to compare legislation and determine whether the chosen law deprives the employee of the protection afforded to him by the law otherwise applicable. As it has been previously discussed regarding consumer contracts, one of the main problems of the preferential law approach is the comparison between the legal systems involved. First, article 8(1) Rome I does not exclude the accumulation of benefits under both laws at stake. That is, if the law chosen provides compensation as a remedy for wrongful dismissal and the law objectively applicable provides instead for reinstatement, the employee would enjoy 'double protection'. However, this approach is rejected.[70] The 'cherry-picking' technique, which would lead to maximum advantages to the employee, consisting in choosing the best single provisions of each legal system, must therefore be rejected. It is

---

[67] Ibid., p. 145.

[68] Franzen and Gröner (2015), p. 224.

[69] Grusic (2015), p. 148.

[70] For example: Franzen and Gröner (2015), p. 225; Grusic (2015), p. 149.

considered to be unjust since no legal system provides for such a protection, and legal certainty would be impaired.[71] Second, the comparison of the legal systems in general is also rejected since it does not seem possible to compare the overall quality of a legal system. It would be considered as arbitrary and even disrespectful for the countries to judge the general quality of a legal system.[72] Thus, the most logical approach seems to be the comparison of the specific provisions of each legal system applicable to the claim at issue, taking into account the specific facts of the case.[73] That is, if the notice of dismissal period is the issue of the claim, the law prescribing the longer period is the most favourable one for the employee (e.g. country A providing that the employee is entitled to a notice of dismissal of 5 months is more favourable than the law of country B providing for a notice of 3 months in that specific claim). However, provisions from one country are not always the exact equivalent of the provisions from another other country (e.g. the law of country A provides for a shorter period of notice and the right to compensation, but the law of country B does not afford compensation for dismissal). In such cases, the judge must examine whether the employee in that case would benefit more from one solution or the other, even taking into account the employee's situation and opinion.[74]

The uncertainties around the manner of comparison has been one of the main criticisms of this technique, together with the fact that it implies a two-step process (i.e. determination of the objectively applicable law and comparison with the chosen law), which increases information costs.[75] However, it also brings many advantages: firstly, the acceptance of choice of law as a connecting factor in individual employment contracts enhances predictability of results and legal certainty; secondly, the limitation provided by the preferential law approach ensures that the employee receives the minimum protection; in addition, the employer is also benefited since this approach allows the standardisation of the legal relationships with its employees.[76]

---

[71] Franzen and Gröner (2015), p. 225, also referring to other authors such as Martiny, in *Internationales Vertragsrecht*, para 4846.

[72] Gardeñes Santiago (2008), pp. 405,406; Franzen and Gröner (2015), p. 225.

[73] In this regard, Gardeñes Santiago even suggested that, despite this being the obvious and adequate interpretation, it would be convenient to clarify the issue in article 8(1) Rome I in order to avoid the possibility of an unrealistic global comparison between laws. Gardeñes Santiago (2008), p. 424.

[74] Grusic (2015), p. 152.

[75] Palao Moreno (2016), pp. 585, 586.

[76] Ibid., p. 583.

3.2.2 *The Law Applicable in the Absence of Choice: Objective Connecting Factors*

When the parties have not chosen the law applicable to their contract, the law applicable to the individual employment contract will be determined by the conflict rules contained in paragraphs 2, 3 and 4 of article 8 Rome I. These provisions determine an objective connection to the employment relationship, and they fulfil a double function: first, the determination of the law applicable when parties have not chosen the applicable law and, second, the ascertainment of the legal system whose minimum protection provided by its mandatory provisions is applicable to the employment relationship even when the parties have chosen the applicable law.

The connecting factors provided by article 8(2) and 8(3) Rome I are to be applied alternatively, meaning that when the connecting factor of article 8(2) Rome I (i.e. habitual place of work) can be ascertained, the application of article 8 (3) Rome I (which refers to the place of business through which the employee was engaged) is not required. Thus, article 8(3) Rome I works as a secondary connecting factor.[77] In addition, article 8(4) Rome I constitutes an exceptional provision that states that where the general circumstances indicate that the contract is most closely connected to another country, the law of that country shall be applicable.

3.2.2.1 Article 8(2) Rome I: Place Where the Employee Habitually Carries Out His Work

Article 8(2) Rome I provides:

> To the extent that the law applicable to the individual employment contract has not been chosen by the parties, the contract shall be governed by the law of the country in which or, failing that, from which the employee habitually carries out his work in performance of the contract. The country where the work is habitually carried out shall not be deemed to have changed if he is temporarily employed in another country.

The *lex loci laboris* is the principal connecting factor in determining the law applicable to the individual contract of employment in the absence of choice of law. The same connecting factor was used by the Rome Convention as well as in the different Member States. The law of the place where the employee habitually carries out his work is considered to be the most closely connected to the contract, and its applicability is predictable by the parties. This law will be familiar to the employee since the place where the worker habitually works is usually his habitual residence as well, and it also favours the interests of the employer since all the workers of the

[77] See Case C-384/10 *Jan Voogsgeerd v Navimer SA* [2011] *ECR* I-13275, para. 32.

establishment, independently of the nationality of the worker, will be governed by the same law (i.e. the law of their habitual place of work).[78] This connecting factor is generally supported, especially from the perspective of the internal market, because it treats all the employees working in the same country in an equal manner, regardless of their nationality.

It has to be noticed that the rule refers to the country 'in' or 'from which' the employees habitually carry out their work. The corresponding provision in the Rome Convention (article 6 Rome Convention) only referred to the place in which employees habitually carry out their work, and the ECJ clarified that this expression was to be interpreted as the place 'where or from which the employee principally discharges his obligations towards his employer' or where he 'has established the effective centre of his working activities and where, or from which, he in fact performs the essential part of his duties vis-à-vis his employer'.[79] Thus, the ECJ allowed for a broader interpretation of the connecting factor contained in article 6 Rome Convention, now reflected in article 8 Rome I. In the majority of the cases, employees will carry out their work in a specific single country. However, there are also cases of 'mobile' labour relationships, in which in most of the cases there is a fixed base from which the employees work. Those cases are covered by article 6 (2) Rome I.

The identification of the habitual place of work is easy in the majority of the cases where the work is performed by the employee in one single place, like in the case of local employees or employees transferred to another country. Cases involving migrant workers, frontier workers or workers who are employed by a foreign employer do not normally bring special difficulties since the work is typically performed in one country, and thus the habitual place of work is easy to determine. However, there are circumstances under which the determination of such a place becomes more complicated, especially when the worker carries out activities in more than one place. Cases involving transnational occupations, such as transport workers, and cases regarding posting of workers abroad deserve a closer look.

'Transnational Occupations'

There are some occupations that are transnational by nature, such as commercial representatives or international transport workers. In these cases, where the employee performs his work in different countries, difficulties might arise regarding the determination or existence of the habitual place of work. The ECJ has clarified the meaning of the place where or from which the work is habitually carried out in several cases.

[78] Palao Moreno (2016), p. 587.

[79] Case C-383/95 *Petrus Wilhelmus Rutten v Cross Medical* Ltd [1997] ECR I-00057.

The question was first brought in the *Mulox* case[80] regarding the interpretation of article 5(1) Brussels Convention 1968. This case concerned a dispute between Mulox, an English company, and Mr. Geels, a Dutch national with French domicile. Mr. Geels, employed as a commercial representative, used his French home as an office and base of operations. In the first 14 months of his employment, he sold products in Germany, Belgium, the Netherlands and Scandinavia but not in France. Following his dismissal, he started proceedings in France. The employer argued that French courts did not have jurisdiction since it was not the habitual place of work. In response to a preliminary ruling, the ECJ held that where the work was performed in more than one country, the multiplication of courts having jurisdiction should be avoided.[81] Jurisdiction should not be conferred on the courts of each Member State in which the work was performed. Jurisdiction over the whole dispute should be concentrated at the place where or from which the employee principally discharges his obligations towards the employer. The most important factor determining this place is that 'the work entrusted to the employee was carried out from an office . . . from which he performed his work and to which he returned after each business trip'.[82] Thus, the ECJ concluded that 'the case of a contract of employment in pursuance of which the employee performs his work in more than one Contracting State, the place of performance of the obligation characterizing the contract, within the meaning of that provision, is the place where or from which the employee principally discharges his obligations towards his employer'.

The *Rutten* case[83] involved a similar situation. Mr. Rutten, a commercial representative with domicile in the Netherlands, started proceedings in the Netherlands against Cross Medical, his English employer. In this case, Mr. Rutten performed 2/3 of his work in the Netherlands and the rest divided among the UK and other countries. The work was carried out from an office that Mr. Rutten had established in his home in the Netherlands. The ECJ, referring to the *Mulox* case, held that habitual place of work was 'the place where the employee has established the effective centre of his working activities and where, or from which, he in fact performs the essential part of his duties vis-à-vis his employer'.[84]

From these two cases, it can be understood that relevant factors to identify the habitual place of work are the location of the employee's effective centre of working activities or 'office' and the distribution of the working time among various countries.

The *Weber* case[85] concerned an employee who, differing from the previous cases, did not have an office that could constitute the effective centre of his working activities. Mr. Weber was a German national, also domiciled in Germany, employed

[80]Case C-125/92 *Mulox IBC Ltd v Hendrick Geels* [1993] *ECR* I-04075.

[81]*Mulox*, para 21.

[82]*Mulox*, para 25.

[83]Case C-383/95 *Petrus Wilhelmus Rutten v Cross Medical* Ltd [1997] *ECR* I-00057.

[84]*Rutten*, para 23.

[85]Case C-37/00 *Herbert Weber* v *Universal Ogden Services Ltd* [2002] *ECR* I-02013.

as a cook by Universal Ogden Services (Scottish company) on board various vessels and sea installations. It was established that he was first, and most of the time, in the Netherlands and later on in Denmark. The ECJ held:

> [...] Article 5(1) of the Brussels Convention must be interpreted as meaning that where an employee performs the obligations arising under his contract of employment in several Contracting States the place where he habitually works, within the meaning of that provision, is the place where, or from which, taking account of all the circumstances of the case, he in fact performs the essential part of his duties *vis-à-vis* his employer.
>
> In the case of a contract of employment under which an employee performs for his employer the same activities in more than one Contracting State, it is necessary, in principle, to take account of the whole of the duration of the employment relationship in order to identify the place where the employee habitually works, within the meaning of Article 5(1).
>
> Failing other criteria, that will be the place where the employee has worked the longest.
>
> It will only be otherwise if, in light of the facts of the case, the subject-matter of the dispute is more closely connected with a different place of work, which would, in that case, be the relevant place for the purposes of applying Article 5(1) of the Brussels Convention [...].[86]

That is, it is not possible to grant jurisdiction to all courts of the countries where the employee has carried out his work; in the same manner, it is not possible to determine as applicable the laws of several countries. In order to establish the habitual place of work when there are several Member States involved, it is necessary to determine where the employee performs the essential part of his duties. The existence of an effective centre of working activities (i.e. an office from where the employee performs most of his duties) constitutes a presumption. However, when the employee performs for his employer the same activities in more than one Member State, it is required to take into account the duration of the employment relationship and ascertain in which place the employee has worked the longest. However, these presumptions can be overturned if, in the light of the facts of the case, the subject matter of the dispute is more closely connected with a different place of work.[87]

Transport workers were traditionally understood as falling under what now would be article 8(3) Rome I, which reads that

> [w]here the law applicable cannot be determined pursuant to paragraph 2, the contract shall be governed by the law of the country where the place of business through which the employee was engaged is situated.

Nevertheless, the ECJ interprets the habitual place of work of paragraph 2 in such a wide manner that most of the cases of international transport can fall under article 8

[86] *Weber*, para 58.

[87] For example, the case where an employee, having carried out his work in a Member State, goes to permanently work to another Member State, would be understood as a desire to have a new habitual place of work in the latter country, and thus could overturn the presumptions. Palao Moreno (2016), p. 590.

(2) and do not need to invoke article 8(3) Rome I. In the cases *Koelzsch*[88] and *Voogsgeerd*,[89] involving a lorry driver and a seaman, the ECJ made a wide interpretation of 'habitual place of work'.

In the first case, Mr. Koelzsch, domiciled in Germany, signed an employment contract in Luxembourg in 1998 to work as an international heavy goods vehicle driver with Gasa (a subsidiary of Gasa Odense Blomsteramba, a company established under Danish law). The business consisted in the transport of flowers and other plants from Denmark to other European countries, mainly Germany, by means of lorries located in Germany. However, the company did not have a seat or offices in Germany, the lorries were registered in Luxembourg and the drivers were covered by Luxembourg social security. Following his dismissal, Mr. Koelzsch started proceedings against his employer before German courts, which declined jurisdiction, and subsequently before the Luxembourg court. He argued that, notwithstanding the choice of Luxembourg law as the *lex contractus*, the mandatory rules of German law that protect members of works councils were applicable to the dispute, within the terms of Article 6(1) of the Rome Convention, on the ground that the contract would have been governed by German law in the absence of choice by the parties. The preliminary question brought to the ECJ consisted in whether in a situation where the employee works in more than one country but returns systematically to one of them that country must be regarded as that in which the employee habitually carries out his work. The ECJ, in accordance with the case law and the new drafting in article 8(2) Rome I, stated that an extensive interpretation of the place of habitual work should be given, taking into account all the factors that characterise the activity of the employee. The ECJ provided that '[...]in a situation in which an employee carries out his activities in more than one Contracting State, the country in which the employee habitually carries out his work in performance of the contract, within the meaning of that provision, is that in which or from which, in the light of all the factors which characterise that activity, the employee performs the greater part of his obligations towards his employer'. In the case of transport workers, in particular, the relevant factors that need to be taken into account to determine the habitual place of work are the place from which the employee carries out his transport tasks and receives instructions; where his work tools are situated, as well as the place where the transport is principally carried out; where the goods are unloaded; and the place to which the employee returns after working.[90]

In the *Voogsgeerd* case, which involved a seaman, the ECJ also defended an extensive interpretation of the term 'habitual place of work'. In this case, Mr. Voorgsgeerd, the seaman, concluded an employment contract with Navimer, a Luxembourg company, at the headquarters of the company's subsidiary (Naviglobe) in Belgium. The contract contained a choice of law clause indicating the law of Luxembourg. While Mr. Voogsgeerd worked on board ships from Navimer and

[88]Case C-29/10 *Heiko Koelzsch v État* du *Grand Duchy* of *Luxemburg* [2011] *ECR* I-01595.

[89]Case C-384/10 *Jan Voogsgeerd v Navimer SA* [2011] *ECR* I-13275.

[90]*Koelzsch*, paras 39 et seq.

received his salary from that Luxembourg company, he obtained instructions from and reported to the subsidiary in Belgium, where he also commenced and terminated all of his voyages. Mr. Voogsgeerd started proceedings in Belgium against his employer and claimed Belgium law as the law objectively applicable to the contract, while Navimer disagreed arguing that Luxembourg law was the only law applicable to the contract as the chosen law and as a result of article 8(3), since Mr. Voogsgeerd did not have a habitual place of work and the engaging place of business was located in Luxembourg. The issue was referred to the ECJ, which confirmed the extensive interpretation given to the rule of habitual place of work. The ECJ held that 'the national court seised of the case must first establish whether the employee, in the performance of his contract, habitually carries out his work in any one country, which is that in which or from which, in the light of all the aspects characterising that activity, the employee performs the main part of his duties to his employer'.

In addition, the *Voogsgeerd* case is also of relevance with regard to which law should be applicable to an employment contract of a seaman or to an employment contract of an aircrew member. Regarding the employment contract of a seaman, some defended the application of the law of the flag since seamen work on ships, which fall under the jurisdiction of the country of the flag. However, it was argued that it does not seem appropriate since there is no guarantee that the country of the flag of the ship will have a close connection with the employment contract, and thus that country might not be legitimately interested in regulating the employment relationship. Also, such a connecting factor would be unilaterally influenced by the employer. Now the debate has been solved in favour of the law of the country where the employee seaman has his permanent base, where, in the light of all the aspects characterising that activity, the employee performs the main part of his duties to his employer (article 8(2): habitual place of work). When the determination of such a place is not possible, resort can be made to the connecting factor of article 8 (3) Rome I. Regarding aircrew members, some supported the application of the law of the aircraft's registration, while others referred to the law of the engagement place of business (article 8(3)). However, when drafting the Rome I Regulation, the European Commission explained that the wording 'country in which or, failing that, from which' of article 8(2) also covered aircrew personnel working on board an aircraft, if there is a fixed base from which work is organised and where the personnel performs other obligations in relation to the employer (registration, safety checks).[91] The interpretation in the *Voogsgeerd* case matches the Commission's interpretation of article 8(2) Rome I.

More recently, in the *Nogueira* case,[92] the ECJ reaffirmed its position. The case involved employees employed or assigned as aircrew members by an airline. The

[91]Proposal for a Regulation of the European Parliament and the Council on the law applicable to contractual obligations (Rome I) COM(2005) 650 final, 7.

[92]Joined Cases C-168/16 and C-169/16 *Sandra Nogueira and Others v Crewlink Ireland Ltd and Miguel José Moreno Osacar v Ryanair Designated Activity Company* [2017] ECLI:EU:C:2017:688.

preliminary question posed to the ECJ consisted in whether in such cases the concept of 'place where the employee habitually carries out his work', within the meaning of article 19(2)(a) Brussels I Regulation, could be equated to the term 'home base' within the meaning of Annex III to Council Regulation (EEC) No 3922/91 of 16 December 1991 on the harmonisation of technical requirements and administrative procedures in the field of civil aviation, as amended by Regulation (EC) No 1899/2006 of the European Parliament and of the Council of 12 December 2006. The ECJ made reference to the above-mentioned judgments regarding the interpretation of the concept of 'habitual place of work', stating that it must be interpreted broadly and autonomously and as referring to the place where or from which the employee performs the essential part of his duties towards the employer.[93] Several indicia to take into account in this regard were mentioned in the judgments *Koelzsch* (para 49) and *Voogsgeerd* (paras 38 to 41), in particular the place from which the employee carries out his transport-related tasks; the place where he returns after his tasks, receives instructions concerning his tasks and organises his work; and the place where his work tools are to be found.[94] These circumstances are also to be taken into account in the present case, and, as a result, the concept of 'place where, or from which, the employee habitually performs his work' cannot be equated with any concept referred to in another act of EU law.[95] Still, the concept of 'home base' is an important indicium in order to determine the place where the employee habitually carries out his work.

Finally, in reference to offshore workers, we have to distinguish between two situations: when offshore workers work within a country's territorial waters and when they do work on the high seas or above a country's continental shelf. In the first situation, the ECJ held in the above-mentioned *Weber* case that the work that an employee carries out on a fixed or floating installation located on or above the part of the continental shelf adjacent to a Member State, when prospecting or exploiting its natural resources, is to be regarded as work performed in the territory of that Member State.[96] However, when that is not the case and the work is performed on installations on high seas, it is generally agreed that the habitual place of work is not possible to be determined, and thus the law applicable to the employment contract shall be determined by article 8(3) Rome I.[97]

[93] *Nogueira and others*, paras 56–59, 74.

[94] *Nogueira and others*, para 63.

[95] *Nogueira and others*, paras 64, 65.

[96] *Weber*, para 36.

[97] Grusic (2015), p. 167; Palao Moreno (2016), p. 593; Giuliano-Lagarde Report [1980] OJ C282/1, 26.

Temporary Employment in Another Country

Employees are often posted abroad by their employers, either on a temporary basis or for the completion of a specific task or on a permanent basis. They can either be posted to an employer's foreign place of business, branch, subsidiary etc. or to a foreign company with which their employer has a cooperation agreement or other similar agreement in that regard. At the same time, the posting might be the result of a clause already existent in the employment contract (a 'mobility clause'), or it can be the result of a new contract containing the details of the posting abroad. Posting of workers takes place especially within the EU internal market, where freedom of establishment and freedom of movement are guaranteed.

According to article 8(2) Rome I, the habitual place of work does not change when the employee is temporarily employed in another country. There are several reasons underlying this provision stating that the habitual place of work does not change when the employee is temporarily employed in another country, and thus neither does the law applicable to the employment contract: avoiding a possible depeçage of the law applicable to the contract in those circumstances, promoting the application of the most closely connected and predictable law and allowing continuity in the law applicable to the employment relationship when the employee returns to the country of origin.

It is very important to differentiate between a situation where the employee has been transferred to another country (and thus changing his habitual place of work) and a situation where the employee has been temporarily posted to another contract (with no change of habitual place of work). In the latter case, the Posted Workers Directive[98] plays an important role. In order to distinguish between the two mentioned situations, the determination of the duration of the employment seems crucial. Article 8(2) Rome I does not make any reference to the extension of the period to which 'temporary' refers. In this regard, recital 36 Rome I provides:

> As regards individual employment contracts, work carried out in another country should be regarded as temporary if the employee is expected to resume working in the country of origin after carrying out his tasks abroad. The conclusion of a new contract of employment with the original employer or an employer belonging to the same group of companies as the original employer should not preclude the employee from being regarded as carrying out his work in another country temporarily.

Thus, special importance is given to the intentions of the employer and the employee to resume working in the country of origin after the posting abroad. That is, if parties intend the posting to be temporary, then there is no change of

[98]Directive 96/71/EC of the European Parliament and of the Council of 16 December 1996 concerning the posting of workers in the framework of the provision of services (OJ 1997 L 18/1) (Posted Workers Directive).

habitual place of work. The terms of the contract and the circumstances of the case can show those intentions.[99] However, besides the intention of the parties, the duration of the posting abroad can also be taken into account. That is, if the worker is posted abroad for a very significant amount of time, it could be regarded that that country is the habitual place of work even if there was an intention to eventually return to the country of origin. However, only a very long posting, together with the circumstances of the case, could lead to such an exception.[100]

The situation where employment starts or ends with a posting abroad might bring doubts. Recital 36 states that the employee must have had worked in the country of origin before the posting and must resume his work there after the posting abroad. However, when the employment begins with a temporary posting abroad, the first requirement would not be met, and when the employment is expected to end with a temporary posting, the second requirement is not met. However, rather than a literal interpretation, it is generally considered that article 8(2) Rome I should be interpreted in a broad manner and still apply the law of the country of origin in the cases where employment starts or ends with a posting abroad.[101]

In a permanent posting, regarding a dispute brought after the habitual place of work changed for a previously performed task, it is generally agreed that the law applicable is the law of the country where the employee habitually worked when the fact giving rise to the dispute occurred.[102] This solution seems more logical and favours legal certainty since the parties complying with the law applicable in that moment should not be affected adversely by the change of habitual place of work and subsequent change of applicable law.

In addition, there are some employees that, because of the speciality of their tasks, are often posted from country to country. For example, managerial, advisory and specialist staff are usually moved to the countries where the employer is doing business, or construction workers are often posted from country to country in order to complete different construction projects. In these cases, the determination of the habitual place of work (or country of origin) will be determined following the criteria described above regarding ‘transnational occupations’. Thus, according to the criteria of the ECJ, it is necessary to determine where the employee performs the

[99]Employers are obliged to provide information regarding the posting to posted employees (article 4 Council Directive 91/533/ECC), which can be especially useful to determine whether the posting is intended to be temporary or definitive.

[100]In the *Schlecker* case (Case C-64/12 *Anton Schlecker v Melitta Josefa Boedeker* [2013] EU: C:2013:551), Advocate General Wahl gave an example in which he referred to this situation and considered that a very long posting would be over 10 years. Case C-64/12 *Anton Schlecker v Melita Josefa Boedeker*, Opinion of Advocate General Wahl delivered on 16 April 2013, para 43.

[101]Max Planck Institute for Foreign Private and Private International Law (2007), p. 289; Grusic (2015), p. 160.

[102]Grusic (2015), p. 160; Plender and Wilderspin (2015), p. 327; Franzen and Gröner (2015), pp. 231, 232.

essential part of his duties or where he spends most of his working time, unless the circumstances of the case show otherwise.[103]

Finally, notwithstanding article 8 Rome I, a special legal regime regarding temporary posted workers is provided by the Posted Workers Directive. According to article 3 of the Directive, when a labour relationship falls under its scope, Member States must ensure that, whatever the law applicable to the employment relationship is, undertakings guarantee workers posted to their territory some specific terms and conditions of employment laid down in the Member State where the work is carried out. Article 3 refers to the terms and conditions laid down by law, regulation or administrative provisions or by collective agreements or arbitration awards that have been declared universally applicable with regard to maximum work periods and minimum rest periods; minimum paid annual holidays; minimum rates of pay; the conditions of hiring out of workers; health, safety and hygiene at work; protective measures concerning the terms and conditions of employment of pregnant women or women who have recently given birth, of children and of young people; and equality of treatment between men and women and other provisions on non-discrimination. Therefore, even when article 8(2) establishes the law of the country of origin as applicable, some mandatory rules regarding those specific terms and conditions of the law of the Member State of posting listed in article 3 Posted Workers Directive must apply to the working relationship.[104]

In relation to the Posted Workers Directive, it is necessary to refer to the current debate involving its application to transport road workers. While the Posted Workers Directive was mainly adopted to regulate the posting of construction workers and similar sectors, the application of its rules to the highly mobile road transport workers is uncertain. On 14 December 2018, the Dutch Supreme Court referred several preliminary questions to the ECJ to obtain clarity on the application of the Posted Workers Directive to road transport workers (C-815/18). The facts entailed Hungarian post drivers who were posted by a Hungarian company to a Dutch transport company to carry out transport activities from the Netherlands throughout the EU. These transport workers were receiving their salary according to Hungarian law. Although the case is still pending, the Advocate General Bobek provided a substantiated intake in his conclusion of 20 April 2020.[105] AG Bobek concludes, principally relying on the legal basis and wording of the Posted Workers Directive and on the recent EU legislative developments, that the Posted Workers Directive applies to road transport operations.[106] Thus, the minimum salary of the 'temporary country of work' must be guaranteed to road transport workers. Regarding the

---

[103] *Mulox* and *Weber* cases.

[104] For a detailed explanation about the Posted Workers Directive, see Chap. 5.

[105] Case C-815/18 *Federatie Nederlandse Vakbeweging v Van den Bosch Transporten BV, Van den Bosch Transporte GmbH, Silo-Tank kft*, Opinion of the Advocate General [2020] ECLI:EU:C:2020:319.

[106] Paras 37–70. More about the recent legislative development regarding a posting rule for road transport in: Van Overveeke (2020), pp. 9–12.

consideration of 'temporary country of work', the AG states that the worker must have a sufficient connection with such a territory. All the relevant indicia (e.g. the location of the person to whom the services at issue are addressed or the place where the transport operations are organised and the drivers receive their assignments and to which they return after the completion of their work) should be considered together to determine the sufficient connection. Therefore, according to the AG, the criterion of a sufficient link used to interpret article 8 Rome I Regulation (for example in the above-mentioned *Koelzsh* case) is also relevant for determining the temporary country of work within the meaning of the Posting of Workers Directive. The decision of the ECJ will clarify important doubts concerning posted road transport workers, although other uncertainties will remain to be solved.[107]

3.2.2.2 Article 8(3) Rome I: Engaging Place of Business

Article 8(3) Rome I provides:

> *Where the law applicable cannot be determined pursuant to paragraph 2, the contract shall be governed by the law of the country where the place of business through which the employee was engaged is situated.*

That is, when the employee does not carry out his work in any one country, the contract is governed by the law of the country where the place of business through which the employee was engaged is situated.

The ECJ, in the *Voogsgeerd* case, clarified the concepts of 'engaged' and 'place of business'. Regarding the term 'engaged', debate existed regarding whether it could relate to the conclusion of the employment contract (or recruitment of employees) or to the 'organisational integration, internal structuring and internal directives'.[108] The ECJ in *Voogsgeerd* held that the term referred to 'the conclusion of the contract or, in the case of a de facto employment relationship, to the creation of the employment relationship and not to the way in which the employee's actual employment is carried out'.[109] Thus, the term engagement shall be determined by looking at the conclusion of the contract and not with reference to the place at which the employee is effectively organisationally integrated. Regarding the term 'place of business', there were also different interpretations in reference to its meaning. The ECJ expressed that the term 'place of business' covered every stable structure of an undertaking, including a subsidiary, office or branch, even when it did not have a legal personality, on the condition that it had a sufficient degree of permanence and was an integral part of the structure that engaged the employee.[110] A mere agent or

[107] In this regard, see: Van Overveeke (2020) and Houwerzijl (2019).

[108] Palao Moreno (2016), pp. 193–197.

[109] *Voogsgeerd*, para 46.

[110] *Voogsgeerd*, paras 54–57.

representative or a place only used for recruitment purposes is not sufficient. Thus, the place of business in the context of article 8(3) Rome I refers not only to the employer's domicile but also to any establishment, whether or not it possesses legal personality, with a sufficient degree of permanence and set up in accordance with the relevant provisions of the country in which it has been established, from which the employer conducts business and from which he appoints employees.[111]

It is necessary to clarify that the relevant point in time in order to define the place of business through which the employee was engaged must be when the first engagement takes place and not the present moment. If one were to take into account the place of business at the present moment, the applicable law could be unilaterally modified by the employer by deciding on changing the competent place of business through which the employee is engaged.[112] Therefore, article 8(3) refers to the time of the first engagement when determining the place of business through which the employee was engaged.

As it has been explained on the basis of article 8(2) Rome I, the ECJ has made a very extensive interpretation of the term 'habitual place of work', which consequently reduces the role of article 8(3) Rome I in exceptional cases. Only when the court dealing with the case is not in a position to determine the country in which the work is habitually carried out can it resort to the rule of the engaging place of business. Even when the work is performed in more than one country or it requires regular assignments abroad, like in the case of transport workers or sale representatives, it is possible in most of the cases to determine the habitual place of work by attending to the place of effective centre of the activity, the amount of time the employee expends in the countries and other relevant factors. Also, in the case of transport workers, the place of habitual work is determined by the place where, in the light of all the factors characterising that activity, the employee performs the greater part of his obligations towards his employer. Thus, the role of article 8(3) Rome I is reduced to cases in which the employee carries out his work in more than one country and it is not possible by any means to determine the place of habitual work (no centre of activity can be established and the amount of time is not relevant, or the means of travel cannot be attributed to any country in the case of transport workers) and to cases where the place where the employee habitually carries out his work does not belong to any country (stateless territory), such as permanent employment in an oil platform in the ocean.

The use of the engaging place of business as a connecting factor brings several criticisms. First, there is no guarantee that this connecting factor will lead to a law that is actually closely connected to the employment contract, contrary to the law of habitual place of work, and, as a consequence, the country might not be legitimately interested in regulating the employment relationship. Second, the employer would ultimately be the one deciding the law applicable to the employment contract since engagement is within the employer's control. In the context of the EU internal

[111]Grusic (2015), p. 170; Franzen and Gröner (2015), p. 230, 231.

[112]Franzen and Gröner (2015), p. 232.

market, where employers enjoy freedom of establishment and freedom of provision of services, they could easily be able to manipulate the law applicable to the employment contract by engaging the employee from an establishment in the country they wish its rules to apply. As a result, the necessity of the rule of the engaging place of business is questioned. If article 8(3) Rome I was abolished, article 8(4) would step in in cases where the habitual place of work cannot be determined. That is, the law most closely connected to the employment contract taking into account all the circumstances of the case would be applicable. It is argued that the abolition of article 8(3) Rome I would bring legal certainty and foreseeability since an interpretation of the terms 'engaged' and 'place of business' can give rise to a dispute between the parties and can lead to an appeal to a higher court to obtain a favourable interpretation.[113] Moreover, the protection of employees would be enhanced since the employer would not be able to directly manipulate the law objectively applicable to the employment contract. Finally, the law most closely connected to the employment contract would be applicable, which ensures that the designated country will be legitimately interested in regulating that employment relationship. Still, in my opinion, due to the secondary and reduced role of article 8 (3) and the possibility to correct its eventual inappropriate outcome with the escape clause of article 8(4), its downsides are not very apparent, and thus the existence of this rule can only benefit legal certainty.

3.2.2.3 Article 8(4) Rome I: Escape Clause

According to article 8(4) Rome I:

> Where it appears from the circumstances as a whole that the contract is more closely connected with a country other than that indicated in paragraphs 2 or 3, the law of that other country shall apply.

Regardless of the law objectively applicable to the contract, if from all the circumstances there is a more closely connected law to the employment contract, this law shall apply. Article 8(4) Rome I contains a so-called escape clause that offers the possibility of correcting on a case-by-case basis the outcome of the application of the connecting factors of 'habitual place of work' and 'engaging place of business' when the circumstances suggest that the contract is most closely connected to another country. The basis of this provision lies in the difficulty to predict all the exact circumstances that can arise in practice and the need for an appropriate solution in such cases.[114]

Article 8(4) Rome I is an exception to the previous paragraphs. However, the wording of the escape clause of article 8(4) Rome I differs from the escape clause

[113] Grusic (2015), p. 173.

[114] Gardeñes Santiago (2008), p. 416.

contained in article 4(3) Rome I, the latter referring to a law *manifestly* more closely connected and applicable only in truly exceptional circumstances. Thus, it was questioned whether the rule of article 8(4) Rome I should be interpreted as less exceptional and therefore making it easier to depart from the rules of article 8(2) and 8(3) Rome I. In the *Schlecker* case,[115] the ECJ agreed with the opinion of Advocate General Wahl, who, when interpreting the escape clause of article 6(2) Rome Convention, considered that there is no hierarchical relationship between the rules of 'habitual place of work' or 'engaging place of business' on the one hand and the escape clause on the other hand. Therefore, the court has discretion in determining the law most closely connected to the relevant employment relationship. The AG explained that even if the employment contract has been performed in a lasting, continuous and uninterrupted manner in a single country, when that contract is located in a country that is obviously not the habitual place of work, the court can bring the escape clause into operation.[116] The ECJ explained that 'even where an employee carries out the work in performance of the contract habitually, for a lengthy period and without interruption in the same country, the national court may ... disregard the law applicable in the country where the work is habitually carried out'.[117] Therefore, article 8(4) Rome I is drafted in a less strict way than the escape clause of article 4(3) Rome I, giving the judge a wider margin for interpretation.[118]

There are several relevant circumstances to take into account in order to consider the application of article 8(4) Rome I. According to the ECJ, particular significant factors to consider are the payment of taxes in a certain country and the affiliation to social security, pension, sickness insurance and invalidity schemes, as well as other circumstances such as parameters relating to salary determination and other working conditions.[119] Other factors to take into account, although to a lesser degree, can be the common nationality of the parties, habitual residence of the employee, place of establishment of the employer, place of conclusion of the contract, language, place of payment and the currency of the salary or previous relationship between the parties.[120] For example, in many cases, the law applicable to the employment contracts of workers of embassies and consulates could be determined according to article 8(4) Rome I, which leads to the application of the law of their country of 'origin' rather than the law of habitual place of work. It is common that the worker in a foreign embassy is still affiliated to the social security and pension schemes of the country of his employer, as well as enjoying a common nationality and language, factors that also point to the place of establishment of the employer or the place of

[115]Case C-64/12 *Anton Schlecker v Melitta Josefa Boedeker* [2013] EU:C:2013:551.

[116]Case C-64/12 *Anton Schlecker v Melita Josefa Boedeker*, Opinion of Advocate General Wahl delivered on 16 April 2013, para 60.

[117]*Schlecker*, para 44.

[118]Gardeñes Santiago (2008), p. 416.

[119]*Schlecker*, para 41.

[120]Palao Moreno (2016), p. 595; Franzen and Gröner (2015), p. 232.

conclusion of the contract. All these factors are conducted in a different country than the country of habitual place of work.[121]

Also, recital 20 Rome I states that it should be taken into account whether the contract has a very close relationship to another contract (e.g. cases of triangular employment relationships within agency employment or within a corporate group). The majority of factors must altogether point to one legal system different from the one designated by the objective connecting factors. However, the escape clause cannot be used, in its current drafting, to ensure the application of the law with the best employee protection among the laws connected with the employment contract. That is not the intention of this provision, and such a use could result in legal uncertainty and unpredictability.[122] The application of the escape clause should be limited to those situations where another legal system is clearly more closely connected to the employment contract.[123]

3.3 Overriding Mandatory Provisions: Article 9 Rome I

The Rome I Regulation defines overriding mandatory provisions (also known as *lois de police*) in article 9(1) Rome I as

> *provisions the respect for which is regarded as crucial by a country for safeguarding its public interests, such as its political, social or economic organisation, to such an extent that they are applicable to any situation falling within their scope, irrespective of the law otherwise applicable to the contract under this Regulation.*

The conflict rules contained in the Rome I Regulation generally focus on the parties' interests (article 3 Rome I recognises party autonomy; articles 6 and 8 protect the consumer and employee, respectively; etc.), while state interests do not play a central role in the Regulation. However, article 9 Rome I deals with those provisions that are so important for the country that has enacted them that they must be observed

[121]Following the same reasoning, it is of interest a commentary criticising the outcome of a Spanish judgment (Sentencia del Tribunal Superior de Justicia de Madrid (Sección n° 02) de lo Social, 9 de noviembre de 2016) regarding the law applicable to an employment contract of a Spanish worker in an embassy in Qatar: Marchal Escalona (2017).

[122]*Schlecker*, paras 34, 35.

[123]Gardeñes Santiago suggests, placing more importance on the protection of workers, the introduction of a modification in article 8(4) Rome I, which entails adding the possibility of applying the most beneficial law for the worker as long as it has a close connection with the contract and not necessarily the closest connection. Gardeñes Santiago (2008), pp. 415–418. However, article 8 (4) Rome I, in its current drafting, just aims at enabling the judge to apply, taking into account all the circumstances of the case, the law most closely connected to the employment contract, not the most beneficial law for the worker.

even in international situations, irrespective of the law applicable to the contract under the normally applicable conflict rules of the Regulation. Article 9 Rome I deals with those rules whose observance is regarded as essential by a country for the safeguarding of its public interests, such as its political, social or economic organisation. Thus, this provision aims at ensuring, on the one hand, the safeguarding of crucial state interests and, on the other hand, the uniformity of conflict rules among Member States and the admission of party autonomy.[124]

It has to be kept in mind that the operation of article 9 Rome I differs from the rest of conflict rules. Overriding mandatory rules are applicable according to their object and purpose. They do not rest in the same theoretical premises as the multilateral conflict of laws rules, which are the basis of the modern Western Europe PIL and have their origin in the German jurist Friedrich Carl von Savigny. In the nineteenth century, Savigny proposed a new approach to determine which law should be applicable to an international legal relationship. Instead of applying the statutist theories of unilateral rules, which determined the law applicable from a domestic approach, primarily determining the scope of domestic law, Savigny maintained an approach based on the abstract legal relationship, the international legal relationship being the starting point to determine the applicable law through multilateral conflict of laws rules. He rejected the domestic approach and established categories of legal relationships, designing conflict of laws rules that linked these categories to a particular legal system through objective connecting factors.[125] However, it seems that he allowed an exception from this multilateral conflict of laws rules by applying 'strictly mandatory rules' of the *lex fori*. These rules were supposed to function as a correcting mechanism, and Savigny considered that they would eventually be unnecessary within the multilateral conflict of rules theory. Nevertheless, overriding mandatory rules prove to be essential in the contemporary European conflict of laws. The application of overriding mandatory rules is based on their object and purpose instead of on the most appropriate law approach. In other words, both the fundamental nature of this type of rule, essential for the interest of the state, and the need for preventing parties from abusing their party autonomy are the basis of its application.[126] Overriding mandatory rules are an expression of the unilateral approach to solving conflicts of laws. Based on their content and purpose, they unilaterally determine their own applicability. These rules coexist in the Rome I Regulation with the traditional multilateral conflict rules and only prevail over them in exceptional cases.[127]

---

[124]Bonomi (2016), p. 604.

[125]Von Savigny (1849).

[126]Renner (2015), pp. 242, 243.

[127]Marques dos Santos explains in detail how the doctrine of overriding mandatory rules ('normas de aplicaçao imediata') started to be introduced in the doctrine, case law, legislation of PIL in Europe in the second half of the twentieth century, displacing the supremacy of Savigny's multilateral method to an acceptance of a pluralism of methods is PIL: Marques dos Santos (1991a).

Overriding mandatory rules are provisions with a mandatory character which function is to regulate international legal relationships independently from the law applicable, provided that the situation falls within their scope of application and with the objective of protecting a public interest related to the political, social or economic organisation of a Member State.[128] Therefore, their application is not limited to the legal system of the state where they originate, but their application outside their own legal system becomes necessary due to the high interest they seek to protect. For this reason, they prevail over the law applicable as determined by the objective connecting factors or by party autonomy, and as a result their application will be dependent solely on whether the situation falls within their scope of application.[129]

The definition given by article 9 Rome I does not solve all uncertainties concerning these special rules. Referring to their application, two important problems arise: firstly, their identification and, secondly, their application. The analysis of these uncertainties becomes essential in order to ascertain whether article 9 Rome I can be used as a mechanism of protection of weaker contracting parties: Can the protection of consumers as employees be considered 'crucial by a country for safeguarding its public interests, such as its political, social or economic organisation'? If so, can the rules deriving from the EU consumer and employment directives be considered as having an overriding mandatory character? In this context, this section will first focus on the identification of overriding mandatory rules, including their definition and whether provisions protecting consumers and employees can fall within that definition, and the possible legal sources of overriding mandatory rules, including EU directives. Second, the applicability of the overriding mandatory rules of the forum and third countries will be described (article 9(2) and 9(3) Rome I). Finally, the relationship between article 9 Rome I and articles 6 and 8 Rome I as concerns consumer and employee protection will be analysed.

3.3.1 Identification of Overriding Mandatory Provisions

3.3.1.1 Definition

Article 9 Rome I includes a definition of overriding mandatory provisions in its paragraph 1:

[128] Belohlávek (2011), pp. 1479–1480; Carrascosa González (2009), p. 119; Gardeñes Santiago (1999), pp. 105–110.

[129] In this sense, Preamble 37 Rome I states: 'Considerations of public interest justify giving the courts of the Member States the possibility, in exceptional circumstances, of applying exceptions based on public policy and overriding mandatory provisions. The concept of overriding mandatory provisions should be distinguished from the expression 'provisions which cannot be derogated from by agreement' and should be construed more restrictively.' Kuipers (2012), p. 67; Van Bochove (2014), p. 148.

> provisions the respect for which is regarded as crucial by a country for safeguarding its public interests, such as its political, social or economic organisation, to such extent that they are applicable to any situation falling within their scope, irrespective of the law otherwise applicable to the contract.

The origin of this definition is to be found in the ECJ joined cases *Arblade* (C-369/96) and *Leloup* (C-376/96) of 23 November 1999.[130] At the same time, this definition originates from legal doctrine, especially from Phocion Francescakis and his writings in the 1960s on 'lois d'application immediate'.[131]

According to the definition of article 9(1) Rome I, three conditions have to be satisfied for a rule to qualify as overriding mandatory: (a) the provision must have a mandatory character, (b) its observance should be crucial for the safeguarding of the public interests of a country and (c) the rule should be applicable irrespective of the law that otherwise governs the contract.

Mandatory Character: Difference Between Overriding Mandatory Provisions and Provisions That Cannot Be Derogated from by Agreement (Domestic Mandatory Provisions)

As evident from the definition, only mandatory provisions can be characterised as overriding mandatory provisions. However, not all provisions with a mandatory character can be characterised as overriding mandatory rules. The introduction of the definition in Rome I has been very useful for distinguishing overriding mandatory provisions from provisions that cannot be derogated from by agreement. As expressed in recital 37,

> the concept of 'overriding mandatory provisions' should be distinguished from the expression 'provisions that cannot be derogated from by agreement' and should be construed more restrictively.

The introduction of the terminology 'overriding mandatory rules' in the Rome I Regulation has been chosen in order to avoid confusion of both terms since in the

[130]Joined cases C-369/96 *Jean-Claude Arblade and Arblade & Fils SARL* and C-376/96 *Bernard Leloup, Serge Leloup and Sofrage SARL* [1999] ECRI-8453, where para 30 states: '(...) *that term must be understood as applying to national provisions compliance with which has been deemed to be so crucial for the protection of the political, social or economic order in the Member State concerned as to require compliance therewith by all persons present on the national territory of that Member State and all legal relationships within that State*'.

[131]For example, Francescakis (1966, 1967). An extensive study regarding the origin and comparative analysis of the definition of overriding mandatory rules is contained in: Marques dos Santos (1991b), pp. 693–943.

Rome Convention both types of rules were referred to as 'mandatory rules'.[132] The Rome Convention maintained certain ambiguity between both concepts. In fact, the expression 'mandatory rules' was used with different meanings in several articles of the Convention: while in articles 3(3) Rome Convention (internal contracts with no cross-border elements), 5(2) Rome Convention (consumer contracts) and 6(1) Rome Convention (employment contracts) the term was used as a limitation to the party autonomy of the parties and referred to rules that cannot be departed from by agreement, the same term appeared in article 7 Rome Convention, which covered mandatory rules with an overriding mandatory character, which have to be applied irrespective of the law governing the contract. The formulation led to confusion, and it was especially noticeable in some linguistic versions of the Rome Convention, which used literally the same legal term for both types of rules (e.g. in English 'mandatory rules', in German 'zwingende Vorschriften' or in Spanish 'disposiciones imperativas').

Where overriding mandatory provisions are aimed at protecting the public interests of the Member State in question and therefore require an international application, provisions that cannot be derogated from by agreement are the provisions of a legal order whose mandatoriness is only domestic and not international, aimed at protecting private interests, specifically those intended to protect the weaker party or prevent third parties from suffering any harm.[133] Provisions that cannot be derogated from by agreement are part of the domestic legal system. They are the opposite of default rules, which are applicable when parties have not reached an agreement about a specific legal matter. Normally, provisions that cannot be derogated from by agreement, or domestic mandatory rules, are national rules that have a mandatory character and thus cannot be derogated from by the parties when choosing another state law. They must be complied with in purely domestic situations and in international situations, when they belong to the law applicable to the contract.[134] The Rome I Regulation, in its article 3(3), limits party autonomy by stating that

> where all other elements relevant to the situation at the time of the choice are located in a country other than the country whose law has been chosen, the choice of the parties shall not prejudice the application of provisions of the law of that other country which cannot be derogated from by agreement.

In addition, the Rome I Regulation also recognises the existence of 'internal' mandatory rules at EU level. Article 3(4) Rome I provides that

> where all other elements relevant to the situation at the time of the choice are located in one or more Member States, the parties' choice of applicable law other

[132]Both article 3(3) Rome Convention and Article 7 Rome Convention (predecessor of article 9 Rome I) used the terminology 'mandatory rules' when referring to two different concepts.

[133]Guardans Cambó (1992), pp. 314–316.

[134]Gardeñes Santiago (2017), p. 167.

> than that of a Member State shall not prejudice the application of provisions of Community law, where appropriate as implemented in the Member State of the forum, which cannot be derogated from by agreement.

In this context, when referring to 'provisions of Community law that cannot be derogated from by agreement'—or EU mandatory law—the EU is seen as a state, and these type of provisions are mandatory internally, within the EU legal system. Their meaning can be understood better if we relate them to the Rome I provisions regarding consumer contracts (article 6 Rome I) and employment contracts (article 8 Rome I), which also limit party autonomy by ensuring the application of the provisions that cannot be derogated from by agreement of the law objectively applicable. These articles refer to those provisions as the limit to respect when there is a choice of law, in the sense that the choice of law cannot diminish the protection that the consumer or employee receives from the domestic mandatory provisions of the law that would have been applicable in the absence of choice.[135] The protective character of the weaker contracting party, as well as the internal mandatoriness, proves apparent.[136]

The mandatory character of internal EU mandatory provisions should be mainly determined by the legislator's intention. That is, the national or European legislator can refer expressly to this character, or in the absence of that statement, it has to be established by the adequate legal technics and with reference to the intention of the specific provision. More precisely, the mandatory character will be determined by the intention of the provision to serve private interests or protect the weaker contracting party.[137] Again, this character is mandatory at an internal or European level and not at an international one. That is the reason why the Rome I Regulation in article 3(3) and 3(4) only provides for the application of these rules to objectively internal and intra-EU situations, respectively.

In order to be applicable in all situations irrespective of the law applicable to the contract, a rule must have an overriding mandatory character, i.e. crucial for the safeguarding of public interests. There is an unbreakable connection between the objective crucial for the safeguarding of public interests of the country to which the rule belongs and the scope of application of the rule. That is, overriding mandatory rules are characterised by their willingness to apply regardless of the law applicable to the contract.[138]

National courts of the Member States should therefore restrain the temptation to attribute the character of overriding mandatory provisions to all mandatory rules and thus derogate from the conflict rules of the Rome I Regulation. Member State courts will be required to provide an appropriate justification when they decide to qualify a

---

[135] Garcimartín Alférez (2008), p. 65.

[136] Ibid., p. 65.

[137] Renner (2015), pp. 246, 247; Rühl (2007), p. 153.

[138] Gardeñes Santiago (2017), p. 167.

rule as overriding mandatory, specifying that it pursues an objective essential for the country and that its application is necessary to achieve that result.[139]

Crucial for the Safeguarding of Public Interests: Can Rules Protecting the Weaker Party Fall Within This Category?

It is clear from the definition of article 9(1) Rome I that overriding mandatory rules involve crucial public interests for a country, such as its political, social or economic organisation. However, how is it determined whether a provision is essential for the political, social or economic organisation of a state? It is quite unlikely that these elements result from the wording of the rule itself. The court will have to assess the general structure of the provision and the circumstances under which it was adopted.[140]

Typical examples are antitrust legislation, rules against unreasonable restraint of trade and commercial embargoes, rules on the import and export of goods and services, provisions on the access and exercise of specific trades or professions, rules restricting credit in the interest of currency stability etc.[141] These are provisions not concerned with the protection of the private interests of a contractual party, but they directly aim to safeguard the public interests of a state.

However, controversy arises as to whether that definition should be interpreted restrictively and, therefore, exclude those rules aiming at the protection of the considered contractual weaker parties or whether a broader view of the definition of overriding mandatory rules should be contemplated and, therefore, cover rules that as such protect the interests of private individuals although indirectly affecting interests of a public nature. The distinction of whether a rule is primarily aimed at the protection of a weaker party or also serves a public interest is difficult. In fact, every provision aimed at the protection of the weaker party could be understood as also aiming to protect a higher interest.[142] Article 9(1) Rome I offers no definition of public interests, but it merely explains that they include the political, social or economic organisation of the state.

With regard to the inclusion in the definition of article 9 Rome I of certain provisions protecting the weaker contracting parties, neither doctrine nor jurisprudence among Member States shares a common approach in this respect.[143] For example, on the one hand, the doctrine and jurisprudence of Germany interpret in a very restrictive manner the concept of overriding mandatory provisions. German doctrine distinguishes between two types of mandatory rules: *Eingriffsnormen*, or

[139]Bonomi (2008a), p. 289.

[140]Case C-184/12 *United Antwerp Maritime Agencies (Unamar) NV v Navigation Maritime Bulgare [2013]* EU:C:2013:663, para. 50. Bonomi (2016), p. 621.

[141]Ibid., p. 621.

[142]Kuipers (2012), pp. 93, 94.

[143]Bonomi (2008a), p. 292.

ordo-political rules (which pursue objectives of public interest, such as protection of competition), and *Parteischutzvorschriften* (which pursue the equilibrium between the parties of a contract, such as consumer and employee protection provisions). Only the former type of rules falls under the category of overriding mandatory rules.[144] This point of view of the German doctrine has influenced German courts. For example, the Federal Labour Court (*Bundesarbeitsgericht*) refused to apply some German rules protecting employees against abusive dismissal based on this restrictive interpretation of article 7 Rome Convention (more exactly, of article 34 (2) *Einführungsgesetz zum Bürgerlichen Gesetzbuch* (EGBGB) implementing article 7 Rome Convention).[145] Also, for a clearer example, the *Bundesgerichtshof* (German Federal Supreme Court) in a decision on 13 December 2005, explicitly stated that provisions concerning the protection of contractual weaker parties do not fall under the category of overriding mandatory provisions in article 34(2) EGBGB, even if they also promote, indirectly, public interests.[146] Thus, a provision can serve either the individual interests of a weaker party or public interests, these objectives being mutually exclusive. Those supporting this view highlight that reference to public interests in article 9 should not be ignored and leads to a restrictive interpretation of the provision, which would only be referring to ordo-political rules and excluding those rules aimed at the protection of weaker parties; article 9 Rome I is not a provision destined to protect consumers, employees, commercial agents or other weaker parties.[147]

On the other hand, others consider that the protective provisions of specific individual groups can also have essential relevance to the political, social and economic organisation of a country and, therefore, may fall under the category of overriding mandatory rules. French doctrine distinguishes between *lois de police de direction* (as comparable to the *Eingriffsnormen*) and *lois de police de protection* (equivalent to the *Parteischutzvorschriften*), but the vast majority agree that both can be classified as overriding mandatory rules.[148] This approach can be seen in the case of *Agintis*,[149] where the *Cour de Cassation* (French Supreme Court) held that the French law provisions at stake, under which a subcontractor can seek direct redress against the master of the works in the case of default of the main contractor, were *lois de police*, in the sense of both article 3(1) French Civil Code and articles 3 and 7 Rome Convention. According to the Advocate General, those provisions were aimed at serving both the interests of the French state in ensuring French competition

[144]Bonomi (2016), p. 622, referring to Mankowski, *RIW- Kommentar* (1996), 8 et seq, and Martiny, in*: Münchener Kommentar*, para. 13.

[145]Bundesarbeitbericht, 29 October 1992, in: IPRax 1994, p. 123.

[146]*Bundesgerichtshof,* 13 December 2005- XI ZR 82/05, in: IPRax 2006, p. 272. See Bonomi (2008a); Garcimartín Alférez (2008), p. 77.

[147]Garcimartín Alférez (2008), p. 77; von Bar and Mankowski (2003), p. 267; Kropholer (2006), pp. 493–496.

[148]For example: Dominique and Watt (2007), pp. 558–562; Mayer and Heuzé (2004), p. 89.

[149]Cour de Cassation, 30 November 2007, 06-14006.

(ensuring equal competition for all subcontractors operating in the French market) and the protection of the subcontractor as the weaker party.[150]

In the Netherlands, rules protecting socially or economically weaker parties can be generally considered, according to the doctrine, overriding mandatory rules as long as they are partially intended to protect common higher interests, although there is no full agreement.[151] In practice, in the *Sorensen/Aramco* decision[152] of the Dutch *Hoge Raad*, the application of a Dutch employment law provision was imposed on an employment contract governed by the law of Texas on the ground that the provision aimed both at protecting the employees against a socially unjustified termination of contract and at protecting the Dutch labour market.[153] The *Hoge Raad* explained that the socio-economic relations in the Netherlands were involved to such an extent that the interests protected by the provision were higher than the interest in fully applying the law objectively applicable to the employment contract. The involvement of the Dutch labour market justified the consideration of the Dutch provision as an overriding mandatory rule rather than a protection of the individual employee.[154] This approach has been confirmed more recently in the *Nuon Personeelsbeheer decision,*[155] *regarding the same provision of Dutch law.*[156] *Thus, the applicability of this provision regarding unfair dismissal depends* on the extent to which the interests of the Dutch labour market are involved in the employment contract. The *Hoge Raad* added that the importance of the Dutch labour market must largely be equated with the interests of the individual employee against unjustified dismissal. On the other hand, in Belgium, the idea that provisions aimed primarily at protecting individual interests of weaker parties can qualify as overriding mandatory provisions in the sense that the abuse of weaker parties could be regarded as a threat to civil society, although they do not serve a specific state interest, is particularly strong.[157]

---

[150]McParland (2015), pp. 691, 692; Kuipers (2012), p. 131.

[151]Kuipers (2012), p. 154, referring also to other authors, such as: Strikwerda and Schaafsma (2005), p. 72; Bertrams and Kruisinga (2007), p. 58. However, in the opposite opinion: Roelvink (1993), p. 224.

[152]Hoge Raad 23 October 1987, NJ 1988/842 (Sorensen/Aramco).

[153]In this case, the Dutch provision in question was article 6 *Buitengewoon Besluit Ardbeidsverhoudingen* (BBA) which required employers to have prior consent from an employment office before proceeding to the termination of an employment relationship.

[154]Henckel (2016), p. 286; Verhagen (2002), p. 144.

[155]Hoge Raad 24 February 2012, LJN BU8512 (*Nuon Personeelsbeheer/X*).

[156]Article 6 BBA (Buitengewoon Besluit Arbeidsverhoudingen 1945).

[157]Belgian provisions on the protection of the commercial agent and distributors are traditionally regarded as overriding mandatory rules (see, for example, the position of Belgium in the *Unamar* case: C-184/12 *United Antwerp Maritime Agencies* (*Unamar*) *NV v Navigation Maritime Bulgare [2013]*).

Finally, the Giulano-Lagarde Report identified consumer protection rules as a category falling within the scope of article 7(2) Rome Convention (the predecessor of article 9 Rome I).[158]

The ECJ Position

The ECJ left the door open for an extensive discussion on the inclusion of weaker party protection rules in the definition of overriding mandatory rules in the *Ingmar* judgment[159] regarding the consideration of the provisions protecting the commercial agent as overriding mandatory rules. In *Ingmar v Eaton,* the ECJ, although it did not address explicitly whether the provisions at stake were to be regarded as overriding mandatory rules in the sense of the Rome I Regulation, gave some guidelines for its determination as such.

Ingmar, a commercial agent with domicile in the United Kingdom, initiated a claim against Eaton, its principal established in California, for the payment of commission and compensation of damages caused by the termination of their agency contractual relationship. Ingmar was performing its services exclusively in the UK and Ireland. The parties had chosen Californian law to govern their contract. Nevertheless, Ingmar's claims were based on the Commercial Agents Regulation of 8 December 1993, the transposition in English law of the Commercial Agents Directive.[160] The Court of Appeal of England and Wales (Civil Division) requested a preliminary ruling from the ECJ regarding whether articles 17 and 18 of the Commercial Agents Directive, on which the claims of the agent were based, would be applicable when the commercial agent performs its activities within a Member State, regardless of the establishment of the principal on a third state and the choice of a third state law to govern their contract. Articles 17 and 18 of the Commercial Agents Directive define the circumstances under which a commercial agent, upon termination of the contract, is entitled to claim compensation for the damages suffered because of the termination of the contractual relationship with the principal. At the same time, article 19 of the Directive states that

> parties may not derogate from articles 17 and 18 to the detriment of the agent before the agency contract expires.

[158]Giuliano-Lagarde Report [1980] OJ C282/1. Following a similar approach, the Spanish doctrine, contrarily to the German approach, considered that there was no problem in applying national consumer protection legislation through article 7 Rome Convention. Calvo Caravaca and Carrascosa González (1997), pp. 116–118.

[159]Case C-381/98, *Ingmar GB Ltd v Eaton Leonard Technologies Inc*. [2000] *ECR* I-9305.

[160]Council Directive 86/653/EEC of 18 December 1986 on the coordination of the laws of the Member States relating to self-employed commercial agents (OJ 1986 L 382/17).

The ECJ concluded that the purpose these provisions serve requires their application where the situation is closely connected with the EU, irrespective of the law chosen by the parties to govern their contract.[161]

It has to be noticed that the Commercial Agents Directive protects the private interests of a special category of individuals (the commercial agents). Nevertheless, it aims to harmonise the conditions of competence within the internal market and therefore contribute to the proper functioning of the internal market. The ECJ did not base its decision on the objective of the Directive to protect a weaker party but referred to its wide objective of economic policy. That is, the ECJ explained that the aim of articles 17 to 19 of the Directive is to protect the freedom of establishment and to circumvent distorted competition within the internal market, promoting at the same time the certainty of commercial transactions.[162] Companies, both European and international, that hire agents in order to commercialise their products within the EU must be aware of and respect the fact that they are trading in an internal market environment and, as a result, cannot benefit from a legal diversity that may distort the competence of the internal market.[163] Furthermore, although the *Ingmar* decision only refers to articles 17 to 19 of the Commercial Agents Directive, a wider meaning could be inferred from its reasoning. The ECJ formulated its decision by referring to the freedom of establishment and undistorted competition within the internal market as the aims of these provisions, and since from the recitals of the Directive it is implied that these objectives are present in more provisions, those other provisions of the Directive could be regarded also as applicable *irrespective of the law by which the parties intended the contract to be governed.*[164]

Consequently, following this line of reasoning, many authors agree that a provision that only aims to protect a weaker party would not be considered as an overriding mandatory rule, but it definitely could be as long as it also aims to promote a higher political, social or economic interest that justifies the priority of this provision in an international scenario.[165] Although the definition of overriding mandatory provisions in article 9 Rome I does not provide sufficient clarity, there is no suggestion that shows that the EU legislator intended to overturn *Ingmar*. Therefore, it has been widely considered that the ECJ contemplates that article 9 Rome I also covers those provisions that protect the interests of weaker parties provided their application proves crucial for the safeguarding of a public interest essential for the Member State in question.

---

[161] *Ingmar*, para. 25.

[162] *Ingmar*, paras. 23–24. In that respect, Case C-215/97 *Barbara Bellone v Yokohama SpA* [1998] *ECR* I-2191, already considered in para. 17, regarding preamble 2 of the Commercial Agents Directive, that the referred objectives of protection of the internal market, freedom of establishment and circumvention of distorted competition, were the aims pursued by it.

[163] Font i Segura (2009), pp. 265–266; Aguilar Grieder (2007), pp. 64–65.

[164] Verhagen (2002), p. 138.

[165] For example, among others, Kuipers (2012), p. 200; Aguilar Grieder (2006), p. 53; Carrascosa González (2012); Verhagen (2002), p. 136.

However, it is questionable whether the overriding effect given in *Ingmar* of the provisions of the Commercial Agents Directive could also be extended to consumers and employees, which already enjoy a limited choice of law under the Rome I Regulation. Moreover, the *Ingmar* case is widely considered as giving rise to more questions than answers.[166] The ECJ held that the provisions in question (originated in the Commercial Agents Directive and aimed at the protection of the rights of the agent) were aimed at ensuring the freedom of establishment and undistorted competition in the internal market and, therefore, were to be considered essential for the EU. The safeguard of the internal market in this case seemed subsidiary to the protection of the agent in this case, and thus it is generally understood that the position taken is that provisions primarily protecting weaker parties can be considered overriding mandatory provisions as long as they aim at protecting an essential state (or EU) interest, even in a subsidiary manner. However, it has to be kept in mind that the ECJ did not refer to the Rome Convention in this case, nor to the concept of overriding mandatory rules, but rather made an autonomous interpretation determining the scope of the Directive on the basis of its nature and purpose (although it is true that Rome Convention was not temporarily applicable in this case and the ECJ also did not have at that time the competence to interpret the Rome Convention).[167] Therefore, there are still authors who do not consider that the ECJ has taken this position and authors who, even though they consider that the ECJ has taken this position, criticise it on the basis of several grounds.

Firstly, within the Rome I Regulation (and also before in the Rome Convention), special protective conflict rules are already provided in order to protect higher interests at stake originating from the weaker position of some contracting parties (i.e. articles 6 and 8 Rome I for employment and consumer contracts, respectively). It is true that the overriding mandatory rules of article 9 Rome I may be still a form of recourse to protect those special individual interests in areas of contract law not covered by special conflict rules, such as the interests of commercial agents. But whereas the need for the protection of consumers and employees is clear, the consideration of commercial agents as weaker parties is disputed as, depending on the situation, they will not be necessarily in a weaker bargaining position, and therefore such a protection is not required.[168]

Secondly, it seems reasonable that party autonomy may be limited in some cases in order to protect important EU interests, such as the freedom of establishment and undistorted competition within the internal market, as the ECJ explained in its judgment. Nevertheless, it is also true that the imposition of the provisions of the Commercial Agents Directive in this case does not seem really essential for the proper functioning of the internal market but rather corresponds more with the protection of the rights of the agent against the foreign choice of law. It is criticised that the ECJ assumed too straightforwardly that the provisions of the Directive aimed

---

[166] Regarding other discussions concerning the case, see Sects. 4.1.1.4, 4.3.2 and 6.2.2.

[167] Kuipers (2012), p. 199.

[168] Verhagen (2002), p. 145; Bonomi (2008a), p. 293.

at the protection of such high interests in a manner that even when the principal was established outside the EU, the required application and party autonomy should be bypassed.[169] The impact that these rules have on fair competition and freedom of establishment is considered too indirect as to contravene the law chosen by the parties.[170] Indeed, the ECJ seemed more worried about a uniform application and interpretation of the EU instruments.

It has to be mentioned that in France, a few days after the *Ingmar* decision, it was declared that the provisions protecting the commercial agents do not have an overriding mandatory character but are just internally mandatory.[171] The ECJ seems to fail to make a distinction between domestic mandatory rules (or, in the terminology of the Rome I Regulation, 'provisions that cannot be derogated from by agreement') and overriding mandatory rules. If the criterion for the international mandatoriness of a provision is that it aims somehow to help the proper functioning of the internal market, almost every directive would be classified as internationally mandatory. As a result, party autonomy, the cornerstone of the Rome I Regulation, would be seriously undermined. It seems that whereas party autonomy is supported by the court when it allows individuals to take advantage of the internal market, and therefore a strict test is imposed upon national overriding mandatory provisions that could affect that right, on the other hand the court is less reluctant to limit that party autonomy in order to guarantee the application of EU law.[172] The concept of overriding mandatory provisions seems to be interpreted more widely than what traditionally some Member States did in order to ensure the application of EU secondary law, which blurs the distinction between the provisions that cannot be derogated from by agreement and overriding mandatory rules and leaves them to the exclusion of party autonomy. Moreover, in my opinion, it also has to be added that the ECJ in this case provided for the application of the Commercial Agents Directive provisions 'irrespective of the law chosen by the parties'. Thus, it does not provide for their applicability 'irrespective of the law otherwise applicable to the contract', which means that if the third country law was applicable as a result of the general conflict rules in the absence of choice of law, the provisions of the Directive would not require applicability. Although in the Rome Convention overriding mandatory rules were not defined, in the Rome I Regulation they are defined as applicable 'irrespective of the law otherwise applicable to the contract'. Thus, it seems indeed that there is some confusion between provisions that cannot be derogated from by agreement and overriding mandatory rules.

---

[169]Kuipers (2009), p. 1520; Verhagen (2002), p. 148.

[170]Verhagen (2002), pp. 148–150; Sonnenberger (2016), p. 121.

[171]Nine days after the *Ingmar* judgment, the French *Cour de Cassation* on 28 November 2000 (no. 98-11.335) held that the Commercial Agents Directive does not provide overriding mandatory character to the French implementing legislation. This also seemed to be the position taken by the Netherlands previous to the Ingmar judgment, where the *District Court Arnhem* (The Netherlands), on 11 July 1991, held that the Dutch commercial agency provisions implementing that Directive sis not have overriding mandatory character.

[172]Kuipers (2012), p. 201; Kuipers (2009), p. 1524.

To sum up, it is generally presumed that article 9 Rome I, according to the interpretation of the ECJ, will also include those provisions that, although protecting a structural weaker party, mainly serve to protect higher interests that are so essential that their priority over the law chosen by the parties is justified, including significant EU interests. However, it is up to each Member State to determine which national rules are considered essential for their interests and thus overriding mandatory. Member States have to restrain themselves and be cautious when they define their protective rules as overriding mandatory. Indeed, article 9 Rome I requires that they must be classified *as crucial by a country for safeguarding its public interests, such as its political, social or economic organization*, and the Member State would have to justify it.

The same conclusion can be inferred from the *Unamar* judgment.[173] In this case, a preliminary ruling was referred to the ECJ asking whether the mandatory rules of the *lex fori* (in this case the Belgium agency rules), which offer wider protection than the minimum laid down by the Commercial Agents Directive, could be applied even when the law chosen by the parties is the law of another Member State in which the minimum protection provided by the Directive has also been implemented (in this case Bulgarian law). The ECJ concluded that despite the fact that the Commercial Agents Directive was correctly transposed into Bulgarian law, the Belgium Court had discretion to qualify its own national provisions as overriding mandatory rules in the sense of article 7 Rome Convention (now article 9 Rome I) and therefore apply them irrespective of the otherwise applicable law.[174]

Therefore, it seems that, although article 9 Rome I refers to public interests, it does not lead a priori to the exclusion of all protective rules. Another argument that supports this approach can be inferred from the *Arblade* case[175] and the *Mazzoleni* case,[176] in which the ECJ used the notion 'overriding mandatory rules' in reference to national rules on employee's protection. This view seems to be supported by the

---

[173]Case C-184/12 *United Antwerp Maritime Agencies (Unamar) NV v Navigation Maritime Bulgare [2013]* EU:C:2013:663.

[174]The ECJ in *Unamar* concluded: *Articles 3 and 7(2) of the Convention on the law applicable to contractual obligations opened for signature in Rome on 19 June 1980 must be interpreted as meaning that the law of a Member State of the European Union which meets the minimum protection requirements laid down by Council Directive 86/653/EEC of 18 December 1986 on the coordination of the laws of the Member States relating to self-employed commercial agents and which has been chosen by the parties to a commercial agency contract may be rejected by the court of another Member State before which the case has been brought in favour of the law of the forum, owing to the mandatory nature, in the legal order of that Member State, of the rules governing the situation of self-employed commercial agents, only if the court before which the case has been brought finds, on the basis of a detailed assessment, that, in the course of that transposition, the legislature of the State of the forum held it to be crucial, in the legal order concerned, to grant the commercial agent protection going beyond that provided for by that directive, taking account in that regard of the nature and of the objective of such mandatory provisions.*

[175]Joined cases C-369/96 *Jean-Claude Arblade and Arblade & Fils SARL* and C-376/96 *Bernard Leloup, Serge Leloup and Sofrage SARL* [1999] ECRI-8453.

[176]Case C-165/98 *Mazzoleni and ISA* [2001] ECR I-2189.

European legislator, which also attributes an overriding mandatory character to provisions protecting the weaker party in certain EU directives. In the Posting of Workers Directive, for example, certain protective norms of the state to which an employee is posted are given the nature of overriding mandatory rules. Therefore, apparently, the tendency of the EU is to accept that rules aimed at the protection of weaker parties can also qualify as overriding mandatory rules.[177] Nevertheless, this does not mean that all protective rules can have such a character, but only when it is regarded as crucial for the safeguarding of the country's interests. The rule must have a dual purpose: the protection of weaker parties and the promotion of public interests. This extensive approach to the meaning of article 9 Rome I leaves enough autonomy to the legislators and courts of the Member States to determine their own crucial interests.

Applicable Irrespective of the Law That Otherwise Governs the Contract

Overriding mandatory rules, because of their particular purpose and content, demand to be applied in all circumstances falling within their scope, irrespective of the law that otherwise governs the contract. The overriding reach of a provision can be indicated by an express delimitation of its scope, or it can result from its wording. However, in general, overriding mandatory provisions do not specifically refer to their overriding reach or determine their own scope. Courts would have to, in those cases, determine the provision's scope by attending to the content and objectives of the rule.[178]

3.3.1.2 Sources of Overriding Mandatory Rules

Overriding mandatory rules are normally originated from the national law of a country. Sometimes, also public international law can be qualified as overriding mandatory, such as measures adopted by the United Nations Security Council, like trade embargoes or other personal or economic sanctions; these rules are applicable in the law of the Member States when they are in force, normally as a result of transposition by EU regulations, and can prevail over the law otherwise applicable when they meet the definition of article 9 Rome I.[179]

EU law can also be qualified as overriding mandatory. In the case of EU law rules, the application of article 9 Rome I supposes the objective of safeguarding the public interests of the EU.[180] EU treaties or EU regulations already enjoy direct applicability, and their application within the EU does not depend on their classification as

[177] Bonomi (2016), p. 624.

[178] *Unamar*, para 50.

[179] Schmidt-Kessel (2015), p. 328; Bonomi (2016), p. 616.

[180] Schmidt-Kessel (2015), pp. 328, 329.

overriding mandatory rules, but in any case they have priority over the national law of the Member States. The principles of primacy and territoriality solve the conflicts between national law and EU law. According to the principle of territoriality, all EU legislation is applicable within the EU territory in the same manner that national law applies within national territory. By reason of the principle of primacy, EU law takes precedence over national law when the two conflict. This is the case when the law applicable to the contract is the law of a Member State; however, when the law of a non-Member State governs the contract, EU law rules are not directly applicable and need a basis for their application under the Rome I Regulation. When a non-Member State law is applicable to the contract, EU rules can only prevail over the law applicable to the contract if they are considered overriding mandatory rules under article 9 Rome I.[181]

The situation regarding rules originated in EU directives is different. Overriding mandatory provisions can have their origin in EU directives. However, directives have to be implemented into national law. Directives do not enjoy a horizontal effect, and therefore private parties cannot rely directly on the provisions of a directive against other individuals when they are not properly transposed. Thus, they have to be transposed into national law, becoming part of national law and having the same hierarchy as any other national provision. This means that, in order to be considered as overriding mandatory rules, the provisions of EU directives, in the same manner as any other provision of domestic law, must fall under the definition of article 9 (1) Rome I. In order to determine whether the provisions of a directive are aimed at protecting public interests, a restrictive interpretation is defended in this study since, to some extent, all EU legislation is aimed at the proper functioning of the internal market.[182]

Some directives ask Member States to establish overriding mandatory provisions. For example, article 3 of the Posted Workers Directive (96/71/EC) states that Member States shall ensure that employees posted to their territory enjoy certain terms and conditions of employment, whatever the law applicable to the employment relationship is.[183] According to some authors, the clauses included in some EU consumer directives (which provide for the application of the protection provided in the directive when parties chose the law of a third state but the situation is closely connected to the EU) also have the effect of conferring an overriding mandatory character to the relevant substantive rules.[184] However, this affirmation is very arguable, and it will later be discussed that such rules should not generally be interpreted as asking Member States to establish overriding mandatory

[181] Bonomi (2016), pp. 615, 616.

[182] Such restrictive interpretation will be justified and defended regarding EU consumer directives in Chap. 4, regarding EU employment directives in Chap. 5 and regarding directives involving other weaker parties in Chap. 6.

[183] The nature of article 3 PWD is analysed and discussed in Sect. 6.3.2.2.

[184] Bonomi (2016), p. 616.

provisions.[185] According to the definition of overriding mandatory rules, three elements are needed for a rule to be considered overriding mandatory: to have a mandatory character, to be crucial for the safeguarding of public interests, and to be applicable irrespective of the law that otherwise governs the contract. It has been submitted that not all rules with mandatory character can have an overriding mandatory character. In order to be overriding mandatory, the rule must be essential for protecting specific public interests. Provisions protecting a weaker party are still possible to become overriding mandatory if at the same time they pursue the protection of a crucial public interest. I consider that provisions deriving from EU directives protecting weaker contracting parties do not have, as a general rule, an overriding mandatory character. In my opinion, they usually have the character of provisions that cannot be derogated from by agreement in the sense of article 3(3), 3 (4), 6 or 8 Rome I. However, if exceptionally a specific (implemented) directive provision mainly serves public interests, its qualification as an overriding mandatory provision in the sense of article 9 is not excluded.[186]

3.3.2 Application of Overriding Mandatory Provisions

Article 9 Rome I governs overriding mandatory rules in the area of contracts. This means that it provides for the possible applicability of overriding mandatory provisions that have an effect on the formation, validity or interpretation of a contract or on the rights or duties of the parties to the contract. Moreover, in accordance with the universal scope of application of the Rome I Regulation, the overriding mandatory provisions referred to by article 9 are applicable whether or not they are part of the law of a Member State.

After having determined what an overriding mandatory rule is according to article 9(1) Rome I, article 9(2) and 9(3) describes the legal effect of overriding mandatory rules. Article 9(2) covers the overriding mandatory provisions of the forum, and article 9(3) gives effect to those of the law of the country where the contractual obligations have to be or have been performed.

Article 9(2) Rome I explicitly makes reference to the law of the forum. It provides that

> *nothing in this Regulation shall restrict the application of the overriding mandatory provisions of the law of the forum.*

---

[185] In that regard, see Sect. 4.3.1. In the same opinion: Magnus (2016), pp. 23–25; Schmidt-Kessel (2015), p. 331.

[186] This affirmation will be object of analysis in Chaps. 4, 5 and 6 specifically regarding consumer, employment and other weaker contracting parties' directives.

The provisions of the law of the forum within the category of overriding mandatory rules prevail over the *lex contractus*. Once a provision is classified as an overriding mandatory rule, the question is whether it would be applicable to the specific case at hand.

Article 9(2) Rome I does not present a mayor problem: the application of the overriding mandatory rules of the law of the forum is perceived as self-evident. Still, some circumstances need some clarification. In a situation where the law applicable to the contract is the law of the forum and the overriding mandatory provision also belongs to that law, is it automatically applicable? That is, are they applicable as part of the governing law regardless of whether the situation falls within its scope? This question seems to be resolved differently by the Member States. While in Germany and the Netherlands overriding mandatory rules have to justify their own application regardless of whether the law governing the contract is already the law of the forum, in France there is no reluctance towards the use of overriding mandatory provisions as part of the law applicable to the contract in those cases.[187]

The application of foreign overriding mandatory provisions is more controversial. Article 9(3) states that

> *effect may be given to the overriding mandatory provisions of the law of the country where the obligations arising out of the contract have to be or have been performed, in so far as those overriding mandatory provisions render the performance of the contract unlawful. In considering whether to give effect to those provisions, regard shall be had to their nature and purpose and to the consequences of their application or non-application.*

The possibility of applying foreign overriding mandatory rules is narrower than under article 7 Rome Convention, which referred to a close connection with the country rather than to the country where the obligations arising out of the contract have to be or have been performed. The final solution adopted in article 9(3) is the result of the compromise of the Member States regarding this concept.[188] During the conversion of the Rome Convention into the Rome I Regulation, the application of foreign overriding mandatory rules was the object of a large debate. The possibility of applying foreign overriding mandatory rules was already accepted by the Dutch *Hoge Raad* in the *Alnati* case (1966), wherein it was held that a foreign state might have such an interest in the application of its mandatory law outside its territory that its provisions would have to be respected by Dutch courts in such cases, even though the parties had chosen the application of Dutch law.[189] This is the rationale incorporated already in the Rome Convention. However, there were many grounds of criticism to this approach: it required analysing foreign policies, it entailed splitting up the applicable law and it restricted party autonomy and brought legal uncertainty

---

[187]Kuipers (2012), pp. 76, 77, with further references.

[188]Oró Martínez (2008), pp. 542–544.

[189]Hoge Raad 13 May 1966, NJ 1967, 3. Kuipers (2012), pp. 58, 59.

to the conflict of laws process.[190] The first two arguments could also be used against the application of the overriding mandatory rules of the forum. The principal criticism consisted in the idea that it would create a large amount of legal uncertainty. Still, article 7 Rome Convention did not refer to every potential legal system, but it limited the application of foreign overriding mandatory rules when the situation had a sufficient close connection with the legal system where the overriding mandatory rules belonged. Besides this criticism, article 7 Rome Convention was defended on the ground that it was the way to respect and give effect to the public interests of foreign states and uphold each other's sociological and economic interests. Some Member States made a reservation on this clause, which was allowed in the light of all the controversies, and even the states that did not make a reservation were not very keen on its application.[191] Thus, during the conversion of the Rome Convention into the Rome I Regulation, there was a long debate over the drafting of this clause. There were several ideas. It was first proposed by the Commission to redraft the wording of article 7 Rome Convention, which became one of the key objections against Rome I. The European Parliament suggested to delete the article altogether on the basis that its 'discretionary nature, the uncertainty of the criteria which it employs and its potential breadth could detract from legal certainty and encourage speculative attempts to evade contractual obligations, thereby increasing uncertainty and risk for economic operators and entailing higher costs'.[192] The final version was a compromise, allowing the application of foreign overriding mandatory rules but narrowing the reach compared to article 7 Rome Convention: effect may be given to the overriding mandatory rules of *the lex loci solutionis*.[193]

Article 9(3) Rome I refers to the place of performance as a particular close connection and only applies to cases of unlawfulness of performance that contravenes an overriding mandatory rule. While this solution has not been very welcomed by some scholars who consider it a step backwards, others consider the modification as necessary and even rest relevance to the differences in practice between both provisions.[194]

[190]For a description of the traditional grounds of criticism to this approach, see: Dickinson (2007), pp. 56–63.

[191]Article 22(1)(a) Rome Convention allowed Member States to make a reservation to this application of article 7(1), and seven Member States (specifically Germany, Slovenia, Ireland, Latvia, Luxembourg, Portugal and the UK) made use of it, mainly on the basis of the concerns about legal uncertainty. However, in the context of the Rome Regulation, being an EU Regulation, there was no possibility to make reservations, and, as a result, it seemed very difficult to keep the same controversial drafting of article 7(2) Rome Convention. Oró Martínez (2008), p. 544.

[192]Amendment 26, European Parliament Draft Report on COM (2005) 650, PE274.427.

[193]Oró Martínez (2008), pp. 543, 544.

[194]For example, Bonomi has criticised the new solution of article 9(3) Rome I, defending the previous connecting factor and considering that the modification does not enhance legal certainty and can be described as arbitrary (Bonomi (2016), pp. 637, 642; Bonomi (2008a), pp. 297–299; also, Kuipers (2012), pp. 85–89). On the other hand, others consider the modification as necessary, mainly due to the political controversy around it, and even highlight the similarity of results in

The wording 'effect may be given' provides the court with a wide discretion to apply such a rule or not.[195] When considering giving effect to it, the court shall look at the nature and purpose of the provision and the consequences of its (non)-application. It seems that the court has the freedom to strictly apply foreign law or to only take it into account on a substantive level. While the application of the rule would mean the application of the legal consequences of such rule to the specific case covered by it, the 'giving effect to the rule' means taking the rule into account but does not necessarily require the application of such legal consequences, or it can even consist of the application of only some of them.[196] In addition, the court could take into account the foreign rule as a legal rule, or could take it into account as a fact, integrating it within the law applicable to the contract.[197] The ECJ has recently addressed the scope and effect of article 9(3) Rome I in the *Nikiforidis* case.[198] The case concerned an employment contract governed by German law, in which the employee was a teacher at a Greek school in Germany, employed by Greece. The question was whether Greek legislation involving a reduction on the payment of public employees, implemented as a result of the economic crisis, would apply to the contract of Mr. Nikiforidis. According to the ECJ, article 9(3) Rome I should not be given a wide interpretation, allowing only the application as legal rules of the overriding mandatory provisions of the state where the obligations arising out of the contract had to be or had been performed (which, in the present case, was Germany and not Greece). However, the ECJ also concluded that it is allowed, provided that the law applicable to the contract allows so, for a court to take into account other overriding mandatory provisions as matters of fact.

The ECJ also clarified that article 4(3) Treaty on European Union (TEU) providing for the principle of sincere cooperation does not change the conclusion reached. That is, since the principle does not allow a Member State to circumvent the obligations that are imposed upon it by EU law, it is accordingly not capable of allowing a court to disregard the fact that the list of overriding mandatory provisions that may be given effect as legal rules according to article 9(3) Rome I is exhaustive and only includes those of the law of the country where the obligations arising out of the contract had to be or had been performed.[199]

---

practice resulting from the application of both provisions, Hellner (2009), pp. 464–466, 470; Lando and Nielsen (2008), p. 1721.

[195]See, in general, Guardans Cambó (1992), pp. 548–562.

[196]Gardeñes Santiago (2017), pp. 178, 179.

[197]Ibid., p. 179.

[198]Case C-135/15 *Republik Griechenland v Grigorios Nikiforidis* [2016] ECLI:EU:C:2016:774.

[199]*Republik Griechenland v Grigorios Nikiforidis*, para 54.

3.3.3 The Relationship Between Overriding Mandatory Provisions and the Protective Conflict Rules of the Rome I Regulation

As it has been described, overriding mandatory provisions are an exception to the normal operation of the conflict of laws mechanism and have been narrowly defined by article 9(1) Rome I.

Although they conventionally aim to protect state interests, they can also sometimes play a role in the protection of weaker parties. It has been previously submitted that provisions protecting weaker parties can be considered overriding mandatory rules as long as they also pursue the protection of essential public interests, fulfilling the definition of article 9(1) Rome I. The Rome I Regulation already provides for protective conflict rules regarding weaker parties (i.e. article 6 Rome I relative to consumer contracts and article 8 Rome I relative to individual employment contracts). The main question would be whether the Rome I Regulation provides for two cumulative mechanisms of protection of weaker contracting parties.

Since it seems generally accepted that article 9 Rome I can be used as a mechanism to protect the weaker contracting party (in exceptional circumstances, when public interests are at stake),[200] it is necessary to analyse its relationship with the protective conflict rules contained in the Rome I Regulation regarding consumer contracts (article 6 Rome I) and individual employment contracts (article 8 Rome I).

3.3.3.1 The Relationship Between Article 9 Rome I and Article 6 Rome I: Consumer Contracts and Overriding Mandatory Provisions

Article 6 Rome I provides that a consumer contract shall be governed by the law of the place where the consumer has his habitual residence

> *provided that the professional: (a) pursues his commercial or professional activities in the country where the consumer has his habitual residence, or (b) by any means, directs such activities to that country or to several countries including that country, and the contract falls within the scope of such activities.*

Parties can choose the law applicable to the contract if the law chosen provides for the same or more protection to the consumer than the law applicable in the absence of choice (law of habitual residence of the consumer). In a situation where the consumer expects his own law to apply, he is protected against the imposition of another law. In this regard, article 6 Rome I intends not to raise the substantive level of consumer protection but just to protect the consumer against the negative consequences of a choice of law. Article 6 Rome I ensures the application of the

[200] See above Sect. 3.3.1.1.

mandatory rules of the country of habitual residence of the consumer and only allows the application of other laws chosen by the parties if the mandatory rules protecting the consumer offer him the same or a better protection. Article 6 Rome I refers to 'rules that cannot be derogated from by agreement', which are a wider set of rules than overriding mandatory rules. However, their mandatory character is of a national character and not international, and thus they are limited to the legal system where they come from. Provisions that cannot be derogated from by agreement, thus, cannot be derogated by the parties when choosing another state law. They are applicable in purely domestic situations and in international situations when they belong to the law applicable to the contract and therefore cannot be departed from by choosing a different law as applicable to the contract. On the other hand, overriding mandatory provisions are a more limited category within the group of mandatory rules. They are applicable in international situations and not limited to the legal system where they come from, and thus they can be applied regardless of the law applicable to the contract (whether it is the result of a choice of law or on the basis of the objective connecting factors). Mandatory rules protecting the consumer belonging to the law of the country of habitual residence of the consumer are already ensured by article 6 Rome I, regardless of whether they have the character of internally mandatory or overriding mandatory rules.

We can distinguish two different types of situations concerning the relationship between article 6 Rome I and article 9 Rome I.

The first situation is when the consumer contract falls within the scope of article 6 Rome I, and therefore the application of the mandatory rules of the country of habitual residence of the consumer is ensured by that article but, at the same time, the forum (which can be a different country) is interested in the application of the forum's consumer protection rules as overriding mandatory provisions. According to articles 17–19 Brussels I bis Regulation, jurisdiction over disputes regarding consumer contracts is conferred on either the courts of the country of habitual residence of the consumer or the courts of the country of habitual residence of the professional (only in case the consumer decides to sue the professional there). Choice of court is limited to certain scenarios (i.e. parties agreed on it after the dispute has arisen; the choice of court agreement allows the consumer to bring proceedings in a court different from the court of the consumer or professional habitual residence; or the consumer and professional have habitual residence in the same Member State at the time of the conclusion of the contract, and they choose the courts of that Member State, provided that such a choice is not contrary to the law of that Member State). Therefore, there is the possibility that the forum court is not the court of the place of habitual residence of the consumer, and thus this court would have an interest in the application of the overriding mandatory provisions of the forum. However, it seems very rare that a country where the consumer does not even have his habitual residence would have an interest in applying its consumer protection provisions and especially that the application of these provisions would be regarded as crucial for the safeguarding of the public interests of that country. Also, in these cases, the application of overriding mandatory rules is hard to justify since the mandatory protection offered by the country of habitual residence of the consumer is already given effect by article 6 Rome I, and there is no reason why a higher protection should be ensured by an overriding mandatory rule when the weaker position of the consumer has already been compensated by the operation of article 6 Rome I. Thus, overriding mandatory rules should not be applicable when the weaker party already enjoys the security of a protective connecting factor. Article 9 Rome I should not play a role in this situation since article 6 Rome I already contains a protective conflict rule benefiting the consumer.

A second situation is when the consumer contract at hand falls outside the scope of the protective conflict rule of article 6 Rome I. That is, it falls *rationae materiae* under article 6 Rome I but not under the circumstances required by that provision to be applicable. As it is known, not all consumer contracts fall within the scope of article 6 Rome I: the consumer who approaches the professional on his own initiative is excluded (it is required that the professional pursue or direct his commercial activities to the country of habitual residence for the consumer). Also, several consumer contracts are excluded from article 6(4) Rome I. In these cases, the general rules of the Rome I Regulation would be applicable. It makes sense that when the consumer approaches the professional in the country of habitual residence of the professional, voluntarily leaving his jurisdiction and without any targeting activity from part of the professional's business, applying the law of the place of habitual residence of the consumer is not deemed as necessary anymore. That is, article 6 Rome I aims to undo the bias towards the stronger party of the contract (the professional) which is created by the objective conflict rules of Rome I. The test of the characteristic performance of article 4 Rome I, in the case of consumer contracts, favours the stronger party since the law of the habitual place of residence of the professional would become applicable, going against the expectations of the consumer who was targeted in his own home country. When it is the consumer approaching the professional in the professional's place without having been targeted by the professional, that presumption of bias towards the professional is vanished.[201] That is why the application of the law of the place of habitual residence of the consumer is not required anymore. Ensuring the application of the mandatory rules protecting the consumer belonging to his country of habitual residence is not necessary in those situations. For example, when article 6 Rome I does not apply to a consumer contract because the professional did not target his activities to the Member State of habitual residence of the consumer, the general rules of Rome I being applicable, it does not seem possible that the Member State of habitual residence of the consumer would have interest in the application of its protective rules as essential for the public interests of the state. However, following this broad understanding of article 9 Rome I, this provision could play a role in the protection of other weaker contracting parties that do not enjoy a special protective conflict rule under Rome I. This would be the case of commercial agents, for example. Also, in the case of insurance contracts or contracts of carriage, since their special conflict rules do not insist on the application of mandatory rules, the broad understanding of

[201] Kuipers (2012), pp. 106–108.

article 9 Rome I could play a role as the cumulative protection of the weaker party does not occur.

However, there are some situations where article 6 Rome I is not applicable but still the interests of the consumer should be taken into account. For instance, imagine a case where a Dutch consumer purchases some goods in Germany. In this case, the Dutch consumer cannot expect that Dutch consumer law be applicable. Instead, he can reasonably expect that German consumer law apply to their contract. However, the contract might contain a choice of another country law, which could provide a lower level of consumer protection. The Dutch consumer would be subject to a lower level of consumer protection than a German consumer operating in the German market (since the mandatory consumer protection of German law would still be ensured by article 3(3) Rome I as it is a purely internal situation) and than a Dutch consumer operating in the Dutch market. Another example would be the 'holiday' consumer. Imagine a case where a company established in Morocco directs some of its activities to tourists in the south of Spain, organising tours together with sales events. A German consumer on a holiday in Málaga (Spain) takes part in a tour and purchases some goods offered to him during the sales event. In this case, if the contract provides for a choice of Moroccan law, the German consumer would not be under the protection of article 6 Rome I since the activities were directed not to his country of habitual residence but to Spain. However, a Spanish tourist could rely on the protection of article 6 Rome I, and Spanish mandatory rules on consumer law would be applicable. The German tourist could only rely on the protection of article 6 Rome I if the Moroccan company was also targeting Germany (e.g. approaching them in German language, terms and conditions drafted in German etc.), but it is not. The law applicable in the absence of choice would be Moroccan law, and the German tourist operating within the EU internal market would be deprived of the mandatory protection provided by the EU consumer directives. This situation will be the object of a detailed analysis in the following chapter.

In these cases, when the interests of the consumer have not been taken into account since the consumer contract is excluded from the protective conflict rule of article 6 Rome I, article 9 Rome I could play a role. However, there is no agreement regarding this subsidiary application of article 9 Rome I. Under the Rome Convention, the situation was uncertain and different positions were taken. The Giuliano-Lagarde Report[202] mentioned some rules on consumer protection as examples of provisions that could be mandatory within the meaning of article 7 (2) Rome Convention. This implied that there was no objection to apply these rules when the conditions of the application of article 5 Rome Convention (predecessor of article 6 Rome I) were not met, although the Report was silent on this specific matter.[203] In the Rome Convention Green Paper, the Commission expressed: 'There are those who express doubts about the combination between the mandatory provisions of Article 5 and those of Article 7: they argue that Article 5 is a special

[202]Giuliano-Lagarde Report [1980] OJ C282/1.

[203]Plender and Wilderspin (2009), p. 352.

application of Article 7 as the two aim to displace the normally applicable law. Accordingly, when the conditions of Article 5 are not met, Article 7 would also be inoperative. This interpretation would deprive a mobile consumer, who already does not enjoy the protection of Article 5, of the safety valve offered by the public order acts.'[204] Those against the application of article 7 Rome Convention as a safety valve considered that article 5 Rome Convention regulated exhaustively the application of protective mandatory rules regarding consumer contracts since this provision dealt specifically with the extent to which the mandatory rules of a law other than the objectively applicable law were to be applied to the contract, and additional application of mandatory rules of other laws would be unjust.[205] This restrictive view was supported in Germany. In the Gran Canaria cases, the *Bundesgerichtshof* held that, since the consumer contract had not been concluded in one of the circumstances required by article 5, it was not possible to apply the mandatory rules of the forum as article 5 Rome Convention was a *lex specialis* which ousted the potential application of article 7 Rome Convention. The facts of these cases were similar to the example of the 'holiday consumer' above: German tourists in Spain, targeted in Spain and not in their own country and the contract containing a choice of Manx law. The German provisions allowing the consumer to withdraw from the contract (which were the implementation of an EU directive and thus also implemented into Spanish law) could not be invoked as mandatory rules of habitual place of residence of the consumer (since the contract was outside the circumstances of article 5 Rome Convention) but neither applicable as overriding mandatory rules of the forum (since the German court said it was not possible).[206] In contrast, the Luxembourg court in *Hames v Spaarkrediet*,[207] in which article 5 Rome Convention was not applicable to the consumer contract in question, the court did not apply Luxembourg consumer law as overriding mandatory rules not because article 5 Rome Convention precluded that possibility but because the consumer provisions in question were considered not as overriding mandatory rules but internally mandatory.[208]

However, I consider that this discussion, in the context of the Rome Convention, was dominated by the confusion existent between mandatory rules and overriding mandatory rules. In the current context, it seems that when article 6 Rome I is not applicable, mandatory consumer protection rules could be applicable as overriding mandatory rules under article 9 Rome I as long as the provision in question could be classified as overriding mandatory. Of course, not all the consumer protection provisions would be applicable, but guaranteeing some essential consumer mandatory

---

[204]Green Paper on the conversion of the Rome Convention of 1980 on the law applicable to contractual obligations into a Community instrument and its modernisation (COM(2002) 654 final) 33.

[205]Lasok and Stone (1987), p. 378.

[206]The Gran Canaria cases will be object of further debate in Chap. 4, since they involve interaction of article 6 Rome I and implementation of EU Directive.

[207]Judgment of July 15, 1992 of the Cour d'appel de Luxembourg in the case *Hames v Spaarkrediet*.

[208]Plender and Wilderspin (2009), pp. 352,353.

protection as overriding mandatory rules would be a possibility as long as the provisions fall within the definition of article 9 Rome I and can be classified as essential for the safeguarding of the interests of the country. Thus, the discussion would be more focused on the possibility of considering weaker party protection rules as overriding mandatory rules rather than article 6 Rome I being *lex specialis* and ousting the potential application of article 9 Rome I. Article 6 Rome I operates on a different basis and concerns a different matter than article 9 Rome I, which does not make it look like *lex specialis*. Also, when article 9(2) starts with the wording 'Nothing in this Regulation shall restrict...' in such a categorical affirmation, it does not make it look like it is subordinated to article 6 Rome I either.[209]

Finally, it remains to clarify that overriding mandatory rules having other goals than protecting the consumer are applicable irrespective of the law governing the consumer contract (e.g. embargo measures, even if they affect a consumer contract).[210]

3.3.3.2 The Relationship Between Article 9 Rome I and Article 8 Rome I: Overriding Mandatory Provisions and Individual Employment Contracts

Article 8(1) Rome I states that the choice of law of the parties to an individual employment contract is effective on the condition that it provides the same or more protection than the mandatory rules of the law that, in the absence of choice, would have been applicable pursuant to paragraphs 2, 3 and 4 of this article. Article 8 (2) Rome I states that, in the absence of choice of law, the law applicable will be the law of the country in which or, failing that, from which the employee habitually carries out his work in the performance of the contract. The country where the work is habitually carried out shall not be deemed to have changed if he is temporarily employed in another country. Article 8(3) provides that where the law applicable cannot be determined pursuant to paragraph 2, the contract shall be governed by the law of the country where the place of business through which the employee was engaged is situated. Article 8(4) applies where it appears from the circumstances as a whole that the contract is more closely connected with a country other than that indicated.

In the same manner as article 6 Rome I regarding consumer contracts, two situations can be distinguished concerning the interaction of article 8 Rome I regarding employment contracts and article 9 Rome I regarding overriding mandatory provisions.

Firstly, article 8 Rome I also leaves some gaps in employee protection. Especially, it leaves some gaps regarding posted workers. Article 8(2) Rome I provides that the habitual place of work does not change when the employee temporarily

[209] In the same opinion: Ibid., p. 354; Merrett (2011), pp. 239, 240; Kuipers (2012), pp. 106–108.

[210] Bonomi (2016), pp. 610–612.

carries out his work in another country. Therefore, although the work is temporary carried out outside, the Member State of origin is still presumed to be the country having the closest connection with the employment contract. However, this does not mean that the state to where the employee is posted does not have an essential interest (e.g. prevention of social dumping or fair competition) in the application of their labour law. Overriding mandatory rules can play a role in those cases. In fact, article 3(1) of the Posted Workers Directive requires the application of certain rules of the country of destination.[211] Articles 8 and 9 Rome I are not intended to be exhaustive.[212] The line of argument is the same as with regard to articles 6 and 9 Rome I in the context of consumer contracts discussed above: overriding mandatory rules can fill the gap left by article 8 Rome I but exceptionally, when talking about provisions essential for public interests.

Mandatory rules protecting the employee belonging to the law of habitual place of work, which is considered as the one having the closest connection and the biggest interest in its application, are already ensured by article 8 Rome I. Overriding mandatory provisions covered by article 9 Rome I are a much narrower category of mandatory rules within the mandatory law that would already be ensured through article 8 Rome I when the forum and the law objectively designated by article 8 Rome I are the same country. However, a second situation would consist in a real conflict between these provisions: article 8 Rome I is applicable, and the forum thus has to ensure the application of the mandatory employment law of the country of habitual place of work, but at the same time it is required by the forum law to apply to the situation a mandatory rule of the forum (which provided for a lower level of protection). For this situation to happen, the law whose mandatory rules were designated by article 8 Rome I has to be different from the *lex fori* and the *lex fori* rule would have to be classified as overriding mandatory. This seems like a very unlikely situation, especially since the Brussels I bis Regulation provisions determining jurisdiction and article 8 Rome I determining the law applicable are coordinated in this regard, leading to the same country. Like in the case of consumer contracts, in these type of situations, the application of overriding mandatory rules is hard to justify since the mandatory protection offered by the country of habitual place of work is already given effect by article 8 Rome I, and there is no reason why a higher protection should be ensured by an overriding mandatory rule when the weaker position of the employee has already been compensated by the operation of article 8 Rome I. However, the interest of the state plays a much higher role in employment contracts than consumer contracts, which means that the forum state can consider certain rules as overriding mandatory and be applicable, superseding the provisions of the law determined by article 8 Rome I. Still in this type of situation where the law designated by article 8 Rome I provides for higher protection than the overriding mandatory rule, in practice it is probable that the overriding mandatory rule would not result in the non-application of the foreign law that is more beneficial.

[211] In this regard, Sect. 5.3.

[212] Merrett (2011), pp. 239, 240; Kuipers (2012), pp. 111, 112.

That is, in practice, both rules could be respected: e.g. an employee whose employment contract is governed by the law of country A is sent to work to country B and, according to the law of country A, the minimum salary is doubled than the minimum salary required by country B; even if the worker receives the amount as the minimum salary of country A, it does not mean that the overriding mandatory rule requiring the minimum salary of country B is being neglected. In such a case, both rules are being respected.[213]

Again, in the case of overriding mandatory rules, provisions having other goals than protecting the employee are applicable irrespective of the law applicable to the employment contract (e.g. embargo measures).

3.4 The Protection Clause of EU Mandatory Law in Intra-EU Situations: Article 3(4) Rome I

Article 3(3) and article 3(4) Rome I ensure the application of domestic and EU mandatory laws, respectively, in cases where all the relevant elements to the situation are located in a place other than the country whose law has been chosen. Both provisions constitute a limit on the freedom of choice of law by the parties and can serve as a mechanism of protection of weaker contracting parties.

Article 3(3) Rome I Regulation, following its predecessor, article 3(3) Rome Convention, provides for a limit on party autonomy intended to protect the domestic mandatory rules of contract law from being avoided in a purely domestic situation. Article 3(3) reads:

> *Where all other elements relevant to the situation at the time of the choice are located in a country other than the country whose law has been chosen, the choice of the parties shall not prejudice the application of provisions of the law of that other country which cannot be derogated from by agreement.*

In addition to the limit on choice of law in purely domestic situations, the Rome I Regulation introduces a new provision under which the application of EU law is ensured in the case of purely intra-EU situations, and as a result, the protection afforded by the provisions of EU law protecting weaker contracting parties can be ensured. This new provision is article 3(4) Rome I, which provides:

> *Where all other elements relevant to the situation at the time of the choice are located in one or more Member States, the parties' choice of applicable law other than that of a Member State shall not prejudice the application of provisions of Community law, where appropriate as implemented in the Member State of the forum, which cannot be derogated from by agreement.*

[213]Gardeñes Santiago (2017), p. 172.

In other words, where all the relevant elements of a contract are objectively connected with the Member States yet the parties choose the law of a third state, that choice is valid and that law will be applicable to the contract, although on one condition: it cannot elude the application of the 'provisions of Community law which cannot be derogated from by agreement' that are applicable to the case. Since in our study we focus on the protection of weaker contracting parties at EU level, I will focus on the analysis of article 3(4) Rome I, although similar reflexions can be made regarding article 3(3) Rome I at a domestic level.

Article 3(4) Rome I is new in the Rome I Regulation, and it is the result of the increasing necessity of coordination between the general conflict of laws rules determining the law applicable to the contract and EU secondary law or, broadly speaking, the necessity of compatibility within the European legal system. The Rome Convention did not provide for any provision dealing with the situation of a choice of a foreign law in a purely intra-EU contract. Some authors defended an analogic application of article 3(3) Rome Convention, which provides that in a purely internal situation where the contract is just connected with a single Member State, parties cannot elude the application of the national mandatory rules of that Member State.[214] Nevertheless, the EU did not consider sufficient that analogic application as an *ad hoc* provision for intra-EU situations, whose requirements differed from those of article 3(3), was required.[215]

Article 3(4) Rome I is intended to protect the interests of the EU and ensure the application and respect of mandatory EU law when all the relevant elements of the contractual relationship are located within one or several Member States (intra-EU situations) but the parties chose a third country law as the law applicable to their contract.[216] Therefore, it guarantees the application of the 'provisions of Community law which cannot be derogated from by agreement'—mandatory EU law—in situations where, due to the choice of law of the parties, those provisions could be eluded. Hence, article 3(4) Rome I is considered a mechanism for fighting abuse of law at EU level.[217] It seems completely justifiable that in an intra-EU situation, contract parties should be prevented from avoiding the application of mandatory EU secondary law, which aims precisely to establish a common ground between market participants established in the EU.[218]

The respective EU mandatory law derived from directives would be applicable, as implemented by the law of the Member State of the forum, rather than the closest connected law or the law applicable in the absence of choice. This option, despite being more convenient for the judge, could result in forum shopping and lead to less predictable results in cases where directives are of a minimum harmonisation nature

[214]Lando (1987), pp. 181, 182; Aguilar Grieder (2006), pp. 54, 55; Aguilar Grieder (2011), p. 30.

[215]In this sense, see Aguilar Grieder (2006), pp. 54–57; Bonomi (2008b), pp. 172, 173; Max Planck Institute for Foreign Private and Private International Law (2007), pp. 240–243.

[216]Belohlávek (2011), pp. 707–711; Carrascosa González (2009), pp. 151, 152.

[217]Lagarde (2006), p. 337.

[218]Verhagen (2002), p. 140.

and thus transposed differently among the Member States.[219] However, since EU law regards the laws of the Member States as equivalent, the law of the forum, which is more pragmatic and reduces costs for the judge, was chosen over the other possible (and more coherent with the Rome I Regulation system) connecting factors.[220]

Article 3(4) Rome I refers not to the so-called overriding mandatory provisions or *lois de police* of article 9 Rome I previously defined but to the provisions of EU origin in which mandatoriness is restricted to the internal scope of each Member State. Accordingly, the majority of the provisions contained in the EU directives aiming at the protection of weaker contracting parties fall under article 3(4) Rome I. The category of mandatory rules covered by article 3(4) Rome I is wider than the category of overriding mandatory rules of article 9 Rome I, the latter only covering those mandatory provisions whose application is essential for the safeguarding of public interests, such as the political, social or economic organisation of a country. As a result, provisions of EU directives regarding weaker parties that do not apply as a result of article 6, article 8 or article 9 Rome I can still be applicable according to article 3(4) Rome I.

However, article 3(4) Rome I only becomes applicable when all relevant elements are located within the EU (purely intra-EU situations).[221] But which elements are to be considered relevant in this regard? The silence of the legislator confers a wide margin of discretion, which at the same time may disturb the legal certainty. The Giuliano/Lagarde Report on the Rome Convention can be of guidance. The Report described situations related to conflict of laws as 'situations which involve one or more elements foreign to the internal social system of a country (for example, the fact that one or all of the parties to the contract are foreign nationals or persons habitually resident abroad, the fact that the contract was made abroad the fact that one or more of the obligations of the parties are to be performed in a foreign country, etc.)'.[222] Similarly, some authors consider that the connecting factors determining the law applicable to the contract contained in the Rome I Regulation could be understood as relevant elements. Following this latter interpretation, when we contemplate the clauses referring to a 'manifestly closest connection', every element

219 Calliess (2015a), p. 108; Mankowski (2016), p. 235.

220 Mankowski (2016), p. 235. In addition, because of the coordination between the Brussels I bis Regulation concerning jurisdiction and the Rome I Regulation, the forum country will most probably be the same country to which the conflict rule in the absence of choice of law would have referred to and/or the closest connected to the contract.

221 Article 3(4) Rome I cannot be used to justify the application of European provisions when all relevant elements are not located within the European Union. Article 3(4) Rome I has been questioned as it does not fulfil I its purpose of coordination and protection against abuse of law, since it does not cover any extra-EU situation. Within the EU secondary law there are no different mandatory provisions for intra-EU and extra-EU situations, but they become applicable provided the situation falls within its scope of application, which can happen even if not all the relevant elements are within the EU. As a result, either article 3(4) Rome I is not adapted to the requirements of the EU secondary law, or the EU secondary law is not adapted to the Rome I Regulation system.

222 Giuliano-Lagarde Report [1980] OJ C282/1, 10.

could be interpreted in this sense as relevant, which would not be feasible.[223] The determination of the objective factors of the contract as relevant elements seems more feasible. Hence, the place of performance or the place of conclusion of the contract is definitely considered as relevant elements for the situation. In the same manner, the place of habitual residence of the parties shall also be considered as such.[224] On the other hand, nationality becomes less important to the situation. It should not be a relevant element for determining a situation as extra-EU, for example a case where a consumer with non-EU nationality but with habitual residence in a Member State for a long time concludes a contract within the EU with an EU professional. It could become more relevant if both parties are non-EU nationals.[225] Similarly, elements as the currency or language of the contract should not be considered as relevant to contemplate a contract as extra-EU. However, when several of these elements appear together within the same contractual relationship, they could justify a legitimate interest in a foreign choice of law.[226]

Finally, it is required to pay special attention to the choice of court of the parties in case they have chosen a non-EU court as competent to solve their eventual disputes. Preamble 15 Rome I, in reference to article 3(3) Rome I, explains that the rule should be applicable regardless of whether there is a choice of court or tribunal. Following the same interpretation, it should be understood in the context of article 3(4) Rome I that in a situation where all the relevant elements are located within the EU, a foreign choice of court clause should not transform an intra-EU situation into an extra-EU situation as the choice of forum does not require that the facts relevant to the substantive law be objectively connected with the EU, and accordingly the mandatory provisions of EU law should be applicable.[227]

Accordingly, the existence of relevant elements outside the EU will be determined by the existence of a legitimate interest of the parties with regard to the foreign choice of law. In this manner, where none of the objective elements of the contract concur (e.g. habitual residence, place of performance etc.), that interest should be determined on a case-by-case basis, avoiding the non-application of mandatory provisions of EU law when it is actually necessary.

[223]Specifically, articles 4(3), 5(3), 7(2), 8(4) Rome I, which state that 'where it is clear from all the circumstances of the case that the contract is manifestly more closely connected with a country (...) the law of that other country shall apply'; Belohlávek (2011), p. 703.

[224]Plender and Wilderspin (2009), p. 164.

[225]Belohlávek (2011), p. 703.

[226]Leible (2011), pp. 234–235; Plender and Wilderspin (2009), p. 164.

[227]Garcimartín Alférez (2008), p. 65.

References

Aguilar Grieder H (2006) La Voluntad de Conciliación con las Directivas Comunitarias Protectoras en la Propuesta del Reglamento Roma I. In: La Unión Europea ante el Derecho de la Globalización. Colex, Madrid, pp 45–61

Aguilar Grieder H (2007) La Protección del Agente en el Derecho Comercial Europeo. Colex, Madrid

Aguilar Grieder H (2011) El Impacto del Reglamento Roma I en el Contrato Internacional de Agencia. Cuadernos de Derecho Transnacional 3:24–46

Belohlávek AJ (2011) Rome convention - Rome I regulation. Juris Publishing, Inc., Huntington

Bertrams RIVF, Kruisinga SA (2007) Overeenkomsten in het internationaal Privaatrecht en het Weens Koopverdrag. Wolters Kluwer, Deventer

Bonomi A (2008a) Overriding mandatory provisions in the Rome I regulation on the law applicable to contracts. In: Sarcevic P et al (eds) Yearbook of private international law. Sellier, European Law Publishers and Swiss Institute of Comparative Law, München, pp 285–300

Bonomi A (2008b) The Rome I regulation on the law applicable to contractual obligations: some general remarks. In: Yearbook of international private law. Sellier, European Law Publishers and Swiss Institute of Comparative Law, München, pp 165–176

Bonomi A (2016) Article 9: overriding mandatory provisions. In: Magnus U, Mankowski P (eds) Rome I regulation - commentary. Verlag Dr. Otto Schmidt, Köln, pp 597–661

Calliess G-P (2015a) Article 3. Freedom of choice. In: Calliess G-P (ed) Rome regulations. Commentary, 2nd edn. Kluwer Law International, Alphen aan den Rijn, pp 76–108

Calliess G-P (2015b) Article 6. Consumer contracts. In: Calliess G-P (ed) Rome regulations. commentary, 2nd edn. Kluwer Law International, Alphen aan den Rijn, pp 155–193

Calvo Caravaca AL, Carrascosa González J (1997) El Convenio de Roma sobre la Ley aplicable a las obligaciones contractuales del 19 de junio de 1980. In: Contratos Internacionales. Tecnos, Madrid, pp 41–143

Carrascosa González J (2009) Ley Aplicable a los Contratos Internacionales: el Reglamento Roma I. Colex, Madrid

Carrascosa González J (2012) La Autonomía de la Voluntad Conflictual y la Mano Invisible en la Contratación Internacional. Diario La Ley 7847:2

Dickinson A (2007) Third-country mandatory rules in the law applicable to contractual obligations: so long, farewell, Auf Wiedersehen, Adieu? J Priv Int Law 3:53–88

Dominique B, Watt HM (2007) Droit International Privé- partie générale. Presses Universitaires de France, Paris

Font i Segura A (2009) Reparación Indemnizatoria tras la Extinción del Contrato Internacional de Agencia Comercial: Imperatividad Poliédrica o el Mito de Zagreo (STJCE de 9 de noviembre de 2000, As. C-381/98, Ingmar Gb Ltd c. Eaton Leonard Technologies Inc.). Revista de Derecho Comunitario Europeo 5:259–279

Francescakis P (1966) Quelques Precisions sur les 'Lois d'Application Immediate' et leurs Rapports avec les Règles sur les Conflits de Lois. Revue critique de droit international privé 55:1–18

Francescakis P (1967) Lois d'Application Immediate et Règles de Conflit. Rivista di diritto internazionale privato e processuale 3:691–697

Franzen M, Gröner N (2015) Article 8. Individual employment contracts. In: Calliess G-P (ed) Rome regulations. Commentary, 2nd edn. Kluwer Law International, Alphen aan den Rijn

Garcimartín Alférez FJ (2008) The Rome I regulation: much ado about nothing? Eur Legal Forum:61–80

Garcimartín Alférez FJ (2009) The Rome I regulation: exceptions to the rule on consumer contracts and financial instruments. J Priv Int Law 5:85–103

Gardeñes Santiago M (1999) La Aplicación de la Regla de Reconocimiento Mutuo y su Incidencia en el Comercio de Mercancías y Servicios en el Ámbito Comunitario e Internacional. Eurolex, Madrid

Gardeñes Santiago M (2008) La Regulación Conflictual del Contrato de Trabajo en el Reglamento Roma I: una oportunidad perdida. Anuario Español de Derecho Internacional Privado 8:387–424
Gardeñes Santiago M (2017) Derecho Imperativo y Contrato Internacional de Trabajo. Revista de Ministerio de Empleo y Seguridad Social 132:163–188
Grusic U (2015) The European private international law of employment. Cambridge University Press, Cambridge
Guardans Cambó I (1992) Contrato Internacional y Derecho Imperativo Extranjero. Aranzadi, Pamplona
Hellner M (2009) Third country overriding mandatory rules in the Rome I regulation: old wine in new bottles? J Priv Int Law 5:447–470
Henckel KC (2016) Cross-border transfers of undertakings. Ulrik Huber Institute for Private International Law, Ees, The Netherlands
Houwerzijl M (2019) The analysis of the posting of workers Directive(s) with a specific focus on EU cross-border road transport. In: Zwanenburg A, Bednarowicz B (eds) Cross-border employment and social rights in the EU road transport sector. Eleven International Publishing, The Hague, pp 71–111
Kropholer J (2006) Internationales Privatrecht, 5th edn. Mohr Siebeck, Tübingen
Krvavac M, Belovic J (2014) Communitarisation of private international law rules on party autonomy in European Union. Int J Bus Humanit Technol 4:54–68
Kuipers J-J (2009) Party autonomy in the Brussels I regulation and Rome I regulation and the European Court of Justice. German Law J 10:1505–1525
Kuipers J-J (2012) EU law and private international law: the interrelationship in contractual obligations. Martinus Nijhoff Publishers, Leiden
Lagarde P (2006) Remarques sur la Proposition de Règlement sur la Loi Applicable aux Obligations Contractuelles (Rome I). Revue critique de droit international privé 95:331–349
Lando O (1987) The ECC convention on the law applicable to contractual obligations. Common Market Law Rev 24:159–214
Lando O, Nielsen PA (2008) The Rome I regulation. Common Market Law Rev 45:1687–1725
Lasok D, Stone P (1987) Conflict of laws in the European Community. Professional Books Ltd, London
Leible S (2011) La Importancia de la Autonomía Conflictual para el Futuro del Derecho de los Contratos Internacionales. Cuadernos de Derecho Transnacional 3:214–233
Magnus U (2016) Introduction. In: Magnus U, Mankowski P (eds) Rome I regulation - commentary. Verlag Dr. Otto Schmidt, Köln, pp 6–51
Mankowski P (2016) Article 3: freedom of choice. In: Magnus U, Mankowski P (eds) Rome I regulation - commentary. Verlag Dr. Otto Schmidt, Köln, pp 87–263
Marchal Escalona N (2017) De la Protección del Personal Laboral al Servicio de las Embajadas Españolas. Bitácora Millennium DIPr: Derecho Internacional Privado 6:1–27
Marques dos Santos A (1991a) As Normas de Aplicaçao Imediata no Direito Internacional Privado. Livraria Almedina, Coimbra
Marques dos Santos A (1991b) As Normas de Aplicaçao Imediata no Direito Internacional Privado. Livraria Almedina, Coimbra
Max Planck Institute for Foreign Private and Private International Law (2004) Comments on the European Commission's Green Paper on the conversion of the Rome Convention of 1980 on the law applicable to contractual obligations into a Community instrument and its modernization. RabelsZ 68:1–118
Max Planck Institute for Foreign Private and Private International Law (2007) Comments on the European Commission's Proposal for a Regulation of the European Parliament and the Council on the law applicable to contractual obligations (Rome I). RabelsZ Bd71
Mayer P, Heuzé V (2004) Droit International Privé, 8th edn. Librairie générale de droit et jurisprudence, Paris

McParland M (2015) The Rome I regulation on the law applicable to contractual obligations. Oxford University Press, Oxford

Merrett L (2011) Employment contracts in private international law. Oxford University Press, Oxford

Mills A (2018) Party autonomy in private international law. Cambridge University Press, Cambridge

Oró Martínez C (2008) Del Artículo 7 del Convenio de Roma al Artículo 9 del Reglamento 'Roma I': Algunas Implicaciones para el Derecho de la Competencia. Anuario Español de Derecho Internacional Privado 8:531–554

Palao Moreno G (2016) Article 8: individual employment contracts. In: Magnus U, Mankowski P (eds) Rome I regulation - commentary. Verlag Dr. Otto Schmidt, Köln, pp 577–599

Plender R, Wilderspin M (2009) The European private international law of obligations, 3rd edn. Sweet & Maxwell, London

Plender R, Wilderspin M (2015) The European private international law of obligations, 4th edn. Sweet & Maxwell, London

Ragno F (2009) The law applicable to consumer contracts under the Rome I regulation. In: Ferrari F, Leible S (eds) Rome I regulation. Sellier, European Law Publishers, München

Renner M (2015) Article 9. Overriding mandatory provisions. In: Calliess G-P (ed) Rome Regulations. Commentary, 2nd edn. Kluwer Law International, Alphen aan den Rijn, pp 242–261

Roelvink HLJ (1993) Artikel 6:2 BW en het Nederlandse IPR. In: Van Rijn van Alkemade J (ed) Grensoverschrijdend privaatrecht: een bundel opstellen over privaatrecht in internationaal verband: aangeboden aan Mr. J. van Rijn van Alkemade bij gelegenheid van zijn afscheid als raadadviseur bij het Ministerie van Justitie. Kluwer, Deventer, p 219 ff

Rühl G (2007) Party autonomy in the private international law of contracts: transatlantic convergence and economic efficiency. In: Gottschalk E et al (eds) Conflict of laws in a globalized world. Cambridge University Press, Cambridge

Rühl G (2011) Consumer protection in choice of law. Cornell Int Law J 44:569–601

Sánchez Lorenzo S (2018) El Principio de Coherencia en el Derecho Internacional Privado. Revista Española de Derecho Internacional 70:17–47

Schmidt-Kessel M (2015) Article 9. In: Ferrari F (ed) Rome I regulation. Pocket commentary. Sellier, European Law Publishers, München, pp 320–354

Sonnenberger HJ (2016) Overriding mandatory provisions. In: Leible S (ed) General principles of European private international law. Wolters Kluwer, Alphen aan den Rijn, pp 117–128

Strikwerda L, Schaafsma SJ (2005) Inleiding tot het Nederlandse Internationaal Privaatrecht. Wolters Kluwer, Alphen aan den Rijn

Van Bochove LM (2014) Overriding mandatory rules as a vehicle for weaker party protection in European private international law. Erasmus Law Rev 7:147–157

Van Overveeke F (2020) Posting drivers in the EU road transport sector. ERA Forum:1–12

Verhagen HLE (2002) The tension between party autonomy and European Union Law: some observations on IngmarGB Ltd v Eaton Leonard Technologies Inc. Int Comp Law Q 51:135–154

Von Bar C, Mankowski P (2003) Internationales Privatrecht Band 1: Allgemeine Lehren, 2nd edn. C.H. Beck, Munich

von Savigny FC (1849) System des Heutigen Römischen Rechts. Veit und Comp, Berlin

Wilderspin M (2016) Article 6: consumer contracts. In: Magnus U, Mankowski P (eds) Rome I regulation - commentary. Verlag Dr. Otto Schmidt, Köln, pp 453–490

Chapter 4
The Relationship and Coordination Between EU Consumer Directives and the Rome I Regulation

This chapter aims to clarify the incoordination existent between the Rome I Regulation and the EU consumer directives. Conflict of laws regarding consumer protection has been an object of debate among European private international law scholars during the last decades due to the several inconsistencies around it.[1] Besides the discussions regarding gaps and contradictions deriving from the interaction of those instruments, the arising of EU law has brought back basic conflict of laws questions, which in our specific case are translated in: When should EU consumer directives be applicable? Should the existent EU conflict rules—the Rome I Regulation—determine their applicability? Should instead the directives themselves determine their own applicability? How would their interaction with the existent conflict rules then be? It can be observed that the debate goes back to the eternal PIL dispute between a multilateral conflict of laws method and a unilateral conflict of laws approach. While the Rome I Regulation mainly follows a multilateral approach, containing in its majority multilateral conflict rules, plus some modern principles such as party autonomy, protection of weaker contracting parties or the concept of overriding mandatory rules, the autonomous determination of scope of application by the directives themselves would result in a unilateral approach since they would indicate their own scope of application while ignoring the application of foreign law.

Regarding the existent gaps and inconsistencies relative to the conflict of laws on consumer contracts, these derive from different intended reaches between the Rome I Regulation and the EU consumer directives. On the one hand, the Rome I Regulation contains a protective conflict rule that determines the law applicable to consumer contracts: article 6 Rome I. This rule covers consumer contracts where the consumer is an individual acting outside its trade or profession (not acting for business purposes), the professional party acts in the course of its trade or profession

[1] For example: Jayme and Kohler (1995); De la Rosa (2003), p. 139 et seq.; Francq (2005, 2006); De la Rosa (2007); Kramer (2015).

M. Campo Comba, *The Law Applicable to Cross-border Contracts involving Weaker Parties in EU Private International Law*,
https://doi.org/10.1007/978-3-030-61481-2_4

and the contract must fall within the scope of the professional's activities. Moreover, the contract will be regarded as a consumer contract under article 6 Rome I when the professional pursues his commercial or professional activities in the country where the consumer has his habitual residence or by any means directs such activities to that country or to several countries, including that country. Also, some consumer contracts are explicitly excluded by article 6(4) Rome I. Thus, the protective conflict rule of article 6 Rome I applies not to all consumer contracts but to active and 'mobile' consumers, and consumers explicitly excluded are outside its scope of application.[2] Of course, there are situations in which a consumer could not reasonably expect the law of the country of his habitual residence to apply, like in the case of active consumers: when a Dutch citizen goes on holiday to Mexico and purchases an item in a souvenir shop there, he cannot reasonably expect that in case of any conflict arising, Dutch consumer law would be applicable.

On the other hand, EU consumer directives seem to intend to apply their standards of protection to more situations than covered by article 6 Rome I. In fact, several EU consumer directives contain a so-called scope rule that refers to the application of their standards; an example is article 6(2) Unfair Contract Terms Directive:[3]

> *Member States shall take the necessary measures to ensure that the consumer does not lose the protection granted by this Directive by virtue of the choice of law of a non-Member State as the law applicable to a contract if the latter has a closest connection with the territory of the Member States.*

The only requirement of a close connection with the EU for the application of the standards of the Directive covers more situations than those of article 6 Rome I. However, as it will be shown in this chapter, the existence of scope rules interferes with the Rome I Regulation system since it uses a unilateral approach to determine the applicability of the instrument which determines the scope of the instrument without referring to foreign law, clashing with the multilateral nature of the Rome I Regulation. Furthermore, if the Rome I Regulation aims to unify the conflict of laws of the different Member States regarding contractual obligations, the fact that scope rules are spread around directives disrupts that aim. The consumer would probably be better protected in a coherent system that ensures legal certainty. Moreover, the broad drafting of scope rules gives place to different understanding when implementing these rules among the national laws of the Member States, which add more uncertainty to the situation.

In addition, not all the EU consumer directives contain scope rules defining their application, but some refer the conflict of laws issue to the Rome I Regulation. This seems to be the current trend followed by the European legislator; however, the

---

[2]For a deeper analysis of article 6 Rome I, see Chap. 3.

[3]Council Directive 93/13/EEC of 5 April 1993 on unfair terms in consumer contracts (OJ L 95/29) (*Unfair Contract Terms Directive*).

existence of scope rules in other directives makes the whole system inconsistent. Also, if we were to follow this new trend, would the protection provided by the consumer directives be ensured in all situations the directives intend to cover?

In this regard, it is important to bear in mind that EU law and PIL have different starting points and aims. While EU consumer directives pursue the well-functioning of the internal market and a consumer protection standard common in all Member States, PIL is based on different values. The traditional multilateral approach entails solving a conflict of laws by bringing the legal relationship home, with a neutral conflict rule that would find the legal systems most closely connected to the legal relationship. In that manner, international harmony of decisions would be achieved, meaning that the outcome would be the same regardless of the jurisdiction where the proceedings were brought, which would prevent limping legal relationships and would promote legal certainly for the parties involved. The EU PIL and the Rome I Regulation follow this approach, although some other values and principles are involved: in order to protect important social values of substantive law, such as consumer protection, conflict rules refer to the country that should have the strongest interest in the application of its law (e.g. article 6 Rome I referring to the law of habitual residence of the consumer); also, the principle of party autonomy has become increasingly accepted, especially in the area of contract law, which means that another connecting factor is the one that refers to the law of the country that the parties have chosen (which, in some cases such as consumer contracts, needs to be limited to avoid abuse).[4] However, values regarding a single EU area of justice and the functioning of the EU internal market are not sufficiently reflected in the Regulation. Therefore, this can be the underlying problem concerning the incapacity of the Rome I Regulation to correctly designate the law applicable to consumer contracts when the application of the EU consumer directives is at stake. It may be that some conflict rules of the Rome I Regulation need to take into account the internal market objectives in order to ensure coordination between PIL and EU law.

Regarding the never-ending debate between multilateralism and unilateralism, in this case relative to the scope of application of the EU consumer directives, the existence of scope rules in some of the directives has been interpreted in different manners from PIL point of view and has brought back the traditional discussion. On the one hand, those supporting a unilateralist method of PIL have defended that every act of EU law, and thus the EU consumer protection directives, determines, implicitly or explicitly, its own scope of application and claim a return of the unilateralist approach.[5] Below, it will be seen that a unilateral approach could be considered a more pragmatic solution to protect the EU objectives, with the big downside of probably becoming a protectionist system that imposes as a rule the application of its law over the foreign law.

[4] De Boer (1996), p. 279.

[5] For example, Stéphanie Francq in: Francq (2005, 2006). Also, recognising the unilateralism existent in different EU instruments and the necessity of it: Bucher (2011), p. 82 et seq.; Symeonides (2005).

On the other hand, those defending the persistence of the multilateral approach try to fit the scope rules within the existent multilateral conflict of laws system of the Rome I Regulation and defend the new trend of the EU legislator of referring the conflict of laws issue to the rules of the Regulation.[6] Under a PIL multilateral approach, a consumer contract between a Dutch consumer and a German professional is not different from a consumer contract between a Dutch consumer and a Brazilian professional. However, from the point of view of EU law, the situations completely differ from each other: while in the first case the application of the EU standards is generally ensured, in the second case there is the possibility that the EU standards are not applied when the EU intended to, disrupting the well-functioning of the internal market. In this intra-EU/extra-EU discussion, one reflexion has to be taken into account: when different legal systems share common or similar legal values, like in the case of the Member States, conflict of laws should definitely promote equality between these different national legal systems through neutral conflict rules; however, when legal systems do not share similar legal values and important interests are at stake, should the application of foreign law be decided by neutral conflict rules?

Thus, considering rejecting the idea that PIL methodological purity, on the basis that it does not seem possible that a single method, neither multilateral nor unilateral, can solve all conflict of laws issues and, furthermore, taking into account the notion that the functioning of the internal market should be respected and thus the EU consumer protection should be ensured when necessary, a solution regarding the incoordination existent between the Rome I Regulation and the EU consumer directives should be achieved.

In that context, this chapter will:

- Firstly, describe the existent inconsistencies and gaps regarding the relationship between EU consumer directives and the Rome I Regulation. The problems arising from the first generation of EU consumer directives, silent about their scope of application, and the second generation of consumer directives, containing a scope rule, in relation to the EU conflict of laws regime, will be discussed. Then the final solution adopted by the Rome I Regulation and the current trends of the European legislator regarding EU consumer directives and conflict of laws will be described. Finally, the current chaotic situation regarding all the existent gaps will be analysed.
- Secondly, focus on the issues regarding intra-EU conflicts of law related to EU consumer directives. Two different issues will be discussed: on the one hand, the different understanding arising from the implementation of the scope rules of the directives into the national law of the Member States, which brings more uncertainty to an already confusing system and, on the other hand, whether, in cases where forum law grants a better level of protection as a result of the minimum

[6] Kuipers (2012) and Piir and Sein (2016).

harmonising nature of some of the directives, the forum law should impose its standards against the law of another Member State.

- Thirdly, focus on EU consumer directives and extra-EU conflicts of law, especially referring to the international scope of the EU consumer directives in PIL terms. Thus, the possibilities of fitting the scope rules of the EU consumer directives within the Rome I Regulation system, defending that conflict of laws regarding consumer contracts regulated by EU consumer directives should be solved through the Rome I Regulation, will be discussed. Moreover, a unilateral PIL approach in this regard will be debated, considering the advantages and disadvantages of determining the scope of application of EU consumer directives in an autonomous manner using a unilateral approach. Finally, some reflexions will be made regarding the application of foreign law, considering several issues influencing the use of a multilateral or unilateral method.
- Finally, suggest several modifications in the current system to coordinate the interaction of the Rome I Regulation and the EU consumer directives, taking into account all the considerations discussed in the chapter.

4.1 The Existence of Scope Rules in EU Consumer Directives and Its Relation to the Rome I Regulation

During the eighties and nineties of the twentieth century, the EU started to enact consumer protection directives containing common standards of consumer contract law to be implemented among the national laws of the different Member States.[7] At the same time, the notion of consumer protection was reflected in the private international law area of the EU: regarding the law applicable to consumer contracts, article 5 Rome Convention on the law applicable to contractual obligations[8] provided for a special protective conflict rule regarding some consumer contracts.

However, it was soon noticed that article 5 Rome Convention had been too narrowly considered and did not respond to the necessities that EU consumer directives required. The Gran Canaria cases, where some EU consumer protection provisions ought to be applicable but following the Rome Convention were not, proved some of the existing gaps in article 5 Rome Convention. As a solution to this problem, some EU consumer directives enacted since the nineties started to contain a so-called scope rule that ensured the applicability of the respective directive when the parties had chosen the law of a non-EU country. However, this technique proved to be disruptive for the conflict of laws system since it led to inconsistencies regarding the regime of the Rome Convention, as well as different interpretations

[7] Kramer (2015), p. 261.

[8] *Convention 80/934/EEC on the law applicable to contractual obligations opened for signature in Rome on 19 June 1980 [1980] (OJ L 266).*

of these scope rules among the different national laws of the Member States.[9] The Rome Convention was an international instrument inspired in the classical PIL multilateral approach with a view of the world divided into different states, without taking into account the specialties of the territory of the EU.[10]

The conversion of the Rome Convention into the Rome I Regulation was the perfect opportunity to coordinate the EU consumer directives with the conflict rules regarding consumer protection. Several proposed solutions were considered during this process. However, the Rome I Regulation did not achieve this goal: article 6 Rome I and article 3(4) Rome I, even though they cover more situations than the Rome Convention, are still insufficient to ensure the application of the EU consumer directives in all the situations these directives intend to cover. Moreover, article 23 Rome I gives priority to conflict rules dealing with specific matters over the conflict rules of the Rome I Regulation. Thus, scope rules of the consumer protection directives could have priority over the conflict rules of the Regulation. On the other hand, the EU consumer directives most recently enacted do not contain any scope rule but rather refer the conflict of laws issue to the Rome I Regulation. As a result, the current situation seems chaotic.[11]

This section will describe the existent inconsistencies and gaps regarding the relationship between EU consumer directives and the Rome I Regulation. Firstly, the problems arising among the Rome Convention and the first generation of EU consumer directives (silent about their scope of application) and the second generation of consumer directives (containing a scope rule) will be discussed. Secondly, the proposed solutions for this incoordination and the final solution adopted by the Rome I Regulation will be described. Then the current trends of the EU legislator regarding EU consumer directives and conflict of laws will be explained. Finally, the chaotic situation regarding all the existent inconsistencies and gaps will be summarised in order to be able to understand the different possible interpretations and solutions from private international law point of view in the following sections.

4.1.1 The First and Second Generations of EU Consumer Directives: Covering the Insufficiencies of the Rome Convention Regarding Consumer Protection

During the eighties and nineties of the twentieth century, the EU increased its interest on consumer protection and took over the area of consumer law as a part of the

[9] Añoveros Terradas (2003); De Miguel Asensio (2005), pp. 79, 80.

[10] Paredes Pérez (2006), p. 92.

[11] The situation of co-existence of these scope rules and article 6 Rome I has also been described as 'unsatisfactory', 'confusing', 'irritating' or 'unnecessary'. Magnus (2016), pp. 23, 24; Weller (2015), pp. 422, 423.

necessary measures to complete the internal market.[12] As a result, a number of directives on consumer contracts were adopted establishing mandatory provisions regarding information requirements, right of withdrawal etc., establishing a common consumer protection standard among all Member States.[13]

Consumer protection directives pursue a double objective: on the one hand, to adapt to the specific needs of the internal market in order achieve a well-functioning internal market; thus, it is required to approximate or harmonise the conditions of competition within the EU while ensuring that fundamental freedoms, like the freedom of provision of services, are safeguarded, and, on the other hand, to protect the consumer, which is the weaker contracting party in this case.[14] A minimum standard of protection of the consumer is to be safeguarded by the consumer directives.

These minimum standards, in order to fulfil the purpose of the directives, need to be ensured not only in situations where all the elements are inside the EU but also sometimes when the professional is located in a non-EU country, for example. The created consumer rights have to be protected when necessary in an international situation.[15] They conform to a minimum scope of protection. In those cases, conflict of laws enters into play since if the law applicable to a consumer contract is not the law of a Member State, the minimum scope of protection of the directive would not be ensured; in the same manner, since many of the consumer protection directives are minimum harmonisation directives, the application of the law of a Member State might be more beneficial or detrimental to the consumer than the law of another Member State.

Therefore, the approach of consumer protection was also present in the area of private international law (PIL), where it was first established by the 1968 Brussels Convention[16] (now Brussels I Regulation recast)[17] concerning jurisdiction and then followed, regarding conflict of laws, by Article 5 of the 1980 Rome Convention on the law applicable to contractual obligations (now article 6 Rome I Regulation).

---

[12] The Maastricht Treaty (1992) introduced Article 129a, later Article 153 EC Treaty, and currently Article 169 TFEU, which provides that 'in order to promote the interests of consumers and to ensure a high level of consumer protection, the Union shall contribute to protecting the health, safety and economic interests of consumers as well as to promoting their right to information, education and to organise themselves in order to safeguard their interests'.

[13] A more detailed description of this process can be found, for instance, in: Micklitz (2009).

[14] Aguilar Grieder (2012), pp. 29, 30.

[15] Micklitz (2009), p. 76.

[16] 1968 Brussels Convention on jurisdiction and the enforcement of judgments in civil and commercial matters (OJ 1972 L 299/32).

[17] Regulation (EU) No 1215/2012 of the European Parliament and of the Council of 12 December 2012 on jurisdiction and the recognition and enforcement of judgments in civil and commercial matters (OJ L 351/1).

4.1.1.1 The First Generation of EU Consumer Directives: Silence Regarding Its Scope of Application

The first generation of EU consumer directives enacted during the eighties include the Doorstep Selling Directive 85/577/ECC,[18] the Consumer Credit Directive 87/102/ECC[19] and the Package Travel Directive 90/314/ECC.[20] The Doorstep Selling Directive, now replaced by the Consumer Rights Directive,[21] set minimum standards of protection for the consumer in case of contracts concluded away from the business premises of the trader, for which it is frequent that the consumer is unprepared, unable to compare the quality or price of the product with other offers, and as a result the element of surprise creates a disadvantage.[22] In these cases, the consumer was granted with a right of cancellation of at least seven days (article 5), which, as it was a minimum harmonisation directive, could be extended by the Member States in their national laws when implementing the Directive. On the other hand, the Consumer Credit Directive, replaced by Directive 2008/48/EC of the European Parliament and of the Council of 23 April 2008 on credit agreements for consumers,[23] laid down minimum standards for consumer credit arrangements within the EU, which consisted especially in information requirements. Again, the terms of a credit might turn out disadvantageous to the consumer, and therefore a better protection of consumers could be achieved by adopting certain requirements. This was also a minimum harmonisation directive, and Member States could decide for a better protection than the minimum required in the Directive. The Package Travel Directive, now replaced by the new version (Directive 2015/2302/EU),[24] aimed to approximate the laws of the Member States regarding packages sold or

---

[18]Council Directive 85/577/EEC of 20 December 1985 to protect the consumer in respect of contracts negotiated away from business premises (OJ 1985 L 372/31) (Doorstep Selling Directive).

[19]Council Directive 87/102/EEC of 22 December 1986 for the approximation of the laws, regulations and administrative provisions of the Member States concerning consumer credit (OJ 1987 L 42/48) (Consumer Credit Directive).

[20]Council Directive 90/314/ECC of 13 June 1990 on package travel, package holidays and package tours (OJ 1990 L 158/59) (Package Travel Directive).

[21]Directive 2011/83/EU of the European Parliament and of the Council of 25 October 2011 on consumer rights, amending Council Directive 93/13/EEC and Directive 1999/44/EC of the European Parliament and of the Council and repealing Council Directive 85/577/EEC and Directive 97/7/EC of the European Parliament and of the Council, (OJ 2011 L 304/64) (Consumer Rights Directive).

[22]Recitals 4 and 5 of the Doorstep Selling Directive.

[23]Directive 2008/48/EC of the European Parliament and of the Council of 23 April 2008 on credit agreements for consumers and repealing Council Directive 87/102/EEC (OJ 2008 L 133/66).

[24]Directive 2015/2302 of the European Parliament and of the Council of 25 November 2015 on package travel and linked travel arrangements, amending Regulation (EC) No 2006/2004 and Directive 2011/83/EU of the European Parliament and of the Council and repealing Council Directive 90/314/EEC (OJ 2015 L 326/1).

offered for sale in the territory of the Community (article 1) since tourism plays an essential role in the achievement of a complete internal market, and the approximation of these issues would help the freedom of provision of services and avoid distortions on competition, as well as benefit consumer protection.

The aforementioned directives were silent about the conflict of laws issue; they only regulated substantive law.[25] In that moment, it was believed that the harmonisation process would eventually set aside PIL issues and, while that was not the case, the Rome Convention could ensure the protection of the consumers in the EU when necessary.[26] However, as it will be explained below, these assumptions proved to be wrong.

The role of determining the law applicable to cross-border consumer contracts was left to the Rome Convention on the law applicable to contractual obligations. Article 5 Rome Convention contained a protective conflict rule for certain consumer contracts, which, in the absence of choice of law, determined as applicable the law of the country in which the consumer has his habitual residence, and in case parties chose the law applicable to the contract, the chosen law could not result in depriving the consumer of the protection afforded to him by the mandatory rules of the law of the country in which he has his habitual residence.[27]

[25]Regarding the Package Travel Directive 90/314, some doubts existed in this regard since article 1 refers to the approximation of the laws in relation to 'packages sold or offered for sale in the territory of the Community'. Some authors have interpreted that reference as a scope rule determining that the directive determines its scope of application through a rigid connecting factor, and it is applicable when the conclusion of the contract takes place on the territory of the Community or when an offer was made in the Community. Fallon and Francq (2000), pp. 159–160.

[26]De la Rosa (2003), p. 154.

[27]Article 5 Rome Convention, covering 'certain consumer contracts' read:

1. This Article applies to a contract the object of which is the supply of goods or services to a person ('the consumer') for a purpose which can be regarded as being outside his trade or profession, or a contract for the provision of credit for that object.
2. Notwithstanding the provisions of Article 3, a choice of law made by the parties shall not have the result of depriving the consumer of the protection afforded to him by the mandatory rules of the law of the country in which he has his habitual residence:

   - if in that country the conclusion of the contract was preceded by a specific invitation addressed to him or by advertising, and he had taken in that country all the steps necessary on his part for the conclusion of the contract, or
   - if the other party or his agent received the consumer's order in that country, or
   - if the contract is for the sale of goods and the consumer travelled from that country to another country and there gave his order, provided that the consumer's journey was arranged by the seller for the purpose of inducing the consumer to buy.

3. Notwithstanding the provisions of Article 4, a contract to which this Article applies shall, in the absence of choice in accordance with Article 3, be governed by the law of the country in which the consumer has his habitual residence if it is entered into in the circumstances described in paragraph 2 of this Article.
4. This Article shall not apply to:

   (a) a contract of carriage;

Article 5 Rome Convention, as well as the other conflict rules of the instrument, aimed at creating legal certainty and security in cross-border transactions, avoiding forum shopping through the uniform conflict rules, enhanced in combination with the Brussels Convention. However, the solutions provided by the Convention were not oriented towards internal market integration.[28] It was soon discovered that article 5 Rome Convention presented important deficiencies. Firstly, article 5 Rome Convention covered a narrow material scope. Article 5 Rome Convention covered certain consumer contracts the object of which was

> the supply of goods or services to a person ('the consumer') for a purpose which can be regarded as being outside his trade or profession, or a person for the provision of credit for that object.

This definition was not only imprecise, but this material scope covered by the article led to several inconsistencies as well, which became more apparent with the generalisation of electronic commerce.[29] Of course, it seems obvious that since the Rome Convention was published in 1980, it focused on the traditional commercial models existing before the thriving of the Internet. Also, several contracts on financial services were not included as a result of the reference to the supply of goods and services in the definition, as well as independent loans not connected to the purpose of financing the supply of goods or services and timeshare agreements on immovable property.[30]

Secondly, regarding its territorial scope, article 5 Rome Convention applied to contracts concluded in one or more of these three specific circumstances: when in the country of habitual residence of the consumer the conclusion of the contract was preceded by a specific invitation addressed to him or by advertising and he had taken in that country all the steps necessary on his part for the conclusion of the contract, when the other party or his agent received the consumer's order in the country of habitual residence of the consumer or when, in the case of a contract for the sale of goods, the consumer travelled from his country of habitual residence to another country to place his order, provided that the consumer's journey was arranged by the seller for the purpose of inducing the consumer to buy. Therefore, article 5 Rome Convention did not protect the 'active' consumer, the consumer that has its own

---

(b) a contract for the supply of services where the services are to be supplied to the consumer exclusively in a country other than that in which he has his habitual residence.

5. Notwithstanding the provisions of paragraph 4, this Article shall apply to a contract which, for an inclusive price, provides for a combination of travel and accommodation.

[28] De la Rosa (2003), pp. 152–156; De la Rosa (2015), p. 60.

[29] Riefa (2004).

[30] Leible (2015), p. 40; Max Planck Institute for Foreign Private and Private International Law (2004), p. 51; Stone (2014), pp. 344, 345.

initiative to enter in a foreign market, but safeguarded only the 'passive' consumer, who is targeted in his home market by the principal. Moreover, specific connections with the country of habitual residence of the consumer were required. However, by stipulating that all the necessary steps for the conclusion of the contract had to be taken in the country of habitual residence of the consumer, article 5 could be easily eluded by the deliberate signing of the contract in another country.

As a result, the requirements of article 5 Rome Convention led to the exclusion of a big number of cross-border consumer contracts, which were then governed by the general conflict rules of the Convention, and therefore not protected against the possible choice of a less favourable law by the principal, or a non-Member State law (which lacked the protection granted by the directives). The most important rule of the Rome Convention was the party autonomy principle (article 3 Rome Convention), which allowed the parties to choose the law applicable to their contract; in the absence of choice, article 4 Rome Convention referred to the law of the country of habitual residence of the party executing the characteristic performance of the contract, according to which in the event that the contract is entered into in the course of that party's trade or profession, *that country shall be the country in which the principal place of business is situated or, where under the terms of the contract the performance is to be effected through a place of business other than the principal place of business, the country in which that other place of business is situated.* Thus, when a consumer contract fell outside the scope of application of article 5 Rome Convention, it was governed by the law defined by article 3 or 4 Rome Convention.

The consumer protection directives required more protection than provided by the Rome Convention. The well-known Gran Canaria cases decided on the German courts constitute the perfect example of the deficiencies of article 5 Rome Convention. In the first generation of the cases, German tourists on holiday in Canary Islands (Spain) were approached in German language to purchase household goods from a German firm acting through an agent in Spain. The contract, drafted in German language, was signed by the parties while on their holiday in Spain. The firm was concluding transactions away from business premises, and the goods were to be delivered to the German tourists once back in Germany. These consumers were to be protected by the minimum standards of the Doorstep Selling Directive, which granted them the right of cancellation. However, in most of the cases, the contract contained a choice of law clause designating Spanish law as applicable, and at the material time Spain had not transposed the Directive into its national law. The circumstances of these consumer contracts did not fall within the material and territorial requirements of article 5 Rome Convention, and therefore German mandatory provisions could not be applied (in case the situation would have fallen within the scope of article 5 Rome Convention, the chosen law could not have resulted in depriving the consumer of the protection afforded to him by the mandatory rules of the law of the country of his habitual residence). Spanish law was applicable as a result of the materiality of article 3 Rome Convention, which allows party autonomy, and as the Spanish law had not transposed the Directive yet, the right of withdrawal was not guaranteed to the consumers.[31] Thus, in these cases, the Rome Convention failed to guarantee the application of the mandatory provisions of the Directive when necessary.

In the second generation of cases, German tourists also on holiday in Canary Islands (Spain) were persuaded to enter into a contract for the acquisition of an interest in real property on a timeshare basis in Spain from companies established in the Isle of Man. Upon their return to Germany, the tourists refused to pay and claimed that German law implementing the Doorstep Selling Directive granted them the right to withdraw from the contract. However, the contract contained a choice of law clause referring to Manx law. The contract did not fall within the requirements of article 5 Rome Convention, and therefore Manx law was applicable as a result of the general rule of freedom of choice of law of the Rome Convention (article 3 Rome Convention). As a result, when the buyers wished to cancel their contracts, this right ensured by the Directive was not granted as Manx law was applicable.[32] If these consumer contracts would have been under the scope of application of article 5 Rome Convention, this right would have been ensured as implemented by German law because the choice of law cannot deprive the consumer from the mandatory rules of his country of habitual residence.[33] Again, the aim of the Directive was to protect the consumer from a Member State in this type of situations, and the protection was not granted.

Therefore, it soon became apparent that the conflict rule designed for consumer protection of the Rome Convention had been narrowly conceived.[34] Article 5 Rome Convention was likely to apply to a small amount of cross-border consumer contracts initiated in the European Community, and as a result the protection provided by the consumer directives was easily circumvented because of the normal operation of the general conflict rules of the Rome Convention.

4.1.1.2 The Second Generation of EU Consumer Directives: Introduction of Scope Rules

The lacunae revealed by the Gran Canaria cases, where German consumers who were approached to enter into consumer contracts in Spain could not enjoy the minimum protection granted by the Doorstep Selling Directive, was tackled by the European legislator in a peculiar manner. As the Rome Convention could not ensure

[31]Francq (2005), pp. 336–339; Wilderspin (2016), p. 484; Francq (2006), pp. 340, 341; Basedow (2004), pp. 276–278.

[32]Wilderspin (2016), p. 484; Francq (2006), pp. 340–341; Kuipers (2012), pp. 212–214.

[33]Although other courts suggested applying the mandatory consumer protection of German law, the *Bundesgerichtshof*, following the Rome Convention, rejected those attempts (BGH 19.3.1997, IPRspr. 1997 no. 34). Max Planck Institute for Foreign Private and Private International Law (2004), p. 53.

[34]Morse (1992), p. 11; Leible (2015), p. 39.

the application of the national mandatory rules implementing the standards of the directives when necessary, the European Community introduced a different approach: since the early nineties, mainly in the area of consumer law, directives started specifically to refer to their own territorial scope of application. Consumer protection directives introduced a specific 'conflict rule' defining the spatial scope of application of the instrument.[35] The provisions differed in their drafting but followed the same method: they determined the scope of application of the respective directive while remaining silent about the application of foreign law. In the Netherlands, these provisions are called 'scope rules'.[36]

The first directive containing this type of rule was the Unfair Contract Terms Directive.[37] This Directive, still in force, approximates the laws of the Member States regarding unfair terms in contracts concluded between a seller or supplier and the consumer (article 1), and it constitutes one of the pillars of consumer protection in the EU.[38] Unfair terms in consumer contracts might cause a significant imbalance to the detriment of the consumer and are contrary to the requirement of fairness. Thus, the Unfair Contract Terms Directive stipulates that standard terms of consumer contracts (excluding the price and the subject matter) can be challenged as unfair by the consumers.[39] Besides regulating substantive aspects, it introduces for the first time a rule determining its international scope of application. Article 6 (2) provides:

> *Member States shall take the necessary measures to ensure that the consumer does not lose the protection granted by this Directive by virtue of the choice of law of a non-Member State as the law applicable to a contract if the latter has a closest connection with the territory of the Member States.*

This provision imposes the application of the Unfair Contract Terms Directive when a contract has a closest connection with one or more Member States, in order to ensure the protection provided to the consumer, when the parties chose the law of a

[35] Wilderspin (2016), p. 485; Kuipers (2012), p. 181 et seq.

[36] See below Sect. 4.3.1 for further explanation and definitions of 'scope rules'.

[37] Council Directive 93/13/EEC of 5 April 1993 on unfair terms in consumer contracts (OJ L 95/29) *(Unfair Contract Terms Directive)*.

[38] Belohlávek (2011), p. 1093.

[39] Regarding choice of law clauses and the Unfair Contract Terms Directive, the ECJ in the Amazon case (C-191/15 *Verein für Konsumenteninformation v Amazon EU Sàrl* [2015] ECLI:EU:C:2016:612) concluded that article 3(1) Unfair Contract Terms Directive should be interpreted 'as meaning that a term in the general terms and conditions of a seller or supplier which has not been individually negotiated, under which the contract concluded with a consumer in the course of electronic commerce is to be governed by the law of the Member State in which the seller or supplier is established, is unfair in so far as it leads the consumer into error by giving him the impression that only the law of that Member State applies to the contract, without informing him that under Article 6(2) of Regulation No 593/2008 he also enjoys the protection of the mandatory provisions of the law that would be applicable in the absence of that term, this being for the national court to ascertain in the light of all the relevant circumstances'.

third country as applicable. Thus, it aims at preventing the parties from circumventing the protection granted by the Directive by choosing the law of a non-Member State.

Similar rules, with slightly different formulation, were provided in article 12 (2) Distance Selling Directive[40] (now repealed by the Consumer Rights Directive[41]), article 7(2) Consumer Sales Directive[42] (amended but not repealed by the Consumer Rights Directive), article 12(2) Distance Marketing of Consumer Financial Services Directive[43] (amended but not repealed by Payment Services Directive 2015/2366[44]) and article 22(4) Consumer Credit Directive.[45] The Distance Selling Directive, aiming at approximating the consumer rules of the Member States regarding distance contracts between consumers and suppliers, contained minimum harmonisation rules on information duties, right of withdrawal and payment possibilities in the case of distance consumer sales contracts. The Consumer Sales Directives cover and harmonise parts of consumer contract law on the sale of goods, which include legal guarantees and, in a lesser extent, commercial guarantees, ensuring, for example, that the goods comply with the description, quality, purpose etc. expected and ensuring the liability of the sellers to remedy the defects existent. The Distance Marketing of Consumer Financial Services Directive includes rules for the marketing of financial services by suppliers to consumers within the EU, which impose on the consumer pre-contractual information obligations to the supplier and the right of withdrawal from the contract within 14 days, and prevents abusive marketing practices. The Consumer Credit Directive (which repealed Council Directive 87/102/EEC, which was silent about its scope of application) contains common rules on credit agreements for consumers, granting information rights and the right

---

[40] Directive 1997/7/EC of the European Parliament and of the Council of 20 May 1997 on the protection of consumers in respect of distance contracts (OJ 144/19) (Distance Selling Directive).

[41] Directive 2011/83/EU of the European Parliament and of the Council of 25 October 2011 on consumer rights, amending Council Directive 93/13/EEC and Directive 1999/44/EC of the European Parliament and of the Council and repealing Council Directive 85/577/EEC and Directive 97/7/EC of the European Parliament and of the Council, (OJ 2011 L 304/64) (Consumer Rights Directive).

[42] Directive 1999/44/EC of the European Parliament and of the Council of 25 May 1999 on certain aspects of the sale of consumer goods and associated guarantees (OJ L171/12) (Consumer Sales Directive).

[43] Directive 2002/65/EC of the European Parliament and of the Council of 23 September 2002 concerning the distance marketing of consumer financial services and amending Council Directive 90/619/EEC and Directives 97/7/EC and 98/27/EC (OJ L 271/16) (Distance Marketing of Consumer Financial Services Directive).

[44] Directive (EU) 2015/2366 of the European Parliament and of the Council of 25 November 2015 on payment services in the internal market, amending Directives 2002/65/EC, 2009/110/EC and 2013/36/EU and Regulation (EU) No 1093/2010, and repealing Directive 2007/64/EC (OJ L 337/35) (Payment Services Directive).

[45] Directive 2008/48/EC of the European Parliament and of the Council of 23 April 2008 on credit agreements for consumers and repealing Council Directive 87/102/EEC (OJ L 133/66) (Consumer Credit Directive).

of withdrawal from the credit agreement within 14 days to the consumer, and granted the possibility of early payment of credit at any time. As a commonality, these consumer protection directives contain a rule imposing the application of their standards of protection when in the consumer contract there is a choice of a non-Member State law and the situation has a close link with the territory of the Member States.

The scope rules contained in the above-mentioned consumer protection directives do not specify which law should be applicable, meaning that they do not refer to the application of the standards of the directive as implemented by the law of the Member State of habitual residence of the consumer, the law of the forum, or whether one should just rely on the minimum standards of the directive, for example. Furthermore, these rules do not preclude the application of the third country law chosen by the parties when this law does not prevent the consumer from the protection granted by the directive.[46] Moreover, they only cover cases where the application of non-Member State law is the result of a choice of law, which means that the consumer would not enjoy the protection of the directives when he travels to another Member State and concludes a consumer contract there with a professional established in a third country.[47]

On the other hand, the Timeshare Directive (Directive 2008/122/EC in the protection of consumers in respect of certain aspects of time-share, long-term holiday product, resale and exchange contracts, replacing Directive 94/47/EC) includes a more specific scope rule. The Timeshare Directive establishes certain obligations regarding information requirements that the vendor of timeshare rights must comply with, and which the Member States must ensure; grants the right of withdrawal from timeshare contracts to the consumer within 14 days after signing the contract; and prohibits advance payments during that period to the consumer.

Article 12(2) Timeshare Directive provides:

> Where the applicable law is that of a third country, consumers shall not be deprived of the protection granted by this Directive, as implemented in the Member State of the forum if (1) any of the immovable properties concerned is situated within the territory of a Member State, or, (2) in the case of a contract not directly related to immovable property, the trader pursues commercial or professional activities in a Member State or, by any means, directs such activities to a Member State and the contract falls within the scope of such activities.

Unlike the other scope rules contained in the other consumer protection directives, this rule specifies which law should apply, referring to the law of the forum implementing the Directive, and it ensures the application of the protection granted by the Directive regardless of whether the third country law is applicable as a result of a choice of law or of the connecting factors used in the absence of choice of law. The forum law would ensure the minimum mandatory protection provided by the Directive.

---

[46] Kuipers (2012), pp. 188, 189.

[47] In the absence of choice of law, article 4 Rome Convention would have led to the law of the country where the professional has his principal place of business.

Therefore, we can differentiate between two categories of directives in regard to their scope rules: those directives with scope rules that entail a flexible connection and those with scope rules that require a rigid connection. That is, the first set of directives that we referred to (Unfair Contract Terms Directive, Distance Sales Directive etc.) has a scope rule with a flexible connection since it does not require any specific connecting factor in the territory of a Member State. This type of scope rules only requires a 'close connection' to the territory of the Member States. On the contrary, the second type of scope rule, which is found in the Timeshare Directive, requires a rigid connection since the scope rule specifies the element of the situation that needs to be in the territory of a Member State in order for the situation to fall under the scope of application of the directive.[48] In the case of the Timeshare Directive, this is when (1) *any of the immovable properties concerned is situated within the territory of a Member State, or,* (2) *in the case of a contract not directly related to immovable property, the trader pursues commercial or professional activities in a Member State or, by any means, directs such activities to a Member State and the contract falls within the scope of such activities.*

4.1.1.3 Evaluation of the Role and Function of Scope Rules Contained in EU Consumer Directives

It has to be noticed that all the aforementioned scope rules contained in consumer protection directives were not enacted to solve a conflict of laws, but they merely aimed to ensure the application of the protection provided by the respective directive when a choice of a non-Member State law could lead to the non-application of the minimum standards of protection of the consumer when the situation is closely connected with the Community.[49] Therefore, to avoid confusions, these types of rules are better referred to as 'scope rules' since they are special applicability rules trying to ensure the effective application of the respective instrument.[50]

Scope rules did not intend to set aside the system of conflict rules established by the Rome Convention. However, they introduced a complementary complex system that required to consider both the Rome Convention and the national rules implementing the scope rules in order to determine the law applicable to consumer contracts. This leads to the existence of as many ways to determine the law

[48] Mathieu (2015), pp. 129, 130.

[49] In the case *Commission v Spain* (Case C-70/03 *Commission v Spain* [2004] ECR I-9657), para 30, the ECJ said: 'As is clear from the 22nd recital of the preamble to Directive 93/13, that provision seeks to avert the risk that, in certain cases, the consumer may be deprived of Community protection by the designation of the law of a non-Member country as the law applicable to the contract. For that purpose, it provides that the protection granted by the directive to consumers in contractual relationships within the Community is to be maintained for contractual relationships involving non- Member countries, as long as the contract has close ties with the territory of the Member States.'

[50] See below Sect. 4.3 for a discussion regarding the nature of scope rules in PIL terms.

applicable to consumer contracts as Member States are. Still, some justify the adequacy of a disperse model on the special needs derived from EU sectorial directives, considering it appropriate to reach the objective of EU market integration.[51] The correct functioning of the internal market as an objective served as a justification for the introduction of scope rules. Sometimes, it is necessary that all market participants are subject to the same rules, which means that EU secondary law should define its spatial scope of application.[52]

The specific purpose of these provisions was to complement the protective conflict rule of the Rome Convention by filling the gaps that article 5 Rome Convention seemed to leave on consumer protection.[53] As it was mentioned, the scope covered by the directives was wider than the scope covered by article 5 Rome Convention, which meant that some situations where consumers were supposed to enjoy the protection provided in the directives were in fact not covered by article 5 Rome Convention, leading to the application of the general connecting factors of the Rome Convention and, sometimes, to the application of a non-Member State law more detrimental to the consumer. For example, while the applicability requirements of article 5 Rome Convention refer to the activities of the professional taking place in (or addressed to) the country of habitual residence of the consumer, article 12 (2) Timeshare Directive declares the protection of the directive applicable when the professional directs his activities to any Member State, not to the Member State of habitual residence of the consumer. Also, in *Commission v Spain*,[54] where Spain was found accountable from failing to correctly implement article 6(2) Unfair Contract Terms Directive into national law, the Commission argued that

> article 6(2) of the directive seeks to ensure that all consumers are protected under all contracts entered into with a seller or supplier, while Article 10a of amended Law 26/1984 *[Spanish law]* affords such protection only for certain types of contracts, that is to say those referred to in Article 5(1) of the Rome Convention, and only when certain conditions are satisfied, namely those laid down in Article 5(2). Those conditions are more restrictive than the sole requirement provided for in Article 6(2) of the directive that 'the [contract] has a close connection with the territory of the Member States'.[55]

The European Court of Justice (ECJ) agreed with the Commission that the term 'close connection' was deliberately vague in order to make it possible to adapt to the circumstances of the case and, as a result, covered more situations than those referred

---

[51] De la Rosa (2007), p. 415.

[52] Ibid., p. 411.

[53] Tenreiro and Karsten (1999), pp. 247–251.

[54] Case C-70/03 *Commission v Spain* [2004] ECR I-9657.

[55] *Commission v Spain* para. 28.

to in article 5 Rome Convention.[56] It is clear therefore that the protection intended by the directives went beyond the scope of application covered by article 5 Rome Convention.[57]

However, scope rules were not very welcomed.[58] First of all, they were unrelated to the system of the Rome Convention.[59] The connecting factor used by the scope rules contained in directives generally referred to a close connection with the territory of a Member State, which differed from the connecting factors contained in the Convention. Although the general expression was intended to make it possible to attend to several links depending on the circumstances of the case,[60] it was inconsistent with the specific connecting factors contained in the Rome Convention. Moreover, questions arise as to when a closest connection occurs or which factors are to be taken into account (place of conclusion of the contract, habitual residence of the parties, place of performance of the contract etc.): Should a contract be subject to EU law whenever it has any type of connection with the EU? Could this connection be, for example, that the consumer is a national of a Member State? Is it necessary that a company directs its activities to the Member States in order to have a close connection?[61]

Such a vague term could also give rise to different implementation in the national law of the Member States since, as long as it is according to the purposes of the directive, each Member State can implement the rule as they wish, which would naturally lead to inconsistencies.[62] In this regard, the directives did not define the law on which Member State should be applicable: Could Member States determine the law applicable to the consumer contract in those cases? Was it possible for the

[56]The ECJ held that 'as regards ties with the Community, Article 6(2) of the directive merely states that the contract is to have "a close connection with the territory of the Member States". That general expression seeks to make it possible to take account of various ties depending on the circumstances of the case.' The judgment continues: 'Although concrete effect may be given to the deliberately vague term "close connection" chosen by the Community legislature by means of presumptions, it cannot, on the other hand, be circumscribed by a combination of predetermined criteria for ties such as the cumulative conditions as to residence and conclusion of the contract referred to in Article 5 of the Rome Convention' (*Commission v Spain*, paras. 22–23).

[57]See below Sect. 4.2.1.2 for a further commentary about this case. Also, in this regard: Paredes Pérez (2006), pp. 97–100; De la Rosa (2005); Vilà Costa and Gardeñes Santiago (2002), pp. 296–302.

[58]Ragno (2009), pp. 188, 189; Jayme and Kohler (1995). Even in the Commission's Green Paper regarding the conversion of the Rome Convention into the Rome I Regulation, it was commented that the proliferation of these rules were a source of concern, referring to problems such as the transposition of the state or the dispersion of conflict rules among different instruments (Green Paper on the conversion of the Rome Convention of 1980 on the law applicable to contractual obligations, COM (2002) 654 final, 17, 18).

[59]For a more extensive explanation in this regard, see Jayme and Kohler (1995).

[60]*Commission v Spain* para. 32.

[61]De la Rosa (2015), p. 61; Francq (2006), pp. 346, 347.

[62]Which, in fact, it did. In this regard, see Sect. 4.2.1 referring to the implementation of scope rules in the national law of the Member States; also, Max Planck Institute for Foreign Private and Private International Law (n 22) 13–14, referring, for further explanation in note 42, to Bitterich (2003), pp. 522–533; Klauer (2002), pp. 267–330.

Member States to submit all consumer contracts with close connections with the EU to the law of the forum?[63] It is also noticeable that the wording of the different scope rules of the directives, although similar, contained some unnecessary terminological variants.[64] For example, while some provisions referred to a close connection with the 'territory of *one or more* Member States',[65] others referred to the 'territory of *the Member States*',[66] creating doubt as to whether the connection with just one Member State is sufficient. On the other hand, it is true that the scope rule found in the Timeshare Directive, article 12(2), does not lead to different implementation among the Member States since it determines exactly in which circumstances the Directive should apply and according to which law (the law of the forum).[67]

Furthermore, the unilateral approach of the scope rules, determining the scope of the instrument without referring to foreign law, clashed with the multilateral nature of the Rome Convention. The Rome Convention mainly followed the traditional multilateral conflict of laws method, with conflict rules that designated the applicable law through connecting factors based on the abstract legal relationship, regardless of whether the designated law was the law of the forum or a foreign law. The main exception to this multilateral method was through the application of overriding mandatory rules, which applied regardless of the law applicable to the contract. Introducing an old-fashioned unilateral approach that did not fit within the system that only determined the scope of the instrument and ignored foreign law seemed disrupting for the normal operation of the conflict of laws system.

Moreover, the relationship between the scope rules of the consumer protection directives and the Rome Convention also created doubts. It is commonly admitted that the application of the scope rules preceded the application of the Rome Convention on the ground that article 20 Rome Convention gave priority to the conflict rules

> which are or will be contained in acts of the institutions of the European Communities or in national laws harmonized in implementation of such acts.

In fact, most considered this provision the reflexion of the maxim *lex specialis derogat legi generali*, which would lead to the same result.[68] However, there was no agreement on this, leaving doubt on whether the conflict rules of the Rome

---

[63]De la Rosa (2015), p. 61.

[64]De la Rosa (2003), pp. 136, 137.

[65]E.g. Article 12(2) Directive 97/7/EC (Distance Selling Directive); article 12(2) Directive 2002/65/EC (Distance Marketing of Consumer Financial Services Directive).

[66]E.g. Article 6(2) Directive 93/13/EC (Unfair Contract Terms Directive); article 7(2) Directive 1999/44/EC (Consumer Sales Directive).

[67]See above Sect. 4.1.1.2. De la Rosa (2015), pp. 67, 68.

[68]Francq (2006), p. 354; Kramer (2015), p. 9.

Convention should operate in advance since the definition of these scope rules as conflict of law rules was not certain.[69]

Also, the existence of scope rules in the directives frustrated one of the aims of the Rome Convention, which was the unification of conflict of laws for contractual obligations, since Member States implemented the scope rules of the directives in their national laws in very diverse manners, tending to favour their own territory rather than the territory of the Community.[70] If the aim is to unify the conflict rules among the EU countries, the existence of disperse and diverse scope rules among the Member States interrupts such objective. Finally, it is necessary to mention the complication of the task of the legal practitioner that dispersed conflict rules entail. All these issues put in doubt whether the scope rules would fulfil their aim of enhancing consumer protection or whether all the complications deriving from their operation would at the end become detrimental to consumers.

4.1.1.4 A New Approach for the Earlier Directives Lacking a Scope Rule: The *Ingmar* Case

Besides the specific conflict rules contained in consumer protection directives enacted since the nineties, judge-made scope rules were introduced by the ECJ, aiming to repair the deficiency from older directives that did not contain a scope rule. In the *Ingmar* case,[71] the ECJ introduced a scope rule for the Commercial Agents Directive, which was silent about its scope of application. Although that is not a consumer protection directive, the result could easily be extended to the consumer protection directives enacted before the nineties.

The *Ingmar* case involved the claim of a commercial agent, Ingmar, domiciled in the UK, against its principal established in California, claiming some rights deriving from the termination of its contract on the basis of the English law transposing the Commercial Agents Directive.[72] While Ingmar was performing its services exclusively in the UK and Ireland, there was a choice of law in the contract for Californian law. The ECJ was asked in a preliminary ruling to clarify whether some provisions of the Commercial Agents Directive were applicable when a commercial agent performs its activities within a Member State, regardless of the establishment of the principal on a third state and the choice of a third state law to govern their contract.

[69]Magnus U, Mankowski P (2002) Joint Response to the Green Paper on the conversion of the Rome Convention on the Law Applicable to Contractual Obligations into a Community Instrument and its Modernisation (COM 2002) 654 final, p. 6.

[70]Ibid., p. 6.

[71]Case C-381/98, *Ingmar GB Ltd v Eaton Leonard Technologies Inc.* [2000] *ECR* I-9305. Regarding the influence of Ingmar on the interpretation of overriding mandatory rules and weaker party protection, see Sect. 3.3.1.1; also, for a more extensive description of the judgment regarding commercial agency contracts, see Sect. 6.2.2.

[72]For a general commentary regarding the Ingmar case, see: Font i Segura (2009); also, Verhagen (2002).

The ECJ concluded that the purpose these provisions serve requires their application where the situation is closely connected with the Community, irrespective of the law chosen by the parties to govern their contract.[73] According to the ECJ, a close link with the EU exists when the agent carries on his activity within one Member State, regardless of the establishment of the principal in a third country and the choice of a third state law. The reasoning relied on the nature and purpose of the Commercial Agents Directive as decisive factors in determining its international scope of application, as in the event that the situation is closely connected to the EU, the application of the provisions of the Directive becomes essential for the undistorted competition and the security of commercial transactions within the internal market.[74]

From the ECJ ruling followed the idea that directives might implicitly determine their own scope of application.[75] In the case of consumer protection directives, this approach would have affected the directives enacted before the nineties that did not contain a specific scope rule (i.e. the Doorstep Selling Directive, Consumer Credit Directive and Package Travel Directive). It was argued that these directives clearly covered some situations, e.g. contracts concluded between a consumer with habitual residence in a Member State and a professional established in another Member State, while they clearly did not aim to cover other situations, e.g. a contract between a Mexican consumer and a Brazilian professional.[76] These limitations on their scopes would mean, according to some authors, that the directives themselves delimit their own scope of application, even though they do not include an explicit scope rule.[77]

However, besides the criticisms that the specific conflict rules existent in directives received, the existence of judge-made conflict rules and implicit scope rules in directives added the factor of the unknown and thus legal uncertainty to the already confusing system.[78] As a result of the *Ingmar* case, the focus of the discussion was around the excessive mandatoriness of the provisions of EU secondary law against the application of a foreign non-EU law in extra-EU situations.[79] However, the confusing scope of application of the consumer protection directives, and their difficult interaction with the Rome Convention, also needed to be redefined, which was expected with the conversion of the Rome Convention into a Community instrument: the Rome I Regulation.

---

[73] *Ingmar*, para. 25.

[74] *Ingmar*, paras. 23 and 25.

[75] Francq (2006), p. 343.

[76] Ibid., p. 341.

[77] Ibid., p. 341; Van Bochove (2014), p. 154; Roth (2002), p. 381.

[78] See Sect. 4.1.1.3 regarding the general criticisms referring to the existence of scope rules in consumer protection directives. Regarding the specific discussion about judge-made and implicit scope rules, Magnus U, Mankowski P (2002) Joint Response to the Green Paper on the conversion of the Rome Convention on the Law Applicable to Contractual Obligations into a Community Instrument and its Modernisation (COM 2002) 654 final, pp. 7, 8.

[79] Some literature in this regard: Kramer (2015), Van Bochove (2014), Sánchez Lorenzo (2010), Verhagen (2002) and Fallon and Francq (2000).

4.1.2 *From the Rome Convention to the Rome I Regulation: The Expected Solution to the Problem?*

4.1.2.1 The Long Discussion and the Multiple Proposals Regarding a New Consumer Contract Conflict Rule in the Rome I Regulation and Coordination with EU Consumer Directives

The controversy surrounding article 5 Rome Convention, the protective conflict rule for consumer contracts, was evidenced by the many proposals of the European Commission, and private international law scholars suggested for the redrafting of this provision during the conversion of the Rome Convention into the Rome I Regulation, which will be the object of analysis below. Besides the change of legal nature to transform the Convention into a community instrument, the intention was to take advantage of this transformation and modernise its most controversial provisions. In fact, it has been affirmed that the most controversial provision contained in the Rome Convention was article 5 Rome Convention.[80] Firstly, because of its narrow material and territorial scope, it leaves without protection situations in which a Member State consumer is supposed to be protected. The scope of article 5 Rome Convention is confined to certain types of contracts, concluded in very precise circumstances, which, for example, in most of the cases would not include mobile consumers (e.g. Gran Canaria cases). Secondly, and related to the previous reason, the controversy also arose because of the difficult relationship of the provision with EU consumer directives. Consumer protection directives, in order to remedy the insufficient protection of article 5 Rome Convention, started to include scope rules determining their own scope of application. The proliferation of these type of rules contained in sectoral instruments of Community secondary law was subject to extensive comments and criticism, mainly focused on the different nature of the scope rules compared with the traditional conflict rules, which may distort the conflict of laws system, and on the diverse transposition by the Member States of these scope rules, which sometimes were transposed as to delimit the scope of national law.

As a result, the Commission in the *Green Paper on the conversion of the Rome Convention of 1980 on the law applicable to contractual obligations into a Community instrument and its modernisation*, after summarising the aforementioned issues regarding article 5 Rome Convention, developed a number of alternatives for the new drafting of the provision to be subject to discussion.[81] Bearing in mind the general concerns regarding consumer protection and the balance of the interests

[80] Magnus U, Mankowski P (2002) Joint Response to the Green Paper on the conversion of the Rome Convention on the Law Applicable to Contractual Obligations into a Community Instrument and its Modernisation (COM 2002) 654 final, p. 23.

[81] Green Paper on the conversion of the Rome Convention of 1980 on the law applicable to contractual obligations into a Community instrument and its modernisation (COM(2002) 654 final).

of the parties and aiming to develop clear, general and broad rules, the Green Paper considered eight different alternatives for the drafting of the new conflict rule on consumer contracts.[82] The suggested options included the following:

(1) Maintain article 5 Rome Convention as it was, adding a clause guaranteeing the Community minimum standards. The clause that the Commission was referring to was a similar clause to article 3(3) Rome Convention but for intra-EU cases, that is a clause that provided that the parties cannot circumvent the minimum standards imposed by a directive by choosing as applicable the law of a third country for contracts purely internal to the Community. Even if this solution was not the one taken by the Rome I Regulation, since article 5 Rome Convention was modified, such a clause for intra-EU cases was eventually introduced in article 3(4) Rome I as a limit to party autonomy. However, this clause does not determine itself the applicable law but only limits party autonomy. The mechanism is different from conflict rules. Also, it only ensures the application of EU directives when all the elements of the contract are located in the EU.
(2) Maintain article 5 but enlarge its scope in order to include mobile consumers and maybe the types of contracts excluded. However, this solution has as a starting point the adequacy of article 5 Rome Convention to determine the law applicable, and the only modification required pertains to the scope of application.
(3) Generalise the application of articles 3 and 4 Rome Convention (the general conflict rules) to cover consumer contracts but combine them with the mandatory rules of the country of habitual residence of the consumer. This solution will result in the application of the law of the place where the business is established but combined with the application of the mandatory rules of protection of the law of the consumer's habitual place of residence. Despite the foreseeability this option would bring, there are several practical downsides, such as the increase of the cases of depeçage of the contract. Also, would all the consumer contracts be included (i.e. also the ones including active consumers)?

Both options (2) and (3) involve the task of identifying the mandatory provisions of the country of habitual residence of the consumer.

(4) For matters harmonised at the Community level, apply the chosen law; for matters not harmonised, the consumer should not be deprived of the protection provided by the mandatory rules of the country of his habitual residence. Thus, in matters harmonised by the EU directives, party autonomy is completely allowed. Such a solution is based on the ground that a minimum mandatory standard of protection exists in all Member States, and therefore it does not matter that parties choose the law of another Member State since that minimum standard of protection is ensured. This solution would require, however, to differentiate between intra-EU cases, in which party autonomy is allowed, and extra-EU cases, where the choice of a third state law should be limited, in the

[82]Green Paper para. 3.2.7.3 i–viii at pp. 30–32.

same manner as it is limited in cases of areas that are not harmonised at EU level. Although this option reflects the needs of the EU in consumer protection and regarding the application of EU directives, it seems very complicated at first sight.

(5) Apply the law of the country of habitual residence of the consumer, that is, a complete exclusion of party autonomy in the case of a consumer contract falling under the scope of the specific rule. This option has been seriously taken into account since several jurisdictions around the world exclude freedom of choice of law regarding consumer contracts (e.g. article 120(2) of the Swiss Act on Private International Law).[83] On the one hand, this solution would avoid the depeçage of the contract and the difficulty of determining which mandatory rules should apply. Thus, it enhances legal certainty and reduces litigation costs. In addition, it respects the expectations of the consumer of having his own law applied. On the other hand, the professional would find it more burdensome to trade among the different Member States since he would have to adapt his business to every consumer law of every Member State. As a result, he would be more reluctant to conduct his business in a different Member State, and the additional effort of adapting to a foreign law can also be reflected in the costs and final price of the service or product. Besides the increase of the final cost, the exclusion of party autonomy also might affect the consumers since they are deprived of the possible choice of law that is more beneficial to them.[84] Even if the legislator considered this option, it would still be necessary to review the conditions of application of the conflict rule.

(6) Follow the drafting of article 15 Brussels I Regulation (regarding the conditions of application of the rule). The consumer would be under the protective rule when the professional directs his professional activities to the country of habitual residence of the consumer. Most of the authors supported the implementation of a provision parallel to article 15 Brussels I Regulation in order to keep a parallelism between jurisdiction and the applicable law.[85] At this point, it has to be noticed that consumer claims are usually small claims, and therefore it would be exceedingly costly and inefficient for a judge to apply (systematically) a foreign law; thus, the synchronisation between the rules on jurisdiction and applicable law seemed like the logical solution.[86]

(7) Follow the drafting of article 15 Brussels I Regulation, adding the condition that the law of the country of habitual residence of the consumer could only be applicable if the supplier was or should have been aware of it.

---

[83] See Sect. 2.4.1.1.

[84] About the debate regarding party autonomy in consumer contracts, see Sect. 2.4.1.

[85] To cite some: Max Planck Institute for Foreign Private and Private International Law (2004), p. 52 et seq.; Magnus U, Mankowski P (2002) Joint Response to the Green Paper on the conversion of the Rome Convention on the Law Applicable to Contractual Obligations into a Community Instrument and its Modernisation (COM 2002) 654 final, p. 24; Bernardeau (2003), p. 85.

[86] Max Planck Institute for Foreign Private and Private International Law (2004), pp. 54–56.

(8) Have a complete change of approach, making the rule applicable to all consumers but only allowing a very limited freedom of choice of law, such as only allowing the choice of the law of the country where the professional is established.[87] Still, it would have to be proved that the consumer had made an informed choice (including information on all rights and obligations conferred on him by the law of the business' habitual residence). Otherwise, the law applicable would be the law of the consumer's habitual residence or the mandatory provisions of that law. This option would only be applicable to businesses domiciled in Member States, while those with domicile in a third country would be subject to the mandatory provisions of the country of habitual residence of the consumer when they choose another applicable law since within the EU the minimum standards of protection are ensured. However, this option brings several downsides. First, it is complex to determine which information is necessary to provide, and, second, even if all the relevant information about consumer law was provided, it is still unlikely that consumers would read it or, in some cases, fully understand it. It does not seem reasonable to expect consumers to compare their own law with the chosen law.[88]

The solution suggested in the Proposal for the Rome I Regulation was a combination of some of the aforementioned.[89] The most surprising change was the complete exclusion of party autonomy. Instead of a restricted choice of law, article 5 Proposal Rome I did not consider that possibility at all. Instead, the law applicable to consumer contracts was systematically the law of the country of habitual residence of the consumer.[90] As it has been previously explained, the complete elimination of party autonomy avoids the complications of the 'preferential law' approach: the judge does not need to identify and compare the law chosen by the parties and the law of the habitual place of residence of the consumer, and the possible depeçage of the contract is avoided. It avoids the complex process of identifying the relevant mandatory rules and compares them, and promotes predictability. In addition, from an economic perspective, it seems more 'fair' that the internationalisation costs of the contract are assumed by the professional since consumers effectuate cross-border transactions for only a limited amount of time, while professionals do it on a frequent basis. It seems more equitable that the cost of 'internationalisation' is assumed by the professional, which effectuates more transactions and thus is able spread those costs.[91] Nevertheless, despite the advantages it brings, I already submitted that it brings several downsides: professionals could be more reluctant to cross-border

[87]Green Paper para. 3.2.7.3 i–viii at pp. 30–32.

[88]Tang (2007), pp. 115–117.

[89]Proposal for a Regulation of the European Parliament and the Council on the law applicable to contractual obligations (Rome I), COM(2005) 650 final.

[90]Article 5(1) Proposal Rome I: '1. Consumer contracts within the meaning and in the conditions provided for by paragraph 2 shall be governed by the law of the Member State in which the consumer has his habitual residence.'

[91]Explanatory Memorandum Proposal Rome I COM(2005) 650 final (p. 6).

trade, the final cost of the product could be incremented because of the effort of adapting to a foreign law and the exclusion of party autonomy also might affect the consumers since they are deprived of the possible choice of law that is more beneficial to them.[92] In addition, such a solution does not take into account the harmonisaton efforts within the EU. Consumers are supposed to enjoy a minimum mandatory protection level within the EU, and thus it should not matter if the contract provides for a choice of law of another Member State since consumers can only benefit from that.

Regarding the scope covered by the provision, it included the targeted activity test, in the same manner that the current article 6 Rome I provides, and thus it was parallel to article 15 Brussels I Regulation.[93] Besides that, it included in paragraph 2 the 'awareness test' ('unless the professional did not know where the consumer had his habitual residence and this ignorance was not attributable to his negligence'), which, in fact, did not add any change to the provision since in cases where the professional directs his activities to a Member State, it seems obvious that he is aware that the consumer has his habitual place there.[94] Finally, like the current provision, it included a list of excluded consumer contracts.[95] Without any doubt, the scope covered by the provision was wider than article 5 Rome Convention. The definitions of consumer and professional were clarified; the material scope covered all consumer contracts that complied with the definition of consumer and professional, except the ones specified in the exceptions in paragraph 3; and the territorial scope was defined by the targeted activity test. The main criticism regarding its scope was that it only covered consumers with habitual residence in a Member State, taking therefore a unilateral approach when it comes to protection. As a result, a consumer with habitual residence in a non-Member State contracting in the territory of the Community, even targeted by EU professionals, would not be protected by the special conflict rule of article 5 Proposal Rome I. That distinction between Member

---

[92]Section 2.4.1.1.

[93]Article 5(2) Proposal Rome I: 'Paragraph 1 shall apply to contracts concluded by a natural person, the consumer, who has his habitual residence in a Member State for a purpose which can be regarded as being outside his trade or profession with another person, the professional, acting in the exercise of his trade or profession. It shall apply on condition that the contract has been concluded with a person who pursues a trade or profession in the Member State in which the consumer has his habitual residence or, by any means, directs such activities to that Member State or to several States including that Member State, and the contract falls within the scope of such activities, unless the professional did not know where the consumer had his habitual residence and this ignorance was not attributable to his negligence.'

[94]For a more detailed explanation, see Max Planck Institute for Foreign Private and Private International Law (2007), pp. 273–276.

[95]Article 5(3) Proposal Rome I: 'Paragraph 1 shall not apply to: (a) a contract for the supply of services where the services are to be supplied to the consumer exclusively in a country other than that in which he has his habitual residence; (b) contracts of carriage other than contracts relating to package travel within the meaning of Directive 90/314/EEC of 13 June 1990; (c) contracts relating to a right in rem or right of use in immovable property other than contracts relating to a right of user on a timeshare basis within the meaning of Directive 94/47/EC of 26 October 1994.'

State consumers and non-Member State consumers was considered by the majority of authors as unjustified and discriminatory since there was no background to deny consumers from outside the EU the protection granted to them by their own laws.[96] Whether consumers from outside the EU should fall under the scope of the protective conflict rules of the EU must be the subject of analysis. The protective rule of the Rome I Proposal only covered consumers with habitual residence in the EU who were targeted by a professional in order to enter into a consumer contract. Thus, active consumers with habitual residence in the EU and all types of consumers with no habitual residence in the EU (both purchasing actively and targeted by a professional) would be subject to the general rules. The law applicable to the latter cases would be the law of habitual residence of the professional or, in the case of a choice of law clause, the law chosen. Consumers that contract on their own initiative are excluded regardless of their place of habitual residence. Thus, in order to discern whether there is an unjustified and discriminatory treatment towards non-EU consumers, we need to focus on the non-EU consumer that is targeted by a professional in a Member State:

The Rome instruments have a universal character (*erga omnes*) to determine the law applicable to a contract, according to which the conflict rules will design the law applicable to the contract regardless of whether it is a law from a Member State or a third state. However, article 5 Proposal Rome I introduces a unilateral approach. Instead of using a multilateral conflict rule such as 'the law applicable to a consumer contract is the law of the place of habitual residence of the consumer', regardless of whether that is a law from a Member State or a third state, article 5 Proposal Rome I provided something like 'the law of the Member State of habitual residence of the consumer will be applicable when...'.[97] Since consumers from outside the EU are receiving a different treatment, such differentiation should be justified in order to be compatible with the universal character of the instrument and its multilateral nature, as well as to not be considered discriminatory. Although the legislator did not provide for any explanation in this regard, the unilateral approach favouring EU consumers seems to have its basis on EU internal market integration purposes.[98] However, while EU integration purposes might justify different treatment in specific cases (e.g. when dealing with EU consumer directives, a possible differentiation could be made between intra-EU and extra-EU consumer contracts), it does not seem to justify the conflict rule of article 5 Proposal Rome I, under which the condition for application is the habitual residence of the consumer in a Member State. First, it is necessary to take into account the fact that the specialty of the protective conflict rule in consumer contracts is based on the need for protecting the consumer against the normal operation of conflict rules to compensate his weaker position in the contract, and EU integration purposes should be an addition rather than the main purpose of

---

[96] In this regard, see for example: Añoveros Terradas (2006), p. 386 et seq.; Lagarde (2006), p. 342; Max Planck Institute for Foreign Private and Private International Law (2007), p. 48.

[97] Lagarde (2006), p. 342.

[98] Añoveros Terradas (2006), pp. 388, 389.

the rule. Second, which is the EU objective that requires that non-EU consumers are excluded from the protective conflict rule? When the consumer is not a resident of the EU and the professional is also from a non-EU country, the only link with the EU is probably that it was the place where the contracting took place. When the consumer's habitual residence is not in a Member State but the professional who is targeting him is from a Member State, the EU professional sees himself benefited by the exclusion of the non-EU consumer from the protective conflict rule since the law applicable would be the law of the place of the professional (i.e. a Member State law) or maybe a low consumer protection chosen law. The EU companies would not have to deal with a different or more protective consumer law from the country of habitual residence of the consumer. In addition, they would not have to deal with the extra information and adaptation costs to a foreign law.[99] In this case, the protective conflict rule of article 5 Rome I Proposal benefits EU companies to the detriment of non-EU consumers. From a unilateral PIL approach, this technique is justified since conflict of laws is solved from the point of view of the forum without taking into account foreign law. There is nothing that ensures that the conflict rules of a non-EU country provide that when a company of their country targets a consumer from a Member State, the law of the Member State of the consumer would be applied by their courts. I consider that a unilateral approach is justified when important interests are at stake and, thus, could even be justified in certain cases to ensure the application of the protection of EU consumer directives.[100] Nevertheless, since the unilateral technique of article 5 Rome I Proposal only discriminates non-EU consumers while benefiting EU professionals, I do not think that EU integration purposes, or legal certainty, justify that different treatment. An EU professional who is targeting consumers from a foreign market can reasonably predict and expect that the consumer law of the country of the consumer might apply to a possible claim.

Still, the aforementioned scenario is not very likely to happen in practice. Imagine a US citizen going on a holiday to Spain and targeted at the airport in the US by a Spanish company. If he wishes, the US citizen can sue the company in Spanish courts. Brussels I Regulation (now Brussels I bis) cannot give judicial competence to courts of non-Member States, but it does not require for the consumer to have habitual residence in a Member State in order to point a Member State court as competent. A US citizen can sue a Spanish company in Spanish courts since that is the place of habitual residence of the defendant. In practice, it seems more practical that the consumer with habitual residence in the US would sue the company back in the US in the consumer's home jurisdiction, but he has the option of starting proceedings in Spain.

Regarding the relationship between the consumer conflict rules and the scope rules contained in some consumer protection directives, article 22 Proposal Rome I is of interest. Article 22 Proposal Rome I aimed to clarify the relationship between the Regulation and some European directives, giving specific conflict rules priority

---

[99] On the same opinion, Ibid., p. 392.

[100] In this regard, see below Sect. 4.3.3.

over the provisions of the Regulation and referring to Annex I, which included a list of directives containing conflict rules. However, only four directives were on the list of Annex I: Return of Cultural Objects Directive,[101] Posted Workers Directive,[102] Second Non-life Insurance Directive[103] and Second Life Assurance Directive.[104] Consumer protection directives were not listed. It is true that, since article 5 Proposal Rome I excluded party autonomy and the scope rules of directives only claimed application of the instrument when there was a choice of law, the scope rules on consumer protection directives could turn irrelevant.[105] However, the scope of consumer protection covered by the directives was still wider than the scope covered by article 5 Proposal Rome I, which meant that the situation remained unsolved.[106]

Still, article 3(5) Proposal Rome I provided that when there was a choice of a non-Member State law,

> *that choice shall be without prejudice to the application of such mandatory rules of Community law as are applicable to the case.*

This provision aimed to ensure the application of mandatory Community law when applicable to the case, and it would have covered the situations that claimed application according to the scope rules of the directives. However, instead of achieving this conciliating aim, it would have caused more uncertainty to the situation because of all the problems that its broad wording would have caused. For example, first of all, it would have covered intra-EU and extra-EU situations, without determining which is the connection necessary in order to apply mandatory EU law in extra-EU situations. Thus, the scope rules of the consumer protection directives would still be necessary so as to determine the connection necessary with the EU. Second, article 3(5) Proposal Rome I did not clarify which law would be applicable for the application of the mandatory rules of Community law: the law most closely connected to the case, the law of the forum, the law applicable in the absence of choice of law etc. Hence, this provision would not improve the situation

[101] Council Directive 93/7/EEC of 15 March 1993 on the return of cultural objects unlawfully removed from the territory of a Member State (OJ L 74/1), now replaced by Directive 2014/60/EU of the European Parliament and of the Council of 15 May 2014 on the return of cultural objects unlawfully removed from the territory of a Member State and amending Regulation (EU) No 1024/ 2012 (Recast) (OJ L 159/1).

[102] Directive 96/71/EC of the European Parliament and of the Council of 16 December 1996 concerning the posting of workers in the framework of the provision of services (OJ L 18/1).

[103] Second Council Directive 88/357/EEC of 22 June 1988 on the coordination of laws, regulations and administrative provisions relating to direct insurance other than life assurance and laying down provisions to facilitate the effective exercise of freedom to provide services and amending Directive 73/239/EEC [*1988*] (OJ L 1 72/1), as amplified and amended by Directives 49/1992/EC and 13/2002/EC.

[104] Directive 619/1990/EEC of 8.1.1990 as amplified and amended by Directives 96/1992/EC and 12/ 2002/EC.

[105] Weller (2015), pp. 419, 420.

[106] Kuipers (2012), p. 210 et seq.

regarding the scope of application of consumer protection directives but rather would make the system more confusing due to its various possible interpretations.[107] Legal certainty is not benefited from such approach.

Therefore, we can say that the Proposal for Rome I, although improving consumer protection on conflict of laws by extending the scope of the protective conflict rule, did not solve the problem on the relationship between the consumer protective conflict rules and the existent scope rules in consumer protection directives.

4.1.2.2 The Final Solution: Article 6 Rome I, Article 3(4) Rome I and Article 23 Rome I as Mechanisms of Coordination Between Rome I and the Scope Rules on EU Consumer Directives

Regarding the final draft of the Rome I Regulation, after the numerous suggestions, discussions and comments, the end result failed to solve one of its most controversial problems, in particular the relationship between article 5 Rome Convention (now article 6 Rome I) and the scope rules contained in some consumer protection directives.

As it has been explained in the previous chapter, article 6 Rome I has brought a number of modifications compared with its predecessor, and without any doubt it improved consumer protection at the conflict of laws level.[108]

First, unlike Proposal Rome I, it provides protection to both EU and non-EU consumers regardless of the place of habitual residence of the parties (i.e. universal

---

[107] Aguilar Grieder (2006), p. 58; Oprea (2010), pp. 4–7; Max Planck Institute for Foreign Private and Private International Law (2007), pp. 240–243.

[108] Article 6 Rome I reads:

> 1. Without prejudice to Articles 5 and 7, a contract concluded by a natural person for a purpose which can be regarded as being outside his trade or profession (the consumer) with another person acting in the exercise of his trade or profession (the professional) shall be governed by the law of the country where the consumer has his habitual residence, provided that the professional:
>
>   (a) pursues his commercial or professional activities in the country where the consumer has his habitual residence, or
>   (b) by any means, directs such activities to that country or to several countries including that country,
>
>   and the contract falls within the scope of such activities.
>
> 2. Notwithstanding paragraph 1, the parties may choose the law applicable to a contract which fulfils the requirements of paragraph 1, in accordance with Article 3. Such a choice may not, however, have the result of depriving the consumer of the protection afforded to him by provisions that cannot be derogated from by agreement by virtue of the law which, in the absence of choice, would have been applicable on the basis of paragraph 1.
> 3. If the requirements in points (a) or (b) of paragraph 1 are not fulfilled, the law applicable to a contract between a consumer and a professional shall be determined pursuant to Articles 3 and 4.
> 4. Paragraphs 1 and 2 shall not apply to:

scope of application), and therefore all consumer contracts within its material and territorial scope of application are governed by the law determined by this provision rather than by the general conflict rules of Rome I (i.e. articles 3 and 4 Rome I).

Regarding its material scope, the consumer must be an individual acting outside its trade or profession (not acting for business purposes); the professional party must be acting in the course of its trade or profession, and the contract must fall within the scope of the professional's activities. Hence, the material scope is just determined by the definition of consumer and professional, rather than covering specific consumer contracts, making it wider. Contrarily, article 6(4) Rome I includes a list of excluded contracts.

Regarding the territorial scope, it is defined by the targeted activity test and thus is kept parallel to the Brussels I Regulation (now Brussels I recast). In order to ensure that the consumer is guaranteed the protection offered by the law of his country of habitual residence only in cases where the contract or the supplier has a sufficient connection with that country, the contract will be regarded as a consumer contract under article 6 Rome I only when the professional pursues his commercial or professional activities in the country where the consumer has his habitual residence or, by any means, directs such activities to that country or to several countries, including that country. This criterion of targeted activities allows to accommodate within the provision the specialties required by the electronic commerce.[109] If the consumer contract falls within the above-mentioned requirements, the applicable law in the absence of choice of law would be the law of the country of habitual residence of the consumer. However, unlike Proposal Rome I, this provision admits a restricted choice of law: article 6(2) provides that it is effective with the condition that the law chosen provides for the same protection as or more protection than the mandatory rules of the country of habitual residence of the consumer (the so-called preferential law approach).

(a) a contract for the supply of services where the services are to be supplied to the consumer exclusively in a country other than that in which he has his habitual residence;

(b) a contract of carriage other than a contract relating to package travel within the meaning of Council Directive 90/314/EEC of 13 June 1990 on package travel, package holidays and package tours;

(c) a contract relating to a right *in rem* in immovable property or a tenancy of immovable property other than a contract relating to the right to use immovable properties on a timeshare basis within the meaning of Directive 94/47/EC;

(d) rights and obligations which constitute a financial instrument and rights and obligations constituting the terms and conditions governing the issuance or offer to the public and public take-over bids of transferable securities, and the subscription and redemption of units in collective investment undertakings in so far as these activities do not constitute provision of a financial service;

(e) a contract concluded within the type of system falling within the scope of Article 4(1) (h).

[109]Leible (2015), p. 42.

Therefore, article 6 Rome I extends its scope of application, covering more consumer contracts than its predecessor. However, the material and territorial scope of application is still narrow in comparison with the intended scope of application of the consumer protection directives. For example, the directives cover more consumer contract types than those covered by article 6 Rome I because of the exclusions provided in article 6(4) Rome I. Several contracts excluded by article 6(4) Rome I could fall within the definition of consumer contract under article 6(1) Rome I, but instead they are excluded from the operation of the protective conflict rule contained in the provision, for example contracts for the supply of services in which the service is exclusively provided in a country other than the country of habitual residence of the consumer, contracts relating to a right in rem in immovable property or contracts of carriage (except for package travel contracts).

Furthermore, for the purposes of article 6(1) Rome I, active consumers and mobile consumers (who move to another Member State on their own initiative and conclude there a contract with a professional from a third country that does not direct his activities to the Member State of habitual residence of the consumer) are not protected. In the case of active consumers, the final solution does not seem completely satisfying from the EU consumer protection point of view. For example, in the case of a Dutch consumer travelling to Barcelona and purchasing some items there in his own initiative, the Dutch consumer cannot expect that Dutch rules would apply to that transaction. However, since the consumer is acting within the EU internal market, wouldn't he expect the minimum EU protection to be applicable?[110] However, according to the Rome I Regulation, article 3 Rome I would allow the choice of any foreign law, and mandatory EU consumer protection would only be applicable if all the relevant elements of the situation are located in the EU (article 3 (4) Rome I). Although most probably all the relevant elements of the contract are located in Spain or the Netherlands, if that is not the case, then the Dutch consumer could lose the EU consumer protection.

The case of mobile consumers who are targeted by a professional in a Member State different from the Member State of their habitual residence is also not solved in the Rome I Regulation. For instance, imagine a case where a company established in Morocco directs some of its activities to tourists in the south of Spain, organising tours together with sales events. A German consumer on holiday in Málaga (Spain) takes part of the tour and purchases some of the household appliances offered to him during the sales event. In this case, if the contract provides for a choice of Moroccan law, the German consumer would not be under the protection of article 6 Rome I since the activities were directed not to his country of habitual residence but to Spain. However, a Spanish tourist could rely on the protection of article 6 Rome I, and Spanish mandatory rules on consumer law would be applicable. The German tourist could only rely on the protection of article 6 Rome I if the Moroccan company was also targeting Germany (e.g. approaching them in German language, terms and conditions drafted in German etc.). Thus, 'holiday' or 'mobile' consumers are

[110] Lagarde (2006), p. 317; Añoveros Terradas (2006), p. 393.

excluded from the territorial scope of article 6 Rome I. When the consumer contract is not covered by article 6 Rome I, the law applicable is determined by articles 3 and 4 Rome I. It can be said that the excluded consumer is treated in the same manner that a professional would be treated, without any type of special protection whatsoever.[111] According to article 3 Rome I, parties are free to choose the law applicable to the contract, and article 4 Rome I will normally, in the absence of choice, determine as applicable the law of the country where the professional is established. Could that consumer with habitual residence in a Member State and contracting in another Member State after being targeted there by a professional legitimately expect a minimum level of EU consumer protection to be applicable to that consumer contract? Although, formally, this consumer is contracting outside his own country and could be considered an active consumer, he is still contracting with the EU market and has been targeted within the EU market.[112] The free movement of goods, services and people within the internal market, besides ensuring the right of a consumer to move to obtain a product or service, also guarantees consumer freedom to choose between the different offer of products and services among the Member States under the same conditions as the consumers who are habitual resident of the specific Member State.[113] It is not compatible with the EU objectives to deny the EU consumer directives protection to a consumer from a Member State that acquired products or services in another Member State. Indeed, EU consumer directives aim to guarantee a standard of consumer protection within the EU, which, in this case, article 6 Rome I does not ensure.[114]

On the other hand, some of the deficiencies of article 6 Rome I would be covered by article 3(4) Rome I when there is a choice of a non-Member State law and all the relevant elements of the situation are located within the Member States. Article 3 (4) Rome I was introduced with the intention of helping the coordination between the general conflict of laws rules determining the law applicable to the contract and the specific rules of PIL contained in EU secondary law, or, broadly speaking, the necessity of compatibility within the European legal system. To the extent that the rules of the consumer protection directives are mandatory, their application would be ensured against a choice of a non-Member State law when all the relevant elements are located within the EU. Three elements are essential for the application of article 3 (4) Rome I: a choice of law of a third country law, all elements located in the EU and mandatory rules. However, even when not all the elements are located within the EU, the scope rules contained in the directives claim the application of their protection since they only require a close connection with the EU. Hence, article 3

[111]Van Bochove (2014), p. 151.

[112]Espiniella Menéndez (2014), pp. 298, 299.

[113]Añoveros Terradas (2006), p. 394.

[114]It has sometimes been assumed that, in such a case, the Member State in question can ensure the application of the EU consumer protection deriving from EU directives as overriding mandatory rules through article 9 Rome I. Espiniella Menéndez (2014), p. 299. However, that is not—in most occasions—the case. See, in this regard, below in this Sect. 4.3.1 and Sect. 3.3.1.1.

(4) fails to coordinate article 6 Rome I and the scope rules of the directives, since the directives claim for a broader scope of application, and thus fails to guarantee the application of scope rules.

Therefore, once it is clear that the intended scope of application of the consumer protection directives is broader than the scope covered by the protective conflict rules available for consumer contracts in Rome I, it remains to clarify which of the rules would prevail. Following article 20 Rome Convention, article 23 Rome I provides that

> with the exception of Article 7, this Regulation shall not prejudice the application of provisions of Community law which, in relation to particular matters, lay down conflict-of-law rules relating to contractual obligations.

Therefore, article 23 Rome I provides for the prevalence of the scope rules contained in the consumer protection directives upon the Rome I provisions, if we were to understand scope rules as conflict rules.

The Rome I Regulation rejected to leave behind the existent scope rules of the directives, failing to solve the problem of coordination between the instruments involved. In fact, the recast of the Consumer Credit Directive, which was passed two months before the Rome I Regulation was enacted, did include a scope rule determining its scope of application. Some say that the reason for not repealing the scope rules contained in the consumer protection directives when enacting the Rome I Regulation is simply found in the distribution of internal competences inside the Commission; while the General Directorate Home and Justice is just responsible for the Rome I Regulation, the responsibility for consumer protection rests on the other General Directorates.[115] Regardless of the reason behind, the result is that the Rome I Regulation failed to resolve one of the most controversial matters around the conflict rule on consumer protection, which is the coordination between article 6 Rome I and the scope rules contained in some of the consumer protection directives, leaving this issue as an object of debate among scholars.

4.1.3 The Most Recent EU Consumer Directives: Reconsidering the Existence of Scope Rules

Contrasting with the trend followed since the nineties, the most recently adopted consumer protection directives include a provision stating that they do not contain conflict rules and thus refer the conflict of laws issue regarding consumer contracts to the Rome I Regulation. This is the case of the Consumer Rights Directive (2011/83/

---

[115]Mankowski (2016), p. 847.

EU)[116] and the new Package Travel Directive (2015/2302/EU).[117] This new trend raises the questions of whether the EU legislator is reconsidering his approach regarding scope rules in EU secondary law and whether there is still a need for scope rules.

The Consumer Rights Directive modernises consumer law in the fields of distance and off-premises contracts and contracts including digital content on a non-tangible medium and amends some aspects of the Unfair Contract Terms Directive and Consumer Sales Directive. It is a maximum harmonisation directive regulating information duties, rights of withdrawal and payment conditions in the aforementioned fields. Regarding its relationship with the conflict of laws process, recital 10 of the Consumer Rights Directive reads:

> [t]his Directive should be without prejudice to Regulation (EC) No 593/2008 of the European Parliament and of the Council of 17 June 2008 on the law applicable to contractual obligations (Rome I).

Moreover, to dissipate any doubt, recital 58 states that

> [t]he consumer should not be deprived of the protection granted by this Directive. Where the law applicable to the contract is that of a third country, Regulation (EC) No 593/2008 should apply, in order to determine whether the consumer retains the protection granted by this Directive.

Thus, any conflict of laws issue would be solved by the Rome I Regulation. The Consumer Rights Directive gives up the inclusion of scope rules interfering with PIL and relies on the Rome I Regulation.[118]

The initial idea of the Consumer Rights Directive was to remedy the problems resulting from the different interpretations due to the minimum harmonisation nature of the Consumer Sales Directive, the Unfair Contract Terms Directive, the Distance Selling Directive and the Doorstep Selling Directive. At the end, it only replaced the Distance Selling Directive and the Doorstep Selling Directive and just modified certain aspects of the Consumer Sales Directive and Unfair Contract Terms Directive. Thus, the two last ones, with a minimum harmonisation nature and including scope rules, remain in force. As a result, the material scope covered by the Directive

---

[116] Directive 2011/83/EU of the European Parliament and of the Council of 25 October 2011 on consumer rights, amending Council Directive 93/13/EEC and Directive 1999/44/EC of the European Parliament and of the Council and repealing Council Directive 85/577/EEC and Directive 97/7/EC of the European Parliament and of the Council, (OJ 2011 L 304/64) ('Consumer Rights Directive').

[117] Directive (EU) 2015/2302 of the European Parliament and of the Council of 25 November 2015 on package travel and linked travel arrangements, amending Regulation (EC) No 2006/2004 and Directive 2011/83/EU of the European Parliament and of the Council and repealing Council Directive 90/314/EEC (OJ 2015 L 326/1) ('Package Travel Directive').

[118] Weller (2015), p. 422.

is not as broad as intended. EU consumer directives including scope rules and with a minimum harmonisation nature are still in the scene.

Following the same maximum harmonisation principle, the new Package Travel Directive entered into force on 31 December 2015.[119] It includes more information requirements, cancellation rights and clarity on liability and on consumer rights. In the same trend as the Consumer Rights Directive, it provides in recital 49 that

> this Directive is without prejudice to rules on the protection of personal data laid down in Directive 95/46/EC of the European Parliament and of the Council and to the Union rules on private international law, including Regulation (EC) No 593/2008 of the European Parliament and of the Council [Rome I Regulation].

Thus, it lacks a scope rule and refers the conflict of laws issues to the Rome I Regulation.

Since the Consumer Rights Directive and the Package Travel Directive follow the principle of maximum harmonisation, intra-EU conflicts lose their importance in their context as the same level of protection is guaranteed to the consumer throughout the EU. It is irrelevant therefore whether Spanish law or Dutch law is applicable since they both would provide the same protection required by the Consumer Rights Directive and the Package Travel Directive. In intra-EU situations, regarding matters covered by maximum harmonisation directives, the fact that the parties choose the law of another Member State does not matter in practice: article 6(2) Rome I ensuring the application of the mandatory consumer protection offered to the consumer in his country of habitual residence when there is a choice of law is not relevant anymore for these type of situations.

The absence of a scope rule (as well as, in this case, the fact that the directives have a maximum harmonisation nature) avoids the different interpretations and implementation into the national law of the Member States of such a rule, which used to lead to inconsistencies and a forum-centred regulation from some Member States.[120] Moreover, in intra-EU conflicts, the debate around 'gold-plating' provisions is avoided. Gold-plating situations happen as a result of the minimum harmonisation nature of some EU consumer directives, which creates a level playing field allowing the Member States to improve the minimum standards set by the Directive when transposing it on its national law. Therefore, a Member State could either transpose in its national legal order the minimum standards of protection required by the Directive or gradually improve the level of protection offered by it.[121] Since the Consumer Rights Directive and the Package Travel Directive require the implementation of its protection in the same manner among the Member States, this debate is avoided.

---

[119] The Member States had to transpose it by 1 January 2018 and it has been applicable from 1 July 2018.

[120] In this regard, see below Sect. 4.2.1.

[121] See below Sect. 4.2.2.

Furthermore, the absence of scope rules and reference to the Rome I Regulation in resolving any conflict of laws issue helps to maintain the coherence of the conflict of laws system of the Rome I Regulation, which aims at the unification of conflict of laws for contractual obligations. Dispersed conflict or scope rules around other instruments prejudice this aim.

Nevertheless, regarding extra-EU situations, where the law of a third country could be applicable and threaten the protection provided by the directive, the question is whether the Rome I Regulation system itself would be sufficient in order to ensure the applicability of the mandatory rules of the directive when necessary, without the help of scope rules. The gaps on article 6 Rome I have been described, and it has also been submitted that article 3(4) Rome I is not sufficient since it only ensures the application of mandatory rules when all the elements of the situation are located in the EU. The Rome I Regulation does not ensure in all cases the protection intended by the directives, as it has been previously submitted, for example regarding active consumers and mobile consumers. However, it might be overall more beneficial for consumer protection the absence of scope rules since it avoids intra-EU problems and debates, and it enhances the coherence of the conflict of laws system and legal certainty. While some authors agree with this, this author included, I also believe that there might be better solutions that would guarantee consumer protection while at the same time ensure a coherent system of conflict of laws in the EU.[122]

Thus, even if the EU seems to be reconsidering its approach towards the existence of scope rules on consumer protection directives, the still existent 'gaps' of article 6 Rome I, covering a narrower scope than the one intended by the consumer directives, creates doubt as to which approach should be better. What is clear is that the mixture between directives determining their scope of application and directives referring to Rome I are not the best option regarding clarity, legal certainty and, at the end, consumer protection and internal market objectives.

4.1.4 The Current Situation Regarding EU Consumer Directives and Rome I Regulation: Inconsistencies, Gaps and Criticisms

Since the multiple developments and approaches explained above make the present situation somehow chaotic, it seems necessary to summarise the current state of affairs regarding the relation between EU consumer directives and the Rome I Regulation:

[122] On the view that scope rules are unnecessary and the Rome I Regulation system should prevail: Piir and Sein (2016). On the other hand, arguing for a change since article 6 Rome I is not sufficient: Leible (2015).

- Regarding the Rome I Regulation, article 6 Rome I is the protective conflict rule that determines the law applicable to consumer contracts. The main gaps that can be derived from this provision are, with regard to its material scope, the exclusions provided in article 6(4) Rome I. Regarding its territorial scope, active consumers and 'holiday consumers' also seem to be excluded from its application since the provision incorporates the targeted activity test and becomes applicable when the professional performs or directs his commercial activities to the country of habitual residence of the consumer. Article 3(4) Rome I was created to prevent abuse of law and ensures the application of EU mandatory law (e.g. EU consumer directives) when all the relevant elements of the situation are located in the EU. However, it seems that in some situations, EU consumer directives would need to be applicable even when not all the relevant elements are located in the EU.[123]
- Regarding the consumer protection directives, there are, on the one hand, directives containing a conflict rule determining its scope of application and, on the other hand, directives lacking a scope rule or directives referring directly the conflict of laws issue to the Rome I Regulation. Article 6(2) Unfair Contract Terms Directive, article 12(2) Distance Marketing of Consumer Financial Services Directive, article 7(2) of the Consumer Sales Directive and article 22(4) of the Consumer Credit Directive provide for the application of the protection of the respective rules when the contract is closely connected with the EU and parties chose the law of a non-Member State. Moreover, article 12(2) Timeshare Directive ensures the application of the protection granted by the Directive regardless of whether the third country law is applicable as a result of a choice of law or of the connecting factors used in the absence of choice of law. Thus, these are the directives that contain a scope rule and are in force nowadays and, according to article 23 Rome I, prevail over the conflict rules of the Rome I Regulation.

The main criticisms arising from the existence of scope rules are, first of all, related to the uncertainty around them: scope rules contained in the above-mentioned consumer protection directives do not stipulate which law should be applicable (the directive as implemented by the law of the Member State of habitual residence of the consumer, the law of the forum etc.), with the exception of the Timeshare Directive. Moreover, also with the exception of the latter, they only cover cases where the application of non-Member State law is the result of a choice of law, which means that the consumer would not enjoy the protection of the directives when he travels to another Member State and concludes a consumer contract there with a professional established in a third country. Furthermore, the implementation of scope rules into the national law of the different Member States creates different national implementation and understanding and thus adds more uncertainty to the system. Also, uncertainties and different possible interpretations arise as to when a close connection occurs.

[123] See below Sect. 4.4 for a proposal regarding article 3(4) Rome I.

Second, in their current drafting, scope rules are unrelated and disrupt the current conflict of laws system of the Rome I Regulation. Introducing the unilateral approach of the scope rules, which determine the scope of the instrument without referring to foreign law, clashes with the multilateral nature of the Rome I Regulation. In fact, it reopened the debate among European private international law scholars regarding the adequacy of multilateralism or unilateralism resolving conflicts of laws.[124] Furthermore, it has been submitted that if the Rome I Regulation tries to unify the conflict of laws of the different Member States in contractual obligations, the fact that scope rules are spread around directives and prevail over the Rome I Regulation disrupts that aim; the legal practitioner sees himself lost. The consumer would probably be better protected in a coherent system that ensures legal certainty.

On the other hand, the most recent consumer directives give us the hint that the EU legislator might be changing its approach on the inclusion of scope rules. The Consumer Rights Directive and Package Travel Directive refer the conflict of laws issue to the Rome I Regulation. While this approach avoids all the aforementioned inconveniences arising from the existence of scope rules, it has to be assessed whether the conflict rules of the Rome I Regulation ensure the international applicability of the EU consumer directives when necessary since there are indeed inconsistencies regarding consumer protection in the protective conflict rules of the Rome I Regulation.

As a result, the whole situation regarding the protection of consumers in EU conflict of laws seems at least chaotic, in both intra-EU and extra-EU situations. It has to be considered whether the scope rules of the consumer directives are still necessary in order to ensure the application of their mandatory protection, whether the Rome I Regulation should be the sole instrument dealing with conflict of laws regarding consumer contracts or whether a new approach balancing conflict of laws and internal market objectives should be determined.

4.1.5 General Remarks Regarding the Concepts of Scope of Application, Mandatory Character and Conflict Rules

There is sometimes confusion regarding the concepts and the relationship between the application of a rule or statute, the mandatory character of a rule or statute and conflict of laws, which must be clarified.

As it is known, conflict rules are legal provisions determining the law applicable to the legal relationship in question. According to the contemporary understanding of PIL in Europe, the application of a statute in an international situation is the result of the operation of the conflict rules applicable to the case. It has been suggested that

---

[124] See below Sect. 4.3.

the opposite view would be a mistake and a fall back in time to the medieval statutist thinking, according to which the applicability of a statute was determined by its own desirability to apply.[125] In the current European PIL thinking, it is understood that if a legal system has been determined as applicable by the conflict rules, then the statutes of that legal system shall apply to the situation (as long as the situation falls within the scope of application of the statute in question). The judge will follow the forum conflict rules that will point to the applicable law rather than apply a statute of the forum without previously resorting to the conflict rules. That is the starting point according to the multilateral conflict of laws method followed nowadays. Contrarily, from a unilateral theory point of view, every statute determines its own international scope of application; the statute is applicable because it has determined itself its applicability in an international situation.

Originally, multilateral conflict rules identified the 'seat' of the legal relationship. Nowadays, it is generally considered that the 'seat' of the legal relationship leads to the legal order that is most closely connected to the legal relationship. Although in principle this process would take place regardless of the substantive content of the designated law, some conflict rules contain connecting factors designed to complete certain substantive objectives (e.g. article 6 Rome I). On the other hand, unilateralism implies that the content and aim of substantive rules determine their international applicability and take part in the conflict of laws process.[126]

The mandatory character of a rule or a statute refers to the degree of intensity with which the rule or statute requires its application. Nowadays, we distinguish between dispositive rules, internal mandatory rules (or rules that cannot be derogated from by agreement) and overriding mandatory rules (which prevail over the designated applicable law).[127] From a current EU PIL perspective, in the context of the Rome I Regulation, the international applicability of a statute can only be imposed over the normal operation of conflict rules through the mechanism of overriding mandatory rules. International applicability can be related then to the international mandatory character of the provision. Only provisions considered as overriding mandatory can delimit their international scope of application and have a direct effect in the conflict of laws process. Other rules giving indications about their territorial scope of application but lacking an overriding mandatory character do not have a direct effect in the conflict of laws process. As a result, the existence of a scope rule does not imply the overriding mandatory character of a directive.

The imperative character of the directives can be understood differently if we interpret it in a unilateral method or multilateral method context. According to the unilateral theory, rules determine their own scope of application; according to the multilateral theory, they do not. For our current PIL system, to establish internal

---

[125] Bisping refers to this as the 'statutist trap'. Bisping (2012a), p. 44.

[126] Francq (2006), pp. 349–353.

[127] Dispositive rules and internal mandatory rules are applicable because of the objective operation of connecting factors, the latter not being subject to be derogated from by a choice of a different law.

mandatory character parties cannot derogate from the rule by choosing another law. However, in order to ensure the international applicability of a rule regardless of the law objectively applicable, that rule has to have an overriding mandatory character. EU directives containing scope rules cannot be understood as being conferred with an overriding mandatory character. The EU legislator, aiming to achieve a specific social or economic aim, provides for 'scope rules' making a spontaneous and, to a certain extent, unintentional use of a unilateral method of PIL.[128] Nowadays, I consider that scope rules should not be understood as directly conferring an overriding mandatory character or delimiting the international scope of application of a directive prevailing as a specific conflict rule over the Rome I Regulation but rather as helping to establish their degree of mandatory character.[129]

It is necessary to clearly distinguish between overriding mandatory rules, unilateral conflict rules and scope rules. The mechanism of unilateral conflict rules and overriding mandatory rules can be comparable to a certain extent. On the one hand, overriding mandatory rules are the typical and more widespread example of unilateralism in contemporary PIL. As previously discussed in Chap. 3 and as defined by the ECJ (*Arblade* decision)[130] and later codified in article 9(1) Rome I, overriding mandatory rules are characterised by three elements: first, they fix their own scope of application (implicitly or explicitly); second, their application and scope derive from their nature and purpose, which aims at protecting essential public interests; and, third, that purpose justifies their overriding mandatory character and need to derogate from the general conflict rules. Thus, overriding mandatory rules constitute an expression of the link between the aim of a statute and its international scope of application.[131]

Unilateral conflict rules delimit the scope of forum law, ensuring its application to the situations covered, without referring to the hypothesis of application of foreign law.[132] Similarly, scope rules determine the scope of a specific set of rules, such as a domestic statute. The scope of an instrument has various elements (temporal, material, spatial). It is the spatial (or territorial) scope that can be relevant for PIL purposes. This (spatial) scope rule might identify the situations covered by the instrument regarding its connections with the country or legal system to which the rule belongs. It will determine when a specific statute applies to an international situation. Scope rules, if understood as defining the applicability of a statute in a conflict of laws situation, are unilateral conflict rules, but while the latter determine the hypothesis of application of an unlimited amount of provisions (such as provisions regarding divorce, for example), scope rules refer to a limited set of

---

[128]Francq (2017), pp. 1789, 1790.

[129]In this regard, see the discussion below in Sect. 4.3.

[130]Joined Cases C-369/96 and C-376/96 *Criminal proceedings against Jean Claude Arblade and Arblade & Fils SARL* and *Bernard Leloup, Serge Leloup and Sofrage SARL* [1999] ECR I-8453.

[131]Francq (2017), p. 1789.

[132]Normally, they will delimit the scope of unlimited amount of provisions (like the rules on divorce) of the forum law, rather than the scope of a specific statute.

provisions (such as the provisions of a specific domestic statute). Also, it is necessary to distinguish between scope rules that can affect PIL (like the ones present in the EU consumer directives mentioned above) and 'scope rules' that are territorial scope rules that are only relevant after the law to which they belong has been determined as applicable in order to clarify the territorial scope of an instrument (e.g. article 1 (1) of the CISG (United Nations Convention of 11 April 1980 on Contracts for the International Sale of Goods), which states that the Convention applies to international sales contracts when the two parties are established in contracting states).[133]

In a similar way to overriding mandatory rules, unilateral conflict rules delineate the scope of forum law and ensure its application to the situation covered, without deciding on the application of foreign law. However, the provisions designated by unilateral conflict rules do not necessarily have a mandatory character or an overriding mandatory character. In the same way, scope rules may determine the scope of mandatory provisions, overriding mandatory provisions or simply dispositive provisions.[134]

The mandatory character of overriding mandatory rules, which makes these rules prevail over party autonomy and the objective applicable law, has sometimes led to confusion with regard to scope rules. It has sometimes been assimilated that the existence of a scope rule directly brings overriding mandatory character to the provisions covered.[135] However, it is fundamental to distinguish between the scope of application of a statute and its (overriding) mandatory character.[136]

4.2 EU Consumer Directives and Intra-EU Conflicts of Laws

Within the EU legal order, we can distinguish three types of situations regarding the existence of foreign elements: 1) the situation involves only one Member State (all the elements are located within the frontiers of one Member State); 2) the situation involves two or more Member States, but still all the elements are located within the EU; 3) the situation involves one (or more) Member State(s) and also one (or more) third state(s). From an EU point of view, the two first situations would be characterised as internal and the third situation as international. The first situation

[133]Fernández Rozas and Sánchez Lorenzo (1999), pp. 172, 173.

[134]Guardans Cambó (1992), p. 333. The confusion regarding these concepts was already object of study and matter of confusion among doctrine in the second half of the twentieth century with the arising of the doctrine of overriding mandatory rules. Authors debated about the scope of application of a rule and imperative or overriding imperative character, or the scope of application of a statute and conflict of laws; among others: Ibid., pp. 328–359; Danson (1964); De Nova (1966); Kelly (1969). Nowadays, despite the confusion derived from the complexity of these concepts, the distinction among them is clear. Magnus (2016), pp. 23–25.

[135]Bonomi (2017), p. 616.

[136]Magnus (2016), pp. 23–25; Francq (2005), pp. 575, 576.

is purely internal within a national legal order, and the second one is internal within the EU (intra-EU).

When talking about intra-EU conflicts of law, we refer to the situation where the application of the laws of two or more Member States is at stake. We refer to purely intra-EU situations where both the consumer and the professional party are located in the EU, and all the elements related to the consumer contract also take place in the EU. Relevant elements to be taken into account in this regard are the place of habitual residence of the parties, place of performance or conclusion of the contract etc.[137]

When talking about harmonised areas, such as consumer law harmonised by EU directives, there is no specific regime to deal with intra-EU conflicts, but, in the case of consumer contracts, the applicable law will be decided through the conflict rules of the Rome I Regulation.

Regarding conflict of laws between Member States related to EU consumer directives, two different issues arise, which will be dealt with within this section. Firstly, directives have to be implemented into the national law of the Member States; it follows that the scope rules contained in some of the EU consumer directives also have to be implemented. As a result, different national implementation of the already confusing scope rules arise among the different Member States, creating an uncertain system parallel to the Rome I Regulation system. The EU legislator obviates the fact that when introducing a scope rule on an EU directive, the national legislator is confronted with the difficulty of implementing this type of rules.[138] Secondly, most of the EU consumer directives are minimum harmonisation directives, which allow Member States to improve the minimum standards required by the directive itself; as a result, different levels of protection exist among the Member States, which raises the question of whether, in this so-called gold-plating situations, the Member State of the forum that grants a better level of protection should impose its standards against the law of another Member State that, according to the normal operation of the Rome I Regulation, is applicable to the contract.

4.2.1 *The Difficult Implementation of the Scope Rules of EU Consumer Directives into the National Law of the Member States*

One of the main practical inconveniences regarding scope rules contained in consumer directives regards its implementation into the national law of the different Member States. Since directives are not applicable as such but have to be implemented by the Member States into their national law, the implementation of the scope rules will have an influence on the conflict of laws. In fact, several

[137] See Sect. 3.4 regarding the definition of relevant elements in relation to article 3(4) Rome I.

[138] Francq (2005), p. 422.

difficulties arise regarding the different implementation and interpretations by Member States of the scope rules, especially regarding the reference of the scope rules to the territory of the Member States and the term close connection.

4.2.1.1 Reference to the Territory of the Member States

Scope rules provide for the application of the specific directive when the situation has a close link with the territory of the EU or the territory of a Member State. Such reference is difficult to implement correctly by a Member State. While it makes sense from the perspective of the EU that an EU directive is determining its own scope by referring to the frontiers of the EU legal system, this leads to national implementation focused instead on the territory of the own Member State, determining the applicability of the law of the forum while ignoring the law of other Member States.[139]

For example, regarding the implementation of the Unfair Contract Terms Directive, in which article 6(2) provides that

> Member States shall take the necessary measures to ensure that the consumer does not lose the protection granted by this Directive by virtue of the choice of law of a non-Member State as the law applicable to a contract if the latter has a closest connection with the territory of the Member States,

German law provided for the application of German law when the contract had a close connection with Germany, without saying anything about a close connection with other Member States.[140] Thus, as an implementation of a scope rule ensuring the standards of the Unfair Contract Terms Directive, there was a rule taking a unilateral approach ensuring the application of national law. This rule, although

---

[139] Fallon and Francq (2000), p. 166; Kuipers (2012), p. 188.

[140] Law of 19 July 1996, BGBI. 1996, I, 1013, article 1: '*Unterliegt ein Vertrag ausländischem Recht, so sind die Vorschriften dieses Gesetzes gleichwohl anzuwenden, wenn der Vertrag einen engen Zusammenhang mit dem Gebiet der Bundesrepublik Deutschland aufweist. Ein enger Zusammenhang ist insbesondere anzunehmen, wenn 1. der Vertrag auf Grund eines öffentlichen Angebots, einer öffentlichen Werbung oder einer ähnlichen im Geltungsbereich dieses Gesetzes entfalteten geschäftlichen Tätigkeit des Verwenders zustande kommt und 2. der andere Vertragsteil bei Abgabe seiner auf den Vertragsschluß gerichteten Erklärung seinen Wohnsitz oder gewöhnlichen Aufenthalt im Geltungsbereich dieses Gesetzes hat und seine Willenserklärung im Geltungsbereich dieses Gesetzes abgibt*' ['If a contract is subject to foreign law, then the provisions of this act are nevertheless applicable if the Contract has a close connection with the territory of the Federal Republic Germany. A close connection is to be assumed in particular if 1. the contract based on a public offer, a public offer Advertising or similar in scope this law unfolded business activity of the user comes about and 2. the other party to the contract on the conclusion of the contract residence or ordinary residence Stay within the scope of this law has and his declaration of intent within the scope of this law write'] (translation by author).

ensuring the minimum protection required by the Directive by imposing the application of national law, was unilaterally imposing the application of German law.[141]

Also, there was controversy regarding the implementation of the scope rule contained in article 12(2) of the Timeshare Directive, which provides that

> [w]here the applicable law is that of a third country, consumers shall not be deprived of the protection granted by this Directive, as implemented in the Member State of the forum if (1) any of the immovable properties concerned is situated within the territory of a Member State, or, (2) in the case of a contract not directly related to immovable property, the trader pursues commercial or professional activities in a Member State or, by any means, directs such activities to a Member State and the contract falls within the scope of such activities.

For example, German law implementing the Timeshare Directive[142] provided for the applicability of German law when the immovable property was located on the

[141]Later on, by a Law of 27 June 2000, article 29a was introduced in the EGBGB (Introductory Law to the Civil Code), introducing a rule implementing article 6(2) Unfair Contract Terms, article 9 Timeshare Directive and article 12(2) Distance Sales Directive. Later, it also included article 7 (2) Consumer Sales Directives and article 12(3) Distance Marketing of Consumer Financial Services Directive. Article 29a EGBGB followed the drafting of the scope rules of the Directives and provided in paragraph 1 that if, as a result of a choice of law, a contract is not governed by the law of a Member State but the contract has a close connection with the territory of one of those States, the national legislation of that Member State implementing the Consumer Protection Directives should apply ('*Unterliegt ein Vertrag auf Grund einer Rechtswahl nicht dem Recht eines Mitgliedstaats der Europäischen Union oder eines anderen Vertragsstaats des Abkommens über den Europäischen Wirtschaftsraum, weist der Vertrag jedoch einen engen Zusammenhang mit dem Gebiet eines dieser Staaten auf, so sind die im Gebiet dieses Staats geltenden Bestimmungen zur Umsetzung der Verbraucherschutzrichtlinien gleichwohl anzuwenden*'). This provision was later repealed when the Rome I Regulation entered into force in 2009.

[142]Law of 20 December 1996, BGBI. 1996, I, P. 2154: '§ *8 Kollisionsregel. Unterliegt ein Vertrag über die Teilzeitnutzung von Wohngebäuden oder ein Vertrag zur Finanzierung des Erwerbs eines Teilzeitnutzungsrechts (§ 6) ausländischem Recht, so sind die Vorschriften dieses Gesetzes gleichwohl anzuwenden, wenn 1. das Wohngebäude im Hoheitsgebiet eines Mitgliedstaates der Europäischen Union oder eines Vertragsstaates des Abkommens über den Europäischen Wirtschaftsraum belegen ist oder 2. der Vertrag auf Grund eines öffentlichen Angebotes, einer öffentlichen Werbung oder einer ähnlichen geschäftlichen Tätigkeit zustandekommt, die der Veräußerer in einem Mitgliedstaat der Europäischen Union oder in einem anderen Vertragsstaat des Abkommens über den Europäischen Wirtschaftsraum entfaltet, und wenn der Erwerber bei Abgabe seiner auf den Vertragsabschluß gerichteten Erklärung seinen Wohnsitz oder gewöhnlichen Aufenthalt in einem Mitgliedstaat der Europäischen Union oder in einem anderen Vertragsstaat des Abkommens über den Europäischen Wirtschaftsraum hat*' ['If a contract on the part-time use of residential buildings or a contract to finance the acquisition of a timeshare (§ 6) is governed by foreign law, the provisions of this Act shall nevertheless be applicable if: 1. the dwelling is located in the territory of a Member State of the European Union or of a Contracting State to the Agreement on the European Economic Area, or 2. the contract is concluded on the basis of a public offer, a public advertisement or a similar business activity which the transferor has in a Member State of the European Union or in another Contracting State to the Agreement on the European Economic Area and if the transferee, upon submission of his contract declaration of

territory of a Member State; therefore, a German court would apply German law to a contract between a Belgium consumer and a Dutch company regarding a property located in Spain.[143] On the other hand, the French law implementing the Directive[144] determined the law of the Member State where the immovable is located as applicable, indicating at the same time that French law would apply in the absence of implementation provisions in that law, ensuring therefore the minimum protection of the Directive.

The Italian implementation of scope rules is also interesting.[145] To give an example, article 12(2) Distance Marketing of Financial Services Directive provides:

> Member States shall take the measures needed to ensure that the consumer does not lose the protection granted by this Directive by virtue of the choice of the law of a non-member country as the law applicable to the contract, if this contract has a close link with the territory of one or more Member States.

However, the Italian provision provided for the applicability of Italian law to all cases in which the parties have chosen a different law.[146] Moreover, one of the final provisions of the Italian Consumer Code (containing both substantive consumer law and conflict rules implementing scope rules) provided that if parties have chosen a law other than Italian law as applicable, the consumer should still enjoy the minimum protection provided by the Italian Consumer Code.[147]

In the Spanish case, the implementation of directives was done in different texts, and, as a result, rules on consumer protection were disperse. Like in the previous cases, the implementation did not correspond with the drafting of the scope rules of the directives. For example, the implementation of article 7(2) Consumer Sales Directive provided for the application of the Spanish protective rules regardless of

---

residence or habitual residence in a Member State of the European Union or in another Contracting State to the Agreement on the European Economic Area'] (translation by author).

[143] Later on, article 29a EGBGB provided in paragraph 3 that the provisions of the Civil Code on timeshare contracts shall apply to a contract that is not governed by the law of a Member State of the European Union or of another Contracting State to the Agreement on the European Economic Area if the dwelling is in the territory of one of these states. It did not change that approach.

[144] Law no 98-566 of 8 July 1998, JO(RF) 9 July 1998, p. 10486.

[145] For a more detailed explanation on the implementation of scope rules by Italian law, Ragno (2009), pp. 159–161.

[146] Article 67*octiesdecies* Italian Consumer Code paragraph 2 stated that when parties chose as applicable a law different from Italian law, the consumer would still receive the protection provided by the same section (which was the transposition of the rules of the Directive): '*Ove le parti abbiano scelto di applicare al contratto una legislazione diversa da quella italiana, al consumatore devono comunque essere riconosciute le condizioni di tutela previste dalla presente sezione.*'

[147] Article 143(2) of the Italian Consumer Code: '*Ove le parti abbiano scelto di applicare al contratto una legislazione diversa da quella italiana, al consumatore devono comunque essere riconosciute le condizioni minime di tutela previste dal codice*' ['If the parties have chosen to apply a different legislation to the contract than the Italian one, the consumer must still be recognized the minimum conditions of protection provided by the code'] (translation by author).

the law chosen by the parties.[148] Also, the implementation of article 12(2) Distance Sales Directive provided for the application of the rights conferred by the act even when the law applicable was other than Spanish law.[149] These rules impose the application of the Spanish consumer rules even when parties choose the law of another Member State or even when the law of another Member State is applicable.[150]

Thus, in general, national rules transposing scope rules impose the application of the national consumer law with the objective of ensuring the application of the protection of the EU consumer directive in question, but they do it unilaterally, imposing the application of national law even when the law of another Member State (which also ensures the minimum of the Directive) is applicable.

The different implementation of the Member States with regard to the territory covered by the rules derives in a kind of intra-EU conflict of laws system parallel to the Rome I Regulation. A big number of scope rules are implemented by the Member States as unilateral conflict rules, imposing the application of national law even against other Member States and thus preventing the consumer from benefitting from a better protection provided by the law of another Member State. This parallel system interferes with article 6 Rome I, for example when the consumer contract falls under the requirements of article 6 Rome I and the parties chose the law of another Member State. According to article 23 Rome I, the provisions of the Regulation

[148]Law 23/2003 of 10 July 2003. Article 13: '*Las normas de protección de los consumidores contenidas en esta ley serán aplicables, cualquiera que sea la Ley elegida por las partes para regir el contenido cuando el bien haya de utilizarse, ejercitarse el derecho o realizarse la prestación en alguno de los Estados miembros de la unión Europea, o el contrato se hubiera celebrado total o parcialmente en cualquiera de ellos, o una de las partes sea ciudadano de un Estado miembro de la Unión Europea o presente el negocio jurídico cualquier otra conexión análoga o vínculo estrecho con el territorio de la Unión Europea*' ['The rules of consumer protection contained in this law will be applicable, whatever the law chosen by the parties to govern the content is, when the good is to be used, the right to be exercised or the service be performed in any of the Member States of the European Union, or the contract has been concluded in whole or in part in any of them, or one of the parties is a citizen of a Member State of the European Union or the legal transaction presents any other analogous connection or close link with the territory of the European Union'] (translation by author).

[149]Law 47/2002 of 19 December 2002, modifying Law 7/1996. Article 48: '*Cuando el comprador sea un consumidor (...), los derechos que el presente capítulo le reconoce serán irrenunciables y podrán ser ejercidos por los mismos aunque la legislación aplicable al contrato sea otra distinta de la española, si el contrato presenta un vínculo estrecho con el territorio de cualquier Estado miembro de la Unión Europea*' ['When the buyer is a consumer (...) the rights granted to him by the present section cannot be derogated from and can be exercised despite the law applicable to the contract is other than Spanish law, if the contract presents a close link with the territory of any Member State of the European Union'] (translation by author).

[150]More about the Spanish implementation of 'scope rules' in: De la Rosa (2007).

> shall not prejudice the application of provisions of Community law which, in relation to particular matters, lay down conflict-of-law rules relating to contractual obligations.

However, to the extent that these national conflict rules do not reflect the rationale behind the directives, which did not intend at any moment to impose the application of a national law over the law of other Member States, they should not prevail over the provisions of Rome I.[151] Also, it is submitted that the principle of minimum harmonisation of the majority of the EU consumer directives should operate only on a substantive law level but not on a conflict of laws level, meaning that the Member States should implement the scope rules as provided for in the respective directive and not extend or modify their scope.[152]

4.2.1.2 The Term Close Connection

The term 'close connection' seems to be included in the scope rules as a flexible concept, allowing the courts to interpret whether the consumer contract is closely connected to a Member State taking into account all the circumstances of the case. The notion of 'close connection' brings difficulties since many elements can be taken into consideration in that regard. In the context of the EU, in the Rome Convention and Rome I Regulation, the concept of 'closest connection' is used as a connecting factor, included in an 'escape clause' either when the contract is most closely connected to a different one than the law designated or when the law applicable cannot be determined by the other connecting factors (article 4(3) and 4 (4) Rome I). The legislator did not refer to a list of factors to take into account, and thus a catalogue of the specific relevant circumstances does not exist. Generally, doctrine agrees that the place of performance of the contract and the common habitual residence of the parties are elements with some weight, while factors such as nationality, language and a choice of forum clause do not play a very important role.[153] However, the understanding of the term in the context of article 4 Rome I differs from the one contained in the directives. In the Rome I Regulation, 'closest connection' is used in an escape clause or in a subsidiary rule, and thus in an exceptional manner, and it is not applicable with regard to consumer contracts falling under article 6 Rome I. However, in the directives, the scope rule requires the application of the consumer protection rules contained in the respective directive when there is a close connection with one or more Member States. Other authors suggested different possibilities. For example, seeking coordination and harmonisation between instruments, Jayme and Kohler suggested that close connection could be deemed to exist when the Rome Convention, in the absence of choice

[151] In the same opinion, Ragno (2009), p. 161.

[152] Ibid., p. 159.

[153] Gebauer (2015), pp. 125, 126.

of law, would have designated the law of a Member State as applicable to the consumer contract.[154] On the other hand, Esteban de la Rosa suggested that since one of the objectives behind the EU consumer directives was, besides consumer protection, the effective functioning of the internal market and, therefore, to avoid distortions of the competition existent in the market, a close connection with the market would be when the application of the directive is necessary in order to avoid a distortion on competition within the internal market.[155]

Regarding the implementation of the term 'close connection' contained in the scope rules of the directives within the national law of the Member States, we can difference two trends.

The first one corresponds to a more rigid rule in which the national law determines when a close connection occurs. We find several examples: in French law, when implementing the Unfair Contract Terms Directive, the term 'close connection' was transposed as reference to the residence of the consumer when the offer was made in that state or the contract was concluded or performed in that state. In fact, the current French Consumer Code contains a rule (article L231-1) defining when a close connection occurs, followed by several rules indicating the applicability of some EU consumer directives when such a close connection with the EU occurs (article 232-1–5). Article L231-1 French Consumer Code establishes as factors indicating a close connection the conclusion of the contract in the Member State of habitual residence of the consumer, the professional directing his activities towards the Member State of habitual residence of the consumer, a special offer or advertising preceding the contract and the acts performed by the consumer necessary for the conclusion of this contract taking place in a Member State and the conclusion of the contract in a Member State where the consumer has given in to a proposal of travel or stay made, directly or indirectly, by the seller to encourage him to conclude the contract.[156]

In German law,[157] several factors were included as presumptions that might constitute a close connection, such as the residence of the consumer or elements of the contract covering an offer or advertisement, but without prejudice to the fact that

[154]Jayme and Kohler (1995), p. 20.

[155]De la Rosa (2003), pp. 158–168. Paredes Pérez is of the same opinion, considering that, rather than the habitual residence of the consumer in the EU or the professional directing activities to the EU, the relevant factor to consider there is a close connection is how the internal market is affected by the (non-)application of the directive. Paredes Pérez (2006), pp. 95, 96.

[156]Article L231-1 French Consumer Code: '*un lien étroit avec le territoire d'un Etat membre est réputé établi notamment : 1° Si le contrat a été conclu dans l'Etat membre du lieu de résidence habituelle du consommateur ; 2° Si le professionnel dirige son activité vers le territoire de l'Etat membre où réside le consommateur, sous réserve que le contrat entre dans le cadre de cette activité ; 3° Si le contrat a été précédé dans cet Etat membre d'une offre spécialement faite ou d'une publicité et des actes accomplis par le consommateur nécessaires à la conclusion de ce contrat ; 4° Si le contrat a été conclu dans un Etat membre où le consommateur s'est rendu à la suite d'une proposition de voyage ou de séjour faite, directement ou indirectement, par le vendeur pour l'inciter à conclure ce contrat.*'

[157]Law of 19 July 1996, BGBI. 1996, I, 1013.

the court could consider other circumstances of the case.[158] While the French rule seems to be more rigid, stating the specific conditions, the German rule states some presumptions and leaves room for the court to consider more circumstances.[159]

The Spanish transposition of the term close connection also included in some cases presumptions, such as in the rule implementing article 7(2) Consumer Sales Directive, which stated that the provisions should be applicable (regardless of the choice of law by the parties) when the good is to be used, the right is exercised or the service is performed in a Member State or the contract has been concluded in a Member State or any of the parties to the contract is a citizen of a Member State or the legal relationship presents any analogous connection or close link with the territory of the EU.[160] The current legal act dealing with consumer protection rules (including those transposing EU Directives)—*Ley General para la Defensa de los Consumidores y Usuarios*—also provides for the application of the rules when there is a close connection with the territory of the EU, understanding that there is a close connection when the aforementioned circumstances take place.[161]

The second trend consists in the interpretation of the 'close connection' term as having a direct effect, meaning that it would be the court that would decide in every specific case whether there is a close link with the territory attending to the circumstances of the case. For example, regarding the implementation of the Unfair Contract Terms Directive, Italy and Portugal followed this trend.[162]

It is also interesting to mention that the first transposition of article 6(2) Unfair Contract Terms Directive by Spanish law provided that the consumer protection rules against unfair contract terms were to be applicable, irrespective of the law

158 Later on, article 29a EGBGB, regarding the scope of several consumer directives and now repealed since the Rome I Regulation entered into force, provided that '(2) A close connection is to be assumed in particular if 1.the contract is concluded on the basis of a public offer, a public advertisement or a similar business activity, which is carried out in a Member State of the European Union or another Member State of the Agreement on the European Economic Area, and 2.the other party has his habitual residence in a Member State of the European Union or another Contracting State to the Agreement on the European Economic Area when making his declaration for the purpose of the conclusion of the contract'.

159 Fallon and Francq (2000), pp. 167–168.

160 See above in Sect. 4.2.1.1.

161 Article 67(3) Real Decreto Legislativo 1/2007, de 16 de noviembre, por el que se aprueba el texto refundido de la Ley General para la Defensa de los Consumidores y Usuarios y otras leyes complementarias: '*(...) Se entenderá, en particular, que existe un vínculo estrecho cuando el bien haya de utilizarse, ejercitarse el derecho o realizarse la prestación en alguno de los Estados miembros de la Unión Europea, o el contrato se hubiera celebrado total o parcialmente en cualquiera de ellos, o una de las partes sea ciudadano de un Estado miembro de la Unión Europea o presente el negocio jurídico cualquier otra conexión análoga o vínculo estrecho con el territorio de la Unión Europea.*'

162 Law no 52 of 6 February 1996 (*Gazz. Uffic.*, 10 February 1996); Law no 220/95 of 31 January 1995 (*Diario da Republica*, 31 August 1995). Fallon and Francq (2000), p. 168. Also, the Spanish transposition of article 12 97/7/CE Distance Consumer Sales referred to a close connection with any Member State of the EU (article 48 Law 7/1996 15 January 1996, introduced by law 47/2002 of 19 December).

chosen by the parties, under the conditions provided for in article 5 Rome Convention establishing the law applicable to consumer contracts.[163] However, the ECJ in *Commission v Spain*[164] ruled that Spain had failed to transpose article 6(2) Unfair Contract Terms Directive and held that the term 'close connection', deliberately vague in order to make it possible to adapt to the circumstances of the case, covered more situations than those referred to in article 5 Rome Convention.[165] Nevertheless, the ECJ did not take this opportunity to clarify the doubts arising from the interpretation and transposition of scope rules.[166]

Therefore, different rules deriving from the different national implementation exist among the different Member States, especially when Member States implement the term through a rigid rule with specific conditions, which leads again to inconsistencies among the different implementation and does not help in the achievement of a coherent and harmonised conflict of laws system.

Besides the different existent national implementation, other issues arise from the term 'close connection' included in scope rules. The most obvious issue is the legal uncertainty derived from the fact that it is a term open to interpretation, created with the intention to cover the necessary circumstances of every case. While the vagueness of the concept is intentional as to cover the necessary situations in the specific case, it necessarily brings legal uncertainty to the conflict of laws process. Depending on which Member State court the claim is brought, this court might consider whether there is a close connection with the EU or not and thus might apply the respective EU consumer protection rules or not, which promotes forum shopping.

Furthermore, it is a requirement not familiar with the traditional PIL. According to article 6 Rome I, the consumer directives would be applicable when the consumer

---

[163]Law 7/1998 of 13 April 1998 on general terms in contracts, *Boletín Oficial del Estado* No 89 of 14 April 1998, p. 12304 ('Law 7/1998'), amending General Law 26 of 19 July 1984 providing for consumer protection, *Boletín Oficial del Estado* No 176 of 24 July 1984, p. 21686 ('amended Law 26/1984'), article 10 bis 3: '*Las normas de protección de los consumidores frente a las cláusulas abusivas serán aplicables, cualquiera que sea la Ley que las partes hayan elegido para regir el contrato, en los términos previstos en el artículo 5 del Convenio de Roma de 1980, sobre la Ley aplicable a las obligaciones contractuales.*'

[164]Case C-70/03 *Commission of the European Communities v Kingdom of Spain* [2004] ECR I-9657. See above Sect. 4.1.1.3.

[165]The ECJ held that 'as regards ties with the Community, Article 6(2) of the directive merely states that the contract is to have "a close connection with the territory of the Member States". That general expression seeks to make it possible to take account of various ties depending on the circumstances of the case.' The judgment continues: 'Although concrete effect may be given to the deliberately vague term "close connection" chosen by the Community legislature by means of presumptions, it cannot, on the other hand, be circumscribed by a combination of predetermined criteria for ties such as the cumulative conditions as to residence and conclusion of the contract referred to in Article 5 of the Rome Convention' (*Commission v Spain*, paras. 22–23). In this regard: Paredes Pérez (2006), pp. 97–100; De la Rosa (2005). Also, in a previous commentary regarding the Spanish provision, the incompatibility confirmed by the ECJ was already predicted: Vilà Costa and Gardeñes Santiago (2002), pp. 296–302.

[166]Paredes Pérez (2006), p. 100.

is approached by the professional in the country of habitual residence of the consumer. Moreover, it would not be possible to circumvent their protection through a choice of a third country law when the protection provided by them is more beneficial than the law chosen. In case the situation would be outside the scope of article 6 Rome I, in case of active or mobile consumers (or in case the situation is not covered by the material scope of article 6 Rome I neither), as a result of article 4 Rome I, the directives would still be applicable when the professional is established in a Member State (test of characteristic performance) and no choice of law has been made. Furthermore, when all the relevant elements are located within the EU, the application of the consumer directives is ensured through article 3 (4) Rome I. Also, it has been criticised that it is difficult to determine that a close connection between the contract and the territory of a Member State exists when the professional does not pursue or direct its commercial activity towards the Member State.[167] That is true when the situation is covered by the material and territorial scope of article 6 Rome I; however, the close connection test was more intended to cover the gaps of that provision (the former article 5 Rome Convention). Still, it would have made more sense to include in the scope rules another more familiar connecting factor—such as the targeted activity test—rather than the requirement of close connection.

In conclusion, as a result of the implementation of the scope rules of EU consumer directives into the national law of the Member States, first, a parallel system to the Rome I Regulation appears regarding the scope of application of EU consumer directives in intra-EU situations. While scope rules refer to the application of the directive when the situation has a close link with the territory of the EU, some national laws refer instead to the application of the consumer law when the situation is closely connected to the territory of that country. Thus, they create a unilateral conflict rule that claims the application of national law, even in intra-EU situations (i.e. against the law of another Member State), without referring to the law of other Member States or any foreign law.

Second, the different implementation rules regarding the requirement of 'close connection' bring even more uncertainty than the vague concept itself. Some Member States adopt rigid rules with specific requirements, which contradicts the purpose of the concept (i.e. to allow a case-by-case interpretation of the circumstances), as well as leads to different requirements depending on each Member State law. Moreover, the unfamiliarity of the 'close connection' requirement with the PIL connecting factors regarding consumer protection disturbs the conflict of laws system, bringing up the question of why a close connection rather than any other known requirement (such as the targeted activity test of article 6 Rome I).

Finally, regarding intra-EU conflict of laws, it becomes obvious that scope rules bring more legal uncertainty and disturb the aim of the Rome I Regulation regarding the unification of conflict of laws in contractual obligations.

---

[167] Max Planck Institute for Foreign Private and Private International Law (2004), p. 56.

4.2.2 Gold-Plating Situations: Minimum Harmonisation, Maximum Protection?

Most of the EU consumer directives, except the most recent ones (Consumer Rights Directive and Package Travel Directive), have a minimum harmonising nature. As a result, a level playing field is created allowing the Member States to improve the minimum standards set by the directive when transposing it on its national law. Therefore, a Member State can either transpose in its national legal order the minimum standards of protection required by the directive or gradually improve the level of protection offered by it—a phenomenon known as gold plating.[168]

When the consumer contract falls within the scope of article 6 Rome I and a choice of another Member State law has been made, article 6(2) Rome I ensures that the most beneficial law to the consumer will be applicable: either the law of habitual residence of the consumer or the law chosen by the parties. Thus, according to this so-called preferential law approach, the court should only apply the law chosen by the parties if the mandatory provisions of that law do not deprive the consumer from the protection offered by the mandatory provisions of the law of the country of habitual residence. The court shall identify the mandatory provisions of the law of the country of habitual residence of the consumer and compare them with the mandatory provisions of the law chosen by the parties. Although this approach imposes a burdensome task on the judge, it provides the consumer with the higher protection available while respecting party autonomy. Regarding gold-plating situations, the preferential law approach will lead to the application of the law that, when implementing the respective directive, improved more the standards of protection, this being the law of the Member State of habitual residence of the consumer or the Member State law chosen by the parties.

In the cases excluded from the scope of article 6 Rome I, such as mobile and active consumers, or the specific material exceptions, it is already known that, generally, the law applicable will be determined by articles 3 and 4 Rome I, which will lead to the law chosen by the parties or, in the absence of choice, to the law of the place of establishment of the professional party. The protection of the EU consumer directives as transposed by the *lex fori* is ensured against the choice of a third country law when all relevant elements are located within the EU (article 3 (4) Rome I). However, if parties choose as applicable the law of a Member State, what happens if the *lex fori* provides for a better protection than a Member State law chosen by the parties? Provided that the Member State has implemented the directive correctly, the minimum protection granted by it is ensured. But could the provisions of the law of the forum that provide for a better level of protection be applied?

On the one hand, it is submitted that as the standards set by the directives are mandatory EU law, the 'excessive' protection provided by a national law could in

[168] Van Bochove (2014), p. 155.

the same way be regarded as national mandatory law.[169] In such a case, its application is only ensured when a situation is purely internal (article 3(3) Rome I). As a result, under this line of reasoning, the application of the provisions of the law of the forum that exceed the level of protection of the respective directive would not prevail over the Member State law chosen by the parties, unless we are in a purely internal situation of article 3(3) Rome I.

On the other hand, the opposite conclusion can be achieved by following the reasoning of the ECJ in the *Unamar* judgment.[170] In this case, a preliminary ruling was referred to the ECJ asking whether the mandatory rules of the *lex fori* (in this case, the Belgium agency rules), which offered wider protection than the minimum laid down by the Commercial Agents Directive, could be applied even if the law chosen by the parties was the law of another Member State in which the minimum protection provided by the Directive had also been implemented (in this case Bulgarian law). The ECJ concluded that despite the fact that the Commercial Agents Directive was correctly transposed in Bulgarian law, the Belgium Court had discretion to qualify its own national provisions as overriding mandatory rules in the sense of article 7 Rome Convention (now article 9 Rome I) and therefore apply them irrespective of the otherwise applicable law.[171] Nevertheless, it is necessary to note that the *Unamar* case does not deal exactly with a gold-plating situation since it concerns a type of agency contract not included in the Commercial Agents Directive (i.e. the Belgium provisions involved extended the scope of application of the provisions of the Directive, rather than improving the protecting standards).[172]

In any case, such a broad interpretation of overriding mandatory rules can undermine the principle of party autonomy. Also, this interpretation would affect the harmonising effect of the directives, and legal certainty would turn out impaired since it would be up to each national court to decide whether or not its gold-plating provisions are to be regarded as overriding mandatory rules and applicable in any

[169] Kramer (2015), p. 267.

[170] Case C-184/12, *United Antwerp Maritime Agencies (Unamar) NV v Navigation Maritime Bulgare* [2013] ECLI:EU:C:2013:663.

[171] The ECJ in *Unamar* concluded that: *Articles 3 and 7(2) of the Convention on the law applicable to contractual obligations opened for signature in Rome on 19 June 1980 must be interpreted as meaning that the law of a Member State of the European Union which meets the minimum protection requirements laid down by Council Directive 86/653/EEC of 18 December 1986 on the coordination of the laws of the Member States relating to self-employed commercial agents and which has been chosen by the parties to a commercial agency contract may be rejected by the court of another Member State before which the case has been brought in favour of the law of the forum, owing to the mandatory nature, in the legal order of that Member State, of the rules governing the situation of self-employed commercial agents, only if the court before which the case has been brought finds, on the basis of a detailed assessment, that, in the course of that transposition, the legislature of the State of the forum held it to be crucial, in the legal order concerned, to grant the commercial agent protection going beyond that provided for by that directive, taking account in that regard of the nature and of the objective of such mandatory provisions.*

[172] Van Bochove (2014), p. 156.

situation regardless of the law chosen by the parties, which would lead again to an uncertain and uncoordinated situation.[173]

Since the majority of the provisions of the directives are intended to be mandatory provisions, rather than overriding mandatory provisions, they should also be considered as such when implemented within the law of the Member States, respecting thus the intention and purpose of the directive.[174] I consider that in order to ensure the predictability of outcomes and respect as much as possible party autonomy, two possibilities arise: either the more protective provisions of the *lex fori* should be applied but according to a specific conflict rule designed to deal with intra-EU harmonised areas or the Member State law chosen by the parties should be respected since at the end that law ensures the minimum protection required by the respective directive. The first option entails that if a preferential approach is going to be adopted within the system of the Rome I Regulation regarding gold-plating provisions of the *lex fori*, the complexity carried by these situations should be addressed by conflict of laws rules specialised in harmonised fields.[175]

However, I do not consider such a preferential approach necessary in intra-EU situations: since at least the same minimum standards are shared, multilateral conflict rules should be promoted in intra-EU conflicts. It is inherent in our current PIL method that conflict rules should promote equality between the different legal systems. Of course, this is not completely possible when important interests or values are at stake, hence the existence of rules ensuring the applicability of mandatory rules and overriding mandatory rules when necessary. However, in intra-EU situations, EU consumer directives impose common legal standards among the Member States, which are mandatory at EU level. Moreover, it has to be taken into account that the same situation happens in other areas of contract law (e.g. commercial agency contracts). This EU mandatory set of rules might need to be ensured against the application of a foreign law but not against the law of Member States that share the same EU mandatory provisions. The situation can be understood as an interstate conflict of laws.

Therefore, I consider that the gold-plating provisions of a Member State should not be imposed against the choice of another Member State law since both Member States share the mandatory EU provisions. I agree, however, with the idea that maybe conflict rules focused on EU harmonised areas could be included in the Rome I Regulation in order to make possible a clear differentiation between intra-EU and extra-EU situations.

---

[173] Ibid., p. 156.

[174] See below Sect. 4.3.1 regarding the debate over the classification of the provisions of EU consumer directives as mandatory rules or overriding mandatory rules.

[175] In this opinion, see Sánchez Lorenzo (2010), p. 76.

4.3 EU Consumer Directives and Extra-EU Conflicts of Laws: The International Scope of the EU Consumer Directives in PIL Terms

The EU has used several methods in order to determine the international applicability of EU consumer directives in extra-EU situations where the eventual applicability of a foreign law might spoil the objectives of a consumer protection directive. Firstly, the first generation of consumer directives enacted during the eighties did not contain any scope rule; from the point of view of PIL, this method did not create any special problem since the conflict of laws would have been solved by the PIL rules contained in the Rome I Regulation. Secondly, the second generation of consumer directives already introduced scope rules with the close connection requirement and covering just the cases where there is a choice of a non-Member State law. Moreover, the Timeshare Directive included a more rigid and specific scope rule, determining the law of the forum as applicable where the situation is closely connected with the EU, the applicable law is that of a third country, and the immovable property is located in the EU or the professional directed his activities towards a Member State. The two latter methods that come as a reaction on the gaps in consumer protection in the conflict rules of the Rome Convention are the ones that interfere with the conflict of laws system regulated in these cases by the Rome I Regulation. Finally, the most recent method used by the EU regarding the international applicability of the consumer directives is the reference to the conflict rules of the Rome I Regulation, which, from a PIL point of view, seems ideal since it avoids any confusion. However, it is also necessary to find out which method could respect the aim of the conflict rules and thus ensure legal certainty and, at the same time, guarantee the application of the protection required by the EU consumer directives when necessary.

As it is known, conflict of laws aims to determine the law applicable to international situations to ascertain which law a national judge will apply when cross-border elements are involved. The determination of the law applicable to a cross-border situation has been solved through history, in very general terms, with the application of two theories: unilateralism and multilateralism. The unilateral theory is historically the oldest and was used exclusively with its different variants until the nineteenth century. Substituted by the multilateral theory, the unilateral method is nowadays an exception in Europe and finds its principal expression through the existence of overriding mandatory rules. Is there a place for unilateralism in EU secondary law?

The existence of scope rules in the EU consumer directives, as well as in other instruments of secondary EU law, has been understood in different manners from a PIL point of view. On the one hand, those supporting a unilateralist method of PIL have defended that every act of EU law, and thus the EU consumer protection directives, determines, implicitly or explicitly, its own scope of application and claim a return of the unilateralist approach. There is a thorough study that has exclusively aimed to explain that EU secondary law is a manifestation of a modern unilateralist theory of PIL (Francq 2005).[176] On the other hand, those defending the persistence of the multilateral approach deny the previous statement and try to fit the scope rules within the existent multilateral conflict of laws system of the Rome I Regulation. Therefore, the question would be how and where the applicability of the secondary EU law, and the EU consumer protection directives, is to be determined: through traditional conflict of laws mechanisms following the Rome I Regulation or through the instruments themselves, depending on their nature and purpose, as it was done in the past before the prevalence of multilateralism.

Thus, this section will firstly argue the possibilities of fitting the scope rules of the EU consumer directives within the Rome I Regulation system, preserving thus the point of view that also conflict of laws regarding consumer contracts regulated by EU consumer directives should be solved through the Rome I Regulation. Secondly, however, the opposite point of view will be analysed, describing the possibility of determining the scope of EU consumer directives autonomously using a unilateral approach, discussing its advantages and disadvantages. Finally, a general reflexion on the application of foreign law will be made, listing few issues to take into account regarding the use of a unilateral approach over a multilateral method to solve conflicts of laws.

4.3.1 The Scope of EU Consumer Directives According to the Rome I Regulation System and the Prevalence of Multilateralism

If the scope rules of the directives are understood in the light of the traditional method of PIL and fit within the Rome I Regulation system, they should be considered not as general conflict of law rules but merely as mechanisms to guarantee the application of mandatory EU secondary law. Conflict rules and scope rules fulfil different functions: conflict rules aim to determine the law applicable to an international situation, while scope rules aim to ensure that the mandatory protection provided by an instrument is not circumvented.[177] At the same time, they both address the application of EU secondary law. According to Fallon and Francq, an 'applicability rule'—or, as we call it, a scope rule—'aims only at defining the spatial scope of a set of substantive rules, the mandatory character of which requests them to be applied irrespective of the law designated by the choice of law rule'.[178] According to Symeonides, 'localizing rules'—scope rules—are rules that '*expressly* delineate the spatial reach of the particular statute so as to ensure its applicability to certain multistate cases'.[179] In the Green Paper on the Conversion of the Rome

[176] Francq (2005).

[177] Kuipers (2012), pp. 221–223.

[178] Fallon and Francq (2000), p. 156.

[179] Symeonides (2014), p. 294.

Convention into the Rome I Regulation, the Commission referred to these rules as provisions that, although not being conflict rules, are 'rules that determine the scope of territorial application of community law and therefore having an impact on the applicable law'.[180]

As a result of the deficiencies of the Rome Convention, the EU legislator was forced to include scope rules in order to ensure that the minimum protection of the consumer protection directives was not avoided in situations the directive aimed to protect. It is true that they constitute a unilateral inroad but should not be seen as unilateral conflict rules as such; they operate similarly to overriding mandatory rules, trying to ensure the application of other rules.

In fact, the question whether rules contained in the consumer protection directives could be classified as overriding mandatory rules has been the object of intense debate. Some authors have defended that scope rules determine the overriding mandatory character of the provisions contained in the EU consumer directives.[181] If they were classified as such, the directive would be applicable according to article 9 Rome I (which ensures the applicability of overriding mandatory rules irrespective of the law applicable to the contract) and not through the scope rule and operation of article 23 Rome I. Thus, it would constitute a way to coordinate the existence of scope rules within the Rome I Regulation system. Overriding mandatory rules are the only mechanism that the Rome I Regulation provides for rules that delimit their international scope of application and prevail over the normal operation of conflict rules.

Overriding mandatory rules constitute a unilateral inroad within the mostly multilateral approach, followed by the European PIL, including the Rome I Regulation. Even Savigny, when describing his multilateral PIL method, recognised the existence of some rules that require their applicability regardless of the law applicable to the situation; the question was not which rule is applicable to a certain legal relationship but rather whether a legal rule of the forum law should be applicable to a case involving foreign elements where foreign law is applicable.[182] Nowadays, overriding mandatory rules are defined as rules crucial for the safeguarding of public interests, such as the political, social or economic organisation of a country, and are applicable regardless of the law designated as applicable.[183]

---

[180] Green Paper on the conversion of the Rome Convention of 1980 on the law applicable to contractual obligations into a Community instrument and its modernisation (COM(2002) 654 final), Sect. 3.1.1.1.

[181] Plender and Wilderspin (2015), pp. 268, 377–379; Fallon and Francq (2000), pp. 156–157; Bonomi (2016), p. 616; Sánchez Lorenzo (2003), pp. 374, 375.

[182] von Savigny (1849), (see in English: von Savigny (1869), pp. 34–37.). See also Sonnentag (2017), pp. 1609–1615.

[183] For example, in the Rome I Regulation, the definition of article 9 Rome I is as follows: 'Overriding mandatory provisions are provisions the respect for which is regarded as crucial by a country for safeguarding its public interests, such as its political, social or economic organisation, to such an extent that they are applicable to any situation falling within their scope, irrespective of the law otherwise applicable to the contract under this Regulation.'

However, overriding mandatory rules should be used as an exception to the normal operation of the conflict of laws in order to avoid a situation where every country that has an interest in the situation would try to impose the application of their national rules through the mechanism of overriding mandatory rules. Therefore, not every provision contained in the consumer protection directives can be classified as crucial for the safeguarding of the political, social or economic organisation of the country.[184] It is true that overriding mandatory rules are a matter of national law: each state decides which are overriding mandatory rules since article 9(2) Rome I just states that the provisions of the Regulation do not restrict the application of the overriding mandatory provisions of the forum, and therefore it is the Member State of the forum that has to decide which national rules are overriding mandatory. However, when that national rules are rules implementing the same or better standards of the EU directives, a consistent interpretation towards the objectives of the directive must be followed. As a result, what is crucial for the EU should be determined by the EU.[185] In this regard, it is true that the ECJ, especially concerning the Unfair Contract Terms Directive, has in some occasions referred to the protection of consumers as a purpose related to 'public interest'.[186] However, none of the cases concern a private international law discussion about the overriding mandatory character of these rules in order to ensure their application, but they mainly concern the procedural implications of the Unfair Contract Terms Directive. Also, the ECJ referred in those cases to the objective of consumer law to balance the interest of the parties to the contract and to the weaker position of the consumer. In the context of PIL, and in the Rome I Regulation, to determine that a provision is related to 'public interest' might have big implications since it can determine the difference between mandatory rules and overriding mandatory rules. A wide interpretation of what is an overriding mandatory rule would seriously damage the principles of party autonomy and decisional harmony of the Regulation.[187] Although in some cases of consumer protection public interests are involved, a large part of consumer law provisions is mainly aimed at the protection of private interests. That is, provisions regarding contracting or control of contract terms are primarily aimed at protecting the consumer as the weaker party to the contract; then by regulating those contracts, the consumer market is also regulated.[188] Thus, although the protection of consumers can be considered as related to 'public interest', it should not generally be regarded as 'crucial' for the public interest of a country or the EU in terms of article

---

[184]Regarding article 9 Rome I as a possible mechanism of protection of weaker contracting parties, see Sect. 3.3.

[185]Kuipers (2012), pp. 203–204.

[186]For example, see cases C-168/05 *Elisa María Mostaza Claro v Centro Móvil Milenium SL* [2006] ECR I-10421, para 38; C-243/08 *Pannon GSM Zrt. v Erzsébet Sustikné Győrfi* [2009] ECR I- 04713 paras 25, 31; C-26/13 *Árpád Kásler and Hajnalka Káslerné Rábai v OTP Jelzálogbank Zrt* [2014] para 78.

[187]Bisping (2012b), p. 251.

[188]Ibid.

9 Rome I. In order to not completely exclude party autonomy, the difference between mandatory rules and overriding mandatory rules has to be kept in mind.

If one were to interpret the rules of the directives as overriding mandatory, party autonomy would be completely excluded, they would be applicable regardless of the law otherwise applicable and it would not be relevant whether that applicable law resulted from the normal operation of the connecting factors or the choice of law by the parties. However, most of the scope rules contained in the EU consumer directives, with the exception of the Timeshare Directive, indicate that the provisions of the directive cannot be circumvented when a choice of the law of a non-Member State has been made and a close connection with the EU exists. This means that the rules of these directives are mandatory rules in the sense of article 6(2) Rome I and article 3(4) Rome I (or, as referred to in the latter article, 'provisions of Community law which cannot be derogated from by agreement'), not overriding mandatory rules that are applicable in any case.[189] The only exception is the Timeshare Directive: while the scope rules of the other directives indicate that their rules cannot be avoided by a choice of a foreign law when a close link with the EU exists, article 12(2) Timeshare Directive states that the consumer cannot be deprived of the protection of the Directive *regardless of the law applicable* when the immovable property is located in the EU or the professional directs its activities to the EU.[190] Thus, the rules of this Directive (specifically the national rules implementing this directive) could be interpreted as overriding mandatory rules.[191]

As a result, not all the EU consumer protection rules can be classified as overriding mandatory rules since not all of them are crucial for the safeguarding of the public interests of the EU and intend to be applicable regardless of the law otherwise applicable, but they rather only intend to ensure that they do not become circumvented as a result of a choice of a third country law.[192]

---

[189] Symeonides, when explaining the existence of unilateral inroads within a multilateral system, divides the different unilateral inroad rules into four types of rules:

(1) 'Localizing rules' contained in substantive statutes (other than choice-of-law codifications). These rules *expressly* delineate the spatial reach of the particular statute so as to ensure its applicability to certain multistate cases;
(2) 'Rules of immediate application' or 'mandatory rules.' These rules have the same effect as localizing rules, even in the absence of such express language;
(3) Unilateral choice-of-law rules contained in PIL codifications; and
(4) Certain multilateral rules that, despite their multilaterality and resulting appearance of neutrality, are designed to lead to the application of the *lex fori* in the majority of cases and thus to ensure compliance with important public policies of the enacting state.

He later classifies the scope rules contained in the EU consumer directives as 'localizing rules' rather than in the second category, which equals what we understand as overriding mandatory rules, supporting therefore the same position. Symeonides (2014), pp. 294, 296.

[190] Italics provided by the author.

[191] Kuipers (2012), pp. 223–224.

[192] In this regard, Basedow also claimed that the characterisation of these rules from a traditional PIL point of view as overriding mandatory rules would not fit with the fact that a choice of law is required for their application. However, he reasoned that the importance for the forum of an

Still, it is defended that the application of EU consumer directives should not be determined outside the system of the Rome I Regulation. The EU legislator, seeing that the Rome Convention contained gaps and was unable to accommodate the EU needs regarding consumer protection, started to lay down criteria for the application of the consumer directives through scope rules. At the time, it was seen as the only mechanism for the EU to guarantee the application of mandatory EU law. Thus, rather than unilateral conflict rules, these rules should be understood as scope rules that, more that determining the applicability of the directives, declare the level of mandatory nature of their provisions. They should be interpreted as rules facilitating the task of determining the degree of mandatoriness of the provisions of the instrument and not as conflict rules as such. Some of them could prevail over the multilateral conflict rules of Rome I through article 9 Rome I if they are to be classified as overriding mandatory rules, which would not happen in most of the cases. However, they should not prevail over article 23 Rome I because they would not be considered as conflict of laws rules.[193]

If we follow this approach, the Rome I Regulation system is respected, and the advantages deriving from the use of a (mostly) multilateral system are safeguarded. A multilateral approach requires a choice between the different state laws by connecting the legal relationship to the law of a state according to objective criteria. With this approach, equality between the forum law and foreign law is promoted, as well as predictability and respect for the expectations of the parties involved. This approach aims to achieve uniformity of results. Since a system completely based on value-free conflict rules is not sufficient in order to protect certain values essential for the forum, the Rome I Regulation includes, for example, special protective conflict rules for weaker contracting parties, with protective connecting factors and limits on party autonomy, and the doctrine of overriding mandatory rules.

However, this system is not able to differentiate between intra-EU situations and extra-EU situations. Under a PIL multilateral approach, a consumer contract between a Dutch consumer and a German professional is not different from a consumer contract between a Dutch consumer and a Brazilian professional. However, from the point of view of EU law, the situations completely differ from each other: while in the first case the application of the EU standards is ensured, in the second case there is the possibility that the EU standards are not applied when the

overriding mandatory rule depends on both the content and the connection of the situation with the forum country, being therefore possible that scope rules could have the character of overriding mandatory rules. Basedow (2006), p. 153. However, that being said, I still consider that not every directive on consumer protection can be classified as crucial for the safeguarding of the political, social or economic organisation of the EU, and the different drafting between article 12 (2) Timeshare Directive and the rest of the scope rules, the former requiring the application of the rules *regardless of the law applicable*, evidences the different level of mandatoriness existent between the named directives.

[193] Kuipers (2012), p. 224. On the contrary, considering scope rules prevail over the conflict rules of Rome I through article 23 Rome I since they are conflict rules of community origin, even though considering the situation as complex and unsatisfactory: Weller (2015), pp. 421–424; Mankowski (2016), p. 847.

EU intended to, disrupting the well-functioning of the internal market. The EU does not want that, as a result of the operation of conflict rules, difficulties to the functioning of the internal market are created, while the current PIL system does not properly reflect that desire, as it has been shown in this case regarding consumer protection.

4.3.2 *The Scope of EU Consumer Directives According to a Unilateral Approach: The Return of Unilateralism?*

In contrast to multilateralism, which focuses on the legal relationship in order to determine the law applicable, unilateralism focuses on the legal acts themselves and defends that each law determines its own scope of application. The first paradigm of unilateralism rests on the notion that laws prescribe their own scope of application, which derives from the content and purposes of the rule. As a result, the second paradigm of unilateralism is that each legal order would itself determine when and to which extent its rules would be applicable to international situations. Therefore, following a unilateral approach, every EU consumer protection directive determines its own international scope of application.

It has been explained that only some consumer protection directives contain explicit scope rules that impose the application of the minimum standards of the directive when the situation is closely connected to the territory of the Member States and a choice of law of a non-Member State has been made. However, following a unilateral approach, every directive, even implicitly, determines its scope of application.[194] Francq defends that every act of EU secondary law fixes implicitly or explicitly its own scope of application in the function of its objectives and substantive content.[195] Even when a directive does not include an explicit scope rule, it does not mean that it does not determine its own scope of application. Its scope of application can be inferred from its nature and purpose, a classical interpretation method. In this sense, all the substantive provisions of the directive should be taken into account to determine the scope that the directive aims to cover, as well as the recitals and preparatory works, which can be significant in order to ascertain the purpose of the directive. In fact, under this line of reasoning, even when the consumer protection directives contain an explicit scope rule, it could be necessary to take into account the purpose and nature of the instrument as well. For example, in order to interpret the vague term 'close connection' that these scope rules contain, it might be necessary to interpret the provisions of the directive and ascertain when a specific situation could be considered as closely connected to the territory of the EU for the purposes of that directive.[196] According to Francq, directives determine their

194 Francq (2006), p. 339.

195 Francq (2005), p. 479.

196 Francq (2006), pp. 346–348.

own scope of application just because they are rules of law, and rules of law necessarily define their territorial scope of application.[197] The author explains that the EU secondary law would adhere to the unilateralist theory of Quadri, according to which substantive rules always contain criteria of applicability because they are a manifestation of the will of the legislator.[198] According to Quadri, rules should be understood as commands, and thus they would include the indication of their addressees. All rules, as a result of specific experiences, include their own limits of application, at least in an implicit way.[199] Still, Francq states that the EU legal system conforms to the unilateralist theory, although it does not constitute a unilateral system.[200]

Those supporting a unilateral approach also find support on the reasoning of the ECJ in the previously mentioned *Ingmar* case.[201] In this case, the ECJ, in order to determine the international scope of application of the Commercial Agency Directive, interpreted it in the light of its nature and purpose. The Commercial Agency Directive, as the consumer protection directives enacted during the eighties, was silent about its international scope of application. Because of the choice of a non-Member State law (Californian law) where the principal was established, the commercial agent established in the UK, and performing all his activities in the UK and Ireland, did not have the protection provided for in the Commercial Agency Directive. The ECJ referred in his reasoning to the purposes of the Directive, which were 'to eliminate restrictions on the carrying-on of the activities of commercial agents, to make the conditions of competition within the Community uniform and to increase the security of commercial transactions'.[202] Moreover, the ECJ also based his decision on the provisions of the Directive at stake: articles 17 and 18 of the Commercial Agents Directive define the circumstances under which a commercial agent, upon termination of the contract, is entitled to claim compensation for the damages suffered by him because of the termination of his contractual relationship with the principal. At the same time, article 19 of the Directive states that

[197]Francq (2005), p. 479.

[198]Ibid., p. 479.

[199]Quadri (1967), p. 199. On the contrary, Mathieu (2015), pp. 78, 79: although recognising some legitimacy behind the statement that rules enacted by a legislator are a result of a sociological observation where the scope is limited to a given population, Mathieu has submitted that, firstly, the 'cultural context' is not capable of providing applicability criteria that are precise enough to be useful and, secondly, that sociological observations can remain relevant across the borders of a specific country. For example, the sociological observations behind the enactment of French and Belgian rules on contract law are not so different.

[200]Francq (2005), p. 599. In addition to Francq, several authors recognise the unilateralism existent in EU instruments, and the necessity of such approach, such as Bucher (2011), p. 82 et seq.; Symeonides (2005).

[201]Case C381/98 *Ingmar GB Ltd v Eaton Leonard Technologies Inc.* [2000] ECR I-9305.

[202]*Ingmar*, para. 23.

> parties may not derogate from articles 17 and 18 to the detriment of the agent before the agency contract expires.

The ECJ concluded that the nature and purpose that these provisions serve require their application where the situation is closely connected with the Community, irrespective of the law chosen by the parties to govern their contract.[203] Although the *Ingmar* decision only refers to articles 17 to 19 of the Commercial Agents Directive, a wider meaning could be inferred from its reasoning. The ECJ formed its decision by referring to the freedom of establishment and undistorted competition within the internal market as aims of these provisions, and as from the recitals of the Directive it is implied that these objectives are present in more provisions, those other provisions of the Directive could be regarded also as applicable *irrespective of the law by which the parties intended the contract to be governed.*[204] Therefore, the ECJ determined that the Directive applies when the situation has a close connection with the EU, which is presumed when the agent carries out his activities in a Member State. It is observed that the ECJ determines the international scope of application of a directive that lacks an explicit scope rule based on its nature and purpose.

Thus, following this reasoning, the criteria for applicability would always be included in the instrument itself, but they would not always be presented as such.[205] Inclusion of the criteria for territorial applicability in the instrument and silence about the application of foreign law are characteristics of the unilateral method. If we understood that the EU is following a unilateral approach, the directives would always determine their own scope according to their purpose while being silent about the application of foreign law. The existence of explicit scope rules would thus be justified as rules helping to define the international scope of the directive, and the reasoning followed by the ECJ in the *Ingmar* case, which received many criticisms, would also be justified as it follows traditional methods of interpretation in order to determine the scope of the directive. Since article 23 Rome I states that the provisions of the Rome I do not

> prejudice the application of provisions of Community law which, in relation to particular matters, lay down conflict-of-law rules relating to contractual obligations,

the unilateral conflict rules laid down in the directives would prevail over the conflict rules of the Rome I Regulation. Since this provision is the reflection of the principle *lex specialis* over *lex generalis*, and thus the special unilateral rules of the directives take precedence as a general principle, both explicit and implicit scope rules would prevail over the provisions of the Rome I Regulation.[206]

---

[203] *Ingmar*, para. 25.

[204] Ibid.

[205] Francq (2006), p. 348.

[206] Following this line of reasoning, Ibid., pp. 354, 355.

If we were to accept the prevalence of unilateralism in the determination of the international scope of EU law, could the EU objectives be better achieved? Following the postulates of unilateralism developed during the twentieth century, mainly supported in Europe by the writings of Jean-Paul Niboyet, Rolando Quadri or Alexander Pilenko, the reason why the determination of the scope of application of a law is an inherent part of it lies in the postulate that laws are not universal (i.e. they are territorial) but are created to fulfil specific aims of a society, and as such they have a specific reach.[207] For example, according to the view of Quadri, a complete unilateralist thinker who rejected and attacked multilateralism and even the concept of conflict rules, rules always contain limits of their own efficiency, since they command the activities and actions of the individuals, and thus must identify their addressees as well. Laws are a product of social experience.[208] Then a legal instrument, understood according to its purpose, would be considered as an instrument that regulates social and economic life, and thus enacted based on specific political or economic aims, or the special needs of a society. Therefore, the modern unilateralist thinking would be based on the understanding of law as fulfilling the purposes of regulating specific social or economic needs of the society rather than aiming neutrality or justice, and because of that it limits its own application.[209] EU law serves the social and economic needs of the EU, necessary to establish an internal market.[210] The EU aims to maintain and develop an area of freedom, security and justice, and in order to achieve that goal, it is necessary to regulate the economic activities that affect the market. Thus, EU law is created in order to achieve the ideal economic development of the market, taking into account the

[207] Niboyet (1952), Quadri (1967) and Pilenko (1954).

[208] Quadri (1967).

[209] In contrast, multilateralism differs in its conception of law. Both unilateral and multilateral theories, besides solving a conflict of laws, include a certain conception of the general nature of the rules of law. The majority of multilateral thinkers agree that rules of law are neutral and universal, since they are the result of rationality. They understand the law as a model of social conduct and an answer a judge gives when a certain behaviour is presented to him, and thus can be used by the judge to all the cases presented to him regardless of the place where the facts took place or where the persons come from. The rule of law is understood as the type of legal solution appropriate for when certain facts occur, and as such is virtually universal. Mathieu (2015), p. 75; Francq (2017), p. 1786.

[210] Article 3(3) TEU explains the EU objectives, both economic and social:

> The Union shall establish an internal market. It shall work for the sustainable development of Europe based on balanced economic growth and price stability, a highly competitive social market economy, aiming at full employment and social progress, and a high level of protection and improvement of the quality of the environment. It shall promote scientific and technological advance.
>
> It shall combat social exclusion and discrimination, and shall promote social justice and protection, equality between women and men, solidarity between generations and protection of the rights of the child.
>
> It shall promote economic, social and territorial cohesion, and solidarity among Member States.
>
> It shall respect its rich cultural and linguistic diversity, and shall ensure that Europe's cultural heritage is safeguarded and enhanced.

respect for certain social values. In the same manner, the consumer protection directives pursue specific economic and social objectives, necessary for the well-functioning of the internal market.[211] The EU legislator, when making use of scope rules, is making sure that those objectives are not spoiled. As a result, the use of a unilateral approach could be seen as a more pragmatic manner of ensuring that the aims of the consumer protection directives are fulfilled. EU secondary law determining its own scope of application cannot be made to completely conform to overriding mandatory rules, and therefore the EU legislator makes use of the unilateral method thinking in functional terms. The EU legislator aims to achieve specific social or economic objectives, and indications on the international scope of the instrument are sometimes provided in order to ensure those objectives.[212]

A priori, taking a unilateral approach turns out to be more attractive, even as a general PIL system for EU law, but several points are to be taken into account.

The well-known major criticism of unilateralism is with regard to the conflict created when two or more legal orders claim application to the situation and when none of them does. Although at this stage every unilateral theory differs in its proposed solutions (e.g. Currie resorted to the forum non conveniens theory, some modern unilateralists resort to multilateralism at this stage, and others, like Quadri, searched for the law that in practice is more effective and corresponds to the expectation of the parties),[213] this is known as the most problematic issue of unilateralism, and no definitive solution has been generally accepted. Regarding the lacuna, when no legal order claims application, most have opted for the application of the *lex fori*, although different approaches can be found in this regard as well.[214]

Also, if the decision needs to be recognised or enforced in a different country, that country would be more reluctant to recognise and enforce the foreign decision when the forum judge unilaterally applied the forum law to an international situation with no objective connections to the forum country.

Moreover, since the unilateral approach only gives room for the application of foreign law once it is determined that the situation is not covered by the substantive forum law, it is considered as a forum-centred approach. It would be inconsistent to

[211] According to the European Parliament research service, 'European consumer policy is a vital element of a well-functioning internal market. It aims to guarantee consumers rights vis-à-vis merchants and to provide additional protection, for example for vulnerable consumers. Empowering consumers and effectively protecting their safety and economic interests have become essential goals of European policy in the area of consumer protection. Research carried out for the European Parliament indicates that effective consumer protection policy is essential for an efficient and well-functioning European market. Improved transparency and better informed transactions resulting from well implemented consumer policy results in better solutions for consumers and greater market efficiency.' Mariusz Maciejewski and Sarabjeet Hayer, "Consumer policy: principles and instruments", *Fact sheets of the European Union*, March 2017, available in: http://www.europarl.europa.eu/atyourservice/en/displayFtu.html?ftuId=FTU_5.5.1.html.

[212] Francq (2017), pp. 1789, 1790.

[213] Ibid., pp. 1784, 1785.

[214] Ibid., pp. 1784, 1785.

maintain that EU law depends on its own applicability criteria and impose its application and to ignore at the same time that foreign law might do the same. One of the main PIL principles in our current PIL system is the equal treatment between forum law and foreign law, which unilateralism does not respect. While the principle of supremacy applies to relationships between national Member States law and EU law, when a foreign law comes into play, the EU is not the sovereign. Since the EU legislator is not the sole legislator, it should not impose its law over foreign law.[215]

It can also be added that legal certainty is not benefited from a unilateral approach: instead of defining the circumstances under which a Member State law applies and under which foreign law applies, it would only be determined when EU law applies; moreover, the practice of finding the purpose of a legal act might be difficult and adds uncertainty to the process of determining the applicable law. In that sense, unilateralism might be seen more as an approach rather than as a specific PIL system.[216]

To sum up, the advantages of following a unilateral approach regarding EU law in general are a more pragmatic and better protection of the EU objectives. However, this would result in a protectionist system that imposes the application of its law over foreign law, completely contradictory with the current PIL approach. In my opinion, a general unilateral approach should be rejected, although it will be discussed below whether, for specific sectors of EU law, consumer protection in this case could be considered not as a general approach but as an exception to multilateralism.

4.3.3 General Reflexions Regarding the Interaction Between Multilateral and Unilateral Methods in the EU PIL

As a general reflexion, taking into account the PIL values, the need of protection of weaker contracting parties such as the consumers and the special needs of the internal market, several points might be taken into account in terms of a future change of approach of EU PIL. In this regard, it has to be noticed that regarding the PIL method, methodological purity (i.e. purely multilateral method or unilateral method) is not realistic nor desirable; no contemporary conflict of laws system is purely multilateral or purely unilateral.[217] Also, both methods should not be understood as opposite, but combined together they might produce a better PIL system. Since European PIL history has shown us that a multilateral method brings more

[215]Kuipers (2012), p. 215. As Rühl explains, one of the principal characteristics of our modern PIL system is the openness to the application of a foreign law, rather than requiring courts to systematically apply law of the forum in cross-border situations. Rühl (2017), p. 1383.

[216]Francq (2017), p. 1786; Basedow (2017), p. 1401.

[217]Symeonides (2005), pp. 433–434.

advantages than a unilateral method does, we could then analyse which situations might require the introduction of a unilateral inroad.

4.3.3.1 Interrelationship Among Countries and Similarity of Legal Values

The traditional approach of PIL since Savigny and until nowadays has been to solve a conflict of laws from the point of view of the legal relationship, with a neutral conflict rule that would find the legal systems most closely connected to the legal relationship. In that manner, international harmony of decisions would be achieved, meaning that the outcome would be the same regardless of the jurisdiction where the proceedings were brought, which would prevent limping legal relationships and would promote legal certainty.[218]

Having this in mind, one reflexion can be made: it makes sense that when different legal systems share common or similar legal values, conflict of laws rules should definitely promote equality between these different national legal systems through neutral conflict rules; however, when legal systems do not share similar legal values and important interests are at stake, should the application of foreign law be decided by neutral conflict rules?

It has been suggested to understand the application of foreign law by imagining a sliding scale (scale of Ten Wolde): on the one end of the scale are states with which no basic values or principles are shared, against which the forum state would desire to apply its own law, and on the other end are states that are so integrated with each other that they share the same legal values and principles, and thus there would be neutrality regarding the application of the forum law or foreign law.[219] Of course, it is difficult to imagine countries at the far end of the scale, which do not share basic values or legal principles whatsoever and do not have any interaction among other countries. On the other side of the scale, we can have the EU Member States (depending on which area of law) or the American states or the Spanish provinces, for example; they are completely interconnected societies that share the same or very similar legal values and can, therefore, easily apply neutral conflict rules to resolve conflicts of laws within them.[220]

The interrelationship between the countries involved becomes one of the factors that PIL should take into account in order to determine the application of foreign law.

---

[218]It is necessary to put Savigny's multilateral theory and his 'community of law among independent states' in context: the conclusion to apply the same principles to conflict laws between independent states and to conflict laws between interstate conflicts is related to the geographical and legal situation he lived: in 1849, Prussia consisted on several regions where, at the same time, different laws were into force; moreover, Prussia belonged to a confederation of German States, for which Savigny considered the existence of a common law among the various German states. von Savigny (1869), p. 25 et seq.

[219]Ten Wolde (2013), p. 576.

[220]Ibid., p. 576.

The more the countries are interrelated, the more legal values they would share and, therefore, the more eager they would be to use neutral conflict rules. However, in the opposite case, the more the countries are on the other side of the scale, the more need for a unilateral approach ensuring the application of the forum law.

4.3.3.2 The Mandatory Character of the Forum Rules

The importance of the interconnection between countries and the legal values shared among them in order to determine the application of foreign law varies in the different areas of law. In contract law, a mostly value-free area where the free will of the parties prevails, the existence of common principles among the countries involved does not seem to be so relevant as compared, for example, to family law, where the cultural differences among the countries are evident in the legal system of each country. Therefore, the use of a multilateral method should be more extended in more value-free areas of law, while in other areas of law with a stronger mandatory character, it would be required to introduce more unilateral inroads in order to ensure their legal values.

Still, in the area of contract law, there might be important values at stake, such as the protection of consumers, employees etc. Therefore, it is necessary to differentiate between rules with an overriding mandatory character, rules with a mandatory character and rules with regulatory character. Then in contract law, regarding rules with a regulatory character (which are the majority of rules in this field), it makes sense that conflict rules promoting neutrality between legal systems prevail since relevant values are not at stake. When talking about rules with a mandatory character, for example in the areas of contract law that aim to protect contractual weaker parties (e.g. consumer law), the state needs to protect these values, and thus the conflict rules are not that neutral but conditioned to ensure these values of the forum state when necessary. In the case of overriding mandatory rules, essential for the organisation of a state, the forum state would like to ensure the application of these rules unconditionally.[221]

Even in a mostly value-free area such as contract law, the existence of mandatory rules and overriding mandatory rules can require to introduce, as an exception to multilateralism, some unilateral-based rules. Then multilateralism would be the general rule and unilateralism the exception.

4.3.3.3 The Special Situation of the European Union

In the case of the EU Member States, regarding intra-EU conflicts, we could place them almost at the end of the scale, where the societies are so interconnected that

[221] An extensive reflexion in this regard is found in: Marques dos Santos (1991).

they almost share the same legal values. Again, this depends on which area of law, but, in general, multilateral conflict rules should prevail.

Moreover, there are many fields that are harmonised among the EU. The more harmonised an area of law is, the less need for unilateral conflict rules since all Member States would share the same (minimum) standards.

In our case, regarding consumer protection, we can differentiate between minimum harmonisation directives and maximum harmonisation directives. While the first ones impose minimum protection standards that the Member States have to implement, and moreover improve, the latter impose the same standards among the Member States. Since at least the same minimum standards are shared, multilateral conflict rules should be used in intra-EU conflicts.

Regarding extra-EU situations, in harmonised areas of law such as consumer law, the Member States should be understood as a single legal order, in which sometimes, in order to defend their values, they should require the application of EU mandatory rules against a foreign legal order and thus make use of a more unilateral approach when necessary, according to the circumstances described above.

4.4 Achieving a Better Consumer Protection in the EU While Respecting PIL Values: Some Proposals

Some suggestions to coordinate the interaction of the Rome I Regulation and the EU consumer directives with regard to their international scope will be submitted on the basis of two starting points: first, on the basis of the idea that PIL methodological purity is rejected (and has been rejected in Europe for more than 50 years) since it does not seem possible that a single method, neither multilateral nor unilateral, can solve all conflict of laws issues[222] and, second, on the basis of the notion that the EU area of justice and the correct functioning of the internal market should be respected and thus EU consumer protection should be ensured when necessary. Indeed, the PIL method should respect and reflect the changing needs of society.

The Rome I Regulation includes a review clause in article 27 Rome I, according to which the Commission should have submitted a report on the application of the Regulation, including a study on the law applicable to insurance contracts and an evaluation on the application of article 6 Rome I, especially concerning its coherence with EU law in the area of consumer protection.[223] While a report regarding

[222]Fernández Rozas (2000); Jacquet (2010), p. 36; Marques dos Santos (1991); Batiffol (1973).

[223]Article 27(1) Rome I provides: 'By 17 June 2013, the Commission shall submit to the European Parliament, the Council and the European Economic and Social Committee a report on the application of this Regulation. If appropriate, the report shall be accompanied by proposals to amend this Regulation. The report shall include:

(a) a study on the law applicable to insurance contracts and an assessment of the impact of the provisions to be introduced, if any; and insurance contracts was submitted,[224] a report regarding an explicit evaluation of article 6 Rome I and its interaction with the EU consumer directives has not been released up to the date of writing, even if it was due by mid-June 2013. On the other hand, an extensive review of EU consumer law (Fitness Check) took place in 2017, aiming to analyse aspects such as effectiveness, efficiency, coherence, relevance and efficient achievement of objectives of several EU consumer directives; however, this Fitness Check explicitly excludes the evaluation of the Rome I Regulation on the basis that 'EU consumer law instruments are also without prejudice to the existing EU rules of private international law, in particular Regulation (EC) No 593/2008 of the European Parliament and of the Council of 17 June 2008 on the law applicable to contractual obligations (Rome I) and Regulation (EC) No 1215/2012 on jurisdiction and the recognition and enforcement of judgments in civil and commercial matters (recast). This Fitness Check does not, therefore, extend to these instruments.'[225] While a report regarding the function of article 6 Rome I and the interaction of the Rome I Regulation with the EU consumer directives would be desirable, the exclusion of this topic from the Fitness Check, together with the most recently enacted directives, gives us a hint that the new pattern of the EU is to refer any conflict of laws issue deriving from the consumer protection directives to the coverage of Rome I Regulation.

Considering that the 'new trend' of the EU legislator is to dispense with the scope rules of the consumer directives and determine the law applicable to a consumer contract exclusively through the conflict rules of the Rome I Regulation, some improvements could be made regarding the Rome I Regulation system to accommodate it to the needs of the EU consumer protection.

4.4.1 Elimination of Scope Rules from EU Consumer Directives

In my opinion, scope rules contained in EU consumer directives should be eliminated since the uncertainty they create might be even prejudicial to the consumer, whom they seek to protect: that is, uncertainty around its nature and function and with regard to their interaction with the Rome I Regulation; vagueness in their drafting, causing a difficult and possible diverse implementation in the national law of the Member States; disruption of the EU conflict of laws system based on

---

(b) an evaluation on the application of Article 6, in particular as regards the coherence of Community law in the field of consumer protection.'

224 Final Report of the Commission Expert Group on European Insurance Contract Law, *European Commission, Doctorate-General for Justice (2014), available at: http://ec.europa.eu/justice/contract/files/expert_groups/insurance/final_report_en.pdf.*

225 European Commission Evaluation and Fitness Check (FC) Roadmap (REFIT Fitness Check of consumer law) (December 2015), available in: http://ec.europa.eu/smart-regulation/roadmaps/docs/2016_just_023_evaluation_consumer_law_en.pdf.

the Rome I Regulation regarding contractual obligations; and legal uncertainty when rules somehow affecting conflict of laws are dispersed in different instruments (in this regard, as recital 40 Rome I states,

> 'a situation where conflict-of-law rules are dispersed among several instruments and where there are differences between those rules should be avoided').

The possibility of introducing a list of EU consumer directives into the Annex of the Rome I Regulation as instruments including specific conflict rules prevailing over the general conflict rules of the Rome I Regulation has been considered during the transformation of the Rome Convention into the Rome I Regulation. The Rome I Proposal included in Annex I a list of instruments laying down conflict rules relating to contractual obligations and which should prevail over the conflict rules of the Rome I (article 22 Proposal Rome I). Although this list did not include the EU consumer directives, it was defended that if the list of the Annex were to be in the final version of the Regulation, it should also include the scope rules of the consumer directives.[226] This solution has been rejected since that would impose a continuous necessity for adaptation in order to include new consumer directives.[227] However, if directives were to keep including scope rules and the legislator indeed aimed for them to prevail over the general conflict rules of the Rome I Regulation, the inclusion of such list would increase legal certainty and facilitate the task of the legal operator and would constitute the only manner of coordinating the existence of such rules with the Rome I Regulation and at the same time allow each directive to design its own international scope. Still, in my opinion, such a solution would tip the balance excessively in favour of a unilateral method of PIL.

4.4.2 *Protection of EU Mobile Consumers Against a Non-EU Choice of Law When Necessary: Distinguishing Between Intra-EU and Extra-EU Situations in Article 6 Rome I*

'Holiday consumers' or mobile consumers (i.e. a consumer from Member State A who while on a short stay in Member State B is approached by a non-Member State company that is targeting its activities to Member State A) are excluded from the protection of article 6 Rome I in case of a choice of a third country law since article

[226]Max Planck Institute for Foreign Private and Private International Law (2007), pp. 339–344.

[227]For example, this option was completely rejected by the responses to the proposal in Magnus U, Mankowski P (2002) Joint Response to the Green Paper on the conversion of the Rome Convention on the Law Applicable to Contractual Obligations into a Community Instrument and its Modernisation (COM 2002) 654 final, p. 8; Max Planck Institute for Foreign Private and Private International Law (2004), pp. 15, 16.

6 Rome I requires that the professional directs his activity to the Member State of habitual residence of the consumer in order to ensure the application of the mandatory provisions of the law of the state of habitual residence of the consumer. It is not logical that a consumer from Member State A would lose the EU consumer law protection just because he is on holiday on Member State B and at the same time not enjoying the protection of Member State B; it is more in line with the objectives of EU consumer protection and the normal functioning of the internal market that, for example, a Dutch consumer travelling to Spain enjoys the same protection as a Spanish consumer vis-à-vis a non-EU professional, even when the latter does not target the Dutch market. The effectiveness of EU consumer protection directives would be threatened if a professional established in a non-Member State could target EU consumers who are temporarily staying in another Member State without being bound to the EU consumer requirements, being able to circumvent them by a simple choice of a third country law. Instead of solving this gap through scope rules contained in the directives themselves, a novelty could be incorporated within article 6 Rome I: in the case of legislation implementing EU consumer directives, the different Member States could be seen as a single jurisdiction; the EU should be seen as a single state in this regard.[228] Article 6 Rome I would be able to differentiate between intra-EU and extra-EU cases.

It is true that until now article 6 Rome I is a protective conflict rule that does not discriminate or differentiate between forum law and foreign law and, in this case, between EU consumer law and non-EU consumer law. Following the basic notion of our current PIL that legal orders should be treated equally, article 6 Rome I provides for the application of the law of habitual residence of the consumer and ensures that the application of its mandatory provisions against a choice of law of another country, regardless of the habitual residence of the consumer (and thus the law applicable), is in a Member State or in a third country. Although introducing a protective connecting factor favouring consumers, article 6 Rome I is a multilateral conflict rule, non-discriminating against foreign law and respecting the legitimate expectations of the parties and legal certainty. Moreover, the fact that scope rules contained in directives took a unilateral approach and determined the scope of the directive ignoring the application of foreign law and the Rome I Regulation system has been criticised previously in this chapter.[229]

However, the proposed solution would entail taking a unilateral inroad and favouring EU consumer law: whenever a professional directs his activities to a Member State, the application of the minimum requirements of EU consumer directives should be ensured, regardless of the Member State of habitual residence of the consumer. In my opinion, this little exception to the multilateral nature of the provision could be justified. First, the specific conflict of laws issue deriving from the international application of EU directives calls for a special solution: it does not seem outrageous to consider the EU as a single jurisdiction for international cases when

[228] In the same opinion: Kuipers (2012), p. 220.

[229] See in this Chapter 4.1. Also, Magnus (2016), pp. 23, 24; Weller (2015), pp. 422, 433.

the mandatory provisions we are talking about are also EU made. The situation 'EU mandatory law vs. foreign country law' can be treated as equal to 'forum mandatory law vs. foreign country law', and thus a choice of foreign law should not result in depriving the EU consumer of the protection granted by EU consumer law.

This modification will mean a PIL adaptation to the EU requirements. For the EU, a conflict between a German consumer and a Spanish consumer is considered internal, while a conflict between a German consumer and a Moroccan professional is considered international; from a PIL point of view, both are international. By treating the EU as a 'country' in cases where the application of EU directives is at the stake, the Rome I Regulation would be adapting to the EU necessities. Moreover, the legal expectations of the parties are better served since 'holiday consumers' or mobile consumers would be protected, and, regarding the professional, it can be expected that when targeting the EU market, the EU standards are to be applicable. That is, in harmonised areas, an intra-EU conflict of laws situation would be comparable to an intra-regional conflict of laws situation.

The Max Planck Institute, in its Comments on the Green Paper for the Conversion of the Rome Convention in the Rome I Regulation, already proposed a similar addition to the conflict rule on consumer contracts involving mobile consumers: *If a supplier residing in a non-Member State directs his business activities to one or more Member States, the choice of law of a non-Member State as the law applicable to a contract falling into the scope of such activities does not deprive a consumer who, at the time of the conclusion of the contract, is habitually resident in a Member State of the protection afforded by the relevant Directives; in this case, the provisions of the relevant Directives apply as implemented in the domestic law of the Member State in which the consumer concluded the contract.*[230]

I propose that the same or a very similar rule, ensuring the application of the protection of the relevant EU consumer directives when a non-EU professional targets the EU market, be included in article 6 Rome I following article 6(3) Rome I. Article 6(3) Rome I provides:

> If the requirements in points (a) or (b) of paragraph 1 are not fulfilled, the law applicable to a contract between a consumer and a professional shall be determined pursuant to Articles 3 and 4.

With the introduction of the new proposed provision, in cases where the territorial requirements of article 6(1) Rome I are not fulfilled, the choice of law resulting from the application of the general rule of article 3 Rome I should not deprive the consumer of the protection granted by the relevant EU consumer directives in the case that a non-EU professional directed his activities to the internal market. I consider the introduction of a similar provision as a better manner of ensuring the application of EU consumer directives since it fulfils the function of scope rules (i.e. ensuring that the mandatory EU consumer protection is not circumvented by a

[230] Max Planck Institute for Foreign Private and Private International Law (2004), p. 15.

foreign choice of law) but at the same time does not disrupt the whole EU conflict of laws system with dispersed conflict rules in different instruments, ensuring legal certainty and respecting the legitimate expectations of the parties. The PIL values are respected; it only adapts the needs of EU law in PIL terms: in the same manner that consumer protection provided by the country of habitual residence of the consumer cannot be circumvented by a choice of foreign law, EU consumer protection provided by the EU directives cannot be circumvented by a choice of law when a consumer has habitual residence in a Member State.

4.4.3 Protection of Some Consumer Contracts Not Covered by Article 6 Rome I: Extending the Scope of Article 3(4) Rome I

If we were to include the aforementioned provision in article 6 Rome I, it seems logical that the material exceptions contained in article 6(4) Rome I would still be applicable: article 6 Rome I only applies to consumer contracts not excluded by article 6(4) Rome I, and the number of contracts recognised by the EU consumer directives is more extensive. The most controversial exception is the first one:

> (a) *Contracts for the supply of services where the services are to be supplied to the consumer exclusively in a country other than that in which he has his habitual residence*

(e.g. accommodation in a hotel, a language course etc.). The rationale behind this exclusion is to respect the legitimate expectations of the professional, and since the contract is supposed to be more connected with the country where the service is supplied, the consumer could not reasonably expect the law of the country of his habitual residence to apply.[231] However, because of this exclusion, the consumer is treated as if he were a professional since there are no restrictions on the choice of law, meaning that he can also be deprived of the protection afforded to him by the law of the country where the services are provided. An example is a case where a French resident enters into a consumer contract for an English language course held in Ireland and the contract contains a choice of a foreign law and he does not receive the protection of French law nor Irish law. The consumer could expect French mandatory law to not be applicable since the English course completely takes place in Ireland. But could he expect that other laws apply in this situation?

If one were to keep the material exceptions of article 6(4) Rome I, since there is a rationale behind them, but still palliate the effects of some minor gaps resulting from the material scope limitations of article 6 Rome I, that might be sorted out by article 3 (4) Rome I. Article 3(4) Rome I provides:

---

[231]Garcimartín Alférez (2008), p. 72.

Where all other elements relevant to the situation at the time of the choice are located in one or more Member States, the parties' choice of applicable law other than that of a Member State shall not prejudice the application of provisions of Community law, where appropriate as implemented in the Member State of the forum, which cannot be derogated from by agreement.

This provision becomes applicable when all relevant elements are located within the EU (intra-EU situations).[232] However, in this case, we would require a provision that ensures the application of EU consumer directives even if not all the relevant elements are located in the EU since, for instance, in the example above the professional might be a company established in China focused on Chinese nationals but with habitual residence in a Member State. It could be considered the introduction of the close connection test that scope rules provided rather than the 'all relevant elements to the situation' requirement. It is true that 'a close connection with the territory of one or more Member States' is a vague term; however, maybe presumptions to facilitate its interpretation could be included. Moreover, this general expression was originally intended 'to make it possible to take account of various ties depending on the circumstances of the case'.[233] In the directives, this constituted legal uncertainty and inconsistencies since directives are to be transposed into national law and might give rise to as many interpretations as there are Member States. However, this would not be the case if we include this concept in article 3 (4) Rome I. In the case of consumer contracts, it would be ensured that, in the case of consumer contracts not covered by article 6 Rome I, the consumer (for example a consumer falling under the exception of article 6(4)(a)), is not treated as a professional, but the application of the EU consumer protection standards is ensured through this provision. Moreover, it does not preclude the application of foreign law but only ensures the application of EU mandatory law when the situation is most closely connected with the EU.

Finally, one reflexion regarding all the modifications suggested is that even if they suppose a limitation in the exercise of party autonomy, they do not eliminate it. I consider that a systematic application of the law of habitual residence of the consumer, although it is true that it avoids the task of analysing the applicable mandatory rules of the chosen law and the law of habitual residence of the consumer and brings some legal certainty, it would also mean that the protective rules of the consumer's habitual residence would apply to any case (e.g. mobile consumers, active consumers etc.), which might negatively affect the market and would not be

[232] Article 3(4) Rome I cannot be used to justify the application of European provisions when all relevant elements are not located within the European Union. Article 3(4) Rome I has been questioned as it does not fulfil its purpose of coordination and protection against abuse of law, since it does not cover any extra-EU situation. EU mandatory law becomes applicable provided all the relevant elements are within the EU (but rather just require a close connection with the Member States). As a result, either article 3(4) is not adapted to the requirements of the EU secondary law, or the EU secondary law is not adapted to the Rome I Regulation system.

[233] *Commission v Spain* (para. 32).

according to the expectations of the parties.[234] In my opinion, the advantages that party autonomy brings can be coordinated with the needs of consumer law and EU consumer law without completely setting aside party autonomy, but just limiting it. Also, in case of consumer directives that seem to require to be applicable irrespectively whether a foreign law is applicable as a result of a choice of law or of the normal operation of the connecting factors (i.e. the Timeshare Directive), their provisions, if they are to be regarded as essential for the organisation of a state (or of the EU), can be ensured through article 9 Rome I since the existence of overriding mandatory rules in EU consumer directives, rather than normal mandatory rules, seems exceptional.[235]

4.5 Closing Remarks

In order to better understand the existent inconsistencies regarding the relationship between EU consumer directives and the Rome I Regulation, and the implications of this relationship in the EU conflict of laws system, several reflexions and conclusions can be highlighted from this chapter.

First, regarding the current inconsistencies, these derive from the different protective reach that article 6 Rome I and the EU consumer directives intend to cover. With the enactment of the first generation of consumer directives in the eighties, it was evident that the protective conflict rule of the Rome Convention (article 5 Rome Convention regarding some consumer contracts) left outside its scope many situations the directives intended to apply to. This became evident with the Gran Canaria cases, where simply a choice of a third country law set aside the EU mandatory consumer provisions in cases where they clearly should have been applicable. In order to avoid the circumvention of the application of EU mandatory consumer law, the EU legislator started to introduce in the second generation of consumer directives scope rules that provided for the application of the standards of the directive whenever there was a choice of a non-Member State law and the situation was closely connected with the EU. Although article 6 Rome I broadened its scope of

[234]The Max Planck Institute, in its comments to the Green Paper for the conversion of the Rome Convention, agreed with this statement. Max Planck Institute for Foreign Private and Private International Law (2004), p. 54. However, later on, when commenting on the Rome I Proposal eliminating party autonomy in this regard, it embraced the modification on the basis of avoiding a complicated interaction between the choice of law and mandatory rules, bringing more legal certainty. Max Planck Institute for Foreign Private and Private International Law (2007), pp. 269, 270.

[235]In a different opinion, Magnus and Mankowski consider that to distinguish between cases where a choice of law has been made and where no choice of law has been made would be unsuccessful, since the aim would be to protect the EU standards and this aim applies irrespective of a choice of law. Magnus U, Mankowski P (2002) Joint Response to the Green Paper on the conversion of the Rome Convention on the Law Applicable to Contractual Obligations into a Community Instrument and its Modernisation (COM 2002) 654 final, pp. 8, 9.

application and covers more consumer contracts, there are still gaps on its regulation, such as 'mobile consumers'.

Thus, it is questioned whether there is still a need for scope rules in order to ensure the application of consumer directives when necessary. It is submitted that the existence of scope rules does more harm than good: first, their drafting is too broad; in general, they do not stipulate which law should be applicable (the directive as implemented by the law of the Member State of habitual residence of the consumer, the law of the forum etc.), and the requirement of a close connection is difficult to interpret. As a result, the implementation of scope rules into the national law of the different Member States creates different interpretations and thus adds more uncertainty to the system; since Member States implement into their national law different drafting of the scope rules, sometimes even taking a unilateral approach ensuring the application of national law, a sort of parallel intra-EU conflict of laws system is created. Second, scope rules are unrelated and disrupt the current conflict of laws system of the Rome I Regulation. Introducing the unilateral approach of the scope rules, which determines the scope of the instrument without referring to foreign law, clashes with the multilateral nature of the Rome I Regulation. Moreover, if the Rome I Regulation tries to unify the conflict of laws of the different Member States in contractual obligations, scope rules disrupt that aim. The consumer is most certainly better protected in a coherent system that ensures legal certainty, and therefore a preference for an integrated Rome I approach is defended. Moreover, this seems to be the new trend followed by the EU legislator since the most recent consumer directives refer the conflict of laws matter to the rules of the Rome I Regulation.

Second, it is debated whether the Rome I Regulation traditional approach is preferred to a change of approach towards a unilateral method in order to determine the scope of application of EU consumer directives. According to a unilateral approach, every directive determines its own scope of application; even if it does not contain an explicit scope rule, every directive, even implicitly, determines its own scope according to its purpose and nature. In fact, this point of view finds support in the *Ingmar* decision of the ECJ, in which the court determined the international applicability of the Commercial Agency Directive, which lacks an explicit scope rule, based on the nature and purpose of the directive. A unilateral thinking would justify the existence of scope rules of directives as well as the *Ingmar* decision. Since the modern unilateralist thinking is based on the understanding of law as fulfilling the purposes of regulating specific social or economic needs of the society, rather than aiming neutrality or justice as multilateralism defends, and EU law serves the social and economic needs of the EU necessary to establish an internal market, those objectives would be easily promoted by the use of a unilateralist approach. The use of a unilateral approach can be seen as a more pragmatic manner of ensuring that the aims of the consumer protection directives are fulfilled. Nevertheless, apart from the problems inherent to a unilateral approach (i.e. the conflict created when two or more legal orders claim application to the situation and when none of them does, as well as being a forum-centred approach that does not consider the application of foreign law), other disadvantages arise if we were to use this approach to determine the application of EU consumer directives autonomously.

First, it would be inconsistent to maintain that EU law depends on its own applicability criteria and imposes its application and at the same time ignore the fact that foreign law might do the same; the principle of supremacy applies to relationships between national Member States law and EU law, but when a foreign law comes into play, the EU is not the sovereign. It is submitted that the EU legislator should not impose its law over foreign law. Second, legal certainty is not benefited from a unilateral approach: instead of defining the circumstances under which a Member State law applies and under which foreign law applies, it would only be determined when EU law applies; also, the practice of finding the purpose of a legal act is a burdensome task and adds uncertainty to the process. Therefore, it is concluded that an autonomous approach entailing the EU directives determining its own scope of application through a unilateral method would result in a protectionist system that imposes the application of its law over foreign law, contrary to the current PIL approach.

On the other hand, according to the multilateral approach followed by the Rome I Regulation, a choice between the different state laws is made by connecting the legal relationship to the law of a state according to objective criteria. With this approach, equality between the forum law and foreign law is promoted, as well as predictability and respect for the expectations of the parties involved. This approach aims to achieve uniformity of results. Of course, since a system completely based on value-free conflict rules is not always sufficient in order to protect certain values essential to the forum, the Rome I Regulation includes in this case special protective conflict rules for weaker contracting parties, with protective connecting factors and limits on party autonomy, and the doctrine of overriding mandatory rules. The applicability of the EU consumer directives (as transposed to the national law of the Member States) is decided according to the conflict rules of the Regulation. According to this approach, the existent scope rules, rather than unilateral conflict rules, should be understood as rules that, more than solving a conflict of laws, declare the level of mandatory nature of the provisions of the respective directive. They should be interpreted as rules facilitating the task of determining the degree of mandatoriness of the provisions of the instrument and not as conflict of laws rules as such. In this regard, the provisions of the majority of EU consumer directives should not be understood as overriding mandatory rules essential for the safeguarding of the political, social or economic organisation of the country. Although overriding mandatory rules are a matter of national law and it is the Member State of the forum that has to decide which national rules are overriding mandatory, when that national rules are rules implementing the standards of the EU directives, a consistent interpretation towards the objectives of the directive must be followed. As a result, what is crucial for the EU should be determined by the EU. Also, while overriding mandatory rules completely set aside party autonomy, most of the scope rules contained in the EU consumer directives, with the exception of the Timeshare Directive, indicate that the provisions of the directive cannot be circumvented when a choice of the law of a non-Member State has been made and a close connection with the EU exists. Thus, as a general consideration, the provisions of the EU consumer directives are, a priori, EU mandatory provisions and not overriding mandatory provisions. This means that, with regard to the Rome I Regulation system, some exceptional provisions of EU consumer directives that should be considered as overriding mandatory rules would prevail over the law designated by the Regulation according to article 9 Rome I; however, normally, since they are considered as EU mandatory law, they would not prevail over the law designated by the Rome I Regulation.

As a disadvantage, the Rome I Regulation system is not able to differentiate between intra-EU situations and extra-EU situations. From an EU point of view, in the first case the application of the EU standards is ensured, while in the second case there is the possibility that the EU standards are not applied when the EU intended to, disrupting the well-functioning of the internal market.

As a result, both methods—multilateral and unilateral—have their advantages and disadvantages, and it is submitted that the intended objectives will be better achieved combining both, ensuring the prevalence of PIL values while adapting them to the internal market needs. Methodological purity in a modern PIL system is rejected. In this regard, several factors can be taken into account in order to understand the situations in which a unilateral approach is justified: when different legal systems share common or similar legal values, like in the case of the Member States, conflict of laws rules should definitely promote equality between these different national legal systems through neutral conflict rules; however, when legal systems do not share similar legal values and important interests are at stake, the rules determining the law applicable to an international situation shall not be that neutral. The interrelationship between the countries involved and the mandatory nature of the applicable rules are factors to be taken into account when building a conflict of laws system. In our specific case, we are dealing with EU mandatory rules common to the European Member States. Therefore, it should be necessary to differentiate between intra-EU conflicts of law and extra-EU conflicts of law. In intra-EU conflicts of law, the use of a multilateral method should be promoted in regard to consumer contracts since the same or similar standards are shared among the Member States, even in gold-plating situations. However, in extra-EU conflict of laws, the Member States could be understood as a single legal order that needs to ensure the application of its EU mandatory rules against a foreign legal order, and thus the use of a more unilateral approach when necessary can be justified and considered regarding future European PIL reforms.

Finally, some short-term improvements to coordinate the interaction of the Rome I Regulation and the EU consumer directives regarding their international scope are submitted. First, as it has been explained, scope rules that are spread around some EU consumer directives create more harm than good when it comes to consumer protection due to the uncertainty around their functioning, and therefore they should be eliminated.

Second, article 6 Rome I should take a unilateral inroad and favour EU consumer law, being able thus to difference between intra-EU consumer contracts and extra-EU consumer contracts. Whenever a professional directs his activities to a Member State, the application of the minimum requirements of EU consumer directives should be ensured, regardless of the Member State of habitual residence of the consumer. The situation 'EU mandatory law vs. foreign country law' can be treated as equal to 'forum mandatory law vs. foreign country law', and thus a choice of foreign law should not result in depriving the EU consumer of the protection granted by EU consumer law. A rule similar to the one suggested by the Max Planck Institute in its Comments on the Green Paper for the Conversion of the Rome Convention in the Rome I Regulation should then be introduced, maybe following article 6 (3) Rome I:

> *If a supplier residing in a non-Member State directs his business activities to one or more Member States, the choice of law of a non-Member State as the law applicable to a contract falling into the scope of such activities does not deprive a consumer who, at the time of the conclusion of the contract, is habitually resident in a Member State of the protection afforded by the relevant Directives; in this case, the provisions of the relevant Directives apply as implemented in the domestic law of the Member State in which the consumer concluded the contract.*[236]

Lastly, some consumers not covered by article 6 Rome I could still be better protected if the scope of article 3(4) Rome I was extended. Article 3(4) Rome I ensures the application of EU mandatory law against the choice of a non-Member State law but only when all relevant elements are located within the EU. The requirement of all relevant elements within the EU could be modified as to include, for example, the close connection test that scope rules provided. Although a close connection with the territory of one or more Member States is a vague term that might affect legal certainty as well as the legitimate expectations of the parties, presumptions to facilitate its interpretation could be included. Also, even a most favourable law approach like in article 6(2) Rome I, according to which the application of the provisions of EU mandatory law would only be applicable if they are more beneficial than the mandatory provisions of the chosen law, could be considered, not depriving then the consumer of a possible more favourable regime.

Therefore, I consider that the applicability EU consumer directives, as implemented by the national laws of the Member States, should be determined by the Rome I Regulation system since legal certainty is better ensured by a unified EU conflict of laws regime. However, the Rome I Regulation needs to adapt to the EU requirements in order to promote the well-functioning of the internal market, and in that regard some unilateral inroads can be included in order to differentiate between intra-EU conflicts of law and extra-EU conflicts of law in consumer contracts, ensuring therefore the application of EU consumer mandatory law when necessary.

[236]Max Planck Institute for Foreign Private and Private International Law (2004), p. 15.

References

Aguilar Grieder H (2006) La Voluntad de Conciliación con las Directivas Comunitarias Protectoras en la Propuesta del Reglamento Roma I. In: La Unión Europea ante el Derecho de la Globalización. Colex, Madrid, pp 45–61

Aguilar Grieder H (2012) Desafíos y Tendencias en el Actual Derecho Internacional Privado Europeo de los Contractos. Cuadernos de Derecho Transnacional 4:23–48

Añoveros Terradas B (2003) Los Contratos de Consumo Intracomunitarios. Marcial Pons, Madrid

Añoveros Terradas B (2006) Consumidor Residente en la Unión Europea vs. Consumidor Residence en un Estado Tercero: A Propósito de la Propuesta del Reglamento Roma I. Anuario Español de Derecho Internacional Privado 6:379–401

Basedow J (2004) Consumer contracts and insurance contracts in a future Rome I-Regulation. In: Meeusen J et al (eds) Enforcement of international contracts in the European Union: convergence and divergence between Brussels I and Rome I. Intersentia, Antwerp; New York

Basedow J (2006) Conflicto de Leyes y Armonización del Derecho Privado Material en la UE. Anuario Español de Derecho Internacional Privado 6:141–159

Basedow J (2017) Private international law, methods of. In: Basedow J et al (eds) Encyclopedia of private international law. Edward Elgar Publishing, Cheltenham, pp 1402–1407

Batiffol H (1973) Le Pluralisme des Méthodes en Droit International Privé. Collect Courses Hague Acad Int Law 139:75–148

Belohlávek AJ (2011) Rome Convention - Rome I Regulation. Juris Publishing, Inc., Huntington

Bernardeau L (2003) Droit international privé et services financiers de détail - 2e partie : les conflits de lois. Euredia 1:59–114

Bisping C (2012a) Avoid the statutist trap: the international scope of the Consumer Credit Act 1974. J Priv Int Law 8:35–62

Bisping C (2012b) European consumer protection - theory and practice. Cambridge University Press, Cambridge

Bitterich K (2003) Die Neuregelung des Internationalen Verbrauchervertragsrechts in Art. 29a EGBGB. Peter Lang, Frankfurt/M et al

Bonomi A (2016) Article 9: overriding mandatory provisions. In: Magnus U, Mankowski P (eds) Rome I Regulation - commentary. Verlag Dr. Otto Schmidt, Köln, pp 597–661

Bonomi A (2017) Article 9 Rome I. In: Magnus U, Mankowski P (eds) European commentaries on private international law. Commentary. Rome I Regulation, vol II. Sellier European Law Publishers, p 616

Bucher A (2011) La Dimension Sociale du Droit International Privé : cours général. Brill, Leiden

Danson AS (1964) Territorially limited statutes and choice of law process. Harv J Legis 1:115–143

De Boer TM (1996) Facultative choice of law: the procedural status of choice-of-law rules and foreign law. Collect Courses Hague Acad Int Law 257:223–427

De la Rosa FE (2003) La Protección de Consumidores en el Mercado Interior Europeo. Comares, Granada

De la Rosa FE (2005) La Inadecuación del Sistema Español de Derecho Internacional Privado de las Cláusulas Abusivas al Derecho Comunitario: Claves para una Nueva Transposición y Propuesta Legislativa. La Ley: Revista jurídica española de doctrina, jurisprudencia y bibliografía 2:1932–1942

De la Rosa FE (2007) El Sistema Europeo y Español de Ley Aplicable a los Contratos de Consumo Transfronterizos: el Modelo de Dispersión Normativa para el Derecho Privado de la Integración. Revista Agenda Internacional 13:409–441

De la Rosa FE (2015) La Determinación del Derecho Aplicable a los Contratos de Consumo Transfronterizos: perspectiva europea y española. In: De la Rosa FE (ed) La Protección del Consumidor en Dos Espacios de Integración: Europa y América. Tirant lo Blanch, Valencia, pp 57–85

De Miguel Asensio P (2005) Conflictos de Leyes e Integración Jurídica: Estados Unidos y Unión Europea. Anuario Español de Derecho Internacional Privado 5:43–102

De Nova R (1966) Conflict of laws and functionally restricted substantive rules. Calif Law Rev 54:1569–1574

Espiniella Menéndez Á (2014) Contratos de Consumo en el Tráfico Comercial UE- Terceros Estados. Anuario Español de Derecho Internacional Privado 14–15:277–303

Fallon M, Francq S (2000) Towards internationally mandatory directives for consumer contracts? In: Basedow J (ed) Private law in international arena. Liber Amicorum K. Siehr. Asser Instituut, The Hague, pp 155–178

Fernández Rozas JC (2000) Orientaciones de Derecho Internacional Privado en el Umbral del Siglo XXI. Revista Mexicana de Derecho Internacional Privado 9:7–32

Fernández Rozas JC, Sánchez Lorenzo S (1999) Derecho Internacional Privado. Civitas, Madrid

Font i Segura A (2009) Reparación Indemnizatoria tras la Extinción del Contrato Internacional de Agencia Comercial: Imperatividad Poliédrica o el Mito de Zagreo (STJCE de 9 de noviembre de 2000, As. C-381/98, Ingmar Gb Ltd c. Eaton Leonard Technologies Inc.). Revista de Derecho Comunitario Europeo 5:259–279

Francq S (2005) L'Applicabilité du Droit Communautaire Dérivé au Regard des Méthodes du Droit International Privé. LGDJ, Bruxelles/Paris

Francq S (2006) The scope of secondary community law in the light of the methods of private international law- or the other way around? In: Sarcevic P et al (eds) Yearbook of private international law. Sellier, European Law Publishers and Swiss Institute of Comparative Law, pp 333–374

Francq S (2017) Unilateralism. In: Basedow J et al (eds) Encyclopedia of private international law. Edward Elgar Publishing, Cheltenham, pp 1179–1791

Garcimartín Alférez FJ (2008) The Rome I Regulation: much ado about nothing? Eur Leg Forum:61–80

Gebauer M (2015) Article 4. Applicable law in the absence of choice. In: Calliess G-P (ed) Rome Regulations. Commentary, 2nd edn. Kluwer Law International, The Netherlands

Guardans Cambó I (1992) Contrato Internacional y Derecho Imperativo Extranjero. Aranzadi, Pamplona

Jacquet J-M (2010) La Aplicación de las Leyes de Policía en Materia de Contratos Internacionales. Anuario Español de Derecho Internacional Privado 10:35–48

Jayme E, Kohler C (1995) L'interaction des Règles de Conflit contenues dans le Droit Dérivé de la Communauté Européenne et des Conventions de Bruxelles et de Rome. Revue critique de droit international privé 1:11–36

Kelly DSL (1969) Localising rules and differing approaches to the choice of law process. Int Comp Law Q 18:249–274

Klauer S (2002) Das europäische Kollisionsrecht der Verbraucherverträge zwischen Römer EVÜ und EG-Richtlinien. Mohr Siebeck, Tübingen

Kramer XE (2015) The interaction between Rome I and mandatory EU private rules- EPIL and EPL: communicating vessels? In: Stone P, Farah Y (eds) Research handbook on EU private international law. Edward Elgar Publishing, Cheltenham, pp 248–284

Kuipers J-J (2012) EU law and private international law: the interrelationship in contractual obligations. Martinus Nijhoff Publishers, Leiden

Lagarde P (2006) Remarques sur la Proposition de Règlement sur la Loi Applicable aux Obligations Contractuelles (Rome I). Revue critique de droit international privé 95:331–349

Leible S (2015) Article 6 Rome I and conflict of laws in EU directives. J Eur Consum Mark Law 4:39–44

Magnus U (2016) Introduction. In: Magnus U, Mankowski P (eds) Rome I Regulation - commentary. Verlag Dr. Otto Schmidt, Köln, pp 6–51

Mankowski P (2016) Article 23: relationship with other provisions of community law. In: Magnus U, Mankowski P (eds) Rome I Regulation - commentary. Verlag Dr. Otto Schmidt, Köln, pp 846–853

Marques dos Santos A (1991) As Normas de Aplicaçao Imediata no Direito Internacional Privado. Livraria Almedina, Coimbra

Mathieu B (2015) Directives Européennes et Conflits de Lois. LGDJ, Issy-les-Moulineaux
Max Planck Institute for Foreign Private and Private International Law (2004) Comments on the European Commission's Green Paper on the conversion of the Rome Convention of 1980 on the law applicable to contractual obligations into a Community instrument and its modernization. RabelsZ 68:1–118
Max Planck Institute for Foreign Private and Private International Law (2007) Comments on the European Commission's Proposal for a Regulation of the European Parliament and the Council on the law applicable to contractual obligations (Rome I). RabelsZ Bd71
Micklitz H-W (2009) The targeted full harmonisation approach: looking behind the curtain. In: Howells GG, Schulze R (eds) Modernising and harmonising consumer contract law. Sellier, European Law Publishers, München, pp 47–84
Morse CGJ (1992) Consumer contracts, employment contracts and the Rome Convention. Int Comp Law Q 41:1–21
Niboyet J-P (1952) Territoriality and universal recognition of rules of conflict of laws. Harv Law Rev 65:582–596
Oprea A (2010) Le Article 3.4 du Reglement Rome I sur la Loi Applicable aux Relations Contractuelles et les Contrats Intracommunautaires. Babes-Bolyai Studia Jurisprudentia 3:1–10
Paredes Pérez JI (2006) La Necesidad de Una Nueva Norma de Conflicto Bilateral Sobre Contratos de Consumo. Propuesta de Lege Ferenda. Anuario Español de Derecho Internacional Privado 6:87–114
Piir R, Sein K (2016) Law applicable to consumer contracts. Interaction of the Rome I Regulation and EU-directive-based rules on conflict of laws. Juridica International 24:63–70
Pilenko A (1954) Droit Spatial et Droit International Privé. Ius Gentium 5:35–59
Plender R, Wilderspin M (2015) The European private international law of obligations, 4th edn. Sweet & Maxwell, London
Quadri R (1967) Lezioni di diritto internazionale privato. Liguori, Napoli
Ragno F (2009) The law applicable to consumer contracts under the Rome I Regulation. In: Ferrari F, Leible S (eds) Rome I Regulation. Sellier, European Law Publishers, München
Riefa C (2004) Article 5 of the Rome Convention on the law applicable to contractual obligations of 19 June 1980 and consumer E-contracts: the need for reform. Inf Commun Technol Law 13:59–73
Roth W-H (2002) Case C-381/98, Ingmar GB Ltd v. Eaton Leonard Technologies Inc. judgment of the Court (Fifth Chamber) of 9 November 2000. [2000] ECR I-9305. Common Mark Law Rev 40:369–383
Rühl G (2017) Private international law, foundations. In: Basedow J et al (eds) Encyclopedia of private international law. Edward Elgar Publishing, Cheltenham
Sánchez Lorenzo S (2003) La Unificación del Derecho Contractual Europeo Vista desde el Derecho Internacional Privado. In: Derecho Patrimonial Europeo. Thomson-Aranzadi, Cizu Menor (Navarra), pp 363–381
Sánchez Lorenzo S (2010) Choice of law and overriding mandatory rules in international contracts after Rome I. In: Sarcevic P et al (eds) Yearbook of private international law. Sellier, European Law Publishers, Germany, pp 67–93
Sonnentag M (2017) Savigny, Friedrich Carl Von. In: Basedow J et al (eds) Encyclopedia of private international law. Edward Elgar Publishing, Cheltenham, pp 1609–1615
Stone P (2014) EU private international law, 3rd edn. Edward Elgar Publishing, Cheltenham
Symeonides SC (2005) Accommodative unilateralism as a starting premise in choice of law. In: Rasmussen-Bonne H et al (eds) Balancing of interests: Liber Amicorum Peter Hay. Verlag Recht und Wirtschaft GmbH, pp 417–434
Symeonides SC (2014) Codifying choice of law around the world: an international comparative analysis. Oxford University Press, New York
Tang ZS (2007) Parties' choice of law in E-consumer contracts. J Priv Int Law 3:113–136
Ten Wolde MH (2013) The relativity of legal positions in cross-border situations: the foundations of private interregional law, private intra-community law and private international law. In: A

commitment to private international law- essays in honour of Hans van Loon. Intersentia, Cambridge, pp 569–581
Tenreiro M, Karsten J (1999) Unfair terms in consumer contracts: uncertainties, contradictions and novelties of a directive. In: Schulte-Nölke H, Schulze R (eds) Europäische Rechtsangleichung und nationale Privatrechte. Nomos Verlagsgesellschaft, pp 223–276
Van Bochove LM (2014) Overriding mandatory rules as a vehicle for weaker party protection in European private international law. Erasmus Law Rev 7:147–157
Verhagen HLE (2002) The tension between party autonomy and European Union law: some observations on Ingmar GB Ltd v Eaton Leonard Technologies Inc. Int Comp Law Q 51:135–154
Vilà Costa B, Gardeñes Santiago M (2002) Comentario Disposición Adicional 1ª Tres. In: Comentarios a la Ley sobre Condiciones Generales de la Contratación. Civitas, Madrid, pp 296–302
von Savigny FC (1849) System des Heutigen Römischen Rechts. Veit und Comp, Berlin
von Savigny FC (1869) Private international law. A treatise on the conflict of laws, and the limits of their operation in respect of place and time (trans: Guthrie W). T. & T. Clark, Edinburgh
Weller M (2015) Article 23. Relationship with other provisions of community law. In: Calliess G-P (ed) Rome Regulations. Commentary, 2nd edn. Kluwer Law International, The Netherlands
Wilderspin M (2016) Article 6: consumer contracts. In: Magnus U, Mankowski P (eds) Rome I Regulation - commentary. Verlag Dr. Otto Schmidt, Köln, pp 453–490

Chapter 5
The Relationship and Coordination Between EU Employment Directives and the Rome I Regulation

How does the Rome I Regulation relate to the application of EU directives regarding employment matters? Do the existent conflict rules respond to the needs of the EU employment directives? Can the analysis regarding the relationship between Rome I and EU consumer directives also apply to EU employment directives? This chapter aims to analyse the coordination between the Rome I Regulation and the application of EU directives in the context of individual employment matters. Since the same analysis has been conducted in the previous chapter with regard to EU consumer directives, it will be examined whether the same examination and conclusions can, to a certain extent, be applied regarding cross-border employment issues.

Employment contracts with cross-border elements are very common nowadays, especially within the EU, where freedom of provision of services and freedom of movement of workers facilitate access to the market of other Member States. Thus, within the EU, there are every time more situations involving cross-border employment relationships: workers commuting to a place of work in their neighbouring country, employers posting workers to another Member State, companies seeking out employees abroad, relocation after a cross-border transfer of an undertaking, workers whose job is of a cross-border nature etc.

Article 8 Rome I regulates the law applicable to individual employment contracts in cross-border situations. Article 8 Rome I does not present the same type of problems as article 6 Rome I regarding consumer contracts since article 8 does not provide for specific requirements for its application but applies to all individual employment contracts.[1] Article 8(1) Rome I allows the parties to choose the law applicable to the contract as long as the provisions of the chosen law are not prejudicial to the employee in comparison to the mandatory provisions of the law objectively applicable. The law objectively applicable is generally the law of the place in which or from which the employee habitually works (article 8(2) Rome I);

[1]Definition provided in Sect. 2.1.2.2.

M. Campo Comba, *The Law Applicable to Cross-border Contracts involving Weaker Parties in EU Private International Law*,
https://doi.org/10.1007/978-3-030-61481-2_5

when the habitual place of work cannot be determined, the law of the country where the place of business through which the employee was engaged is situated will apply (article 8(3) Rome I). Article 8(4) Rome I contains an escape clause stating that if from the circumstances as a whole the contract is more closely connected with a country other than that indicated in paragraph 2 or 3, the law of that other country shall apply. Article 8 Rome I clarifies that the habitual place of work is not deemed to have changed if the employee is temporarily posted to another country. As is known, the Rome I Regulation has a universal scope of application, meaning that whether the law designated by the conflict rule is the law of a Member State or the law of a third country, the Member State court will have to apply it. Article 8 Rome I ensures that as long as the habitual place of work of an employee is a Member State, then the law of that Member State, and, as a result, the protection provided by the EU directives applicable to the situation, applies, except when the contract is most closely connected with a non-Member State (article 8(4) Rome I). Although article 8 Rome I provides for several connecting factors, it has been determined in Chapter III that the majority of the times the law applicable in the absence of choice will be the law of the habitual place of work. Identification of the habitual place of work is easy in the majority of cases, where the work is performed by the employee in one single place, like in the case of local employees or employees transferred to another country. Cases involving migrant workers, frontier workers or workers who are employed by a foreign employer do not normally bring special difficulties since the work is typically performed in one country, and thus the habitual place of work is easy to determine. The European Court of Justice (ECJ) has made a very extensive interpretation of the term 'habitual place of work', which consequently reduces the role of article 8(3) Rome I in exceptional cases.[2]

In the area of labour law, the EU, in accordance with article 153 Treaty on the Functioning of the European Union (TFEU), adopts directives that set minimum requirements regarding working and employment conditions and informing and consulting of workers. Generally, EU directives dealing with employment matters are of a minimum harmonising nature. Therefore, Member States, when transposing into their national law the provisions of the corresponding directive, are able to provide a higher level of protection (e.g. the Working Time Directive[3] entitles workers to an annual paid leave of 20 days, but several Member States have opted for a more beneficial regime). The existent diversity among the Member States regarding social and labour policies and realities constitutes an impediment against a unified EU social policy going beyond minimum standards accepted by all Member States.[4] EU employment law just covers regulatory aspects of employment law, and even in this regard there are central issues (such as unfair dismissal) that are

---

[2]Case C-29/10 *Heiko Koelzsch v État* du *Grand Duchy* of *Luxemburg* [2011] *ECR* I-01595 and Case C-384/10 *Jan Voogsgeerd v Navimer SA* [2011] *ECR* I-13275; in that regard, Sect. 3.2.2.

[3]Directive 2003/88/EC of the European Parliament and of the Council of 4 November 2003 concerning certain aspects of the organisation of working time (OJ 2003 L 299/9).

[4]Riesenhuber (2012), p. 169, 170.

regulated by national law. That is, EU employment law is quite fragmented and mainly composed of minimum harmonisation directives that complement the policies of Member States. Sometimes, they even leave a big amount of discretion with regard to the minimum standard. Therefore, since national employment laws in the EU are still very disparate, PIL is still essential even in intra-EU scenarios.

Regarding the relationship of the Rome I Regulation and the EU employment directives, it can already be anticipated that article 8 Rome I Regulation ensures most of the times the application of the mandatory employment provisions of the specific directives when necessary. This is because most EU employment directives do not interfere with PIL and just lay down a minimum substantive protection that Member States have to implement. However, there are some directives (Acquired Rights Directive[5] and Posted Workers Directive[6]) that directly deal with cross-border employment situations and contain rules that interfere with PIL, which relationship with the Rome I Regulation requires specific attention.

Thus, on the one hand, EU employment directives generally do not intend to deal with cross-border situations but just lay down (minimum) substantive rights for employees that Member States have to implement into their national employment legislation. Workers in the EU enjoy that minimum protection. Every worker in the EU has certain minimum rights established by EU employment directives relating to health and safety at work, equal opportunities for women and men, protection against discrimination and working conditions regarding part-time work, fixed-term contracts, working hours or informing and consulting of employees.[7] Most of the directives in this regard do not create any special issue for PIL. As it was previously discussed, under our current PIL system and, specifically, under the Rome I Regulation, the conflict rules will determine which law is applicable to the case. The provisions of the specific directive will be applicable as implemented by the Member State law determined by the Rome I Regulation.

On the other hand, we also find EU employment directives that directly involve cross-border situations. These are directives that involve situations where there is a change in the country of place of work of the employee, either permanent or temporary, due to a cross-border transfer of undertaking involving a relocation of the workforce or due to a temporary posting of workers. We refer to the Acquired Rights Directive and Posted Workers Directive. Both directives deserve a closer analysis.

---

[5]Council Directive 2001/23/EC of 12 March 2001 on the approximation of the laws of the Member States relating to the safeguarding of employees' rights in the event of transfers of undertakings, businesses or parts of undertakings or businesses *(OJ 2001 L 82/16)*.

[6]Directive 96/71/EC of the European Parliament and of the Council of 16 December 1996 concerning the posting of workers in the framework of the provision of services (OJ L 1996 18/1); *also:* Directive (EU) 2018/957 of the European Parliament and of the Council of 28 June 2018 amending Directive 96/71/EC concerning the posting of workers in the framework of the provision of services (OJ 2018 L 173/16).

[7]For a comprehensive study on those topics, Riesenhuber (2012).

The Acquired Rights Directive aims at preserving employees' rights in the case of a transfer of undertaking, protecting a business' employees in the event of a change of employer; when the transfer is across the borders of a country, the habitual place of work of employees also shifts, changing the law applicable to their contract. In addition, it contains a rule referring to its territorial scope, which should be the object of analysis in PIL terms. Article 1(2) of the Acquired Rights Directive states that the

> directive shall apply where and in so far as the undertaking, business or part of the undertaking or business to be transferred is situated within the territorial scope of the Treaty.

How is this rule reconciled with the Rome I Regulation? Are the conflict rules of the Rome I Regulation enough to ensure the aims of the Acquired Rights Directive in a cross-border transfer of undertaking?

Regarding the Posted Workers Directive, it is applicable to temporary cross-border postings of workers in the context of an intra-EU provision of services. The Directive tries to promote the freedom of provision of services as well as to ensure the protection of workers who are temporarily posted to other Member States. Although article 8 Rome I provides that the habitual place of work does not change upon a temporary posting and thus the law of the Member State of habitual place of work remains applicable, article 3 of the Posted Workers Directive requires to extend the application of some provisions of the law of the Member State of posting regarding certain areas to workers who are temporarily posted there. In addition, the revised version of the Directive adds a provision requiring the application of all the applicable terms and conditions of employment of the law of the Member State of posting after 12 (or 18) months of posting. Are the requirements of the Posted Workers Directive ensured through the Rome I Regulation? The relationship between the Posted Workers Directive and the rules of the Rome I Regulation must be the object of analysis.

Thus, this chapter will first analyse the coordination of the Rome I Regulation and the general EU employment directives that do not directly deal with cross-border situations and do not interfere with the PIL rules. Second, it will focus on the interaction of the rules of the Rome I Regulation and the Acquired Rights Directive, which contains a 'scope rule' similarly to some of the EU consumer directives. A similar analysis to the one conducted in the previous chapter regarding the scope of consumer directives is conducted in the context of the Acquired Rights Directive. Finally, this chapter will deal with the law applicable to employment contracts in the context of a temporary posting of workers. The original Posted Workers Directive and the new Posted Workers Directive, as well as the Enforcement Directive, are object of brief analyses. Then focus will be on the issues deriving from the requirements of article 3 Posted Workers Directive and the provisions applicable to the posted worker. It can be advanced that article 9 Rome I regarding overriding mandatory provisions plays an important role in that regard.

5.1 The Rome I Regulation and EU Employment Directives That Do Not Directly Interfere with PIL

Most of the existent EU employment directives lay down minimum substantive provisions that Member States have to implement into their national employment law, with the opportunity to improve the protection required by the directive. The majority of the employment directives do not intend to deal with issues related to cross-border employment contracts but just aim to ensure that workers in a Member State enjoy the minimum rights required by the respective directives. The most typical scenario is internal: a person working in a Member State with no international elements related to the employment contract. The national law, which has implemented the EU minimum employment standards, ensures that the worker enjoys that substantive rights provided by the directives. However, there are many cases that involve cross-border elements: employees transferred to another country, cases involving migrant workers, frontier workers or workers who are employed by a foreign employer, a worker carrying out activities in more than one place, cases involving transnational occupations etc. Therefore, coordination between those directives and their applicability to individual employment contracts involving cross-border elements are discussed.

Aside from directives on health and safety (e.g. Directive 89/391/EEC on safety and health of workers at work[8]) or on non-discrimination (e.g. Directive 2000/43/EC against discrimination on grounds of race and ethnic origin;[9] Directive 2000/78/EC against discrimination at work on grounds of religion or belief, disability, age or sexual orientation;[10] Directive 2006/54/EC equal treatment for men and women in matters of employment and occupation;[11] etc.), which are essential for the respect of EU fundamental rights, one of the main areas covered by EU employment law is working conditions. This comprises provisions regarding working time, part-time and fixed-term work, temporary workers or the posting of workers. Directives such as Directive 91/533/EEC on employer's obligation to inform of the individual employment conditions,[12] Directive 1999/70/EC on fixed-term work,[13] Directive

[8]Council Directive 89/391/EEC of 12 June 1989 on the introduction of measures to encourage improvements in the safety and health of workers at work (OJ 1989 L 183/1).

[9]Council Directive 2000/43/EC of 29 June 2000 implementing the principle of equal treatment between persons irrespective of racial or ethnic origin (OJ 2000 L180/22).

[10]Council Directive 2000/78/EC of 27 November 2000 establishing a general framework for equal treatment in employment and occupation (OJ 2000 L 303/16).

[11]Directive 2006/54/EC of the European Parliament and of the Council of 5 July 2006 on the implementation of the principle of equal opportunities and equal treatment of men and women in matters of employment and occupation (recast) (OJ 2006 L 204/23).

[12]Council Directive 91/533/EEC of 14 October 1991 on an employer's obligation to inform employees of the conditions applicable to the contract or employment relationship (OJ 1991 L 28/32).

[13]Council Directive 1999/70/EC of 28 June 1999 concerning the framework agreement on fixed-term work concluded by ETUC, UNICE and CEEP (OJ 1999 L 175/43).

97/81/EC on part-time work,[14] Directive 2008/104/EC on temporary agency work,[15] Directive 2003/88/EC on working time[16] etc. lay down provisions regarding the working conditions of employees in the EU. Member States must have implemented into their national law the minimum rights and conditions required by these directives. Besides the specific objectives of each directive in every area of employee protection, the EU employment directives generally aim to avoid social dumping and improve the conditions of the workers and life within the EU.[17]

These directives do not contain conflict rules or references to PIL. They do not deal with cross-border situations but establish substantive rights and ensure that Member States apply minimum working protection to the employees working in that Member State. Therefore, the directives will apply when the national law of a Member State is applicable because it is a purely internal situation or, in a cross-border situation, as a result of the conflict rules of the Rome I Regulation. In our current EU PIL approach, it is understood that if a law has been determined as applicable by the conflict rules, then the statutes of that legal system shall apply to the situation (as long as the situation falls within the scope of application of the statute in question). That is, the national judge, when a situation involves cross-border elements, is expected to follow the forum conflict rules which will point to the applicable law rather than apply a statute of the forum without previously resorting to the conflict rules. In the case of an individual employment relationship with cross-border elements, when the case regards any of the areas regulated by an EU directive, the forum judge will determine the law applicable to the contract in accordance with article 8 Rome I. Then the application of the EU directive is ensured through the application of the determined Member State law, which has implemented (and maybe improved) the terms and conditions required by the directive.

EU employment directives establish terms and conditions regarding employees working within the EU. In such cases, the application of the mandatory provisions of the EU directives are (mostly) ensured through the Rome I Regulation since the main connecting factor of article 8 Rome I is the habitual place of work.[18]

In this sense, the EU employment directives and article 8 Rome I are coordinated. The directives lay down substantive law and the Rome I Regulation determines which national law will be applicable in a cross-border situation. The mandatory provisions of the habitual place of work are ensured by article 8 Rome I, and if the

[14] Council Directive 97/81/EC of 15 December 1997 concerning the Framework Agreement on part-time work concluded by UNICE, CEEP and the ETUC—Annex: Framework agreement on part-time work (OJ 1998 L 14/9).

[15] Directive 2008/104/EC of the European Parliament and of the Council of 19 November 2008 on temporary agency work (OJ 2008 L 327/9).

[16] Directive 2003/88/EC of the European Parliament and of the Council of 4 November 2003 concerning certain aspects of the organisation of working time (OJ 2003 L 299/9).

[17] Regarding EU employment policy, see Sect. 2.3.1.2.

[18] The exceptions to these situations are dealt with in the following sections regarding temporary posting of workers and acquired employment rights in a transfer of undertaking.

habitual place of work is a Member State, then the provisions of the respective directive are ensured. The majority of these directives, in general, do not have any interest in being applicable to workers outside the EU. The relevant criterion is therefore the place of work. None of the directives refer to factors such as nationality or place of residence.[19] Unlike the EU consumer directives, they do not make any reference to a 'close connection to the Community' or any other extra-EU elements. In general, they intend to improve the conditions of life and work within the EU. That aim can be inferred from their wording. Many directives refer specifically to the workers of the EU. For example, Directive 89/391/EEC on safety and health of workers at work refers to the responsibility of Member States of promoting the health and safety of the workers in their place of work.[20] Directive 2002/44/CE refers to 'all Community workers'.[21] Directive 2003/88/EC on working time is also directed to 'Community workers'.[22] For example, the latter directive lays down minimum working time requirements that Member States have to implement into their national law. It does not include any PIL rules or scope rules interfering with PIL. Therefore, the provisions of the Directive regarding working time will apply when the law of a Member State applies as implemented by that national law. One of the objectives of the Directive is that Member States implement or improve its minimum requirements, and, as a result, all the employees working in all the EU countries enjoy a minimum protection.

Article 8(1) Rome I follows the preferential law approach when there is a choice of law. In terms of the protection provided by the Directive, this is relevant when the choice is a non-Member State law or when the choice is a less beneficial Member State law. Article 8(1) Rome I ensures the application of the mandatory provisions of the law otherwise applicable (in most scenarios, the law of the habitual place of work) that are more beneficial for the employee in comparison with those of the law chosen. The provisions deriving from the EU employment directives, as provisions protecting the weaker party, entail mandatory character. They belong to a category of 'provisions of Community law that cannot be derogated from by agreement'—or EU mandatory law—and these types of provisions are mandatory internally within the EU legal system. Provisions that mainly aim at protecting the weaker contracting party (in this case employees) fall within that category.[23] As a result of article 8 (1) Rome I, if parties have chosen the law of a Member State that has just implemented the minimum protection required by the specific directive while the

[19]Francq (2005), pp. 384–386.

[20]See, for example, Recital 2 ('Whereas it is known that workers can be exposed to the effects of dangerous environmental factors at the work place during the course of their working life') and recital 7 ('Whereas Member States have a responsibility to encourage improvements in the safety and health of workers on their territory').

[21]Recital 3 reads: '(...) These measures are intended (...) also to create a minimum basis of protection for all Community workers in order to avoid possible distortions of competition.'

[22]Recital 5 states that '(...) Community workers must be granted minimum daily, weekly and annual periods of rest and adequate breaks'.

[23]In this regard, see discussion in Sect. 3.3.1.

Member State of habitual place of work has improved the requirements of the directive applicable to the specific case at hand, the more beneficial mandatory rules will be applicable.

While in majority of the cases the application of mandatory rules is ensured by article 8 Rome I, there might be situations in which that is not the case.[24] Although provisions of the EU employment directives are mainly aimed at the protection of the employee, it has to be taken into account that the interests of the state, and, in some cases, the interest of the EU, play a much higher role in employment contracts than in consumer contracts. Therefore, in some specific cases, the application of certain employment provisions can be so essential for the public interests of the EU or of a state that it justifies their application over the designated applicable law as overriding mandatory rules (article 9 Rome I).[25]

5.2 Coordination Between the Acquired Rights Directive and the Rome I Regulation

Cross-border transfers of undertakings comprise all the different elements of an undertaking being transferred (assets, contracts, employees, rights etc.) from one country to another, which constitutes a complex and often uncertain process. Employees of the undertaking being transferred might be subject to a negative impact as a result of the agreement on the transfer, in which they have not participated. Employees are not the direct participants of this transaction but might be the ones suffering the negative consequences if the labour conditions stipulated between the former employer and the new employer are agreed upon with the intention of reducing the costs of the transfer.

Council Directive 2001/23/EC of 12 March 2001 on the approximation of the laws of the Member States relating to the safeguarding of employees' rights in the event of transfers of undertakings, businesses or parts of undertakings or businesses (Acquired Rights Directive) is aimed at preserving employees' rights in the case of a transfer of undertaking and thus protecting a business' employees in the event of a change of employer. It harmonises the national laws of the Member States in that regard in order to ensure comparable protection of employees' rights in the Member States and to approximate the obligations that the rules of protection place on undertakings in the EU.

Acquired Rights Directive also covers cross-border transfers of undertakings. Any cross-border transfer from one Member State to another Member State is subject to the provisions of the Directive. In addition, the Directive refers to the place of origin of the business unit to be transferred, covering situations where the

[24]For example, see below Sect. 5.2 regarding the Acquired Rights Directive.

[25]Regarding the relationship between article 8 and article 9 Rome I concerning the application of overriding mandatory rules, see Sect. 3.3.3.2.

undertaking to be transferred is located in a Member State—even when it is transferred outside the territory of the EU. However, the Directive does not directly deal with PIL issues nor refers to any PIL instrument for the cases of cross-border transfers of undertakings. The Commission Report[26] on the Directive in 2007 pointed out that some national transposition rules regarding cross-border transfers could give rise to problems for which the Directive did not provide a solution since, contrarily to the Commission Proposal of 1974, the Directive did not contain any provisions dealing with conflict of laws.

The purpose of the Acquired Rights Directive consists in preserving acquired employment rights, ensuring, among other measures, that the transferee (new employer) has the same rights and obligations arising from an employment contract as the transferor (former employer). The laws of the Member States differ in the application of the Directive, and they also differ regarding employment rights. How are these rights preserved in a cross-border transfer of the undertaking? For example, the law of the Member State of origin provides for the right of an employee to not be unfairly dismissed: How is that right preserved when employees are transferred from that Member State to a Member State with a different regulation regarding dismissal?

According to the prevailing opinion, the transfer of undertakings can be classified within the conflict of laws category for individual employment contracts.[27] Issues such as whether the transferee automatically takes over the employment relationships of the employees concerned and the dismissal or modification of contract terms and conditions are to be decided according to the law applicable to the employment contract.[28] Therefore, article 8 Rome I will apply. The applicable law is determined by the restricted choice of the parties (article 8(1) Rome I) and the habitual place of work (article 8(2) Rome I) and, more exceptionally, by the engaging place of business (article 8(3) Rome I) or the country to which the employment contract is more closely connected (article 8(4) Rome I). The habitual place of work, however, changes with the transfer of undertaking when the transfer involves a simultaneous or subsequent relocation of the undertaking and its employees. It is generally considered that in the case of a cross-border transfer of undertaking, the law

[26]Commission Report on Council Directive 2001/23/EC of 12 March 2001 on the approximation of the laws of the Member States relating to the safeguarding of employees' rights in the event of transfers of undertakings, businesses or parts of undertakings or businesses [SEC(2007) 812] (COM/2007/0334 final).

[27]However, there are different conflict of laws theories regarding the law applicable to a transfer of undertaking: there are opinions claiming for a separate category for transfer of undertakings and opinions defending that each effect of a transfer of undertaking shall be judged separately and shall fall in different conflict of laws categories. This study will not focus on the classification of transfer of undertakings as a conflict of laws category. The analysis of the Acquired Rights Directive will be done based on the prevailing opinion; i.e., the rights and obligations deriving from a transfer of undertaking are governed by the law regulating individual contract of employment. For a discussion on the different perspectives in that regard: Henckel (2016), pp. 221–237.

[28]CMS Employment Practice Area Group, Study on the Application of Directive 200/23/EC to Cross-border Transfer of Undertakings (2006) 64.

applicable normally changes because the habitual place of work of the affected employees changes.[29] The change in applicable law will affect those employees who are transferred to the new location of the undertaking in a different country since only for them that the habitual place of work actually changes.[30] As to the date relevant for the change in the applicable law, the CMS Study on the application of the Acquired Rights Directive refers to the date of the transfer agreement or the date on which the employee starts working on the new location.[31]

On the other hand, there is a provision in the Acquired Rights Directive that, although it is not a conflict rule as such, might affect PIL: Article 1(2) Acquired Rights Directive states that the

> directive shall apply where and in so far as the undertaking, business or part of the undertaking or business to be transferred is situated within the territorial scope of the Treaty.

That is, the Directive establishes that it is applicable when the undertaking to be transferred is a Member State. This seems to be the territorial scope covered by the Directive. However, is article 1(2) Acquired Rights Directive a scope rule affecting PIL? The way the provision is drafted and the different national implementations that Member States have made of this rule bring up that question. A lot of discussions regarding scope rules in a PIL context take place regarding EU consumer directives, probably because of the specialty of these scope rules, which are focused on preventing the strong party of the contract from abusing party autonomy to avoid the application of EU mandatory consumer protection. In my opinion, article 1 (2) Acquired Rights Directive has a different aim, which is clarifying the territorial scope of the Acquired Rights Directive. Scope rules of EU consumer directives refer to a close connection with the EU and to a limitation of party autonomy, while the rule of article 1(2) Acquired Rights Directive merely makes a reference to the territorial application of the instrument. However, the drafting of the rule brings doubts regarding its intention since it could also be understood as intending to ensure that in a conflict of laws situation, the provisions of the Directive are applicable whenever the undertaking to be transferred is located in the EU, fulfilling the function of a scope rule. The different national implementations by the Member States bring more uncertainty to the situation. What seemed to be a clarification of the territorial scope of the Directive has opened a debate as to the possible existence

---

[29]The change in the applicable law is not retroactive. That is, rights, obligations and facts occurring before the change of the habitual place of work shall be governed by the laws of the former place of work, while those occurring after the change in applicable law will be governed by the law of the new place of work. Claims arising from the continuing employment contract (leave, pension etc.) are governed by the new law. Henckel (2016), pp. 270, 271.

[30]See Sect. 3.2.2.1 for an analysis of the connecting factor of habitual place of work of article 8 (2) Rome I.

[31]CMS Employment Practice Area Group, Study on the Application of Directive 200/23/EC to Cross-border Transfer of Undertakings (2006) 65.

of a scope rule in PIL terms. As a result, if so, the same questions as concerning scope rules in EU consumer directives arise in this case: How does this rule relate to the Rome I Regulation system? Shall it be considered as a separate conflict rule that takes precedence over the Rome I Regulation according to article 23 Rome I? Do Member States (adequately) transpose the scope rule into their national law? Does the scope rule require the application of the protection of the Directive whenever the undertaking to be transferred is located in the territory of a Member State regardless of the law applicable to the situation?

To answer these questions, this section will first point out the inconsistencies existent in the national implementations of article 1(2) Acquired Rights Directive, to then try to discern how this rule is reconciled with the conflict rules of the Rome I Regulation and whether the Rome I Regulation ensures the application of the provisions of the Acquired Rights Directive when necessary.

5.2.1 Implementation of Article 1(2) Acquired Rights Directive into the National Law of the Member States

As it was previously argued regarding scope rules in the EU consumer directives, the implementation of 'scope rules' is problematic since Member States take different approaches due to the minimum harmonisation nature of the Directive. While from the perspective of the EU it seems justified that an EU directive determines its own territorial scope by referring to the frontiers of the EU legal system, this approach can result in different and inconsistent national implementations (e.g. implementations focused on the territory of the own Member State, determining the applicability of the law of the forum as a 'scope rule' while ignoring the law of other Member States).[32] That seems to be the case of the Acquired Rights Directive.

Different ways to implement article 1(2) Acquired Rights Directive can be observed among the Member States.[33] The first one entails a literal transposition of the provision ensuring the application of the national acquired rights provisions when the undertaking to be transferred is located in a Member State *(a)*. The second transposition provides only for the application of the national acquired rights provisions if the undertaking to be transferred is located in the territory of the Member State in question *(b)*. Finally, some Member States do not transpose the scope rule into their national laws.[34] For example, the French[35] implementation and Dutch[36]

[32] Fallon and Francq (2000), p. 166; Kuipers (2012), p. 188.

[33] For an extensive study on the implementation of the Directive by the different Member States, see Study on the Application of Directive 200/23/EC to Cross-border Transfer of Undertakings, CMS Employment Practice Area Group (2006).

[34] Henckel (2016), p. 318.

[35] L1224-1–L1224-4 Code du Travail.

[36] Articles 7:662–7:666 Dutch Civil Code.

implementation of the Acquired Rights Directive do not require the undertaking to be established on their territories for their legislation to be applicable. As in the case of the majority of Member States, they do not contain an explicit rule implementing article 1(2) Acquired Rights Directive:

(a) Regarding those countries transposing article 1(2) Acquired Rights Directive, we find on the one hand implementations such as the Greek and Danish, which follow the first transposition mentioned in the above paragraph: they limit the application of their national acquired rights provisions to the transfer of an undertaking when the undertaking to be transferred is located within the territorial scope of the Treaty establishing the European Economic Area (EEA) or within the area to which the Treaty is applied.[37] That is, when the court of a Member State has jurisdiction over a case, the application of its provisions are ensured whenever the undertaking to be transferred is situated in the territory of a Member State.

(b) On the other hand, the second transposition mentioned above is the more problematic, to the point that it has been argued whether it complied with the Acquired Rights Directive.[38] Where article 1(2) Acquired Rights Directive states that the Directive

> shall apply where and in so far as the undertaking, business or part of the undertaking or business to be transferred is situated in the territorial scope of the Treaty,

some Member States provide for the application of their national acquired rights provisions where and in so far as the undertaking, business or part of the undertaking and business to be transferred is situated within the territory of the Member State. For example, the UK had followed that type of transposition. The transposed scope rule focused on the territory of the own country. The scope rule becomes a unilateral rule determining the application of national law. For example, the Transfer of Undertakings Regulation[39] (the UK regulation that implemented the Acquired Rights Directive) expressly provided that it is applicable to a transfer of undertaking where the undertaking to be transferred is established in the UK. Also, the Regulation does not allow the parties to contract out the provisions. Outbound transfers, where the business being transferred is transferred from the UK to another state, are covered by the Regulation, and the UK provisions on acquired rights are applicable. However, inbound transfers, where the business is transferred from another country to the UK, are not covered. In these type of cases, the protection provided by the Acquired Rights Directive would still be applicable when the business is transferred from a Member State since the Member State of origin also implements the minimum protection required by the Acquired Rights Directive.

---

[37] Henckel (2016), p. 318, 319.

[38] Ibid., p. 319.

[39] The Transfer of Undertakings (Protection of Employment) Regulations 2006, no 246.

Still, the existing differences in the national implementations of 'scope rules' could disturb the conflict of laws process. Including a rule such as article 1 (2) Acquired Rights Directive in a directive has different consequences than the existence of a similar rule in a treaty or even a regulation. In the latter case, a rule determining the territorial scope of the instrument will merely do so, and since the instruments are directly applicable as uniform law, there is no room for different national implementations of such a rule. However, in the case of directives, the existence of such a rule, especially when drafted as article 1(2) Acquired Rights Directive, can be implemented and understood differently depending on the Member State. In addition, from a PIL perspective, the existence of rules determining the territorial scope of a directive can logically be related to the existing debate regarding the relationship of scope rules in EU secondary law instruments and PIL instruments. An EU law expert might read and understand such rules in a different way than a PIL expert. The different national implementations of scope rules lead to the application of different national laws applying in different Member States, creating a parallel and non-harmonised intra-EU conflict of laws system. The purpose of the Acquired Rights Directive is to safeguard the rights of the employees in a transfer of undertaking through the harmonisation of minimum protection rules among Member States. Member States should ensure that the minimum protection is applicable in a cross-border transfer when the Directive requires so (i.e. whenever the undertaking to be transferred is situated in the territorial scope of the Treaty). However, that substantive protection will only be applicable when the relevant PIL rules determine that the law of a Member State is applicable to the situation.

5.2.2 *How Is Article 1(2) Acquired Rights Directive Reconciled with the Rome I Regulation?*

Although the national implementation of article 1(2) Acquired Rights Directive is unclear, the rule unmistakably indicates that the acquired rights provisions of a Member State are applicable when the undertaking to be transferred is located within the territory of the Treaty. The objective connecting factor of article 8(2) Rome I leads to the application of the law of the habitual place of work of the employee. That is, the provisions of the Acquired Rights Directive will generally apply as implemented by the law of the Member State of the habitual place of work of the employee. Even if there is a choice of law of a non-Member State, the application of the mandatory provisions of the Acquired Rights Directive as implemented by the law of the habitual place of work shall be ensured as provisions that cannot be derogated from by agreement (article 8(1) Rome I). However, problems can arise when the location of the place of establishment of the undertaking differs from the place where the employee habitually carries out his or her work or when the employment contract is most closely connected to a country different from the country of habitual place of work. For example, the *American Pilots* case[40] concerned a transfer of a Berlin-based aviation business from Pan American World Airways to Berliner Lufthansa Airport. The undertaking transferred was located in Germany before and after the transfer, while the law applicable to the employment contract was the law of New York as the law chosen and as the law applicable in the absence of choice because of being the law most closely connected to the contract. In such scenarios, the law applicable as a result of the operation of article 8 Rome I would not lead to the application of the Acquired Rights Directive, even when the undertaking to be transferred is located within the EU. Should article 1(2) Acquired Rights Directive, as a scope rule, take precedence over article 8 Rome I? If so, how? Or should article 8 Rome I be applicable regardless of the existence of the scope rule of article 1(2) Acquired Rights Directive? The existence of possible inconsistencies urges the necessity of clarifying the nature and relationship of scope rules of EU employment directives and the conflict rules of the Rome I Regulation. Such clarification is essential in order to know when and how the rules of an EU employment directive, and, in this specific case, the rules of the Acquired Rights Directive, are applicable. Different understandings are possible from a PIL point of view in this regard. On the one hand, a radical return to a unilateral conflict of laws approach to determine the scope of the directives would be a possibility if the scope rule of article 1(2) Acquired Rights Directive is understood as a unilateral conflict rule. However, that would imply a turn in the current understanding of EU PIL, and it does not necessarily lead to a more advantageous system. On the other hand, in coordination with the current Rome I Regulation system, article 8 Rome I determining the law applicable to the employment contract does not cover all the situations where article 1(2) Acquired Rights Directive intends to apply. Therefore, it has to be determined whether other mechanisms of Rome I, such as article 9 regarding overriding mandatory rules, can ensure the application of the Acquired Rights Directive.

5.2.2.1 Article 1(2) Acquired Rights Directive as a Separate Unilateral Conflict Rule?

If article 1(2) Acquired Rights Directive was considered as a separate unilateral conflict rule, it could prevail over article 8 Rome I by operation of article 23 Rome I, which states that

> (. . .) this Regulation shall not prejudice the application of provisions of Community law which, in relation to particular matters, lay down conflict-of-law rules relating to contractual obligations.

[40] *BAG 29 October 1992*, in IPRspr. 1992, pp. 142 et seq.

Article 1(2) Acquired Rights Directive, if considered a conflict rule, would be one of a unilateral nature since it determines the scope of the instrument itself rather than referring to the legal system where the legal relationship 'belongs'. Contrarily to multilateralism, which determines the law applicable focusing on the legal relationship, unilateralism focuses on the legal acts themselves and defends that each legal instrument determines its own scope of application. It has been previously mentioned that some have defended that the scope rules existent in the EU consumer directives are to be considered as unilateral conflict rules and that the application of EU directives is or should be determined by a unilateral PIL method.[41] Although the 'scope rule' of article 1(2) Acquired Rights Directive differs from the scope rules of EU consumer directives, which are more involved with PIL rather than merely referring to the territorial scope of the directive, the discussion can be similar.

According to a unilateral approach, every directive, even implicitly, determines its scope of application.[42] Francq defended that every act of EU secondary law fixes implicitly or explicitly its own scope of application according to its objectives and substantive content.[43] If we understood that the EU legislator is following a unilateral approach, the directives would always determine their own scope according to their nature and purpose while being silent about the application of foreign law. The same reasoning regarding EU consumer directives is to be followed in this regard. In both cases, we are dealing with the applicability of EU secondary law protecting weaker parties. In both cases, the rules of the directives have to be transposed into national law, and in most of the times, Member States can choose to improve the minimum level required by the directive, resulting in diverse national rules among Member States.[44]

As discussed regarding EU consumer directives, the use of a unilateral method to determine the applicability of EU directives might seem attractive at first since it ensures the applicability of the EU instrument and the protection provided by it in all the cases the EU instrument wishes to apply.[45] However, such a method in its purity is not desirable. The unilateral approach is obviously a forum-centred approach, which imposes the application of forum law and ignores the applicability of foreign law. The EU legislator cannot impose the application of all EU employment protection in every international situation. Moreover, legal certainty would be impaired if only the application of EU law is determined instead of defining the circumstances under which a Member State law applies and under which foreign law applies. In addition, the exercise of finding the purpose of the legal act might be difficult and adds uncertainty to the process of determining the applicable law.

---

[41]Francq (2005, 2006), Bucher (2011), p. 82 et seq.; Symeonides (2005), Cremona and Micklitz (2016), p. 91.

[42]Francq (2006), p. 339.

[43]Francq (2005), p. 479.

[44]Regarding the difficulties derived from the national implementation of this type of rules, see Sects. 4.2.1 and 4.2.2.

[45]The same reasoning regarding EU consumer directives and unilateralism applies. See Sect. 4.3.2.

Finally, the advantage of having unified PIL rules codified in the Rome I Regulation would be lost, as well as the advantages deriving from the use of a (mostly) multilateral system. A multilateral approach requires a choice between the different state laws by connecting the legal relationship with the law of a state according to objective criteria. With this approach, equality between the forum law and foreign law is promoted, as well as predictability and respect for the expectations of the parties involved.[46]

Therefore, although the use of a unilateral conflict of laws approach in EU employment directives would ensure the applicability of their protection and, in this case, ensure the application of the Acquired Rights Directive whenever the undertaking to be transferred is located within the EU, the imposition of EU law over foreign law in a unilateral way is contradictory to the contemporary PIL approach, and such a protectionist system should be rejected. It is possible, as we will see, to ensure the application of the protection of the EU employment directives in international situations following a different method. Ensuring the application of EU secondary law through unilateral conflict rules does not fit within the current EU PIL system of the Rome I Regulation, mainly conformed by multilateral conflict rules with the exception of the application of overriding mandatory rules.

Article 1(2) Acquired Rights Directive should not be considered a unilateral conflict rule as such: first, it does not directly affect the conflict of laws; second, it does not even determine which law should apply (since the Directive is to be transposed into national law); third, it is an ambiguous provision and Member States disagree on the way it should be transposed into national law and only a few Member States actually expressly translate article 1(2) Acquired Rights Directive into their acquired rights provisions.[47] In the previous chapter, the similarities and disparities between unilateral conflict rules, scope rules and overriding mandatory rules were discussed.[48] In a few words, the application and scope of an overriding mandatory provision are based on its mandatory character, which derives from the purpose of the provision. Contrarily, unilateral conflict rules delineate the scope of forum law and ensure its application to the situation covered without referring to foreign law, but the provisions covered do not necessarily have a mandatory character. Finally, scope rules may determine the scope of mandatory provisions, overriding mandatory provisions or dispositive provisions. However, we should distinguish between those scope rules in a PIL sense, which try to ensure the application of an instrument in an international situation (e.g. scope rules in some EU consumer directives),[49] and those rules that are only relevant after the law to which they belong has been determined as applicable in order to clarify the territorial scope of an instrument. This latter category is very common in treaties and international conventions

[46] In this regard, see reflexion on PIL methods and directives in Sect. 4.3.3.

[47] Henckel (2016), p. 329.

[48] See Sect. 4.1.5. In that regard, Francq (2017), p. 1788, 1789; Francq (2006), pp. 349–353; Bisping (2012), pp. 40–47.

[49] See Sect. 4.1.1.

(e.g. article 1(1) of the United Nations Convention on Contracts for the International Sale of Goods (CISG) provides that that the Convention applies to international sales contracts when the two parties are established in contracting states). Although article 1(2) Acquired Rights Directive is indeed provided for in a directive, the intention of the EU legislator merely seems to have been to clarify the territorial scope of the directive rather than to have any influence on the cross-border application of the Directive from a PIL point of view. While article 1(2) Acquired Rights Directive is included under the heading 'Scope and Definitions', scope rules of EU consumer directives are under the heading 'Binding Nature' (article 7(2) Consumer Sales Directive[50]) or 'Imperative Nature of This Directive's Provisions' (e.g. article 12 (2) Distance Marketing of Consumer Financial Services Directive,[51] article 22 (4) Consumer Credit Directive[52]) or 'Imperative Nature of the Directive and Application in International Cases' (article 12(2) Timeshare Directive).[53]

5.2.2.2 Article 1(2) Acquired Rights Directive in Coordination with the Rome I Regulation System

Article 8 Rome I generally determines the law applicable to a transfer of undertaking in relation to an individual employment contract. As it is known, the connecting factors of the rules contained in article 8 Rome I benefit the employee as the weaker contracting party, as well as limit party autonomy taking the so-called preferential law approach. The application of the Acquired Rights Directive is ensured as long as the law applicable to the employment contract is the law of a Member State according to article 8 Rome I.[54] However, when that is not the case but an undertaking is to be transferred to a Member State, article 8 does not ensure the application of the Acquired Rights Directive. For example, if the habitual place of work is in the US and the undertaking is to be transferred to Germany, why would that situation involving the workers in the US and a US undertaking require the protection of the

[50]Directive 1999/44/EC of the European Parliament and of the Council of 25 May 1999 on certain aspects of the sale of consumer goods and associated guarantees (OJ L171/12) (Consumer Sales Directive).

[51]Directive 2002/65/EC of the European Parliament and of the Council of 23 September 2002 concerning the distance marketing of consumer financial services and amending Council Directive 90/619/EEC and Directives 97/7/EC and 98/27/EC (OJ L 271/16) (Distance Marketing of Consumer Financial Services Directive).

[52]Directive 2008/48/EC of the European Parliament and of the Council of 23 April 2008 on credit agreements for consumers and repealing Council Directive 87/102/EEC (OJ L 133/66) (Consumer Credit Directive).

[53]Directive 2008/122/EC of the European Parliament and of the Council of 14 January 2009 on the protection of consumers in respect of certain aspects of timeshare, long-term holiday product, resale and exchange contracts (OJ L 33/10) (Timeshare Directive).

[54]On the basis of the majoritarian opinion that the rights and obligations deriving from a transfer of undertaking are governed by the law regulating individual contract of employment and thus, in our case, by article 8 Rome I. Henckel (2016), pp. 221–237.

Acquired Rights Directive? However, in cases similar to the above-mentioned *American Pilots* case, where the undertaking to be transferred is located in a Member State (and thus the habitual place of work of the employees was a Member State) but the law applicable to the employment contract as a result of the closest connection test is a non-Member State law, should the protection of the Acquired Rights Directive be applicable? The first example would fall outside the territorial scope of the Acquired Rights Directive according to article 1(2) since it covers undertakings located in the EU that are to be transferred. Indeed, trying to extend the application of acquired rights provisions to undertakings that are not even established in the territory of the EU would seem like a step too far from the EU legislator. Undertakings not established in the EU cannot predict the application of EU law. In addition, if the EU legislator imposes the application of the EU in an excessive extraterritorial way, it faces the risk that legislators from other countries would react in the same way, which would impair EU undertakings. However, the application of EU law is sometimes necessary for the sake of the EU workers. The second example includes an undertaking located in the territory of the EU that is to be transferred. The objective of the Directive seems to involve the protection of acquired rights to EU workers in the case of a transfer of undertakings. Since article 8 Rome I might not always ensure the application of the Acquired Rights Directive when necessary, does the Rome I Regulation provide for other mechanisms to ensure that application?

Article 3(4) Rome I

Article 3(4) Rome I was introduced into the Regulation with the objective of ensuring that the application of mandatory provisions originated in EU instruments. When this article was drafted, it was done with the intention of dealing with the necessity of coordination between EU secondary law instruments and the conflict rules of the Rome I Regulation. Article 3(4) provides that when all the relevant elements of the contractual relationship are located within one or several Member States (purely intra-EU situations) but the parties chose a non-Member State law as the law applicable to their contract, the mandatory provisions deriving from EU instruments shall be applicable.[55] Therefore, it guarantees the application of the 'provisions of Community law which cannot be derogated from by agreement'—mandatory EU law—when, due to the choice of law of the parties, those provisions could be eluded. Article 3(4) Rome I only becomes applicable when all relevant elements are located within the EU (purely intra-EU situations) and thus cannot be used to justify the application of mandatory EU law when some of the elements of the situation are non-EU.[56] It does not cover any extra-EU situation, while numerous secondary EU law instruments with a mandatory character intend to apply to certain extra-EU situations.

[55]Belohlávek (2011), pp. 707–711; Carrascosa González (2009), p. 151, 152.

[56]For a definition of relevant elements, see Sect. 3.4.

Article 3(4) Rome I is not suitable to coordinate the scope of the Acquired Rights Directive with the Rome I Regulation. It would not cover the situation if the undertaking is to be transferred to another Member State, for example. Article 3 (4) Rome I ensures the application of mandatory EU instruments whenever there is a choice of a non-Member State law but only in purely intra-EU situations. Thus, in situations where article 8 Rome I would not lead to the application of a Member State law (and, as a result, to the Acquired Rights Directive protection), article 3(4) Rome I would not be applicable. Article 8 Rome I can only lead to the application of a non-Member State law in an extra-EU situation or when parties have chosen a non-Member State law as applicable, in which case, if it is a purely intra-EU situation, the law objectively applicable would be the law of a Member State, and therefore the mandatory acquired rights provisions are already ensured as a result of article 8 Rome I.

Thus, article 3(4) Rome I does not really succeed in the objective of coordinating EU secondary law instruments with the Rome I Regulation, and the application of the Acquired Rights Directive is not ensured through article 3(4) Rome I.

Article 9 Rome I

The ECJ, in the *Ingmar* judgment,[57] although it did not address explicitly whether the provisions at stake were to be regarded as overriding mandatory rules in the sense of the Rome I Regulation, gave some guidelines for its determination as such. The *Ingmar* case regarded the application of some specific provisions of the Commercial Agents Directive. The ECJ concluded that the purpose those provisions served required their application where the situation is closely connected with the EU, irrespective of the law chosen by the parties to govern their contract.[58] Following the *Ingmar* judgment, the provisions of the Commercial Agents Directive were to be considered as overriding mandatory and prevailed over the law applicable to the contract. The ECJ based its decision on the freedom of establishment and undistorted competition within the internal market rather than on weaker party protection objectives. As a result, many authors agree that a provision protecting weaker parties, such as employees, can be considered as an overriding mandatory provision as long as it also aims to promote a higher political, social or economic interest that justifies the priority of this provision in an international scenario.[59] That is, the provisions of EU directives can be classified as overriding mandatory rules as long as they serve crucial EU interests.[60]

---

[57] Case C381/98 *Ingmar GB Ltd v Eaton Leonard Technologies Inc.* [2000] ECR I-9305.

[58] *Ingmar*, para. 25.

[59] For example, Kuipers (2012), p. 200; Aguilar Grieder (2006), p. 53; Carrascosa González (2012); Verhagen (2002), p. 136.

[60] For a discussion on overriding mandatory rules as a possible mechanism for the protection of weaker parties in the Rome I Regulation, see Sect. 3.3.

However, various important questions arise in this regard in relation to the Acquired Rights Directive. First, does the existence of a scope rule directly give overriding effect to the provisions of the Directive? Second, do the provisions of the Acquired Rights Directive fall under the definition of overriding mandatory rules in article 9(1) Rome I and, as a result, apply irrespective of the objectively applicable law? Third, can the doctrine of overriding mandatory rules be applied in gold-plating situations?

Does the Existence of Article 1(2) Acquired Rights Directive Directly Give Overriding Effect to the Provisions of the Directive?

If it is concluded that the existence of an explicit scope rule directly gives overriding effect to the provisions of the Directive, then there is no need to discuss whether these rules are to be classified as overriding mandatory under the definition of article 9(1) Rome I. That is, regardless of whether the provisions of the Directive (or, better said, the national implementation provisions of the Member States) are classified as overriding mandatory rules, they would prevail over the law applicable to the contract.

Regarding EU consumer directives containing scope rules, some authors consider that scope rules have the immediate effect of conferring an overriding mandatory character on the provisions of the directive itself.[61] The same could be said about article 1(2) Acquired Rights Directive. That assuming, the existence of scope rules is coordinated with the conflict of laws system of the Rome I Regulation. The provisions of the Acquired Rights Directive would be applicable whenever the undertaking to be transferred is located within the territory of the treaty through the operation of article 9 Rome I, even when the law applicable to the employment contract is not the law of a Member State according to article 8 Rome I.

Under Dutch private international law, for example, Dutch courts are obliged to apply Dutch law when a situation falls under the scope of a Dutch scope rule. That is, when an instrument of national law contains a scope rule and the situation falls under that scope, the provisions of that instrument should be applied by the Dutch court regardless of whether a provision is considered as overriding mandatory or not.[62]

If the same reasoning is followed with regard to article 1(2) Acquired Rights Directive and article 9 Rome I, this would mean that every Member State court would apply their national acquired rights provisions whenever the situation falls within their scope, irrespective of and without the determination of the law that would otherwise govern the situation. National acquired rights provisions would directly apply whenever the undertaking to be transferred was located in the territory of a Member State. In my opinion, this would not be the ideal scenario since a sort of intra-EU parallel PIL system would be created, as it was criticised above regarding the consideration of the scope rule as a unilateral conflict rule. This reasoning ignores

---

[61] Bonomi (2016), p. 616; Fallon and Francq (2000), p. 156, 157.

[62] Explanatory Memorandum to the Dutch Code of Private International Law (Book 10 BW). Henckel (2016), p. 312.

article 8 Rome I, which could (maybe as a result of the preferential law approach or the connecting factor of 'most closely connected law') point to an applicable law different from the forum law and which transposition of acquired rights might be more beneficial for the employee. Also, in case the overriding mandatory character of national acquired rights provisions derived directly from the scope rule of article 1 (2) Acquired Rights Directive, that overriding mandatory character should then be limited to the minimum protection provided by the Directive. If national law provides for a better or wider protection, that extra-protection should then only be considered as overriding mandatory if the provisions fall under the definition of overriding mandatory rules of article 9(1) Rome I (*Unamar* case).[63]

However, article 9 Rome I was designed as an escape mechanism or exception to the normal operation of the multilateral conflict rules of Rome I. If EU directives could impose the application of their rules through the mechanism of article 9 Rome I in any case, regardless of whether they are falling under the definition of article 9 (1) or not, then they would be adhering to the above-mentioned unilateral approach and ignoring the functioning of our current PIL system. If one were to generally understand the rules of the directives protecting weaker parties as overriding mandatory, party autonomy would be completely excluded, the provisions of the directive would be applicable regardless of the law otherwise applicable and it would not be relevant whether that applicable law resulted from the normal operation of the connecting factors or the choice of law by the parties.

Thus, in my understanding, scope rules should not generally be interpreted as asking Member States to apply the provisions of the respective directive as overriding mandatory provisions in every case.[64] It is essential to distinguish between the scope of application of a statute and its mandatory character.[65] The provisions designated by scope rules do not necessarily have a mandatory character or an overriding mandatory character but may determine the scope of mandatory provisions, overriding mandatory provisions or simply dispositive provisions. That is, article 1(2) Acquired Rights Directive should not be understood as automatically conferring an overriding mandatory character on the protection provided by the directive. Instead, I consider that for the provisions of the Acquired Rights Directive to be applied as overriding mandatory rules, they should fall under the definition of article 9(1) Rome I.

Do the Provisions of the Acquired Rights Directive Fall Under the Definition of Overriding Mandatory Rules of Article 9(1) Rome I and Are as a Result Applicable Irrespective of the Objectively Applicable Law?

Besides the differences among the Member States as to the doctrine of overriding mandatory rules and its role in the protection of weaker parties, it is generally agreed at EU level, especially on the basis of the judgments of *Ingmar* and *Unamar*, that

[63]C-184/12 *United Antwerp Maritime Agencies (Unamar) NV v Navigation Maritime Bulgare* [2013] EU:C:2013:663.

[64]In the same opinion: Magnus (2016), pp. 23–25; Schmidt-Kessel (2015), p. 331.

[65]Magnus (2016), pp. 23–25; Francq (2005), p. 575, 576.

article 9(1) Rome I also covers those provisions that protect weaker parties as long as they mainly aim to protect higher interests, which are so essential that their priority over the law applicable is justified.[66] That is, besides protecting weaker parties, the provisions have to be classified as 'crucial by a country for safeguarding its public interests, such as its political, social or economic organization'. In the case of provisions stemming from an EU directive, they should protect interests crucial for the EU. Thus, even though article 9 Rome I refers to public interests, it does not lead a priori to the exclusion of all protective rules. For example, in the *Arblade* case and the *Mazzoleni* case, the ECJ used the notion 'overriding mandatory rules' in reference to national rules on employee protection.

On the one hand, part of the doctrine considers that the rules of the acquired rights provisions are provisions that can fall under the concept of overriding mandatory rules on the basis that they pursue a public interest related to the economic and social organisation of a state. Specifically, regarding the Acquired Rights Directive, the overriding mandatory character is defended.[67] The mandatory character of the Acquired Rights Directive has been recognised by the ECJ. In *Celtec*,[68] the ECJ referred to the provisions of the predecessor of the current directive as mandatory, not being possible to derogate from them in a manner that is unfavourable to the employees.[69] In the same line, in *Temco*,[70] the ECJ referred to the mandatory character of the acquired rights provisions and specified that 'the implementation of the rights conferred on employees by the directive may not be made subject to the consent of either the transferor or the transferee nor the consent of the employees' representatives or the employees themselves'.[71] However, it does not look like the ECJ was referring to the overriding mandatory character of the provisions of the directive as applicable regardless of the law otherwise applicable, but in my opinion, it looks more like it was referring to the mandatory character as provisions that cannot be derogated from by agreement (in this case, EU mandatory character). Doctrine and courts from certain jurisdictions have the tendency to interpret overriding mandatory rules in a more extensive manner and thus could easily consider the acquired rights provisions, as well as other weaker party protection legislation, as overriding mandatory rules, even when the provision is not that crucial for the

[66]See Sect. 3.3.1.

[67]Moreau and Trudeau (2000), p. 932, 933; Sabido Rodríguez (2010), p. 253, 254.

[68]C-478/03 *Celtec Ltd v John Astley and Others* [2005] ECR I-04389.

[69]*Celtec*, para 42: 'the Court considered that to allow the transferor or transferee the possibility of choosing the date from which the contract of employment or employment relationship is transferred would amount to allowing employers to derogate, at least temporarily, from the provisions of Directive 77/187, whereas those provisions are mandatory, and it is thus not possible to derogate from them in a manner unfavourable to employees (*Rotsart de Hertaing*, paragraphs 17 and 25).'

[70]C-51/00 *Temco Service Industries SA v Samir Imzilyen and Others* [2002] ECR I-00969.

[71]*Temco*, para 35.

safeguarding of public interest.[72] It is up to every Member State to determine which national provisions are overriding mandatory, but in order to be considered as such, they should fall under the definition of article 9(1) Rome I. However, Member States should not make a too extensive interpretation of overriding mandatory rules since it would undermine the meaning of article 9 Rome I. Having complete freedom to decide which are national overriding mandatory rules but without justifying their application based on the strict definition of article 9(1) Rome I would be a danger to the legal certainty of the parties to the contract and to the legal predictability regarding the law applicable to a contract. In addition, the acceptance of such extensive interpretations as a general rule entails the risk of promoting a different PIL method in the determination of the law to be applied by a Member State. That is, Member States usually resort to a 'method of introvert unilateralism',[73] like in the case of article 27 of the Belgian Law of 13 April 1995 on commercial agency contracts.[74] The judge of the forum could then apply the provisions protecting weaker contracting parties as overriding mandatory rules (not only regarding commercial agency but also consumers, employees, distributors, franchisees etc.), undermining all the Rome I Regulation system.

In the EU level, for the Acquired Rights Directive to be considered as overriding mandatory, its application should be considered essential for the achievement of specific EU public interests. And that EU overriding mandatory character should only have an effect regarding the application of a non-Member State law since in an intra-EU conflict where the law of a different Member State is applicable, the minimum protection of the Directive (which would be the one considered as EU overriding mandatory) would be ensured by the national transposition of the Member State. Regarding intra-EU situations, the national implementation of the Acquired Rights Directive that exceeds the minimum required by the Directive would have to be considered as overriding mandatory for the Member State in question (at a national level and not EU overriding mandatory) in order to prevail over the applicable law of another Member State.[75]

The provisions stemming from the Acquired Rights Directive mainly aim at preserving employees' rights in the case of a transfer of undertaking. In addition,

---

[72] For example, countries such as France, Belgium or Spain. See, for example, Moreau and Trudeau (2000), Sabido Rodríguez (2010), Fallon and Francq (2000), Sánchez Lorenzo (2003).

[73] We find this concept in Calvo Caravaca and Carrascosa González (2013), pp. 328–330, as well as in Cebrián Salvat (2014), p. 364 (*método del unilateralismo introverso*). These authors describe it as a method according to which a country would establish the spatial scope of its substantive rules in a unilateral and independent manner. As a result, conflict rules would only cover cases regulated by the substantive law of that country. This method is against the current understanding of PIL since this type of unilateral rules would result in forum shopping and diversity in the private international law solutions of the countries (which is the opposite of what Rome I Regulation aims).

[74] Article 27 reads: 'Without prejudice to the application of international conventions to which Belgium is a party, any activity of a commercial agent whose principal place of business is in Belgium shall be governed by Belgian law and shall be subject to the jurisdiction of the Belgian courts.' See *Unamar*, para 13.

[75] See below in this section (iii) a discussion on gold-plating situations and article 9 Rome I.

as most directives, especially those regarding employee protection, the Acquired Rights Directive is also based on the interest of the functioning of the internal market. In addition, it concerns the transfer of rights and obligations originated in collective agreements as well as the preservation of the position of employee representatives. Still, it is very doubtful that the provisions of the Acquired Rights Directive would be determined as crucial for the safeguarding of essential EU interests since the primary aim is not the protection of specific public interests but the protection of the rights of employees.[76] Internal market interests and collective employment considerations could be used to justify the overriding mandatory character of the Acquired Rights Directive, although I consider that a stricter interpretation should be followed since the main aim of the rules is the protection of employees. The rules of the Acquired Rights Directive seem to fall under the category of provisions that cannot be derogated from by agreement (i.e. mandatory rules) rather than overriding mandatory rules of article 9 Rome I. In the *American Pilots* decision,[77] the *Bundesgerichtshof*, in the case of an employment contract governed by New York state law, indicated that they would have applied German employment legislation on acquired rights if it was regarded as overriding mandatory law, which was not the case.[78] However, other Member States, as previously mentioned, interpret overriding mandatory rules in a more extensive manner (e.g. France, Spain, Belgium etc.), and an interpretation of the ECJ in this regard concerning the Acquired Rights Directive is yet to come.[79]

Gold-Plating Situations
Due to the minimum harmonising character of the Acquired Rights Directive, a level playing field is created allowing Member States to improve the minimum standards set by the Directive when transposing it on their national law. Member States, when transposing the directive into their national laws, can exceed the minimum protection afforded by the instrument by extending the material scope of the directive, by offering more protection or by implementing the optional provisions. The phenomenon is known as gold plating.

The issue regarding article 9 Rome I and gold-plating situations is that when the *lex fori* provides for a better protection than the law applicable, the Member State of the forum might wish to apply its own national implementation of the Directive as overriding mandatory. In *Unamar*, the ECJ concluded that despite the Commercial Agents Directive being correctly transposed under Bulgarian law, the Belgian Court had discretion to qualify its own national provisions as overriding mandatory rules in

[76]Henckel (2016), p. 334.

[77]*BAG 29 October 1992*, in IPRspr. 1992, pp. 142 et seq.

[78]Plender and Wilderspin (2009), p. 353, 354.

[79]Although the ECJ in *Ingmar* and *Unamar* considered that the provisions of the Commercial Agents Directive were overriding mandatory because they aim at ensuring the freedom of establishment and undistorted competition of the internal market, it does not mean that the role of the provisions of the Acquired Rights Directive is so crucial for internal market interests and collective employment considerations as to be considered overriding mandatory.

the sense of article 7 Rome Convention (now article 9 Rome I) and apply them irrespective of the otherwise applicable law. It follows from this judgment that Member State provisions that provide for a better protection than those in the Directive can be considered as overriding mandatory rules if they are essential to the public interests of the Member State in which they originate.[80] Since they go over the minimum rules of the Directive, the national implementation rules that surpass the minimum standard would have to justify their overriding mandatory character not only according to EU law objectives but also based on national law objectives.

Thus, the national implementation of the Acquired Rights Directive that exceeds the minimum required by the Directive would have to be considered essential for the safeguarding of the public interests of the Member State where they originate in order to be considered as overriding mandatory and apply over the law applicable to the employment contract. However, the determination of the provisions related to the Acquired Rights Directive as overriding mandatory rules, even when exceeding the minimum of the Directive, seems difficult. In a situation like this, where article 8 and article 9 Rome I 'conflict', the application of overriding mandatory rules is hard to justify since the mandatory protection ensured by the Member State of habitual place of work, including the implementation of the minimum requirements of the Acquired Rights Directive, is already given effect by article 8 Rome I, and there is no reason why a higher protection should be ensured by an overriding mandatory rule when the weaker position of the employee has already been compensated by the operation of article 8 Rome I. As explained above, provisions stemming from the Acquired Rights Directive mainly aim at preserving employees' rights in the case of a transfer of undertakings. In the same manner that it seems very doubtful that they would be considered essential for the safeguarding of the public interests of the EU, it also seems doubtful that the extra-protection would be considered essential for the safeguarding of the public interests of a single Member State. If that was the case, the law of the forum Member State would most probably already be the law applicable according to article 8 Rome I. In addition, in any case, in order to justify the overriding character of the extra-protection, it has to be noticed that it is not always easy to distinguish between national acquired rights provisions originated in the directive and national acquired rights originated in national law exceeding the requirements of the directive.

Although from the *Unamar* judgment it is generally understood that national courts can consider as overriding mandatory rules the national provisions exceeding the minimum protection of a directive and thus apply them over the *lex causae* (which already provides for the minimum required by the directive), I consider that this decision should be understood in a very restrictive manner. Of course, it is up to each national court to decide which national provisions are overriding mandatory, but it should be done according to the definition of article 9(1) Rome I. Otherwise, an extensive interpretation would affect the harmonising effect of the directives, and legal certainty would be impaired since it would be up to each national court to

[80] *Unamar*, para 50.

decide whether or not its gold-plating provisions are to be regarded as overriding mandatory rules and applicable in any situation regardless of the law chosen by the parties, which would lead again to an uncertain and uncoordinated situation.[81] In a recent case (*Republik Griechenland v Grigorios Nikiforidis*),[82] the ECJ has emphasised that the protection offered by article 8 Rome I to the employee should not be prejudiced by the application of overriding mandatory rules. In reference to our discussion, it could be inferred a hint regarding the role of overriding mandatory rules and protection of employees. The ECJ, logically, attributes the protection of the employee to the mandatory rules of the law of the habitual place of work. It follows that since article 8 Rome I is aimed at the protection of the private interests of employees, then article 9 Rome I cannot attend to the same kind of interests. However, the line between private and public is not always clear-cut, especially in the cases of our concern.[83] For example, the French Cour de Cassation, in a sentence of 30 November 2007,[84] answered to the question of whether the provisions on subcontract were weaker party protection provisions or protected competition. The court opted for the second option. Similarly, the Dutch Supreme Court on 23 October 1987[85] answered whether the rules on termination of employment were protecting the interest of the employee or were essential for the Dutch labour market, opting also for the second option (and later confirmed in the decision of the Dutch Supreme Court on 24 February 2012).[86] That is, higher public interests can always be involved in contractual provisions, especially regarding employment law. That is why an extensive interpretation may lead to the argument that all weaker contracting party provisions protect public interests, and thus the application of national provisions through article 9 Rome I would always be justified.[87] That is not the intention of article 9 Rome I, which definition is more restrictive.[88] Again, national acquired rights provisions are most probably outside the definition of article 9(1) Rome I.

As it was concluded in the previous chapter regarding gold-plating provisions of EU consumer directives, when at least the same minimum standards are shared, multilateral conflict rules should be promoted in intra-EU conflicts. In intra-EU situations, EU employment directives impose upon the Member States common legal standards that are mandatory at EU level. This EU mandatory set of rules might

---

[81] Van Bochove (2014), p. 156.

[82] Case C-135/15 *Republik Griechenland v Grigorios Nikiforidis* [2016] ECLI:EU:C:2016:774.

[83] Carrillo Pozo (2017), p. 11, 12; Kuipers (2012) 112 et seq.

[84] Cour de Cassation, 30 November 2007, 06-14006 (*Agintis*).

[85] Hoge Raad 23 October 1987, NJ 1988/842 (*Sorensen/Aramco*).

[86] Hoge Raad 24 February 2012, LJN BU8512 (*Nuon Personeelsbeheer/X*).

[87] On that line of argument, Bonomi (2008), p. 230 et seq.

[88] The reference to public interests in the definition of article 9(1) Rome I entails a restrictive interpretation of article 9 Rome I, under which not every mandatory rule can be applicable but only those with overriding mandatory character that aim at the protection of public interests. This excludes those rules that are mainly aimed at the protection of the weaker party in a contract since article 9 Rome I is not designed to protect the employees, commercial agents, consumers etc. Garcimartín Alférez (2012), p. 353.

need to be ensured against the application of a foreign law, but not among the Member States that share the same EU mandatory provisions. Therefore, I consider that the gold-plating provisions of a Member State should not easily be imposed against the choice of another Member State law since both Member States share the mandatory EU provisions.

5.2.3 Reflexion

It is submitted that the Acquired Rights Directive and the conflict rules of the Rome I Regulation are not always easy to reconcile.

First, article 1(2) Acquired Rights Directive provides that the Directive

> shall apply where and in so far as the undertaking, business or part of the undertaking or business to be transferred is situated within the territorial scope of the Treaty.

The determination of the nature and function of this rule from a PIL point of view is conflicting. From a PIL perspective, the existence of rules determining the territorial scope of a directive can logically be related to the existing debate regarding the relationship of scope rules in EU secondary law instruments (such as the case of numerous EU consumer directives) and PIL instruments. The scholar debate has not reached an agreement on this regard. In my opinion, although article 1(2) Acquired Rights Directive is included in a directive, the intention of the EU legislator in this case seems to have been to clarify the territorial scope of the directive rather than to have any influence on the cross-border application of the Directive from a PIL point of view. The drafting of article 1(2) Acquired Rights Directive and the drafting of the scope rules included in certain EU consumer directives clearly differ. However, the existence of this 'scope rule' in the Acquired Rights Directive leads to confusion, especially regarding the national implementation of the provision and among PIL scholars. However, even if it was understood as a scope rule in the PIL sense, and in the same manner as described regarding scope rules of EU consumer directives, it can be considered that scope rules in EU secondary law instruments should be considered not as conflict rules as such but as provisions that help to determine the level of mandatoriness that the provisions of the directive have.

Second, article 8 Rome I will most probably indicate the law of the habitual place of work as the law applicable to the employment contract. Even when parties choose another law as applicable, the mandatory provisions of the law of the habitual place of work are applicable if they offer a better protection to the employee. However, it is generally understood that when there is a cross-border transfer of undertaking, the habitual place of work changes, and as a result, the law applicable to the employment contract also changes. If the undertaking is relocated from a Member State to another Member State (intra-EU transfer), the application of the provisions of the Acquired Rights Directive is ensured since the law applicable is the law of a Member State.

Also, when the undertaking is relocated from a Member State to a non-Member State, article 8 Rome I ensures the application of the (at least) minimum protection of Acquired Rights Directive before the employee moves to his or her new habitual place of work. However, when the law applicable to the employment contract is not a Member State law (e.g. the contract is most closely connected to a non-Member State), the application of the Acquired Rights Directive is not ensured, regardless of whether the undertaking is located in the EU. In the mentioned *American Pilots* case, the situation involved a transfer of a Berlin-based aviation business from Pan American World Airways to Berliner Lufthansa Airport. The undertaking transferred was located in Germany before and after the transfer. However, the law applicable to the employment contract was the law of New York as the law chosen and as the law applicable in the absence of choice, being the law most closely connected to the contract. In those cases, how can a Member State court ensure the application of the Acquired Rights Directive?

On the one hand, one could read article 1(2) Acquired Rights Directive as a scope rule in the PIL sense and could consider that the Acquired Rights Directive determines its own unilateral application in accordance with that provision, which would be understood as a unilateral conflict rule. If considered as a separate conflict rule, it could prevail over the rules of the Rome I Regulation through article 23 Rome I. The solution would be to ignore altogether the current conflict of laws system provided in this case in the Rome I Regulation and adhere to a unilateral conflict of laws approach. The majoritarian opinion does not support this approach. Although it would ensure the application of the Directive, it brings more downsides than benefits. A return to a unilateral approach, besides the inherent disadvantages to a unilateral PIL system, would be a return to the past that is not justified. It is inconsistent to maintain that EU law depends on its own applicability criteria and imposes its application and at the same time to ignore that foreign law might do the same. Under our current PIL thinking, neutrality between legal systems should be respected with only some exceptions. The EU legislator should not aim at imposing the application of the directives without regard to the PIL system in force. Indeed, legal certainty is not benefited from such an approach since a parallel conflict of laws would be created imposing the application of the rules of the Directive when determined by the scope rule, without even determining which national law is applicable. It seems more consistent that the EU legislator respects the current PIL thinking. Moreover, not all non-Member States would have a lack of protection of acquired rights that would 'justify' the use of a unilateral approach, but, in fact, many non-Member States have a very similar acquired rights regulation than the EU.[89] Finally, in any way, article 1(2) Acquired Rights Directive should not even be read in the same way as the scope rules of EU consumer directives. The intention of the EU

[89]For example, Switzerland, in article 333 Federal law concerning the Amendment to the Swiss Civil Code (Part Five: Code of Obligations) (*Bundesgesetz betreffend die Ergänzung des Schweizerischen Zivilgesetzbuches (Fünfter Teil: Obligationenrecht)* or South Africa, in Section 197 Labour Relations Act (No. 66 of 1995). Henckel (2016), p. 342.

legislator seems to have been to clarify the territorial scope of the Directive rather than to have any influence on the cross-border application of the Directive from a PIL point of view. As such, when drafting EU secondary law instruments, regard should be paid to the possible (and undesired) influences of the current PIL system.

On the other hand, respect for the current PIL system is sought, and the application of the Acquired Rights Directive should be ensured through the other mechanisms available in the Rome I Regulation. Article 3(4) Rome I, aimed at coordinating the application of mandatory EU secondary law provisions with the Rome I Regulation, is not suitable to ensure the application of the provisions of the Acquired Rights Directive. Article 3(4) Rome I is only applicable to purely intra-EU situations and when the parties have chosen a non-Member State law. Those situations are already covered by article 8 Rome I.

Article 9 Rome I could ensure the application of the provisions of the Acquired Rights Directive when required provided they are considered as overriding mandatory rules. If the provisions of the Acquired Rights Directive are overriding mandatory rules, then they are applicable regardless of the law applicable to the employment contract. However, it is submitted that it is highly doubtful that acquired rights provisions are essential to EU public interests; they might be important for internal market purposes, but are they essential? The doctrine of overriding mandatory rules is intended for provisions that protect public interests, while provisions protecting weaker parties are mainly intended to balance the interests of the parties to the contract. Although the Acquired Rights Directive has some function regarding the internal market, the main objective is to protect the interests of employees upon a transfer of undertaking.

Another option consists in understanding that the 'scope rule' directly gives overriding effect to the provisions of the Directive. Regardless of whether the provisions of the Directive are classified as overriding mandatory rules according to the definition of article 9(1) Rome I, they would be considered as such as a result of the scope rule and they would prevail over the law applicable to the contract. Although such consideration would a priori ensure the application of the Acquired Rights Directive, it has to be kept in mind that it is the national implementation of the Acquired Rights Directive that has to be determined as overriding mandatory. However, Member States have implemented the scope rule of article 1(2) Acquired Rights Directive in different and contradicting ways, which would make very difficult the classification of the rules as overriding mandatory because of the scope rule. Also, this solution would not be much different than the first option (i.e. the unilateral approach). Overriding mandatory rules are the unilateral exception to our mainly multilateral PIL system. If used in such an extensive way, they would not be an exception anymore, and the current PIL system becomes endangered. Moreover, regarding gold-plating situations, the scope rule would not give an overriding mandatory character to the provisions exceeding the protection of the Directive, but that character would have to derive from the definition of article 9 (1) Rome I. However, the difficulty separating the national provisions exceeding the minimum protection with those that do not would make this distinction blurred and burdensome.

It can definitely be submitted that the Acquired Rights Directive and the conflict rules of the Rome I Regulation, according to the current drafting and above-mentioned understanding of the concepts and rules involved, are not entirely coordinated. As I stated regarding scope rules in EU consumer directives, the current drafting of scope rules and the existence of different national implementations and approaches in that regard brings more uncertainty to the system. If the issue of transfer of undertakings is to be classified under the category of conflict rules for individual employment contracts, then the law applicable is to be determined by article 8 Rome I, which already contains protective conflict rules for the benefit of employees. Article 8 Rome I will ensure, most of the times, the application of the mandatory provisions of the law of the habitual place of work of the employee. Thus, an employee with habitual place of work in a Member State will have his or her rights protected according to the Acquired Rights Directive upon a transfer of undertaking. However, when the connecting factors of article 8 lead to a different law than the *lex loci laboris*, which happens to be a non-Member State law, Member States might still wish to apply the provisions of the Acquired Rights Directive. A modification of article 8(4) Rome I has been suggested, not only consisting in covering 'closest connected' situation but also taking into account the protection of workers.[90] The modification would consist in adding the possibility of applying the most beneficial law for the worker as long as it has a close connection with the contract—even if it is not the closest connection.[91] This rule would give a wide margin of interpretation to the judge, allowing him or her to consider all the relevant circumstances of the case and the need for protection of the worker.

However, it is true that in most of the cases where article 8 Rome I leads to the application of a foreign law, that law would be the most 'interested' in being applicable to the employment contract. Indeed, there is generally no reason why EU law should be imposed on a transfer of a US undertaking and on his or her employees habitually carrying out their work in the US, even if they are eventually being transferred to a Member State. US law would be more interested in protecting (or not) the rights of the employees habitually carrying out their work in their territory. The imposition of the Acquired Rights Directive to such situations can be seen as an excessive imposition from the EU legislator. However, there are cases that are more involved with a Member State, such as the previously mentioned situation where the employees involved in the transfer habitually carry out their work in a Member State. Article 9 Rome I is the only possible mechanism to ensure the application of the Directive in such scenarios but, as stated above, not an ideal mechanism. Many options have been suggested by different scholars in this regard.[92] For example, Henckel has suggested the introduction of a multilateral conflict rule to deal with cross-border transfer of undertakings that points to the law of the Member

[90]Gardeñes Santiago (2008), pp. 415–418; Gardeñes Santiago (2017), p. 184.

[91]Gardeñes Santiago (2008), p. 417, 418; Gardeñes Santiago (2017), p. 184.

[92]Some of the theories and solutions are discussed in Henckel (2016), pp. 337–357.

State in which the undertaking to be transferred is located as being applicable.[93] Such a multilateral conflict rule would be in accordance with the requirements of article 1(2) Acquired Rights Directive. However, it also has to be submitted that it would not come without complications, especially because of the difficulty regarding the categorisation and differentiation of the different situations that a transfer of undertakings involves.

One final reflexion from the PIL point of view can be submitted. If article 8 Rome I, which is the rule that Rome I provides for the law applicable to employment contracts and which favours the employee, leads to the application of a non-Member State law, that law is the one 'interested' in having their mandatory rules applied to the situation. If article 8 does not lead to the law of a Member State, even when employees habitually carry out their work there, because the employment contract is more closely connected to a different legal system, then article 8 Rome I assumes that the law most closely connected to the contract is the one 'interested' in applying its mandatory rules protecting the employee. Thus, in that scenario, the protection to the employee comes from the law most closely connected to the employment contract. The interest in the application of the law of the habitual place of work in that case should only be justified on the basis of protection of essential public interests, not on the application of protective provisions to the employee.

5.3 Temporary Posting of Workers in the EU: The Posted Workers Directive and the Rome I Regulation

When a worker carries out work in the territory of another country (host country) where he or she usually works (home country) for a limited period of time, he/she is considered as a posted worker. Cases involving the posting of workers inevitably involve cross-border elements and therefore private international law issues. According to the Rome I Regulation, for applicable law purposes, the country where the work is habitually carried out shall not be deemed to have changed if the worker is temporarily employed in another country (article 8(2) Rome I). Employees will be covered by the law of the country where they habitually carry out their work, even when they are temporarily posted to another country. As a consequence, without any correcting mechanism, the working conditions would differ among workers employed at the same place since the local workers would be protected by the local provisions while the posted workers would be protected according to the provisions of their home state. As a result, undertakings established in 'low-cost' countries would be at a comparative advantage, which could affect negatively the employment conditions in the host state (phenomenon known as social dumping). 'High-cost' countries might want, given that situation, to make

[93] Ibid., p. 356.

applicable their employment protection rules to all labour performed within their territory.[94] On the other hand, the opposite solution entailing the application of the law of the host state as a general rule would lead to a disadvantage to the home undertaking, which would be forced to fulfil both the standards of the host state and the standards of the home state, depriving it at the same time of the comparative advantage. Nowadays, the rules of the Posted Workers Directive, together with the Rome I Regulation, aim at avoiding the aforementioned scenarios.

When a service provider established in a Member State posts workers from one Member State to another Member State, important interests become confronted. According to article 45 TFEU, the free movement of workers is ensured in the EU. A worker in one Member State is entitled to move to another Member State to work. A service provider posting workers to another Member State is exercising its freedom to provide services guaranteed by article 56 TFEU. Normally, this company intends to make use of its cheaper costs to provide services in another country. However, employee organisations of the host state would be afraid that local employees will be at a disadvantage in comparison with posted workers. Also, local companies, which have to comply with the more restrictive employment law provisions, will consider that the competition with foreign companies posting workers is unfair since not complying with the most restrictive rules is cheaper for a company. This situation could result in a 'race to the bottom', in which countries lower their employment protection rules for the benefit of competition.[95] At the same time, the competitive advantage would be undermined if more restrictive employment provisions were applicable to the posted employees, potentially restricting the freedom of providing services. Thus, a balance is necessary between the protection of posted workers fight against social dumping and equal treatment between local companies and companies from another Member States in the provision of services.

In the well-known *Rush Portuguesa* case,[96] the ECJ expressed its view regarding the freedom of provision of services and posted workers. When Portugal became a new Member of the EC in 1986, the Portuguese company Rush Portuguesa entered into a subcontract with a French company for the construction of a railway line in France. For that purpose, workers from Portugal were posted to France, who, due to the transitional arrangements for the accession of Portugal to the EC, were treated as third country nationals. French authorities established that Rush Portuguesa had not complied with the French requirements of the Labour Code for services performed by non-nationals in France. Answering to the question of whether it was compatible with EU law to impose conditions on the freedom of provision of services, the ECJ stated that the Treaty precluded a Member State from banning a service provider established in another Member State from moving freely on its territory, including its staff, and from making restrictions to the movement of the staff, such as a condition as to engagement in situ or an obligation to obtain a work permit. Such conditions

---

[94]Van Hoek (2014), p. 166, 167.

[95]Merrett (2011), p. 264.

[96]Case C-113/89 *Rush Portuguesa Ld^a v Office national d'immigration* [1990] ECR *I-01417.*

discriminate against the service provider from another Member State in relation to the competitors of the host country, whose staff is not subject to restrictions.[97] However, the ECJ also added that EU law does not preclude a Member State from extending national legislation to any person temporarily employed in its territory regardless of the country in which the employer is established.[98]

The judgment of *Rush Portuguesa* triggered in Member States that are usually host countries for posted workers the adoption of national legislation extending national employment standards to posted workers.[99] These Member States saw the necessity to safeguard their labour system and protect it against fair competition as well as to ensure decent working conditions for posted workers.[100] The *Rush Portuguesa* case and the reactions of the Member States eventually triggered the adoption of the Posted Workers Directive in 1996.[101]

5.3.1 The Posted Workers Directive, Enforcement Directive and the Revised Posted Workers Directive

The Posted Workers Directive (PWD) aims to promote the freedom of provision of services as well as to ensure the protection of posted workers.[102] The PWD is applicable to cross-border posting of workers in the context of an intra-EU provision of services. Thus, the PWD limits its own territorial scope of application to an intra-EU temporary posting of workers. Since the territorial scope of the Directive is limited to intra-EU situations, the previous problem regarding the Acquired Rights Directive is mostly avoided. The PWD covers situations involving undertakings established in a Member State that, in the framework of the transnational provision of services, post workers to another Member State (a) under a contract concluded between the undertaking making the posting and the party for whom the services are supplied or (b) by posting them to an establishment or to an undertaking owned by the same group or (c) by posting them via an employment agency.[103] Member States implement the provisions of the Directive within their national law. In an intra-EU posting of workers, the law of a Member State—or, at least, the core mandatory provisions—is ensured by article 8 Rome I. Therefore, the application of the

[97]*Rush Portuguesa*, para. 12.

[98]*Rush Portuguesa*, para. 18. Gardeñes Santiago (2012), pp. 257–259.

[99]For example, Germany adopted the Posting of Workers Act (*Arbeitnehmerentsendegesetz*) in 1996.

[100]Grusic (2015), p. 263; Riesenhuber (2012), p. 195.

[101]Directive 96/71/EC of the European Parliament and of the Council of 16 December 1996 concerning the posting of workers in the framework of the provision of services (OJ 1996 L 18/1).

[102]Liukkunen (2004), p. 229.

[103]Article 1(3) Posted Workers Directive.

provisions of the PWD is also ensured if the conditions of application of the Directive are fulfilled.

The PWD also provides that undertakings established in a non-Member State cannot be given a more favourable treatment than undertakings from Member States (article 1(4) PWD). A posted worker is defined as a worker that carries out his or her work in the territory of a Member State other than the state in which he/she normally works (article 2(1) PWD). For the purposes of the PWD, the definition of 'worker' is that one established by the law of the host Member State (article 2(2) PWD), and thus no problem of classification arises from the PIL perspective. The core provision of the PWD is article 3 PWD, which imposes the obligation on the host Member State to extend its provisions in specific areas of labour law (listed in the article) to workers who are temporarily posted to their territory. The other articles of the Directive relate to exchange of information, enforcement, implementation and review.

The determination of what should be understood as a 'temporary posting' becomes relevant in order to prevent abusive and fraudulent practices involving the so-called letterbox companies, which do not have a real activity in the country of origin but just pretend so in order to avoid the application of the law of the 'host' country, and to differentiate between a permanent transfer and a temporary posting. While the original PWD remained silent in this regard, the Rome I Regulation gives special importance to the intentions of the employer and employee to resume working in the home country once the temporary posting abroad comes to an end. Recital 36 Rome I provides:

> As regards individual employment contracts, work carried out in another country should be regarded as temporary if the employee is expected to resume working in the country of origin after carrying out his tasks abroad. The conclusion of a new contract of employment with the original employer or an employer belonging to the same group of companies as the original employer should not preclude the employee from being regarded as carrying out his work in another country temporarily.

The terms of the contract and the circumstances of the case can show those intentions.[104]

In order to avoid situations of abuse involving letterbox companies and fake temporary postings and with the objective of improving the practical application of

[104]Employers are obliged to provide information regarding the posting to posted employees (article 4 Council Directive 91/533/ECC), which can be especially useful to determine whether the posting is intended to be temporary or definitive, according to article 4 Council Directive 91/533/ECC (OJ L 288/22), which will be repealed from 1 August 2022 and substituted by Directive (EU) 2019/1152 of the European Parliament and of the Council of 20 June 2019 on transparent and predictable working conditions in the European Union (OJ L 186/105), also providing for the obligation of information to posted workers in article 7.

the PWD, the Enforcement Directive on Posted Workers (Directive 2014/67/EU)[105] was adopted in 2014. The Enforcement Directive includes a provision on the interpretation of temporary posting, according to which all factual elements characterising the work and the situation should be taken into account in order to assess whether a worker is temporarily posted to another Member State. The provision includes a non-exhaustive list of elements to take into account: work carried out for a limited period of time in another Member State, date of start of the posting, posting taking place in a country other than the habitual place of work according to Rome I, the posted worker returning to or being expected to resume work in the home country after the completion of the work or tasks for which he or she was posted, the nature of the activities, travel-related expenses and accommodation provided or reimbursed by the employer who is posting the worker, previous periods during which the post was filled by the same or by another (posted) worker (article 4(3) Enforcement Directive).[106]

In order to complement the Enforcement Directive on Posted Workers, the Commission proposed a revision of the PWD. The new PWD (Directive 2018/957/EU)[107] was adopted on 28 June 2018 and was transposed into the national laws of the Member States by 30 July 2020, not being applicable before that date. In the same manner as the original PWD, the revision aims at facilitating the free movement of services while ensuring fair competition and the rights of posted workers. More specifically, the new PWD aims at ensuring fair wages and a level playing field in the host country between posting and local companies. Regarding the concept of a genuine posting and the interpretation of the term ‘temporary posting’, the new PWD refers to the provision of the Enforcement Directive.[108] However, one of the relevant changes introduced by the new PWD is the duration of the posting, extending the application of the additional terms and conditions of the host country to postings lasting longer than 12 months or, where applicable, 18 months.[109] However, those ‘longer’ postings are still considered temporary postings. The duration of the posting does not normally affect its consideration as being temporary.

[105]Directive 2014/67/EU of the European Parliament and of the Council of 15 May 2014 on the enforcement of Directive 96/71/EC concerning the posting of workers in the framework of the provision of services and amending Regulation (EU) No 1024/2012 on administrative cooperation through the Internal Market Information System (‘the IMI Regulation’) [2014] OJ L 159/11.

[106]On the Enforcement Directive, mobile workers and the Rome I Regulation, see Houwerzijl and van Hoek (2016).

[107]Directive (EU) 2018/957 of the European Parliament and of the Council of 28 June 2018 amending Directive 96/71/EC concerning the posting of workers in the framework of the provision of services (OJ 2018 L 173/16).

[108]More regarding genuine posting and the concept of ‘temporary’ posting in Gómez Abelleira (2018).

[109]Article 3(1a) and Recitals 9–11 of the new PWD.

Only a very long posting, together with the circumstances of the case, could lead to an exception.[110]

5.3.2 *Article 3 PWD and the Rome I Regulation: Application of the Core Provisions of the Law of the Host Member State*

The heart of the PWD is article 3. This provision requires the host country to extend the application of the provisions of the law of the host state regarding certain areas to workers who are temporarily posted there.

According to article 3(1) PWD, Member States must ensure that the undertakings of the host state guarantee to the workers posted to their territory certain terms and conditions of employment that are laid down in that Member State concerning:[111]

- Maximum work periods and minimum rest periods.
- Minimum paid annual holidays.
- Minimum rates of pay, including overtime rates (excluding supplementary occupational retirement pension schemes). The revised version of the PWD, however, refers to remuneration rather than to minimum rates of pay. At the moment, the employer is only obliged to comply with the minimum salary of the host country, but the revised version of the PWD requires that the remuneration of posted workers should be at the same level as the salary of the local workers, including the same additional salary elements such as bonuses or allowances (equal pay for equal work). The inclusion of this provision responds to the needs exposed by the impact assessment conducted by the European Commission[112] regarding posting of workers and the need for an improvement in the legislation, which showed that, while the number of workers who are sent from one Member State to another Member State for a limited period of time had extensively increased, these 'posted workers' often earned substantially less than what local workers receive for the same work.
- The conditions of hiring out of workers, in particular the supply of workers by temporary employment undertakings.
- Health, safety and hygiene at work.

[110]In the *Schlecker* case (Case C-64/12 *Anton Schlecker v Melitta Josefa Boedeker* [2013] EU:C:2013:551), Advocate General Wahl gave an example in which he referred to this situation and considered that a very long posting would be over 10 years. Case C-64/12 *Anton Schlecker v Melita Josefa Boedeker*, Opinion of Advocate General Wahl delivered on 16 April 2013, para 43.

[111]Laid down by law, regulation or administrative provision, and/or by collective agreements or arbitration awards universally applicable, in the host Member State.

[112]European Commission, *Impact Assessment accompanying the document Proposal for a Directive of the European Parliament and the Council amending Directive 96/71/EC concerning the posting of workers in the framework of the provision of services SWD* (2016) 52 final.

- Protective measures with regard to the terms and conditions of employment of pregnant women or women who have recently given birth, of children and of young people.
- Equality of treatment between men and women and other provisions on non-discrimination.[113]

The revised version of the PWD adds two more areas to the list:

- Workers' accommodation was provided by the employer to workers away from their regular place of work.
- Allowances or reimbursement of expenditure covering travel, board and lodging expenses were also made available for workers away from home for professional reasons.

However, article 3 PWD does not prevent the application of terms and conditions of employment that are more favourable to the employees (e.g. in case the law of the home state as the law applicable to the employment contract provides for higher protection to the employee in the case at hand).[114] It ensures a minimum level of protection. It does not harmonise substantive law, but it provides that all areas of protection mentioned must be considered to apply to all workers posted to the territory. Therefore, the PWD lays down terms and conditions governing the employment relationship during a transnational provision of services, including a nucleus of mandatory rules of the host country law containing minimum protection for the workers who are temporarily posted there. However, the ECJ has made a restrictive interpretation of article 3 PWD, which shall be the object of brief analysis. Moreover, the relationship between article 3 PWD and the Rome I Regulation shall be discerned.

5.3.2.1 Restrictive Interpretation of the ECJ

The PWD aims at promoting the provision of services within the EU in the context of fair competition and at the same time to guarantee the rights of employees involved in these cross-border situations. However, the balance between these objectives is not easy, and it has been subject to ECJ interpretation several times. It is necessary to make a brief reference to the restrictive interpretation that the ECJ makes of the Posted Workers Directive in defence of the freedom of provision of services under article 56 TFEU to fully understand the objectives of the directive. The principal cases in this regard are the well-known ECJ judgments *Viking*, *Laval*, *Rüffert* and *Luxembourg*. The *Viking* case,[115] dealing with the freedom of establishment in the

[113]This list is non-exhaustive, and Member States may extend it according to the conditions set in article 3(10).

[114]Article 3(7) PWD.

[115]Case C-438/05 *International Transport Workers' Federation and Finnish Seamen's Union v Viking Line ABP and OÜ Viking Line Eesti* [2008] ECR *I-10779.*

EU, is not directly related to the topic at hand and thus will not be the object of analysis, although it is worthy to mention that it sets the principles on which the *Laval* case is built.[116]

The *Laval* case[117] involved Latvian workers posted to work temporarily in Swedish building sites, whose contract was governed by collective agreements between Laval and the Latvian trade union and who earned 40% less than the Swedish workers. Following a collective action taken by the Latvian trade union, Laval commenced proceedings against the relevant trade union, claiming that the collective action trying to force a foreign company to apply the Swedish collective agreement to posted workers breached article 56 TFEU. The main question referred to the ECJ was whether the collective action taken by the trade union in the form of blockade breached article 56 TFEU on the freedom of provision of services. In this case, the relevant collective agreement provided for more favourable conditions than those required by the PWD. The ECJ referred to the settled case law on the freedom of provision of services, which allows the host Member State to apply its legislation and collective agreements to a foreign service provider, provided that such rules are adequate for the protection of workers and do not go beyond what is required.[118] The ECJ considered that the implementation of the PWD in Sweden, under which the payment rates were established on a case-by-case basis rather than by a general legislation, led to a climate of unfair competition between national workers and posted workers.[119] The ECJ concluded that the attempt of a trade union by means of a collective action of forcing an undertaking from a Member State providing services in another Member State to sign a collective agreement with more favourable conditions than those required by the relevant legislative provision and including other terms not even referred to in article 3 PWD was not in accord with article 56 TFEU and article 3 PWD.[120] For the purposes of this study, it is relevant that the ECJ claimed that the host Member State cannot go beyond the terms and conditions required by article 3 PWD—article 3 PWD is the minimum and maximum protection that the host Member State can apply to posted workers.[121] According to the

---

[116]Barnard (2008).

[117]Case C-341/05, *Laval un Partneri Ltd v Svenska Byggnadsarbetareförbundet* [2007] ECR I-11767.

[118]*Laval*, para 56.

[119]*Laval*, paras 70, 71.

[120]'In the light of the foregoing, the answer to the first question must be that Article 49 EC and Directive 96/71 are to be interpreted as precluding a trade union, in a Member State in which the terms and conditions of employment covering the matters referred to in Article 3(1), first subparagraph, (a) to (g) of that directive are contained in legislative provisions, save for minimum rates of pay, from attempting, by means of collective action in the form of a blockade ("blockad") of sites such as that at issue in the main proceedings, to force a provider of services established in another Member State to enter into negotiations with it on the rates of pay for posted workers and to sign a collective agreement the terms of which lay down, as regards some of those matters, more favourable conditions than those resulting from the relevant legislative provisions, while other terms relate to matters not referred to in Article 3 of the directive.' *Laval*, para 111.

[121]*Laval*, paras 80, 81.

Advocate General (AG) of the case, a measure considered incompatible with the PWD would eventually be considered incompatible with article 56 TFEU since the PWD is intended to implement the terms of that article.[122]

A similar conclusion was reached by the ECJ in *Rüffert*.[123] The construction industry in Germany was governed by a collective agreement that provided for a general minimum wage (in accordance with article 3(1)(c) PWD). However, there were also more specific collective agreements within the construction industry in certain territories that also set wages (particularly, the case concerned a German federal state of Lower Saxony (Land Niedersachsen) law on the award of public contracts). In this case, the legitimacy of requiring compliance with such specific German law requiring higher wages was questioned. According to the ECJ, since the collective agreement at hand only covered public contracts (and did not include private contracts) and had not been declared universally applicable, it could not be considered as establishing a minimum rate of pay to be imposed in the context of a transnational provision of services involving posted workers within the meaning of Article 3(1)(c) PWD.[124] Although article 3(7) PWD provides that the previous paragraphs of the provision do not prevent the application of terms and conditions of employment that are more favourable to workers, the ECJ states that this provision should not be interpreted as allowing the host Member State to require the observance of terms and conditions of employment that go beyond the mandatory rules for minimum protection regarding the provision of services in its territory. That is, article 3(1) PWD in (a) to (g) already lays down the degree of protection for posted workers that the host Member State is entitled to require foreign undertakings to observe.[125] Again, the ECJ made clear that the terms indicated in article 3(1) PWD must be applied to posted workers but also constitute a limit to the mandatory protection that the host state can apply. The application of mandatory rules beyond the terms of article 3(1) PWD goes against the free movement of services.[126] Article 3(7), when providing that the previous paragraphs do not prevent the application of terms and conditions of employment that are more favourable to workers, is referring to cases where posted workers already enjoy a more favourable protection from their home state or it results from the employer's own accord.

In *Commission v Luxembourg*,[127] the ECJ examined the implementation of the PWD by Luxembourg. The Luxembourg implementation provided that all laws, regulations and administrative provisions and those resulting from collective agreements that have been declared universally applicable or an arbitration decision with a scope similar to that of universally applicable collective agreements regarding

[122]Opinion Advocate General Mengozzi delivered on 23 May 2007, para 149.

[123]Case C-346/06, *Dirk Rüffert v Land Niedersachsen* [2008] ECR I-01989.

[124]*Rüffert*, paras 29–31.

[125]*Rüffert*, para 33.

[126]*Rüffert*, para 34.

[127]Case C-319/06 *Commission of the European Communities v Grand Duchy of Luxemburg* [2008] ECR I-04323.

matters listed in article 3(1) PWD, plus other areas not covered by that provision or going beyond it, constituted mandatory provisions involving national public policy in the sense of article 7 Rome Convention (now article 9 Rome I Regulation). Luxembourg relied on the exception in article 3(10) PWD allowing for the application of terms and conditions on matters going beyond the ones required in the case of public policy provisions. However, the ECJ, making reference to the *Arblade* case regarding the definition of overriding mandatory rules, held that such rules shall be deemed to be so crucial for the safeguarding of the political, economic or social interests of the Member State concerned as to require their application. As to article 3 (10) PWD, the ECJ clarified that it must be interpreted strictly, and the notion of public policy in an EU context can only be used when there is a genuine and serious threat to a fundamental interest of the society, which shall be supported by appropriate evidence or by an analysis of the proportionality of the measure taken.[128]

These judgments were extensively commented by the doctrine, and doubts arose as to whether the PWD was achieving its mixed objectives, i.e. promoting the provision of services and at the same time guaranteeing fair competition and respect for the rights of workers.[129] The existence of abusive and fraudulent practices supported those doubts. Host Member States had problems with the application of the PWD related to the existence of the so-called letterbox companies, which do not have a real activity in the country of origin, or of false self-employed persons. The Enforcement Directive and the new PWD aim at solving these issues by clarifying the concept of temporary posting and introducing new measures to avoid abusive practices and fake postings.

5.3.2.2 Relationship Between Article 3 PWD and Rome I Regulation

The interaction between article 3 PWD and the Rome I Regulation needs clarification. Article 3 PWD requires that the minimum provisions in the areas mentioned of the Member State where the worker is temporarily working apply. The Rome I Regulation determines the law applicable to the employment contract, which will most probably be the law where the employee habitually carries out his or her work. How do the mechanisms of the Rome I Regulation ensure the application of the PWD requirements? As it has been previously discussed, article 23 Rome I provides that a specific conflict rule stemming from EU law can take precedence over the conflict rules of the Regulation. Is article 3 PWD a specific conflict rule? The relationship of the PWD with article 8 Rome I will also be the object of discussion since article 8 Rome I determines the law applicable to the employment contract. The important role of article 9 Rome I and overriding mandatory rules will also be analysed. Finally, a reference to a novelty of the new PWD regarding posting

[128] *Luxembourg*, paras 50, 51.

[129] Gardeñes Santiago (2012), pp. 255–278.

exceeding 12 to 18 months will also be discussed since it affects the relationship between the PWD and Rome I.

Consideration of PWD as *Lex Specialis*

Is article 3(1) PWD a separate conflict rule independent from the Rome I Regulation system? Recital 11 PWD makes reference to article 20 Rome Convention (predecessor of article 23 Rome I Regulation), which provided for the precedence of EU law over the Rome Convention. Article 23 Rome I states that

> this Regulation shall not prejudice the application of provisions of Community law which, in relation to particular matters, lay down conflict-of-law rules relating to contractual obligations.

In the Proposal for Rome I, article 22 referred to an Annex listing the EU instruments whose conflict rules took priority over those of the Regulation. The Annex included the Posted Workers Directive. Thus, article 3(1) PWD was understood as a separate conflict rule that took preference over the conflict rules of the Rome I Regulation.[130]

Difficulties arise in order to classify article 3(1) PWD as a conflict rule. Article 3 (1) PWD is not a multilateral conflict rule since it does not contain a connecting factor designating a law applicable. It could then fall under the category of unilateral conflict rule, which establishes the spatial scope of the instrument. However, what article 3(1) PWD does is requiring the host country to extend the application of the provisions of the host state regarding the specific listed areas. It would then have to fall under a third category of conflict rules, which are independent or substantive conflict rules, which rather than referring to a particular law or being a demarcation rule, regulate a particular question of law,[131] that is a conflict rule that has substantive content. Thus, the specific conflict rule of the PWD would take precedence over the Rome I Regulation according to article 23 Rome I.

However, Recital 34 Rome I provides that

> the rule on individual employment contracts should not prejudice the application of the overriding mandatory provisions of the country to which a worker is posted in accordance with Directive 96/71/EC of the European Parliament and of the Council of 16 December 1996 concerning the posting of workers in the framework of the provision of services.

Following from this recital, article 3 PWD would fall under article 9 Rome I on overriding mandatory provisions rather than under article 23 Rome I.

---

[130] Weller (2015), p. 419.

[131] Regarding the types and structure of conflict rules: Ten Wolde and Henckel (2012), pp. 13–16.

The application of article 23 Rome I as a rule of precedence would only be necessary when a court has to decide whether to apply the rules of the PWD or the rules of Rome I. Thus, reference to article 23 Rome I would be unnecessary if article 3 PWD did not conflict with those of the Rome I Regulation and simply added a group of mandatory rules complementary to the ones in article 8 Rome I.[132] In fact, the Preamble of the PWD refers to several articles of the Rome Convention, and thus it seems unreasonable to assume that the intention of the PWD is to deviate from the rules of the Regulation rather than complementing them.[133] Recital 10 PWD somehow refers to the rules laid down by the PWD as a form of an overriding mandatory rule under article 7 Rome Convention (now article 9 Rome I):

> Whereas Article 7 of the said Convention lays down, subject to certain conditions, that effect may be given, concurrently with the law declared applicable, to the mandatory rules of the law of another country, *in particular the law of the Member State within whose territory the worker is temporarily posted.*[134]

In addition, Recital 13 PWD refers to a nucleus of mandatory rules providing for a minimum protection that must be observed in the host country regarding posted workers.

Thus, article 3 PWD should not be directly considered as a separate conflict rule or *lex specialis* taking precedence over the Rome I Regulation system.[135] On the contrary, the PWD shall be related to the rules of the Rome I Regulation. Article 23 Rome I provides that

> this Regulation shall not prejudice the application of provisions of Community law which, in relation to particular matters, lay down conflict-of-law rules relating to contractual obligations.

However, it is submitted that the PWD does not lay down special conflict rules that conflict with the Rome I Regulation. The PWD requires the application of the core provisions of the host state, irrespective of the law applicable to the contract and provided they are not less favourable than the core provisions of the law determined by the Rome I Regulation. Recital 34 Rome I states that the provision regarding individual employment contracts should not prejudice the overriding mandatory provisions of the country to which a worker is posted according to the Posted Workers Directive. Rather than laying down a specific conflict rule, it is helping to identify the core provisions of the law of the host state that require application. Still, both perspectives could be reconciled if article 3(1) PWD is understood as a special

---

[132] Plender and Wilderspin (2015), p. 335.

[133] Liukkunen (2004), p. 231. See Recitals 7 to 10 PWD.

[134] Emphasis added.

[135] On the contrary, merely submitting that article 3 PWD prevails as a conflict rule through article 23 Rome I: Palao Moreno (2016), p. 592; Riesenhuber (2012).

substantive conflict rule of EU law giving overriding mandatory character to the set of rules listed, falling under article 9 Rome I, if article 23 Rome I is not *lex specialis.*[136]

Relationship with Article 8 Rome I

Article 8(2) Rome I provides that the law applicable to an employment contract in the absence of choice is the law of the country in which or from which the employee carries out his or her work (habitual place of work), and such place does not change when the worker is temporarily posted to another country. Article 8(1) Rome I allows the parties to choose the law of the employment contract as long as it does not deprive the employee of the protection provided by the mandatory rules of the law otherwise applicable. It follows that in a situation where the worker is temporarily posted to another country, the protection provided by the internal mandatory rules of employment of the country where the worker habitually works (the home country) is applicable. As it is already known, these internal mandatory rules or 'provisions that cannot be derogated from by agreement' are to be distinguished from the narrower category of overriding mandatory provisions of article 9 Rome I. Article 8(1) Rome I only refers to the provisions of the law objectively applicable that parties cannot exclude by agreement and only those concerning the protection of the employee.[137] While labour legislation in most of the EU countries constitutes one of the most important sources of mandatory provisions and, in general, provisions against wrongful dismissal, protection of employees in a business transfer etc. fall within that category, only provisions in very specific areas can fall within the narrower category of overriding mandatory provisions.[138]

Is article 3 PWD providing for the internal mandatory character of the host state core rules on employment protection in the sense of article 8(1) Rome I? Article 3 (7) PWD contains a 'most favourable law' rule according to which article 3 PWD does not prevent the application of terms and conditions of employment that are more favourable to workers. Could it be understood in a similar way as the most favourable law rule in article 8(1) Rome I, according to which the choice of law may not have the result of depriving the employee of the protection afforded to him or her by provisions that cannot be derogated from by agreement of the law objectively applicable?[139] In this regard, it has to be noticed that the PWD imposes the application of the core provisions of the host state, identifying the subject matter and restricting its extent to the matters listed in article 3(1) PWD, while article 8 (1) Rome I does not identify the contents but just requires the application of all the mandatory employee provisions of the law otherwise applicable.

Also, Recital 34 Rome I provides that

---

136 Weller (2015), p. 419.

137 Grusic (2015), p. 145.

138 Franzen and Gröner (2015), p. 224.

139 Liukkunen (2004), pp. 231–233.

> the rule on individual employment contracts should not prejudice the application of the overriding mandatory provisions of the country to which a worker is posted in accordance with Directive 96/71/EC of the European Parliament and of the Council of 16 December 1996 concerning the posting of workers in the framework of the provision of services.

Thus, it is making clear that rules in the areas listed in article 3(1) PWD can take precedence over article 8 Rome I as overriding mandatory provisions under article 9 (2) Rome I. The rules of the host state in the areas listed in article 3(1) PWD are given overriding mandatory character. Still, if the law applicable to the employment contract as a result of article 8 Rome I provides for better conditions to the employee than those provided by the law of the host country, the Directive does not prejudice those worker rights (article 3(7) PWD).

Consequently, the situation might involve three potentially applicable laws: the chosen law by the parties (article 8(1) Rome I), the law objectively applicable (article 8(2), (3) or (4) Rome I) and the law of the host country where the employee is temporarily posted (article 3 PWD and article 9 Rome I). For example, a situation where the contract contains a choice of law clause determining Dutch law as applicable, the employee's habitual place of work is located in Spain and he or she is temporarily posted to France would be a complex situation where three potentially applicable laws are involved. In such a scenario, the law applicable to the contract would be Dutch law as the law chosen by the parties, but without prejudice to the application of more beneficial national mandatory rules of the law otherwise applicable (Spanish law, which is the law of the country of habitual place of work) and without prejudice to the application of the overriding mandatory rules falling under the scope of article 3 PWD of French law, which is the law of the country where the employee is temporarily posted to. The overriding mandatory provisions of French law should only be applicable if they are more beneficial to the employee (article 3 (7) PWD). Contrarily to some suggestions by some authors, the law of the host country may apply in full when, for example, parties have chosen that law and the mandatory provisions of that law are more beneficial for the worker than the law of the home country.[140] That is, there is no home country control rule that submits the posted worker to the law where the employer is established, disallowing the application of more favourable provisions derived from article 8(1) Rome I.

[140]Some authors have understood the interpretation of the ECJ mentioned above in section 3.2.1 regarding article 3(7) as a country of origin rule, drawing a parallel between this situation and the circumstances of the *eDate* decision of the CJEU 25 October 2011, C-509/09 and C-161/10. In that regard, Fornasier and Torga (2013), p. 364. However, it is submitted that the situations are fundamentally different and the application of the country of origin rule does not make sense with regard to the present situation. For a more extensive explanation: Van Hoek (2014), p. 168.

Relationship with Article 9 Rome I

Overriding mandatory rules are defined in article 9(1) Rome I as

> provisions the respect for which is regarded as crucial by a country for safeguarding its public interests, such as its political, social or economic organisation, to such an extent that they are applicable to any situation falling within their scope, irrespective of the law otherwise applicable to the contract under this Regulation.

It is submitted that the mandatory rules of the host Member State in the areas of protection mentioned in article 3 PWD (minimum wage, non-discrimination, safety and health, maximum working time) must be considered as overriding mandatory rules that apply to all workers posted from another Member State to the territory of the host Member State.[141] The rules in the areas referred to in article 3 PWD prevail not only over the chosen law (like in the case of national mandatory rules required by article 8(1) Rome I) but also over the objectively applicable law. Article 3 PWD is providing them with an overriding mandatory character.

However, do these rules concerning the protection of employees fall under the definition of article 9(1) Rome I? Are they essential for the safeguarding of the political, social or economic organisation of the host Member State where the employee is posted to? The position of the courts and the doctrine of the different Member States differ regarding the inclusion in the definition of article 9 Rome I of certain provisions protecting the weaker contracting parties, as it has been previously discussed in Chapter III. Traditionally, German courts have been more reluctant to consider provisions concerning weaker party protection as overriding mandatory rules, contrary to the extensive French approach. However, following the interpretation of the ECJ in cases such as *Ingmar* and *Unamar*, we generally understand that article 9 Rome I also includes those provisions that, in addition to protecting a structural weaker party, mainly serve to protect higher interests, which application is essential for the country. However, as previously stated, Member States have to restrain themselves and be cautious when they define their protective rules as *crucial by a country for safeguarding its public interests, such as its political, social or economic organization*, and justify its application.[142]

The Article 3(1) PWD rule helps the conflict of laws process by clarifying the level of mandatoriness of certain rules. Overriding mandatory rules demand applicability in all circumstances falling within their scope because of their particular purpose and content. The overriding reach of a provision can be indicated by an express delimitation of its scope, or it can result from its wording. However, very

---

[141] Houwerzijl and Hoek (2016), pp. 219–224; Liukkunen (2004), pp. 233–235; Weller (2015), p. 419; McParland (2015), p. 682; Garcimartín Alférez (2008), p. 76; Gardeñes Santiago (2017), p. 167, 168.

[142] Section 3.3.1.1.

often, overriding mandatory provisions do not specifically refer to their overriding reach or determine their own scope, but courts have to determine the provision's scope by attending to the content and objectives of the rule.[143] In the case of the PWD, the EU legislator facilitates the process by providing in article 3(1) PWD the overriding mandatory character and scope of specific rules.[144]

The listed matters in article 3(1) PWD are maximum work periods and minimum rest periods; minimum annual holidays; minimum rate of pay (remuneration in the new PWD); conditions of hiring out of workers; health, safety and hygiene at work; protective measures with regard to the terms and conditions of employment of pregnant women or women who have recently given birth, of children and of young people; non-discrimination; and, in the new PWD, conditions regarding accommodation and travel-related expenses. However, relevant employment law matters such as unfair dismissal, sick pay (except regarding the protection of special groups of workers listed in article 3(1)(g), e.g. pregnant woman) or minimum notice periods are excluded. The matters listed are considered of 'immediate interest' during the period of posting: they are essential to ensuring fair competition and the fundamental freedom of provision of services. Thus, besides ensuring a minimum protection to posted workers, the application of the rules concerning the matters listed is crucial for the safeguarding of the public interests of the host Member State and, especially, of the EU. If, for example, posted workers were not ensured the same minimum pay rate as with local workers, a situation of unfair competition would take place between local companies and companies from the host country since not complying with the most restrictive rules is cheaper for the latter. However, employment provisions not listed in article 3(1) PWD are primarily aimed at protecting the employee and are not essential for the safeguarding of public interests in the case of a temporary posting.

Therefore, employment measures of the host Member State cannot be regarded in its entirety as overriding mandatory rules. In *Commission v Luxembourg*, the ECJ made clear that in order for the matters listed outside article 3(1) PWD to be applicable as 'public policy provisions' under article 3(10) PWD, as exceptions from the list in article 3(1) PWD and a derogation from the freedom of provision of services, they have to be interpreted strictly and their scope could not be possibly determined unilaterally by the Member States.[145] The ECJ's restrictive interpretation shows that provisions on matters outside the list of article 3(1)PWD are most probably not falling under the exception in article 3(10) PWD and thus cannot be applicable as overriding mandatory provisions.

Article 9(2) Rome I provides for the application of the overriding mandatory provisions of the forum. However, the rules on jurisdiction of Brussels I bis, when the employee is the claimant, will usually point to the courts where the employer is domiciled or where the habitual place of work is. The country of origin, rather than the host country, will generally be the forum. Therefore, the application of the host

---

[143] *Unamar*, para 50.

[144] Gardeñes Santiago (2017), p. 167, 168.

[145] *Commission v Luxembourg*, paras 30, 31.

country overriding mandatory rules according to the Rome I Regulation can be through article 9(3) Rome I. Article 9(3) Rome I provides that

> Effect may be given to the overriding mandatory provisions of the law of the country where the obligations arising out of the contract have to be or have been performed, in so far as those overriding mandatory provisions render the performance of the contract unlawful. In considering whether to give effect to those provisions, regard shall be had to their nature and purpose and to the consequences of their application or non-application.

The host Member State falls under the requirements of the provision since it is the country where the posted worker carries out the obligations arising from the employment contract. Also, article 6 PWD gives jurisdiction to the host Member State in order to enforce the rights derived from article 3 PWD:

> In order to enforce the right to the terms and conditions of employment guaranteed in Article 3, judicial proceedings may be instituted in the Member State in whose territory the worker is or was posted, without prejudice, where applicable, to the right, under existing international conventions on jurisdiction, to institute proceedings in another State.

Temporary Posting Exceeding 12 (or 18) Months

The new PWD introduces a new provision that affects the mandatory application of the terms and conditions of the host country when the posting exceeds 12 months: it provides that, in addition to the terms and conditions of employment referred to in the list of article 3(1) PWD, all the applicable terms and conditions of employment of the law of the host Member State shall be applicable after 12 (or 18) months of posting.[146] That is, after 12 (or 18) months of posting, all national mandatory labour law provisions of the host country where the employee is temporary working will be applicable (except the rules regarding the termination of contract and supplementary occupational retirement pension schemes).[147] The new provision also clarifies that in

[146]The period of 12 months can be extended to 18 months by the Member State where the service is provided where the service provider submits a motivated notification (3(1a) third subparagraph new PWD).

[147]The new PWD adds the following provision in article 3(1) PWD: 'a. Where the effective duration of a posting exceeds 12 months, Member States shall ensure, irrespective of which law applies to the employment relationship, that undertakings as referred to in Article 1(1) guarantee, on the basis of equality of treatment, workers who are posted to their territory, in addition to the terms and conditions of employment referred to in paragraph 1 of this Article, all the applicable terms and conditions of employment which are laid down in the Member State where the work is carried out:

- by law, regulation or administrative provision, and/or
- by collective agreements or arbitration awards which have been declared universally applicable or otherwise apply in accordance with paragraph 8.

the case of replacement of a posted worker by another posted worker performing the same task at the same place, the duration of the posting periods of both posted workers involved shall be cumulative for the purposes of the aforementioned provision.

The new provision is one of the measures introduced by the new PWD in order to avoid abuses such as rotational posting or the practices of 'letterbox companies', which exploited loopholes of the original PWD to circumvent employment and social security legislation and engage in operations in other Member States. It can be said that the concept of 'temporary posting', as understood until now, is now limited to 12 (or 18) months. Companies posting workers for a long-term period shall comply with the mandatory employment law of the host country.

The new clause is welcome since it aims at preventing abuse of law by the companies. However, this provision seems to conflict with the Rome I Regulation system. Article 8(2) Rome I provides that the law applicable to the contract does not change when the worker is temporarily posted to another country (i.e. the habitual place of work does not change). According to article 8(1) and (2) Rome I, the law applicable to the employment contract is the law of the habitual place of work, and parties can choose the law applicable but the mandatory protection of the habitual place of work is ensured. Then the listed matters of article 3(1) PWD of the host country law apply as overriding mandatory provisions through article 9 Rome I. However, the new clause requires the application of all internal mandatory employment protection of the host country to the worker. How do the mechanisms of the Rome I Regulation ensure that protection?

The first possibility would be through article 8 Rome I. It could be considered that the new provision of the PWD affects the meaning of temporary posting in a way that a posting exceeding 12 or 18 months is not a temporary posting anymore also in the light of article 8. That is, habitual place of work, after 12 (or 18) months, would turn to be the country where the employee is posted. This option does not benefit transparency since such a change would then have to be made in article 8 Rome I. More importantly, this is not what the new provision of the PWD intends: first, the new article3(1) PWD already clarifies that some provisions of the law of the country of posting are not applicable (e.g. regarding termination of contract), implying that those provisions are applicable as a result of the law objectively applicable (most probably the home state law). Second, it follows from the understanding of the PWD that workers who are posted longer than 12 (or 18) months can still be considered temporary posted workers since they are not excluded from the protection provided by the provisions of the Directive. Finally, article 3(1)a clearly provides that

The first subparagraph of this paragraph shall not apply to the following matters:

(a) procedures, formalities and conditions of the conclusion and termination of the employment contract, including non-competition clauses
(b) supplementary occupational retirement pension schemes. (. . .).'

> [W]here the effective duration of a posting exceeds 12 months, Member States shall ensure, irres*pective of which law applies to the employment relationship* (...),[148]

making clear that the objective applicable law to the contract is not the law of the Member State of posting.

The other possible mechanism to ensure the application of the terms and conditions required by article 3(1)a of the new PWD is article 9 Rome I. However, the obvious impediment in that regard is that general employment terms and conditions of a national law are largely national mandatory provisions—or provisions that cannot be derogated from by agreement. As provisions primarily aimed at protecting the weaker party, they do not fall under the definition of overriding mandatory provisions. Within the context of temporary posting of workers, it was considered that only those core provisions listed in article 3(1) PWD were classified as overriding mandatory for the host state because of the higher interests involved. Provisions falling outside the categories listed in article3(1) PWD would generally just have internal mandatory character and, therefore, cannot be applicable irrespective of the law applicable to the employment contract. Nevertheless, the new article 3(1)a PWD provides that the general terms and conditions of the country of posting shall be applicable irrespective of the law applicable to the contract when the posting exceeds 12 (or 18) months. It could be considered that, because of the specific circumstances, the general terms and conditions that normally aim primarily to protect the employee become essential for the protection of higher interests. Article 3.1.a would then be suggesting that after 12 (or 18) months, the general terms and conditions of the host country become applicable as overriding mandatory provisions, in addition to the provisions derived from article 3(1). The essential higher interests to be protected could be founded on the objective of preventing abuse of law within the EU and defending fair competition between the Member States. That is, an overriding mandatory character could be justified on the basis of prevention of abusive and fraudulent practices involving letterbox companies and fake 'temporary' postings that affect negatively the correct functioning of the internal market. However, it can still be debatable whether such a specific objective can justify that every time that a posting exceeds 12 or 18 months, most of the terms and conditions of the contract would have to be adapted to the law of the host country.

5.3.3 Posting of Workers in Extra-EU Situations

The provisions of the PWD are only applicable to intra-EU posting of workers. In the case of an extra-EU posting (i.e. workers posted to a Member State from an undertaking established in a non-Member State or vice versa), the rules of the

---

[148] Emphasis added.

PWD do not require application. Still, even though the situations mentioned below do not fall under the scope of PWD, I will make a brief reference to the posting of workers in extra-EU situations.

When a worker is temporarily posted from a Member State to a non-Member State, the Member State court will determine as applicable the law of the habitual place of work. The minimum EU mandatory protection is ensured. However, the provisions of the PWD are not applicable unless the Member State had extended in its national implementation of the Directive its application to extra-EU postings.

From an internal labour market point of view of a Member State, the situation where a worker is posted from a non-EU country to temporarily work in a Member State is more interesting. In case a Member State court claims jurisdiction over the dispute, the law applicable to the employment contract as a result of article 8 Rome I would most likely be the law of the habitual place of work (i.e. a non-Member State law). A foreign law does not necessarily provide for rules similar to those of the PWD, which provide for the application of the core provisions of the host country. However, most certainly, the law of the Member State provides for the application of some national law employment provisions as overriding mandatory rules. Although it is a matter of national law to determine which labour legislation shall be considered as overriding mandatory in those cases of temporary posting, we can wonder whether the same restrictive interpretation deriving from the PWD should be applicable. That is, we can question whether the matters outside the list of article 3 PWD could and should be considered as overriding mandatory provisions and apply according to article 9 Rome I.

In the case of intra-EU posting of workers, according to the ECJ, the PWD, in combination with the provisions of the TFEU on the freedom of provision of services, precludes the host state from imposing non-listed matters in article 3 PWD as overriding mandatory rules. However, that restrictive interpretation is based on respect for the freedom of provision of services in the EU and does not apply to an extra-EU posting. When workers are posted by a non-EU undertaking, the Member State where the worker is temporarily posted to could impose the application of rules in other areas of individual employment law listed outside article 3 PWD, resulting in a different treatment between workers posted from a Member State and workers posted from outside the EU.[149] Such an outcome will depend on the interpretation of the concept of overriding mandatory rules by the Member State involved. As to the areas involved in individual employment law regarding posting of workers' situations that can be regarded as overriding mandatory rules, in my opinion, it seems logical to follow the same restrictive interpretation of article 9 Rome I as regards the PWD, even when the situation follows outside its scope

[149] Grusic (2015), p. 290. Grusic also submits that the different treatment between workers posted from a Member State and workers posted from outside the EU is in accordance with the intention of the Posted Workers Directive, which principal objective is to improve the operation of the internal market rather than protecting posted workers.

of application. Recital 37 Rome I also highlights the exceptional character of article 9 Rome I when stating that

> considerations of public interest justify giving the courts of the Member States the possibility, in exceptional circumstances, of applying exceptions based on public policy and overriding mandatory provisions (. . .).

Also, the definition of article 9(1) Rome I of overriding mandatory provisions derives from the *Arblade* case. This case concerned derogations from the fundamental freedom of provision of services, and from this it is understood that the concept of overriding mandatory provisions is narrow. An extensive interpretation of the concept and an unrestricted application of employment legislation concerning other postings in the host country would undermine the conflict of laws process and the system of the Rome I Regulation, leading to less predictable and uniform results. The ECJ, in *Unamar*, stated that the national court has the discretion to qualify its own national provisions as overriding mandatory rules, but it has to do so on the basis of a detailed assessment showing that the application of those provisions is crucial for the safeguarding of the public interests of the country. As previously stated, Member States have followed different interpretations of the concept of overriding mandatory rules, but, following the definition of article 9(1) Rome I and the ECJ, it should generally be considered that provisions protecting the weaker party, in order to be considered as overriding mandatory rules, should have to be essential for the protection of a public interest as well (e.g. the provisions listed in article 3(1) PWD minimum pay: besides protecting the employee, the main objective is to avoid unfair competition). However, provisions regarding areas outside the list, such as unfair dismissal provisions, are generally not considered as crucial for the safeguarding of the political, social or economic organisation of a country since, although important for it, they are primarily aimed at the protection of the employee.[150] However, it is indeed up to each national Member State legislator and courts to determine which national rules are to be considered as overriding mandatory.

5.4 Closing Remarks

First, it is concluded that, in most of the cases, article 8 Rome I ensures the application of the EU employment directives when necessary. The area of EU employment law does not cover as many fields of national law as EU consumer law does. EU employment law is quite fragmented and mainly composed of

[150]Ibid., pp. 212–214. The German Federal Labour Court (*Bundesarbeitsgericht*) refused to apply some German rules protecting employees against abusive dismissal based on a restrictive interpretation of article 7 Rome Convention (Bundesarbeitbericht, 29 October 1992, in IPRax 1994, p. 123).

minimum harmonisation directives that complement the policies of Member States. Therefore, the role of EU PIL is essential in this area. The majority of EU employment directives in the area of contract law do not contain rules interfering with PIL (except for the Acquired Rights Directive and Posted Workers Directive). In general, EU employment directives establish substantive rights trying to ensure that Member States apply the minimum working protection required by the instrument at hand. The provisions of the directives, when dealing with an individual employment contract, will apply when the national law of a Member State is applicable because it is a purely internal situation or, in a cross-border situation, as a result of article 8 of the Rome I Regulation. In our current EU PIL approach, reflected in the Rome I Regulation, it is understood that if a law has been determined as applicable by the conflict rules, then the statutes of that legal system shall apply to the situation (as long as the situation falls within the scope of application of the statute in question), with the only exception of overriding mandatory provisions. Article 8 (2) Rome I ensures that the protection provided by the mandatory rules of the place of habitual work is applied (unless the law chosen by the parties provides for a better protection). Therefore, when the place of habitual work is in a Member State, the application of the requirements laid down by the EU employment directives are ensured. It has been submitted that the majority of these directives do not have any interest in being applicable to workers outside the EU and indeed intend their protection to apply to workers working in the EU. As a result, the generality of EU employment directives and article 8 Rome I on the law applicable to individual employment contracts are coordinated, dealing separately with substantive issues and PIL issues and having as relevant criterion the place of work.

However, there are exceptions to the previous statements. It is generally considered that a transfer of undertakings can be classified within the conflict of laws category for individual employment contracts. The Acquired Rights Directive, which aims at preserving employees' rights in the case of a transfer of undertaking, covers also cross-border transfer of undertakings and contains a 'scope rule' that could affect PIL. Article 1(2) provides that the directive

> shall apply where and in so far as the undertaking, business or part of the undertaking or business to be transferred is situated within the territorial scope of the Treaty.

To a certain extent, the same analysis regarding scope rules and EU consumer directives has been conducted. It has been considered whether this rule could be understood as a unilateral conflict rule taking precedence over the Rome I Regulation and thus whether the directive establishes its own scope under a unilateral PIL approach. Similar to the conclusion reached regarding EU consumer directives, I consider that the EU legislator should not aim at imposing the application of the directives without regard to the PIL system in force and should be careful with the inclusion of rules such as article 1(2) Acquired Rights Directive referring to the territorial scope of a directive in such a way that might lead to confusion from a PIL perspective. Legal certainty would be impaired by the creation of a parallel conflict of laws mechanism imposing the application of the rules of the Directive when established by the scope rule, without even determining according to which national law is applicable, especially when the implementation of the Member States of the scope rule is so inconsistent. Thus, linking the application of the Acquired Rights Directive provisions to the Rome I Regulation is preferred. Article 8 Rome I ensures the application of the mandatory provisions of the law of the habitual place of work of the employee. However, the habitual place of work changes when the employee is transferred to the new location. Also, when the law applicable is the result of the closest connection escape mechanism (a situation like that in the *American Pilots* case), the application of the Acquired Rights Directive is not ensured. Article 9 Rome I is the only possible mechanism to ensure the application of the Directive in such scenarios, although it has been concluded that it is not ideal. Although it could be understood that the 'scope rule' directly gives an overriding mandatory character, I think that should not be the case because a similar parallel unilateral PIL system as the one described would be created and, more importantly, the provisions of the Acquired Rights Directive should not generally be considered as having an overriding mandatory character since they are mainly aimed at protecting the employee.

The current formulation of scope rules in directives and the different national implementations and approaches in that regard create legal uncertainty from a PIL point of view. Regarding EU consumer directives, it was submitted that a solution would be to adapt article 6 Rome I to the needs of the EU directives. However, rather than concluding that article 8 Rome I should be adapted to the necessities of Acquired Rights Directive in this case, as it was concluded regarding article 6 Rome I and EU consumer directives, I consider that the application of the Acquired Rights Directive is ensured by article 8 Rome I when the employee requires that protection. When article 8 Rome I does not ensure the application of the directive because it designates a foreign law as applicable, the only manner that the Acquired Rights Directive would need to apply is not justifiable under employee protection reasons, but it would be because a public interest is at stake.

Finally, the situation of temporary posting of workers to other Member States also deserves special attention. In this regard, the Posted Workers Directive, the Enforcement Directive and the revised version of the Posted Workers Directive aim to promote the freedom of provision of services and to ensure the protection of posted workers where an undertaking established in a Member State posts an employee to work in another Member State on a temporary basis. According to article 8 Rome I, the habitual place of work does not change when the posting to another country is temporary, and therefore the law applicable to the individual employment contract would continue to be the law of the country of habitual place of work (home country). However, article 3(1) of the Posted Workers Directive provides that Member States must ensure that the undertakings of the host state guarantee to the workers posted to their territory certain terms and conditions of employment that are laid down in that Member State regarding maximum work periods and minimum rest periods, remuneration, health and safety conditions etc. The ECJ clarified that in the protection of the freedom of provision of services, the provisions of the country of posting in the areas listed in article 3(1) PWD must be applied to posted workers and also constitute a limit to the mandatory protection that the country of posting can apply. The matters listed are considered of 'immediate interest' during the period of posting: they are essential to ensuring fair competition and the fundamental freedom of provision of services. In relation to the rules of the Rome I Regulation, the provisions referred to in article 3(1) PWD, besides ensuring a minimum protection to posted workers, are considered crucial for the safeguarding of the public interests of the host Member State and of the EU and thus constitute overriding mandatory provisions in accordance with article 9 Rome I. Article 3(1) PWD determines the overriding mandatory character and scope of specific rules. Finally, it is also debated whether the new provision stating that, in addition to the terms and conditions of employment referred to in the list of article 3(1) PWD, all the applicable terms and conditions of employment of the law of the host Member State shall be applicable after 12 (or 18) months of posting can also be applicable under article 9 Rome I. As provisions primarily aimed at protecting the weaker party, they do not fall under the definition of overriding mandatory provisions. However, it has been submitted that, because of the specific circumstances, the general terms and conditions that normally aim primarily to protect the employee might become essential for the protection of higher interests. Article 3(1)(a) PWD would then be suggesting that after 12 (or 18) months, the general terms and conditions of the host country become applicable as overriding mandatory provisions in addition to the provisions derived from article 3 (1). The essential higher interests to be protected could be founded on the objective of preventing abuse of law within the EU and defending fair competition between the Member States. However, reconciling the application of the new provision under the doctrine of overriding mandatory rules in article 9 Rome I could be debatable as being a bit too extensive.

References

Aguilar Grieder H (2006) La Voluntad de Conciliación con las Directivas Comunitarias Protectoras en la Propuesta del Reglamento Roma I. In: La Unión Europea ante el Derecho de la Globalización. Colex, Madrid, pp 45–61

Barnard C (2008) Viking and laval: an introduction. Cambridge Yearb Eur Legal Stud 10:463–492

Belohlávek AJ (2011) Rome Convention - Rome I Regulation. Juris Publishing, Inc., Huntington

Bisping C (2012) Avoid the statutist trap: the international scope of the consumer credit act 1974. J Priv Int Law 8:35–62

Bonomi A (2008) Le Régime des Règles Impératives et des Lois de Police dans le Règlement 'Rome I' sur la Loi Applicable aux Contrats. In: Cashin Ritaine E, Bonomi A (eds) Le Nouveau Règlement Européen 'Rome I' relatif à la Loi Applicable aux Obligations Contractuelles. Schulthess, Zurich, pp 217–240

Bonomi A (2016) Article 9: overriding mandatory provisions. In: Magnus U, Mankowski P (eds) Rome I Regulation - Commentary. Verlag Dr. Otto Schmidt, Köln, pp 597–661

Bucher A (2011) La Dimension Sociale du Droit International Privé: cours général. Brill, Leiden

Calvo Caravaca AL, Carrascosa González JM (2013) Derecho Internacional Privado. Comares, Granada

Carrascosa González J (2009) Ley Aplicable a los Contratos Internacionales: el Reglamento Roma I. Colex, Madrid
Carrascosa González J (2012) La Autonomía de la Voluntad Conflictual y la Mano Invisible en la Contratación Internacional. Diario La Ley 7847
Carrillo Pozo LF (2017) El Tratamiento de las leyes de policía de terceros Estados. (A propósito de la sentencia del TJUE de 18 de octubre de 2016). Bitácora Millennium DIPr: Derecho Internacional Privado 5:1–23
Cebrián Salvat MA (2014) Agencia Comercial, Leyes de Policía y Derecho Internacional Privado Europeo. Cuadernos de Derecho Transnacional 6:357–366
Cremona M, Micklitz H-W (eds) (2016) Private law in the external relations of the EU. Oxford University Press, Oxford
Fallon M, Francq S (2000) Towards internationally mandatory directives for consumer contracts? In: Basedow J (ed) Private law in international Arena. Liber Amicorum K. Siehr. Asser Instituut, The Hague, pp 155–178
Fornasier M, Torga M (2013) The posting of workers: perspective of the sending state. Europäische Zeitschrift für Arbeitsrecht 6:356–365
Francq S (2005) L'Applicabilité du Droit Communautaire Dérivé au Regard des Méthodes du Droit International Privé. LGDJ, Bruxelles/Paris
Francq S (2006) The scope of secondary community law in the light of the methods of private international law- or the other way around? In: Sarcevic P et al (eds) Yearbook of private international law. Sellier, European Law Publishers and Swiss Institute of Comparative Law, pp 333–374
Francq S (2017) Unilateralism. In: Basedow J et al (eds) Encyclopedia of private international law. Edward Elgar Publishing, Cheltenham, pp 1179–1791
Franzen M, Gröner N (2015) Article 8. Individual employment contracts. In: Calliess G-P (ed) Rome regulations. Commentary, 2nd edn. Kluwer Law International, The Netherlands
Garcimartín Alférez FJ (2008) The Rome I Regulation: much ado about nothing? Eur Legal Forum:61–80
Garcimartín Alférez FJ (2012) Derecho Internacional Privado. Thomson Reuters, Pamplona
Gardeñes Santiago M (2008) La Regulación Conflictual del Contrato de Trabajo en el Reglamento Roma I: una oportunidad perdida. Anuario Español de Derecho Internacional Privado 8:387–424
Gardeñes Santiago M (2012) Le Détachement Transnational des Travailleurs dans le Cadre des Prestations de Services: un Sujet Spécialement Difficile pour le Marché Intérieur. In: Liber Amicorum: Mélanges en l'honneur du Professeur Joël Molinier. LGDJ, pp 255–278
Gardeñes Santiago M (2017) Derecho Imperativo y Contrato Internacional de Trabajo. Revista de Ministerio de Empleo y Seguridad Social 132:163–188
Gómez Abelleira FJ (2018) Desplazamiento Transnacional Laboral Genuino y la Ley Aplicable al Contrato de Trabajo. Cuadernos de Derecho Transnacional 10:213–232
Grusic U (2015) The European private international law of employment. Cambridge University Press, Cambridge
Henckel KC (2016) Cross-border transfers of undertakings. Ulrik Huber Institute for Private International Law, Ees, The Netherlands
Houwerzijl M, van Hoek A (2016) Where do EU mobile workers belong, according to Rome I and the (E)PWD. In Verschueren H (ed) Residence, employment and social rights of mobile persons: on how EU law defines where they belong. Intersentia, Cambridge, pp 215–253
Kuipers J-J (2012) EU law and private international law: the interrelationship in contractual obligations. Martinus Nijhoff Publishers, Leiden
Liukkunen U (2004) The role of mandatory rules in international labour law- A comparative study in the conflict of laws. Talentum Media Oy, Helsinki
Magnus U (2016) Introduction. In: Magnus U, Mankowski P (eds) Rome I Regulation - Commentary. Verlag Dr. Otto Schmidt, Köln, pp 6–51

McParland M (2015) The Rome I Regulation on the law applicable to contractual obligations. Oxford University Press, Oxford

Merrett L (2011) Employment contracts in private international law. Oxford University Press, Oxford

Moreau M-A, Trudeau G (2000) Les Normes du Droit du Travail Confrontées à l'Èvolution de l'Èconomie: De Nouveaux Enjeux pour l'Espace Régional. Journal de Droit International 4:915–948

Palao Moreno G (2016) Article 8: individual employment contracts. In: Magnus U, Mankowski P (eds) Rome I Regulation - Commentary. Verlag Dr. Otto Schmidt, Köln, pp 577–599

Plender R, Wilderspin M (2009) The European private international law of obligations, 3rd edn. Sweet & Maxwell, London

Plender R, Wilderspin M (2015) The European private international law of obligations, 4th edn. Sweet & Maxwell, London

Riesenhuber K (2012) European employment law. a systematic exposition. Intersentia, Cambridge

Sabido Rodríguez M (2010) Algunas Cuestiones que Plantea en DIPR la Tutela de los Trabajadores Afectados por Reestructuraciones de Empresas. Cuadernos de Derecho Transnacional 2:233–260

Sánchez Lorenzo S (2003) La Unificación del Derecho Contractual Europeo Vista desde el Derecho Internacional Privado. In: Derecho Patrimonial Europeo. Thomson-Aranzadi, Cizu Menor (Navarra), pp 363–381

Schmidt-Kessel M (2015) Article 9. In: Ferrari F (ed) Rome I Regulation. Pocket commentary. Sellier, European Law Publishers, München, pp 320–354

Symeonides SC (2005) Accommodative unilateralism as a starting premise in choice of law. In: Rasmussen-Bonne H et al (eds) Balancing of interests: Liber Amicorum Peter Hay. Verlag Recht und Wirtschaft GmbH, pp 417–434

Ten Wolde MH, Henckel KC (2012) European private international law- a comparative perspective on contracts, torts and corporations. Hephaestus Publishers, Groningen

Van Bochove LM (2014) Overriding mandatory rules as a vehicle for weaker party protection in European private international law. Erasmus Law Rev 7:147–157

Van Hoek AAH (2014) Private international law: an appropriate means to regulate transnational employment in the European Union? Erasmus Law Rev 7:157–169

Verhagen HLE (2002) The tension between party autonomy and European Union law: some observations on IngmarGB Ltd v Eaton Leonard Technologies Inc. Int Comp Law Q 51:135–154

Weller M (2015) Article 23. Relationship with other provisions of community law. In: Calliess G-P (ed) Rome regulations. Commentary, 2nd edn. Kluwer Law International, The Netherlands

Chapter 6
Other Possible Weaker Contracting Parties and the Rome I Regulation

Consumers and employees are the most characteristic but not the only possible weaker parties to a contract. Under EU private international law (PIL), consumers and employees constitute the paradigmatic example of structural weaker parties, and special protective conflict rules limit party autonomy and provide for special connecting factors for their benefit. However, to a lesser extent, EU PIL, and specifically the Rome I Regulation, extends the protection to passengers and some insurance policyholders. Moreover, even when special rules protecting weaker contracting parties in the Rome I Regulation only include consumers, employees, insurance policyholders (or other beneficiaries) and passengers (articles 5–8 Rome I), other contractual parties can often have a weaker contracting position in their contract (such as franchisees, distributors or commercial agents).

Contracts of carriage of passengers and contracts of insurance are excluded from the protection provided to consumer contracts in article 6 Rome I. According to Recital 32 Rome I, the particular nature of these contracts call for specific provisions ensuring an adequate level of protection of passengers and policyholders. The protection provided by article 5(2) Rome I to passengers and by article 7 Rome I to policyholders differs from the protection provided by articles 6 and 8 Rome I to consumers and employees, respectively. Party autonomy is limited, but in a way that only allows the choice of law that has some connection with the contract. The choice of law is limited to a number of legal systems that are connected to the contract or parties to the contract. The rationale behind it is that the weaker party is protected when a qualified link between the contract and the law chosen is required.[1] However, it is not ensured that the legal system chosen, even if connected with the contract, would have certain level of protection to the passenger or policyholder. In the context of the EU, there are several EU secondary law instruments that provide for substantive rules regarding contracts for the carriage of passengers and insurance

[1] López de Gonzalo (2017), pp. 269–270.

M. Campo Comba, *The Law Applicable to Cross-border Contracts involving Weaker Parties in EU Private International Law*,
https://doi.org/10.1007/978-3-030-61481-2_6

contracts. Since the application of the minimum mandatory rules of the place of habitual residence of the weaker party in these cases is not ensured through the limitation of party autonomy (like in the case of consumers and employees), how are EU passengers and policyholders protected against a non-Member State choice of law? Does the protection of the directives and regulations need to apply in those cases? And, if so, how? An analysis of the relationship between the rules of the Rome I Regulation and the EU secondary law regarding insurance contracts and carriage of passengers contracts will be conducted in this chapter in order to answer these questions. Since the same analysis has already been conducted regarding consumer and individual employment contracts, which are the most paradigmatic examples of contracts involving weaker parties and receive the most protection, the analysis regarding insurance contracts and contracts for the carriage of passengers will be brief. Also, since article 7 Rome I regarding insurance contracts has been introduced in order to unify the disperse conflict rules existent among the EU insurance directives, it will be analysed whether the technique applied by this provision could be of use regarding the disperse scope rules among EU consumer directives.

As we have seen, within the Rome I Regulation in the context of party autonomy, we can differentiate between four special contracts involving presumably weaker parties (articles 5–8 Rome I), which somehow limit the freedom of choice of law of the parties, and all other contracts, for which the general rule is party autonomy. Then, of course, party autonomy can always be limited by article 3(3) and 3(4) Rome I (when all the elements of the situation are located within one Member State or within the EU and parties choose a foreign or a non-EU law, respectively), article 9 Rome I (application of overriding mandatory provisions) and article 21 (public policy exception). These exceptions to party autonomy are not designed to protect the weaker party of a contract since already special protective provisions are laid down with that intention. Besides the four contracts involving presumably weaker parties recognised by the Rome I Regulation, there are other parties to a contract that find themselves often in a weaker contracting position. Franchisees, distributors or commercial agents usually have less bargaining and economic power and information than their counterparties and can see themselves in a similar position than that of a consumer or an employee in respect of their counterparties. For example, the franchisee can be in a similar position to a consumer as regards their bargaining power: in a franchise contract between Dunkin Donuts, a US corporation based in Massachusetts (US), and an individual Dutch franchisee, the US big corporation could include in the contract a choice of law clause selecting the law of a third country with no consumer or franchisee protection and then include in the contract a clause allowing the franchisor to terminate the contract unilaterally under some circumstances that would have not been allowed under Massachusetts or Dutch law. In that case, the Rome I Regulation would find that the law governing the contract is the law chosen by the parties in the franchise contract.[2] In the case of a commercial agency contract, for example, the situation of the agent can be in some occasions similar to that of an employee: when a commercial agent is a natural person mainly depending on one principal, the principal can easily impose a foreign choice of law clause in the contract and then be able to terminate the contract unilaterally without having to compensate the commercial agent, for example. However, these parties are not always in a dependent position in which they have to accept the contractual provisions imposed by a big company, but they can also be medium or big corporations with sufficient bargaining power and resources. Thus, the Rome I Regulation does not include special conflict rules limiting party autonomy for these type of contracts, despite the existence of substantive protection for them in many jurisdictions. It provides for specific connecting factors in the absence of choice of law for franchise and distribution contracts (article 4(1)(e) and 4(1)(f) Rome I), but it does it within the general rule of article 4, with presumable objectives of weaker party protection and also legal certainty and closest connection.[3] At EU level, the Commercial Agents Directive provides for protection to commercial agents operating within the EU. Can this protection be circumvented with a choice of law of a non-Member State? Does the Rome I Regulation provide for mechanisms for the application of the Commercial Agents Directive when necessary? And if not, should it? The ECJ in the previously analysed *Ingmar* judgment has dealt with the applicability of the Commercial Agents Directive, although before the entering into force of the Rome I Regulation.

This chapter aims to analyse the interaction between special (and less protective) conflict rules and general conflict rules of the Rome I Regulation with the EU secondary law instruments that contain mandatory provisions protecting weaker parties other than consumers and employees. Does the Rome I Regulation provide for other mechanisms of protection for these weaker parties? On the other hand, as it has been described in previous chapters, several questions arise with regard to the interaction and coordination of these different instruments: Do the relevant EU secondary law instruments provide for specific conflict rules prevailing over Rome I through article 23 Rome I? Do some other directives provide for scope rules like in the case of EU consumer directives? If so, what would be their role? Does article 9 Rome I (application of overriding mandatory rules) play a role in the application of these EU secondary law to compensate the effects of party autonomy? In order to answer these questions, it will first be analysed the interaction between the conflict rules of the Rome I Regulation protecting the weaker party, although to a lesser extent, and the EU secondary law providing for substantive protection. Since the same type of analysis has been conducted in the previous chapters, this chapter will only focus on the specialties that can be highlighted from the named contracts. Specifically, the special conflict rules of article 7 Rome I regarding insurance contracts will be described, to then briefly examine how they are coordinated with

[2] Symeonides (2010), p. 534.

[3] García Gutiérrez (2008), p. 235; Ancel (2008), pp. 226, 227. Also, see below in this Sect. 6.2.1.

the EU insurance directives. In addition, it will be considered whether a provision with a similar technique would be suitable in the case of consumer contracts. Also, the special conflict rules regarding contracts of carriage of passengers of article 5 Rome I will be studied, as well as their relationship with EU secondary law instruments providing for protection to passengers. Second, this chapter will deal with contracts where party autonomy is not limited through the Rome I Regulation (franchise, distribution and commercial agency contracts). Special attention will be paid to the commercial agency contract since the Commercial Agents Directive provides for substantive rights for commercial agents and the ECJ has reflected on the application of these rights and party autonomy.

6.1 Other Weaker Parties of the Rome I Regulation: Insurance and Carriage of Passengers Contracts and Interaction with EU Secondary Law

6.1.1 Law Applicable to Insurance Contracts (Article 7 Rome I) and Applicability of EU Insurance Directives

Article 7 Rome I contains special conflict rules regarding insurance contracts. However, not all insurance policyholders are in the position of weaker contracting parties. EU PIL distinguishes between contracts where the policyholder needs special protection and contracts where there is no need for such protection.

Article 7 Rome I provides for three different levels of protection based on limits to party autonomy and special conflict rules in the absence of choice. First, in insurance contracts for large risks, parties enjoy complete party autonomy, as provided for by the general rule of article 3 Rome I (article 7(2) Rome I). Insurance contracts for large risks are mostly business-to-business (B2B) contracts relating to large industrial or transport business operations.[4] The policyholder is not in a weaker position in that contract since it is a company with sufficient bargaining power, information and resources to negotiate the contract and the choice of law clause. In the absence of choice of law, the law applicable is the law of the country of habitual residence of the insurer (article 7(2) Rome I). It is not a special protective connecting factor but follows the general approach referring to the country of habitual residence of the party effectuating the characteristic performance.

[4]The definition of large risks, according to article 7, is to be found in in Article 5(d) of the First Council Directive 73/239/EEC of 24 July 1973 amended by Directive 2005/68/EC of the European Parliament and of the Council (OJ 2005 L 323/1), and now repealed by Directive 2009/138/EC of the European Parliament and of the Council of 25 November 2009 on the taking-up and pursuit of the business of Insurance and Reinsurance (OJ 2009 L 335/1) (Solvency II), where large risks are defined now in article 13(27).

Second, in insurance contracts that do not qualify as large risks, normally known as contracts for mass risks, article 7 (3) Rome I provides for more specific rules. These type of contracts are regulated by article 7 to the extent that the mass risks are located in the EU. This category might involve both business-to-consumer (B2C) and B2B contracts. Customers insuring smaller risks are more likely to be small businesses or private persons, who find themselves in a weaker contractual position. Party autonomy is limited to several Member States connected with the insurance contract or the policyholder.[5] In the absence of choice of law, the law applicable is the law of the Member State in which the risk is situated at the time of conclusion of the contract.

Third, article 7(4) Rome I contains a special rule for mandatory insurance contracts, i.e. insurance contracts covering risks for which a Member State imposes an obligation to take out insurance. The insurance contract must comply with the specific provisions relating to that insurance laid down by the Member State that imposes the obligation (7(4)(a) Rome I), and, derogating from paras. 2 and 3, a Member State may require that the insurance contract be governed by the law of the Member State that imposes the obligation to take out insurance. Mandatory insurance contracts are therefore the most protected category by article 7, allowing Member States to completely derogate from party autonomy and imposing the application of the law of the Member State that imposes the obligation to take out insurance. Besides the interests of the policyholder, this rule aims at protecting the public interests of Member States which underlie the decision to impose a mandatory insurance.

Regarding the relationship of the Rome I Regulation and insurance directives, the introduction of article 7 Rome I (as compared with the previous situation) is welcome since, previously, the conflict rules regarding insurance contracts were not unified in the Rome Convention but were dispersed over the different insurance directives and the Rome Convention. Basically, when the insured risk was located in the EU and covered by an EU insurer, the relevant insurance directives and its conflict rules would apply.[6] However, directives did not cover cases where the

[5]According to article 7(3) Rome I: 'In the case of an insurance contract other than a contract falling within paragraph 2, only the following laws may be chosen by the parties in accordance with Article 3:

(a) the law of any Member State where the risk is situated at the time of conclusion of the contract; (b) the law of the country where the policy holder has his habitual residence; (c) in the case of life assurance, the law of the Member State of which the policy holder is a national; (d) for insurance contracts covering risks limited to events occurring in one Member State other than the Member State where the risk is situated, the law of that Member State; (e) where the policy holder of a contract falling under this paragraph pursues a commercial or industrial activity or a liberal profession and the insurance contract covers two or more risks which relate to those activities and are situated in different Member States, the law of any of the Member States concerned or the law of the country of habitual residence of the policy holder.'

[6]The Rome Convention provided in article 1(3) and 1(4) that the Convention did not apply to insurance contracts, other than reinsurance, covering risks situated within the European Community.

insured risk was located outside the EU. In those cases, the general conflict rules of the Rome Convention were applicable. The Rome Convention did not include a special provision for insurance contracts comparable to article 7 Rome I. There was even a third situation where neither the conflict rules of the insurance directives nor the ones of the Rome Convention were applicable, but national conflict rules of the Member States had to determine the applicable law. This was in cases where the risk was located in the EU but was covered by an insurer not established in a Member State.[7]

Insurance directives contained actual conflict rules, not 'scope rules' as in consumer or employment directives. For example, article 7 of the Second Non-life Insurance Directive (88/357/EEC)[8] or article 32 Directive on Life Assurance (2002/83/EC)[9] laid down diverse connecting factors to determine the law applicable to the insurance contract. These conflict rules laid down in the directives were excessively complex. The law applicable depended on whether a contract concerned a life or non-life insurance and, in the case of the latter, whether the risk was small or large and whether the risk was located in the EU. In general, choice of law was possible depending on the Member State law applicable. Moreover, directives are subject to implementation by national law, leaving room for a diverse implementation. As a consequence, the conflict rules were not completely unified among the Member States.[10] As a result, the insurance conflict of laws regulation was fragmented and lacked transparency. The situation left room for gaps and inconsistencies.

After intense discussions, the conflict rules of the insurance directives were incorporated in article 7 Rome I Regulation. Article 7 Rome I conceals and unifies the previously scattered conflict rules, but it does not introduce significant changes. The provision has been a subject of criticism due to the complexity of its conflict rules. During the negotiations for the introduction of a special rule for insurance contracts in the Rome I Regulation, several proposals were suggested and special consultations were conducted. Due to the difficulty of the issue, article 7 Rome I has been considered just a 'complex compromise'.[11] However, it brings more legal certainty to the law applicable to insurance contracts. According to article 23 Rome I, article 7 Rome I supersedes the conflict of laws rules in the individual directives. Thus, conflict rules of the directives lost their relevance. Indeed, as stated by Recital 40,

---

[7]Kramer (2008), p. 25; Kuipers (2012), pp. 118, 119.

[8]Second Council Directive 88/357/EEC of 22 June 1988 on the coordination of laws, regulations and administrative provisions relating to direct insurance other than life assurance and laying down provisions to facilitate the effective exercise of freedom to provide services and amending Directive 73/239/EEC (OJ 1988 L 172/1).

[9]Directive 2002/83/EC of the European Parliament and of the Council of 5 November 2002 concerning life assurance (OJ 2002 L 345/1).

[10]Kramer (2008), p. 24. For a thorough analysis of the implementation of conflict rules in Belgium, France, Germany, Italy, The Netherlands, Spain and the UK, see: Frigessi Di Rattalma (2003).

[11]Kramer (2008), p. 41.

> [a] situation where conflict-of-law rules are dispersed among several instruments and where there are differences between those rules should be avoided (...).

However, apparently, this statement only affects insurance contracts since no difference was made regarding, for example, the scope rules of consumer directives.[12] Concerning the scope rules of EU consumer directives, we can wonder whether introducing a detailed provision with specific conflict rules as article 7 Rome I would have worked with regard to consumer contracts. That is, whether the issue of coordination between the Rome I Regulation and the scope rules of consumer directives dealt with in Chap. 4 could have been resolved if article 6 Rome I incorporated the different scope rules as specific and detailed conflict rules in it. I do not think that such a complex rule would be necessary in relation to consumer contracts. First, the scope rules of EU consumer directives do not point to a specific law applicable as insurance directives rules did. Second, the scope rules of EU consumer directives refer to the same scope of application, sharing similar wording, instead of referring to different applicable laws as insurance directives did. That is, because of the differences in the protection necessary for the different insurance contracts, directives provided for different unilateral conflict rules; however, the scope rules of directives refer to a similar scope, without distinguishing between different levels of protection. Generally, EU consumer directives claim the application of their provisions when the situation is closely connected with the EU (with the exception of article 12(2) Directive 2008/122/EC in the protection of consumers in respect of certain aspects of timeshare, long-term holiday products, resale and exchange contracts, replacing Directive 94/47/EC—Timeshare Directive).[13] The different existing levels of protection for consumer contracts is provided by the Rome I Regulation itself, distinguishing between consumer contracts falling under the protective provision of article 6 Rome I and consumer contracts that do not fall under that provision. No further distinctions, and hence no further specific conflict rules, seem to be required or specifically introduced in a single conflict rule.[14] Another way to follow the technique of article 7 Rome I would be to introduce in article 6 Rome I a specific conflict rule for every consumer contract that is now excluded from the specific protective conflict rule (e.g. active consumers, contract for the supply of services to be supplied entirely outside the consumer's country of habitual residence etc.), distinguishing between different levels of protection and the limits on party autonomy. However, these contracts are already covered by the general rules of the Regulation (articles 3 and 4 Rome I) or by specific conflict rules because of their specialities (e.g. contracts for the carriage of passengers).

[12]Although scope rules are not conflict rules, the debate they generated in the context of the Rome Convention and the drafting of the Rome I Regulation calls for some clarification or specific reference that the Rome I Regulation lacks.

[13]Regarding the existent scope rules in EU consumer directives, see Sect. 4.1.1.2.

[14]In fact, the suggested modifications (see Sect. 4.4) would already adequately coordinate EU consumer directives and Rome I Regulation, without the need of introducing a specific rigid provision.

These distinctions are justified and are not based on the requirements of EU consumer directives, but they simply do not need the special PIL protection of article 6.[15] To include these distinctions within article 6 Rome I would be excessively complex since they mostly can be covered by the general conflict rules of Rome I. Also, they would not have any impact on the coordination of the scope rules of the directives with the Rome I Regulation, which do not share the same distinctions.

As regards the current situation with EU insurance directives, the Solvency II Directive[16] modified and repealed 13 insurance directives, codifying in one instrument both general rules and rules specific for certain types of insurance. According to article 2(1) Solvency II Directive, it applies to direct life and non-life insurance undertakings established in the territory of a Member State (or that wish to become established there) and to reinsurance undertakings established in the territory of a Member State (or wish to become established there) conducting only reinsurance activities. The instrument makes several references to the Rome I Regulation. Following from article 7 and article 23 Rome I, the law applicable to insurance contracts is determined by the Rome I Regulation. When the rules of the Rome I Regulation lead to the application of a Member State law, the protection of the Solvency II Directive is ensured. When the policyholder is a private person in a weak contractual position comparable to a consumer, some general EU consumer law rules will also be applicable to that contract if the law applicable as a result of the Rome I Regulation is the law of a Member State. For example, in B2C insurance contracts, the general rules of consumer contract law of the Distance Marketing of Financial Services Directive and the Unfair Contract Terms Directive can also be applicable.

Party autonomy is not limited by article 7 Rome I in the same manner as in article 6 Rome I regarding consumer contracts. Policyholders in a weaker contractual provision do not enjoy the same protective conflict rules as consumers falling under article 6 Rome I. However, the type of contracts where the policyholder can be in a weaker contractual provision (i.e. mass risks) are regulated by article 7 (3) only when the risk is located in the EU, which only allows the choice of several Member State laws related to the contract or the law of the country of habitual residence of the policyholder. Therefore, it offers enough protection to the policyholder in a weaker contractual position. In fact, it offers more protection than the (non-)protection enjoyed by a consumer falling outside the scope of article 6 Rome I. In case the risk is not located in a Member State, the general provisions of the Rome I Regulation apply (articles 3, 4 and, exceptionally, 6 Rome I in the case of an insurance B2C contract falling under the requirements of article 6 Rome I). Article 3 or 4 Rome I can lead to the application of a non-Member State law, and thus in

[15]See Sect. 3.1.1.

[16]Directive 2009/138/EC of the European Parliament and of the Council of 25 November 2009 on the taking-up and pursuit of the business of Insurance and Reinsurance (Solvency II) (recast) (OJ 2009 L 335/1).

those cases it is considered that the rules of the directive do not need to apply. The rules are complex but coordinated.

In the case of article 7(4) Rome I and mandatory insurance contracts, the provision is only applicable if the mandatory insurance contract covers a risk located within the EU. When the risk is located outside the EU, if the Member State imposing the obligation to take out insurance needs to apply these rules, it can be done under article 9 Rome I only if public interests are involved.[17]

6.1.2 Law Applicable to Contracts for the Carriage of Passengers (Article 5(2) Rome I) and Application of EU Passenger Regulations

Article 5(2) Rome I contains a special provision determining the law applicable to contracts for the carriage of passengers. This rule was newly introduced by the Rome I Regulation. In the Rome Convention, contracts for the carriage of passengers were excluded from article 4(4) Rome Convention, which only applied to carriage of goods, and were also excluded from the special provision on consumer contracts (article 5(4)(a) Rome Convention). The general rule on party autonomy under article 3 Rome Convention and the general rule in the absence of choice of law under article 4(2) Rome Convention determined the law applicable to contracts for the carriage of passengers. There was complete freedom of choice of law, and in its absence, article 4(2) would generally require the application of the law of habitual residence of the carrier. Passengers did not enjoy any special protection.[18]

The Rome I Regulation introduced article 5(2) Rome I as a compromise between the need for protection of the passengers as consumers and the interests of the carrier.[19] In the absence of choice of law, the provision favours the application of the law of the country of habitual residence of the passenger, as long as either the place of departure or the place of destination is located in that country. Otherwise, the law of the country of habitual residence of the carrier applies. When the contract is most closely connected to another country, the law of such country applies (article 5(3) Rome I). Choice of law is limited, but in a different manner than article 6 Rome I regarding consumer contracts. Parties can choose among the law of the country where (a) the passenger has his habitual residence, (b) the carrier has its habitual residence, (c) the carrier has its place of central administration, (d) the place of departure is located, or (e) the place of destination is located. The limitation of party

---

[17] Gruber (2015), p. 199.

[18] A more consumer friendly solution was desired, and the close connection exception was the only option to apply, in case of absence of choice, the law of the place of the passenger/consumer if possible.

[19] For a general discussion, Plender and Wilderspin (2015), pp. 222–232; Fentiman (2016); Schulze (2015), pp. 127–153.

autonomy ensures that the law chosen has some connection with the contract. On the side of the carrier, this provision allows the carrier to choose the law of its place of residence or central administration, avoiding the application of many different laws depending on the passengers. If the mandatory provisions of the law of habitual residence of every passenger were to be applicable, this would mean that an air carrier, for example, would have to apply a different regime for every flight passenger, which would be very burdensome and impractical. On the side of the passenger, the level of protection offered by the limit on party autonomy only ensures that the carrier does not deliberately choose a law with a very low level of consumer protection. However, the application of a minimum level of protection is not ensured. In addition, the carrier could choose to establish its place of habitual residence or central administration in a country with a poor level of consumer/ passenger protection and then choose this law as applicable. Generally, contracts for the carriage of passengers contain a choice of law clause for the law of the country where the carrier has its habitual residence or place of central administration, which means that the passenger will rarely see the provisions of his place of habitual residence applied in accordance to article 5(2) Rome I.[20]

Contracts of carriage of passengers are excluded from the protection by article 6 Rome I of consumers (article 6(4)(b) Rome I), even when the carrier directed its activities to the country of habitual residence of the passenger. If article 6 Rome I would apply to contracts of carriage of passengers, there would be, for example, many consumers booking their flight, bus or train online, which would have the protection of the mandatory provisions of their country that are applied to the contract.[21] Only contracts relating to package travel are included in article 6 Rome I.[22] It is clear that the protection offered by article 6 Rome I is more beneficial than

---

[20]Steennot (2014), p. 2.

[21]Many carriers' websites contain information in different languages, show the prices in the consumer's currency, allow to choose as a place of departure the country of the consumer etc. Ibid., p. 6.

[22]The definition of contract for package travel is to be found it article 3(2) Package Travel Directive (Directive (EU) 2015/2302 of the European Parliament and of the Council of 25 November 2015 on package travel and linked travel arrangements, amending Regulation (EC) No 2006/2004 and Directive 2011/83/EU of the European Parliament and of the Council and repealing Council Directive 90/314/EEC (OJ 2015 L 326/1)):

> 'package' means a combination of at least two different types of travel services for the purpose of the same trip or holiday, if:
>
> (a) those services are combined by one trader, including at the request of or in accordance with the selection of the traveller, before a single contract on all services is concluded; or (b) irrespective of whether separate contracts are concluded with individual travel service providers, those services are: (i) purchased from a single point of sale and those services have been selected before the traveller agrees to pay, (ii) offered, sold or charged at an inclusive or total price, (iii) advertised or sold under the term 'package' or under a similar term, (iv) combined after the conclusion of a contract by which a trader entitles the traveller to choose among a selection of different types of travel services, or (v) purchased from separate traders through linked online booking processes where the traveller's name, payment details and e-mail address are transmitted from the trader with whom the first

that by article 5(2) Rome I. While the application of the mandatory provisions of the law of the country of habitual residence of the consumer is ensured by article 6 Rome I, article 5(2) Rome I, as described above, does not ensure the same protection for passengers. In the case of consumer contracts covered by article 6 Rome I, the reasoning underlying the application of the mandatory provisions of the country of habitual residence of the consumer is based on the targeted activities test: the professional directs its activities to a specific country, so it can expect the consumer protection of that country to be applicable to their residents. In the case of contracts for the carriage of passengers, there is no difference between passengers acting within the course of their commercial activities and those acting outside the scope of their commercial activities (i.e. private purposes). In the latter case, there is no difference between a passenger actively purchasing a ticket from a foreign carrier and a passenger being targeted in his country of residence by a foreign carrier. The rule of article 5(2) Rome I was drafted in a 'simple' way. It would be very burdensome to make a difference between passengers buying a ticket acting within the scope of their commercial activities and passengers acting for private purposes, making the second distinction, on which article 6 Rome I is based, even more difficult. Still, curiously, passengers that would not fall under the conditions of article 6(2) Rome I (targeted activities test) enjoy more protection than consumers falling outside the scope of article 6(2) Rome I.[23]

Generally, it is submitted that international conventions on the transport of passengers prevail over article 5(2) Rome I. The relevant conventions are incorporated into the national law and lay down uniform rules that are applicable by the law of the forum, eliminating the conflict of laws issue, since they are a uniform law, and thus reducing the role of the Rome I Regulation.[24] There are numerous conventions in which the Member States are part (the Athens Convention Relating to the Carriage of Passengers and Their Luggage by Sea, Montreal Convention, International Convention for the Carriage of Passengers and Luggage by Rail (CIV), Convention on the Contract for International Carriage of Passengers and Luggage by Road (CVR 1973) etc.). When these conventions contain conflict rules, resulting in the existence of different conflict rules in the Member States concerning the determination of the

---

contract is concluded to another trader or traders and a contract with the latter trader or traders is concluded at the latest 24 hours after the confirmation of the booking of the first travel service.

A combination of travel services where not more than one type of travel service as referred to in point (a), (b) or (c) of point 1 is combined with one or more tourist services as referred to in point (d) of point 1 is not a package if the latter services:

(a) do not account for a significant proportion of the value of the combination and are not advertised as and do not otherwise represent an essential feature of the combination; or (b) are selected and purchased only after the performance of a travel service as referred to in point (a), (b) or (c) of point 1 has started.

[23]Consumer contracts not falling within the conditions of article 6(2) Rome I do not enjoy any special protection and are governed by the general conflict rules of the Rome I.

[24]Plender and Wilderspin (2015), p. 227; Schulze (2015), p. 140; Fentiman (2016), p. 446.

law applicable to the transport contract (i.e. the conflict rule of the convention and article 5 Rome I), Article 25 Rome I establishes precedence over Rome I in the application of international conventions to which one or more Member States are parties and which lay down conflict rules relating to contractual obligations. Thus, article 5 Rome I is to be displaced by numerous transport international conventions pursuant to article 25 Rome I when different conflict rules are into play.[25]

Regarding the relationship with EU secondary law, the majority of EU provisions on the carriage of passengers are laid down by regulations rather than by directives. The provisions of EU regulations become applicable in a uniform way in all Member States. The existence of conflict rules in EU regulations is less problematic than in directives since the risk of a different implementation by the different Member States due to the minimum harmonising nature of the majority of the directives is avoided. In the case of a conflict rule laid down by a regulation, there is one uniform conflict rule for all Member States. Also, in intra-EU scenarios, it is not relevant which Member State law is applicable since the protection offered by the regulation is implemented by all Member State laws. The level of protection offered by the conflict rules is relevant when there is a choice of law of a non-Member State or when the carrier is established in a non-Member State. Article 23 Rome I establishes the precedence of specific conflict rules laid down in EU instruments. Contrarily to the situation regarding insurance contracts, the provision on contracts for the carriage of passengers does not supersede the possible conflict rules laid down in EU instruments regarding the carriage of passengers. Do these instruments contain their own conflict rules and prevail over the Rome I Regulation through article 23 Rome I? Do they merely contain scope rules similarly to consumer directives? Does article 5(2) Rome I ensure their application?

The Regulation on Rail Passengers Rights and Obligations (1371/2007)[26] aims to offer better protection to rail passengers. It establishes rules on information that rail operators must provide to passengers (about the conclusion of transport contracts or availability of tickets, for example), rules on the liability of the rail operator in certain circumstances, rules regarding compensation (because of delays or cancellation), complaint mechanisms etc. The Regulation implemented within the EU the provisions of the Uniform Rules Concerning the Contract for International Carriage of Passengers and Luggage by Rail (CIV) into the Convention Concerning International Carriage by Rail (COTIF) of 9 May 1980, as modified by the Protocol for the modification of the Convention Concerning International Carriage by Rail of 3 June 1999 (1999 Protocol).

Article 2(1) provides that

> [t]his Regulation shall apply to all rail journeys and services throughout the Community provided by one or more railway undertakings licensed in

[25]Schulze (2015), p. 140.

[26]Regulation (EC) No 1371/2007 of the European Parliament and of the Council of 23 October 2007 on rail passengers' rights and obligations (OJ 2007 L 315/14).

accordance with Council Directive 95/18/EC of 19 June 1995 on the licensing of railway undertakings.

This rule seems to merely refer to the scope of the Regulation, with no intention to interfere with PIL, since it is contained in article 2 of the Regulation with the headline 'scope'. The Regulation should apply to rail journeys within the EU. More importantly, article 4 provides that the conclusion and performance of a transport contract and the provision of information and tickets shall be governed by the provisions of Title II and Title III of Annex I to the Regulation. Article 4 is a unilateral conflict rule, according to which the conclusion and performance of a transport contract are not to be decided according to the rules of a Member State according to external PIL rules, but it is to be decided according to the provisions of Title II and Title III of Annex I to the Regulation. The application of the provisions of the Regulation is mandatory and cannot be derogated from by agreement.

European Regulation No 261/2004 (Airline Passengers Regulation)[27] provides for rules concerning airline passengers' rights in the case of denied boarding, cancellation or delay. Article 3(1) provides:

> This Regulation shall apply: (a) to passengers departing from an airport located in the territory of a Member State to which the Treaty applies; (b) to passengers departing from an airport located in a third country to an airport situated in the territory of a Member State to which the Treaty applies, unless they received benefits or compensation and were given assistance in that third country, if the operating air carrier of the flight concerned is a Community carrier.

That is, article 3(1) establishes territorial criteria for the application of the Airline Passengers Regulation: passengers departing from the airport of a Member State and passengers departing to an airport located in a Member State when the air carrier is from a Member State. This rule falls under the category of scope rule rather than being considered as a conflict rule as such.[28] On the other hand, article 12 Airline Passengers Regulation establishes that the Regulation applies without prejudice to a passenger's right to further compensation. That is, if a third-country applicable law provides for a better compensation, this should be granted to the passenger. The Airline Passengers Regulation is open to the possibility of applying a third law, which confirms that article 3(1) should be read not as a unilateral conflict rule but as a scope rule.

According to article 15,

---

[27]Regulation (EC) No 261/2004 of the European Parliament and of the Council of 11 February 2004 establishing common rules on compensation and assistance to passengers in the event of denied boarding and of cancellation or long delay of flights, and repealing Regulation (EEC) No 295/91 (OJ 2004 L 46/1).

[28]Kuipers (2012), p. 240. This rule is placed under the heading of article 3: 'scope'.

> [o]bligations vis-à-vis passengers pursuant to this Regulation may not be limited or waived, notably by a derogation or restrictive clause in the contract of carriage.

In addition, in a similar way as the Posted Workers Directive, the Airline Passengers Regulation aims to ensure the application of some minimum standards to the passengers, but without prejudice to more beneficial standards available (article 13). However, instead of referring to a situation where two (or more) Member States are involved, the Airline Passengers Regulation refers to a situation of EU standard versus third country law. I do not consider that the Airline Passengers Regulation resolves conflicts of laws, but rather it contains a scope rule that tries to ensure that passengers with specific connections with the EU are protected. If we were to consider that the Regulation does not prevail over article 5 Rome I through article 23 Rome I, because it does not contain a conflict rule as such, then the only way to ensure the application of the Regulation in the scenarios defined by its scope rule is through article 9 Rome I. Member States would apply the rules of the Regulation regardless of a choice of a non-Member State law in the transport contract on the basis of their overriding mandatory character. However, this view can also be controversial: Is the application of the Passengers Rights Regulation essential for the public interests of the EU? The Regulation intends to protect the passenger as a weaker party, but the public interest should also be at stake in order to determine the Regulation as overriding mandatory. There seems to be no debate regarding the possibility of a choice of law setting aside the application of the Regulation, and thus there is an agreement regarding the precedence of the provisions of the Passengers Rights Regulation over article 5(2) Rome I. Some assume that the Regulation prevails over article 5(2) Rome I through article 23 Rome I, based on the existence of a scope rule, and thus article 5(2) only applies in situations outside the scope of the Regulation. For example, in the case of a flight departing from a third country with destination in a Member State but operated by a foreign carrier, article 5(2) Rome I would be applicable since the situation falls outside the scope described by article 3(1) Airline Passengers Regulation.[29] On the other hand, those who do not consider that the Regulation prevails through article 23 Rome I submit that it should apply through article 9 Rome I as overriding mandatory rules.[30] If the application of the Passengers Rights Regulation is to be considered essential for the protection of EU interests going beyond the protection of the passenger as a consumer, I agree with that point of view.

Finally, many EU consumer directives are relevant regarding the protection of passengers (e.g. Unfair Contract Terms Directive, Consumer Rights Directive etc.). Even when the passenger is in the position of a consumer as defined by the Rome I Regulation, a valid choice of law according to article 5(2) Rome I can easily avoid the application of the mandatory provisions of the EU consumer directives.[31]

[29] Schulze (2015), p. 140.

[30] Fauvarque-Cosson and Mazeaud (2008), p. 116; Steennot (2014), p. 4.

[31] See discussion in Chap. 4 regarding the application of EU Consumer Directives.

To conclude, it seems clear that article 5(2) Rome I, opposite to article 7 Rome I regarding insurance contracts, was not drafted in coordination with the different EU secondary instruments on carriage of passengers. The provision merely limits party autonomy, and the protection provided to the passengers can thus be criticised. On the other hand, it is not that relevant because it is agreed that a big number of international conventions and EU secondary law on the carriage of passengers precede the application of article 5(2) Rome I, through either article 23 Rome I or article 9 Rome I. As a result, article 5(2) Rome I only applies when there is a gap not covered by those international conventions or EU regulations.

6.2 Other 'Weaker' Contracting Parties with No Special Protection in Rome I: Franchise, Distribution and Commercial Agency Contracts

6.2.1 Franchise and Distribution Contracts: Party Autonomy and Law Applicable in the Absence of Choice

National substantive rules and EU legal instruments harmonising or unifying substantive rules of private law provide for special protective rules to other contracting parties, such as franchisees, distributors, commercial agents and even some small businesses.

From a PIL perspective, the structural weaker contracting parties are consumers possessing the characteristics provided by article 6 Rome I and employees. To a lesser extent, the weaker position of passengers and policyholders is also recognised since party autonomy is somehow limited to contracts for the carriage of passengers and insurance contracts.

Franchise contracts and distribution contracts are classified in the Rome I Regulation as contracts for services (Recital 17 Rome I), but specific rules within the general provision in the absence of choice of law, article 4 Rome I, are provided regarding the law applicable in the absence of choice. Since specific rules are provided, it can mean that more importance was placed on other factors rather than on the characteristic performance general rule of article 4 Rome I.

Article 4(1)(e) Rome I establishes the law of habitual residence of the franchisee as the law applicable to the contract of franchise. The introduction of this specific rule puts an end to the previous debate regarding the law applicable to the franchise contract in the absence of choice of law since there was disagreement as to who is the party carrying out the characteristic performance in that contract.[32] Therefore, one of the main objectives of this rule is to obtain legal certainty. According to Recital 16 Rome I, conflict rules should be 'highly foreseeable'. The choice for the place of

[32]García Gutiérrez (2008), p. 235.

habitual residence of the franchisee rather than the place of habitual residence of the franchisor has different justifications. Besides being considered by some as the place of characteristic performance, and as the 'market affected by the contract', reasons of weaker party protection seem to be behind this special rule.[33] Between the parties to a franchise agreement, there are information and bargaining inequalities. Although the franchisee is a company in the same position as any other business of similar side, the relationship with a franchisor is characterised by the existence of a standard-form contract to which the franchisee has to agree (almost) with a non-negotiating margin.[34] It is true that the position of consumers or employees, in connection with their information and bargaining power, is weaker in comparison with that of the franchisee. However, Recital 23 Rome I refers in general to the protection of weaker contracting parties by conflict rules, without specifically naming consumers and employees. Thus, there might be more conflict rules in the Rome I with that intention. Several legal instruments of substantive law recognise the weaker contractual position of franchisees, and this need is somehow reflected by article 4(1)(e) Rome I.[35] Still, this rule also refers to the habitual place of residence of the franchisee on the basis that it is assumed as the habitual place where he carries out his activities, making it generally the law most closely connected to the contract.

Even when article 4(1)(e) Rome I is beneficial to the franchisee, if parties have chosen the law applicable to the contract, article 3(1) Rome I applies and the law chosen by the parties would govern the contract. Franchisors can easily elude the application of the law of the place of the franchisee by choosing any other law, related or not to the contract, as applicable. Therefore, substantive protective provisions of the law of the country of habitual residence of the franchisee enacted with the intention of protecting the franchisee can be circumvented by a choice of law. The only possible mechanism that the Rome I Regulation provides for the protection of this national imperative provisions are articles 3(3), 3(4) and 9 Rome I. Article 3(3) and 3(4) Rome I would ensure the application of mandatory national or Community rules, respectively, only when all the relevant elements of the situation are located within a country in the EU. The application of article 9 Rome I is only possible if the franchise contract provisions would fall under the definition of article 9(1) Rome I concerning overriding mandatory rules, which seems highly unlikely.

Similarly, in the case of distribution contracts, article 4(1)(f) Rome I puts an end to the previous discussions regarding the law applicable to distribution contracts in the absence of choice of law.[36] Article 4(1)(f) Rome I provides for the law of the habitual place of residence of the distributor as applicable. Again, legal certainty is the main aim of the rule, besides being considered as the law most closely connected to the distribution contract. The protection of the distributor as a weaker party in the

---

[33] Ibid., p. 238; Gebauer (2015), pp. 116, 117.

[34] García Gutiérrez (2008), p. 239.

[35] Ibid., p. 240.

[36] For an overview of this discussion under the Rome Convention, Martínez Luna (2016), pp. 258–268.

contract can also be behind the conflict rule, although it is questionable.[37] Like in the case of a franchisee (which in a general understanding of the concept of contract of distribution could be considered as a distributor), the distributor can be in a weaker bargaining position against the grantor of the merchandise. However, both the distributor and his counterparty are independent companies, and the possible weaker position is not comparable to the one of the consumer or the employee. Some have questioned the weaker party argument and justify article 4(1)(e) on the grounds of predictability and closest connection to the contract of distribution.[38] In any way, the law of habitual place of the distributor might not be the most protective law, but it is the most familiar for the distributor. However, this law can be circumvented by the parties through article 3(1) Rome I.

6.2.2 Commercial Agency Contracts: Interaction Between the Rome I Regulation and the Commercial Agents Directive

Finally, there is a type of contract involving a generally recognised weaker contracting party that does not enjoy any specific protective rule in the Rome I Regulation: the commercial agency contract.

The introduction of a specific conflict rule for commercial agency contracts was suggested during the process of conversion of the Rome Convention into the Rome I Regulation. Even a rule limiting party autonomy in a similar way that was granted for employees was proposed.[39] Although this suggestion was rejected, the Rome I Proposal provided for a specific provision regarding commercial agents in a similar way to the current provisions on distribution and franchise contracts, under which party autonomy fully applied.[40] However, finally, no specific provision regulating

[37]The weaker position of the distributor was mentioned in the Proposal for Rome I (COM (2005) 650 final) as a justification for the introduction of the new rule, although this aim is not explicitly mentioned in the Recitals of Rome I and many authors have doubted that was the rationale behind the rule. Indeed, if the aim was to protect a weaker party, party autonomy should then be limited. Ancel (2008), pp. 226, 227; Lagarde (2006), p. 339.

[38]For example, Martínez Luna (2016) and Ancel (2008).

[39]In Max Planck Institute for Foreign Private and Private International Law (2004), the introduction of an extra paragraph in article 6 regarding employment contracts was suggested. The rationale behind it was that both commercial agents and employees were a weaker contracting party in a similar position to their employer or principal. The proposal of article 6(4) read: *In an agency contract between a principal and a self-employed commercial agent, a choice of law made by the parties shall not have the effect of depriving the agent of the protection afforded to him by the internally mandatory rules of the law which would be applicable under Article 4.*

[40]Proposal for a Regulation of the European Parliament and the Council on the law applicable to contractual obligations (Rome I) (COM(2005) 650 final) [Proposal for Rome I] provided for an article 7 with the heading 'Contracts Concluded by an Agent', which stated: *In the absence of a choice under Article 3, a contract between principal and agent shall be governed by the law of the*

the law applicable to commercial agency contracts was introduced in the final version of the Rome I Regulation. The law applicable to an agency contract is to be determined according to the general rules of Rome I. Thus, the commercial agency contract shall be governed by the law chosen by the parties (article 3 (1) Rome I), and in the absence of choice, article 4(1) Rome I will generally apply the law of the country of habitual residence of the agent. The agent enjoys a similar position as the distributor or franchisee: there is no limitation on party autonomy, and in the absence of choice, the law of his country of habitual residence will generally be applied.

On the other hand, the EU provides protection to the commercial agent at a substantive level. The Council Directive 86/653/EEC of 18 December 1986 on the coordination of the laws of the Member States relating to self-employed commercial agents (Commercial Agents Directive)[41] harmonises the rules regarding agency contracts in order to improve the conditions of competition while facilitating the conclusion and performance of these contracts across the borders. It was considered that the previously existing different levels of protection afforded by the different national laws within the EU to the agents might have resulted in a disadvantage to the business in some areas or in distortions of competition within the EU.[42] The Directive defines in article 1 the commercial agents as intermediaries with a permanent authorisation to negotiate the sale or purchase of goods in the name and on behalf of another person (the principal). The Commercial Agents Directive defines the rights and obligations of both commercial agents and their principals and establishes rules regarding the remuneration of the commercial agent and the conclusion and termination of the agency contract, with emphasis on the compensation of the agent.[43] It is a minimum harmonisation directive, leaving to the Member States the possibility of improving the minimum standards set.

Besides the objective of harmonising the conditions of competence within the internal market, the Commercial Agents Directive also sets a minimum level of protection to the commercial agents operating in the EU. Still, the level of protection needed by commercial agents differs from the protection needed by consumers and employees. Agents are generally better informed and experienced, and it is common in the current international practice that they are organised as corporations having more than one principal. However, when the commercial agent is a natural person with only one principal, the contractual situation is comparable to that between the employee and the employer.[44] There is often an imbalance in the bargaining power

country in which the agent has his habitual residence, unless the agent exercises or is to exercise his main activity in the country in which the principal has his habitual residence, in which case the law of that country shall apply.

[41]Council Directive 86/653/EEC of 18 December 1986 on the coordination of the laws of the Member States relating to self-employed commercial agents (OJ 1986 L 382/17).

[42]Randolph and Davey (2010), p. 1.

[43]Aguilar Grieder (2011), p. 27.

[44]Verhagen (2002), p. 153; Kuipers (2012), p. 217.

and information between the agent and the principal. The principal, aware of the legal diversity in this area, may wish to elude the national legislation that affords a level of protection to the agent in order to be more economically efficient and become more competitive within its operating market. Therefore, the agency contract may contain a choice of law clause referring to a non-Member State law that does not set the minimum standards of protection in favour of the agent as the Commercial Agents Directive does. As a consequence of this behaviour, it can be considered that the internal market may suffer a negative impact as it promotes distorted competition. Furthermore, the direct consequence would be for the commercial agents as they will be unprotected against eventual abuses from their principal. These were precisely the negative effects that the Commercial Agents Directive aimed to eradicate.

The Commercial Agents Directive does not contain any conflict rule or scope rule, and thus the law applicable to the agency contract is supposed to be determined by the Rome I Regulation. However, the ECJ in the already mentioned *Ingmar* judgment[45] established the application of the Commercial Agents Directive in situations closely connected with the Community (i.e. when the commercial agent carries out his activity within a Member State), irrespective of the law by which the parties intended the contract to be governed. According to the ECJ, '[t]he purpose served by the provisions in question requires that they be applied where the situation is closely connected with the Community (...) irrespective of the law by which the parties intended the contract to be governed'.[46] The phrasing is similar to the scope rules contained in EU consumer directives.

This case involved the following situation: Ingmar, a commercial agent with domicile in the United Kingdom, filed a claim against Eaton, its principal established in California for the payment of commission and compensation of the damages caused by the termination of their agency contract. Ingmar performed his obligations under the contract exclusively in the UK and Ireland. The contract included a choice of law clause determining Californian law as governing the agency contract. However, the claims of the agent were based on the Commercial Agents Regulation of 8 December 1993, the transposition in English law of the Commercial Agents Directive. The preliminary ruling requested from the ECJ asked whether articles 17 and 18 of the Commercial Agents Directive, on which the claims of the agent are based, are applicable when the commercial agent performs its activities within a Member State, regardless of the establishment of the principal on a third state and the choice of a third state law to govern their contract. Articles 17 and 18 of the Commercial Agents Directive define the circumstances under which a commercial agent, upon the termination of the contract, is entitled to claim compensation for the damages suffered by him because of the termination of the contractual relationship with the principal. Article 19 of the Directive states that

[45]Case C-381/98 *Ingmar GB Ltd v Eaton Leonard Technologies Inc.* [2000] ECR I-9305.

[46]*Ingmar*, para. 25.

parties may not derogate from articles 17 and 18 to the detriment of the agent before the agency contract expires.

The ECJ concluded that the purpose these provisions serve requires their application where the situation is closely connected with the Community, which is presumed when the commercial agent carries out his activity within a Member State, irrespective of the law chosen by the parties to govern their contract.[47]

The Commercial Agents Directive, besides protecting the private interests of commercial agents, aims at harmonising the conditions of competence within the internal market and contributing to the proper functioning of the internal market. The ECJ explained that the aim of articles 17–19 of the Commercial Agents Directive is to protect the freedom of establishment and to circumvent distorted competition within the internal market, promoting at the same time the certainty of the commercial transactions.[48] From the recitals of the Directive, it is implied that these objectives are present in more provisions, and thus those other provisions of the Directive could also be regarded as applicable *irrespective of the law by which the parties intended the contract to be governed.*[49] Companies, both European and international, that hire agents in order to commercialise their products within the EU must be aware and respect the fact that they are trading in an internal market environment and, as a result, cannot benefit from a legal diversity that may distort the competence of the internal market.[50]

From the *Ingmar* judgment, it follows that the ECJ determined the international application of the Commercial Agents Directive through a scope rule similar to those existing in some EU consumer directives, determining that whenever the situation is closely connected to the EU, the provisions of the Commercial Agents Directive cannot be circumvented by choosing a non-Member State law. In the moment when the ECJ ruled in this case (2000), the Rome I Regulation still did not exist, and although the provisions of the Rome Convention were similar to those of Rome I, they were not applicable because the contract fell outside the temporal scope of the Convention. However, rather than interpreting the Directive in the light of the conflict rules of the Rome Convention seeking for coordination, the ECJ did not refer to any PIL instrument. The same inconsistencies as regarding the scope rules of the EU consumer directives arise regarding the *Ingmar* judgment and the Commercial Agents Directive. How does this judgment fit within the conflict of laws system of the Rome I Regulation?

---

[47] *Ingmar*, para. 25.

[48] *Ingmar*, paras. 23–24. In that respect, the Judgment of the Court of 30 April 1998, case C-215/97, *Barbara Bellone v Yokohama SpA* [1998] ECR I-2191, in regard to Recital 2 of the Commercial Agents Directive, referred to the objectives of protection of the internal market, freedom of establishment and circumvention of distorted competition of the Directive.

[49] Verhagen (2002), p. 138.

[50] Font i Segura (2009), pp. 265, 266; Aguilar Grieder (2007), pp. 64, 65.

If the application of the rules of EU directives is going to be determined on the basis of the nature and purpose of the directive rather than on the basis of the Rome I Regulation, parties will not be able to choose the applicable law to the contract since the provisions of the directive will become mandatory when the facts fall under its material scope.[51] In any case, it is still argued by some authors that *Ingmar should* be interpreted as establishing an implicit scope rule, which is aimed at determining the international scope of the provisions of the Commercial Agents Directive, and as such it should prevail over the Rome I Regulation according to article 23 Rome I.[52] In other words, the traditional conflict of laws mechanism should be ignored, and the determination of the international scope of the Commercial Agents Directive should be based upon an (implicit) unilateral conflict rule. But if we were to follow this reasoning, it would be inconsistent if, for example, the scope of application of some European directives (e.g. E-Commerce Directive, Services Directive etc.), which specifically state that they do not provide for special conflict of law rules and do not affect the application of the Rome I Regulation, would be determined by the Rome I Regulation while, at the same time, the application of directives silent about their scope of application, such as the Commercial Agents Directive, would be determined autonomously as laying down an implicit scope rule.[53]

On the contrary, the reasoning used in *Ingmar* can still fit within the Rome I Regulation through article 9 Rome I.[54] The application of the provisions of the Commercial Agency Directive whenever the situation is closely connected to the EU and the parties have chosen the law of a non-Member State to govern their contract can be ensured through article 9 Rome I. For that, they should fall under the definition of overriding mandatory provisions in article 9(1) Rome I. Following the ECJ reasoning, the application of the provisions of the Commercial Agents Directive was based on the nature and purpose of the provisions, which entails protecting the freedom of establishment and avoided distorted competition within the internal market. In order to be covered by the definition of article 9(1), the provisions have to be essential for the protection of public interest, in this case EU interest. Besides protecting the commercial agent, the application of these rules is to be considered essential for the internal market.[55]

Although in this case the ECJ took the approach of applying the commercial agent provisions based on the purposes and nature of the provisions and the directive

---

[51] Aguilar Grieder (2007), p. 207.

[52] Van Bochove (2014), p. 154; Francq (2006), pp. 354, 355.

[53] Kuipers (2012), p. 205.

[54] Although ECJ did not refer in its judgment to the Rome Convention (it was not temporary applicable), the Advocate General did refer to the Rome Convention as a guidance useful to supplement the interpretation of the Directive, which may be derived from its content. Opinion Advocate General on *Ingmar*, para. 64; Verhagen (2002), p. 140.

[55] In Chap. 3, when discussing regarding overriding mandatory rules and provisions protecting the weaker parties, it was submitted that provisions protecting weaker parties can generally qualify as overriding mandatory rules as long as they mainly aim, at the same time, at protecting an essential public interest of the country where they originate.

itself, it does not mean that implicit or explicit scope rules on EU directives are always applicable in that way or are directly considered as overriding mandatory rules. The existence of scope rules in directives was discussed during the drafting of the Rome I Regulation, and in case the EU legislator wanted that result, it could have easily been achieved through a slightly different drafting of article 3(4) Rome I. Instead of ensuring the application of EU mandatory provisions in situations where all the relevant elements are located within the EU, the connecting factor could have been where there is a close connection with the EU. In fact, the drafting of the Rome I Proposal would have ensured the application of the directives against a choice of law:

> Where the parties choose the law of a non-member State, that choice shall be without prejudice to the application of such mandatory rules of Community law as are applicable to the case (article 3(5) Rome I Proposal).

However, the final version does not ensure the application of EU mandatory law where parties choose a non-Member State law in all situations, but only when all the elements of the situation are located within the EU. The non-coordination with the ECJ approach in *Ingmar* and with the scope rules of the directives shows that the legislator did not intend to achieve that result with the Rome I Regulation. As it was previously discussed in this book, the majority of the provisions protecting weaker contracting parties have a mandatory character but not overriding mandatory character.[56] The existence of a scope rule does not automatically give an overriding mandatory character and immediate applicability to the provisions of a directive, but they have to fall under the definition of article 9(1) Rome I. The conclusion of the *Ingmar* case in the light of article 9 Rome I would then be that the ECJ considered the application of the provisions of the Commercial Agents Directive as essential to avoid distorted competition in the EU and ensure freedom of establishment (i.e. EU public interests) whenever the situation is closely connected to the EU. Even if the decision determining the international scope and applicability of the Commercial Agents Directive' provisions can be fit within article 9 Rome I, it is criticised that the *Ingmar* decision is difficult to reconcile with the system of the Rome I Regulation.[57] According to some authors, the ECJ assumed too straightforwardly that the provisions of the Directive aimed at the protection of such high interests, in a manner that even when the principal was established outside the EU, required application and party autonomy should be bypassed.[58] The impact that these rules have on fair competition and freedom of establishment is too indirect as to contravene the law chosen by the parties.[59] In this regard, I also consider that a more restrictive and careful interpretation of public interest should be conducted.

[56] Section 3.3.1.

[57] Verhagen (2002), p. 151.

[58] Kuipers (2009), p. 1520; Verhagen (2002), p. 148.

[59] Verhagen (2002), pp. 148–150.

However, this approach of the ECJ has been confirmed in the *Unamar* judgment,[60] although in an intra-EU scenario and regarding the commercial agency provisions of a Member State. In this case, a preliminary ruling was referred to the ECJ asking whether the mandatory rules of the *lex fori* (in this case the Belgium agency rules) that offer wider protection than the minimum laid down by the Commercial Agents Directive could be applied even if the law chosen by the parties is the law of another Member State in which the minimum protection provided by the Directive has also been implemented (in this case Bulgarian law). The ECJ concluded that despite the fact that the Commercial Agents Directive was correctly transposed in Bulgarian law, the Belgium Court had discretion to qualify its own national provisions as overriding mandatory rules in the sense of article 7 Rome Convention (now article 9 Rome I) and therefore apply them irrespective of the otherwise applicable law.[61] However, the provisions have to be essential to the public interest of the country in order to be applicable as overriding mandatory rules, and thus they should not be applicable merely because they offer a better protection to the commercial agent.

Both *Ingmar* and *Unamar* have served as precedents for the application of the Commercial Agents Directive and national commercial agents legislation as overriding mandatory rules. Recently, for instance, the Austrian Supreme Court (*Oberster Gerichtshof*) ruled in March 2017 that claims under the Austrian Commercial Agents Act (*Handelsvertretergesetz*) could be brought before an Austrian court despite the existence of an arbitration clause in the agency contract, which was governed by the law of New York.[62] The Austrian Supreme court based its reasoning on the overriding mandatory character of the provisions of the Austrian Commercial Agents Act. However, the court merely justified that overriding mandatory character on the basis of the reasoning of the ECJ that such provisions can be considered national overriding mandatory law when their application is crucial for the relevant legal order, but without further explanation. The introduction of a specific definition of the overriding mandatory rules of article 9(1) Rome I aims at restricting the

[60]C-184/12 *United Antwerp Maritime Agencies (Unamar) NV v Navigation Maritime Bulgare* [2013] EU:C:2013:663.

[61]The ECJ in *Unamar* concluded: '*Articles 3 and 7(2) of the Convention on the law applicable to contractual obligations opened for signature in Rome on 19 June 1980 must be interpreted as meaning that the law of a Member State of the European Union which meets the minimum protection requirements laid down by Council Directive 86/653/EEC of 18 December 1986 on the coordination of the laws of the Member States relating to self-employed commercial agents and which has been chosen by the parties to a commercial agency contract may be rejected by the court of another Member State before which the case has been brought in favour of the law of the forum, owing to the mandatory nature, in the legal order of that Member State, of the rules governing the situation of self-employed commercial agents, only if the court before which the case has been brought finds, on the basis of a detailed assessment, that, in the course of that transposition, the legislature of the State of the forum held it to be crucial, in the legal order concerned, to grant the commercial agent protection going beyond that provided for by that directive, taking account in that regard of the nature and of the objective of such mandatory provisions.*'

[62]OGH 1.3.2017, 5 Ob 72/16y.

interpretation of national rules as overriding mandatory rules without measure. National EU courts should make a restrictive interpretation of this definition and justify the use of article 9 Rome I in order to prevent the imposition of national rules against the party autonomy of the parties to a contract, which in that case affected international arbitration but can also put in danger the functioning of the conflict of laws system of the Rome I Regulation.

Finally, regarding the application of the Commercial Agents Directive, an opposite type of situation has been recently addressed by the ECJ and deserves mention. The case *Agro Foreign Trade & Agency Ltd v Petersime NV*[63] involved a contract between an agent established in Turkey and a principal established in Belgium. Their contract contained a choice of law in favour of Belgian law. However, the Belgian legislation transposing the Commercial Agents Directive provides for a limited scope of application, restricting its territorial scope to agents operating in Belgium.[64] As a result, the Turkish agent could not enjoy the protection provided by the Commercial Agents Directive since, being outside the scope of the specific agency contract legislation, the default contract law rules of Belgian law applied to the contract. The preliminary question that was referred to the ECJ asked whether the Belgian law is in accordance with the Commercial Agents Directive when limiting its scope to commercial agents whose principal place of business is in Belgium, and therefore not applying when a principal established in Belgium and an agent established in Turkey have explicitly chosen Belgian law. The ECJ referred to the *Ingmar* case and confirmed that where a situation is closely connected with the EU, in particular where the commercial agent carries out his activity in the territory of a Member State, the provisions of the Directive cannot be circumvented.[65] However, the current situation involving an agent carrying out his activities outside the EU does not amount to a situation closely connected to the EU, and as a result, the purposes of fair competition within the EU do not justify the application of the minimum protection of the Commercial Agents Directive. Since the commercial agent carrying out commercial activities in Turkey does not fall within the scope of application of the Directive, regardless of the fact that the principal is established in a Member State, it is not necessary that he benefits from the protection provided by that Directive to commercial agents. Therefore, Belgian law is in accordance with the Commercial Agents Directive in that regard.[66]

Two important reflexions, which can be extended to situations involving EU consumer or employment directives as well, can be made following this judgment: first, the ECJ confirmed the *Ingmar* approach regarding the scope of application of

---

[63] Case C-507/15 *Agro Foreign Trade & Agency Ltd* v *Petersime NV* [2017] ECLI:EU:C:2017:129.

[64] *Wet betreffende de handelsagentuurovereenkomst* (Law on commercial agency contracts) of 13 April 1995 (*Moniteur belge* of 2 June 1995, p. 15621), provides in article 27: 'Without prejudice to the application of international conventions to which Belgium is a party, any activity of a commercial agent whose principal place of business is in Belgium shall be governed by Belgian law and shall be subject to the jurisdiction of the Belgian courts.'

[65] *Agro Foreign Trade*, para 32.

[66] *Agro Foreign Trade*, paras. 33–36.

the Commercial Agents Directive, which cannot be circumvented by a choice of law when the situation is closely connected with the EU. Again, no references to the Rome Convention or the Rome I Regulation are made in this regard. Second, the technique used by the Belgian legislation, unilaterally determining its scope of application and limiting it to commercial agents whose principal place of business is in Belgium, although allowed by the ECJ, can be criticised. Besides the argument regarding the respect for the legitimate expectations of the parties—in this case the Turkish agent—when choosing a Member State law, I would like to draw attention to what the situation would be if the commercial agent's place of operation is another Member State and parties have chosen Belgian law as applicable. Falling outside the scope of application of the specific Belgian legislation but falling under the scope of application of the Commercial Agents Directive, which national law should the Commercial Agents Directive apply (the Member State of habitual place of residence of the commercial agent or the Member State of chosen law)? The protection of the Commercial Agents Directive needs to be applicable because the agent is carrying out his activity in a Member State. But then should the protection of the law of the place of habitual residence of the agent apply according to article 9 Rome I as overriding mandatory rules? The inconsistencies that can result from these types of rules, such as this scope rule of Belgian law, when implementing an EU directive are very disruptive to our current conflict of laws system, as it was previously discussed in Chaps. 4 and 5 regarding the scope rules of EU consumer and employment directives.

6.3 Closing Remarks

Party autonomy is the cornerstone of the Rome I Regulation and brings numerous advantages to the parties involved. Therefore, the limitations to party autonomy are restricted to situations where it is really necessary (the protection of structural weaker parties, the application of overriding mandatory rules or avoiding abuse of law). Because of the specialties of insurance contracts and the carriage of passengers contracts, party autonomy is restricted in a different manner than required in consumer and employment contracts. In the case of insurance contracts, a complex provision was introduced in the Rome I Regulation in order to incorporate the conflict rules previously scattered in several EU insurance directives. Article 7 Rome I determines the law applicable to insurance contracts, and if the law applicable is the law of a Member State, then the national implementation of the relevant directive will, as a consequence, apply. The situation regarding contracts for the carriage of passengers differs. While the conflict rule is simple, allowing the choice of law from a series of legal systems related to the contract (article 5(2) Rome I), the application of the relevant EU regulations is less obvious. It is widely agreed that the EU mandatory provisions protecting the passenger as a consumer are applicable as required by the regulations and regardless of a choice of law. However, when the regulation does not contain a conflict rule but merely includes a scope rule, such as the Airline Passengers Regulation, it should not prevail over the conflict rules of Rome I on the basis of article 23 Rome I. Thus, its applicability should be through article 9 Rome I, and then the provisions of the regulation should fall under the definition of overriding mandatory rules (i.e. essential for the safeguarding of a public interest (of the EU in this case)).

While consumers and employees should be protected against an abuse of a choice of law, the need of protection of distributors, franchisees and commercial agents is far less obvious. Focusing on the latter, a commercial agent will generally be better informed and experienced in comparison with a consumer or employee since it is his professional activity. Still, his bargaining position can often be weaker in comparison with that of his counterparty, especially when the commercial agent is an individual working only for one principal. From the approach of the Rome I Regulation, parties to a commercial agency contract are free to choose the law applicable to their contract (article 3(1) Rome I). Thus, the protection provided to the agent as a weaker party by the Commercial Agents Directive can be circumvented through a choice of a non-Member State law. When concluding a contract with a choice of law clause for a non-Member State law, the commercial agent is giving up the protection provided by EU law. It is up to the commercial agent, on the basis of individual freedom and responsibility, to decide how to best protect its own interests as a professional.[67] Nevertheless, the application of the rights and obligations deriving from the Commercial Agents Directive whenever the agent is carrying out his activities within the EU has been required by the ECJ in *Ingmar* on the grounds of avoiding unfair competition and protecting freedom of establishment in the EU. That is, the application of the protective provisions of the Directive was not justified based on the need for protection of the commercial agent as a weaker party. In the context of the Rome I Regulation, the provisions of the Directive were interpreted as overriding mandatory provisions under article 9 Rome I, and their scope of application was whenever the contract is closely connected with the EU (i.e. the commercial agent carries out his activities within the EU). While it might seem that the application of the directive provisions is not that essential for the avoidance of unfair competition and the protection of freedom of establishment, it is up to every legal system (in this case the EU) to decide which rules have the character of overriding mandatory rules. However, Member State courts should always justify the consideration of their national rules as overriding mandatory for the sake of party autonomy and the system of the Rome I Regulation.

In relation to other directives, the *Ingmar* decision has had some consequences regarding the interaction between the Rome I Regulation and the EU directives. Since the judgment, it has very often been assumed that the existence of a scope rule in a directive either works as a conflict rule and thus prevails over the conflict rules of the Rome I Regulation or directly gives an overriding mandatory character to the

---

[67] Kuipers (2012), p. 215.

directive. As it has been explained in the previous chapters, that is not the case.[68] First, the ECJ did not resolve the *Ingmar* case on the basis of the Rome I Regulation because it was before its entry into force or on the basis of the Rome Convention because it was not temporarily applicable to the contract. Second, if we put the judgment in the context of the Rome system, and in coordination with it, the ECJ decided the application of the directive based on the essential public interests of the EU (overriding mandatory character) and then clarified when it should be applicable for the protection of those public interests with the scope rule. This is confirmed by the recent *Agro Foreign Trade & Agency Ltd v Petersime NV* judgment. This should not be distorted in that the overriding mandatory character follows from every scope rule of a directive; first, the provisions of the directive would have to fall under the definition of article 9(1) Rome I.

References

Aguilar Grieder H (2007) La Protección del Agente en el Derecho Comercial Europeo. Colex, Madrid

Aguilar Grieder H (2011) El Impacto del Reglamento Roma I en el Contrato Internacional de Agencia. Cuadernos de Derecho Transnacional 3:24–46

Ancel M-E (2008) The Rome I regulation and distribution contracts. In: Sarcevic P et al (eds) Yearbook of private international law. Sellier, European Law Publishers and Swiss Institute of Comparative Law, München, pp 221–232

Fauvarque-Cosson B, Mazeaud D (eds) (2008) European contract law: materials for a common frame of reference: terminology, guiding principles, model rules. Sellier, European Law Publishers, München

Fentiman R (2016) Article 5: contracts of carriage. In: Magnus U, Mankowski P (eds) Commentary - Rome I regulation. Verlag Dr. Otto Schmidt, Köln, pp 441–452

Font i Segura A (2009) Reparación Indemnizatoria tras la Extinción del Contrato Internacional de Agencia Comercial: Imperatividad Poliédrica o el Mito de Zagreo (STJCE de 9 de noviembre de 2000, As. C-381/98, Ingmar Gb Ltd c. Eaton Leonard Technologies Inc.). Revista de Derecho Comunitario Europeo 5:259–279

Francq S (2006) The scope of secondary community law in the light of the methods of private international law- or the other way around? In: Sarcevic P et al (eds) Yearbook of private international law. Sellier, European Law Publishers and Swiss Institute of Comparative Law, München, pp 333–374

Frigessi Di Rattalma M (ed) (2003) The implementation provisions of the EC choice of law rules for insurance contracts. A commentary. Kluwer Law International, The Hague

García Gutiérrez L (2008) Franchise contracts and the Rome I regulation on the law applicable to international contracts. In: Sarcevic P et al (eds) Yearbook of private international law. Sellier, European Law Publishers and Swiss Institute of Comparative Law, München, pp 233–244

Gebauer M (2015) Article 4. Applicable law in the absence of choice. In: Calliess G-P (ed) Rome regulations. Commentary, 2nd edn. Kluwer Law International, Alphen aan den Rijn

Gruber UP (2015) Article 7. Insurance contracts. In: Calliess G-P (ed) Rome regulations. Commentary, 2nd edn. Kluwer Law International, Alphen aan den Rijn

[68]See Chap. 4 regarding EU consumer directives and Chap. 5 concerning EU employment directives.

Kramer XE (2008) The new European conflict of law rules on insurance contracts in Rome I: a complex compromise. Icfai Univ J Insur Law 6:23–42

Kuipers J-J (2009) Party autonomy in the Brussels I regulation and Rome I regulation and the European Court of Justice. German Law J 10:1505–1525

Kuipers J-J (2012) EU law and private international law: the interrelationship in contractual obligations. Martinus Nijhoff Publishers, Leiden

Lagarde P (2006) Remarques sur la Proposition de Règlement sur la Loi Applicable aux Obligations Contractuelles (Rome I). Revue critique de droit international privé 95:331–349

López de Gonzalo M (2017) Carriage of passengers. In: Basedow J et al (eds) Encyclopedia of private international law. Edward Elgar Publishing, Cheltenham, pp 269–278

Martínez Luna WF (2016) Applicable law to distribution contracts in the European Regulation 593/2008 (Rome I). Int Law Revista Colombiana Derecho Internacional (28):247–282

Max Planck Institute for Foreign Private and Private International Law (2004) Comments on the European Commission's Green Paper on the conversion of the Rome Convention of 1980 on the law applicable to contractual obligations into a Community instrument and its modernization. RabelsZ 68:1–118

Plender R, Wilderspin M (2015) The European private international law of obligations, 4th edn. Sweet & Maxwell, London

Randolph F, Davey J (2010) The European law of commercial agency, 3rd edn. Hart Publishing, Oxford

Schulze R (2015) Article 5. Contracts of carriage. In: Calliess G-P (ed) Rome regulations. Commentary, 2nd edn. Kluwer Law International, The Hague

Steennot R (2014) The protection of consumers in cross-border airline's contracts of carriage at the level of private international law. In: Liber Amicorum Johan Erauw. Intersentia, Antwerpen, pp 175–188

Symeonides SC (2010) Party autonomy in Rome I and Rome II from a comparative perspective. In: Boele-Woelki K et al (eds) Convergence and divergence in private international law- Liber Amicorum Kurt Siehr. Eleven International Publishing, The Hague, pp 513–550

Van Bochove LM (2014) Overriding mandatory rules as a vehicle for weaker party protection in European Private International Law. Erasmus Law Rev 7:147–157

Verhagen HLE (2002) The tension between party autonomy and European Union Law: some observations on IngmarGB Ltd v Eaton Leonard Technologies Inc. Int Comp Law Q 51:135–154

Chapter 7
Conclusion

The interaction between the existent EU conflict rules and the EU directives on weaker contracting parties can be defined as, at least, complicated. As a result, in practice, consumers or employees might see themselves in situations where expected applicable rights derived from EU instruments are, in fact, not applicable to their cases. On the other side of the balance, the other party to the contract could see how unexpected obligations derived from EU instruments are imposed on him. For example, the case where a consumer from a Member State is temporarily in another Member State (e.g. on holiday) and gets targeted there by a foreign professional is not covered by the special protective conflict rules of article 6 Rome I. Consequently, the application of the relevant provisions derived from EU consumer directives might not be ensured. Or, on the other side of the balance, in the case of employment contracts, an employer might have to comply with EU legislation in case of a transfer of undertakings even when article 8 Rome I does not lead to the application of a Member State law, on the ground of extensive interpretation of article 9 Rome I regarding overriding mandatory provisions. This study aimed at answering whether EU conflict rules and the EU directives on weaker contracting parties are well coordinated and, if not, how they can achieve a mutual understanding. In order to answer that question, three main inquiries were posed: (1) How do traditional principles of conflict of laws relate to the requirements of the internal market for the realisation of the EU objectives regarding the protection of weaker parties such as employees, consumers etc.? (2) When and how should PIL ensure the applicability of EU directives on weaker party protection? (3) Are the current EU PIL conflict of laws rules and PIL method adequate to ensure the EU objectives regarding weaker contracting parties, or is there a call for a different PIL method? These questions have been tackled along this book. However, I will now specifically provide a reflexion and answers to them on the basis of the findings of this research.

M. Campo Comba, *The Law Applicable to Cross-border Contracts involving Weaker Parties in EU Private International Law*,
https://doi.org/10.1007/978-3-030-61481-2_7

7.1 How Do Traditional Principles of Conflict of Laws Relate to the Requirements of the Internal Market for the Realisation of the EU Objectives Regarding the Protection of Weaker Parties Such as Employees, Consumers Etc.?

Savigny's multilateral PIL approach is the starting point of the European conflict of laws system as we understand it nowadays. EU choice of law rules generally contain abstract connecting factors that link the legal relationship to the jurisdiction that is factually most closely connected (e.g. the place of habitual residence of the parties, the location of the real property etc.). While the original multilateral method is based on neutrality, composed of value-neutral conflict rules, nowadays other principles and doctrines have been added to adapt it to our current legal context. The EU PIL method is defined as 'eclectic method' or 'methodpluralism' since different doctrines and principles live together in the multilateral approach developed by Savigny. However, to which extent are EU objectives behind our current EU PIL approach?

The most important principle regarding the law applicable to contractual obligations is nowadays party autonomy. Party autonomy is the cornerstone of the Rome I Regulation. However, party autonomy is limited in some cases:

- One limitation is provided by article 3(4) Rome I on the benefit of EU mandatory law. Article 3(4) Rome I limits party autonomy with the objective of ensuring the application of EU mandatory law. It is the only provision in the Rome I Regulation with a clear EU-focused objective. Article 3(4) Rome I was introduced with the aim of helping the coordination between the general conflict of laws rules determining the law applicable to the contract and the applicability of EU secondary law. This provision should be able to solve most of the problems encountered within this study regarding the application of EU directives protecting weaker contracting parties. However, it does not. As it has been described, article 3(4) Rome I just ensures the application of EU mandatory rules when parties have chosen the law of a third country and all the relevant elements of the situation are located in the EU (purely intra-EU situations). It has been considered as insufficient to ensure the application of EU mandatory law protecting weaker parties. In cases where article 6 Rome I does not ensure the application of EU consumer directives when necessary or in cases of EU directives regarding other weaker parties, article 3(4) Rome I does not complement those needs. In the case of consumer and employment contracts, if all the elements are located within the EU, the application of the directives is already ensured by the special provisions of articles 6 and 8 Rome I. However, the intended international scope of EU mandatory law is not always exclusively limited to purely intra-EU situations. For example, the scope rules contained in consumer directives or the interpretation of the ECJ in *Ingmar* regarding the Commercial Agents Directive ask for a broader scope of application (closest connection with the EU) of their provisions. Thus, article 3(4) Rome I limits party autonomy in the benefit of EU objectives, constituting a mechanism for fighting abuse of law at EU level, but it is not sufficient to ensure the application of EU mandatory law since it is limited to purely intra-EU situations.

- Party autonomy, as well as the use of the general connecting factors, is also affected by the principle of weaker party protection. Articles 6 and 8 Rome I limit the choice of law of the parties to avoid a possible abuse from the stronger party to the contract. Instead of completely eliminating the possibility to choose the law applicable to the contract, they use the preferential law approach, under which the choice cannot deprive the consumer or employee of the protection provided by the mandatory provisions of the law applicable in the absence of choice. The law applicable in the absence of choice is, in the case of consumer contracts falling under article 6 Rome I, the law of the habitual residence of the consumer and, in the case of individual employment contracts of article 8 Rome I, the law of the habitual place of work (or, if not possible to determine, the law of the country of the place of business through which the employee was engaged) or the law most closely connected to the employment contract. These articles, although making use of a connecting factor that favours the weaker contracting party, still make use of a multilateral PIL method, connecting the abstract legal relationship to a legal system through the connecting factor, regardless of whether it points to the law of the forum or any foreign law. They do not differentiate between national and foreign laws or between Member State law and non-Member State law. Thus, although adapted to the principle of weaker party protection, they are not particularly concerned with EU internal market objectives. The aim of articles 6 and 8 is not 'material' justice but avoiding a potential abuse from the stronger party and to equilibrate the positions of the contract. However, indeed, when the law applicable in the absence of choice of law is the law of a Member State, the application of EU mandatory provisions derived from EU consumer and employment directives is ensured through these articles. The problem lays where those articles do not ensure the application of EU mandatory provisions but they still should or intend to apply to the situation.

In the case of consumer contracts, the main 'gaps' that can be derived from article 6 Rome I are, regarding its material scope, originated on the exceptions of article 6 (4) Rome I and, regarding its territorial scope, 'holiday' consumers or mobile consumers (i.e. a consumer from Member State A who, while on a short stay in Member State B, is approached by a non-Member State company that is targeting its activities to Member State A). The latter are excluded from the protection of article 6 Rome I in case of a choice of a third country law, since the provision incorporates the targeted activity test, and becomes applicable when the professional performs or directs his commercial activities to the country of the habitual residence of the consumer. In those cases, the general conflict rules apply and the application of EU consumer directives is not ensured. However, it is not in line with the objectives of the EU on consumer protection and the correct functioning of the internal market that a consumer from Member State A can lose all the EU consumer law protection just because he is on holiday on Member State B. That is, a Dutch consumer travelling to Spain should enjoy the same minimum EU consumer protection than a Spanish consumer vis-à-vis a non-EU professional, even when the latter does not target the Dutch market. It has been submitted that the effectiveness of EU consumer directives would be threatened if a professional established in a non-Member state could target EU consumers who are temporarily staying in another Member State without complying with EU consumer rights. Thus, instead of incorporating 'scope rules' in EU consumer directives, which bring legal uncertainty to our conflict of laws system, article 6 Rome I should be adapted to the EU objectives involved. I suggest that, in the case of legislation implementing EU consumer directives, the different Member States should be seen as a single jurisdiction: the EU. The specific suggestion involves including a unilateral PIL exception in favour of EU consumer law: whenever a professional directs his activities to a Member State, the application of the minimum requirements of EU consumer directives should be ensured, regardless of the Member State of habitual residence of the consumer. This should be seen as an exception, justified by the importance that consumer law holds for the EU internal market. In my opinion, this exception to the multilateral nature of the provision in favour of an EU objective is justified since the specific conflict of laws issue deriving from the international application of EU directives calls for a special solution. Since the mandatory provisions involved are of EU origin, it follows that the EU can be considered as a single jurisdiction in international cases when referring to the international application of those provisions. The situation 'EU mandatory law vs. foreign country law' can be treated as equal to 'forum mandatory law vs. foreign country law', and thus a choice of foreign law should not result in depriving the EU consumer from the protection granted by EU consumer law. In addition, the legal expectations of the parties are better served since 'holiday consumers' or mobile consumers would enjoy the expected protection when acting within the internal market, and, at the same time, regarding the professional, it can be expected that the EU standards are to be applicable when targeting consumers acting within the EU market.

Regarding the consumers intentionally excluded from article 6 by paragraph 4, it has been discussed that there is a rationale behind this exclusion, according to which the consumer, in general, cannot reasonably expect to have the law of his country of habitual residence to apply. That is the case of active consumers, or of consumer contracts 'for the supply of services where the services are to be supplied to the consumer exclusively in a country other than that in which he has his habitual residence' (e.g. accommodation in a hotel, a language course etc.)—article 6(4)(a). In these cases, the consumer is treated in the same way as the professional since there are no restrictions on the choice of law, for example a case where a Dutch resident enters into a consumer contract for a Spanish language course held in Spain and the contract contains a choice of a foreign non-Member State law and he does not receive the protection of Spanish law nor Dutch law and, as a result, not of EU consumer law. In such a case, the consumer could expect Dutch mandatory law to not be applicable since the Spanish course is completely taking place in Spain, but could he expect that other non-EU laws are applicable to this situation? Again, it can be expected that EU consumer protection is to be applicable when acting within the

EU internal market in such cases. While keeping the material exceptions of article 6 (4) Rome I, since there is a rationale behind them, a more EU approach can be achieved in order to ensure the applicability of EU consumer directives when necessary. As previously explained, article 3(4) Rome I was the provision introduced to ensure the application of EU mandatory law when necessary. However, in the above-mentioned example, it would only ensure the application of the relevant EU consumer provisions when all the elements of the situation are located within the EU. If the company offering the Spanish courses is not established in Spain, for example, article 3(4) Rome I would not apply. If the EU legislator considers that EU directives should also apply to this type of cases, rather than resorting to the mechanism of scope rules in directives or (mis)using a posteriori the mechanism of overriding mandatory rules, it could be considered the introduction of the close connection test that scope rules provided rather than the 'all relevant elements to the situation' requirement in article 3(4) Rome I. This general expression was originally intended to make it possible to take into account the different connections depending on the circumstances of the case. In the directives, the expression 'close connection' or similar in scope rules brings legal uncertainty and inconsistencies since directives are to be transposed into national law and might give rise to as many interpretations as Member States are. In addition, this modification of article 3(4) Rome I would not preclude the application of foreign law but would only ensure the application of EU mandatory law when the situation is most closely connected to the EU, allowing the judge to take into account all the circumstances of the case. It is true that the term close connection is a vague term; however, this limit to party autonomy is just an exception to avoid situations of abuse of law to the detriment of EU mandatory law when the normal operation of the conflict rules of the Rome I Regulation does not produce successful result.

In the case of individual employment contracts, article 8 Rome I ensures in most of the cases the application of the EU employment directives when necessary. Contrarily to article 6 Rome I, article 8 Rome I includes all individual employment contracts. When the place of habitual work is in a Member State, the application of the requirements laid down by the EU employment directives are ensured by article 8 Rome I, which primary connecting factor leads to the place of habitual work of the employee. EU employment directives do not have any interest on being applicable to employees working outside the EU and indeed intend their protection to apply to employees working in the EU. As a result, the generality of EU employment directives and article 8 Rome I on the law applicable to individual employment contracts are coordinated, dealing separately with substantive issues and PIL issues and having as relevant criterion the habitual place of work. The area of EU employment law does not cover as many fields of national law as EU consumer law does and is quite fragmented and mainly composed of minimum harmonisation directives that complement the policies of Member States. Although the majority of EU employment directives in the area of contract law do not contain rules interfering with PIL, it has been discussed during this study that such is not always the case and several issues regarding coordination of article 8 Rome I and EU employment directives still arise. The Acquired Rights Directive aims at preserving employees' rights in the case of a transfer of undertaking and covers also cross-border transfer of undertakings. It contains a 'scope rule' that could affect PIL. However, the law applicable to the employment contract should be determined by the Rome I Regulation regardless of the existence of that rule, which provides for the application of the directive whenever the undertaking, business or part of the undertaking or business to be transferred is located within the EU. The EU legislator should not aim at imposing the application of the directives without regard to the PIL system in force and should be careful with the inclusion of rules such as article 1(2) Acquired Rights Directive referring to the territorial scope of a directive in such a way that might lead to confusion from a PIL perspective. Still, the suitability of article 8 Rome I has been object of discussion on the basis that the habitual place of work changes when the employee is transferred to the new location, and in addition, the fact that when the law applicable is the result of the closest connection escape mechanism of article 8(4) Rome I, the application of the Acquired Rights Directive is not ensured. In this regard, rather than concluding that article 8 Rome I should be adapted to the necessities of the Acquired Rights Directive similarly to the conclusion regarding consumer directives and article 6 Rome I, I consider that the application of the Acquired Rights Directive is ensured by article 8 Rome I when the employee requires that protection. When article 8 Rome I does not ensure the application of the directive because it designates a foreign law as applicable—either because the country of habitual place of work or the country most closely connected is a non-EU country—the only manner that the Acquired Rights Directive would need to apply is not justifiable under employee protection reasons, but it would be because a public interest is at stake in the sense of article 9 Rome I.

Regarding the relationship between article 8 Rome I and the Posted Workers Directive (PWD), article 9 Rome I also plays a role. Article 8 Rome I provides that the habitual place of work is not deemed to have changed when the employee is temporarily posted to another country. In intra-EU postings, the Posted Workers Directive provides that Member States must ensure that the undertakings of the host state guarantee to the posted workers to their territory certain terms and conditions of employment that are laid down in that Member State regarding maximum work periods and minimum rest periods, remuneration, health and safety conditions etc. (article 3(1) PWD). The provisions referred to in article 3(1) PWD, besides ensuring a minimum protection to posted workers, are considered crucial for the safeguard of public interests of the host Member State and of the EU and constitute overriding mandatory provisions of article 9 Rome I. The referred terms and conditions are of immediate interest during the period of posting since they are essential to ensuring fair competition and the fundamental freedom of provision of services within the EU. Article 3(1) PWD determines the overriding mandatory character and scope of specific rules. In the case of temporary posting of workers, articles 6 Rome I, 9 Rome I and the Posted Workers Directive complement each other to determine the law applicable to the employment contract.

Concerning other weaker contracting parties, article 5(2) Rome I, regarding contracts for the carriage of passengers, and article 7 Rome I, regarding insurance contracts, also limit party autonomy but in a way that only allows the choice of a law that has some connection with the contract. In these contracts, the choice of law is limited to a number of legal systems that are connected with the contract or the parties of the contract, hence requiring the existence of a qualified link between the contract and the law chosen. In the case of article 5(2) Rome I, concerning contracts for the carriage of passengers, parties can choose among the law of the country where the passenger has his habitual residence, the carrier has his habitual residence, the carrier has his place of central administration, the place of departure is located or the place of destination is located. This provision allows the carrier to choose the law of his place of residence or central administration, avoiding the application of many different laws depending on the passengers, but the level of protection offered by the limit on party autonomy only ensures that the carrier does not deliberately choose a non-related law with a very low level of consumer protection. The application of a minimum level of protection to passengers is not ensured through this provision. Article 5(2) Rome I was not drafted in coordination with the different EU secondary instruments on carriage of passengers. However, it does not have such an impact since a big number of international conventions and EU Regulations regarding the carriage of passengers precede the application of article 5(2) Rome I. As a result, article 5(2) Rome I only applies when there is a gap not covered by those international conventions or EU regulations. Most of the EU legislation regarding carriage of passengers is laid down in regulations and thus is applicable in a uniform way in all Member States. In intra-EU scenarios, it is not relevant which Member State law is applicable since the unified protection offered by the regulation is applied by all Member States laws. However, the level of protection offered by the conflict rules is relevant when there is a choice of law of a non-Member State or when the carrier is established in a non-Member State. In the case of the Regulation on Rail Passengers Rights and Obligations (1371/2007),[1] article 4 contains a unilateral conflict rule, according to which the conclusion and performance of a transport contract is not to be decided according to the rules of a Member State based on external PIL rules, but it is to be decided according to the provisions of Title II and Title III of Annex I to the Regulation. This conflict rule prevails over article 5(2) Rome I, according to article 23 Rome I. On the other hand, the Airline Passengers Regulation (261/2004)[2] does not prevail over article 5 Rome I through article 23 Rome I because it does not contain a conflict rule as such. Thus, the way to ensure the application of the Regulation in the scenarios defined by its scope rule is through article 9 Rome I, provided that the provisions of the Regulation fall under the definition of overriding mandatory rules (i.e. essential for the safeguarding of a public interest (of the EU in this case)).

[1]Regulation (EC) No 1371/2007 of the European Parliament and of the Council of 23 October 2007 on rail passengers' rights and obligations (OJ 2007 L 315/14).

[2]Regulation (EC) No 261/2004 of the European Parliament and of the Council of 11 February 2004 establishing common rules on compensation and assistance to passengers in the event of denied boarding and of cancellation or long delay of flights, and repealing Regulation (EEC) No 295/91 (OJ 2004 L 46/1).

In the case of insurance contracts, a complex provision was introduced in the Rome I Regulation in order to incorporate the conflict rules previously scattered in several EU insurance directives. Article 7 Rome I was drafted in coordination with the existent EU insurance directives and prevails over the conflict rules of EU insurance directives. Article 7 Rome I provides for three different levels of protection with different limits to party autonomy and special conflict rules in the absence of choice. For example, the type of contracts where the policyholder can be in a weaker contractual provision (i.e. mass risks, which are a category that might involve business-to-consumer (B2C) as well as business-to-business (B2B) contracts since customers insuring smaller risks are more likely to be small businesses or private persons, which find themselves in a weaker contractual position) are regulated by article 7(3) only when the risk is located in the EU, which only allows the choice of several Member State laws related to the contract or the law of the country of the habitual residence of the policyholder. Therefore, it offers enough protection to the policyholder in a weaker contractual position. In case the risk is not located in a Member State, the general provisions of the Rome I Regulation apply (articles 3, 4 and, exceptionally, 6 Rome I in the case of an insurance B2C contract falling under the requirements of article 6 Rome I). Article 3 or 4 Rome I can lead to the application of a non-Member State law, and thus in those cases it is considered that rules of the respective directive do not need to apply. The rules are complex but coordinated. Despite article 7 Rome I being subject to criticism due to the complexity of its conflict rules, the rule is the result of a 'complex compromise', reflecting the requirements of the EU directives and bringing more legal certainty to the law applicable to insurance contracts.

- Another limit to party autonomy, and at the same time a big exception to the multilateral PIL system, is the already mentioned article 9 Rome I with the doctrine of overriding mandatory rules. The doctrine of overriding mandatory rules constitutes an expression of unilateralism in our PIL system: provisions qualified as overriding mandatory are applicable regardless of the law chosen by the parties and regardless of the law objectively applicable to the contract. Overriding mandatory rules are applicable according to their object and purpose. Based on their content and purpose, they unilaterally determine their own applicability. And their object and purpose, in order to be considered overriding mandatory, has to be regarded as essential by a country for the safeguard of its public interests, such as its political, social or economic organisation. That means that, first, overriding mandatory rules fix their own scope of application (implicitly or explicitly); second, their application and scope derive from their nature and purpose, which aims at protecting essential public interests; and, third, that purpose justifies their overriding mandatory character and need to derogate from the general conflict rules. Internal market objectives can be ensured through overriding mandatory rules when essential for the safeguard of EU public interests. The EU's interest has to be regarded as essential for the safeguard of a public interest, such as the political, social or economic organisation of the EU.

However, EU objectives regarding the protection of weaker parties such as employees, consumers etc. should not be ensured through article 9 Rome I. The doctrine and courts of different Member States vary as regards their understanding of overriding mandatory rules. While countries such as Germany have traditionally followed a restrictive interpretation under which overriding mandatory rules deal exclusively with public interests and, as a result, rules protecting weaker parties are completely excluded from this category, other countries such as France follow the opposite trend, under which rules protecting weaker parties can easily fall under the category of overriding mandatory rules.[3] However, it is submitted that regardless of the different traditional understandings of the Member States, when talking about EU interest, a common approach should be followed. Following the ECJ position, based on the decision in *Ingmar*, it can be understood that article 9 Rome I will also include those provisions that, although protecting a structural weaker party, mainly serve to protect higher interests, which are so essential that their priority over the law chosen by the parties is justified, including significant EU interests. Following this line of reasoning, a provision that only aims to protect a weaker party would not be considered as an overriding mandatory rule, but it definitely could be as long as it also aims to promote a higher political, social or economic interest which justifies the priority of this provision in an international scenario.[4] Therefore, although article 9 Rome I refers to public interests, it does not lead a priori to the exclusion of all protective rules. This view seems to be supported by the European legislator, which also provides overriding mandatory character to provisions protecting the weaker party in certain EU directives (e.g. Posted Workers Directive). Therefore, the tendency of the EU is to accept that rules aimed at the protection of weaker parties can also qualify as overriding mandatory rules. Nevertheless, again, this does not mean that all protective rules can have such a character, but only when it is regarded as crucial for the safeguarding of the country's interests. The rule must have a dual purpose: the protection of weaker parties plus the promotion of public interests.

This extensive approach for the meaning of article 9 Rome I leaves enough autonomy to the legislators and courts of the Member States to determine their own crucial interests. However, Member States have to restraint themselves when considering provisions as essential for public interest. Otherwise, the meaning of article 9 Rome I would be undermined. For the sake of the legal security of the parties to the contract and for the legal predictability regarding the law applicable to a contract, the application of overriding mandatory provisions has to be justified on the strict definition of article 9(1) Rome I. In order to determine whether the provisions of an EU directive are aimed at protecting public interests, a restrictive interpretation is defended since, to some extent, all EU legislation is aimed at the

---

[3]These two countries represent the two extremes in the position, and in the middle we find countries such as Spain or Belgium with a similar approach to the French or the Netherlands with a more restrictive approach closer to the German view.

[4]Many authors follow this position. For example, among others, Kuipers (2012), p. 200; Aguilar Grieder (2006), p. 53; Carrascosa González (2012); Verhagen (2002), p. 136.

proper functioning of the internal market. Most of the provisions of EU consumer and employment directives are mandatory provisions since they aim at the protection of weaker parties, but not overriding mandatory norms since they are not essential for the protection of a public EU interest. In addition, that overriding mandatory character should only have effect regarding the application of a non-Member State law since in an intra-EU conflict where the law of a different Member State is applicable, the minimum protection of the directive (which would be the one considered overriding mandatory) would be ensured by the national transposition of the Member State.

Therefore, article 9 Rome I is a mechanism that Member States enjoy in order to ensure the application of national provisions or provisions originated in EU law and, as such, is a mechanism that serves the needs of the internal market in order to protect possible public interests involved. However, it is not a mechanism designed for the protection of weaker contracting parties. It can accidentally serve the objective of weaker party protection but only when the provision at stake is primarily aimed at serving a public interest (e.g. fair competition in the internal market, ensuring freedom of provision of services etc.). It is concluded that provisions deriving from EU directives protecting weaker contracting parties do not have, as a general rule, an overriding mandatory character. In my opinion, they usually have the character of provisions that cannot be derogated from by agreement in the sense of article 3(3), 3(4), 6 or 8 Rome I. However, if exceptionally a specific (implemented) directive provision mainly serves public interests, its qualification as an overriding mandatory provision in the sense of article 9 is not excluded.

Finally, the Rome I Regulation provides in its article 23 that, 'with the exception of Article 7, this Regulation shall not prejudice the application of provisions of Community law which, in relation to particular matters, lay down conflict-of-law rules relating to contractual obligations'. This provision intends to coordinate the Rome I Regulation with other EU law providing for conflict rules in particular matters and establishes the priority of the existent specific conflict rules of EU law instruments on specific matters over those of the Rome I Regulation.

7.2 When and How Should PIL Ensure the Applicability of EU Directives on Weaker Party Protection?

During this study, the international applicability of EU directives on weaker party protection has been thoroughly discussed. EU directives are a different legal instrument than which PIL is traditionally used to, especially because, to be applicable, their provisions have to be transposed into the national law of the Member States, and due to the minimum harmonisation technique, this transposition differs from one Member State to another. Thus, there is a common EU standard vs. foreign law and different Member State laws improving or just equalling that standard. Therefore, their international applicability has to be clarified.

First, in order to answer when PIL should ensure the applicability of EU directives on weaker party protection, certain reflexions regarding the application of foreign law are made. The traditional approach of PIL, since Savigny and until nowadays, has been to solve a conflict of laws from the point of view of the legal relationship with a neutral conflict rule that would find the legal systems most closely connected to the legal relationship. In that manner, international harmony of decisions would be achieved, meaning that the outcome would be the same regardless of the jurisdiction where the proceedings were brought, which would prevent limping legal relationships and would promote legal certainty. Nowadays, the prevention of forum shopping seems to be a principal aim. Therefore, the application of foreign law by the forum becomes beneficial. Conflict rules should definitely promote the equality between the different national legal systems through neutral conflict rules. Neutral conflict rules, as well as the principle of party autonomy, generally respect the legal expectations of the parties and promote legal certainty. However, several aspects need to be taken into account regarding the application of foreign law.

Firstly, the more the countries are interrelated, the more legal values they would share and, therefore, the more eager they would be to use neutral conflict rules, regardless of whether the law applicable is national law or foreign law. However, in the opposite case, the more the countries do not share basic values or legal principles, the more the application of foreign law becomes difficult or undesirable (scale of Ten Wolde).[5]

Secondly, the applicability of foreign law varies depending on the area of law. In our case, contract law is a mostly value-free area where the free will of the parties prevails, and as a result, the existence of common principles among the countries involved does not seem to be so relevant as compared to other fields of law, such as family law. However, within contract law there are still values that the law of the forum might need to protect against the application of a foreign law (e.g. weaker party protective rules or public interests). When talking about rules with mandatory character in the areas of contract law that aim to protect contractual weaker parties, the state needs to protect these values, and thus the state is more reluctant to the application of foreign law, aiming to ensure these values of the forum state when necessary. In the case of overriding mandatory rules, essential for the organisation of the state, the forum state would like to ensure the application of these rules unconditionally.

Finally, the special situation of the EU must be taken into account. The EU needs to ensure the correct functioning of the internal market and the achievement of the Area of Justice. While in intra-EU situations between Member States similar legal values are shared, especially in the harmonised areas covered by EU directives, the

[5]Ten Wolde compared this phenomenon to a sliding scale, where in one end of the scale the country would apply exclusively the forum law because the countries involved lacked relationship between them, while on the opposite end of the scale the countries would be neutral regarding the application of forum law or foreign law, since the relationship between the societies is so close that same or similar legal values are shared. Ten Wolde (2013), p. 576.

EU might want to ensure these common values against the application of a foreign (non-Member State) law.

During this study, a separate analysis of the application of consumer, employment and other weaker parties' directives has been conducted. Now, a common reflexion about their applicability will be made.

First, I would like to make a brief reference to the introduction of scope rules in the directives to ensure their application in international situations. Only some specific EU consumer directives contain what we refer to as 'scope rules' from a PIL perspective. EU employment directives are mostly silent in this regard, while article 1(2) Acquired Rights Directive is not the same type of scope rule—it only refers to the territorial scope of the instrument—and article 3 Posted Workers Directive is a rule determining the overriding mandatory character of the provisions referred to in it. The rules contained in the insurance directives, over which article 7 Rome I has now priority, were conflict rules as such. Of all of this type of rules, the most problematic from a PIL point of view are the so-called scope rules, as the ones contained in some EU consumer directives. The introduction of this type of rules was justified on the ground of special needs derived from EU sectorial directives. The correct functioning of the internal market as an objective served as a justification for the introduction of scope rules as a mechanism to originally supplement and fill in the gaps of the Rome Convention in that regard. Sometimes, it is necessary that all market participants are subject to the same rules, which means that EU secondary law should define its spatial scope of application. However, I have already discussed that the introduction of scope rules in directives is not desirable for our EU conflict of laws system. First, there is uncertainty around the specific nature and function of these rules, and regarding their interaction with the Rome I Regulation. Authors do not agree whether these rules prevail over the Rome I Regulation as conflict rules or not. Second, the fact that they have to be implemented into the different national laws of Member States might result in as many conflict of laws rules as Member States are. Vagueness in their drafting causes a difficult and possible diverse implementation in the national law of the Member States. Moreover, they result in a disruption of the EU conflict of laws system based on the Rome I Regulation regarding contractual obligations, affecting the existent unified system. Unified conflict rules prevent forum shopping and enhance legal certainty within the EU. Legal uncertainty is promoted when rules somehow affecting conflict of laws are dispersed in different instruments (in this regard, as recital 40 Rome I states, 'a situation where conflict-of-law rules are dispersed among several instruments and where there are differences between those rules should be avoided'). Thus, I consider that scope rules in directives bring more disadvantages to our conflict of laws system and ultimately will not be serving the internal market, the area of justice and the interests of the weaker parties. In case a directive, because of the speciality of the area covered by it, needs a specific conflict rule different from the ones provided in the Rome I Regulation, it can exceptionally include a specific conflict rule that would prevail over the Rome I Regulation, according to article 23 Rome I. However, in general, the law applicable should be determined by the Rome I Regulation, which, if necessary, should adapt its provisions to the special needs of the EU directives protecting weaker parties.

Second, the possibility of determining the application of EU directives protecting weaker parties using a PIL unilateral approach has been repeatedly discussed during this study. The existence of scope rules in the consumer directives has brought back the discussion regarding the PIL method and the possibility of changing our current PIL method towards a unilateral approach regarding the applicability of EU directives. Since following unilateral approach directives determine their own scope of application and international applicability, the application of their EU mandatory provisions would be ensured in an international situation. According to a unilateral PIL approach, the legal instrument, in this case the directive, determines its own territorial scope of application according to its purpose and nature. The use of a unilateral PIL approach can be seen as a more pragmatic manner of ensuring that the aims of the directives protecting weaker contracting parties are fulfilled since their provisions are applicable in an international situation when required by the same directive. However, the directive would only determine its own application without referring to foreign law. A unilateral PIL method is a forum-centred approach that does not consider the application of foreign law. As a result, it can happen that conflicts are created when two or more legal orders claim application to the situation and when none of them does. But besides the general disadvantages of a unilateral method, other drawbacks arise if we were to use this approach to determine the application of EU directives autonomously. First, the EU legislator should not systematically impose its law over foreign law. It is inconsistent to maintain that EU law depends on its own applicability criteria and imposes its application and at the same time to ignore that foreign law might do the same. While the principle of supremacy applies to relationships between national Member States law and EU law, when a foreign law comes into play, the EU is not the only sovereign. Second, legal certainty is not promoted since, instead of defining the circumstances under which a Member State law applies and under which foreign law applies, it would only be determined when EU law applies. Also, the exercise of finding the purpose of the legal act is a burdensome task and adds uncertainty to the process. In this regard, as previously explained, a multilateral approach promotes legal certainty and respects the legal expectations of the parties. In addition, the directive must be implemented in the national law of the Member States, leading to possible different understandings and interpretations regarding the scope of the instrument. In my opinion, determining the application of the EU directives protecting weaker contracting parties through a unilateral PIL approach systematically and individually would result in a protectionist system that imposes the application of its law over foreign law, contradictory with the current PIL approach and which brings more disadvantages as compared to a multilateral approach.

Following the current multilateral-eclectic EU PIL approach, directives are applicable when the national law of a Member State is applicable, either because it is a purely internal situation or, in a cross-border situation, as a result of the conflict rules of the Rome I Regulation. In our current EU PIL approach, it is understood that if a law has been determined as applicable by the conflict rules, then the statutes of that legal system apply to the situation when the situation at hand falls within the scope of application of the statute in question. That is, the national judge, when a situation involves cross-border elements, is expected to follow the forum conflict rules that will point to the applicable law rather than apply a statute of the forum without previously resorting to the conflict rules. In the case of a cross-border consumer contract, individual employment contract or other contracts involving a weaker party, the forum judge will determine the law applicable to the contract in accordance with the provisions of the Rome I Regulation. Then when the case regards any of the areas regulated by an EU directive, the application of the EU directive is ensured through the application of the determined Member State law, which has implemented (and maybe improved) the terms and conditions required by the directive. Since directives only become applicable when the Rome I Regulation determines as applicable the law of a Member State, the achievement of the objectives and the international application of the directives depends on whether the Rome I Regulation is effectively coordinated with those EU objectives when necessary, hence the importance of interaction and coordination between these instruments.

Therefore, I consider that the application of the EU directives should be determined through the available conflict rules of the Rome I Regulation (subject to certain changes).

7.3 Are the Current EU PIL Conflict of Laws Rules and PIL Method Adequate to Ensure the EU Objectives Regarding Weaker Contracting Parties, or Is There a Call for a Different PIL Method?

As it is known, our current PIL method, as shown in the Rome I Regulation, is mostly based on multilateral conflict rules. The main unilateral exception is the application of overriding mandatory rules. However, we have concluded that overriding mandatory provisions are not a tool per se for the protection of weaker contracting parties. While special conflict rules are provided for the protection of certain weaker parties, limiting party autonomy and providing for special connecting factors, they do not always ensure the application of EU directives when expected. That can be either because the specific conflict rule does not take into account the existence of EU mandatory law or because there are no special conflict rules for some specific weaker parties for which EU directives provide protection. As it has been described above in answer to the first question 'how do traditional principles of conflict of laws relate to the requirements of the internal market for the realisation of the EU objectives regarding the protection of weaker parties such as employees, consumers etc.?', some changes should be introduced in order to ensure the application of the directives when necessary through the Rome I Regulation. In answer to the second research question above, it was indeed concluded that a mostly multilateral system, and specifically the Rome I Regulation as a unified PIL instrument, is preferable to determine the applicability of the provisions of EU directives in comparison to a unilateral PIL approach. The main specific suggestions include the following:

(1) Eliminate scope rules that are spread around some EU consumer directives and refer the conflict of laws question to the Rome I Regulation. Also, avoid the inclusion of rules referring to the territorial scope of a directive drafted in a manner that can be confusing from a PIL point of view, such as article 1 (2) Acquired Rights Directives, since Member States might understand them and implement them in the same way as scope rules or conflict of laws rules.
(2) Adapt article 6 Rome I and article 3(4) Rome I to the requirements of the EU legislator regarding the international application of the EU consumer directives.

Article 6 Rome I shall provide that whenever a professional directs his activities to a Member State, the application of the minimum requirements of EU consumer directives should be ensured, regardless of the Member State of habitual residence of the consumer. The text proposal regarding article 6 Rome I includes the addition of a new text placed following paragraph 3. The new paragraph would read:

> (3) If the requirements in points (a) or (b) of paragraph 1 are not fulfilled, the law applicable to a contract between a consumer and a professional shall be determined pursuant to Articles 3 and 4. *However, when a professional residing in a non-Member State directs his commercial or professional activities to one or more Member States, the choice of law of a non-Member State as the law applicable to a contract falling into the scope of such activities does not deprive a consumer habitually resident in a Member State of the protection afforded by the relevant Directive, which would be applicable as implemented by the law of the Member State in which the consumer concluded the contract.*

In addition, if article 3(4) Rome I is adapted as to include the 'closest connection' connecting factor similar to scope rules, it will also ensure the application of EU mandatory rules deriving from directives protecting other weaker contracting parties against the choice of a third country law, as required by scope rules. Such a rule would also reflect the ECJ decision in *Ingmar* regarding the scope of application of the Commercial Agents Directive, although that scope is justified by the overriding mandatory nature of the provisions rather than by the protection on weaker parties, and it would be the same without the modification of article 3(4). The modification of article 3(4) Rome I would only be necessary if the EU legislator still considers that the international application of EU directives protecting weaker parties should be ensured when the situation is closely connected to the EU, giving up some legal certainty to adapt to the specific circumstances of the case. It is an important adaptation of PIL towards EU objectives since it involves the limitation of the important principle of party autonomy to ensure the application of EU mandatory provisions. Although it can be criticised as giving up some legal certainty of our PIL system, it is a better alternative than trying to use article 9 Rome I and the doctrine of overriding mandatory rules to ensure the application of these rules through a too extensive interpretation of public interests and overriding mandatory provisions.

The text proposal includes a substitution of the current article 3(4) Rome I for the following text:

> *When the contract has a closest connection to the territory of the Member States, the parties' choice of applicable law other than that of a Member State shall not prejudice the application of provisions of Community law, where appropriate as implemented in the Member State of the forum, which cannot be derogated from by agreement.*

(3) Article 9 Rome I includes a definition of overriding mandatory rules that should be respected and interpreted restrictively. Article 9 Rome I is an exception to all the other conflict rules of the Regulation when essential public interests of the Member State in question are at stake. Protection of weaker contracting parties is not a public interest as such, and Member States should not extend the interpretation of 'public interest' as to justify the application of weaker party protection provisions or other provisions they just wish to apply. Provisions protecting weaker parties can only be applicable through article 9 Rome I when the main purpose of the application of the provision is to protect a public interest of the country (e.g. in the case of the Posted Workers Directive, the application of the employment provisions referred to in article 3 PWD are essential to ensuring fair competition within the internal market).

The suggested changes are a short-term reflexion of the following proposed EU PIL approach.

First, within the EU, the unification of EU PIL is desirable. By having common conflict rules determining the law applicable to cross-border contracts codified in the Rome I Regulation, the success of the area of justice, the mutual recognition and enforcement of decisions within the EU, as well as decisional harmony and prevention of forum shopping are promoted. Only when an EU instrument deals with a very specific area that requires the introduction of a very specific conflict rule that an exception can be made.

Regarding the PIL method, the multilateral approach, together with the party autonomy principle, should be, and currently is, the basis. It has been submitted that, in general, a multilateral PIL method brings more advantages than a unilateral approach: legal certainty, legal expectations of the parties and prevention of forum shopping are better promoted though a multilateral PIL method. On the other hand, throughout party autonomy, the parties create the appropriate legal framework for the development of their activities, endowing at the same time their legal relationship with legal certainty, predictability and economic efficiency and adapting their behaviour to that chosen law. As a consequence, international trade becomes more attractive, and international harmony of decisions, by making sure that every court will decide upon the chosen law, is also promoted.

However, methodological purity is not realistic nor desirable. In fact, contemporary conflict of laws systems are not purely multilateral or purely unilateral. Both methods should be understood not as opposite but as a complement to each other, which combined together might produce a better PIL system. The question lies in how this combination should be and which principles or guidelines should be taken into account in order to design that combination. There are several situations that require the use of a unilateral approach and the limit of party autonomy. It has already been submitted that the main factors to take into account when restraining the application of foreign law are the importance of the legal interests involved and the interrelationship between the countries. Regarding the legal interests involved, contract law is an area of law characterised by party autonomy since it is a mostly value-free area. A multilateral approach is preferred since the legal expectations of the parties and legal certainty should prevail over the country's interest to have its own national law applied. However, in our case, we are dealing with contracts involving consumers, employees and other weaker parties. National instruments on consumer and employee protection are usually mandatory contract law (parties cannot change it by agreement, and thus freedom of contract is limited) and differ among states. When the national legislator enacts consumer law or employment law protecting consumers or employees from an abuse of contractual freedom, the substantive rights established in the form of national mandatory law should also be protected in some cross-border situations.

It has been previously said that the more the countries are interrelated, the more legal values they would share and, therefore, the more eager they would be to use neutral conflict rules. Then the use of a multilateral method is preferred. Since contract law is a mostly value-free area, the interrelationship between the countries—and the legal values involved—loses importance and the use of a multilateral method is generally promoted. However, in the specific field of protection of consumers, employees and other weaker contracting parties, where there are national legal values involved, the interrelationship between the countries gains more importance. Thus, a neutral multilateral approach and party autonomy have to be restricted. The Rome I Regulation, so far, reflects this approach.

However, the Rome I Regulation does not sufficiently take into account the specialties deriving from the existence of the EU and an internal market, both regarding the existence of EU legal values and EU mandatory law and regarding the interrelationship between Member States and non-Member States. The existence of the EU modifies the approach towards the legal values involved and the interrelationship between the countries. Not only a national perspective towards the application of foreign law is to be followed, but an EU perspective towards the application of non-EU law has to be added. Therefore, in addition to the current approach, a difference between intra-EU situations and extra-EU situations has to be reflected. Member States, especially in the areas harmonised by the EU directives, share the same legal values. For example, in the area of EU consumer law, Member States share the same minimum level of consumer protection. A multilateral approach is then promoted in an intra-EU scenario, although, since the majority of the directives on weaker party protection are of a minimum harmonising nature and small differences still exist between Member States, the neutral multilateral approach and party autonomy can be restricted to a certain point if desired to take into account national interests. In an extra-EU scenario, when the application of the EU mandatory law deriving from the relevant directives is at stake, the use of a unilateral approach and the restriction of party autonomy can be justified. There are EU interests involved that the EU wishes to protect—although to a lesser extent than public interests—against the application of an eventual non-related and very different foreign law.

For example, in the area of consumer contracts, in which numerous EU directives conform with EU consumer law, a minimum EU consumer protection standard exists. EU consumer law is an important area for the EU internal market, and the application of its mandatory rules needs to be ascertained in certain situations to ensure the well functioning of the market at both economic and social levels. A unilateral conflict rule would ensure the application of EU consumer directives, when necessary, against the possible application of a foreign law with eventual different legal values (e.g. no consumer protection). As suggested above, a specific unilateral conflict rule regarding consumer directives and EU mandatory consumer law, in addition to the current protective multilateral rule, is necessary. The principal condition for the application of the protective conflict rule for consumers is when the professional directs its activities to the country of habitual residence of the consumer. At the EU level, therefore, it should be added that when the professional directs its activities to one or more Member States, the application of the relevant EU consumer directives should be ensured.

It is true that the area of EU consumer law is one of the most harmonised areas in the EU and hence is in need of special attention. Regarding other weaker parties, the same reasoning is to be followed, and a distinction between intra-EU and extra-EU situations, when the application of the relevant EU directives containing mandatory rules is at stake, should be reflected in the instrument. In the case of individual employment contracts, employment law in the EU is less harmonised than consumer law, and national values are still very important. The connecting factor used in the protective conflict rule leads to the law of the country of habitual place of employment of the employee. In an intra-EU situation, this protective multilateral conflict rule and the limit on party autonomy ensure the application of the mandatory rules of the national law interested in applying it (i.e. country where the employee habitually works). If the habitual place of work is a Member State, regardless of the existence of other non-EU elements, the application of the minimum EU employee protection provisions is generally ensured. Normally, EU employment provisions do not have any interest in applying to situations where the employee has its habitual place of work outside of the EU, and, as a result, the existent protective conflict rule seems sufficient by now.

Still, a unilateral approach similar to the case of EU consumer directives could be included: when the worker has its habitual place of work within the EU, the application of EU mandatory law derived from EU employment directives should be ensured. The introduction of this rule would not change much the current situation. It would just have an impact on the cases where the employment contract is most closely connected to a non-Member State, but the employee still has its habitual place of work in a Member State. However, in such cases, it is doubtful that the EU would have a true interest in applying EU mandatory employment law. Another possibility would then ensure the applicability when the habitual place of work is in the EU and the contract is closely connected to the EU. Still, this rule, in the level of harmonisation of EU employment law we are now, does not seem necessary yet.

Regarding other weaker parties that do not receive as much protection as do consumers and employees, principally because they are not always in a weaker contracting position but regarding which there are EU directives with EU mandatory provisions, a more general conflict rule with a unilateral approach to ensure their application in extra-EU situations can be provided. Thus, in order to ensure the application of EU mandatory law, such as the one deriving from other directives protecting other weaker parties, in extra-EU situations, a common general and more flexible conflict rule can be introduced. The suggested modification of article 3 (4) Rome I, according to which the EU mandatory provisions deriving from EU secondary law are applicable if there is a closest connection with the territory of the Member States regardless of the law chosen by the parties, would ensure the protection of EU mandatory law protecting other weaker parties. This provision constitutes a unilateral inroad and a limit to party autonomy. This approach reflects the line followed by the EU legislator in the scope rules of EU consumer directives and by the ECJ in the *Ingmar* judgment.[6] The possibility of making it applicable regardless of the law otherwise applicable, rather than just limiting its application to when there is a choice of law, can also be considered. This second option would indeed constitute a more protective approach, and thus the choice depends on the intentions of the EU legislator. For example, in the case of a commercial agent with habitual residence in Turkey, which works for a Belgian principal and performs its activities within the EU, the law applicable in the absence of choice would be Turkish law. The protective provisions of the Commercial Agent Directive (setting aside for a moment the decision of the ECJ in *Ingmar*) would only apply in this case following the second option since there is no choice of law. Or in the case of an active consumer with habitual residence in a Member State contracting with a non-EU professional from a Member State, the law applicable to the contract would be a non-Member State law (e.g. a Dutch consumer finding some sports shoes on a Chinese website of a Chinese company and, with the help of a Chinese friend to translate and make the transaction, concludes a contract). If the EU legislator aims to apply EU mandatory law in those cases, then the second aforementioned option should be followed. However, in my opinion, that approach seems a step too far, and the EU mandatory rules are more than sufficiently ensured in an international situation when they are applicable when the situation is closely

[6]Although in the *Ingmar* judgment the ECJ justified the application of the Commercial Agents Directive on the objectives of freedom of establishment and undistorted competition (EU public interests), falling under the category of overriding mandatory rules.

connected to the EU and the parties have chosen a non-Member State law as applicable to their contract (but the law otherwise applicable would have ensured the application of the relevant EU mandatory law).

Therefore, I conclude that a more EU-focused PIL method is necessary, but still respecting the current multilateral basis and party autonomy. To the current PIL approach followed by the Rome I Regulation, a difference between intra-EU and extra-EU situations regarding the application of EU directives protecting weaker contracting parties and involving EU mandatory law should be made. Regarding EU mandatory law on weaker party protection, in intra-EU situations a multilateral approach is promoted while, in extra-EU situations, the introduction of a unilateral inroad and limitation of party autonomy are justified. The more harmonised, as well as mandatory, an area of law is, such as EU consumer law, the more necessary and evident should the differentiation be.

References

Aguilar Grieder H (2006) La Voluntad de Conciliación con las Directivas Comunitarias Protectoras en la Propuesta del Reglamento Roma I. In: La Unión Europea ante el Derecho de la Globalización. Colex, Madrid, pp 45–61

Carrascosa González J (2012) La Autonomía de la Voluntad Conflictual y la Mano Invisible en la Contratación Internacional. Diario La Ley 7847

Kuipers J-J (2012) EU law and private international law: the interrelationship in contractual obligations. Martinus Nijhoff Publishers, Leiden

Ten Wolde MH (2013) The relativity of legal positions in cross-border situations: the foundations of private interregional law, private intra-community law and private international law. In: A commitment to private international law- essays in honour of Hans van Loon. Intersentia, Cambridge, pp 569–581

Verhagen HLE (2002) The tension between party autonomy and European Union law: some observations on IngmarGB Ltd v Eaton Leonard Technologies Inc. Int Comp Law Q 51:135–154

Table of Cases

European Court of Justice (ECJ)

Case C-815/18 *Federatie Nederlandse Vakbeweging v Van den Bosch Transporten BV, Van den Bosch Transporte GmbH, Silo-Tank kft*, Opinion of the Advocate General Bobek [2020] ECLI:EU:C:2020:319

Case C-208/18 *Jana Petruchová v FIBO Group Holdings Limited* [2019] ECLI:EU:C:2019:825

Case C-498/16 *Maximilian Schrems v Facebook Ireland Limited* [2018] ECLI:EU:C:2018:37

Case C-507/15 *Agro Foreign Trade & Agency Ltd* v *Petersime NV* [2017] ECLI:EU:C:2017:129

Joined Cases C-168/16 and C-169/16 *Sandra Nogueira and Others v Crewlink Ireland Ltd and Miguel José Moreno Osacar v Ryanair Designated Activity Company* [2017] ECLI:EU:C:2017:688

Case C-135/15 *Republik Griechenland v Grigorios Nikiforidis* [2016] ECLI:EU:C:2016:774

Case C-191/15 *Verein für Konsumenteninformation v Amazon EU Sàrl* [2016] ECLI:EU:C:2016:612

Case C-413/13 *FNV Kunsten Informatie en Media v* Staat der Nederland [2014] ECLI:EU:C:2014:2411

Case C-413/13 *FNV Kunsten Informatie en Media v* Staat der Nederland [2014], Opinion AG Wahl ECLI:EU:C:2014:2215

Case C-26/13 *Árpád Kásler and Hajnalka Káslerné Rábai v OTP Jelzálogbank Zrt* [2014] ECLI:EU:C:2014:282

Case C-508/12 *Walter Vapenik v Josef Thurner* [2013] ECLI:EU:C:2013:790

Case C-218/12 *Lokman Emrek v Vlado Sabranovic* [2013] ECLI:EU:C:2013:666

Case C-184/12 *United Antwerp Maritime Agencies (Unamar) NV v Navigation Maritime Bulgare* [2013] ECLI:EU:C:2013:663

M. Campo Comba, *The Law Applicable to Cross-border Contracts involving Weaker Parties in EU Private International Law*,
https://doi.org/10.1007/978-3-030-61481-2

Case C-64/12 *Anton Schlecker v Melitta Josefa Boedeker* [2013] ECLI:EU:C:2013:551

Case C-64/12 *Anton Schlecker v Melita Josefa Boedeker*, Opinion of Advocate General Wahl [2013] ECLI:EU:C:2013:241

Case C-190/11 *Daniela Mühlleitner v Ahmad Yusufi and Wadat Yusufi* [2012] ECLI:EU:C:2012:542

Case C-29/10 *Heiko Koelzsch v État* du *Grand Duchy* of *Luxemburg* [2011] ECR I-01595

Case C-384/10 *Jan Voogsgeerd v Navimer SA* [2011] ECR I-13275

Joined Cases C-585/08 *Peter Pammer v Reederei Karl Schlüter GmbH & Co. KG* and C-144/09 *Hotel Alpenhof GesmbH v Oliver Heller* [2010] ECR I-12527

Case C-533/07 *Falco Privatstiftung and Thomas Rabitsch v Gisela Weller-Lindhorst* [2009] ECR I-03327

Case C-243/08 *Pannon GSM Zrt. v Erzsébet Sustikné Győrfi* [2009] ECR I- 04713

Case C-438/05 *International Transport Workers' Federation and Finnish Seamen's Union v Viking Line ABP and OÜ Viking Line Eesti* [2008] ECR I-10779

Case C-346/06, *Dirk Rüffert v Land Niedersachsen* [2008] ECR I-01989

Case C-319/06 *Commission of the European Communities v Grand Duchy of Luxemburg* [2008] ECR I-04323

Case C-341/05, *Laval un Partneri Ltd v Svenska Byggnadsarbetareförbundet* [2007] ECR I-11767

Case C-341/05, *Laval un Partneri Ltd v Svenska Byggnadsarbetareförbundet*, Opinion Advocate General Mengozzi [2007] ECR I-11772

Case C-168/05 *Elisa María Mostaza Claro v Centro Móvil Milenium SL* [2006] ECR I-10421

Case C-464/01 *Gruber v Bay Wa AG* [2005] ECR I-439

Case C-256/01 *Debra Allonby v Accrington & Rosendale College et al.* [2004] ECR I-873

Case C-70/03 *Commission of the European Communities v Kingdom of Spain* [2004] ECR I-9657

Case C-334/00 *Fonderie Officine Meccaniche Tacconi SpA v Heinrich Wagner Sinto Maschinenfabrik GmbH (HWS)* [2002] ECR I-07357

Case C-37/00 *Herbert Weber* v *Universal Ogden Services Ltd* [2002] ECR I-02013

Joined Cases C-541/99 *Cape Snc v Idealservice Srl* and C-542/99 *Idealservice MN RE Sas v OMAI Srl* [2001] ECR I-09049

Case C-268/99 *Aldona Malgorzata Jany & Others v Staatssecretaris van Justitie* [2001] ECR I-08615

Case C-165/98 *Mazzoleni and ISA* [2001] ECR I-2189

Case C-381/98, *Ingmar GB Ltd v Eaton Leonard Technologies Inc.* [2000] ECR I-9305

Case C-381/98 *Ingmar GB Ltd v Eaton Leonard Technologies Inc.*, Opinion Advocate General Léger [2000] ECR I-9307

Joined Cases C-369/96 *Jean-Claude Arblade and Arblade & Fils SARL* and C-376/96 *Bernard Leloup, Serge Leloup and Sofrage SARL* [1999] ECR I-8453

Case C-215/97 *Barbara Bellone v Yokohama SpA* [1998] ECR I-2191

Case C-85/96 *María Martínez Sala v Freistaat Bayern* [1998] ECR I-2691
Case C-383/95 *Petrus Wilhelmus Rutten v Cross Medical* Ltd [1997] ECR I-00057
Case C-269/95 *Benincasa v Dentalkit* [1997] ECR *I*-3767
Case C-125/92 *Mulox IBC Ltd v Hendrick Geels* [1993] ECR I-04075
Case C-339/89, *Alsthom Atlantique SA v Compagnie de construction mécanique Sulzer SA* [1991] ECR I-107
Case C-113/89 *Rush Portuguesa Ld[a] v Office national d'immigration* [1990] ECR I-01417
Case C-266/85 *Hassan Shenavai v Klaus Kreischer* [1987] ECR I-239
Case C-66/85 *Lawrie-Blum v Land Baden-Württemberg* [1986] ECR I-2121

Austria

OGH 1 March 2017, 5 Ob 72/16y
OGH 25 October 2000, 8 Nd 502/00

France

Cour de Cassation, 30 November 2007, 06-14006 (*Aginitis*)

Germany

BGH 13 December 2005 - XI ZR 82/05
BGH 19 March 1997- VIII ZR 316/96
BAG 29 October 1992 - 2 AZR 267/92

Netherlands

HR 24 February 2012, LJN BU8512 (*Nuon Personeelsbeheer/X*)
HR 23 October 1987, NJ 1988/842 (*Sorensen/Aramco*)
HR13 May 1966, NJ 1967 (*Alnati*)

Bibliography

Aguilar Grieder H (2006) La Voluntad de Conciliación con las Directivas Comunitarias Protectoras en la Propuesta del Reglamento Roma I. In: La Unión Europea ante el Derecho de la Globalización. Colex, Madrid, pp 45–61

Aguilar Grieder H (2007) La Protección del Agente en el Derecho Comercial Europeo. Colex, Madrid

Aguilar Grieder H (2011) El Impacto del Reglamento Roma I en el Contrato Internacional de Agencia. Cuadernos de Derecho Transnacional 3:24–46

Aguilar Grieder H (2012) Desafíos y Tendencias en el Actual Derecho Internacional Privado Europeo de los Contractos. Cuadernos de Derecho Transnacional 4:23–48

Águila-Real JA (1998) Cláusulas Abusivas, Cláusulas Predispuestas y Condiciones Generales. Anuario Jurídico de La Rioja 4:53–70

Ancel M-E (2008) The Rome I Regulation and distribution contracts. In: Sarcevic P et al (eds) Yearbook of private international law. Sellier, European Law Publishers and Swiss Institute of Comparative Law, München, pp 221–232

Añoveros Terradas B (2003) Los Contratos de Consumo Intracomunitarios. Marcial Pons, Madrid

Añoveros Terradas B (2006) Consumidor Residente en la Unión Europea vs. Consumidor Residente en un Estado Tercero: A Propósito de la Propuesta del Reglamento Roma I. Anuario Español de Derecho Internacional Privado 6:379–401

Arenas García R (1996) Tratamiento Jurisprudencial del Ámbito de Aplicación de los Foros de Protección en Materia de Contratos de Consumidores del Convenio de Bruselas de 1968. Revista Española de Derecho Internacional 48:39–69

Arenas García R (2007) La Regulación de la Responsabilidad Precontractual en el Reglamento Roma II. Anuario Español de Derecho Internacional Privado 7:315–339

Arenas García R (2008) El Derecho Internacional Privado (DIPr) y el Estado en la Era de la Globalización: la vuelta a los orígenes. Cursos de derecho internacional y relaciones internacionales de Vitoria-Gasteiz 19–94

Audit B (1984) Le Caractère Fonctionnel de la Regle de Conflit. Collect Courses Hague Acad Int Law 186:223–397

Barnard C (2008) Viking and Laval: an introduction. Camb Yearb Eur Leg Stud 10:463–492

Basedow J (2004) Consumer contracts and insurance contracts in a future Rome I-Regulation. In: Meeusen J et al (eds) Enforcement of international contracts in the European Union: convergence and divergence between Brussels I and Rome I. Intersentia, Antwerp; New York

M. Campo Comba, *The Law Applicable to Cross-border Contracts involving Weaker Parties in EU Private International Law*,
https://doi.org/10.1007/978-3-030-61481-2

Basedow J (2006a) European private international law of obligations and internal market legislation- a matter of coordination. In: Erauw J et al (eds) Liber Memorialis Peter Sarcevic-universalism, tradition and the individual. Sellier, European Law Publishers, München, pp 13–24
Basedow J (2006b) Conflicto de Leyes y Armonización del Derecho Privado Material en la UE. Anuario Español de Derecho Internacional Privado 6:141–159
Basedow J (2017) Private international law, methods of. In: Basedow J et al (eds) Encyclopedia of private international law. Edward Elgar Publishing, Cheltenham, pp 1402–1407
Basedow J et al (eds) (2012) The Max Planck encyclopedia of European private law. Oxford University Press, Oxford
Basedow J et al (eds) (2017) Encyclopedia of private international law. Edward Elgar Publishing, Cheltenham
Batiffol H (1973) Le Pluralisme des Méthodes en Droit International Privé. Collect Courses Hague Acad Int Law 139:75–148
Beale JH (1914) Bartolus on the conflict of laws. Harvard University Press, Cambridge
Beale JH (1935) A treatise on the conflict of laws. Baker, Voorhis & Co., New York
Belohlávek AJ (2011) Rome Convention - Rome I Regulation. Juris Publishing, Inc., Huntington
Bernardeau L (2003) Droit international privé et services financiers de détail - 2e partie : les conflits de lois. Euredia 1:59–114
Bertrams RIVF, Kruisinga SA (2007) Overeenkomsten in het Internationaal Privaatrecht en het Weens Koopverdrag. Wolters Kluwer, Deventer
Bisping C (2012a) Avoid the statutist trap: the international scope of the Consumer Credit Act 1974. J Priv Int Law 8:35–62
Bisping C (2012b) European consumer protection - theory and practice. Cambridge University Press, Cambridge
Bitterich K (2003) Die Neuregelung des Internationalen Verbrauchervertragsrechts in Art. 29a EGBGB. Peter Lang, Frankfurt/M et al
Boele-Woelki K (2010) Unifying and harmonizing substantive law and the role of conflict of laws. Brill, Leiden
Boele-Woelki K et al (1998) Dutch private international law at the end of the 20th century: pluralism of methods. Netherlands reports to the fifteenth international congress of comparative law (Conference report), pp 203–227
Bonomi A (2008a) Overriding mandatory provisions in the Rome I Regulation on the law applicable to contracts. In: Sarcevic P et al (eds) Yearbook of private international law. Sellier, European Law Publishers and Swiss Institute of Comparative Law, München, pp 285–300
Bonomi A (2008b) The Rome I Regulation on the law applicable to contractual obligations: some general remarks. In: Yearbook of international private law. Sellier, European Law Publishers and Swiss Institute of Comparative Law, München, pp 165–176
Bonomi A (2008c) Le Régime des Règles Impératives et des Lois de Police dans le Règlement 'Rome I' sur la Loi Applicable aux Contrats. In: Cashin Ritaine E, Bonomi A (eds) Le Nouveau Règlement Européen 'Rome I' relatif à la Loi Applicable aux Obligations Contractuelles. Schulthess, Zurich, pp 217–240
Bonomi A (2016) Article 9: overriding mandatory provisions. In: Magnus U, Mankowski P (eds) Rome I Regulation - commentary. Verlag Dr. Otto Schmidt, Köln, pp 597–661
Bucher A (2011) La Dimension Sociale du Droit International Privé : cours général. Brill, Leiden
Cabrelli D (2018) Employment law in context. Oxford University Press, Oxford
Calliess G-P (2015a) Article 6. Consumer contracts. In: Calliess G-P (ed) Rome Regulations. Commentary, 2nd edn. Kluwer Law International, The Netherlands, pp 155–193
Calliess G-P (2015b) Article 3. Freedom of choice. In: Calliess G-P (ed) Rome Regulations. Commentary, 2nd edn. Kluwer Law International, The Netherlands, pp 76–108
Calliess G-P (2015c) Rome Regulations. Commentary, 2nd edn. Kluwer Law International, The Netherlands
Calvo Caravaca AL, Carrascosa González J (1997) El Convenio de Roma sobre la Ley aplicable a las obligaciones contractuales del 19 de junio de 1980. In: Contratos Internacionales. Tecnos, Madrid, pp 41–143

Calvo Caravaca AL, Carrascosa González JM (2013) Derecho Internacional Privado. Comares, Granada
Carrascosa González J (2009) Ley Aplicable a los Contratos Internacionales: el Reglamento Roma I. Colex, Madrid
Carrascosa González J (2012) La Autonomía de la Voluntad Conflictual y la Mano Invisible en la Contratación Internacional. Diario La Ley 7847
Carrillo Pozo LF (2017) El Tratamiento de las leyes de policía de terceros Estados. (A propósito de la sentencia del TJUE de 18 de octubre de 2016). Bitácora Millennium DIPr: Derecho Internacional Privado 5:1–23
Cebrián Salvat MA (2014) Agencia Comercial, Leyes de Policía y Derecho Internacional Privado Europeo. Cuadernos de Derecho Transnacional 6:357–366
Collins H (2001) Justifying European employment law. In: Grundmann S et al (eds) Party autonomy and the role of information in the internal market. De Gruyter, Berlin, New York, pp 205–224
Collins H (2006) A Workers' Civil Code? Principles of European Contract Law evolving in EU social and economic policy. In: Hesselink MW (ed) The politics of a European Civil Code. Kluwer Law International, The Hague, pp 55–71
Collins H (2008) The European Civil Code: the way forward. Cambridge University Press, Cambridge
Collins H (2010) Employment law, 2nd edn. Oxford University Press, Oxford
Collins H et al (2019) Philosophical foundations of labour law. Oxford University Press, Oxford
Cremona M, Micklitz H-W (eds) (2016) Private law in the external relations of the EU. Oxford University Press, Oxford
Cseres KJ (2005) Competition law and consumer protection. Kluwer Law International, The Hague
Currie B (1963) Selected essays on the conflict of laws. Duke University Press, Durham
Danson AS (1964) Territorially limited statutes and choice of law process. Harv J Legis 1:115–143
De Boer TM (1996) Facultative choice of law: the procedural status of choice-of-law rules and foreign law. Collect Courses Hague Acad Int Law 257:223–427
De la Rosa FE (2003) La Protección de Consumidores en el Mercado Interior Europeo. Comares, Granada
De la Rosa FE (2005) La Inadecuación del Sistema Español de Derecho Internacional Privado de las Cláusulas Abusivas al Derecho Comunitario: Claves para una Nueva Transposición y Propuesta Legislativa. La Ley: Revista jurídica española de doctrina, jurisprudencia y bibliografía 2:1932–1942
De la Rosa FE (2007) El Sistema Europeo y Español de Ley Aplicable a los Contratos de Consumo Transfronterizos: el Modelo de Dispersión Normativa para el Derecho Privado de la Integración. Revista Agenda Internacional 13:409–441
De la Rosa FE (2015) La Determinación del Derecho Aplicable a los Contratos de Consumo Transfronterizos: perspectiva europea y española. In: De la Rosa FE (ed) La Protección del Consumidor en Dos Espacios de Integración: Europa y América. Tirant lo Blanch, Valencia, pp 57–85
De Miguel Asensio P (2005) Conflictos de Leyes e Integración Jurídica: Estados Unidos y Unión Europea. Anuario Español de Derecho Internacional Privado 5:43–102
De Nova R (1966) Conflict of laws and functionally restricted substantive rules. Calif Law Rev 54:1569–1574
Devenney J, Kenny M (eds) (2012) European consumer protection. Theory and practice. Cambridge University Press, Cambridge
Dickinson A (2007) Third-country mandatory rules in the law applicable to contractual obligations: so long, farewell, Auf Wiedersehen, Adieu? J Priv Int Law 3:53–88
Dominique B, Watt HM (2007) Droit International Privé- partie générale. Presses Universitaires de France, Paris
Espiniella Menéndez Á (2014) Contratos de Consumo en el Tráfico Comercial UE- Terceros Estados. Anuario Español de Derecho Internacional Privado 14–15:277–303

Fallon M, Francq S (2000) Towards internationally mandatory directives for consumer contracts? In: Basedow J (ed) Private law in international arena. Liber Amicorum K. Siehr. Asser Instituut, The Hague, pp 155–178

Fauvarque-Cosson B, Mazeaud (eds) (2008) European Contract Law: materials for a common frame of reference: terminology, guiding principles, model rules. Sellier, European Law Publishers, München

Fentiman R (2016) Article 5: contracts of carriage. In: Magnus U, Mankowski P (eds) Commentary - Rome I Regulation. Verlag Dr. Otto Schmidt, Köln, pp 441–452

Fernández Rozas JC (2000) Orientaciones de Derecho Internacional Privado en el Umbral del Siglo XXI. Revista Mexicana de Derecho Internacional Privado 9:7–32

Fernández Rozas JC, Sánchez Lorenzo S (1999) Derecho Internacional Privado. Civitas, Madrid

Font i Segura A (2009) Reparación Indemnizatoria tras la Extinción del Contrato Internacional de Agencia Comercial: Imperatividad Poliédrica o el Mito de Zagreo (STJCE de 9 de noviembre de 2000, As. C-381/98, Ingmar Gb Ltd c. Eaton Leonard Technologies Inc.). Revista de Derecho Comunitario Europeo 5:259–279

Fornasier M (2017) Employment contracts, applicable law. In: Basedow J et al (eds) Encyclopedia of private international law. Edward Elgar Publishing, Cheltenham, pp 1679–1703

Fornasier M, Torga M (2013) The posting of workers: perspective of the sending state. Europäische Zeitschrift für Arbeitsrecht 6:356–365

Fotinopouplou Basurko O (2004) Consideraciones en torno al Art. 1.4 del Estatuto de los Trabajadores. Acerca del Sistema de Fuentes del Derecho Internacional Privado. Revista del Ministerio de Trabajo e Inmigración 52:49–60

Francescakis P (1966) Quelques Precisions sur les 'Lois d'Application Immediate' et leurs Rapports avec les Règles sur les Conflits de Lois. Revue critique de droit international privé 55:1–18

Francescakis P (1967) Lois d'Application Immediate et Règles de Conflit. Rivista di diritto internazionale privato e processuale 3:691–697

Francq S (2005) L'Applicabilité du Droit Communautaire Dérivé au Regard des Méthodes du Droit International Privé. LGDJ, Bruxelles/Paris

Francq S (2006) The scope of secondary community law in the light of the methods of private international law- or the other way around? In: Sarcevic P et al (eds) Yearbook of private international law. Sellier, European Law Publishers and Swiss Institute of Comparative Law, pp 333–374

Francq S (2017) Unilateralism. In: Basedow J et al (eds) Encyclopedia of private international law. Edward Elgar Publishing, Cheltenham, pp 1179–1791

Franzen M, Gröner N (2015) Article 8. Individual employment contracts. In: Calliess G-P (ed) Rome Regulations. Commentary, 2nd edn. Kluwer Law International, The Netherlands

Frigessi Di Rattalma M (ed) (2003) The implementation provisions of the EC choice of law rules for insurance contracts. A commentary. Kluwer Law International, The Hague; London; New York

Gamillscheg F (1983) Rules of public order in private international labour law. Collect Courses Hague Acad Int Law 181:285–347

García Gutiérrez L (2008) Franchise contracts and the Rome I Regulation on the law applicable to international contracts. In: Sarcevic P et al (eds) Yearbook of private international law. Sellier, European Law Publishers and Swiss Institute of Comparative Law, pp 233–244

Garcimartín Alférez FJ (2002) La Racionalidad Económica del Derecho Internacional Privado. Cursos de derecho internacional y relaciones internacionales de Vitoria-Gasteiz:87–154

Garcimartín Alférez FJ (2008) The Rome I Regulation: much ado about nothing? Eur Leg Forum:61–80

Garcimartín Alférez FJ (2009) The Rome I Regulation: exceptions to the rule on consumer contracts and financial instruments. J Priv Int Law 5:85–103

Garcimartín Alférez FJ (2012) Derecho Internacional Privado. Thomson Reuters, Pamplona

Gardeñes Santiago M (1999) La Aplicación de la Regla de Reconocimiento Mutuo y su Incidencia en el Comercio de Mercancías y Servicios en el Ámbito Comunitario e Internacional. Eurolex, Madrid

Gardeñes Santiago M (2008) La Regulación Conflictual del Contrato de Trabajo en el Reglamento Roma I: una oportunidad perdida. Anuario Español de Derecho Internacional Privado 8:387–424

Gardeñes Santiago M (2012) Le Détachement Transnational des Travailleurs dans le Cadre des Prestations de Services: un Sujet Spécialement Difficile pour le Marché Intérieur. In: Liber Amicorum: Mélanges en l'honneur du Professeur Joël Molinier. LGDJ, pp 255–278

Gardeñes Santiago M (2017) Derecho Imperativo y Contrato Internacional de Trabajo. Revista de Ministerio de Empleo y Seguridad Social 132:163–188

Gebauer M (2015) Article 4. Applicable law in the absence of choice. In: Calliess G-P (ed) Rome Regulations. Commentary, 2nd edn. Kluwer Law International, The Netherlands

Gómez Abelleira FJ (2018) Desplazamiento Transnacional Laboral Genuino y la Ley Aplicable al Contrato de Trabajo. Cuadernos de Derecho Transnacional 10:213–232

Gómez Pomar F (2008) The harmonization of contract law through European rules: a law and economics perspective. Indret: Revista para el Análisis del Derecho 4:2

González Beilfuss C (2004) Relaciones e Interacciones entre Derecho Comunitario, Derecho Internacional Privado y Derecho de Familia Europeo en la Construcción de un Espacio Judicial Común. Anuario Español de Derecho Internacional Privado 4:117–186

González Campos J (1996) El Paradigma de la Norma de Conflicto Multilateral. In: Estudios Jurídicos en Homenaje al Profesor Aurelio Menéndez. Civitas, Madrid, pp 5239–5270

Gruber UP (2015) Article 7. Insurance contracts. In: Calliess G-P (ed) Rome Regulations. Commentary, 2nd edn. Kluwer Law International, The Netherlands

Grusic U (2015) The European private international law of employment. Cambridge University Press, Cambridge

Guardans Cambó I (1992) Contrato Internacional y Derecho Imperativo Extranjero. Aranzadi, Pamplona

Gutzwiller M (1923) Der Einfluss Savignys auf die Entwicklung des Internationalprivatrechts. Kommissionsverlag : Universitäts-buchh. (Gschwend, Tschopp & Co.), Freiburg

Gutzwiller M (1929) Le Développement Historique du Droit International Privé. Collect Courses Hague Acad Int Law 29:287–400

Hage Chahine N (2012) Culpa in contrahendo in European private international law: another look at Article 12 of the Rome II Regulation. Northwest J Int Law Bus 32:451–540

Halson R, Campbell D (2013) Harmonisation and its discontents: a transaction costs critique of a European Contract Law. In: Devenney J, Kenny M (eds) The transformation of European private law harmonisation, consolidation, codification or chaos? Cambridge University Press, Cambridge, pp 100–130

Hartkamp A, von Bar C (2011) Towards a European Civil Code. Kluwer Law International, Alphen aan den Rijn

Haupt H-G (2004) The history of consumption in Western Europe in the ninetheenth and twentieth centuries. In: Hartmut K (ed) The European way. European societies in the 19th and 20th centuries. Berghahn Books, New York, pp 161–185

Heiss H (2009) Party autonomy. In: Ferrari F, Leible S (eds) Rome I Regulation: the law applicable to contractual obligations in Europe. Sellier, European Law Publishers, München, pp 7–16

Hellner M (2009) Third country overriding mandatory rules in the Rome I Regulation: old wine in new bottles? J Priv Int Law 5:447–470

Henckel KC (2016) Cross-border transfers of undertakings. Ulrik Huber Institute for Private International Law, Ees, The Netherlands

Hesselink MW (2007) European Contract Law: a matter of consumer protection, citizenship, or justice? Eur Rev Priv Law 15:323–348

Hesselink MW (2009) The common frame of reference as a source of European private law. Tulane Law Rev 83:919

Hondius E (1987) Unfair terms in consumer contracts. Molengraaff Instituut voor Privaatrecht, Utrecht

Hondius E et al (2008) Principles of European law: sales contract. Sellier, European Law Publishers, München

Houwerzijl M (2019) The analysis of the posting of workers directive(s) with a specific focus on EU cross-border road transport. In: Zwanenburg A, Bednarowicz B (eds) Cross-border employment and social rights in the EU road transport sector. Eleven International Publishing, The Hague, pp 71–111

Houwerzijl M, van Hoek A (2016) Where do EU mobile workers belong, according to Rome I and the (E)PWD. In: Verschueren H (ed) Residence, employment and social rights of mobile persons: on how EU law defines where they belong. Intersentia, Cambridge, pp 215–253

Jacquet J-M (2010) La Aplicación de las Leyes de Policía en Materia de Contratos Internacionales. Anuario Español de Derecho Internacional Privado 10:35–48

Jansen N, Zimmermann R (2010) A European Civil Code in all but name: discussing the nature and purposes of the Draft Common Frame of Reference. Camb Law J 69:98–112

Jayme E, Kohler C (1995) L'interaction des Règles de Conflit contenues dans le Droit Dérivé de la Communauté Européenne et des Conventions de Bruxelles et de Rome. Revue critique de droit international privé 1:11–36

Juenger FK (1993) Choice of law and multistate justice. Martinus Nijhoff Publishers, Dordrecht, Boston, London

Kahn-Freund O (1967) A note on status and contract in British labour law. Mod Labour Rev 30:635–644

Kelly DSL (1969) Localising rules and differing approaches to the choice of law process. Int Comp Law Q 18:249–274

Klauer S (2002) Das europäische Kollisionsrecht der Verbraucherverträge zwischen Römer EVÜ und EG-Richtlinien. Mohr Siebeck, Tübingen

Koetz HD (2012) Contract law in Europe and the United States: legal unification in the civil law and the common law. Tulane Eur Civil Law Forum 27:1–16

Kramer XE (2008) The new European conflict of law rules on insurance contracts in Rome I: a complex compromise. Icfai Univ J Insur Law 6:23–42

Kramer XE (2015) The interaction between Rome I and mandatory EU private rules- EPIL and EPL: communicating vessels? In: Stone P, Farah Y (eds) Research handbook on EU private international law. Edward Elgar Publishing, Cheltenham, pp 248–284

Krebber S (2000) Conflict of laws in employment in Europe. Comp Labor Law J Policy J 21:501–542

Kropholer J (2006) Internationales Privatrecht, 5th edn. Mohr Siebeck, Tübingen

Krvavac M, Belovic J (2014) Communitarisation of private international law rules on party autonomy in European Union. Int J Bus Humanit Technol 4:54–68

Kuipers J-J (2009) Party autonomy in the Brussels I Regulation and Rome I Regulation and the European Court of Justice. German Law J 10:1505–1525

Kuipers J-J (2012) EU law and private international law: the interrelationship in contractual obligations. Martinus Nijhoff Publishers, Leiden

Lagarde P (2006) Remarques sur la Proposition de Règlement sur la Loi Applicable aux Obligations Contractuelles (Rome I). Revue critique de droit international privé 95:331–349

Lando O (1974) The EC Draft Convention on the law applicable to contractual and non-contractual obligations: introduction and contractual obligations. Rabel J Comp Int Priv Law 38:6–55

Lando O (1987) The ECC Convention on the law applicable to contractual obligations. Common Mark Law Rev 24:159–214

Lando O, Nielsen PA (2007) The Rome I Proposal. J Priv Int Law 3:29–51

Lando O, Nielsen PA (2008) The Rome I Regulation. Common Mark Law Rev 45:1687–1725

Lando O et al (eds) (2003) Principles of European Contract Law. Kluwer Law International, The Hague

Lasok D, Stone P (1987) Conflict of laws in the European Community. Professional Books Ltd, London

Lazić V (2014) Procedural justice for 'weaker parties' in cross-border litigation under the EU regulatory scheme. Utrecht Law Rev 10:100–117

Leible S (2011) La Importancia de la Autonomía Conflictual para el Futuro del Derecho de los Contratos Internacionales. Cuadernos de Derecho Transnacional 3:214–233

Leible S (2015) Article 6 Rome I and conflict of laws in EU directives. J Eur Consum Mark Law 4:39–44

Leighton P (2010) EU employment law: a practical guide. Thorogood Publishing Ltd, London

Liukkunen U (2004) The role of mandatory rules in international labour law- a comparative study in the conflict of laws. Talentum Media Oy, Helsinki

Llobera Vila M (2016) El Artículo 1.4 ET a la Luz de la Jurisprudencia Comunitaria en Materia de Ley Aplicable al Contrato de Trabajo Internacional. Revista de Derecho Social 73:127–148

López de Gonzalo M (2017) Carriage of passengers. In: Basedow J et al (eds) Encyclopedia of private international law. Edward Elgar Publishing, Cheltenham, pp 269–278

Magnus U (2016a) Article 4: applicable law in the absence of choice. In: Magnus U, Mankowski P (eds) Rome I Regulation- commentary. Verlag Dr. Otto Schmidt, Köln, pp 263–441

Magnus U (2016b) Introduction. In: Magnus U, Mankowski P (eds) Rome I Regulation - commentary. Verlag Dr. Otto Schmidt, Köln, pp 6–51

Mandery M (2014) Party autonomy in contractual and non-contractual obligations. Peter Lang, Frankfurt

Mankowski P (2016a) Article 3: freedom of choice. In: Magnus U, Mankowski P (eds) Rome I Regulation - commentary. Verlag Dr. Otto Schmidt, Köln, pp 87–263

Mankowski P (2016b) Article 23: relationship with other provisions of Community law. In: Magnus U, Mankowski P (eds) Rome I Regulation - commentary. Verlag Dr. Otto Schmidt, Köln, pp 846–853

Marchal Escalona N (2017) De la Protección del Personal Laboral al Servicio de las Embajadas Españolas. Bitácora Millennium DIPr: Derecho Internacional Privado 6:1–27

Marques dos Santos A (1991) As Normas de Aplicaçao Imediata no Direito Internacional Privado. Livraria Almedina, Coimbra

Martínez Luna WF (2016) Applicable law to distribution contracts in the European Regulation 593/2008 (Rome I). International Law, Revista Colombiana Derecho Internacional 28:247–282

Mathieu B (2015) Directives Européennes et Conflits de Lois. LGDJ, Issy-les-Moulineaux

Mattei U (1997) A transaction cost approach to the European Code. Eur Rev Priv Law 5:537–540

Maultzsch F (2016) Party autonomy in European private international law: uniform principle or context-dependent instrument? J Priv Int Law 12:466–491

Max Planck Institute for Foreign Private and Private International Law (2004) Comments on the European Commission's Green Paper on the conversion of the Rome Convention of 1980 on the law applicable to contractual obligations into a Community instrument and its modernization. RabelsZ 68:1–118

Max Planck Institute for Foreign Private and Private International Law (2007) Comments on the European Commission's Proposal for a Regulation of the European Parliament and the Council on the law applicable to contractual obligations (Rome I). RabelsZ Bd71

Mayer P (1985) Le Mouvement des Idées dans le Droit des Conflits de Lois. Droits 2:129–143

Mayer P, Heuzé V (2004) Droit International Privé, 8th edn. Librairie générale de droit et jurisprudence, Paris

McParland M (2015) The Rome I Regulation on the law applicable to contractual obligations. Oxford University Press, Oxford

Merrett L (2011) Employment contracts in private international law. Oxford University Press, Oxford

Micklitz H-W (2009) The targeted full harmonisation approach: looking behind the curtain. In: Howells GG, Schulze R (eds) Modernising and harmonising consumer contract law. Sellier, European Law Publishers, München, pp 47–84

Mills A (2018) Party autonomy in private international law. Cambridge University Press, Cambridge

Moreau M-A, Trudeau G (2000) Les Normes du Droit du Travail Confrontées à l'Èvolution de l'Èconomie: De Nouveaux Enjeux pour l'Espace Régional. Journal de Droit International 4:915–948

Morgenstern F (1984) International conflicts of labour law. A survey of the law applicable to the international employment relation. International Labour Office, Geneva

Morse CGJ (1992) Consumer contracts, employment contracts and the Rome Convention. Int Comp Law Q 41:1–21

Moura Vicente D (2013) Culpa in contrahendo in European private international law. Anuario Español de Derecho Internacional Privado 13:53–72

Nadelmann KH (1961) Joseph Story's contribution to American conflicts law: a comment. Am J Leg Hist 5:230–253

Niboyet J-P (1952) Territoriality and universal recognition of rules of conflict of laws. Harv Law Rev 65:582–596

Nolde B (1936) La Codification du Droit International Privé. Collect Courses Hague Acad Int Law 55:299–432

Nygh P (1999a) Autonomy in international contracts. Oxford University Press

Nygh PE (1999b) Autonomy in international contracts. Oxford University Press, Oxford

Oprea A (2010) Le Article 3.4 du Reglement Rome I sur la Loi Applicable aux Relations Contractuelles et les Contrats Intracommunautaires. Babes-Bolyai Studia Jurisprudentia 3:1–10

Oró Martínez C (2008) Del Artículo 7 del Convenio de Roma al Artículo 9 del Reglamento 'Roma I': Algunas Implicaciones para el Derecho de la Competencia. Anuario Español de Derecho Internacional Privado 8:531–554

Ortiz Vidal MD (2012) Ley Aplicable a los Contratos Internacionales y Eficiencia Conflictual. Comares, Granada

Palao Moreno G (2005) Las Normas del Derecho Internacional Privado de Origen Comunitario en Materia de Contrato Individual de Trabajo, ante los Retos de la Integración Europea y la Globalización. Anuario Español de Derecho Internacional Privado 5:309–334

Palao Moreno G (2016) Article 8: individual employment contracts. In: Magnus U, Mankowski P (eds) Rome I Regulation - commentary. Verlag Dr. Otto Schmidt, Köln, pp 577–599

Paredes Pérez JI (2006) La Necesidad de Una Nueva Norma de Conflicto Bilateral Sobre Contratos de Consumo. Propuesta de Lege Ferenda. Anuario Español de Derecho Internacional Privado 6:87–114

Piir R, Sein K (2016) Law applicable to consumer contracts. Interaction of the Rome I Regulation and EU-directive-based rules on conflict of laws. Juridica Int 24:63–70

Pilenko A (1954) Droit Spatial et Droit International Privé. Ius Gentium 5:35–59

Plender R, Wilderspin M (2009) The European private international law of obligations, 3rd edn. Sweet & Maxwell, London

Plender R, Wilderspin M (2015) The European private international law of obligations, 4th edn. Sweet & Maxwell, London

Pocar F (1984) La Protection de la Partie Faible en Droit International Privé. Collect Courses Hague Acad Int Law 188:339–394

Quadri R (1967) Lezioni di diritto internazionale privato. Liguori, Napoli

Ragno F (2009) The law applicable to consumer contracts under the Rome I Regulation. In: Ferrari F, Leible S (eds) Rome I Regulation. Sellier, European Law Publishers, München

Randolph F, Davey J (2010) The European law of commercial agency, 3rd edn. Hart Publishing, Oxford

Remien O (2001) European private international law, the European Community and its emerging area of freedom, security and justice. Common Mark Law Rev 38:53–86

Renner M (2015a) Article 21. Public policy of the forum. In: Calliess G-P (ed) Rome Regulations. Commentary, 2nd edn. Kluwer Law International, The Netherlands

Renner M (2015b) Article 9. Overriding mandatory provisions. In: Calliess G-P (ed) Rome Regulations. Commentary, 2nd edn. Kluwer Law International, The Netherlands, pp 242–261

Riefa C (2004) Article 5 of the Rome Convention on the law applicable to contractual obligations of 19 June 1980 and consumer E-contracts: the need for reform. Inf Commun Technol Law 13:59–73

Riesenhuber K (2012) European employment law. A systematic exposition. Intersentia, Cambridge

Roelvink HLJ (1993) Artikel 6:2 BW en het Nederlandse IPR, in: Van Rijn van Alkemade J, Grensoverschrijdend privaatrecht: een bundel opstellen over privaatrecht in internationaal verband: aangeboden aan Mr. J. van Rijn van Alkemade bij gelegenheid van zijn afscheid als raadadviseur bij het Ministerie van Justitie. Deventer, Kluwer, pp 219 ff

Roth W-H (2002) Case C-381/98, Ingmar GB Ltd v. Eaton Leonard Technologies Inc. judgment of the Court (Fifth Chamber) of 9 November 2000. [2000] ECR I-9305. Common Mark Law Rev 40:369–383

Rühl G (2006) Methods and approaches in choice of law: an economic perspective. Berkeley J Int Law 24:801–841

Rühl G (2007) Party autonomy in the private international law of contracts: transatlantic convergence and economic efficiency. In: Gottschalk E et al (eds) Conflict of laws in a globalized world. Cambridge University Press, Cambridge

Rühl G (2011) Consumer protection in choice of law. Cornell Int Law J 44:569–601

Rühl G (2014) The protection of weaker parties in the private international law of the European Union: a portrait of inconsistency and conceptual truancy. J Priv Int Law 10:335–358

Rühl G (2017) Private international law, foundations. In: Basedow J et al (eds) Encyclopedia of private international law. Edward Elgar Publishing, Cheltenham

Rutgers JW, Sefton-Green R (2008) Revising the consumer acquis: (half) opening the doors of the Trojan horse. Eur Rev Priv Law 16:427–442

Sabido Rodríguez M (2010) Algunas Cuestiones que Plantea en DIPR la Tutela de los Trabajadores Afectados por Reestructuraciones de Empresas. Cuadernos de Derecho Transnacional 2:233–260

Salmerón Hernríquez JA (2016) Freedom of contract, bargaining power and forum seletion in bills of lading. Ulrik Huber Institute for Private International Law, Groningen

Sánchez Lorenzo S (2003) La Unificación del Derecho Contractual Europeo Vista desde el Derecho Internacional Privado. In: Derecho Patrimonial Europeo. Thomson-Aranzadi, Cizu Menor (Navarra), pp 363–381

Sánchez Lorenzo S (2010) Choice of law and overriding mandatory rules in international contracts after Rome I. In: Sarcevic P et al (eds) Yearbook of private international law. Sellier, European Law Publishers, Germany, pp 67–93

Sánchez Lorenzo S (2018) El Principio de Coherencia en el Derecho Internacional Privado. Revista Española de Derecho Internacional 70:17–47

Schmidt-Kessel M (2015) Article 9. In: Ferrari F (ed) Rome I Regulation. Pocket commentary. Sellier, European Law Publishers, München, pp 320–354

Schüller B (2012) The definition of consumers in EU consumer law. In: European consumer protection. Theory and practice. Cambridge University Press, Cambridge

Schulte-Nölke H et al (eds) (2008) EC consumer law compendium. Comparative analysis. Universität, Bielefeld

Schulze R (2015) Article 5. Contracts of carriage. In: Calliess G-P (ed) Rome Regulations. Commentary, 2nd edn. Kluwer Law International, The Netherlands

Siehr K (2017) Private international law, history of. In: Basedow J et al (eds) Encyclopedia of private international law. Edward Elgar Publishing, Cheltenham, pp 1391–1401

Solomon D (2007) The private international law of contracts in Europe: advances and retreats. Tulane Law Rev 82:1709–1740

Sonnenberger HJ (2016) Overriding mandatory provisions. In: Leible S (ed) General principles of European private international law. Wolters Kluwer, Alphen aan den Rijn, pp 117–128

Sonnentag M (2017) Savigny, Friedrich Carl Von. In: Basedow J et al (eds) Encyclopedia of private international law. Edward Elgar Publishing, Cheltenham, pp 1609–1615

Steennot R (2014) The protection of consumers in cross-border Airline's contracts of carriage at the level of private international law. In: Liber Amicorum Johan Erauw. Intersentia, Antwerpen, pp 175–188

Stone P (2014) EU private international law, 3rd edn. Edward Elgar Publishing, Cheltenham

Stone P (2018) Stone on private international law in the European Union, 4th edn. Edward Elgar Publishing, Cheltenham

Story J (1846) Commentaries on the conflict of laws: foreign and domestic, in regard to contracts, rights, and remedies, and especially in regard to marriages, divorces, wills, successions, and judgments, 3rd edn. Little, Brown

Strikwerda L, Schaafsma SJ (2005) Inleiding tot het Nederlandse Internationaal Privaatrecht. Wolters Kluwer

Symeonides SC (2005) Accommodative unilateralism as a starting premise in choice of law. In: Rasmussen-Bonne H et al (eds) Balancing of interests: Liber Amicorum Peter Hay. Verlag Recht und Wirtschaft GmbH, pp 417–434

Symeonides SC (2010) Party autonomy in Rome I and Rome II from a comparative perspective. In: Boele-Woelki K et al (eds) Convergence and divergence in private international law- Liber Amicorum Kurt Siehr. Eleven International Publishing, The Netherlands, pp 513–550

Symeonides SC (2014) Codifying choice of law around the world: an international comparative analysis. Oxford University Press, New York

Symeonides SC (2015) The choice-of-law revolution fifty years after Currie: an end and a beginning. Univ Ill Law Rev 2015:1847–1921

Symeonides SC (2016) Choice of law. Oxford University Press, Oxford; New York

Tang ZS (2007) Parties' choice of law in E-consumer contracts. J Priv Int Law 3:113–136

Tang ZS (2009) Electronic consumer contracts in the conflicts of laws. Hart Publishing, Oxford; Portland, Oregon

Ten Wolde MH (2013) The relativity of legal positions in cross-border situations: the foundations of private interregional law, private intra-community law and private international law. In: A commitment to private international law- essays in honour of Hans van Loon. Intersentia, Cambridge, pp 569–581

Ten Wolde MH, Henckel KC (2012) European private international law- a comparative perspective on contracts, torts and corporations. Hephaestus Publishers, Groningen

Tenreiro M, Karsten J (1999) Unfair terms in consumer contracts: uncertainties, contradictions and novelties of a directive. In: Schulte-Nölke H, Schulze R (eds) Europäische Rechtsangleichung und nationale Privatrechte. Nomos Verlagsgesellschaft, pp 223–276

Twigg-Flesner C (2011) 'Good-bye harmonisation by directives, hello cross-border only regulation?' - a way forward for EU consumer contract law. Eur Rev Contract Law 7:235–256

Twigg-Flesner C (2012) Comment: the future of EU consumer law – the end of harmonisation? In: European consumer protection. Theory and practice. Cambridge University Press, Cambridge, pp 6–20

Twigg-Flesner C (2016) The importance of law and harmonisation for the EU's confident consumer. In: Leczykiewicz D, Weatherill S (eds) The images of the consumer in EU law. Hart Publishing, Oxford; Portland, Oregon, pp 183–202

Van Bochove LM (2014) Overriding mandatory rules as a vehicle for weaker party protection in European private international law. Erasmus Law Rev 7:147–157

Van Hoek AAH (2014) Private international law: an appropriate means to regulate transnational employment in the European Union? Erasmus Law Rev 7:157–169

Van Overveeke F (2020) Posting drivers in the EU road transport sector. ERA Forum:1–12

Veneziani B (2009) The employment relationship. In: Hepple B, Veneziani B (eds) The transformation of labour law in Europe. A comparative study of 15 countries 1945–2004. Hart Publishing, Oxford; Portland, Oregon, pp 99–128

Verhagen HLE (2002) The tension between party autonomy and European Union law: some observations on IngmarGB Ltd v Eaton Leonard Technologies Inc. Int Comp Law Q 51:135–154

Verhulp E (2017) The notion of 'employee' in EU law and national laws. The European Centre of Expertise (ECE) in the field of labour law, employment and labour market policies
Vilà Costa B, Gardeñes Santiago M (2002) Comentario Disposición Adicional 1[a] Tres. In: Comentarios a la Ley sobre Condiciones Generales de la Contratación. Civitas, Madrid, pp 296–302
von Bar C, Mankowski P (2003) Internationales Privatrecht Band 1: Allgemeine Lehren, 2nd edn. C.H. Beck, Munich
von Savigny FC (1849) System des Heutigen Römischen Rechts. Veit und Comp., Berlin
von Savigny FC (1869) Private international law. A treatise on the conflict of laws, and the limits of their operation in respect of place and time (trans: Guthrie W). T. & T. Clark, Edinburgh
Watt HM (2010) "Party autonomy" in international contracts: from the makings of a myth to the requirements of global governance. Eur Rev Contract Law 6:250–283
Weatherill S (2013) EU consumer law and policy, 2nd edn. Edward Elgar Publishing, Cheltenham; Northampton
Weller M (2015) Article 23. Relationship with other provisions of community law. In: Calliess G-P (ed) Rome Regulations. Commentary, 2nd edn. Kluwer Law International, The Netherlands
Wilderspin M (2008) The Rome I Regulation: communitarisation and modernisation of the Rome Convention. ERA Forum:259–274
Wilderspin M (2016) Article 6: consumer contracts. In: Magnus U, Mankowski P (eds) Rome I Regulation - commentary. Verlag Dr. Otto Schmidt, Köln, pp 453–490
Wilhelmsson T (2004) The abuse of the 'confident consumer' as a justification for EC consumer law. J Consum Policy 27:317–337
Willem Vernooij N (2009) Rome I: an update on the law applicable to contractual obligations in Europe. Columbia J Eur Law Online 15:71–76